T0145086

Communications in Computer and Information Science 1474

More information about this series at https://link.springer.com/bookseries/7899

Kadi Bouatouch · A. Augusto de Sousa ·
Manuela Chessa · Alexis Paljic ·
Andreas Kerren · Christophe Hurter ·
Giovanni Maria Farinella ·
Petia Radeva · Jose Braz (Eds.)

Computer Vision, Imaging and Computer Graphics Theory and Applications

15th International Joint Conference, VISIGRAPP 2020
Valletta, Malta, February 27–29, 2020
Revised Selected Papers

Springer

Editors
Kadi Bouatouch
IRISA, University of Rennes 1
Rennes, France

Manuela Chessa
University of Genova
Genova, Italy

Andreas Kerren
Linnaeus University
Växjö, Sweden

Giovanni Maria Farinella (iD)
Università di Catania
Catania, Italy

Jose Braz
Escola Superior de Tecnologia de Setúbal
Setúbal, Portugal

A. Augusto de Sousa
Universidade do Porto
Porto, Portugal

Alexis Paljic
Mines ParisTech
Paris, France

Christophe Hurter
French Civil Aviation University (ENAC)
Toulouse, France

Petia Radeva
Universitat de Barcelona
Barcelona, Spain

ISSN 1865-0929 ISSN 1865-0937 (electronic)
Communications in Computer and Information Science
ISBN 978-3-030-94892-4 ISBN 978-3-030-94893-1 (eBook)
https://doi.org/10.1007/978-3-030-94893-1

This Springer imprint is published by the registered company Springer Nature Switzerland AG
The registered company address is: Gewerbestrasse 11, 6330 Cham, Switzerland

Preface

The present book includes extended and revised versions of a set of selected papers from the 15th International Joint Conference on Computer Vision, Imaging and Computer Graphics Theory and Applications (VISIGRAPP 2020), held in Valletta, Malta during February 27–29, 2020.

VISIGRAPP 2020 received 455 paper submissions from authors in 58 countries, of which 6% were included in this book. The papers were selected by the event chairs and their selection is based on a number of criteria that include the classifications and comments provided by the Program Committee members, the session chairs' assessment, and also the program chairs' global view of all papers included in the technical program. The authors of selected papers were then invited to submit revised and extended versions of their papers having at least 30% innovative material.

The purpose of VISIGRAPP is to bring together researchers and practitioners interested in both theoretical advances and applications of computer vision, computer graphics, information visualization, and human-computer interaction. VISIGRAPP is composed of four co-located conferences, each specializing in at least one of the aforementioned main knowledge areas.

The papers selected to be included in this book contribute to the understanding of relevant trends of current research on computer vision, imaging and computer graphics theory and applications, including the following: deep learning, action recognition, face and gesture recognition, pose estimation, human-aware navigation, mobile robots, dense prediction, pedestrian safety, first-person vision, image-to-image translation, range sensing, high- and super-resolution, fusion methods, human-computer interaction, lighting and appearance, real-time rendering, 3D model repair and scene reconstruction, modeling of natural scenes and phenomena, scene and object modeling, surface modeling, advanced user interfaces, graphical interfaces, virtual and augmented reality, human figure and facial animation, real-time animation and simulation, visual data analysis and knowledge discovery, high-dimensional data and dimensionality reduction, scientific visualization, and text and document visualization.

We would like to thank all the authors for their contributions and also the reviewers who have helped in ensuring the quality of this publication.

February 2020

Kadi Bouatouch
A. Augusto de Sousa
Manuela Chessa
Alexis Paljic
Andreas Kerren
Christophe Hurter
Giovanni Maria Farinella
Petia Radeva
Jose Braz

Organization

Conference Chair

Jose Braz   Escola Superior de Tecnologia de Setúbal, Portugal

Program Co-chairs

GRAPP

Kadi Bouatouch   IRISA, University of Rennes 1, France
A. Augusto Sousa   FEUP/INESC TEC, Portugal

HUCAPP

Manuela Chessa   University of Genoa, Italy
Alexis Paljic   Mines ParisTech, France

IVAPP

Andreas Kerren   Linnaeus University, Sweden
Christophe Hurter   French Civil Aviation University (ENAC), France

VISAPP

Giovanni Maria Farinella   Università di Catania, Italy
Petia Radeva   Universitat de Barcelona, Spain

GRAPP Program Committee

Francisco Abad   Universidad Politécnica de Valencia, Spain
Marco Agus   Hamad Bin Khalifa University, Qatar
Gérard Bailly   GIPSA-Lab, Université Grenoble Alpes/CNRS, France
Francesco Banterle   Visual Computing Lab, Italy
Carla Binucci   Università degli Studi di Perugia, Italy
Fernando Birra   Universidade Nova de Lisboa, Portugal
Kristopher Blom   Virtual Human Technologies, Czech Republic
Benjamin Bringier   Université de Poitiers, France
Dimitri Bulatov   Fraunhofer Institute of Optronics, System Technologies and Image Exploitation, Germany
Maria Beatriz Carmo   Universidade de Lisboa, Portugal
L. G. Casado   University of Almeria, Spain
Dan Casas   Universidad Rey Juan Carlos, Spain
Ozan Cetinaslan   Instituto de Telecomunicações/University of Porto, Portugal

Teresa Chambel	Universidade de Lisboa, Portugal
Parag Chaudhuri	Indian Institute of Technology Bombay, India
Antonio Chica	Universitat Politècnica de Catalunya, Spain
Hwan-gue Cho	Pusan National University, South Korea
Miguel Chover	Universitat Jaume I, Spain
Teodor Cioaca	SimCorp GmbH, Germany
Ana Paula Cláudio	Universidade de Lisboa, Portugal
António Coelho	Universidade do Porto, Portugal
Sabine Coquillart	Inria, France
Vasco Costa	INESC-ID, Portugal
Remi Cozot	LISIC, University of Littoral, France
Carsten Dachsbacher	Karlsruhe Institute of Technology, Germany
Luiz Henrique de Figueiredo	Impa, Brazil
Kurt Debattista	University of Warwick, UK
Paulo Dias	Universidade de Aveiro, Portugal
Elmar Eisemann	Delft University of Technology, The Netherlands
Marius Erdt	Fraunhofer IDM@NTU, Singapore
Petros Faloutsos	York University, Canada
Pierre-Alain Fayolle	University of Aizu, Japan
Francisco R. Feito	University of Jaén, Spain
Dirk Feldmann	Diconium Digital Solutions, Germany
Jie Feng	Peking University, China
António Fernandes	Universidade do Minho, Portugal
Leandro Fernandes	Universidade Federal Fluminense, Brazil
Carla Freitas	Universidade Federal do Rio Grande do Sul, Brazil
Ioannis Fudos	University of Ioannina, Greece
Davide Gadia	Università degli Studi di Milano, Italy
Ignacio García-Fernández	Universidad de Valencia, Spain
Miguel Gea	University of Granada, Spain
Guillaume Gilet	Université de Sherbrooke, Canada
Enrico Gobbetti	CRS4, Italy
Stephane Gobron	HES-SO/Arc, Switzerland
Abel Gomes	Universidade da Beira Interior, Portugal
Alexandrino Gonçalves	Polytechnic of Leiria, Portugal
Daniel Gonçalves	INESC-ID, Portugal
Damiand Guillaume	CNRS/LIRIS, France
Marcelo Guimarães	Federal University of São Paulo/Faculdade Campo Limpo Paulista, Brazil
James Hahn	George Washington University, USA
Vlastimil Havran	Czech Technical University in Prague, Czech Republic
Nancy Hitschfeld	University of Chile, Chile
Sébastien Horna	University of Poitiers, France
Insung Ihm	Sogang University, South Korea
Alberto Jaspe Villanueva	King Abdullah University of Science and Technology, Saudi Arabia

Jean-Pierre Jessel	IRIT, Paul Sabatier University, France
Juan José Jiménez-Delgado	Universidad de Jaen, Spain
Xiaogang Jin	Zhejiang University, China
Cláudio Jung	Universidade Federal do Rio Grande do Sul, Brazil
Josef Kohout	University of West Bohemia, Czech Republic
Maciej Kot	Dfinity, Japan
Alejandro León	University of Granada, Spain
Marco Livesu	Italian National Research Council (CNR), Italy
Helio Lopes	Pontifical Catholic University of Rio de Janeiro, Brazil
Claus Madsen	Aalborg University, Denmark
Luis Magalhães	Universidade do Minho, Portugal
Stephen Mann	University of Waterloo, Canada
Michael Manzke	Trinity College Dublin, Ireland
Maxime Maria	Université de Limoges, France
Demetris Marnerides	University of Warwick, UK
Ricardo Marroquim	Delft University of Technology, The Netherlands
Nelson Max	University of California, USA
Miguel Melo	INESC TEC, Portugal
Daniel Mendes	INESC-ID, Portugal
Daniel Meneveaux	University of Poitiers, France
Paulo Menezes	Universidade de Coimbra, Portugal
Stéphane Mérillou	University of Limoges, France
José Molina Massó	Universidad de Castilla-La Mancha, Spain
Ramon Molla	Universitat Politècnica de València, Spain
Frederic Mora	Université de Limoges, France
David Mould	Carleton University, Canada
João Moura	Universidade de Trás-os-Montes e Alto Douro, Portugal
Adolfo Muñoz	Universidad de Zaragoza, Spain
Rui Nóbrega	Universidade Nova de Lisboa, Portugal
Jean-Marie Normand	Ecole Centrale de Nantes, France
Lidia M. Ortega	University of Jaén, Spain
Afonso Paiva	Universidade de São Paulo, Brazil
Georgios Papaioannou	Athens University of Economics and Business, Greece
Alexander Pasko	Bournemouth University, UK
Gustavo Patow	Universitat de Girona, Spain
Félix Paulano-Godino	University of Jaén, Spain
Aruquia Peixoto	CEFET/RJ, Brazil
João Pereira	INESC-ID, Portugal
João Pereira	Instituto Superior de Engenharia do Porto, Portugal
Sinésio Pesco	Pontifical Catholic University of Rio de Janeiro, Brazil
Christoph Peters	KIT, Germany
Adrien Peytavie	Claude Bernard University Lyon 1, France
Ruggero Pintus	Center for Advanced Studies, Research and Development in Sardinia, Italy
Paulo Pombinho	Universidade de Lisboa, Portugal

Tomislav Pribanic	University of Zagreb, Croatia
Anna Puig	University of Barcelona, Spain
Inmaculada Remolar	Universitat Jaume I, Spain
María Rivara	Universidad de Chile, Chile
Juan Roberto Jiménez	University of Jaén, Spain
Nuno Rodrigues	Polytechnic Institute of Leiria, Portugal
Rui Rodrigues	Universidade do Porto, Portugal
Inmaculada Rodríguez	University of Barcelona, Spain
Przemyslaw Rokita	Warsaw University of Technology, Poland
Teresa Romão	Universidade de Nova Lisboa, Portugal
Luís Romero	Instituto Politecnico de Viana do Castelo, Portugal
Isaac Rudomin	Barcelona Supercomputing Center, Spain
Antonio Rueda	University of Jaén, Spain
Holly Rushmeier	Yale University, USA
Beatriz Santos	University of Aveiro, Portugal
Luis Santos	Universidade do Minho, Portugal
Basile Sauvage	University of Strasbourg, France
Vladimir Savchenko	Hosei University, Japan
Mateu Sbert	Tianjin University, China/Universitat de Girona, Spain
Rafael J. Segura	Universidad de Jaen, Spain
Ricardo Sepulveda Marques	Universitat de Barcelona, Spain
Ana Serrano	Max Planck Institute for Informatics, Germany
Frutuoso Silva	University of Beira Interior, Portugal
Ching-Liang Su	Da-Yeh University, China
Domenico Tegolo	Università degli Studi di Palermo, Italy
Matthias Teschner	University of Freiburg, Germany
Daniel Thalmann	Ecole Polytechnique Federale de Lausanne, Switzerland
Juan Carlos Torres	Universidad de Granada, Spain
Torsten Ullrich	Fraunhofer Austria Research GmbH, Austria
Kuwait University	Kuwait University, Kuwait
Carlos Urbano	Instituto Politécnico de Leiria, Portugal
Anna Ursyn	University of Northern Colorado, USA
Cesare Valenti	Università degli Studi di Palermo, Italy
Andreas Weber	University of Bonn, Germany
Thomas Wischgoll	Wright State University, USA
Skapin Xavier	University of Poitiers, France
Ling Xu	University of Houston-Downtown, USA
Lihua You	Bournemouth University, UK
Rita Zrour	XLIM, France

GRAPP Additional Reviewers

Shaojun Bian	Bournemouth University, UK
Kan Chen	Fraunhofer Singapore, Singapore
Orlando Fonseca	Pontifical Catholic University of Rio de Janeiro, Brazil

Sandra Malpica	Universidad de Zaragoza, Spain
Bernardo Marques	Universidade de Aveiro, Portugal
Francisco Martinez-Gil	Universitat de Valencia, Spain
Viviana Vargas	Brazil
Shuangbu Wang	Bournemouth University, UK
Xingzi Zhang	Singapore

HUCAPP Program Committee

Andrea Abate	University of Salerno, Italy
Yacine Bellik	LIMSI-CNRS, France
Cigdem Beyan	Istituto Italiano di Tecnologia, Italy
Karlheinz Blankenbach	Pforzheim University, Germany
Leon Bodenhagen	University of Southern Denmark, Denmark
Federico Botella	Miguel Hernandez University of Elche, Spain
Eva Cerezo	University of Zaragoza, Spain
Mathieu Chollet	IMT Atlantique, France
Yang-Wai Chow	University of Wollongong, Australia
Cesar Collazos	Universidad del Cauca, Colombia
Damon Daylamani-Zad	Brunel University London, UK
Knut Drewing	Giessen University, Germany
Grégoire Dupont de Dinechin	Mines ParisTech, France
Marc Ernst	Ulm University, Germany
Tom Garner	University of Portsmouth, UK
Juan Enrique Garrido Navarro	University of Lleida, Spain
Valentina Gatteschi	Politecnico di Torino, Italy
Agostino Gibaldi	University of California, Berkeley, USA
Andrina Granic	University of Split, Croatia
Toni Granollers	University of Lleida, Spain
Michael Hobbs	Deakin University, Australia
Michael Hohl	Anhalt University of Applied Sciences, Germany
Wolfgang Hürst	Utrecht University, The Netherlands
Francisco Iniesto	The Open University, UK
Raja Jebasingh	St. Joseph's College of Commerce, Bangalore, India
Alvaro Joffre Uribe Quevedo	University of Ontario Institute of Technology, Canada
Ahmed Kamel	Concordia College, USA
Chee Weng Khong	Multimedia University, Malaysia
Suzanne Kieffer	Université catholique de Louvain, Belgium
Uttam Kokil	Kennesaw State University, USA
Fabrizio Lamberti	Politecnico di Torino, Italy
Chien-Sing Lee	Sunway University, Malaysia
Tsai-Yen Li	National Chengchi University, Taiwan, Republic of China

Régis Lobjois   IFSTTAR, France
Flamina Luccio   Università Ca' Foscari Venezia, Italy
Sergio Lujan Mora   Universidad de Alicante, Spain
José Macías Iglesias   Universidad Autónoma de Madrid, Spain
Guido Maiello   Justus Liebig University Gießen, Germany
Malik Mallem   Université Paris Saclay, France
Troy McDaniel   Arizona State University, USA
Vincenzo Moscato   Università degli Studi di Napoli Federico II, Italy
Ricardo Nakamura   University of São Paulo, Brazil
Keith Nesbitt   University of Newcastle, Australia
Luciano Ojeda   Groupe PSA, France
Nuno Otero   Linnaeus University, Sweden
Oskar Palinko   University of Southern Denmark, Denmark
Evangelos Papadopoulos   National Technical University of Athens, Greece
Florian Pecune   University of Glasgow, UK
Catherine Pelachaud   CNRS, University of Pierre and Marie Curie, France
James Phillips   Auckland University of Technology, New Zealand
Lev Poretski   University of Haifa, Israel
Otniel Portillo-Rodriguez   Universidad Autonóma del Estado de México, Mexico
Soraia Prietch   Universidade Federal de Mato Grosso, Brazil
Rafael Radkowski   Iowa State University, USA
Nitendra Rajput   IBM Research, India
Maria Lili Ramírez   Universidad del Quindío, Colombia
Brian Ravenet   LIMSI-CNRS, Université Paris-Saclay, France
Andreas Riener   Technische Hochschule Ingolstadt, Germany
Juha Röning   University of Oulu, Finland
Andrea Sanna   Politecnico di Torino, Italy
Trenton Schulz   Norwegian Computing Center, Norway
Alessandra Sciutti   Istituto Italiano di Tecnologia, Italy
Jouni Smed   University of Turku, Finland
Fabio Solari   University of Genoa, Italy
Daniel Thalmann   Ecole Polytechnique Federale de Lausanne,
                                 Switzerland
Gouranton Valérie   University of Rennes 1, INSA Rennes, Inria, CNRS,
                                 IRISA, France
Kostas Vlachos   University of Ioannina, Greece
Gualtiero Volpe   Università degli Studi di Genova, Italy
Yingcai Xiao   University of Akron, USA

HUCAPP Additional Reviewers

Flavien Lécuyer   INSA Rennes, France
Guillaume Vailland   University of Rennes 1, INSA Rennes, Inria, CNRS,
                                 IRISA, France

IVAPP Program Committee

Alfie Abdul-Rahman	King's College London, UK
George Baciu	Hong Kong Polytechnic University, Hong Kong
Juhee Bae	University of Skovde, Sweden
Ayan Biswas	Los Alamos National Laboratory, USA
David Borland	University of North Carolina at Chapel Hill, USA
Romain Bourqui	University of Bordeaux, France
Chris Bryan	Arizona State University, USA
Michael Burch	University of Applied Sciences of the Grisons, Switzerland
Maria Beatriz Carmo	Universidade de Lisboa, Portugal
Guoning Chen	University of Houston, USA
Yongwan Chun	University of Texas at Dallas, USA
António Coelho	Universidade do Porto, Portugal
Danilo B. Coimbra	Federal University of Bahia, Brazil
Celmar da Silva	University of Campinas, Brazil
Christoph Dalitz	Niederrhein University of Applied Sciences, Germany
Robertas Damasevicius	Kaunas University of Technology, Lithuania
Mihaela Dinsoreanu	Technical University of Cluj-Napoca, Romania
Georgios Dounias	University of the Aegean, Greece
Soumya Dutta	Los Alamos National Laboratory, USA
Achim Ebert	University of Kaiserslautern, Germany
Danilo Eler	São Paulo State University, Brazil
Kathrin Feige	Deutscher Wetterdienst, Germany
Maria Cristina Ferreira de Oliveira	University of São Paulo, Brazil
Enrico Gobbetti	CRS4, Italy
Randy Goebel	University of Alberta, Canada
Martin Graham	Edinburgh Napier University, UK
Robert Haining	Cambridge University, UK
Jan-Henrik Haunert	University of Bonn, Germany
Christian Heine	Leipzig University, Germany
Torsten Hopp	Karlsruhe Institute of Technology, Germany
Jie Hua	University of Technology Sydney, Australia
Takayuki Itoh	Ochanomizu University, Japan
Stefan Jänicke	University of Southern Denmark, Denmark
Bernhard Jenny	Monash University, Australia
Mark Jones	Swansea University, UK
Daniel Jönsson	Linköping University, Sweden
Ilir Jusufi	Linnaeus University, Sweden
Bijaya Karki	Louisiana State University, USA
Sehwan Kim	WorldViz LLC, USA
Steffen Koch	Universität Stuttgart, Germany
Martin Kraus	Aalborg University, Denmark
Michael Krone	University of Tübingen, Germany

Denis Lalanne	University of Fribourg, Switzerland
Haim Levkowitz	University of Massachusetts Lowell, USA
Giuseppe Liotta	University of Perugia, Italy
Rafael Martins	Linnaeus University, Sweden
Brescia Massimo	INAF, Italy
Krešimir Matkovic	VRVis Research Center, Austria
Eva Mayr	Danube University Krems, Austria
Wouter Meulemans	TU Eindhoven, The Netherlands
Kazuo Misue	University of Tsukuba, Japan
Martin Nöllenburg	TU Wien, Austria
Luis Nonato	Universidade de Sao Paulo, Brazil
Ingela Nystrom	Uppsala University, Sweden
Steffen Oeltze-Jafra	Otto-von-Guericke-Universität Magdeburg, Germany
Benoît Otjacques	Luxembourg Institute of Science and Technology, Luxembourg
Jinah Park	KAIST, South Korea
Fernando Paulovich	Dalhousie University, Canada
Torsten Reiners	Curtin University, Australia
Philip Rhodes	University of Mississippi, USA
Patrick Riehmann	Bauhaus-Universitaet Weimar, Germany
Maria Riveiro	University of Skövde, Sweden
Adrian Rusu	Fairfield University, USA
Filip Sadlo	Heidelberg University, Germany
Beatriz Santos	University of Aveiro, Portugal
Giuseppe Santucci	University of Roma, Italy
Angel Sappa	ESPOL Polytechnic University, Ecuador/Computer Vision Center, Spain
Falk Schreiber	University of Konstanz, Germany/Monash University, Australia
Marcos Serrano	University of Toulouse, France
Juergen Symanzik	Utah State University, USA
Roberto Theron	Universidad de Salamanca, Spain
Christian Tominski	University of Rostock, Germany
Thomas van Dijk	Ruhr-Universität Bochum, Germany
Romain Vuillemot	LIRIS, France
Yunhai Wang	Shandong University, China
Gunther Weber	Lawrence Berkeley National Laboratory/University of California, Davis, USA
Zeng Wei	Shenzhen Institute of Advanced Technology, Chinese Academy of Sciences, China
Jinrong Xie	University of California, Davis, USA
Hsu-Chun Yen	National Taiwan University, Taiwan, Republic of China
Lina Yu	Intel Corporation, USA
Jianping Zeng	Microsoft, USA
Yue Zhang	Oregon State University, USA

IVAPP Additional Reviewers

Subhajit Chakrabarty   University of Massachusetts Lowell, USA
Paulo Dias   Universidade de Aveiro, Portugal

VISAPP Program Committee

Amr Abdel-Dayem   Laurentian University, Canada
Ilya Afanasyev   Innopolis University, Russia
Zahid Akhtar   University of Memphis, USA
Vicente Alarcon-Aquino   Universidad de las Americas Puebla, Mexico
Hamid Al-Asadi   Iraq University College, Iraq
Enrique Alegre   Universidad de Leon, Spain
Hesham Ali   University of Nebraska at Omaha, USA
Dario Allegra   University of Catania, Italy
Hugo Alvarez   Vicomtech, Spain
Pierluigi Vito Amadori   Imperial College London, UK
Petre Anghelescu   University of Pitesti, Romania
Karm Veer Arya   ABV-Indian Institute of Information Technology
    and Management, India
Giuseppe Baruffa   University of Perugia, Italy
Ariel Bayá   CONICET, Argentina
Ardhendu Behera   Edge Hill University, UK
Anna Belardinelli   Honda Research Institute, Germany
Fabio Bellavia   Università degli Studi di Firenze, Italy
Stefano Berretti   University of Florence, Italy
Simone Bianco   University of Milano-Bicocca, Italy
Adrian Bors   University of York, UK
Larbi Boubchir   University of Paris 8, France
Thierry Bouwmans   Université de La Rochelle, France
Lubomír Brancík   Brno University of Technology, Czech Republic
Marius Brezovan   University of Craiova, Romania
Valentin Brimkov   State University of New York, USA
Alfred Bruckstein   Technion, Israel
Arcangelo Bruna   STMicroelectronics, Italy
Vittoria Bruni   Sapienza University of Rome, Italy
Giedrius Burachas   SRI International, USA
Adrian Burlacu   Gheorghe Asachi Technical University of Iasi,
    Romania
Humberto Bustince   Public University of Navarra, Spain
Marco Buzzelli   University of Milano-Bicocca, Italy
Gour C. Karmakar   Federation University Australia, Australia
Alice Caplier   GIPSA-lab, France
Franco Alberto Cardillo   Consiglio Nazionale delle Ricerche, Italy
Dario Cazzato   Université du Luxembourg, Luxembourg
Oya Celiktutan   King's College London, UK

David Fofi   Université de Bourgogne, France
Gian Foresti   University of Udine, Italy
Mohamed Fouad   Military Technical College, Egypt
Antonino Furnari   University of Catania, Italy
Raghudeep Gadde   Max Planck Institute for Intelligent Systems, Germany
Ignazio Gallo   University of Insubria, Italy
Juan Francisco Garamendi   Universitat Pompeu Fabra, Spain
Alba Garcia Seco De   University of Essex, UK
  Herrera
Antonios Gasteratos   Democritus University of Thrace, Greece
Claudio Gennaro   Consiglio Nazionale delle Ricerche, Italy
Riccardo Gherardi   Amazon.com, USA
Enjie Ghorbel   University of Luxembourg, Luxembourg
Dimitris Giakoumis   CERTH-ITI, Aristotle University of Thessaloniki,
                                  Greece
Valerio Giuffrida   Edinburgh Napier University, UK
Herman Gomes   Universidade Federal de Campina Grande, Brazil
Lluis Gomez   Universitat Autònoma de Barcelona, Spain
Luiz Goncalves   Federal University of Rio Grande do Norte, Brazil
Amr Goneid   American University in Cairo, Egypt
Manuel González-Hidalgo   Balearic Islands University, Spain
Nikos Grammalidis   Centre of Research and Technology Hellas, Greece
Michael Greenspan   Queen's University, Canada
Christiaan Gribble   SURVICE Engineering, USA
Kaiwen Guo   Google, China
Levente Hajder   Eötvös Loránd University, Hungary
Daniel Harari   Weizmann Institute of Science, Israel
Walid Hariri   ETIS ENSEA, Université de Cergy Pontoise, France
Irtiza Hasan   Inception Institute of Artificial Intelligence, UAE
Aymeric Histace   ETIS/CNRS, France
Wladyslaw Homenda   Warsaw University of Technology, Poland
Binh-Son Hua   VinAI Research, Vietnam
Hui-Yu Huang   National Formosa University, Taiwan,
                                  Republic of China
Laura Igual   Universitat de Barcelona, Spain
Francisco Imai   Apple Inc., USA
Jiri Jan   University of Technology Brno, Czech Republic
Tatiana Jaworska   Polish Academy of Sciences, Poland
Xiaoyi Jiang   University of Münster, Germany
Soon Ki Jung   Kyungpook National University, South Korea
Paris Kaimakis   University of Central Lancashire, Cyprus
Martin Kampel   Vienna University of Technology, Austria
Kenichi Kanatani   Okayama University, Japan
Benjamin Kenwright   Heriot-Watt University, UK
Etienne Kerre   Ghent University, Belgium
Anastasios Kesidis   University of West Attica, Greece

Sehwan Kim   WorldViz LLC, USA
Seungryong Kim   École Polytechnique Fédérale de Lausanne,
                               Switzerland
Nahum Kiryati   Tel Aviv University, Israel
Sinan Kockara   University of Central Arkansas, USA
Mario Köppen   Kyushu Institute of Technology, Japan
Andrey Kopylov   Tula State University, Russia
Adam Kortylewski   Johns Hopkins University, USA
Constantine Kotropoulos   Aristotle University of Thessaloniki, Greece
Gurunandan Krishnan   Snap Inc, USA
Martin Sagayam   Karunya Institute of Technology and Sciences, India
  Kulandairaj
Martin Lambers   University of Siegen, Germany
Slimane Larabi   University of Science and Technology Houari
                               Boumediene, Algeria
Mónica Larese   CIFASIS-CONICET, National University of Rosario,
                               Argentina
Denis Laurendeau   Laval University, Canada
Isah A. Lawal   Noroff University College, Norway
Marco Leo   Consiglio Nazionale delle Ricerche, Italy
Huei-Yung Lin   National Chung Cheng University, Taiwan,
                               Republic of China
Xiuwen Liu   Florida State University, USA
Giosue Lo Bosco   Università di Palermo, Italy
Liliana Lo Presti   University of Palermo, Italy
Angeles López   Universitat Jaume I, Spain
Cristina Losada-Gutiérrez   University of Alcalá, Spain
Bruno Macchiavello   Universidade de Brasilia, Brazil
Ilias Maglogiannis   University of Piraeus, Greece
Baptiste Magnier   LGI2P, École des mines d'Alès, France
Clement Mallet   LaSTIG, IGN, France
Francesco Marcelloni   University of Pisa, Italy
Lucio Marcenaro   University of Genoa, Italy
Letizia Marchegiani   Aalborg University, Denmark
Emmanuel Marilly   Nokia Bell Labs, France
Marta Marrón-Romera   Alcalá University, Spain
Jean Martinet   University Cote d'Azur/CNRS, France
José Martínez Sotoca   Universitat Jaume I, Spain
Mitsuharu Matsumoto   University of Electro-Communications, Japan
Stephen McKenna   University of Dundee, UK
Javier Melenchón   Universitat Oberta de Catalunya, Spain
Mohamed Arezki Mellal   M'Hamed Bougara University, Algeria
Thomas Mensink   University of Amsterdam, The Netherlands
Radko Mesiar   Slovak University of Technology, Slovak Republic
Leonid Mestetskiy   Lomonosov Moscow State University, Russia
Cyrille Migniot   ImViA, Université de Bourgogne, France

Dan Mikami	NTT, Japan
Steven Mills	University of Otago, New Zealand
Filippo Milotta	University of Catania, Italy
Pedro Miraldo	Instituto Superior Técnico, Lisboa, Portugal
Sanya Mitaim	Thammasat University, Thailand
Pradit Mittrapiyanuruk	Autodesk, Singapore
Birgit Moeller	Martin Luther University Halle-Wittenberg, Germany
Davide Moltisanti	Nanyang Technological University, Singapore
Bartolomeo Montrucchio	Politecnico di Torino, Italy
Davide Moroni	ISTI-CNR, Italy
Peter Morovic	HP Inc., Spain
Kostantinos Moustakas	University of Patras, Greece
Dmitry Murashov	Federal Research Center "Computer Science and Control" of Russian Academy of Sciences, Russian Federation
Armin Mustafa	University of Surrey, UK
Paolo Napoletano	University of Milano-Bicocca, Italy
Shah Nawaz	University of Insubria, Italy
Benjamin Niedermann	University of Bonn, Germany
Mikael Nilsson	Lund University, Sweden
Shohei Nobuhara	Kyoto University, Japan
Nicoletta Noceti	Università di Genova, Italy
Dimitri Ognibene	Università degli studi di Milano-Bicocca, Italy/University of Essex, UK
Yoshihiro Okada	Kyushu University, Japan
Félix Paulano-Godino	University of Jaén, Spain
Marius Pedersen	Norwegian University of Science and Technology, Norway
Francisco José Perales	University of the Balearic Islands, Spain
Fabio Poiesi	Fondazione Bruno Kessler, Italy
Stephen Pollard	HP Labs, UK
Vijayakumar Ponnusamy	SRM IST, Kattankulathur, India
Charalambos Poullis	Concordia University, Canada
Antonis Protopsaltis	University of Western Macedonia, Greece
Giovanni Puglisi	University of Cagliari, Italy
Naoufal Raissouni	ENSA Tétouan, University of Abdelmalek Essaadi, Morocco
Giuliana Ramella	IAC-CNR, Italy
Francesco Rea	Istituto Italiano di Tecnologia, Italy
Ana Reis	Instituto de Ciências Biomédicas Abel Salazar, Portugal
Joao Rodrigues	University of the Algarve, Portugal
Marcos Rodrigues	Sheffield Hallam University, UK
Juha Röning	University of Oulu, Finland
Paolo Rota	Istituto Italiano di Tecnologia, Italy
Ramón Ruiz	Universidad Politécnica de Cartagena, Spain

Silvio Sabatini	University of Genoa, Italy
Farhang Sahba	Sheridan Institute of Technology and Advanced Learning, Canada
Ovidio Salvetti	National Research Council of Italy, Italy
Andreja Samcovic	University of Belgrade, Serbia
Enver Sangineto	University of Trento, Italy
K. C. Santosh	University of South Dakota, USA
Nickolas Sapidis	University of Western Macedonia, Greece
Yann Savoye	Liverpool John Moores University, UK
Gerald Schaefer	Loughborough University, UK
Raimondo Schettini	University of Milano-Bicocca, Italy
Siniša Šegvic	University of Zagreb, Croatia
Kazim Sekeroglu	Southeastern Louisiana University, USA
Jean Sequeira	University of Aix-Marseille, France
Oleg Seredin	Tula State University, Russia
Désiré Sidibé	Université d'Évry-Val-d'Essonne, France
Luciano Silva	Universidade Federal do Parana, Brazil
Seppo Sirkemaa	University of Turku, Finland
Robert Sitnik	Warsaw University of Technology, Poland
Bogdan Smolka	Silesian University of Technology, Poland
Ferdous Sohel	Murdoch University, Australia
Ömer Soysal	Southeastern Louisiana University, USA
Filippo Stanco	Università di Catania, Italy
Liana Stanescu	University of Craiova, Romania
Tania Stathaki	Imperial College London, UK
Mu-Chun Su	National Central University, Taiwan, Republic of China
Girmaw Tadesse	University of Oxford, UK
Ryszard Tadeusiewicz	AGH University of Science and Technology, Poland
Norio Tagawa	Tokyo Metropolitan University, Japan
Domenico Tegolo	Università degli Studi di Palermo, Italy
Yubing Tong	University of Pennsylvania, USA
Ricardo Torres	Norwegian University of Science and Technology, Norway
Andrea Torsello	Università Ca' Foscari di Venezia, Italy
Carlos Travieso-González	Universidad de Las Palmas de Gran Canaria, Spain
Vinh Truong Hoang	Ho Chi Minh City Open University, Vietnam
Du-Ming Tsai	Yuan-Ze University, Taiwan, Republic of China
Aristeidis Tsitiridis	University Rey Juan Carlos, Spain
Cesare Valenti	Università degli Studi di Palermo, Italy
Javier Varona	Universitat de les Illes Balears, Spain
Francisco Vasconcelos	University College London, UK
Javier Vazquez-Corral	University Pompeu Fabra, Spain
Panayiotis Vlamos	Ionian University, Greece
Frank Wallhoff	Jade University of Applied Science, Germany
Tao Wang	BAE Systems, USA

Wen-June Wang	National Central University, Taiwan, Republic of China
Layne Watson	Virginia Polytechnic Institute and State University, USA
Quan Wen	University of Electronic Science and Technology of China, China
Laurent Wendling	Paris Descartes University, France
Christian Wöhler	TU Dortmund, Germany
Stefan Wörz	University of Heidelberg, Germany
Yan Wu	Georgia Southern University, USA
Keiji Yanai	University of Electro-Communications, Tokyo, Japan
Alper Yilmaz	Ohio State University, USA
Sebastian Zambanini	TU Wien, Austria
Pietro Zanuttigh	University of Padua, Italy
Jie Zhang	Newcastle University, UK
Huiyu Zhou	Queen's University Belfast, UK
Yun Zhu	University of California, San Diego, USA
Zhigang Zhu	City College of New York, USA
Peter Zolliker	Empa, Swiss Federal Laboratories for Materials Science and Technology, Switzerland
Ju Zou	University of Western Sydney, Australia

VISAPP Additional Reviewers

Gerasimos Arvanitis	University of Patras, Greece
Kai Brandenbusch	TU Dortmund, Germany
Daniel Helm	TU Wien, Austria
Dominik Kossmann	TU Dortmund, Germany
Xiao Lin	Vicomtech, Spain
As Mansur	Kyushu University, Japan
Marcos Quintana	Vicomtech, Spain
Fernando Rueda	Technische Universität Dortmund, Germany
Eugen Rusakov	TU Dortmund, Germany
Nikos Stagakis	University of Patras, Greece
Thorsten Wilhelm	TU Dortmund University, Germany
Fabian Wolf	TU Dortmund, Germany

Invited Speakers

Matthias Niessner	Technical University of Munich, Germany
Anthony Steed	University College London, UK
Alan Chalmers	University of Warwick, UK
Helen Purchase	University of Glasgow, UK

Contents

Computer Graphics Theory and Applications

Unified Model and Framework for Interactive Mixed Entity Systems. 3
    Guillaume Bataille, Valérie Gouranton, Jérémy Lacoche, Danielle Pelé,
    and Bruno Arnaldi

Skeleton-and-Trackball Interactive Rotation Specification for 3D Scenes 26
    Xiaorui Zhai, Xingyu Chen, Lingyun Yu, and Alexandru Telea

CSG Tree Extraction from 3D Point Clouds and Meshes Using
a Hybrid Approach 53
    Markus Friedrich, Steffen Illium, Pierre-Alain Fayolle,
    and Claudia Linnhoff-Popien

Human Computer Interaction Theory and Applications

Intention Understanding for Human-Aware Mobile Robots: Comparing
Cues and the Effect of Demographics 83
    Oskar Palinko, Eduardo Ruiz Ramirez, Norbert Krüger,
    and Leon Bodenhagen

Tracking Eye Movement for Controlling Real-Time
Image-Abstraction Techniques 103
    Maximilian Söchting and Matthias Trapp

Information Visualization Theory and Applications

Improving Deep Learning Projections by Neighborhood Analysis 127
    Terri S. Modrakowski, Mateus Espadoto, Alexandre X. Falcão,
    Nina S. T. Hirata, and Alexandru Telea

Scalable Visual Exploration of 3D Shape Databases via Feature Synthesis
and Selection 153
    Xingyu Chen, Guangping Zeng, Jiří Kosinka, and Alexandru Telea

Visual Analysis of Linked Musicological Data with the *musiXplora* 183
    Richard Khulusi, Josef Focht, and Stefan Jänicke

A Research-Teaching Guide for Visual Data Analysis
in Digital Humanities. 205
    Stefan Jänicke

Coherent Topological Landscapes for Simulation Ensembles   223
    Marina Evers, Maria Herick, Vladimir Molchanov, and Lars Linsen

Computer Vision Theory and Applications

Efficient Range Sensing Using Imperceptible Structured Light   241
    Avery Cole, Sheikh Ziauddin, Jonathon Malcolm,
    and Michael Greenspan

Hierarchical Object Detection and Classification Using SSD Multi-Loss.   268
    Matthijs H. Zwemer, Rob G. J. Wijnhoven, and Peter H. N. de With

Scene Text Localization Using Lightweight Convolutional Networks.   297
    Luis Gustavo Lorgus Decker, Allan Pinto, Jose Luis Flores Campana,
    Manuel Cordova Neira, Andreza Aparecida dos Santos,
    Jhonatas Santos de Jesus Conceição, Helio Pedrini,
    Marcus de Assis Angeloni, Lin Tzy Li, Diogo Carbonera Luvizon,
    and Ricardo da S. Torres

Early Stopping for Two-Stream Fusion Applied to Action Recognition   319
    Helena de Almeida Maia, Marcos Roberto e Souza,
    Anderson Carlos Sousa e Santos, Julio Cesar Mendoza Bobadilla,
    Marcelo Bernardes Vieira, and Helio Pedrini

RGB-D Images Based 3D Plant Growth Prediction by Sequential
Images-to-Images Translation with Plant Priors.   334
    Tomohiro Hamamoto, Hideaki Uchiyama, Atsushi Shimada,
    and Rin-ichiro Taniguchi

ConvPoseCNN2: Prediction and Refinement of Dense 6D Object Pose   353
    Arul Selvam Periyasamy, Catherine Capellen, Max Schwarz,
    and Sven Behnke

Expression Modeling Using Dynamic Kernels for Quantitative Assessment
of Facial Paralysis.   372
    Nazil Perveen, Chalavadi Krishna Mohan, and Yen Wei Chen

Perceptually-Informed No-Reference Image Harmonisation.   394
    Alan Dolhasz, Carlo Harvey, and Ian Williams

On-board UAV Pilots Identification in Counter UAV Images   414
    Dario Cazzato, Claudio Cimarelli, and Holger Voos

Exploring Tele-Assistance for Cyber-Physical Systems with MAUI.   431
    Philipp Fleck, Fernando Reyes-Aviles, Christian Pirchheim,
    Clemens Arth, and Dieter Schmalstieg

On the Use of 3D CNNs for Video Saliency Modeling   453
   Yasser Abdelaziz Dahou Djilali, Mohamed Sayah, Kevin McGuinness,
   and Noel E. O'Connor

CNN-Based Deblurring of THz Time-Domain Images   477
   Marina Ljubenović, Shabab Bazrafkan, Pavel Paramonov,
   Jan De Beenhouwer, and Jan Sijbers

Thermal Image Super-Resolution: A Novel Unsupervised Approach   495
   Rafael E. Rivadeneira, Angel D. Sappa, and Boris X. Vintimilla

Regression Based 3D Hand Pose Estimation for Human-Robot Interaction . . .   507
   Chaitanya Bandi and Ulrike Thomas

Detection and Recognition of Barriers in Egocentric Images for Safe
Urban Sidewalks   530
   Zenonas Theodosiou, Harris Partaourides, Simoni Panayi,
   Andreas Kitsis, and Andreas Lanitis

Correction to: Regression-Based 3D Hand Pose Estimation for
Human-Robot Interaction C1
   Chaitanya Bandi and Ulrike Thomas

Author Index   545

Computer Graphics Theory and Applications

Unified Model and Framework for Interactive Mixed Entity Systems

Guillaume Bataille[1,2(✉)] , Valérie Gouranton[2], Jérémy Lacoche[1], Danielle Pelé[1],
and Bruno Arnaldi[2]

[1] Orange Labs, Cesson Sévigné, France
guillaume2.bataille@orange.com
[2] Univ. Rennes, INSA Rennes, Inria, CNRS, IRISA, Rennes, France

Abstract. Mixed reality, natural user interfaces, and the internet of things converge towards an advanced sort of interactive system. These systems enable new forms of interactivity, allowing intuitive user interactions with ubiquitous services in mixed environments. However, they require to synchronize multiple platforms and various technologies. Their heterogeneity makes them complex, and sparsely interoperable or extensible. Therefore, designers and developers require new models, tools, and methodologies to support their creation. We present a unified model of the entities composing these systems, breaking them down into graphs of mixed entities. This model decorrelates real and virtual but still describes their interplay. It characterizes and classifies both the external and internal interactions of mixed entities. We also present a design and implementation framework based on our unified model. Our framework takes advantage of our model to simplify, accelerate, and unify the production of these systems. We showcase the use of our framework by designers and developers in the case of a smart building management system.

Keywords: Human-machine interaction · Mixed reality · Natural user interfaces · Internet of things · Mixed interactive systems

1 Introduction

This paper is the sequel of the paper [3] by G. Bataille et al. describing how the DOMIM model and its associated framework support the design and implementation of mixed interactive systems combining mixed reality, natural user interfaces and the internet of things. This revised version introduces the expression *interactive mixed entity system* for convenience, provides additional Figures, and a partial rewriting of the different sections to improve their consistency, update, or clarify them.

In this paper, we aim to enhance the design and implementation of interactive systems blending the paradigms of mixed reality (MR), natural user interfaces (NUI), and the internet of things (IoT). Mixed Interactive Systems (MIS) [12] combine mixed reality, tangible user interfaces, and ambient intelligence. The systems we study are a meta-class of MIS that we name inTeractive mIxed Entity Systems (TIES): NUI does not only cover tangible user interfaces but also gestures, vocal assistants, haptic devices, etc. Also, instead of ambient intelligence, we consider the IoT domain, and more specifically its attempt to connect real entities through the internet (see Fig. 1).

K. Bouatouch et al. (Eds.): VISIGRAPP 2020, CCIS 1474, pp. 3–25, 2022.
https://doi.org/10.1007/978-3-030-94893-1_1

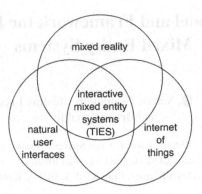

Fig. 1. The Venn diagram of interactive mixed entity systems.

TIES offer new ways for humans to interact with their environment. MR allows users to simultaneously interact with collocated real and virtual worlds. As a part of MR, NUI use the human body as an interface to mediate intuitive interactions with a virtual environment. The IoT provides ubiquitous services to their users. These paradigms are converging to bridge the gap between real and virtual. NUI combined with the IoT are common in our everyday lives. As an example, voice assistants are becoming mainstream products. MR associated to IoT allow users to see the virtual twin of connected objects. Beyond the coupling of NUI and the IoT, MR can inform us about the mixed objects surrounding us. MR could inform us of a broken part of a smart car, how to repair it and help us to order the required spare parts and tools that we are missing.

Blending these domains is still in its infancy and limited to prototypes and proofs of concept. Current techniques like tracking or object recognition constrain this convergence. Their limitations are also due to a lack of dedicated tools. We need to drive the production of TIES from handmade prototypes towards industrial processes. As a contribution, we present in this paper a framework to design and implement TIES. We base this framework on our unified model that we name as the design-oriented mixed-reality internal model (DOMIM). Our DOMIM-based framework offers design and implementation tools to create these systems. Its benefits are simplicity, reusability, flexibility, and swiftness.

In the next section, we present MR, NUI, and the IoT, and work related to hybrid interactions blending these domains. The third section presents our unified model. The fourth section describes our design and implementation framework based on it. The fifth section describes the development of a scenario with our framework to validate our approach. This use case is a smart building TIES for occupants and building managers.

2   Related Work

In this section, we first define MR, NUI, and the IoT as research domains. Then we present work related to hybrid interactive systems blending these domains.

2.1   MR, NUI and the IoT

In 1994 Milgram and Kishino coin the term *Mixed reality* [27] and describe it as "a particular subset of Virtual Reality related technologies that involve the merging of real and virtual worlds somewhere along the "virtuality continuum" which connects completely real environments to completely virtual ones". The Fig. 2 presents the Virtuality Continuum. The Virtuality Continuum is widely used to define Mixed Reality.

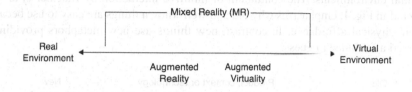

Fig. 2. The Virtuality Continuum (VC) [27].

MR is provided for Coutrix et al. by mixed reality systems composed of mixed objects [10]. A mixed object is composed of a real part described by its physical properties, and a digital part described by its digital properties. A loop synchronizes both parts, as presented in Fig. 3. Current technologies cap this synchronization by restricting the capture of physical properties and the actuation of digital properties.

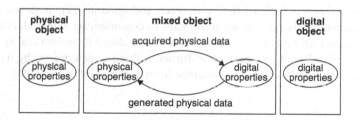

Fig. 3. Based on [10], this figure presents how mixed objects synchronize both their real and virtual properties [3].

Natural user interfaces exploit the human body as an interface to interact with digital content. They address skills that humans acquired since their birth while interacting with the real world [5]. NUI mediate interactions between humans and the virtual by mimicking interactions between humans and their real environment. Sensors track human activity, while actuators render virtual properties [24]. The main interaction modalities used by NUI are vision, voice recognition, and synthesis, touch, haptics, or body motion. For example, users can command voice assistants by speech to listen to music, or manipulate a virtual object by captured gestures. NUI provide what we call in this paper pseudo-natural interactions since they partially succeed in reproducing natural interactions [31].

A key factor of a NUI success is its short learning curve. Users need NUI to be intuitive to adopt them. Gibson [14] defined affordances as: "The affordances of the environment are what it offers the animal, what it provides or furnishes, either for good or ill". Norman clarified this concept by defining affordance as related to the perceived actionable properties of a thing which define its potential uses [29]. Physical affordances are affordances emitted by the physical part of an object. Perceived affordances are generated by rendered feedbacks in charge of providing meaningful cues to potential users [30]. They are both crucial for humans to behave in a mixed environment since they make sense of what we perceive. Therefore, NUI mediate the perceived affordance of virtual environments. The continuum of intuitive interaction by Blackler et al. [4], presented in Fig. 4, emphasizes why old and well-known things are easy to use because of their physical affordance. In contrast, new things use new metaphors providing a perceived affordance to guess.

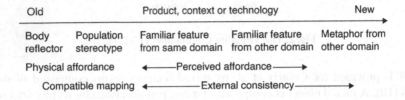

Fig. 4. The continuum of intuitive interaction by Blackler et al. [4].

The Atzori et al. framework provides a Venn diagram based on the core aspects of the *internet of things*, which are things, internet, and semantic [2], as shown in Fig. 5. Semantic provides to things a common language to communicate with each other, while internet furnishes networking capabilities and things afford their own reality by communication channels and languages. For Turner, a thing is determined by its practice while its practice is induced by its affordance from a user point of view [35].

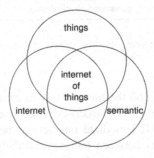

Fig. 5. The internet of things paradigm by Atzori and al. [2].

The IoT connects the physical and digital worlds and transduces their properties to interact with humans [16]. Diverse network services and protocols, like the Z-Wave protocol[1], enable and normalize their network communications.

---

[1] https://z-wavealliance.org/.

Grieves introduced in 2002 the digital twin concept as part of the internet of things in the context of smart and connected product systems [17]. A digital twin is a digital clone of a real product, its physical twin. Both twins are interconnected [15] to provide supervision and control of the physical twin to manufacturers and users [17].

2.2 Hybrid Interactions

In this section, we first introduce software development kits which are useful for the implementation of TIES. Secondly, we study and compare smart building prototypes exploring new interaction techniques. Thirdly, we present models and frameworks aiming at creating MIS more efficiently.

Software Development Kits. Multiple software development kits are available for MR, NUI, and the IoT. They provide developers with an implementation of complex techniques. For example, ARCore[2], ARKit[3] or MixedRealityTookit[4] enable an easy integration of SLAM algorithms [26] in MR applications. They are useful to implement TIES since they save time by providing implemented high-end techniques. However, they do not offer any design or implementation framework and are generally platform-specific.

Smart Building Prototypes. Lin et al. [23] present the Ubii system. This system allows users to command smart devices like a printer with monocular augmented reality goggles. These goggles do not self-locate in their environment. Interaction consists in focusing his gaze on a smart object and interacting with a graphical user interface to control it. This interaction technique allows distant interactions. However, monoscopic goggles bind the perception of the virtual. Furthermore, pointing an infrared beamer to a smart object sensor rapidly becomes difficult when the distance between the user and the smart object grows.

Alce et al. [1] present three interaction techniques combining gaze and hand gestures to control a smart building with an augmented reality device, an optical see-through head-mounted display (OST-HMD). The first technique places icons over real connected objects. The second one is a world in miniature application, displaying the virtual twin of a smart room. The third is a floating menu located over connected objects. All interaction techniques rely on the air-tap technique provided by default by Hololens and only vary in the metaphor used to represent and control connected objects.

Kim et al. [21] study intuitive interactions between a user wearing an OST-HMD and an incarnated smart assistant. The user controls different connected objects in his neighborhood by gesture, voice, or locomotion. But incarnated smart assistants do not provide mixed affordance of connected objects, and the user must know the connected objects he can interact with.

Uimmonen et al. [36] present a mobile augmented reality system enabling the user to interact with a smart building. A large part of their contribution consists in locating

---

[2] https://developers.google.com/ar/.

[3] https://developer.apple.com/augmented-reality/arkit/.

[4] https://github.com/Microsoft/MixedRealityToolkit-Unity.

their system inside the building. This system allows the control of temperature or air-conditioning and shows the convenience of such a system. But natural and pseudo-natural interaction techniques are not exposed or challenged.

The described interaction techniques reduce the gap between virtual and real in the case of smart buildings. They transparently melt virtual and real and enhance the intuitiveness of interactions between users and smart buildings. As a result, they not only provide a more efficient and natural interaction with connected objects but also simplify access to ubiquitous services. These proofs of concept showcase the relevance of TIES. Nevertheless, they are handmade and produce non-reusable and non-interoperable prototypes.

Models and Frameworks. Existing models and frameworks support the design and implementation of interactive systems. They establish methodologies to produce them more efficiently and rapidly. We use the following criterias to compare them:

- real/virtual synchronization: required by both MR and IoT. Both paradigms link real and virtual, MR from the user point of view and IoT from a network perspective,
- distinction between real and virtual: not separating real and virtual is a major source of confusion for designers, developers and users,
- software component libraries dedicated to MR, NUI and the IoT. These tools, which are partly available as mentioned in Sect. 2.2, are important for cost-saving and homogenization during the implementation phase,
- flexibility: this aspect is important to interoperate and extend interactive systems. Flexible systems can adapt to different contexts and environments, and interconnect with other systems for a low cost.

Graphical User Interface Design Models.
These models consider an interface as a composition of interactive objects. The Model-View-Controller (MVC) model [37] and the Presentation-Abstraction-Control (PAC) model [9] date from the 1980s. Each interactive object presents to users its internal state and allows them to operate on this state [18]. MVC separates models, data views, and the controller in charge of user actions. PAC also considers three concepts. Presentation is in charge of user interactions. Abstraction manages data and system functions. Controller links presentation and abstraction. Nevertheless, these models are inappropriate to describe human-machine interactions with mixed environments. They do not distinguish real and virtual.

More recently, approaches like Lacoche et al. [22] propose a model and tools based on PAC to simulate and implement ubiquitous environments combined with virtual reality. Unfortunately, they are not suitable for MR and are therefore not applicable to TIES.

Design and Implementation Frameworks for MIS.
MacWilliams et al. [25] present the DWARF framework. This framework aims at prototyping and offering a connected implementation process. It uses a Petri net editor to implement the behavior of each user interface composing a mixed interactive system. Nevertheless, it does not offer a unified model of these entities or any design framework and is not suitable for TIES creation.

Jacob et al. [19] present a descriptive framework dedicated to the design of new interactions. This is a set of thematic recommendations aiming to understand, compare, and describe emerging interactions. Covered themes are knowledge, physics laws management, body and environment knowledge, and sociability. These recommendations can be useful for designers but do not provide any design model, methodology, or tool.

Dubois et al. [11] propose a model-driven framework for the design of mixed interactive systems. A model graph describing a MIS merges multiple models of this MIS. Models must respect a metamodel that defines modeling rules and syntax. This framework does not provide a unified model of the entities composing a MIS neither describes the behavioral mechanisms of these entities.

Bouzekri et al. [7] present a generic architecture of MIS. It considers user interaction, user interfaces, and a behavioral model of an interface. However, it does not separate real and virtual neither describe their specific behavior. It does not propose any unified model of the different entities composing an interactive system.

Pfeiffer et al. [32] propose a design framework of TIES. It simulates TIES prototypes in virtual reality based on a 360° panoramic picture of a real environment including connected objects. The resulting prototypes can be tested in a simulation of their future environment. Resulting prototypes still require to get implemented.

Implementation Frameworks for the IoT.
Kelaidonis et al. [20] present a framework aiming at virtualizing real objects and managing the cognition of the resulting virtual objects. It combines the virtual objects' functionalities to reply to service requests by users. Virtual objects can recognize a context and decide how to behave depending on it. This approach of the real/virtual interplay is based on semantic in an IoT context. Nevertheless, user interactions are not covered.

Nitti et al. [28] study how virtual objects became a core aspect of the IoT. They are essential to the discovery of connected objects and to service characterization. They are also crucial to complexity and heterogeneity management, and to the scalability of the IoT. However, this study does not cover NUI (Table 1).

Table 1. Comparison between models and frameworks for systems partly similar to TIES [3].

Travaux	Real/virtual synchronization	Real/virtual decorrelation	Platform templates	MR/NUI/IoT libraries	Flexibility
MacWilliams et al. 2003	Yes	Yes	No	No	Static
Kelaidonis et al. 2012	Yes	Yes	No	No	Dynamic
Dubois et al. 2014	Yes	Yes	No	No	Dynamic
Nitti et al. 2016	Yes	Yes	No	No	No
Bouzekri et al. 2018	Yes	No	No	No	No
Pfeiffer et al. 2018	Simulated	Simulated	No	No	No
Lacoche et al. 2019	Yes	Yes	No	No	Static

No related work entirely addresses our modeling and implementation methodology issues for TIES. Still, they present partial clues for partly similar interactive systems. We conclude that no model or framework is currently dedicated to the design and implementation of TIES. We need a model unifying MR, NUI, and the IoT in order to create such a framework and its tools.

3   The Design-Oriented Mixed-Reality Internal Model

TIES are complex to design and implement. This complexity is raising because of the growing amount and the heterogeneity of available NUI combined with the expansion of the IoT. We need to create abstractions, methods, and tools to support TIES design and implementation. We require new models to produce these tools. Our approach consists in providing a common model for NUI, MR, and the IoT. We propose to name this model the design-oriented mixed-reality internal model (DOMIM). We also introduce a framework for designers and developers based on this model.

The resulting framework models a TIES into a graph of interconnected entities. We can split this graph into sub-graphs in order to break the complexity of a TIES. Entities are supported by applications running on different platforms. Each supported platform benefits from an application template. Pre-implemented components are provided by it. They are required during the implementation of TIES including during the integration of available SDKs. This methodology provides simplicity, reusability, flexibility, and swiftness from design to implementation. In the next section, we describe our mixed entity model step by step, before interactions between mixed entities.

3.1   Mixed Entities

MR, NUI, and the IoT mix virtual and real. MR blends real and virtual from a user-centric point of view. NUI mediate intuitive interactions between humans and virtual entities. The IoT allows ubiquitous services. We need to define a transparent relation between the real and the virtual, suitable for MR, NUI, and the IoT.

We first introduce the external model of a mixed entity. This model is composed of a real and a virtual part. Each part behaves in its environment. This model, presented in Fig. 6, is suitable for the entities composing a TIES. These entities are typically users, NUI, and connected objects. Each environment is characterized by specific rules. Both parts of a mixed entity are therefore complementary. This model is useful to decorrelate the virtual and the real properties of a mixed entity. This decorrelation is useful to describe how these properties evolve in their own environment. For example, a virtual fan can get turned on if a humanoid switches it on. And a user can start a fan by pressing its power button.

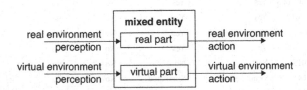

Fig. 6. The mixed entity external model is composed of a real part and a virtual part. Both parts interact with their environment.

The external model of a mixed entity does not describe the internal interactions between its real and virtual parts or the behavior of each part. We propose to complete it with a model of the internal interaction mechanisms of each part. We use the perception-decision-action loop, frequently employed to describe the internal interaction mechanisms of an entity [13].

We also add a synchronization loop between each part. This synchronization loop duplicates or completes the behavior of each part. Typically, smart objects [33, 34] synchronize their virtual and real behaviors in real-time. We present our resulting model in Fig. 7. The internal interactions of a mixed entity occur:

- inside each part of a mixed entity. Sensors, actuators, and controllers capture, transmit and process the properties of the mixed entity,
- between the parts of a mixed entity. They synchronize and complete their knowledge and behavior to generate a mixed behavior.

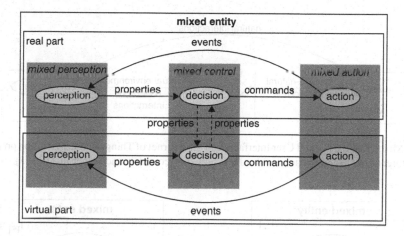

Fig. 7. Our design-oriented mixed-reality internal model of a mixed entity, composed of two synchronized interactions loops [3].

DOMIM enables the coexistence between real and virtual. With DOMIM, the real can affect the virtual and vice versa. In the next subsection, we describe the relations between the mixed entities constituting TIES.

3.2 Interactions Between Mixed Entities

The user-interface-environment interaction graph described in Fig. 8 shows our approach to the interactions occurring between the entities of an MIS. Mixed entities interact externally through natural, pseudo-natural and virtual world interactions in such systems, as shown in Fig. 9:

- between the real part of mixed entities: natural, pseudo-natural or network interactions,
- between the virtual part of mixed entities: virtual world interactions.

DOMIM allows designers and developers to:

- separate the constitutive entities of an MIS. This is useful to design and architect an MIS,
- decorrelate the real and the virtual to design and implement their complementary interactions.

DOMIM supports a simple modeling of mixed humans, NUI, and connected objects and their interactions. The resulting model is flexible since it allows to easily reuse and adapt previous models and their implementation to other mixed entities. Breaking a TIES into pieces is useful to manage its complexity. This property is used by our framework while designing and implementing TIES.

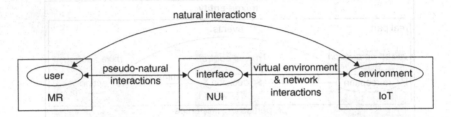

Fig. 8. Mixed Reality, Natural User Interfaces and the Internet of Things interaction graph presents the different types of interaction involved and how they complete each other in TIES [3].

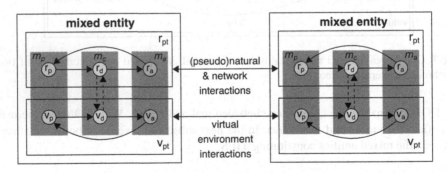

Fig. 9. External and internal interactions in a TIES composed of two mixed entities [3].

4   Design and Implementation DOMIM-Based Framework

TIES interconnect pools of mixed entities and can be considered as distributed user interfaces. These interfaces allow users to interact naturally and intuitively with the mixed entities composing it. TIES are composed of interconnected platforms linked by services. To produce such interfaces, our DOMIM-based framework supports the implementation of interconnected applications in charge of these services. These applications enable the mixed entities of TIES. Platforms like the Hololens run these applications.

Each application implements one or more mixed objects. TIES typically require connected objects management services. For example, one service controls all the Z-Wave-compatible devices of TIES. This service collects sensor events from the connected devices and controls their actuators. It allows synchronizing each application supporting a mixed entity with its real part through the Z-Wave protocol. Simultaneously, a Hololens application supports both the mixed user and the Hololens as a natural user interface.

Our framework requires Unity[5]. Extending supported development environments to the Unreal Engine or even an entirely dedicated development environment represents an important development cost. However, this is still feasible in order to provide a completely independent solution to developers. Our framework provides DOMIM-based application templates for different platforms like Windows, Hololens, or Android devices supporting ARCore. These templates are Unity 2018.4 projects containing:

- a Petri net editor. Our plugin integrates this editor to Unity [6, 8]. Developers easily modify a pre-defined Petri net by connecting the scene graph entities and their behavioral scripts to it. It allows to design software during implementation and is more accessible than coding, noticeably for designers,
- a generic implementation of the DOMIM model as an editable Petri net. Developers complete this generic Petri net in order to configure a mixed entity behavior by clicking on buttons and drop-down lists,
- implemented IoT, NUI, and MR scripts dedicated to TIES' common needs. Developers easily associate these components with the mixed entities composing the scene graph thanks to our Petri net editor.

Our DOMIM-based application templates provide components shown by Fig. 10. For example, we provide implemented gesture recognition components like gaze and tap gesture, tangible touch of virtual objects, and hybrid tangible, in-air, and tactile interactions with virtual objects. Our network synchronization components enable the synchronization of mixed entities' properties. Mixed entities are interconnected in order to produce distributed interactions or synchronize their location. We provide a Z-Wave service based on the Z-Wave .NET library[6]. Other IoT services are under development, like a service based on the LoRa protocol[7].

The semantic analysis component parses the network messages received by a DOMIM-based application. The semantic description component formats the network messages sent by the application, typically to synchronize and distribute the TIES interface. For example, a mixed object and a mixed user need to synchronize their location, in order to interact in the virtual world. The semantic components are crucial to unify the network communications between the mixed entities composing TIES. This homogenization allows better interconnectivity between TIES and consequently enhances the scalability of DOMIM-based TIES. The computer vision component integrates transparently the Vuforia engine[8]. The Vuforia engine is an AR development platform,

---

[5] https://unity.com/fr.

[6] https://github.com/genielabs/zwave-lib-dotnet.

[7] https://lora-alliance.org/.

[8] https://developer.vuforia.com/.

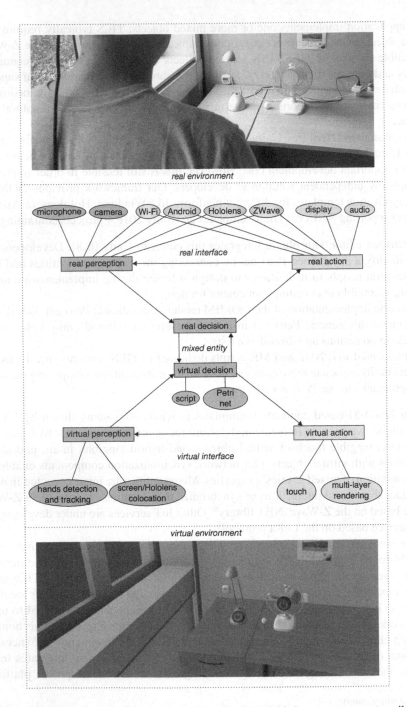

Fig. 10. This Figure is a detailed version of the Fig. 7. Provided components are available in DOMIM application templates. They are easy to connect to the scene graph thanks to our Petri net editor.

providing vision-based pose estimation algorithms. An alternative AR middleware like ARToolKit[9] can be integrated if needed.

We call a Petri net configuration a scenario. A generic DOMIM scenario implements a DOMIM-based mixed entity. This scenario separates the real and virtual parts of the mixed entity, implements for each part its interaction loop, and synchronizes both parts. Figure 11 shows in our Petri net editor a mixed fan scenario based on a generic DOMIM scenario. A real fan wired to a smart plug and an application make up a mixed fan. The application controls the mixed fan behavior. This scenario runs on the Hololens. Developers assign object-oriented methods or properties of the components to the generic scenario transitions. These components belong to the mixed entities of the Unity scene graph:

- set real power state: updates the real fan properties from the virtual ones by calling a method of the mixed fan if the user switched the virtual button of the mixed fan,
- network communication: commands the Z-Wave server to update the real fan state according to its real properties, this commands the smart plug of the mixed fan,

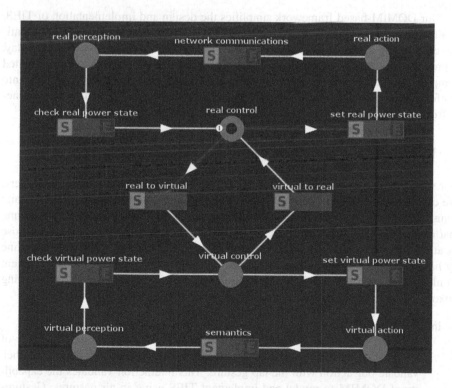

Fig. 11. The Petri net scenario of a mixed fan, provided by our Petri net editor, by Bataille et al. [3]. Orange circles are places. Yellow boxes are transitions, the E letter indicates a transition effector, the S letter indicates a transition sensor. The black dot is the token at its initial place. (Color figure online)

[9] https://github.com/artoolkit.

- check real power state: asks the Z-Wave server the real fan state to update the real properties of the mixed fan, this checks the power state of the smart plug,
- set virtual power state: this transition effector calls a method of the mixed fan. This method updates the virtual fan properties with the real ones,
- semantics: parses messages received from other mixed entities of the TIES, formats the messages to send to these entities, for example, to synchronize their locations,
- check virtual power state: observes if the virtual properties of the mixed fan have changed if the mixed user interacted with the virtual power button of the mixed fan.

The process we just described is the same for any TIES. Developers apply this process to all their TIES applications with the support of our DOMIM-based framework. They declare the properties of each mixed entity. They associate network components with them and tune their communications with other mixed entities composing the TIES. They provide each mixed entity with a 3D model, their virtual twin eventually completed by metaphors as the geometry of their virtual part, and their DOMIM-based behavior description. Finally, they associate each mixed entity with interaction techniques.

Our DOMIM-based framework simplifies the design and implementation of TIES. It allows breaking TIES into comprehensible sub-systems. It distinguishes the entities constituting it, classifies their interactions, and describes their real-virtual interplay. It provides an integrated design and implementation tool which frames implemented components. It allows reusing these implemented components by integrating them into platform-specific templates. During the implementation of new TIES, developers benefit from reusing them rapidly and simply with our Petri net editor.

5   Use Case

Our validation use case is a smart building TIES for occupants and building managers. We chose this use case since a building contains a large number of heterogeneous and connected objects. For this use case, humans interact with a fan and a lamp. We assume that objects are stationary. They are located by detecting the pose of a texture whose location is pre-defined in the building virtual twin. We model rooms and objects offline by hand for rendering performance reasons, but real-time capture of the environment would provide a more dynamic system. This use case aims at controlling and monitoring mixed objects inside or outside the building. We propose the following interactions:

- inside a room:
    - interaction A, in-air gestures: an air tap gesture turns on and off the power of the fan and the lamp. We first focus on a connected object with head gaze, then validate our action with the tap gesture. This interaction validates the capability of DOMIM to model and implement TIES using in-air gestures. Gestures are used to interact in real-time with smart objects surrounding users. They are interpreted into commands sent to mixed objects,
    - interaction B, tangible interactions: touching the fan and the lamp in virtual and real environments turns them on and off. We touch with the index finger the virtual button displayed by the Hololens on the surface of the real fan to

command it. Compared to previous interaction, this implementation validates our framework capability to implement tangible interactions,

– outside the room, interaction C combines tangible, tactile, and in-air gestures. We use a smartphone as a tangible and tactile device in association with a Hololens for stereovision and in-air gestures to:

  • manipulate the virtual twin of a room represented as a world in miniature (WIM),
  • turn on/off the fan and the lamp by touching the smartphone screen.

Compared to previous interactions, this implementation validates our framework capability to use a smartphone as a tangible interface to create hybrid interactions mixing tangible, tactile, and in-air gestural interactions.

We use our DOMIM-based framework while designing and implementing this use case in order to validate our approach.

5.1 Design

We consider in this section the design of our use case TIES. The first step is to enumerate the entities composing the setup, shown in Fig. 12:

– a mixed user enabled by a Hololens and a smartphone Xiaomi Mi8 supporting ARCore,
– a mixed room containing an Alienware Area 51 running a Z-Wave server, a Netgear R6100 wifi router to connect the PC, the Hololens and the smartphone, and a Z-Stick S2 Z-Wave USB antenna plugged to the laptop, making it our ZWave gateway,
– mixed objects, which are a fan plugged into a Fibaro Wall Plug, and a lamp plugged into an Everspring AD142 plug, switching them on and off.

Fig. 12. The mixed environment is composed of a real environment and its virtual twin, by Bataille et al. [3]. On the left, a capture of the use case setup. On the right, a capture of the room's virtual twin.

The architecture of this TIES is presented in Fig. 13.

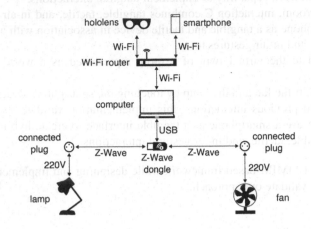

Fig. 13. Architecture of our smart room usecase.

We now detail how our framework provides the claimed services to designers.

Simplicity. DOMIM allows us to segment a TIES complexity into several sub-TIES and to distinguish real and virtual interactions between mixed entities. Figure 14 shows the sub-TIES composed of the mixed user, a Hololens, and the mixed fan. This TIES allows interaction A. Interactions between mixed entities are clearly identified, categorized, and described.

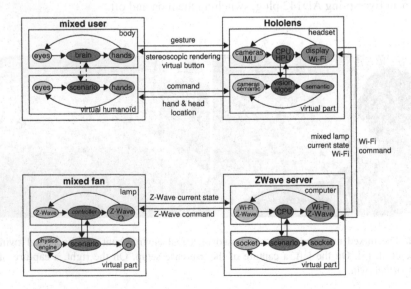

Fig. 14. The external model based on DOMIM of the use case subsystem composed of a user, a Hololens and a mixed fan in the case of interaction A.

Flexibility. DOMIM eases the adaptability of a TIES to its evolutions, thanks to its abstraction capacity. For example, we can replace in the previous sub-TIES a Hololens by a Magic Leap, a mixed fan by a mixed lamp, and a gesture interaction by a voice interaction effortlessly.

Reusability. We now present how to reuse a DOMIM model of TIES. The ability of DOMIM to produce comprehensive models appears here. We keep from Fig. 14 the mixed user, the Hololens, the Z-Wave server, the mixed fan, and their interactions. We complete this sub-MIS with a smartphone and a mixed lamp in order to design interaction C, as described in Fig. 15. Both smartphone and Hololens are self-located, and their locations are synchronized.

The designed and implemented TIES validates the use of DOMIM as a simple, flexible and reusable model.

5.2   Implementation

Interactions inside each mixed entity application produce its behavior. This behavior enables its interactions with other mixed entities composing the TIES. Developers

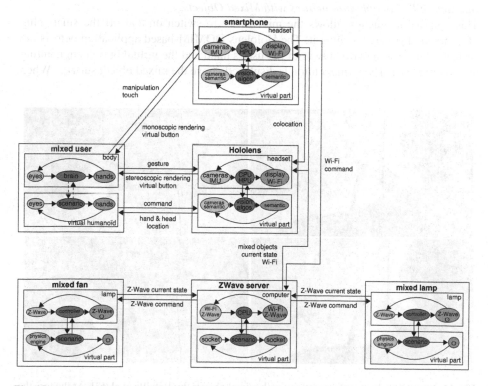

Fig. 15. Interaction C, the DOMIM model of a mixed user enabled by a Hololens and an ARCore smartphone. ARCore provides the location of the smartphone, while the Hololens embeds its own SLAM in order to locate it.

produce the applications supporting each mixed entity by using DOMIM application templates and pre-developed components provided by the DOMIM framework. For each application, developers create their mixed objects graph, declare for each mixed entity its properties, locate them in the virtual twin of the real space, and associate them with pre-developed pseudo-natural and network interactions. Our network components provide inter-platforms communications and IoT-based services like a Z-Wave service. Interaction components offer pseudo-natural interactions, like in-air gestures, described in this subsection and available as components in our framework. The Z-Wave server commands devices and collects their real properties in order to synchronize their virtual part. Typically, the virtual part of a mixed fan knows if its real part is powered or not. The mixed user is supported by this application. The Hololens perceives the mixed user location with its embedded SLAM and tracks his hands with its depth camera. It renders the virtual properties of the mixed objects surrounding him. It detects which mixed object the mixed user observes with gaze tracking, and the in-air tap gesture to switch on and off the mixed object. When the Hololens detects the mixed user intention to switch on and off a mixed object, it communicates to the Z-Wave server the command. The Z-Wave server then switches on/off the smart plug of the mixed object. Figure 16 presents the interaction A.

Interaction B: Tangible Interactions with Mixed Objects.
This tangible interaction allows the mixed user to switch on and off the smart plug of a mixed object by touching it. The Hololens DOMIM-based application detects the collision between the virtual twin of the user's hand and the virtual button augmenting the mixed object. The virtual button is displayed above the mixed object surface. When

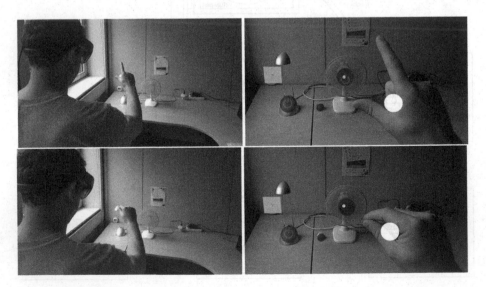

Fig. 16. Interaction A: in-air interactions with mixed objects, by Bataille et al. [3]. At the top, the user's gaze focuses on the virtual power button of the mixed fan. At the bottom, the user uses the tap gesture to switch on the mixed fan.

the user touches the virtual button he also touches the real object, making the virtual part of the mixed object tangible. The mixed user application developed for interaction A is modified by adding this virtual collision detection as an interaction modality in order to command the mixed object. Figure 17 shows interaction B, provided by our framework as a component. This TIES implementation shows the capability of our DOMIM-based framework to design and develop TIES rapidly and efficiently.

Interaction C: Hybrid In-air, Tangible and Tactile Interactions with Tangible Virtual Objects.

This interaction combines two user interfaces, the Hololens, and the smartphone. The smartphone is used as a tangible and tactile interface, a tracking device mediating the virtual world surfaces, but not as a visual rendering device. We can manipulate the virtual twin of the room displayed on the smartphone by manipulating it. The Hololens is aware of its location thanks to its embedded SLAM and of the location of the smartphone thanks to the smartphone ARCore SLAM. The smartphone continuously transmits its location to the Hololens. We synchronize both coordinate systems when the Hololens estimates the smartphone with the Vuforia engine pose when the smartphone displays a texture. When Vuforia detects the texture on the smartphone, it computes the transformation matrix of the smartphone in its own coordinate system. We then estimate a transition matrix, which defines a common coordinate system for both Hololens and smartphone locations. The sum of the Hololens location and the smartphone pose estimated by the Vuforia engine on Hololens is compared to the smartphone location estimated by ARCore in order to provide this transition matrix. Our framework provides this interaction as a component, including the transition matrix estimation. When

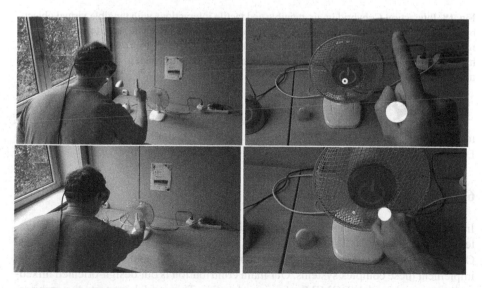

Fig. 17. Interaction B: tangible interactions with mixed objects, by Bataille et al. [3]. At the top, the user is about to touch the virtual power button of the mixed fan. At the bottom, the user touches the virtual button in order to switch on the mixed fan.

the mixed user wants to interact with the virtual twin of a mixed object, the Hololens detects his free hand location and focuses on the closest virtual object twin. When the mixed user touches the tactile screen of the smartphone, the smartphone sends the touch event to the Hololens. The Hololens then sends by the Z-Wave service the command to the focused mixed object. Our framework provides this Z-Wave service hosted by a computer included in this TIES. We show interaction C in Fig. 18.

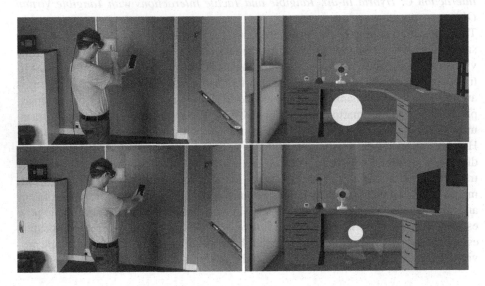

Fig. 18. Interaction C: hybrid in-air, tangible and tactile interactions with tangible virtual objects, by Bataille et al. [3]. At the top, the user manipulates the smartphone in order to manipulate the room's virtual twin displayed by the Hololens, the virtual twin of a mixed lamp is focused by his hand. At the bottom, the user touches the smartphone tactile screen in order to switch on the mixed lamp.

If we want to extend or change a TIES, we complete or change the DOMIM implementation of developed mixed entities, and eventually add new mixed entities based on DOMIM application templates and tune their interactions with the TIES.

6   Conclusion

In this paper, we present our solution for the development of mixed interactive systems blending MR, NUI, and the IoT that we call interactive mixed entity systems. Our approach responds to the need for appropriate models and tools to abstract and implement these complex systems. Our main contribution is our design-oriented mixed-reality internal model (DOMIM) of a mixed entity. This model supports the architecture, design, and implementation of TIES. We used this model to produce our DOMIM-based framework providing simplicity, reusability, flexibility, and swiftness. A DOMIM framework-based project breaks TIES into pieces in order to structure it and segment its complexity. Interactions between different platforms are provided by the network, which enables the interoperability of DOMIM-based TIES. Our framework also allows us to design software during implementation.

For future work, we aim at further investigating how TIES can support hybrid pseudo-natural interactions by exploiting the interconnectivity of NUI. We also want to strengthen our DOMIM-based framework by opening it to a small set of designers and developers in order to develop and strengthen it. Another target is to plug our framework with an existing research-oriented IoT platform for fast TIES prototyping and deployment. That platform supports many IoT-specific aspects like connected objects discovery, service characterization, or advanced security.

References

1. Alce, G., Roszko, M., Edlund, H., Olsson, S., Svedberg, J., Wallergård, M.: [POSTER] AR as a user interface for the internet of things—comparing three interaction models. In: 2017 IEEE International Symposium on Mixed and Augmented Reality (ISMAR-Adjunct), pp. 81 86, October 2017. https://doi.org/10.1109/ISMAR-Adjunct.2017.37
2. Atzori, L., Iera, A., Morabito, G.: The internet of things: a survey. Comput. Netw. **54**(15), 2787–2805 (2010). https://doi.org/10.1016/j.comnet.2010.05.010. http://dx.doi.org/10.1016/j.comnet.2010.05.010
3. Bataille, G., Gouranton, V., Lacoche, J., Pelé, D., Arnaldi, B.: A unified design & development framework for mixed interactive systems. In: VISIGRAPP, GRAPP, the 15th International Joint Conference on Computer Vision, Imaging and Computer Graphics Theory and Applications, Valetta, Malta, pp. 49–60 (2020)
4. Blackler, A., Hurtienne, J.: Towards a unified view of intuitive interaction: definitions, models and tools across the world. MMI-Interaktiv 13 (2007)
5. Blake, J.: The natural user interface revolution. In: Natural User Interfaces in .Net, pp. 1–43. Manning publications edn. (2012)
6. Bouville, R., Gouranton, V., Boggini, T., Nouviale, F., Arnaldi, B.: #FIVE: high-level components for developing collaborative and interactive virtual environments. In: 2015 IEEE 8th Workshop on Software Engineering and Architectures for Realtime Interactive Systems (SEARIS), pp. 33–40. IEEE, Arles, March 2015. https://doi.org/10.1109/SEARIS.2015.7854099. http://ieeexplore.ieee.org/document/7854099/
7. Bouzekri, E., Canny, A., Martinie, C., Palanque, P.: A generic software and hardware architecture for hybrid interactive systems. In: EICS 2018 - Workshop on Heterogeneous Models and Modeling Approaches for Engineering of Interactive Systems, Paris, France, June 2018
8. Claude, G., Gouranton, V., Arnaldi, B.: Versatile scenario guidance for collaborative virtual environments. In: Proceedings of 10th International Conference on Computer Graphics Theory and Applications (GRAPP 2015), Berlin, Germany, March 2015. https://hal-univ-rennes1.archives-ouvertes.fr/hal-01147733
9. Coutaz, J.: PAC: an object oriented model for implementing user interfaces. ACM SIGCHI Bull. **19**(2), 37–41 (1987). https://doi.org/10.1145/36111.1045592. https://dl.acm.org/doi/10.1145/36111.1045592
10. Coutrix, C., Nigay, L.: Mixed reality: a model of mixed interaction. In: Proceedings of the Working Conference on Advanced Visual Interfaces - AVI 2006, p. 43. ACM Press, Venezia (2006). https://doi.org/10.1145/1133265.1133274. http://portal.acm.org/citation.cfm?doid=1133265.1133274

11. Dubois, E., Bortolaso, C., Appert, D., Gauffre, G.: An MDE-based framework to support the development of Mixed Interactive Systems. Sci. Comput. Program. **89**, 199–221 (2014). https://doi.org/10.1016/j.scico.2013.03.007. https://linkinghub.elsevier.com/retrieve/pii/S0167642313000671

12. Dubois, E., Gray, P., Nigay, L.: The Engineering of Mixed Reality Systems. Human-Computer Interaction Series, Springer, Heidelberg (2010). https://doi.org/10.1007/978-1-84882-733-2

13. Fuchs, P., Moreau, G., Guitton, P.: Virtual Reality: Concepts and Technologies. CRC Press (2011)

14. Gibson, J.J.: The theory of affordances. In: Shaw, R.E., Bransford, J. (ed.) Perceiving, Acting, and Knowing: Toward an Ecological Psychology, pp. 67–82. Lawrence Erlbaum Associates, Hillsdale (1977). https://hal.archives-ouvertes.fr/hal-00692033

15. Glaessgen, E., Stargel, D.: The digital twin paradigm for future NASA and US Air Force vehicles. In: 53rd AIAA/ASME/ASCE/AHS/ASC Structures, Structural Dynamics and Materials Conference 20th AIAA/ASME/AHS Adaptive Structures Conference 14th AIAA, p. 1818 (2012)

16. Greer, C., Burns, M., Wollman, D., Griffor, E.: Cyber-physical systems and internet of things. Technical report NIST SP 1900–202, National Institute of Standards and Technology, Gaithersburg, MD, March 2019. https://doi.org/10.6028/NIST.SP.1900-202. https://nvlpubs.nist.gov/nistpubs/SpecialPublications/NIST.SP.1900-202.pdf

17. Grieves, M.W.: Virtually intelligent product systems: digital and physical twins. In: Complex Systems Engineering: Theory and Practice, pp. 175–200 (2019)

18. Hussey, A., Carrington, D.: Comparing the MVC and PAC architectures: a formal perspective. IEE Proc. - Softw. Eng. **144**(4), 224–236 (1997). https://doi.org/10.1049/ip-sen:19971512

19. Jacob, R.J., et al.: Reality-based interaction: a framework for post-WIMP interfaces. In: Proceedings of the SIGCHI Conference on Human Factors in Computing Systems, CHI 2008, pp. 201–210. ACM, New York (2008). https://doi.org/10.1145/1357054.1357089. http://doi.acm.org/10.1145/1357054.1357089

20. Kelaidonis, D., et al.: Virtualization and cognitive management of real world objects in the internet of things. In: 2012 IEEE International Conference on Green Computing and Communications, pp. 187–194. IEEE, Besancon, November 2012. https://doi.org/10.1109/GreenCom.2012.37. http://ieeexplore.ieee.org/document/6468312/

21. Kim, K., Bölling, L., Haesler, S., Bailenson, J., Bruder, G., Welch, G.F.: Does a digital assistant need a body? The influence of visual embodiment and social behavior on the perception of intelligent virtual agents in AR, Munich, pp. 105–114 (2018). https://doi.org/10.1109/ISMAR.2018.00039

22. Lacoche, J., Le Chenechal, M., Villain, E., Foulonneau, A.: Model and tools for integrating iot into mixed reality environments: towards a virtual-real seamless continuum. In: ICAT-EGVE 2019 - International Conference on Artificial Reality and Telexistence and Eurographics Symposium on Virtual Environments. Tokyo, Japan, September 2019. https://hal.archives-ouvertes.fr/hal-02332096

23. Lin, S., Cheng, H.F., Li, W., Huang, Z., Hui, P., Peylo, C.: Ubii: physical world interaction through augmented reality. IEEE Trans. Mob. Comput. **16**(3), 872–885 (2017). https://doi.org/10.1109/TMC.2016.2567378

24. Liu, W.: Natural user interface- next mainstream product user interface. In: 2010 IEEE 11th International Conference on Computer-Aided Industrial Design Conceptual Design 1, vol. 1, pp. 203–205, November 2010. https://doi.org/10.1109/CAIDCD.2010.5681374

25. MacWilliams, A., Sandor, C., Wagner, M., Bauer, M., Klinker, G., Bruegge, B.: Herding sheep: live system development for distributed augmented reality. In: Proceedings of the

2Nd IEEE/ACM International Symposium on Mixed and Augmented Reality, ISMAR 2003, p. 123. IEEE Computer Society, Washington, DC (2003). http://dl.acm.org/citation.cfm? id=946248.946803

26. Marchand, E., Uchiyama, H., Spindler, F.: Pose estimation for augmented reality: a hands-on survey. IEEE Trans. Vis. Comput. Graph. **22**(12), 2633–2651 (2016). https://doi.org/10. 1109/TVCG.2015.2513408. http://ieeexplore.ieee.org/document/7368948/

27. Milgram, P., Kishino, F.: A taxonomy of mixed reality visual displays. IEICE Trans. Inf. Syst. **E77-D** (1994)

28. Nitti, M., Pilloni, V., Colistra, G., Atzori, L.: The virtual object as a major element of the internet of things: a survey. IEEE Commun. Surv. Tutor. **18**(2), 1228–1240 (2016). https:// doi.org/10.1109/COMST.2015.2498304. http://ieeexplore.ieee.org/document/7320954/

29. Norman, D.A.: The Psychology of Everyday Things. (The Design of Everyday Things). Basic Books (1988)

30. Norman, D.A.: Affordance, conventions, and design. Interactions **6**(3), 38–43 (1999). https:// doi.org/10.1145/301153.301168. http://doi.acm.org/10.1145/301153.301168

31. Norman, D.A.: Natural user interfaces are not natural. Interactions **17**(3), 6–10 (2010). https://doi.org/10.1145/1744161.1744163. http://doi.acm.org/10.1145/1744161.1744163

32. Pfeiffer, T., Pfeiffer-Leßmann, N.: Virtual prototyping of mixed reality interfaces with inter net of things (IoT) connectivity. i-com **17**(2), 179–186 (2018). https://doi.org/10.1515/icom-2018-0025. http://www.degruyter.com/view/j/icom.2018.17.issue-2/icom-2018-0025/icom-2018-0025.xml

33. Poslad, S.: Ubiquitous Computing: Smart Devices, Environments and Interactions. Wiley, Hoboken (2011)

34. Sánchez López, T., Ranasinghe, D.C., Harrison, M., Mcfarlane, D.: Adding sense to the internet of things. Pers.Ubiquit. Comput. **16**(3), 291–308 (2012). https://doi.org/10.1007/ s00779-011-0399-8. http://dx.doi.org/10.1007/s00779-011-0399-8

35. Turner, P.: Affordance as context. Interact. Comput. **17**(6), 787–800 (2005). https://doi.org/ 10.1016/j.intcom.2005.04.003

36. Uimonen, M.: Accessing BIM-related information through AR, p. 2 (2018)

37. Walther, S.: ASP.NET 3.5 unleashed. Sams, Indianapolis, Ind (2008). oCLC: ocn180989631

Skeleton-and-Trackball Interactive Rotation Specification for 3D Scenes

Xiaorui Zhai[1] , Xingyu Chen[1,2] , Lingyun Yu[3] , and Alexandru Telea[4(✉)]

[1] Bernoulli Institute, University of Groningen, Groningen, The Netherlands
{x.zhai,xingyu.chen}@rug.nl
[2] School of Computer and Communication Engineering, University of Science and Technology Beijing, Beijing, China
[3] Department of Computer Science and Software Engineering, Xi'an Jiaotong-Liverpool University, Suzhou, China
Lingyun.Yu@xjtlu.edu.cn
[4] Department of Information and Computing Science, Utrecht University, Utrecht, The Netherlands
a.c.telea@uu.nl

Abstract. We present a new technique for specifying rotations of 3D shapes around axes inferred from the local shape structure, in support of 3D exploration and manipulation tasks. We compute such axes by extracting approximations of the 3D curve skeleton of such shapes using the skeletons of their 2D image silhouettes and depth information present in the Z buffer. Our method allows specifying rotations around parts of arbitrary 3D shapes with a single click, works in real time for large scenes, can be easily added to any OpenGL-based scene viewer, and is simple to implement. We compare our method with classical trackball rotation, both in isolation and in combination, in a controlled user study. Our results show that, when combined with trackball, skeleton-based rotation reduces task completion times and increases user satisfaction, while not introducing additional costs, being thus an interesting addition to the palette of 3D manipulation tools.

Keywords: Skeletonization · 3D interaction · Image-based techniques

1 Introduction

Interactive exploration and navigation of 3D scenes is essential in many applications such as CAD/CAM modeling, computer games, and data visualization [26]. 3D rotations are an important interaction tool, as they allow examining scenes from various viewpoints. Two main 3D rotation types exist – rotation around a *center* and rotation around an *axis*. Rotation around a center can be easily specified via classical mouse-and-keyboard [51] or touch interfaces [49] by well-known metaphors such as the virtual trackball [21]. Axis rotation is easy to specify if the axis matches one of the world-coordinate axes. Rotations around arbitrary axes are much harder to specify, as this requires a total of 7 degrees of freedom (6 for the axis and one for the rotation angle around the axis).

© Springer Nature Switzerland AG 2022
K. Bouatouch et al. (Eds.): VISIGRAPP 2020, CCIS 1474, pp. 26–52, 2022.
https://doi.org/10.1007/978-3-030-94893-1_2

For certain tasks, users do not need to rotate around *any* 3D axis. Consider examining a (complex) 3D shape such as a statue: We can argue that a natural way to display this shape is with the statue's head upwards; and a good way to explore the shape from all viewpoints is to rotate it around its vertical symmetry axis while keeping its upwards orientation fixed.

Several methods support this exploration scenario by aligning the shape's main symmetry axis with one of the world coordinate axes and then using a simple-to-specify rotation around this world axis [12]. This falls short when (a) the studied shape does not admit a *global* symmetry axis, although its parts may have local symmetry axes; (b) computing such (local or global) symmetry axes is not simple; or (c) we do not want to first align the shape with a world axis.

To address the above, Zhai *et al.* [50] recently proposed a novel interaction mechanism based on local symmetry axes: The user points at a region of interest (part) of the viewed 3D shape, from which a local symmetry axis is computed. Next, one can rotate the shape around this axis with an interactively specified angle. This method allows an easy selection of parts and automatic computation of their approximate 3D symmetry axes, both done using the shape silhouette's 2D skeleton. The method handles any 3D scene, *e.g.*, polygon mesh or polygon soup, point-based or splat-based rendering, or combination thereof, without preprocessing; and works at interactive rates for scenes of hundreds of thousands of primitives.

Zhai *et al.* mention that their skeleton-based rotation is not to be seen as a replacement, but a *complement*, of classical trackball rotation. Yet, what this precisely means, *i.e.*, how the two rotation mechanisms perform when used in practice, either separately or jointly, is an open question. Also, they mention a formal evaluation of the effectiveness of skeleton-based rotation as an important open research question. In this paper, we extend the work of Zhai *et al.* in the above directions with the following contributions:

- We provide a more detailed technical explanation of the skeleton-based rotation, covering aspects left open by the original paper [50];
- We present the design and execution of a controlled user study aimed at gauging the added value of skeleton-based rotation when used against, but also combined with, trackball rotation;
- We analyze the results of our study to show that, when used together with trackball rotation, skeleton-based rotation brings in added value, therefore being a good complement, and not replacement, of trackball rotation.

The structure of this paper is as follows. Section 2 presents related work on interactive rotation specification and skeleton computation. Section 3 details the skeleton-based rotation presented in [50]. Section 4 presents a formative evaluation aimed at finding out how the skeleton-based rotation is received by users. Section 5 presents an in-depth quantitative and qualitative user study that studies the hypotheses outlined by the formative study. Section 6 discusses the skeleton-based rotation and our findings regarding its best ways of use. Section 7 concludes the paper.

2 Related Work

Rotation Specification: 3D rotations can be specified by many techniques. The trackball metaphor [8] is one of the oldest and likely most popular techniques. Given a 3D

center-of-rotation x, the scene is rotated around an axis passing through x and determined by the projections on a hemisphere centered at x of the 2D screen-space locations p_1 and p_2 corresponding to a (mouse) pointer motion. The rotation angle α is
controlled by the amount of pointer motion. While simple to implement and use, trackball rotation does not allow precise control of the actual axis around which one rotates,
as this axis constantly changes while the user moves the pointer [2,51]. Several usability studies of trackball and alternative 3D rotation mechanisms explain these limitations
in detail [17,23,27,34]. Several refinements of the original trackball [8] were proposed
to address these [24,38]. In particular, Henriksen et al. [21] formally analyze the trackball's principle and its limitations and also propose improvements which address some,
but not all, limitations. At the other extreme, world-coordinate-axis rotations allow
rotating a 3D scene around the x, y, or z axes [26,51]. The rotation axis and rotation
angle are chosen by simple click-and-drag gestures in the viewport. This works best
when the scene is already pre-aligned with a world axis, so that rotating around that
axis yields meaningful viewpoints.

Pre-alignment of 3D models is a common preprocessing stage in visualization [7].
Principal Component Analysis (PCA) does this by computing a 3D shape's eigenvectors
e_1, e_2 and e_3, ordered by their eigenvalues $\lambda_1 \geq \lambda_2 \geq \lambda_3$, so that the coordinate
system $\{e_i\}$ is right-handed. Next, the shape is aligned with the viewing coordinate
system (x, y, z) by a simple 3D rotation around the shape's barycenter [28,42]. Yet,
pre-alignment is not effective when the scene does not have a clear main axis (λ_1 close
to λ_2) or when the major eigenvector does not match the rotation axis desired by the
user.

3D rotations can be specified by classical (mouse-and-keyboard) [51] but also touch
interfaces. Yu et al. [49] present a direct-touch exploration technique for 3D scenes
called Frame Interaction with 3D space (FI3D). Guo et al. [18] extend FI3D with constrained rotation, trackball rotation, and rotation around a user-defined center. [48] used
trackball interaction to control rotation around two world axes by mapping it to single-
touch interaction. Hancock et al. [19,20] use two or three touch input to manipulate 3D
shapes on touch tables and, in this context, highlighted the challenge of specifying 3D
rotations. All above works stress the need for simple rotation-specification mechanisms
using a minimal number of touch points and/or keyboard controls.

Medial Descriptors: Medial descriptors, also known as skeletons, are used for decades
to capture the symmetry structure of shapes [5,39]. For shapes $\Omega \subset \mathbb{R}^n$, $n \in \{2,3\}$
with boundary $\partial\Omega$, skeletons are defined as

$$S_\Omega = \{x \in \Omega) | \exists f_1 \in \partial\Omega, f_2 \in \partial\Omega : f_1 \neq f_2 \wedge ||x - f_1|| = ||x - f_2|| = DT_\Omega(x\} \quad (1)$$

where f_i are called the feature points [32] of skeletal point x and DT_Ω is the distance
transform [10,37] of skeletal point x, defined as

$$DT_\Omega(x \in \Omega) = \min_{y \in \partial\Omega} ||x - y|| \quad (2)$$

These feature points define the so-called *feature transform* [22, 41]

$$FT_\Omega(\mathbf{x} \in \Omega) = \underset{\mathbf{y} \in \partial\Omega}{\operatorname{argmin}} \|\mathbf{x} - \mathbf{y}\|, \tag{3}$$

which gives, for each point $\mathbf{x}$ in a shape Ω, its set of feature points on $\partial\Omega$, or contact points with $\partial\Omega$ of the maximally inscribed disk in Ω centered at $\mathbf{x}$.

Many methods compute skeletons of 2D shapes, described as either polyline contours [33] or binary images [10, 15, 16, 46]. State-of-the-art methods *regularize* the skeleton by removing its so-called spurious branches caused by small noise perturbations of the boundary $\partial\Omega$, which bring no added value, but only complicate further usage of the skeleton. Regularization typically defines a so-called *importance* $\rho(\mathbf{x}) \in \mathbb{R}^+ | \mathbf{x} \in S_\Omega$ which is low on noise branches and high elsewhere on S_Ω. Several authors [10, 15, 16, 33, 46] set ρ to the length of the shortest path along $\partial\Omega$ between the two feature points $\mathbf{f}_1$ and $\mathbf{f}_2$ of $\mathbf{x}$. Upper thresholding ρ by a sufficiently high value removes noise branches. Importance regularization can be efficiently implemented on the GPU [14] using fast distance transform computation [6]. Overall, 2D skeletonization can be seen, from a practical perspective, as a solved problem.

In 3D, two skeleton types exist [41]: *Surface skeletons*, defined by Eq. 1 for $\Omega \subset \mathbb{R}^3$, consist of complex intersecting manifolds with boundary, and hence are hard to compute and utilize [41]. *Curve skeletons* are curve-sets in $\mathbb{R}^3$ that locally capture the tubular symmetry of shapes [9]. They are structurally much simpler than surface skeletons and enable many applications such as shape segmentation [36] and animation [4]. Yet, they still cannot be computed in real time, and require a well-cured definition of Ω as a watertight, non-self-intersecting, fine mesh [40] or a high-resolution voxel volume [15, 35].

Kustra *et al.* [29] and Livesu *et al.* [31] address the above challenges of 3D curve-skeleton computation by using an *image based* approach. They compute an approximate 3D curve skeleton from 2D skeletons extracted from multiple 2D views of a shape. While far simpler and also more robust than true 3D skeleton extraction, such methods need hundreds of views and cannot be run at interactive rates. Our proposal also uses an image-space skeleton computation, but uses different, simpler, heuristics than [29, 31] to estimate 3D depth, and a single view, thereby achieving the speed required for interactivity.

3 Proposed Method

We construct a 3D rotation in five steps (Fig. 1). We start by loading the scene of interest – any arbitrary collection of 3D primitives, with no constraints on topology or sampling resolution – into the viewer (a). Next, the user can employ any mechanisms offered by the viewer, *e.g.* trackball rotation, zoom, or pan, to choose a *viewpoint of interest*, from which the scene shows a detail around which one would like to further rotate to explore the scene. In our example, such a viewpoint (b) shows the horse's rump, around which – for the sake of illustration – we want to rotate to examine the horse from different angles.

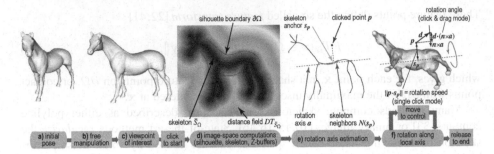

Fig. 1. Skeleton-based rotation pipeline with tool states (blue) and user actions (green). Image taken from [50]. (Color figure online)

3.1 Rotation Axis Computation

From the above-mentioned initial viewpoint, we compute the rotation axis by performing three image-space operations, denoted as A, B, and C next.

A. Silhouette Extraction: This is the first operation in Fig. 1, step (d). We render the shape with Z buffering on and using the *GL_LESS* OpenGL depth-test. Let Ω_{near} be the resulting Z buffer. We next find the silhouette Ω of the shape as all pixels that have a value in Ω_{near} different from the default (the latter being 1 for standard OpenGL settings).

B. Skeleton Computation: We next compute the silhouette skeleton S_Ω (Eq. 1) by the method in [46] (Fig. 1, step (d)). To eliminate spurious skeletal branches caused by small-scale noise along $\partial\Omega$, we regularize S_Ω by the salience-based metric in [43]. This regularization works as follows – see also the sketch in Fig. 2c. For every point $\mathbf{x} \in S_\Omega$ of the full skeleton delivered by Eq. 1, we first compute the importance ρ [46], *i.e.*, the shortest path along $\partial\Omega$ between the two feature points of $\mathbf{x}$ (see also Sect. 2). This path is marked red in Fig. 2c. As shown in [15,41,46], and outlined in Sect. 2, ρ monotonically increases along skeletal branches from their endpoints to the skeleton center, and equals, for a skeleton point $\mathbf{x}$, the amount of boundary which is captured (described) by $\mathbf{x}$.

We next define the *salience* of skeletal point $\mathbf{x}$ as

$$\sigma(\mathbf{x}) = \frac{\rho(\mathbf{x})}{DT_\Omega(\mathbf{x})}, \tag{4}$$

that is, the importance ρ normalized by the skeletal point's distance to boundary. As shown in [43], σ is *overall high* on skeleton branches caused by important (salient) cusps of $\partial\Omega$ and *overall low* on skeleton branches caused by small-scale details (noise cusps) along $\partial\Omega$. Figure 2c shows this for a small cusp on the boundary of a 2D silhouette of a noisy 3D dino shape. As we advance in this image along the black skeleton branch into the shape's rump (going below the grey area in the picture), ρ stays constant, but the distance to boundary DT_Ω increases, causing σ to decrease. Hence, we can regularize S_Ω simply by removing all its pixels having a salience value lower than a fixed threshold σ_0. Following [43], we set $\sigma_0 = 1$. Figure 2 illustrates this regularization by showing the raw skeleton S_Ω and its regularized version

$$\overline{S}_\Omega = \{\mathbf{x} \in S_\Omega | \sigma(\mathbf{x}) \geq \sigma_0\} \tag{5}$$

for the noisy dino shape. Salience regularization (Fig. 2b) removes all spurious branches created by boundary noise, but leaves the main skeleton branches, corresponding to the animal's limbs, rump, and tail, intact. Images (d–g) in the figure show the silhouette Ω, importance ρ, distance transform DT_Ω, and salience σ for a zoom-in area around the shape's head, for better insight. Looking carefully at image (e), we see that ρ has non-zero values also outside the main skeleton branch corresponding to the animal's neck, visible as light-blue pixels. While such details may look insignificant, they are crucial: Thresholding ρ by too low values – the alternative regularization to our proposal – keeps many spurious skeletal branches, see the red inset in Fig. 2a. In contrast, σ is practically zero outside the neck branch (Fig. 2g). So, thresholding σ by $\sigma_0 = 1$ yields a clean skeleton, see the red inset in Fig. 2b. Salience regularization is simple and automatic to use, requiring no free parameters, and hence preferable to ρ regularization which requires careful setting of the threshold for ρ – or to any other skeleton regularization we are aware of. For further details on salience regularization, we refer to [43] and also its public implementation [44].

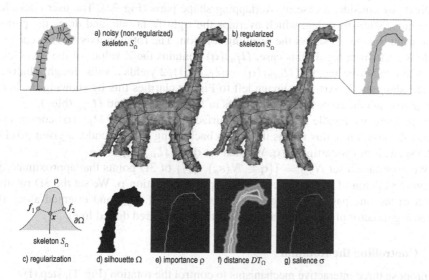

Fig. 2. Raw skeleton S_Ω with (a) noise-induced branches and (b) salience-based regularized skeleton $\overline{S}_\Omega$. c) Principle of salience regularization. (d–g) Details of silhouette, importance, distance transform, and salience values for the noisy dino's head.

C. Rotation Axis Computation: This is step (e) in Fig. 1. Let $\mathbf{p}$ be the pixel under the user-controlled pointer (blue in Fig. 1e). We first find the closest skeleton point $\mathbf{s}_p = \text{argmin}_{\mathbf{y} \in \overline{S}_\Omega} \|\mathbf{p} - \mathbf{y}\|$ by evaluating the feature transform (Eq. 3) $FT_{\overline{S}_\Omega}(\mathbf{p})$ of the regularized skeleton $\overline{S}_\Omega$ at $\mathbf{p}$. Figure 1d shows the related distance transform $DT_{\overline{S}_\Omega}$.

In our case, s_p is a point on the horse's rump skeleton (cyan in Fig. 1e). Next, we find the neighbor points $N(s_p)$ of s_p by searching depth-first from s_p along the pixel connectivity-graph of $\overline{S}_\Omega$ up to a fixed maximal distance set to 10% of the viewport size. $N(s_p)$ contains skeletal points along a single branch in $\overline{S}_\Omega$, or a few connected branches, if s_p is close to a skeleton junction. In our case, $N(s_p)$ contains a fragment of the horse's rump skeleton (red in Fig. 1e). For each $q \in N(s_p)$, we set the depth q_z as the average of $\Omega_{far}(q)$ and $\Omega_{near}(q)$. Here, Ω_{near} is the Z buffer of the scene rendered as described in step A above; and Ω_{far} is the Z buffer of the scene rendered as before, but with front-face culling on, *i.e.*, the depth of the *nearest* backfacing polygons to the view plane.

Figure 3 shows how this works. The user clicks above the horse's rump and drags the pointer upwards (a). Image (b) shows the resulting rotation. As visible in the inset in (a), the rotation axis (red) is centered inside the rump, as its depth q_z is the average of the near and far rump faces. To better understand this, the image left to Fig. 3a shows the horse rendered transparently, seen from above. The depth values in Ω_{near} and Ω_{far} are shown in green, respectively blue. The skeleton depth values (red) are the average of these. Note that, when the rotation ends, the new silhouette skeleton does *not* match the rotation axis – see inset in (b). This is normal and expected. If the user wants to start a new rotation from (b), then the 2D skeleton from this image will be used to compute a new, matching, rotation axis.

Next, we consider a case of overlapping shape parts (Fig. 3c). The user clicks left to the horse's left-front leg, which overlaps the right-front one, and drags the pointer to the right. Image (d) shows the resulting rotation. The rotation axis (red) is centered inside the left-front leg. In this case, $\Omega_{far}(q)$ contains the Z values of the backfacing part of the left-front leg, so $(\Omega_{near}(q) + \Omega_{far}(q))/2$ yields a value roughly halfway this leg along the Z axis. The image left to Fig. 3c clarifies this by showing the horse from above and the respective depth values in Ω_{near} (green) and Ω_{far} (blue).

Separately, we handle non-watertight surfaces as follows: If $\Omega_{far}(q)$ contains the default Z value (one), this means there's no backfacing surface under a given pixel q, so the scene is not watertight at q. We then set q_z to $\Omega_{near}(q)$.

We now have a set $N_{3D} = \{(q \in N(s_p), q_z)\}$ of 3D points that approximate the 3D curve skeleton of our shape close to the pointer location p. We set the 3D rotation axis a to the line passing through the average point of N_{3D} and oriented along the largest eigenvector of N_{3D}'s covariance matrix (Fig. 1e, red dotted line).

3.2 Controlling the Rotation

We propose three interactive mechanisms to control the rotation (Fig. 1), step (f)):

- **Indication:** As the user moves the pointer p, we continuously update the display of a. This shows along which axis the scene *would* rotate if the user initiated rotation from p. If a is found suitable, one can start rotating by a click following one of the two modes listed next; else one can move the pointer p to find a more suitable axis;
- **Single Click:** In this mode, we compute a rotation speed σ equal to the distance $\|p - s_p\|$ and a rotation direction δ (clockwise or anticlockwise) given by the sign of the cross-product $(s_p - p) \times n$, where n is the viewplane normal. We next continuously rotate (spin) the shape around a with the speed σ in direction δ;

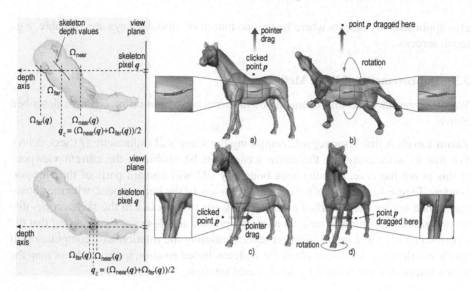

Fig. 3. Depth estimation of rotation axis for (a, b) non-overlapping part and (c, d) overlapping parts. In both cases, the rotation axis (red) is nicely centered in the shape. See Sect. 3.1. (Color figure online)

- **Click and Drag:** Let d be the drag vector created by the user as she moves the pointer p from the current to the next place in the viewport with the control, *e.g.* mouse button, pressed. We rotate the scene around a with an angle equal to $d \cdot (n \times a)$ (Fig. 1e).

We stop rotation when the user release the control (mouse button). In single-click mode, clicking closer to the shape rotates slowly, allowing to examine the shape in detail. Clicking farther rotates quicker to *e.g.* explore the shape from the opposite side. The rotation direction is given by the *side* of the skeleton where we click: To change from clockwise to counterclockwise rotation in Fig. 1, we only need to click below, rather than above, the horse's rump. In click-and-drag mode, the rotation speed and direction is given by the drag vector d: Values d orthogonal to the rotation axis a create corresponding rotations clockwise or anticlockwise around a; values d along a yield no rotation. This matches the intuition that, to rotate along an axis, we need to move the pointer *across* that axis.

The skeleton-based construction of the rotation axis is key to the effectiveness of our approach: If the shape exhibits some elongated structure in the current view (*e.g.* rump or legs in Fig. 1c), this structure yields a skeleton branch. Clicking closer to this structure than to other structures in the same view – *e.g.*, clicking closer to the rump than to the horse's legs or neck – selects the respective skeleton branch to rotate around. This way, the 3D rotation uses the 'natural' structure of the viewed shape. We argue that this makes sense in an exploratory scenario, since, during rotation, the shape parts we rotate around stay *fixed* in the view, as if one 'turns around' them. The entire method requires a *single click* and, optionally, a pointer drag motion to execute. This makes our method simpler than other 3D rotation methods for freely specifiable 3D axes, and also applicable to contexts where no second button or modifier keys are available, *e.g.*, touch screens.

3.3   Improvements of Basic Method

We next present three improvements of the local-axis rotation mechanism described above.

Zoom Level: A first issue regards computing the scene's 2D silhouette Ω (Sect. 3.1A). For this to work correctly, the entire scene must be visible in the current viewport. If this is not the case, the silhouette boundary $\partial\Omega$ will contain parts of the viewport borders. Figure 4a shows this for a zoomed-in view of the horse model, with the above-mentioned border parts marked purple. This leads to branches in the skeleton S_Ω that do not provide meaningful rotation axes. We prevent this to occur by requiring that the entire scene is visible in the viewport before initiating the rotation-axis computation. If this is not the case, we do not allow the skeleton-based rotation to proceed, but map the user's interaction to standard trackball-based rotation.

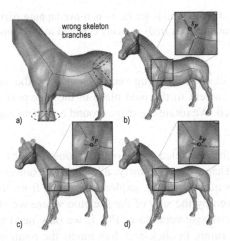

Fig. 4. Two problems of estimating rotation axes from skeletons. (a) Zoomed-in scene. Anchor points close to (c), respectively farther from (b, d) a skeleton junction. See Sect. 3.3. Image taken from [50]. (Color figure online)

Skeleton Junctions: If the user selects p so that the skeleton anchor s_p is too close to a skeleton junction, then the neighbor-set $N(s_p)$ will contain points belonging to more than two branches. Estimating a line from such a point set (Sect. 3.1C) is unreliable, leading to possibly meaningless rotation axes. Figures 4b–d illustrates the problem. The corresponding skeleton points $N(s_p)$ used to estimate the axis are shown in yellow, and the resulting axes in red. When s_p is far from the junction (Figs. 4b,d), $N(s_p)$ contains mainly points from a *single* skeleton branch, so the estimated rotation axes are reliable. When s_p is very close to a junction (Fig. 4c), $N(s_p)$ contains points from all three meeting skeletal branches, so, as the user moves the pointer p, the estimated axis 'flips' abruptly and can even assume orientations that do not match any skeleton branch.

We measure the *reliability* of the axis **a** by the anisotropy ratio $\gamma = \lambda_1/\lambda_3$ of the largest to smallest eigenvalue of N_{3D}'s covariance matrix. Other anisotropy metrics can be used equally well [13]. High γ values indicate elongated structures N_{3D}, from which we can reliably compute rotation axes. Low values, empirically detected as $\gamma < 5$, indicate problems to find a reliable rotation axis. When this occurs, we prevent executing the axis-based rotation.

Selection Distance: A third issue concerns the position of the point **p** that starts the rotation: If one clicks too far from the silhouette Ω, the rotation axis **a** may not match what one expects. To address this, we forbid the rotation when the distance d from **p** to Ω exceeds a given upper limit d_{max}. That is, if the user clicks too far from any silhouette in the viewport, the rotation mechanism does not start. This signals to the user that, to initiate the rotation, she needs to click closer to a silhouette. We compute d as $DT_{\overline{\Omega}}(\mathbf{p})$, where $\overline{\Omega}$ is the viewpoint area outside Ω, *i.e.*, all viewport pixels where Ω_{near} equals the default Z buffer value (see Sect. 3.1A).

We studied two methods for estimating d_{max} (see Fig. 5). First, we set d_{max} to a fixed value, in practice 10% of the viewport size. Using a constant d_{max} is however not optimal: We found that, when we want to rotate around *thick* shape parts, *e.g.* the horse's rump in Fig. 5b, it is intuitive to select **p** even quite far away from the silhouette. This is the case of point $\mathbf{p}_1$ in Fig. 5b. In contrast, when we want to rotate around *thin* parts, such as the horse's legs, it is not intuitive to initiate the rotation by clicking too far away from these parts. This is the situation of point $\mathbf{p}_2$ in Fig. 5b. Hence, d_{max} depends on the scale of the shape part we want to rotate around; selecting large parts can be done by clicking farther away from them than selecting small parts.

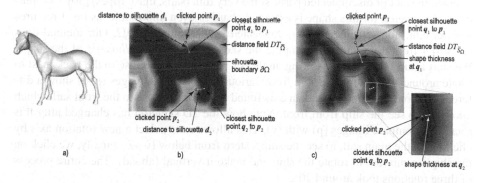

Fig. 5. Improvements of axis-based rotation method. (a) A view of the shape to be rotated. (b) Fixed maximum-distance setting for two clicked points $\mathbf{p}_1$ and $\mathbf{p}_2$. (c) Thickness-based maximum-distance setting for two clicked points $\mathbf{p}_1$ and $\mathbf{p}_2$. Image taken from [50].

We model this by setting d_{max} to the local *shape thickness* (Fig. 5c). We estimate thickness as follows: We find the closest point on the silhouette boundary $\partial\Omega$ to the clicked point **p** as $\mathbf{q} = FT_{\overline{\Omega}}(\mathbf{p})$. The shape thickness at **q** is the distance to the skeleton, *i.e.*, $DT_{\overline{S}_\Omega}(\mathbf{q})$. This is the 2D equivalent of the more general 3D-shape-thickness estimation proposed in [45]. In Fig. 5c, the point $\mathbf{p}_1$ is the farthest clickable point around $\mathbf{q}_1$ to the silhouette that allows starting a rotation around the rump. If we click further from the silhouette than the distance d_{max} from $\mathbf{p}_1$ to $\mathbf{q}_1$, no rotation is done. For the leg part, the farthest clickable point around $\mathbf{q}_2$ must, however, be much closer to the silhouette (Fig. 5c), since here the local shape thickness (distance d_{max} from $\mathbf{p}_2$ to $\mathbf{q}_2$) is smaller.

4   Formative Evaluation

To evaluate our method, we conducted first a *formative* evaluation. In this evaluation, only the authors of this work and a few other researchers, familiar with 3D interactive data visualization, were involved. This evaluation aimed at (a) verifying how the skeleton-based rotation practically works on a number of different 3D shapes; and (b) eliciting preliminary observations from the subjects to construct next a more in-depth evaluation study. We next present the results of this first evaluation phase. Section 5 details the second-phase evaluation designed using these findings.

Figure 6 shows our 3D skeleton-based rotation applied to two 3D mesh models. For extra insights, we recommend watching the demonstration videos [47]. First, we consider a 3D mesh model of a human hand which is not watertight (open at wrist). We start from a poor viewpoint from which we cannot easily examine the shape (a). We click close to the thumb (b) and drag to rotate around it (b–e), yielding a better viewpoint (e). Next, we want to rotate around the shape to see the other face, but keeping the shape roughly in place. Using a trackball or world-coordinate axis rotation cannot easily achieve this. We click on a point close to the shape-part we want to keep *fixed* during rotation (f), near the wrist, and start rotation. Images (g–j) show the resulting rotation.

Figure 6(k-ad) show a more complex ship shape. This mesh contains multiple self-intersecting and/or disconnected parts, some very thin (sails, mast, ropes) [30]. Computing a 3D skeleton for this shape is extremely hard or even impossible, as Eq. 1 requires a watertight, non-self-intersecting, connected shape boundary $\partial\Omega$. Our method does not suffer from this, since we compute the skeleton of the *2D silhouette* of the shape. We start again from a poor viewing angle (k). Next, we click close to the back mast to rotate around it, showing the ship from various angles (l–o). Images (p–u) show a different rotation, this time around an axis found by clicking close to the front sail, which allows us to see the ship from front. Note how the 2D skeleton has changed after this rotation – compare images (p) with (v). This allows us to select a new rotation axis by clicking on the main sail, to see the ship's stern from below (w–z). Finally, we click on the ship's rump (aa) to rotate the ship and make it vertical (ab–ad). The entire process of three rotations took around 20 s.

Figure 7 shows a different dataset type – a 3D point cloud that models a collision simulation between the Milky Way and the nearby Andromeda Galaxy [11, 25]. Its 160K points describe positions of the stars and dark matter in the simulation. Image (a) uses volume rendering to show the complex structure of the cloud, for illustration purposes. We do not use this rendering, but rather render the cloud in our pipeline using 3D spherical splats (b). Image (c) shows the cloud, rendered with half-transparent splats, so that opacity reflects local point density. Since we render a 3D sphere around each point, this results in a front and back buffer Ω_{near} and Ω_{far}, just as when rendering a 3D polygonal model. From these, we can compute the 2D skeleton of the cloud's silhouette, as shown in the figure. Images (d–f) show a rotation around the central tubular

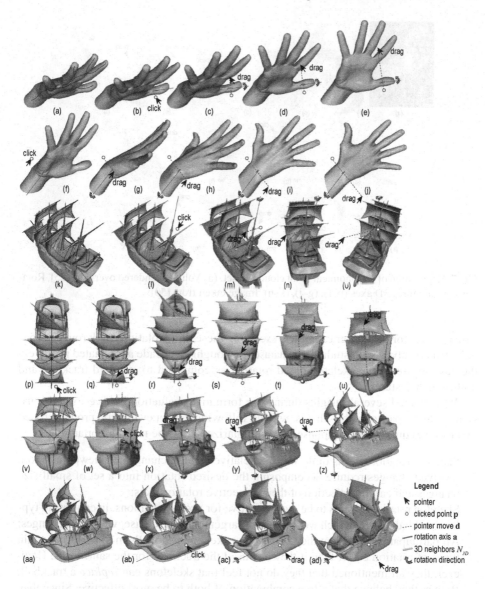

Fig. 6. Examples of two rotations (a–e), (f–j) for the hand shape and four rotations (k–o), (p–u), (v–z), (aa–ad) for the ship model. Image taken from [50].

structure of the cloud, which reveals that the could is relatively flat when seen from the last viewpoint (f). Image (g) shows the new 2D skeleton corresponding to the viewpoint after this rotation. We next click close to the upper high-density structure (f) and rotate around it. Images (h–j) reveal a spiral-like structure present in the lower part of the cloud, which was not visible earlier. To explore this structure better, we next click on its local symmetry axis (l) and rotate around it. Images (l–n) reveal now better this

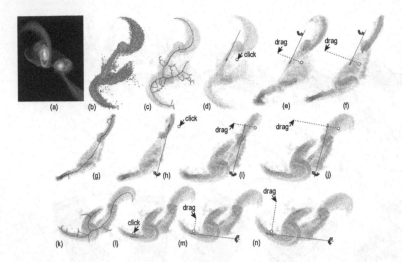

Fig. 7. Exploration of astronomical point cloud dataset. (a) Volume-rendered overview [25]. Rotations around three 3D axes (b–f), (g–j), (k–n). Image taken from [50].

structure. As for the earlier examples, executing these three rotations took roughly 15 s. Scientists involved with studied this dataset for roughly a decade appreciated positively the ease of use of the skeleton-based rotation as compared to standard trackball and multi-touch gestures.

We gathered several insights during our formative evaluation by free-form discussions with the participants – that is, without following a strict evaluation protocol based on tasks and quantitative responses. We summarize below the most important ones:

– Skeleton rotation works quite well for relatively *small* changes of viewpoint; more involved changes require decomposing the desired rotation into a set of small-size changes and careful selection of their respective rotation axes;
– Skeleton rotations seems to be most effective for *precise* rotations, in contrast to typical trackball usage, which works well for larger, but less precise, viewpoint changes;
– All participants stated that they *believe* that skeletons allow them to perform certain types of rotation easier than if they had used the trackball for the same tasks. However, they all mentioned that they do not feel that skeletons can *replace* a trackball. Rather, they believe that a free combination of both to be most effective. Since they could only use the skeleton rotation (in our evaluation), they do not know whether (or when) this tool works better than a trackball;
– All participants agreed that *measuring* the added-value of skeleton rotation is very important for its adoption.

5   Detailed Evaluation: User Study

The formative evaluation (Sect. 4) outlined that there is perceived added-value in the skeleton rotation tool, but this value needs to be actually measured before users would consider adopting the tool – either standalone or in combination with trackball. To deepen our understanding of how skeleton-based rotation works, and to answer the above questions, we designed and conducted a more extensive user evaluation. We next describe the design, execution, and analysis of the results of this evaluation.

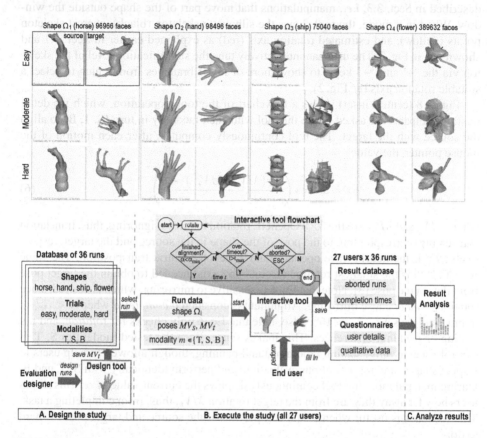

Fig. 8. Top: user evaluation showing the 12 trials for one modality (Sect. 5.1). Each trial consists of a source window in which the user interacts to align the shape to match the target window. Bottom: execution of end-to-end user evaluation. The use of our interactive tool in both design and evaluation modes is shown in red (Sect. 5.2). (Color figure online)

5.1 Evaluation Design

Tool: To assess how the skeleton rotation modality compares with the trackball modality, we designed an experiment supported by an interactive *tool*. The tool has two windows: The *target* window shows a 3D shape viewed from a viewpoint (pose) that is preselected by the evaluation designer. No interaction is allowed in this window. The *source* window shows the same shape, which can be freely manipulated by the user via the skeleton (S), the trackball (T), or both tools (B), activated via the left, respectively right, mouse buttons. Both windows have the same resolution (512^2 pixels), use the same lighting and rendering parameters, and have a fixed position on the computer screen, to simplify usage during the experiment that invokes multiple runs of the tool. Besides rotation, the tool also allows panning and zooming. We also added an option to automatically zoom out to show the full extent of a shape. This eliminates the issues described in Sect. 3.3, *i.e.*, manipulations that move part of the shape outside the window. When in S mode, the tool shows the silhouette skeleton (black), nearest skeleton points (yellow), and estimated rotation axis (red) as explained earlier in Sect. 3.1 and shown *e.g.* in Fig. 3. The user can interactively tune the simplification level of the skeleton via the '+' and '−' keys, to show more or fewer branches from which to select a suitable rotation axis (*cf* Fig. 2).

Figure 8 (central inset) shows a flowchart of the tool's operation, which we detail next. Participants are asked to use the tool with each modality in turn (S, T, B) to align the source with the target. The tool continuously computes, after each motion of the mouse pointer, the value

$$\alpha = \arccos\left(\frac{Tr(MV_s \cdot MV_t^T) - 1}{2}\right), \tag{6}$$

where MV_s and MV_t are the 3×3 OpenGL rotation matrices (ignoring, thus, translation and scaling) corresponding to the pose of the shape in the source and the target, respectively; Tr is the matrix trace operator; and T denotes matrix transposition. The value $\alpha \in [0, 180]$ is the smallest rotation (around any axis) needed to obtain the target pose from the source pose [3]. Note that Eq. 6 is sensitive to mirroring, which is desired, since rotations *cannot* cause mirroring. Alignment is considered *completed* when $\alpha < \alpha_{min}$; in practice, we set $\alpha_{min} = 15°$. Also, note that Eq. 6 only checks for *rotation*, and not scaling or panning, differences. This makes sense, since the tested modalities S, T, B control rotation only; scaling (zooming) and panning, though allowed to help users to inspect shapes, are not part of our evaluation, and perform identically with S, T, and B. During manipulation, the tool continuously displays the current value of α. This shows users how far away they are from the target rotation MV_t, thus, from completing a task. This feedback is useful when visual comparison of the source and target poses is hard to do.

Shapes: We use the alignment tool to evaluate the performance of the S, T, and B modalities on $N = 4$ *shapes* Ω_i, $1 \leq i \leq N$, shown in Fig. 8(top). Shapes were selected so as to be familiar, have a structure that exposes potential local-rotation axes, and have geometric complexity ranging from simple (horse, hand) to complex (ship). The flower shape is of lower complexity than the ship; however, its manifold structure makes it particularly hard to understand and manipulate, since it looks quite similar from many viewpoints. All shapes use identical material properties and no opacity or textures, to favor uniform evaluation. We excluded the more complicated point-cloud shape (Fig. 7) used during formative evaluation (Sect. 4) since no more than five of our recruited subjects had the technical background needed to understand what such data means in the first place.

Task Difficulties: For each shape, we use three target poses MV_t to capture three levels of difficulty of the alignment task:

- *Easy:* Alignment can be done by typically one or two manipulations, such as a rotation around one of the x or y window axes, or a rotation around a clearly-visible symmetry axis of the shape). For example, the blue-framed target in Fig. 8 can be obtained from the green-framed pose (left to it) by a single counterclockwise rotation of the horse with 90° around the y axis or, alternatively, the rump's skeleton;
- *Hard:* Alignment requires multiple rotations around many different rotation axes; it is not easy to see, from the source and target, which would be these axes;
- *Intermediate:* Alignment difficulty is gauged as between the above two extremes.

We call next the combination of shape Ω_i and start-and-end pose (MV_s, MV_t) a *trial*. Using multiple-difficulty trials aims to model tasks of different complexity. Trial difficulty was assessed by one of the authors (who also designed the actual poses MV_t) and agreed upon by the others by independent testing. We verified that all three modalities could accomplish all trials within a time t lower than a predefined timeout $t_{max} = 120$ s.

Figure 8(top) shows the source (left window in each window-pair) and target (right window in same pair) windows for the 12 trials spanning the 4 shapes using the T modality. Source windows show the currently-enabled modality in red text, to remind users how they can interact. We see, for instance, that the *easy* trial would require, in S mode, a simple 90° rotation around the y axis (in T mode) for the ship model, or around the main skeleton branch passing through the horse's rump for the horse model. In contrast, the *hard* task requires several incremental rotations for all modalities. The 12 trials use *identical* initial poses MV_s and target poses MV_t. That is, the user is asked to perform, for each shape, the same alignment $MV_s \rightarrow MV_t$ using all three modalities, thus ensuring that only the target pose (endpoint of manipulation) and, of course, the used modality, affect the measured execution time.

In total, we thus execute 12 trials × 3 modalities = 36 *runs*. For each run, we record the time needed for the user to complete it. If the user fails to perform the alignment within the allowed timeout, the run is considered *failed* and the user moves automatically to the next run. Users can at any time (a) abort a run by pressing 'ESC' to move to the next run; this helped impatient users who did not grasp how to perform a given alignment task and did not want to wait until the timeout; (b) abort the entire evaluation, if something goes entirely wrong; and (c) reset the viewpoint to the initial one (MV_s), to 'undo' all manipulations performed so far if these are deemed unproductive.

Pose Design: The different target poses MV_t were designed in advance by us by using the S and T tools – intermixed – to freely change the shape's pose until obtaining the desired target poses, and stored, as explained, as 3 × 3 OpenGL rotation matrices.

5.2 Evaluation Execution

Subjects: Twenty-seven persons took part in the evaluation. they self-report ages of 9 to 64 years (median: 24, average: 26.9); and gender being male (16) and female (11), see Fig. 9b. To gauge their experience with 3D manipulation, we asked them to report how many times a year they used 3D games and/or 3D design software. Both categories are reported in Fig. 9b as '3D software usage'. Results show a median of 30 times, with

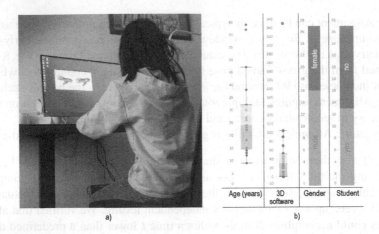

Fig. 9. a) Setup employed during the user evaluation. b) Self-reported characteristics of the experiment participants. See Sect. 5.2.

the minimum being zero (never) and the maximum being basically every day. From these data we conclude that most participants should have a good practical mastery of 3D manipulation. Fromf the 27 participants, 13 were students in fields as diverse as Computer Science, social science, medicine, economy and society, and mathematics; the other 14 were primary or secondary school pupils (6) or employed in various liberal professions (8). All participants reported no color blindness issues. All except one were right-handed. They all reside in the Netherlands or Belgium. Communication during the training and experiment was done in the native language of each participant by a (near-)native speaker. For participants with limited English proficiency, all English material (tutorial, questionnaires) was transcribed by the trainer.

Workflow: Participants followed the evaluation workflow showed in Fig. 8(bottom). First, we created the information needed to execute the 36 runs (Fig. 8(bottom, A)), as explained in Sect. 5.1. Next, participants were given access, prior to the actual experiment, to an web tutorial which describes both S and T tools in general, and also allows users to practice with these tools by running the actual application to execute some simple alignment tasks. No statistics were collected from this intake phase. After intake, users asked if they felt interested in, and able to follow, the tutorial. This intake acted as a simple filter to separate users with interest in the evaluation (and potential ability to do it) from the rest, so as to minimize subsequent effort. Seven persons dropped from the process due to lack of general computer skills (1 user), one too young (6 years), one too old (82 years), and four due to technical problems related to remote-deployment of the tool. These persons are not included in any of the statistics further on, nor in Fig. 9b.

Next, a trainer (role filled by different co-authors) took part in a *controlled session* where they explained to either individual participants or, when social distancing rules due to the Corona pandemy were not applicable, to groups of participants how the tool works and also illustrated it live. The aim of this phase was to refine the knowledge disseminated by the web tutorial and confirm that participants understood well the evaluation process and tooling. Participants and trainers used Linux-based PCs (16 to 32

GB RAM) with recent NVidia cards, wide screens, and a classical two-button mouse. To maximize focus on the experiment, no application was run on screen during the evaluation besides the two-window tool described in Sect. 5.1. Training took both the in-person form (with trainer and user(s) physically together), and via TeamViewer or Skype screen sharing, when social distancing rules mandated separation. Training took between 20 and 40 min per user, and was done until users told that they were confident to use the tool to manipulate both a simple model and a complex one via all three modalities (S, T, B). During this phase, we also verified that the tool runs at real-time framerates on the users' computers so as to eliminate confusing effects due to interaction lag; and that the users did not experience any difficulty in using the keyboard shortcuts outlined in Sect. 5.1.

After training, and confirmation by participants that they understand the evaluation tool and tasks to be done, participants started executing the 36 runs (Fig. 8(bottom, B). They could pause between runs as desired but not change the orders of the runs. Figure 9a shows the setup used during the evaluation by one of the actual participants; notice the two-window interaction tool on the screen. At the end, the results of all 36 runs – that is, either completion time or run failure (either by timeout or user abortion) – were saved in a database with no mention of the user identity. Next, users completed a questionnaire covering both personal and self-assessment data and answers to questions concerning the usability of the tool. Both types of results (timing data and questionnaires) were further analyzed (Fig. 8(bottom, C)), as described in Sect. 5.3.

5.3   Analysis of Results

We next present both a quantitative analysis of the timing results and an analysis of the qualitative data collected via questionnaires.

Analysis of Timing Results. A most relevant question is: How did performance (measured in completion time and/or number of aborted runs) depend on the interaction *modality* and *shape*? Figure 10a shows the average completion time, for the *successful* runs, aggregated (over all users) per modality and next per shape. User identities are categorically color-coded for ease of reading the figure. Median and interquartile ranges for each modality are shown by black lines, respectively gray bands. We see that the S modality is significantly slower than T and S. However, the B modality is faster than T, both as median and interquartile range, and also for each specific shape. This is an interesting observation, as it suggests that, in B mode, users did gain time by using S only for some specific manipulations for which T was hard to use. A likely explanation for this is that the B modality was always used last during the trials. Hence, when in B mode, users could discover the situations when S outperformed T, and switch to S in those cases to gain time. We will analyze thys hypothesis further below.

Figure 10b shows the number of *failed* runs per modality, shape, and user. These are largest for the S modality. This tells again that S cannot be used *alone* as a general-purpose manipulation tool. If we combine this insight with the total times per shape (Fig. 10a), we see that the perceived difficulty of the task varies significantly over both shapes and modalities: T and S behave quite similarly, with *horse* and *ship* being easier

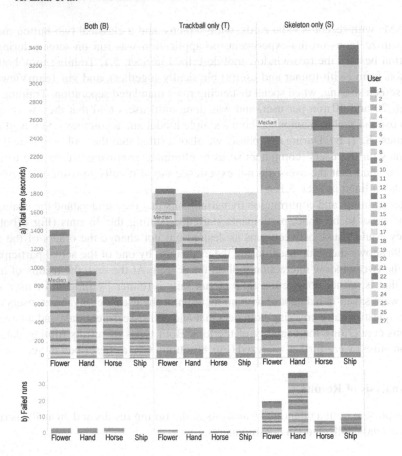

Fig. 10. Completion time (a) and number of failed runs (b) per modality and shape, all users. See Sect. 5.2.

to handle and *flower* being the hardest. In contrast, *hand* seems to be the hardest to handle by the S modality, as it has most aborted runs. Upon a closer analysis, we found that the pose used by the 'hard' trial for *hand* (see the respective image in Fig. 8(top)) is quite easy to achieve with T (and thus also B), but quite difficult to obtain using S, since it implies, at several points, performing a rotation around an axis orthogonal to the hand's palm, for which no skeleton line exists in the silhouette. The second-hardest shape for S is *ship*. Analyzing the users' detailed feedback showed us that *ship*'s complex geometry produces a wealth of potential rotation axes with quite different angles, which makes the users' choice (of the optimal rotation axis) hard. This happens far less for the other simpler-structure shapes. Separately, Fig. 10b shows that the number of aborted runs in B mode is far lower than that in S mode, being practically the same as for T mode. This, and the fact that B mode is fastest, reinforces our hypothesis that users employ the S tool in B mode only for very *specific* manipulations and revert to T for all other operations. Hence, S works best as a complement, not a replacement, of T.

Figure 11a introduces additional information in the analysis by showing how the average times vary over the three task *difficulty* levels (easy, moderate, hard, see Sect. 5.1). For all shapes and modalities, the task labeled easy by us is, indeed, completed the fastest. The other two difficulty levels are, however, not significantly different in execution times. We also see that effort (time) is distributed relatively uniformly over all difficulty levels for all shapes and modalities. This indicates that there is no 'outlier' task or shape in our experiment that would strongly bias our evaluation's insights.

Finally, we examine the data from a *user-centric* perspective. Figure 11b shows the total time per user, split per modality, with the fastest users at the right and the slowest at the left. We see a quite large spread in performance, the fastest user being roughly 2.5 times faster than the slowest one. We see that the T modality does not explain the big speed difference – the red bars' sizes do not correlate with the total time. In contrast, the blue bars show an increase when scanning the chart right-to-left, at the 8th leftmost bar – meaning that the 8 slowest users needed clearly more time to use the B modality as opposed to the remaining 19 users. Scanning the graph right-to-left along its orange bars shows a *strongly* increasing bar-size. That is, the main factor differentiating slow from fast users is their skill in using the S tool. We hypothesized that this skill has to do with the users' familiarity with 3D manipulation tools. To examine this, we show a scatterplot of the average time per user (all trials, all shapes) *vs* the user's self-reported number of days per year that one uses 3D computer games or 3D creation software (Fig. 11c). All points in the plot reside in the lower range of the y axis, *i.e.*, all users report under 100 days/year of 3D tool usage, except user 12 who indicated 3D gaming daily. The computed correlation line shown in the figure ($R^2 = 0.0022$, $p = 0.813$) indicates a negligible inverse correlation of average time with 3D software usage. Hence, our hypothesis is not confirmed. The question what determines the variability in users' average completion times is still open.

Questionnaire Results. As mentioned at the beginning of Sect. 5.2, users completed a questionnaire following the experiment. They were asked to answer 13 questions concerning their experience with each of the three modalities (T, S, B) using a 7-point Likert scale S (1 = strongly disagree, 2 = disagree, 3 = disagree somewhat, 4 = no opinion, 5 = agree somewhat, 6 = agree, 7 = strongly agree). An extra question (Q14) asked which of the three modalities users prefer *overall*. Figure 12(bottom) shows these 14 questions. Here, 'tool' refers to the modality being evaluated. Following earlier studies that highlight that user *satisfaction* is not the same as user *efficiency* or *effectiveness* when using interactive tools [17,34], we included questions that aim to cover all these aspects. Users could also input free text to comment on their perceived advantages and limitations of all three modalities or any other remarks.

Figure 12(top) shows the aggregated answers for Q1..Q13 for each of the three modalities with box-and-whisker plots (box shows the interquartile range; whiskers show data within 1.5 times this range). We see that the S modality ranks, overall, worse than the T modality, except for accuracy (Q5). Accuracy (Q5) can be explained by the fact that users need to control a *single* degree of freedom with S – the rotation angle – but two degrees of freedom with T. In other words, once a suitable rotation axes is chosen, S allows one to precisely specify the rotation angle around this axis. We also see

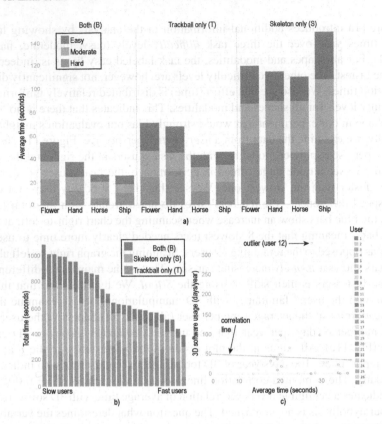

Fig. 11. a) Average completion time per difficulty levels, modality, and shape. b) Total time for all users, from slowest to fastest, split per modality. c) Correlation of average time (all runs) with users' frequency of 3D software usage. See Sect. 5.2.

that S helps completing the task less often than T (Q10), which matches the failure rates shown in Fig. 10b. However, the B modality ranks in nearly all aspects better than both T and S. This supports our hypothesis that S best *complements*, rather than replaces, T. An interesting finding are the scores for Q8 and Q6, which show that B was perceived as less tiring to use, and needing fewer steps to accomplish the task respectively, than both T and S. This matches the results in Fig. 10a that show that B is faster than both T and S – thus, arguably less tiring to use. For Q14, 22 of the 27 users stated that they prefer B overall, while the remaining 5 users preferred T, with none mentioning S as the highest-preference tool. As for the previous findings, this strongly supports our hypothesis that the S and T modalities work best when combined.

From the free text that captures the user's comments on the perceived advantages and limitations of all three modalities, we could distil several salient points. For space constraints, we list only a few below:

– **Trackball (T):** Several users praised T for being "easy to use". However, users also complained about trackball being imprecise for performing fine adjustments;

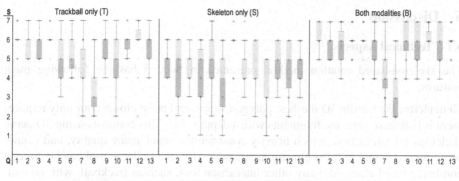

Q1	The tool met my needs for performing the alignment task
Q2	The tool worked as expected (after following the training)
Q3	The tool helped me be more effective than the two other tools
Q4	The tool was easy to use
Q5	The tool was accurate
Q6	The tool requires the fewest steps (compared to the other two) to accomplish my goals
Q7	I felt that I have to think carefully to get a good result with this tool
Q8	The tool was tiring to use
Q9	Both occasional and regular users would like the tool
Q10	I can use the tool successfully every time
Q11	I learned to use the tool quickly
Q12	I easily remember how to use the tool
Q13	I am satisfied with the tool
Q14	Which tool (T, S, or B) do you overall prefer?

Fig. 12. Results of 13-point user questionnaire for the three modalities. Questions are shown below the charts. See Sect. 5.3.

- **Skeleton (S):** This modality was mentioned as better than the other two by only a few users, and specifically for the horse, hand, and flower models, because of their clear and simple skeletons, which allow one to intuitively rotate the shape around its parts ("easy to turn the hand around a finger"; "easy to turn the horse around a leg"; "S helps to turn the flower around its stem"). However, several users mentioned advantages of S when used in combination with T. These are discussed below;
- **Both (B):** Overall, this modality received the most positive comments. It was deemed the "most accurate"; and "feeling quick to use when we have two methods [to choose from]". Specifically, users noted that B is "good for doing final adjustments/fine tuning the alignment" and that "S helps T to getting the desired result easily" and "I started with T and used S for final touches". One user also commented: "I work as a graphic designer with a lot of 3D tools; I see how S helps me by providing a lot of control when rotating, and I would love to have this tool along my other manipulation tools in my software [...] but I would not use it standalone".

Summarizing the above, we see that our initial hypothesis that the S modality helps (complements) T for precision tasks is largely supported by user experience.

6   Discussion

6.1   Technical Aspects

The skeleton-based rotation method presented in Sect. 3 has the following main features:

Genericity: We handle 3D meshes, polygon soups, and point clouds; our only requirement is that these generate fragments with a depth value. This contrasts using 3D curve skeletons for interaction, which heavily constrain the input scene quality, and cannot be computed in real time, as already mentioned. Also, the skeleton tool can be directly combined (used alongside) any other interaction tool, such as trackball, with no constraints.

Reversibility: Since 3D rotation axes are computed from 2D silhouette skeletons, rotations are not, strictly speaking, invertible: Rotating from a viewpoint v_1 with an angle α around a 3D local axis a_1 computed from the silhouette Ω_1 leads to a viewpoint v_2 in which, from the corresponding silhouette Ω_2, a different axis $a_2 \neq a_1$ can be computed. This is however a problem only if the user *releases* the pointer (mouse) button to end the rotation; if the button is not released, the computation of a new axis a_2 is not started, so moving the pointer back will reverse the rotation.

Scalability: Our method uses OpenGL 1.1 (primitive rendering and Z-buffer reading) plus the 2D image-based skeletonization method in [46] used to compute the skeleton S_Ω, its regularization $\overline{S}_\Omega$, and the feature transform $FT_{\overline{S}_\Omega}$. We implemented skeletonization in NVidia's CUDA and C++ to handle scenes of hundreds of thousands of polygons rendered at 1000^2 pixel resolution in a few milliseconds on a consumer-grade GPU, *e.g.* GTX 660. The skeletonization computational complexity is linear in the number of silhouette pixels, *i.e.*, $O(|\Omega|)$. This is due to the fact that the underlying distance transform used has the same linear complexity. For details on this, we refer to the original algorithm [6]. The separate code of this skeletonization method is available at [1]. Implementing the two improvements presented in Sect. 3 is also computationally efficient: The skeleton's distance transform $DT_{\overline{S}_\Omega}$ is already computed during the rotation axis estimation (Sect. 3.1C). The distance $DT_{\overline{\Omega}}$ and feature transforms $FT_{\overline{\Omega}}$ require one extra skeletonization pass of the background image $\overline{\Omega}$. All in all, our method delivers interaction at over 100 frames-per-second on the aforementioned consumer-grade GPU. The full code of our skeleton-and-trackball manipulation tool (Sect. 5.1) is provided online [47].

Novelty: To our knowledge, this is the first time when 2D image-based skeletons have been used to perform interactive manipulations of 3D shapes. Compared to similar view-based reconstructions of 3D curve skeletons from their 2D silhouettes [29,31], our method requires a *single* viewpoint to compute an approximate 3D curve skeleton and is two to three orders of magnitude faster.

6.2   Usability and Applicability

The evaluation described in Sect. 5 confirmed the insights elicited from the earlier formative study (Sect. 4), *i.e.* that skeleton rotation is best for precise, small-scale, final alignment touches; and that skeleton rotation best works as a *complement*, and not replacement, of trackball rotation. The latter point was supported by all types of data from our evaluation – task timing, scores assigned by users to evaluation questions, and free-form text feedback. The same data shows that users rank the combined modality (B) as better than both S and T modalities taken separately. The user scores also show that, overall, the combined modality is easy to learn and use (Fig. 12, Q2-4-8-11-12). Put together, all above support our claim of added value for the skeleton-based rotation technique.

Besides the above results, the user study also unveiled several questions which we cannot fully answer:

User Performance: There is a large variability of user performance, measured as task success rates and completion times (see Fig. 11b and related text). We cannot explain this variability by differences in the experiment setup, previous user familiarity with 3D manipulation, amount of training with the evaluated tool, or other measured factors. This variability may be due to user characteristics which the self-reported variables (Fig. 9b and related text) do not capture; to the high heterogeneity of the user population; but also due to dependent variables which we did not measure, *e.g.*, how often did users use the skeleton simplification level (Sect. 5.1) to produce suitable skeletons for generating rotation axes. Repeating the experiment with a more homogeneous population and more measured variables would help answering this question.

Applicability: An important limitation of our study is that, for the B modality, we did not measure how (much) the task was completed using each *separate* modality, *i.e.*, S and T. The formative study (Sect. 4), textual user feedback for the controlled experiment, and our observation of the users during the experiment jointly show that, in most cases involving moderate or hard tasks, trackball was *first* used to obtain a viewpoint roughly close to the target one, which was next fine-tuned using skeleton. This is fully in line with our initial design ideas (see Fig. 1 and related text) and also with earlier findings on what trackball best works for [21,27,34]. However, understanding more precisely which are the rotation types that skeleton best supports would greatly help to improve the combined modality by *e.g.* suggesting this modality to the user when it appears fit, and/or conversely, blocking this modality when it does not match the task at hand.

Study Limitations: Besides the above-mentioned aspects, our study (Sect. 5) has further limitations: It uses only four shapes that cannot capture the rich distributions of 3D shapes that need manipulation. Also, it only covers the task of rotating from an initial pose to a given final pose. Yet, manipulation is also used for free exploration and/or design actions which do not require reaching a predefined pose. It is unclear how to *quantitatively* measure the added value of interaction tools in such contexts, beyond qualitative user-satisfaction questionnaires [21]. Also, we cannot exclude learning effects between the trials that address the same task with different modalities. Finally, what is the exact added-value of all the rotation-specification improvements (Sect. 3.3) was not currently measured. Exploring all these directions is left to future work.

7 Conclusion

We proposed a method for specifying interactive rotations of 3D scenes around local rotation axes using image skeletons. We compute such axes from the skeleton of the 2D silhouette of the rendered scene, enhanced with depth information from the rendered Z buffer. Specifying such rotation axes requires a single click-and-drag gesture and no additional parameter settings. Our method is simple to implement, using distance and feature transforms provided by modern 2D skeletonization algorithms; handles 3D scenes consisting of arbitrarily complex polygon meshes (not necessarily watertight, connected, and/or of good quality) or 3D point clouds; can be integrated in any 3D viewing system that allows access to the Z buffer; and works at interactive frame-rates even for scenes of hundreds of thousands of primitives.

We measured the added value of the proposed rotation technique by a formative study (to elicit main concerns from users) followed by a controlled user study. Results showed that, when combined with trackball rotation, our method leads to better results (in terms of task completion times) and higher user satisfaction than trackball rotation alone. Also, our method is easy to learn and does not carry a significant learning or execution cost for the users, thereby not increasing the costs of using standard trackball rotation.

Several future work directions are possible. More cues can be used to infer more accurate 3D curve skeletons from image data, such as shading and depth gradients, leading to more precise rotation axes. Such data-driven cues could be also used to better control the rotation, and also suggest to the user which of the two modalities (skeleton-based or trackball rotation) are best for a given context. Separately, we aim to deploy our joint skeleton-and-trackball rotation tool on touch displays (single or multiple input) and evaluate its effectiveness in supporting domain experts to perform 3D exploration for specific applications, such as the astronomical data exploration outlined in Sect. 4.

References

1. Telea, A.: Real-time 2D skeletonization using CUDA (2019). http://www.staff.science.uu.nl/~telea001/Shapes/CUDASkel
2. Bade, R., Ritter, F., Preim, B.: Usability comparison of mouse-based interaction techniques for predictable 3D rotation. In: Butz, A., Fisher, B., Krüger, A., Olivier, P. (eds.) SG 2005. LNCS, vol. 3638, pp. 138–150. Springer, Heidelberg (2005). https://doi.org/10.1007/11536482_12
3. Belousov, B.: Difference between two rotation matrices (2016). http://www.boris-belousov.net/2016/12/01/quat-dist
4. Bian, S., Zheng, A., Chaudhry, E., You, L., Zhang, J.J.: Automatic generation of dynamic skin deformation for animated characters. Symmetry 10(4), 89 (2018)
5. Blum, H.: A transformation for extracting new descriptors of shape. In: Models for the Perception of Speech and Visual Form, pp. 362–381. MIT Press (1967)
6. Cao, T.T., Tang, K., Mohamed, A., Tan, T.S.: Parallel banding algorithm to compute exact distance transform with the GPU. In: Proceedings of ACM SIGGRAPH Symposium on Interactive 3D Graphics and Games, pp. 83–90 (2010)
7. Chaouch, M., Verroust-Blondet, A.: Alignment of 3D models. Graph. Models 71(2), 63–76 (2009)

8. Chen, M., Mountford, S., Sellen, A.: A study in interactive 3D rotation using 2D control devices. Comput. Graph Forum **22**(4), 121–129 (1998)

9. Cornea, N., Silver, D., Min, P.: Curve-skeleton properties, applications, and algorithms. IEEE TVCG **13**(3), 597–615 (2007)

10. Costa, L., Cesar, R.: Shape Analysis and Classification. CRC Press, Boca Raton (2000)

11. Dubinski, J.: When galaxies collide. Astron. Now **15**(8), 56–58 (2001)

12. Duffin, K.L., Barrett, W.A.: Spiders: a new user interface for rotation and visualization of N-dimensional point sets. In: Proceedings of IEEE Visualization, pp. 205–211 (1994)

13. Emory, M., Iaccarino, G.: Visualizing turbulence anisotropy in the spatial domain with componentality contours. Cent. Turbul. Res. Ann. Res. Briefs 123–138 (2014). https://web.stanford.edu/group/ctr/ResBriefs/2014/14_emory.pdf

14. Ersoy, O., Hurter, C., Paulovich, F., Cantareiro, G., Telea, A.: Skeleton-based edge bundling for graph visualization. IEEE TVCG **17**(2), 2364–2373 (2011)

15. Falcao, A., Feng, C., Kustra, J., Telea, A.: Multiscale 2D medial axes and 3D surface skeletons by the image foresting transform. In: Saha, P., Borgefors, G., di Baja, G.S. (eds.) Skeletonization - Theory, Methods, and Applications. Elsevier (2017). Chap. 2

16. Falcão, A., Stolfi, J., Lotufo, R.: The image foresting transform: theory, algorithms, and applications. IEEE TPAMI **26**(1), 19–29 (2004)

17. Frokjaer, E., Hertzum, M., Hornbaek, K.: Measuring usability: are effectiveness, efficiency, and satisfaction really correlated? In: Proceedings of CHI, pp. 345–352 (2000)

18. Guo, J., Wang, Y., Du, P., Yu, L.: A novel multi-touch approach for 3D object free manipulation. In: Chang, J., Zhang, J.J., Magnenat Thalmann, N., Hu, S.-M., Tong, R., Wang, W. (eds.) AniNex 2017. LNCS, vol. 10582, pp. 159–172. Springer, Cham (2017). https://doi.org/10.1007/978-3-319-69487-0_12

19. Hancock, M., Carpendale, S., Cockburn, A.: Shallow-depth 3D interaction: design and evaluation of one-, two- and three-touch techniques. In: Proceedings of ACM CHI, pp. 1147–1156 (2007)

20. Hancock, M., ten Cate, T., Carpendale, S., Isenberg, T.: Supporting sandtray therapy on an interactive tabletop. In: Proceedings of ACM CIII, pp. 2133–2142 (2010)

21. Henriksen, K., Sporring, J., Hornbaek, K.: Virtual trackballs revisited. IEEE TVCG **10**(2), 206–216 (2004)

22. Hesselink, W.H., Roerdink, J.B.T.M.: Euclidean skeletons of digital image and volume data in linear time by the integer medial axis transform. IEEE TPAMI **30**(12), 2204–2217 (2008)

23. Hinckley, K., Tullio, J., Pausch, R., Proffitt, D., Kassell, N.: Usability analysis of 3D rotation techniques. In: Proceedings of UIST, pp. 1–10 (1997)

24. Hultquist, J.: A virtual trackball. In: Graphics Gems, vol. 1, pp. 462–463 (1990)

25. Dubinski, J., et al.: GRAVITAS: portraits of a universe in motion (2006). https://www.cita.utoronto.ca/~dubinski/galaxydynamics/gravitas.html

26. Jackson, B., Lau, T., Schroeder, D., Toussaint, K., Keefe, D.: A lightweight tangible 3D interface for interactive visualization of thin fiber structures. IEEE TVCG **19**(12), 2802–2809 (2013)

27. Jacob, I., Oliver, J.: Evaluation of techniques for specifying 3D rotations with a 2D input device. In: Proceedings of HCI, pp. 63–76 (1995)

28. Kaye, D., Ivrissimtzis, I.: Mesh alignment using grid based PCA. In: Proceedings of CGTA, pp. 174–181 (2015)

29. Kustra, J., Jalba, A., Telea, A.: Probabilistic view-based curve skeleton computation on the GPU. In: Proceedings of VISAPP. SciTePress (2013)

30. Kustra, J., Jalba, A., Telea, A.: Robust segmentation of multiple intersecting manifolds from unoriented noisy point clouds. Comput. Graph. Forum **33**(4), 73–87 (2014)

31. Livesu, M., Guggeri, F., Scateni, R.: Reconstructing the curve-skeletons of 3D shapes using the visual hull. IEEE TVCG **18**(11), 1891–1901 (2012)

32. Meijster, A., Roerdink, J., Hesselink, W.: A general algorithm for computing distance transforms in linear time. In: Goutsias, J., Vincent, L., Bloomberg, D.S. (eds.) Mathematical Morphology and its Applications to Image and Signal Processing. Computational Imaging and Vision, vol. 18, pp. 331–340. Springer, Boston (2002). https://doi.org/10.1007/0-306-47025-X_36

33. Ogniewicz, R.L., Kubler, O.: Hierarchic Voronoi skeletons. Pattern Recog. **28**, 343–359 (1995)

34. Partala, T.: Controlling a single 3D object: viewpoint metaphors, speed, and subjective satisfaction. In: Proceedings of INTERACT, pp. 536–543 (1999)

35. Reniers, D., van Wijk, J.J., Telea, A.: Computing multiscale skeletons of genus 0 objects using a global importance measure. IEEE TVCG **14**(2), 355–368 (2008)

36. Rodrigues, R.S.V., Morgado, J.F.M., Gomes, A.J.P.: Part-based mesh segmentation: a survey. Comput. Graph. Forum **37**(6), 235–274 (2018)

37. Rosenfeld, A., Pfaltz, J.: Distance functions in digital pictures. Pattern Recogn. **1**, 33–61 (1968)

38. Shoemake, K.: ARCBALL: a user interface for specifying three-dimensional orientation using a mouse. In: Proceedings of Graphics Interface (1992)

39. Siddiqi, K., Pizer, S.: Medial Representations: Mathematics, Algorithms and Applications. Springer, Heidelberg (2008). https://doi.org/10.1007/978-1-4020-8658-8

40. Sobiecki, A., Yasan, H.C., Jalba, A.C., Telea, A.C.: Qualitative comparison of contraction-based curve skeletonization methods. In: Hendriks, C.L.L., Borgefors, G., Strand, R. (eds.) ISMM 2013. LNCS, vol. 7883, pp. 425–439. Springer, Heidelberg (2013). https://doi.org/10.1007/978-3-642-38294-9_36

41. Tagliasacchi, A., Delame, T., Spagnuolo, M., Amenta, N., Telea, A.: 3D skeletons: a state-of-the-art report. Comput. Graph. Forum **35**(2), 573–597 (2016)

42. Tangelder, J.W.H., Veltkamp, R.C.: A survey of content based 3D shape retrieval methods. Multimed. Tools Appl. **39**(3) (2008)

43. Telea, A.: Feature preserving smoothing of shapes using saliency skeletons. In: Linsen, L., Hagen, H., Hamann, B., Hege, H.C. (eds.) Visualization in Medicine and Life Sciences II. Mathematics and Visualization, pp. 136–148. Springer, Heidelberg (2011). https://doi.org/10.1007/978-3-642-21608-4_9

44. Telea, A.: Source code for salience skeleton computation (2014). https://webspace.science.uu.nl/~telea001/Shapes/Salience

45. Telea, A., Jalba, A.: Voxel-based assessment of printability of 3D shapes. In: Soille, P., Pesaresi, M., Ouzounis, G.K. (eds.) ISMM 2011. LNCS, vol. 6671, pp. 393–404. Springer, Heidelberg (2011). https://doi.org/10.1007/978-3-642-21569-8_34

46. Telea, A., van Wijk, J.J.: An augmented fast marching method for computing skeletons and centerlines. In: Ebert, D., Brunet, P., Navazo, I. (eds.) Proceedings of Eurographics/IEEE VGTC Symposium on Visualization (VisSym), pp. 251–259. The Eurographics Association (2002)

47. The Authors: Source code and videos of interactive skeleton-based axis rotation (2019). http://www.staff.science.uu.nl/~telea001/Shapes/CUDASkelInteract

48. Yu, L., Isenberg, T.: Exploring one- and two-touch interaction for 3D scientific visualization spaces. In: Posters of Interactive Tabletops and Surfaces, November 2009

49. Yu, L., Svetachov, P., Isenberg, P., Everts, M.H., Isenberg, T.: FI3D: direct-touch interaction for the exploration of 3D scientific visualization spaces. IEEE TVCG **16**(6), 1613–1622 (2010)

50. Zhai, X., Chen, X., Yu, L., Telea, A.: Interactive axis-based 3D rotation specification using image skeletons. In: Proceedings of 15th International Joint Conference on Computer Vision, Imaging and Computer Graphics Theory and Applications - Volume 1: GRAPP, pp. 169–178. SciTePress (2020)

51. Zhao, Y.J., Shuralyov, D., Stuerzlinger, W.: Comparison of multiple 3D rotation methods. In: Proceedings of IEEE VECIMS, pp. 19–23 (2011)

CSG Tree Extraction from 3D Point Clouds and Meshes Using a Hybrid Approach

Markus Friedrich[1($\boxtimes$)], Steffen Illium[1], Pierre-Alain Fayolle[2], and Claudia Linnhoff-Popien[1]

[1] Institute of Informatics, LMU Munich, Oettingenstr. 67, 80538 Munich, Germany
{markus.friedrich,steffen.illium,claudia.linnhoff-popien}@ifi.lmu.de
[2] Division of Information and Systems, The University of Aizu, Aizu-Wakamatsu, Fukushima 965-8580, Japan
fayolle@u-aizu.ac.jp

Abstract. The problem of Constructive Solid Geometry (CSG) tree reconstruction from 3D point clouds or 3D triangle meshes is hard to solve. At first, the input data set (point cloud, triangle soup or triangle mesh) has to be segmented and geometric primitives (spheres, cylinders, ...) have to be fitted to each subset. Then, the size- and shape optimal CSG tree has to be extracted. We propose a pipeline for CSG reconstruction consisting of multiple stages: A primitive extraction step, which uses deep learning for primitive detection, a clustered variant of RANSAC for parameter fitting, and a Genetic Algorithm (GA) for convex polytope generation. It directly transforms 3D point clouds or triangle meshes into solid primitives. The filtered primitive set is then used as input for a GA-based CSG extraction stage. We evaluate two different CSG extraction methodologies and furthermore compare our pipeline to current state-of-the-art methods.

Keywords: 3D computer vision · CSG tree recovery · Deep learning · Evolutionary algorithms · Fitting · RANSAC · Segmentation

1 Introduction

A commonly used technique for CAD (Computer Aided Design) modeling is based on the combination of solid primitives (spheres, cuboids, cylinders, etc.) with intuitive operations, like the set union or the set intersection. The resulting model can be represented as a tree structure with operations in the inner nodes and solid primitives as leaves. This representation is called a CSG (Constructive Solid Geometry) tree.

Several robust techniques exist to convert such a CSG-based model into other representations, like triangle meshes or point clouds. However, the inverse transformation is by far more complex: At first, solid primitives must be detected and extracted from the input representation. We focus on bounded primitives

© Springer Nature Switzerland AG 2022
K. Bouatouch et al. (Eds.): VISIGRAPP 2020, CCIS 1474, pp. 53–79, 2022.
https://doi.org/10.1007/978-3-030-94893-1_3

(instead of, e.g., planes and infinite cylinders, we use spheres, capped cylinders and 4–6 sided convex polytopes, including cuboids as a special case of arbitrary 6-sided convex polytopes), as they simplify the later on reconstructed CSG tree and allow for easier manual editing of the tree after automatic extraction. Then, a CSG tree has to be inferred that best fits the target geometry represented as a point cloud or triangle mesh. Since a given model can be expressed by an infinite number of different CSG trees, it is necessary to define additional quality criteria beyond the expression's geometric fitness. In this work, we therefore focus also on minimal tree size, which is optimized in a final optimization step and completes the proposed pipeline.

This paper is an extension of the work [15] presented at VISIGRAPP 2020. In particular, it makes the following new contributions:

- Support for arbitrary, 4 to 6-sided convex polytopes in the primitive segmentation and fitting stage was added.
- The primitive type detection network was re-implemented and re-trained with noisy point clouds to improve prediction robustness for real-world data sets.
- A new, volume-based, fitness function for shape fitting replaces the former surface-based measure and leads to faster running times and more robust results.
- An additional solid primitive filtering stage was added which removes duplicates and degenerate primitives from the result set.
- A whole new CSG tree extraction step was introduced that takes the fitted solid primitives and creates a size-optimized CSG tree. Based on a detailed analysis of the CSG tree extraction problem, two different approaches were implemented and evaluated.
- The evaluation was extended to include the CSG tree extraction step, a comparison with state-of-the-art methods and new data sets.

The structure of this paper is as follows: We start by reviewing works related to our problem of interest in Sect. 2, followed by a presentation of relevant background material (Sect. 3). We describe our proposed approach in Sect. 4 and present the numerical results obtained from our experiments with this approach in Sect. 5. Finally, we conclude in Sect. 6.

2   Related Work

2.1   Primitive Segmentation and Fitting

Reverse Engineering. Segmentation of the input data set (whether it is a 3D point cloud, a polygonal soup or polygonal mesh) into subsets, primitive detection and fitting to these subsets are necessary steps of any reverse engineering process. See, for example, [2,28,45] and the references therein.

Segmentation in Computer Graphics. Recently, interest to segmentation and fitting arose in the graphics community with applications in geometric modeling and processing. Segmentation of shapes with application to simplification and re-meshing is discussed in [5,23]. Sometimes, segmentation along is insufficient, and there is a need to recover the primitives type or their parameters [1,24,27,34,44].

RANSAC-Based Approaches. A popular approach in graphics is based on RANSAC and its variants: an efficient version of RANSAC for fitting planes, spheres, cylinders, cones and torii is described in [34]. It was later extended in [27] to handle constraints between the fitted primitives, e.g. two planes are parallel, etc. Our approach is also based on RANSAC, however: 1) we apply RANSAC to a pre-clustered (by primitive type) point cloud. It allows us to limit the types of primitive to try and make the process more robust and less parameter sensitive. 2) Unlike RANSAC that fits unbounded primitives, we generate bounded primitives, in particular planes are combined to form general polytopes.

Machine Learning Approaches. Techniques from Machine Learning were applied to the problems of segmentation and fitting. Traditional Machine Learning techniques[1] are used for learning segmentation and labelling in [19] or to fit template shapes corresponding to each part [21].

Deep Learning Approaches. Recently approaches based on Deep Learning have been used to train deep neural networks to perform tasks of segmentation and fitting. PointNet [31] and PointNet++ [32] use deep neural networks for the problem of segmentation and classification of shapes. Li et al. propose an end-to-end learning pipeline for segmenting, detecting and fitting primitives (plane, sphere, cylinder and cone) in 3D point clouds [26]. Approximating the input 3D shape by a collection of cuboids is proposed in [43,47]. Generalizing the used primitives leads to the learning of shape templates [17]. Our segmentation and fitting step is not limited to cuboids and is closer to the approach of Li et al. [26], however we have no limitations on the number of points in the input point cloud, and generate bounded, solid primitives. Similar to our approach, Sharma et al. [40] use a clustering module based on a neural network. Unlike our approach, their fitting module is also based on a neural network similar to [26]. Their approach stops at the fitting stage, and they don't try to reconstruct a CSG solid, as we do.

For a more complete overview of existing works on segmentation and fitting, the reader is also referred to the recent survey by Kaiser et al. [18].

2.2   CSG Extraction

B-Rep to CSG. The related problem of converting a solid defined by its Boundary Representation (B-Rep) to a CSG representation was first investigated by Shapiro and Vossler [36–38], then later improved by Buchele in [3]. In this work, we deal with unstructured point clouds or triangle meshes.

---

[1] By "traditional" we mean methods that are not based on deep neural networks.

Point Cloud to CSG. The problem of converting a point cloud to a CSG representation was first introduced in [41], where strongly typed Genetic Programming (GP) was used for fitting primitives and evolving a CSG expression. It is limited to very simple point clouds. A related approach [10] generates a CSG tree by combining fitted parametric primitives using a GA. In [9] a two stage pipeline is proposed: A segmentation/fitting stage followed by a GP to evolve a CSG tree. The objective function in the GP is constrained to limit the CSG tree size. This approach was further improved in [13] with various algorithmic tricks for accelerating the search.

Wu et al. [46] propose to cluster fitted primitives in groups of intersecting primitives. Each group contains only a few primitives and the CSG expression is generated by brute force. Du et al. use program synthesis [25] to generate CSG expressions in [7]. Their approach relies on CAD triangle meshes (no defect, few and long triangles) as input.

Recent works such as [29,30] rely on functional programming techniques to convert an input triangle mesh to a CSG representation.

Images/Voxels to CSG. Approaches based on deep neural networks have also been used for extracting structured shape descriptions (such as a CSG representation) from input data. In general, these approaches assume as input an image (2D) or voxel data (3D). Sharma et al. propose in [39] to use a deep recurrent neural network to learn the production of CSG expressions from an image (2D) or voxel data (3D). Chen et al. [4] describe a method that learns a BSP (Binary Space Partition) tree from a single view image or voxel data. A BSP tree can be easily converted to a CSG tree. A related approach [6] fits convex shapes as a combination of halfplanes, then define the final solid object as the union of the convex shapes.

Instead of being limited to a CSG description, the approaches described in [8,42] infer 2D/3D graphics programs from voxel input by training a model using a neural program synthesis technique.

3   Background

This section introduces concepts, definitions and background material necessary for understanding the approach described in Sect. 4.

3.1   Evolutionary Algorithms

Evolutionary Algorithms are population-based meta-heuristics for solving optimization problems. They follow principles from evolution theory to evolve a population of solutions to a problem based on a certain fitness criterion. The fitness criterion is formalized as a function that assigns a score value to each solution in the population. This function is then minimized (or maximized) by an iterative process: At each iteration, a subset of ranked solutions is selected and altered using so-called mutation and crossover operators, and combined with newly, randomly generated solutions. The evolved population is then again ranked and the whole process continues until a stopping condition is met.

Evolutionary Algorithms are known for their ability to solve difficult combinatorial optimization problems and in general for problems with a complicated fitness function, which is not necessarily differentiable, and with potentially multiple minima. In this paper, we use a Genetic Algorithm for generating solid primitives (by combining unbounded primitives) and for CSG tree extraction (by combining Boolean operations with solid primitives).

3.2   CSG Trees and Signed Distance Functions

A CSG tree represents a solid by combining simple primitives in the tree leaves with operations (Boolean, rigid transformations) in the tree internal nodes. We represent primitives by the signed distance function (SDF) of their boundary. Thus, to a solid primitive S, corresponds an SDF d_S, which is zero on the boundary ∂S (we assume $d_S < 0$ inside S). Boolean operations are implemented with the min- and max-functions [33]:

- Intersection: $S_1 \cap^* S_2 := \max(d_{S_1}, d_{S_2})$,
- Union: $S_1 \cup^* S_2 := \min(d_{S_1}, d_{S_2})$,
- Complement: $\backslash^* S := -d_S$,
- Difference: $S_1 -^* S_2 := \max(d_{S_1}, -d_{S_2})$.

Note that min- and max-functions are not regularized set-operations in the strict sense [35] but are a sufficient approximation for our purposes.

3.3   The CSG Tree Extraction Problem

In this section, we present a complexity analysis of the CSG tree extraction problem and available simplifications, given a certain set of primitives and a description of the solid surface.

The CSG Tree Search Space. A CSG tree $\Phi(P)$ for a primitive set P is a binary tree. Its inner nodes are operations, its outer nodes (leaves) are primitives. Operations are always binary: $O = \{\cup^*, \cap^*, -^*\}$ (in order to keep things simple, we do not consider here the complement operation $\backslash^*$, which is unary). The number of binary trees with n internal nodes and $n + 1$ leaves is $C(n)$, the so-called Catalan Number, see Fig. 1

$$C(n) = \frac{1}{n+1} \binom{2n}{n} \tag{1}$$

We choose the $n + 1$ leaf labels from P. It is possible to select a leaf label (primitive) more than once. There are $(2|P|)^{n+1}$ possible leaf label configurations

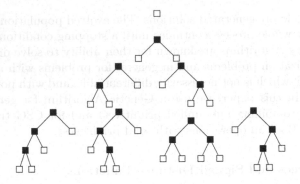

Fig. 1. Number of binary trees for $n \in \{0, 1, 2, 3\}$.

(The factor 2 is needed since a primitive p can also occur as its complement $\backslash^* p$ in the tree). We choose the labels of the n inner nodes (operation nodes) from O. It is possible to select an operation label (operation) more than once. There are $|O|^n$ possible operation node label configurations. Thus, there are

$$E(n) = (2|P|)^{n+1} \cdot |O|^n \cdot C(n) \tag{2}$$

possible CSG trees with $2n + 1$ nodes (see also [22] for various results on enumerating trees).

For a given number of inner nodes, the number of CSG trees is given by (2). In order to get all possible trees for a given set of primitives P, we need to count all possible trees for all possible number of inner nodes between specified minimum and maximum numbers of inner nodes $n_{\min}$ and $n_{\max}$

$$A(n_{\min}, n_{\max}) = \sum_{i=n_{\min}}^{n_{\max}} E(i) \tag{3}$$

In order to define the search space for the combinatorial CSG tree extraction problem, we need to be able to derive (or estimate) $n_{\min}$ and $n_{\max}$ for a given primitive set P:

- For $n_{\min}$, we have $n_{\min} = |P| - 1$, since the tree should contain all primitives at least once (we do not consider the case where P contains redundant or spurious primitives). Thus there should be at least $|P|$ leaves, resulting in at least $|P| - 1$ inner nodes.
- For $n_{\max}$, it is not possible to derive a value, since it is always possible to add new inner nodes and thus leaves (redundancies). Instead, we need to look for possible empirical values for $n_{\max}$. In [14], the estimation for the maximum tree height $h_{\max} \approx \sqrt{\pi/2 \cdot |P| \cdot (|P| - 1)}$ is used ($n_{\max}$ can then be estimated from $h_{\max}$). Experiments revealed that it almost always produces far too high values. A good choice of $n_{\max}$ depends on the size of the primitive set P, the spatial configuration of the primitives as expressed in the intersection graph

(see Fig. 2b for an example) and the overall complexity of the model surface that should be represented by the CSG tree. The latter is difficult to quantify.

Furthermore, the range of values for the CSG tree's height h is:

$$\lceil \log_2(n+1) \rceil \leq h \leq n \tag{4}$$

As shown in [12], the average CSG tree height $\overline{H}_n(\Phi)$ for CSG trees with n inner nodes has the asymptotic behavior

$$\overline{H}_n(\Phi) \sim 2\sqrt{\pi n} \quad \text{as } n \to \infty. \tag{5}$$

Since it is possible to characterize the size of the CSG tree search space for a given set of primitives and an upper bound for the tree size n_{max}, the question is how the size of the search space can be reduced in order to simplify the CSG tree extraction problem.

Fundamental Products and the Disjunctive Canonical Form. Analogous to the disjunctive canonical form (DCF) for Boolean functions one can restrict the tree topology to a set of primitive intersections (so-called fundamental products [36]) that are combined via the set union operator. The result is commonly referred to as a two-level CSG representation [36] and reads

$$\Phi(P) = \bigcup_{k=1}^{2^{|P|}-1} g_1 \cap^* g_2 \cdots \cap^* g_{|P|}, g_i \in \{p_i, \backslash^* p_i\}. \tag{6}$$

The number of non-empty fundamental products n_f is in $[|P|, 2^{|P|}-1]$. It depends on the intersections between primitives which can be formalized using the intersection graph $G = (P, I)$ of the primitives P, where I is the set of edges. Each edge (p_i, p_j) represents an intersection between primitive p_i and p_j with $i, j \in \{1, \ldots, |P|\}$. If G is fully connected, n_f reaches its maximum, if I is empty its minimum. See Fig. 2 for an example with a set of fundamental products and the corresponding intersection graph.

   This formulation reduces the aforementioned search space complexity to $\mathcal{O}(2^{|P|})$ since we only have to check for each non-empty fundamental product if it is inside the target solid S. The downside of this formulation is, however, the excessive size of the resulting tree. A better method to reduce the search space while keeping tree size optimality is described in the next section.

Dominant Halfspaces and Solid Decomposition. Dominant halfspaces $\{d_1, ..., d_n\} \subseteq P$ are primitives that are located either fully inside or fully outside of the target solid S. Thus, they behave essentially like fundamental products but with by far smaller expression sizes. A solid can be decomposed using dominant halfspaces [36]:

$$S = ((...(S_{rem} \oplus d_1) \oplus ...) \oplus d_2) \oplus d_n, \tag{7}$$

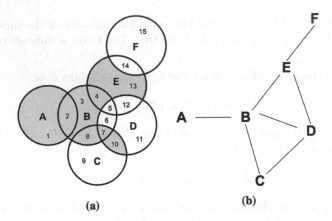

Fig. 2. (a) Example with $P = \{A, B, C, D, E, F\}$ and S, the solid to represent, in grey. Numbers 1–15 identify non-empty fundamental products. (b) The corresponding intersection graph G. Illustration adapted from [11].

where S_{rem} is the remaining solid after decomposition which can be described as an expression containing all non-dominant primitives and $\oplus$ is the difference operator if the following primitive dominates $\backslash^* S$ and the union operator if it dominates S. Decomposition can be applied recursively, making it a powerful tool for search space reduction. Since in the output expression, each dominant halfspace is used exactly once, it is optimal [36]. Considering the run-time complexity of the decomposition algorithm, it is $\mathcal{O}(|P|^2)$. In the worst case, each decomposition iteration results in a single primitive being removed from S. Thus, the first iteration visits each primitive once ($|P|$ visits) to check if it is dominant. Removing the single dominant primitive, the second iteration needs $|P| - 1$ visits and so on, resulting in $\sum_{k=|P|}^{1} k = \frac{|P|^2 + |P|}{2}$ necessary visits in total.

If S_{rem} is not empty after decomposition, it is possible to take the non-dominant remaining primitives and build their intersection graph (see also [13]). For sufficiently large models, this graph is not connected. Thus, a connected component analysis results in a set of sub-intersection graphs. The corresponding expressions for each sub-graph can be extracted independently and the result is then merged. This can be used to further partition the search space. The proposed CSG tree extraction approach (Sect. 4.4) uses decomposition but leaves further intersection graph partitioning for future work.

4   CSG Tree Extraction Pipeline

The CSG extraction pipeline is depicted in Fig. 3. It consists of five major parts: *Input Preparation, Solid Primitive Segmentation and Fitting, Solid Primitive Filtering, CSG Tree Extraction* and *CSG Tree Optimization*.

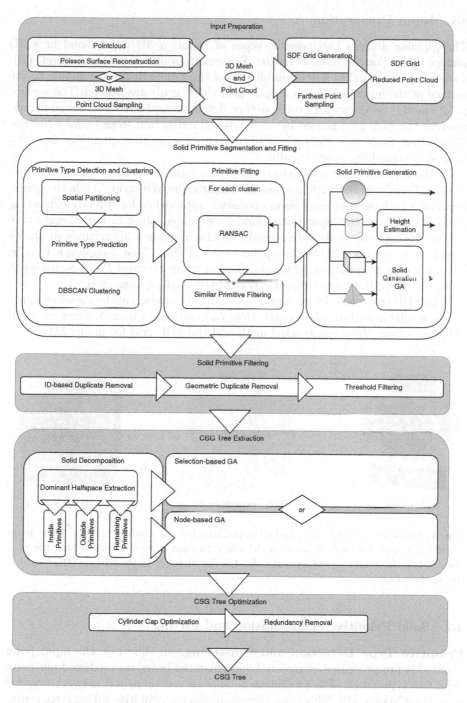

Fig. 3. The pipeline for CSG extraction from point clouds and 3D meshes. The parts in green were added to the pipeline proposed in [15]. (Color figure online)

4.1 Input Preparation

The pipeline accepts two possible types of input: a 3D point cloud or a 3D surface mesh. For the *Solid Primitive Segmentation and Fitting* step (Sect. 4.2), a surface point cloud O and a sampling F of the signed distance function to the surface of the input solid on a regular grid (SDF grid) are needed. The surface point cloud is necessary for primitive type detection and RANSAC-based fitting, whereas the SDF grid is used by all GA-based extraction steps (*solid Primitive Generation, CSG Tree Extraction*) to compute a score that quantifies how well shapes are matching geometrically.

If the input is a 3D point cloud, a surface mesh is extracted using *Poisson Surface Reconstruction* [20] in order to compute the SDF grid. While the generation of a surface mesh may seem excessive, approaches for directly extracting an SDF grid from the input point cloud by weighted point fusion schemes were not producing sufficiently stable results. If the input is a 3D triangle mesh, we sample it to obtain a 3D surface point cloud (*Point Cloud Sampling*). Finally, in both cases, the point cloud is sub-sampled using *Farthest Point Sampling* in order to reduce the computational effort of the next pipeline step.

The SDF grid stores for each grid cell an approximation of the signed distance to the available surface mesh (*SDF Grid Generation*). Figure 4 shows an input 3D point cloud, the reconstructed mesh and the SDF grid for model M1.

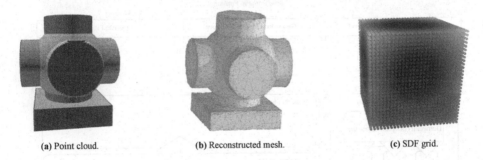

(a) Point cloud.   (b) Reconstructed mesh.   (c) SDF grid.

Fig. 4. Example of input data and data preparation for model M1: The input point cloud (a) is used for mesh generation (b) which in turn is used for computing the SDF grid. In (c), the brightness of a point indicates the distance to the surface (the brighter, the farther away).

4.2 Solid Primitive Segmentation and Fitting

Primitive Type Detection and Clustering. In this step, the input point cloud O is pre-processed, segmented and clustered based on predicted per-point primitive type labels. The prediction is done by a deep neural network inspired from PointNet++ [32]. This clustering simplifies the primitive fitting step, resulting in more stable results with less redundant or incorrectly fitted primitives (see also Fig. 12).

First, O is de-noised and outliers are removed. Then, it is partitioned along the coordinate axes into n^3 boxes, where $n \in \{3, 4\}$ in our experiments. This *Spatial Partitioning* helps the primitive type detection network to generalize to unseen shapes and relaxes the constraint on the network's input point cloud size. The next step performs per-point primitive type prediction for the point-cloud in each partition. It results in a type label for each point (*Primitive Type Prediction*). Due to the input size restrictions of the PointNet++-based prediction model [32], the per-partition point cloud is further down-sampled by *Farthest Point Sampling* (we use $k = 2048$ points).

Then, the per-partition point clouds are merged into a single point cloud, which is clustered by *DBSCAN Clustering*. Each point $o \in O$ has 9 components:

$$o = (p_x, p_y, p_z, n_x, n_y, n_z, t_0, t_1, t_2),$$

where $\mathbf{o}_p = (p_x, p_y, p_z)$ is the point spatial coordinates, $\mathbf{o}_n = (n_x, n_y, n_z)$ is the normal vector to the surface at $\mathbf{o}_p$, and $\mathbf{o}_t = (t_0, t_1, t_2)$ is the 1-hot-encoded primitive type label. See [15] for further details. This 1-hot encoding was selected such that we can use the Euclidean distance as the distance metric for DBSCAN. Based on our experiments, using a custom distance is not as efficient as using the built-in Euclidean distance metric. DBSCAN clustering is applied in two steps: First, on position $\mathbf{o}_p$ and normals $\mathbf{o}_n$ only. Secondly, on each resulting cluster with position $\mathbf{o}_p$ and primitive type label $\mathbf{o}_t$. This combination resulted in the best clustering in our experiments. The output of this step is a set of clusters with each cluster being represented by a point cloud with 6-dimensional points (point coordinates and normal vector).

Primitive Fitting. For each cluster, RANSAC [34] is run multiple times (in our experiments three times) to retrieve a set of primitives and their parameters. Since primitive types that can occur in a cluster are known from the type detection step, it is possible to reduce the search space. E.g., if a cluster contains only planes, it is unnecessary to search for spheres in that particular cluster. This, together with the reduced per-cluster point cloud size, greatly improves the stability of RANSAC, as can be seen in Fig. 12. Since the fitting procedure is applied multiple times in each cluster, a merge procedure that filters similar primitives from the set of all per-cluster primitives is applied to the result (*Similar Primitive Filtering*). This step generates a set of primitives with each primitive having a type, a set of parameters (e.g. radius and center for a sphere) and a point cloud with all points belonging to this primitive (note that the per-primitive point cloud is sub-sampled in order to improve efficiency of the next step). Since RANSAC detects and fits potentially unbounded primitives (planes, infinite cylinders, ...), an additional step is used to produce convex polytopes (from planes) and bounded cylinders (from infinite cylinders and planes), as described next.

Solid Primitive Generation. Given the set of (potentially unbounded) primitives obtained from the previous step, we generate solid (bounded) primitives (bounded cylinders, boxes and general convex polytopes). The strategy choice depends on the primitive type:

- **Spheres:** Spheres don't need any special treatment since they are already bounded.
- **Cylinders:** Cylinders fitted by RANSAC are unbounded. We estimate their height from the cylinder's corresponding point cloud: Its projection along the cylinder's main axis provides a good approximation of its height. Further improvement is conducted in the *CSG Tree Optimization* step, see Sect. 4.5.
- **Cuboids:** Cuboids are a special case of convex polytopes with 6 pair-wise parallel planes. A GA is used to find the best set of cuboids representing the input point cloud. Handling cuboids as a special case allows for faster GA convergence.
- **General Convex Polytopes:** General convex polytopes with 4-6 planes are also generated by a GA.

The GA for generating cuboids and 4–6-sided convex polytopes (in the following, both are simply called polytopes) is shown in Fig. 5. It is an extended and improved version of the method described in [15]. Each individual in the *Population* consists of a set of primitives P. During *Initialization*, the population is filled with sets of randomly generated polytopes. Duplicate polytopes are removed using *ID-based Duplicate Removal*, described in Sect. 4.3. This is followed by the *Ranking* step which computes a score for each individual based on the objective function

$$B(P,O,F) = \alpha \cdot G(P,O) + \beta \cdot V(P,F) - \gamma \cdot \frac{|P|}{n_{P\ max}}, \tag{8}$$

where $G(\cdot)$ is the geometry term, $V(\cdot)$ is the per-primitive geometry term and the last term is a size penalty term with $n_{P\ max}$ being the user-controlled maximum number of primitives in the set of primitives P. O is the input point cloud and F is the SDF of the target solid sampled on a regular grid (SDF grid). The parameters α, β and γ are user-controlled weights. The geometry term counts points that are close to any primitive in P and reads

$$G(P,O) = \frac{1}{|O|} \sum_{o \in O} \begin{cases} 1, & \text{if } \min_{p \in P} |d_p(o)| < \epsilon \\ 0, & \text{otherwise} \end{cases}, \tag{9}$$

where $d_p(\cdot)$ is the signed distance function of primitive $p \in P$ and ϵ is a user-defined epsilon value. This term makes sure that the target solid is well-covered with primitives.

Since it does not prevent primitives from being fully outside of the target solid, an additional per-primitive geometry term is added:

$$V(P,F) = \sum_{p \in P} \frac{1}{|V_p|} \sum_{v \in V_p} \begin{cases} 1, & \text{if } F(o_v) < \epsilon \\ 0, & \text{otherwise} \end{cases}, \tag{10}$$

where V_p is the set of voxels occupying the space of primitive p and o_v is the center of a voxel $v \in V_p$ in world coordinates. After *Ranking*, the best primitives out of all the primitive sets in the population are selected and added as a single primitive set to the population. This *Elite Selection* results in faster convergence. In the following *Selection* process, operands (*Parents*) for the variation operators (*Crossover* and *Mutation*) are selected using Tournament Selection. The *Crossover* operator re-combines two primitive sets from the population by randomly exchanging single primitives. The *Mutation* operator is applied to a single primitive set and corresponds to one of the following modes:

- **Replace:** Replace a randomly selected primitive with a newly created one.
- **Modify:** Modify a randomly selected primitive by exchanging planes randomly.
- **Add:** Add a newly generated primitive to the primitive set.
- **Remove:** Remove a primitive at a randomly selected position.
- **New:** Re-create the whole primitive set.

Mutation modes are selected randomly. The modified individuals (*Offspring*) are combined with the n best primitive sets ($n = 2$ in our experiments) to form the population for the next GA iteration. The GA terminates if a maximum number of iterations has been reached or if the score of the best individual has not changed over a certain number of iterations (*Termination Check*). The *Result* of the GA is the best individual of the last population which is selected in the step *Best Individual Selection*.

4.3   Solid Primitive Filtering

The primitive set generated in the previous step (Sect. 4.2) contains potentially redundant or erroneous primitives. An additional filtering stage is used to remove these primitives. We propose three possible techniques: *Threshold Filtering* is used to remove low quality primitives. In order to filter redundant primitives, we propose two possible approaches: an ID-based method and a geometric method.

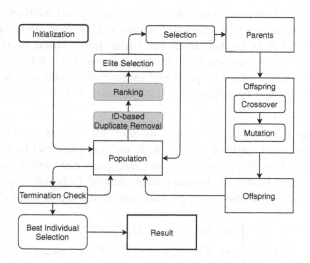

Fig. 5. The GA used for polytope extraction. Diagram adapted from [15] with modified parts in green. (Color figure online)

Threshold Filtering. Primitives with a low per-primitive geometry score (10) are removed from the primitive set. The lower bound can be manually set by the user.

ID-Based Duplicate Removal. All polytopes and capped primitives are a combination of fitted planes and unbounded Quadrics (e.g., a cylinder consists of two capping planes and an infinite cylinder, a polytope consists of a set of planes). Each fitted primitive (plane, infinite cylinder, sphere, ...) has a unique ID. Each solid primitive, obtained from combining fitted primitives, is assigned a unique ID by hashing the IDs of the fitted primitives that defines it. Solid primitives with the same hash can be reduced to a single one. This method is computationally cheap because it only needs to compute hashes on integer IDs. However, it fails to identify duplicates of primitives that are geometrically similar but with different hashes, or it fails to find primitives that are fully contained in another primitive (with all solid primitives entirely contained inside the target solid object). In order to capture these cases, we propose a method that relies on geometric information.

Geometric Duplicate Removal. For each primitive, we check if it is similar to or fully contained in another primitive. If this is the case, we remove it. Given two primitives p_0 and p_1: To check if p_0 is fully contained in p_1, we iterate over each voxel inside p_0 and check if it is also inside the primitive p_1. Note that p_1 needs to be a perfect primitive, i.e. it has a per-primitive geometry score (10) of 1.0 and thus is fully contained in the shape to reconstruct.

4.4 CSG Tree Extraction

The CSG tree extraction process takes a set of generated solid primitives P as input and reconstructs a CSG tree $\Phi(P)$ from it that best describes the input solid S. The solid S is implied from the input point cloud or triangle mesh and represented by the discrete SDF function F (see Sect. 4.1). A perfect fit is obtained when $|\Phi(P)| = S$. The proposed extraction mechanism has two steps: *Decomposition* followed by either the *Selection-based GA* or the *Node-based GA*.

Solid Decomposition. As described in Sect. 3.3, S can be decomposed by removing all dominant halfspaces from it. It reduces the CSG tree search space significantly. In a first step, the *Dominant Halfspace Extraction*, each primitive $p \in P$ is categorized in one of the categories: 'inside' (p is fully contained in S), 'outside' (p is fully contained in $\setminus^* S$) and 'remaining' (p is partially contained in S):

$$L_{(p)} = \begin{cases} \text{`inside'}, & \text{if } N(V_p, F) > t_{\text{inside}} \\ \text{`outside'}, & \text{if } N(V_p, F) < t_{\text{outside}} , \\ \text{`remaining'}, & \text{otherwise} \end{cases} \qquad (11)$$

where V_p is the set of voxels occupying the space of p, t_{inside} (resp. t_{outside}) is the threshold for inside primitives (resp. outside primitives) and $N(\cdot)$ counts the voxels in V_p located inside S:

$$N(V, F) = \frac{1}{|V|} \sum_{v \in V} \begin{cases} 1, & \text{if } F(o_v) < \epsilon \\ 0, & \text{otherwise} \end{cases}, \tag{12}$$

where o_v is the center point of voxel v. This results in three primitive sets P_{in}, P_{out} and P_{rem}. According to (7), S can be expressed as:

$$S = S_{rem} \cup^* P_{\text{in}} -^* P_{\text{out}}, \tag{13}$$

where S_{rem} is the remaining solid for which an expression is to be found using primitives from P_{rem}. We propose two GA-based approaches to find an expression for S_{rem}: A selection-based GA and a node-based GA.

Selection-Based GA. This approach tries to find the optimal selection of primitives in P_{rem} that best fits S_{rem}. These selected primitives are added to the decomposed expression using the union operation. The optimization problem is solved using a GA similar to the one shown in Fig. 5 but without *Elite Selection* and *Duplicate Removal*. An individual in the GA population is described by a bit string T_{rem}, where each bit represents the selection status of a single primitive. *Mutation* and *Crossover* operators are simple bit string manipulation operations. Before *Ranking*, the bit string is converted into an expression and is combined with the decomposed expression to form the individual's expression Ψ:

$$\Psi = \text{decode}(T_{rem}) \cup^* P_{\text{in}} -^* P_{\text{out}}, \tag{14}$$

where

$$\text{decode}(T) = \begin{cases} \text{decode}(T \backslash \{t\}) \cup^* p, & \text{if } T \neq \varnothing \wedge t = 1 \wedge L(p) = \text{'inside'} \\ \text{decode}(T \backslash \{t\}) \backslash^* p, & \text{if } T \neq \varnothing \wedge t = 1 \wedge L(p) = \text{'outside'} \\ \varnothing, & \text{otherwise} \end{cases} \tag{15}$$

with $t \in T$ being the bit and $p \in P_{rem}$ its corresponding primitive. The objective function used by the GA reads

$$M(\Psi, F) = \alpha \cdot Q(\Psi, F) - \beta \frac{\text{size}(\Psi)}{\text{size}_{max}}, \tag{16}$$

where $\text{size}(\cdot)$ is the expression size, size_{max} is the user-defined maximum expression size and $Q(\cdot)$ is a geometry term given by

$$Q(\Psi, F) = \frac{1}{|V_F|} \sum_{v \in V_F} \begin{cases} 1, & \text{if } |F(o_v) - d_\Psi(o_v)| < \epsilon \wedge \nabla F(o_v) \cdot \nabla_\Psi(o_v) \geq 0 \\ 0, & \text{otherwise} \end{cases}, \tag{17}$$

where $\cdot$ is the dot product, $d_\Psi(\cdot)$ is the distance function of the solid $|\Psi|$ and $\nabla_\Psi(\cdot)$ its gradient at voxel position o_v. For this selection problem, the search space is of size $2^{|P_{rem}|}$.

Node-Based GA. This approach searches for the best-fitting and size-optimal tree expression considering all possible trees with primitives P_{rem} (see Sect. 3.3 for a search space characterization). This search is conducted using a GA. The operators *Crossover* and *Mutation* manipulate the trees directly (similar to [9]). The objective function used by this GA is the same as the one described in (16). The difference is that Ψ is directly available since an individual of the population is already a tree expression (applying the decode($\cdot$) method (15) is not necessary).

One advantage of the node-based GA is the support of the intersection operation. Furthermore, more complex expressions, where one primitive needs to appear more than once in order to fit the target shape, are possible. Its main disadvantage is its slower convergence speed compared to the selection-based approach which is due to the larger search space to be considered.

4.5   CSG Tree Optimization

The extracted CSG tree might not be optimal in terms of its size, geometric structure or other characteristics (for an overview, see [16]) since there is an infinite number of CSG trees representing the same geometric shape for a given set of primitives. We try to optimize the extracted tree with two heuristics.

Cylinder Cap Optimization. The height of a cylinder primitive p_{cyl} is estimated from its corresponding point cloud (see Sect. 4.2). The quality of the estimate depends on the point cloud density and distribution. An improvement consists in determining the cylinder's cap planes $\{p_{top}, p_{bottom}\} \in P$ as follows: The intersection points of the cylinder's main axis with its top and bottom caps are computed. Then, for each point the closest plane (from the set of fitted planes) is selected as the top, respectively bottom, cap plane. Finally, the cylinder primitive leaves in the CSG tree containing p_{cyl} are replaced with the sub tree expression $p_{cyl} -^* (p_{top} \cup^* p_{bottom})$.

Redundancy Removal. GA-generated CSG trees tend to contain redundant or unnecessary expressions, such as for example, the union of a primitive with itself or the intersection of non-overlapping sub trees. Finding a size-optimal CSG tree is equivalent to the problem of Boolean function minimization which is NP-hard [36]. However, it is possible to use a simple heuristic to catch a lot of redundancy cases. Let $\varnothing$ be the empty set and W be the universal set. For each node in the binary CSG tree, we check if one of the following rules applies:

- Replace the difference between a sub tree and the sub tree itself with $\varnothing$.
- Replace unions/intersections where both operands are equivalent expressions or only a single operand exists with the expression of one of the operands.
- Replace intersections containing non-overlapping operands with $\varnothing$.
- Replace the complement of a complement with the operand of the inner complement.

$\varnothing$ and W are then replaced by the rules:

- A union with one operand being $\varnothing$ is replaced by the other operand.
- An intersection with one operand being W is replaced by the other operand.
- A union with one operand being W is replaced by W
- Replace differences where the right-hand side is $\varnothing$ with the left-hand side.

The process is repeated until no rule applies anymore. A more detailed description of a sampling-based variant of this technique, as well as other possible techniques for CSG tree optimization, can be found in [16].

5 Evaluation

5.1 Training of the Neural Network for Primitive Type Detection

Data Generation. The data generator described in [15] was enhanced to support the generation of general convex polytopes as well as point coordinates and normal distortion with Gaussian noise. At first, an input triangle mesh or CSG model is sampled and its point cloud clustered using K-Means Clustering. For each cluster, its main point-set orientation axes are derived using Principal Component Analysis (PCA). Then, a primitive of randomly selected type is fitted in the cluster using the cluster's main orientation, center point and point cloud dimensions. The goal here is not to generate an accurate primitive-based approximation of the input model, but to use it as a source for spatial variation and as a loose geometric pattern for the generated point set. See Fig. 6 for an example of a generated point cloud (a) and its corresponding primitive type segmentation (b) as predicted by the trained Neural Network.

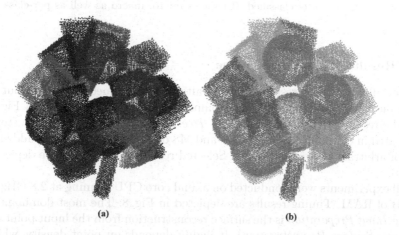

(a)   (b)

Fig. 6. (a) Point cloud generated by the data generator. Colors were used for better visual separation of single primitives and have no deeper meaning. (b) Predicted primitive labels. Colors indicate primitive types (Grey: sphere, orange: plane, red: cylinder). (Color figure online)

Training. Neural network training was conducted with a data set consisting of 1024 point clouds, each having around 50k points. We split each point cloud in partitions of $3 \times 3 \times 3$ equally-sized cubes. From those partitions, 1024 points are sampled in each epoch. For data augmentation, we randomly translate point samples by 0.1% of the bounding box length, change the ordering and scale them to fit into the unit cube. This procedure allows the network to learn a representation, which is able to generalize from the randomly generated training point clouds (see the previous section on data generation) to arbitrary models. After about 25 epochs without further hyperparameter tuning, model performance on our test data set (also randomly generated) reaches almost perfect results (see Fig. 7 for the Confusion Matrix and Receiver Operating Characteristic (ROC) Curves).

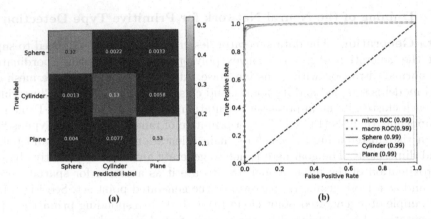

(a)   (b)

Fig. 7. (a) The confusion matrix for 3×3 classes shows that 98.0% of the points in the test set are correctly classified. (b) shows micro, macro as well as per-class ROC curves.

5.2   Results of the Full Pipeline

Figure 9 illustrates the results obtained after each intermediate step of our approach on 8 test models. Note that compared to the results shown in Fig. 6 in [15], the results of the additional *CSG Tree Extraction & Optimization* step are illustrated in column (d). Models M7 and M8 demonstrate the newly added support of arbitrary convex polytopes. Selected resulting CSG trees are depicted in Fig. 10.

All experiments were conducted on a dual core CPU running at 2.8 GHz with 16 GB of RAM. Timing results are depicted in Fig. 8. The most dominant step during *Input Preparation* is the surface reconstruction from the input point cloud (*Poisson Surface Reconstruction*). It highly depends on point density, which is the highest for M1 and M8. During *Solid Primitive Segmentation and Fitting*, the most expensive step is the generation of solid primitives via GA. M6 takes the longest time since it has the largest number of input primitives (see also

Fig. 12). Primitive type prediction is the second most costly task. In step *Solid Primitive Filtering*, the most time-consuming task is the *Geometric Duplicate Removal* which has a runtime complexity of $\mathcal{O}(|P|^2)$ and operates on a per-voxel level. For M6, twice as much solid primitives are generated to be able to capture the whole model (the GA's primitive set size is doubled). Thus, running times are the highest for this model.

Durations for the *CSG Tree Generation* process are significantly lower for all models that do not need to use a GA for tree extraction since they are fully decomposable (all except M4 and M7). For M4 and M7, durations of the *Selection-based GA* (M4, M7) and the *Node-based GA* (M4*, M7*) were compared. Since the search space for the latter is significantly larger (see Sect. 3), it takes approximately around five times longer to converge. Please note that the main advantage of the *Node-based GA* lies in its superior expressiveness since it can also handle intersections and other, more sophisticated operators. Furthermore, it can be used to find results following different optimization criteria (e.g., the shape of the CSG tree), as described in [16].

The *CSG Tree Optimization* step is dominated by the module for removing redundant sub trees from the output tree. There, M2 and M6 need a significant amount of time due to the amount of polytopes to process, followed by M5 and M3.

5.3   Comparison with Related Approaches

In this section, the proposed pipeline is compared to related approaches.

Hybrid Solid Fitting [15]. In this section, we address the limitations of the solid primitive generation and fitting pipeline described in [15] which this work extends:

CSG Tree Extraction. One of the main additions to [15] is the introduction of the *CSG Tree Extraction* step that extracts a CSG model corresponding to the input object from the list of fitted solid primitives. See column (d) in Fig. 9 for meshes obtained from the extracted CSG model and Fig. 10 for some of the corresponding CSG trees.

Tolerance to Noise. With the new primitive type detection network, it is now possible to detect primitives even in noisy point clouds. Figure 11 illustrates the results obtained by the former prediction model (column (a)) and the new prediction model (column (b)) on a noisy point cloud scanned from an object. The object consists only of planes (orange), most of them incorrectly classified with the method used in [15]. On the other hand, our improved model (b) classifies most of the points in the point cloud correctly.

Redundant Primitives. The newly introduced *Solid Primitive Filtering* pipeline step removes redundant primitives completely. In addition, the resulting CSG tree is further optimized by the *CSG Tree Optimization* step.

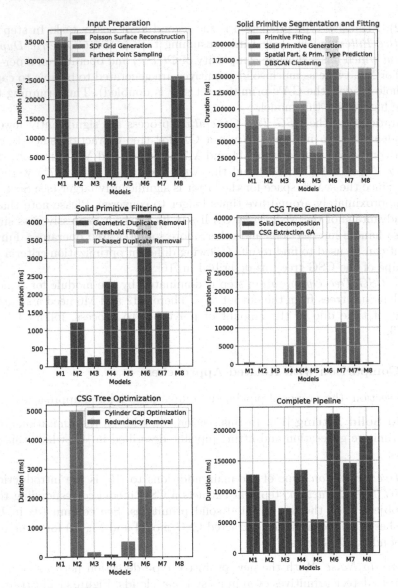

Fig. 8. Benchmark results for models M1–M8 for all pipeline steps.

Missing Details. In rare cases, small details can be missed from the reconstruction. This can be the result of a failure of the segmentation/fitting step to capture them. This problem can be mitigated using more GA iterations, finer point cloud resolutions and different objective function weights in the *Solid Primitive Generation* step. The additional volumetric term (10) is also helping there, since it penalizes erroneous geometry parts more strictly compared to the surface-based term formerly used in [15].

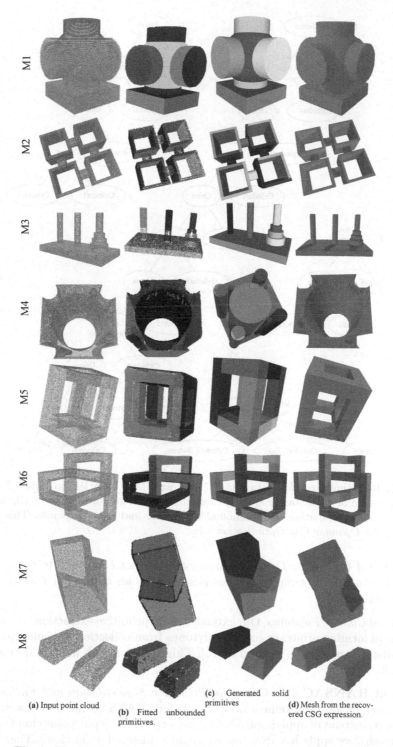

(a) Input point cloud

(b) Fitted unbounded primitives.

(c) Generated solid primitives

(d) Mesh from the recovered CSG expression.

Fig. 9. Pipeline step results. Models M1–M5 were also used in [15].

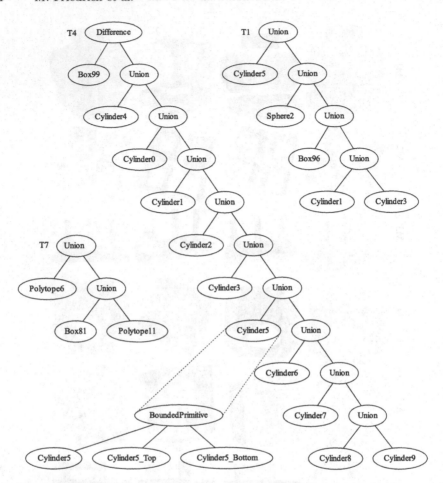

Fig. 10. Resulting trees for data sets M7, M4 and M1 (from left to right). For the tree expression of the data set M4, the expanded expression for cylinder 'Cylinder5' is depicted as a combination of an unbounded cylinder and two cap planes. This is the result of the *Cylinder Cap Optimization* step.

Unconnected Cylinders. The problem of cylinders not connected to other primitives due to poorly sampled regions is solved by an additional *Cylinder Cap Optimization* step.

Support of Convex Polytopes. Our extended solid primitive extraction step is now capable of forming arbitrary convex polytopes from collection of planes (and not only cuboids), unlike the method in [15]. This is shown with models M7 and M8 in Fig. 9.

Efficient RANSAC [34]. Our *Solid Primitive Segmentation and Fitting* step can be seen as an improvement over the efficient RANSAC method described in [34]. First, instead of applying RANSAC directly to the input point cloud (or triangle mesh), we apply RANSAC on an already clustered point cloud. The cluster

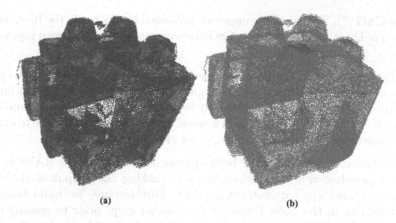

(a)   (b)

Fig. 11. Real-world scan with noise. All parts should be classified as planar (orange). (a) shows the result of [15], (b) shows the almost perfectly detected planes obtained with the newly trained and optimized model (Grey: sphere, orange: plane, red: cylinder). Scanned data set from [27]. (Color figure online)

partitioning has two advantages: 1) It reduces the point cloud size that RANSAC has to work with and 2) it further reduces the problem complexity, since each cluster contains only primitives of the same (known) type. The improvement is visible in Fig. 12, where models containing more than a single primitive type (M1–M4) profit from the clustering step: Primitive set size and size variance are both significantly reduced. In addition, the efficient RANSAC method can fit Quadrics (planes, cylinders, spheres, cones, ...), but compared to our approach, it does not support the fitting of bounded, solid primitives (convex polytopes, bounded cylinders). Finally, our *CSG Tree Extraction* step allows to extract a CSG model from the solid primitives.

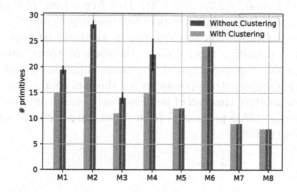

Fig. 12. The effect of clustering on the resulting primitive set size. Black lines indicate variance.

InverseCSG [7]. Similar to the approach proposed in this work, the InverseCSG approach of Du et al. [7] extracts a CSG tree corresponding to a given input data set.

Input Type. Unlike our approach that takes as input either an unstructured point cloud or a triangle mesh (including a triangle soup), InverseCSG [7] takes as input a well formed triangle mesh, with preferably few, long, triangles. This assumption is used in a few steps of their pipeline. In general, one would like to be able to extract a CSG expression from a raw, scanned, point cloud or a triangle soup.

Segmentation and Fitting. While both approaches are based on RANSAC, we rely on a pre-clustering step, which helps in making the output of RANSAC more robust, and less parameter dependent. Furthermore, we build bounded, solid primitives in the *Solid Primitive Generation* step, prior to passing them to the *CSG Extraction* step, instead of forming all possible combinations and passing them to the *CSG Extraction* step. Our *Solid Primitive Generation* step is capable to handle arbitrary convex polytopes and not just cuboids.

CSG Extraction. The generation of a CSG expression in [7] is done by using techniques from program synthesis [25], unlike our approach, which is based on techniques from Boolean expression optimization and evolutionary techniques.

A thorough experimental comparison of both approaches is left for future work.

6   Conclusion and Future Work

In this work, we propose an hybrid approach for recovering CSG models from 3D point clouds or triangle meshes. The *Solid Primitive Segmentation and Fitting* step is an extension of the approach proposed in [15]. It is significantly improved by introducing new primitive types (arbitrary polytopes), a volumetric geometric fitting term for the primitive generation GA and an improved neural network for primitive type detection and clustering. The other steps in the pipeline are either new (*Solid Primitive Filtering, CSG Tree Extraction, Cylinder Cap Optimization*) or adapted from related works (*Redundancy Removal*).

There are several directions in which this work could be improved: the support of additional primitive types (some, like cone or torus, are easy to add, others, like ellipsoid or super-ellipsoid, are more difficult to add), the consideration of additional geometric operations, or the inclusion of conditionals and loops in the modeling tree (instead of just Boolean operations), among others. In particular, inferring "CAD programs" from input data seems a very interesting direction of investigation.

References

1. Attene, M., Falcidieno, B., Spagnuolo, M.: Hierarchical mesh segmentation based on fitting primitives. Vis. Comput. **22**(3), 181–193 (2006)
2. Benkő, P., Martin, R.R., Várady, T.: Algorithms for reverse engineering boundary representation models. Comput. Aided Des. **33**(11), 839–851 (2001)

3. Buchele, S.F., Crawford, R.H.: Three-dimensional halfspace constructive solid geometry tree construction from implicit boundary representations. Comput. Aided Des. **36**(11), 1063–1073 (2004)
4. Chen, Z., Tagliasacchi, A., Zhang, H.: BSP-Net: generating compact meshes via binary space partitioning. arXiv preprint arXiv:1911.06971 (2019)
5. Cohen-Steiner, D., Alliez, P., Desbrun, M.: Variational shape approximation. ACM Trans. Graph. **3**(23), 905–914 (2004)
6. Deng, B., Genova, K., Yazdani, S., Bouaziz, S., Hinton, G., Tagliasacchi, A.: CvxNets: learnable convex decomposition. arXiv preprint arXiv:1909.05736 (2019)
7. Du, T., et al.: InverseCSG: automatic conversion of 3D models to CSG trees. ACM Trans. Graph. **37**(6), 213:1–213:16 (2018)
8. Ellis, K., Nye, M., Pu, Y., Sosa, F., Tenenbaum, J., Solar-Lezama, A.: Write, execute, assess: program synthesis with a REPL. In: Advances in Neural Information Processing Systems, pp. 9165–9174 (2019)
9. Fayolle, P.A., Pasko, A.: An evolutionary approach to the extraction of object construction trees from 3D point clouds. Comput. Aided Des. **74**, 1–17 (2016)
10. Fayolle, P.-A., Pasko, A., Kartasheva, E., Rosenberger, C., Toinard, C.: Automation of the volumetric models construction. In: Pasko, A., Adzhiev, V., Comninos, P. (eds.) Heterogeneous Objects Modelling and Applications. LNCS, vol. 4889, pp. 214–238. Springer, Heidelberg (2008). https://doi.org/10.1007/978-3-540-68443-5_9
11. Feld, S., Friedrich, M., Linnhoff-Popien, C.: Optimizing geometry compression using quantum annealing. In: IEEE Workshop on Quantum Communications and Information Technology 2018 (IEEE QCIT 2018), pp. 1–6 (2018)
12. Flajolet, P., Odlyzko, A.: The average height of binary trees and other simple trees. J. Comput. Syst. Sci. **25**(2), 171–213 (1982)
13. Friedrich, M., Fayolle, P.A., Gabor, T., Linnhoff-Popien, C.: Optimizing evolutionary CSG tree extraction. In: Proceedings of the Genetic and Evolutionary Computation Conference, GECCO 2019, pp. 1183–1191. Association for Computing Machinery (2019)
14. Friedrich, M., Feld, S., Phan, T., Fayolle, P.A.: Accelerating evolutionary construction tree extraction via graph partitioning. In: Proceedings of WSCG 2018 (2018)
15. Friedrich, M., Illium, S., Fayolle, P.A., Linnhoff-Popien, C.: A hybrid approach for segmenting and fitting solid primitives to 3D point clouds. In: Proceedings of the 15th International Conference on Computer Graphics Theory and Applications (GRAPP), vol. 1. INSTICC, SCITEPRESS (2020)
16. Friedrich, M., Roch, C., Feld, S., Hahn, C., Fayolle, P.A.: A flexible pipeline for the optimization of construction trees. In: Proceedings of the 28th International Conference on Computer Graphics, Visualization and Computer Vision (WSCG) (2020)
17. Genova, K., Cole, F., Vlasic, D., Sarna, A., Freeman, W.T., Funkhouser, T.: Learning shape templates with structured implicit functions. arXiv preprint arXiv:1904.06447 (2019)
18. Kaiser, A., Zepeda, J.A.Y., Boubekeur, T.: A survey of simple geometric primitives detection methods for captured 3D data. Comput. Graph. Forum **38**(1), 167–196 (2019)
19. Kalogerakis, E., Hertzmann, A., Singh, K.: Learning 3D mesh segmentation and labeling. ACM Trans. Graph. **29**(4), 102:1–102:12 (2010)
20. Kazhdan, M., Bolitho, M., Hoppe, H.: Poisson surface reconstruction. In: Proceedings of the Fourth Eurographics Symposium on Geometry Processing, vol. 7 (2006)

21. Kim, V.G., Li, W., Mitra, N.J., Chaudhuri, S., DiVerdi, S., Funkhouser, T.: Learning part-based templates from large collections of 3D shapes. ACM Trans. Graph. **32**(4), 70:1–70:12 (2013)
22. Knuth, D.E.: The Art of Computer Programming, Volume 4, Fascicle 4: Generating All Trees. Addison-Wesley Professional (2013)
23. Lavoué, G., Dupont, F., Baskurt, A.: A new CAD mesh segmentation method, based on curvature tensor analysis. Comput. Aided Des. **37**(10), 975–987 (2005)
24. Le, T., Duan, Y.: A primitive-based 3D segmentation algorithm for mechanical cad models. Comput. Aided Geometr. Des. **52**, 231–246 (2017)
25. Lezama, A.S.: Program synthesis by sketching. Ph.D. thesis, U. C. Berkeley (2008)
26. Li, L., Sung, M., Dubrovina, A., Yi, L., Guibas, L.J.: Supervised fitting of geometric primitives to 3D point clouds. In: Proceedings of the IEEE Conference on Computer Vision and Pattern Recognition, pp. 2652–2660 (2019)
27. Li, Y., Wu, X., Chrysathou, Y., Sharf, A., Cohen-Or, D., Mitra, N.J.: GlobFit: consistently fitting primitives by discovering global relations. ACM Trans. Graph. (TOG) **30**(4), 52 (2011)
28. Marshall, D., Lukacs, G., Martin, R.: Robust segmentation of primitives from range data in the presence of geometric degeneracy. IEEE Trans. Pattern Anal. Mach. Intell. **23**(3), 304–314 (2001)
29. Nandi, C., Wilcox, J.R., Panchekha, P., Blau, T., Grossman, D., Tatlock, Z.: Functional programming for compiling and decompiling computer-aided design. Proc. ACM Program. Lang. **2**, 1–31 (2018)
30. Nandi, C., et al.: Synthesizing structured cad models with equality saturation and inverse transformations. In: Proceedings of the 41st ACM SIGPLAN Conference on Programming Language Design and Implementation, PLDI 2020, pp. 31–44. Association for Computing Machinery, New York (2020)
31. Qi, C.R., Su, H., Mo, K., Guibas, L.J.: PointNet: deep learning on point sets for 3D classification and segmentation. In: Proceedings of the IEEE Conference on Computer Vision and Pattern Recognition, pp. 652–660 (2017)
32. Qi, C.R., Yi, L., Su, H., Guibas, L.J.: PointNet++: deep hierarchical feature learning on point sets in a metric space. In: Advances in Neural Information Processing Systems, pp. 5099–5108 (2017)
33. Ricci, A.: A constructive geometry for computer graphics. Comput. J. **16**(2), 157–160 (1973)
34. Schnabel, R., Wahl, R., Klein, R.: Efficient RANSAC for point-cloud shape detection. Comput. Graph. Forum **26**(2), 214–226 (2007)
35. Shapiro, V.: Well-formed set representations of solids. Int. J. Comput. Geomet. Appl. **9**(02), 125–150 (1999)
36. Shapiro, V., Vossler, D.L.: Construction and optimization of CSG representations. Comput. Aided Des. **23**(1), 4–20 (1991)
37. Shapiro, V., Vossler, D.L.: Efficient CSG representations of two-dimensional solids. J. Mech. Des. **113**(3), 239–305 (1991)
38. Shapiro, V., Vossler, D.L.: Separation for boundary to CSG conversion. ACM Trans. Graph. (TOG) **12**(1), 35–55 (1993)
39. Sharma, G., Goyal, R., Liu, D., Kalogerakis, E., Maji, S.: CSGNet: neural shape parser for constructive solid geometry. In: The IEEE Conference on Computer Vision and Pattern Recognition (CVPR), June 2018
40. Sharma, G., Liu, D., Kalogerakis, E., Maji, S., Chaudhuri, S., Měch, R.: ParSeNet: a parametric surface fitting network for 3D point clouds (2020)

41. Silva, S., Fayolle, P.-A., Vincent, J., Pauron, G., Rosenberger, C., Toinard, C.: Evolutionary computation approaches for shape modelling and fitting. In: Bento, C., Cardoso, A., Dias, G. (eds.) EPIA 2005. LNCS (LNAI), vol. 3808, pp. 144–155. Springer, Heidelberg (2005). https://doi.org/10.1007/11595014_15
42. Tian, Y., et al.: Learning to infer and execute 3D shape programs. arXiv preprint arXiv:1901.02875 (2019)
43. Tulsiani, S., Su, H., Guibas, L.J., Efros, A.A., Malik, J.: Learning shape abstractions by assembling volumetric primitives. In: Proceedings of the IEEE Conference on Computer Vision and Pattern Recognition, pp. 2635–2643 (2017)
44. Vanco, M., Brunnett, G.: Direct segmentation of algebraic models for reverse engineering. Computing 72(1), 207–220 (2004)
45. Várady, T., Benko, P., Kos, G.: Reverse engineering regular objects: simple segmentation and surface fitting procedures. Int. J. Shape Model. 3(4), 127–141 (1998)
46. Wu, Q., Xu, K., Wang, J.: Constructing 3D CSG models from 3D raw point clouds. Comput. Graph. Forum 37(5), 221–232 (2018)
47. Zou, C., Yumer, E., Yang, J., Ceylan, D., Hoiem, D.: 3D-PRNN: generating shape primitives with recurrent neural networks. In: Proceedings of the IEEE International Conference on Computer Vision, pp. 900–909 (2017)

Human Computer Interaction Theory and Applications

Intention Understanding for Human-Aware Mobile Robots: Comparing Cues and the Effect of Demographics

Oskar Palinko[✉] , Eduardo Ruiz Ramirez , Norbert Krüger ,
and Leon Bodenhagen

The Maersk Mc-Kinney Moller Institute, University of Southern Denmark, Odense, Denmark
ospa@mmmi.sdu.dk

Abstract. Mobile robots are becoming more and more ubiquitous in our every-day living environments. Therefore, it is very important that people can easily interpret what the robot's intentions are. This is especially important when a robot is driving down a crowded corridor. It is essential for people in its vicinity to understand which way the robot wants to go next. To explore what signals are the best for conveying its intention to turn, we implemented three lighting schemes and tested them out in an online experiment. We found that signals resembling automotive signaling work the best also for logistic mobile robots. We further find that people's opinion of these signaling methods will be influenced by their demographic background (gender, age).

Keywords: Human-aware navigation · Mobile robots · Human-robot interaction

1 Introduction

Mobile robots are becoming more ubiquitous every day. They are being used for many menial tasks quite successfully. They provide flexible solutions in factories and especially in warehouses, replacing more standard automation platforms like conveyor belts. In other areas like elderly and healthcare, they are still struggling to make considerable impact despite their potential for changing the field [1]. They are still facing some challenges even though many of the technologies to overcome these are already available [2]. The challenge in healthcare is that logistic robots might encounter humans on their way through hospital corridors, unless they have special logistics tunnels built for them. Robots not only need to navigate between people, but they also need to make sure not to hurt them, as safety is of paramount importance for automatic devices operating in unconstrained environments with many people. At the same time, they need to function with high reliability, as there is not much space for breakdowns in such busy areas as hospital corridors. One of the basic ways to keep people safe is for the robot to make its intentions easily readable, even to untrained individuals like patients or hospital visitors. If people are informed of the robot's intentions, it can reduce the anxiety of meeting one unexpectedly on the corridor and increase the possibility of its acceptance. Of course,

K. Bouatouch et al. (Eds.): VISIGRAPP 2020, CCIS 1474, pp. 83–102, 2022.
https://doi.org/10.1007/978-3-030-94893-1_4

robots do not have intentions in the human sense, but they could simulate it using light, sound and other modalities to make it easier for people to accept them. In our case these are intentions of turning different ways at crossways, e.g. turning left, turning right or going straight.

This study is a direct extension of a previously published article by Palinko et al. [3]. The next two sections, Related Research and Approach will strongly rely on information published in that article. In Related Research we did not use verbatim quotation, while in Approach at any place we did so, we cited [3] at the end of the paragraph. The subsequent sections (Results, Discussion, Conclusion) rely partially upon the afore mentioned article's findings, but expands those and adds new aspects like investigating demographic perspectives of people's reaction to the robot (e.g. women vs. men, younger vs. older participants might have quite different interpretation of the robot's behavior).

2   Related Research

Robots are becoming more able to function in unconstrained human environments like public spaces or even homes. They are able to constantly adapt to changing situations and re-plan their movements accordingly [4].

It is very important that humans see robots as agents and that they can attribute intention to them. Without this, encounters with robots may lead to conflicting situations and thus reduce people's acceptance of them [5, 6]. In the following subsections we will discuss how humans anticipate intention and how robots can produce it.

2.1   Intention Anticipation by Humans

The successfulness of interaction between two humans in large part depends on mutual understanding of actions and intentions. We use context to make quick assumptions about each other. If somebody is approaching a door with hands full of shopping bags, we might jump to their help because we conclude that they want to enter their apartment building. Context lets us limit uncertainty about the intention of others [7].

If context is unavailable, other sources of intention can be used. For example, gaze could be a source of intention understanding [8]. Another source is body posture and movement: an arm movement can inform about the final intention of a grasping motion [9].

These approaches that inform us about people's intentions can also be applied to robots. Robots can be used twofold: they could try to read and decipher people's intention, or they can exhibit elements of intention to inform and assure us of their goals. We can also use context to figure out the robot's intention: if it is carrying a tray with drinks, we might assume that it will offer us or someone else these beverages. If context is not providing this information, then the robot can do so instead. In the next section we will describe how this can be done using different types of lighting, anticipatory motion, animation techniques, augmented reality, gaze, etc.

2.2 Robots Communicating Intention

Animation techniques are easily used in robotics, as robots might appear as animation characters to a younger audience. These techniques could include squash and stretch (for a falling animated hero), secondary action (putting on jacket while leaving a room) and anticipation (swinging back to throw a ball). Schulz et al. conducted a thorough review of these and other animation techniques which can be very useful in communicating intention.

Studies have found that anticipatory motion can provide a wealth of intention information. Gielniak and Thomaz concluded that such motion can enable participants to prepare for an interactive task with the robot [10]. Ferreira Duarte et al. showed that when a robot overemphasizes a motion the intention of the robotic arm becomes easily predictable [11].

Robots could also use augmented reality to express their intention. e.g. a robot can use a small projector to display an arrow in front of it thus informing people in its environment of its intended path [12]. In their experiment, people found it easy to interpret these arrows and rated the robot more favorably. A robot can also project an exact line representing its intended motion [13]. People in the robot's environment found this approach very useful in understanding the robot's intended path, compared to a baseline setup.

Light is a commonly used device for expressing robots' intentions. Portner et al. used it as a feedback signal on a mobile robot [14]. They associated different colors with different operating modes: active, help needed, error state. The active state was associated with green, 'help needed' was yellow, while red represented an error. These colors can be understood even by people without prior knowledge of robots.

Baraka and Veloso used periodic and non-periodic light to express the robot's state and actions [15]. In their study a robot which used such lights got more help than when it did not use this type of signaling. They also found that the same light increases trust between robots and humans.

Expressive light can also be used in a different context: for drones to communicate their intended flight directions. Szafir et al. asked people to predict the direction of flight of these drones based on light signals, which was completed successfully [16].

Gaze can also be used for communicating intention. Hart et al. made a mobile robot equipped with a virtual head [17]. It drove towards people and signaled lane changes using its gaze. They compared a simple LED signal with gaze signaling and found the gaze to be more useful in preventing collisions between people and the robot. Thus, it can be said that gaze is a more informative channel than using simple LED lights. However, for this to be successful the head of the robot must be visible from all angles, which is not possible when it is shown virtually on a screen. This setup also requires a certain level of anthropomorphism which might not be the most appropriate for mobile robots.

Other robots might already have a high level or anthropomorphism in which situation the usage of gaze is very natural. Mutlu et al. designed a storytelling robot using an Asimo, which used its own gaze to assign certain roles to experiment participants. People were able to understand and interpret these intentional signals very easily [18]. In another experiment by Palinko et al. a drink serving mobile robot was also able to assign conversation roles on bystanders it gazed at [19]. Even when there were multiple people in front of it, most often the person gazed at by the robot answered the robot's question, thus interpreting the agent's intention to talk to her, correctly.

Overall, Fereira Duarte et al., Hart et al., and Szafir et al. suggest that using signals which are well known to humans as gaze will increase the level of understanding of robots' intentions.

In this paper we take inspiration from Szafir et al. [16] in employing a signaling method from the automotive industry and applying it on a mobile robot. We take inspiration also from Portner [14] and Baraka and Veloso [15] in using an animated light in a well-known setting (e.g. blinking). We use anticipatory motion to suggest which way the robot will make its turn as suggested Gielniak and Thomaz [10].

3 Approach

This chapter will cover all aspects of the methodology involved in this study. First, we will describe the technical platform which enables signaling on the robot (Sect. 3.1). Then we will introduce the three experimental conditions (Sect. 3.2). Finally, we will discuss the experimental design used to conduct this study (Sect. 3.3). Since the experimental setup is identical as in [3], some technical details are omitted here.

3.1 The Robot: Experimental Platform

We built the experimental platform on top of a MIR100 mobile robot. We modified the platform to accommodate for four customized LED lights which were used for signaling.

We placed a chest of drawers on top of the MIR platform to simulate the logistic use case for the Health-CAT project. On top of the drawers we installed four rings of LED lights. The MIR base already contained LED strips around its base which served as the bottom lights. Both top and bottom LED arrays are individually addressable which allowed us to create custom signal patterns. The top and bottom LED setups are shown in Fig. 1. All robot movements as well as the application of turning cues have been scripted to achieve reproducible robot behaviors.

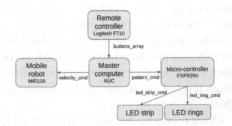

Fig. 1. Robot test platform used for the experiments (left); top view of the robot with standard car light pattern (right) [3].

Fig. 2. Robot system architecture [3].

The system architecture is shown in Fig. 2. The main computer in charge of controlling the setup was an Intel NUC with installed ROS (Robot Operating System). It provided the interface between the MIR and the controller system for the LEDs. We used a Logitech Wireless Gamepad F710 to drive the robot and select different signaling approaches.

The LEDs were controlled using a n ESP8285 microcontroller. For the light control, we programmed the patterns, first, in a way they emulated car lights: white for the headlights, red for the tail lights and yellow for the signal lights (Fig. 3a). Along with the car signals (Fig. 3b), an extra pattern was programmed, showing a LED rotation motion in each of the rings and the base strip in the direction of the turn (Fig. 3d). Further explanation about the robot signals can be found in Sect. 3.2.

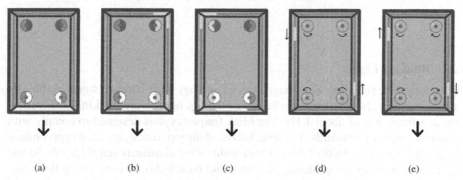

(a)   (b)   (c)   (d)   (e)

Fig. 3. Signaling behaviors. Each image shows a robot top view where the lines in the perimeter represent the bottom LEDs, and the circles inside the rectangle represent the top LED ring arrays. The arrow in the top indicates the front side of the robot. (a) Standard car lights (b) Left blinking signal (c) Right blinking signal (d) Left rotating signal (yellow LEDs move in the arrow direction) e) Right rotating signal (yellow LEDs move in the arrow direction) [3]. (Color figure online)

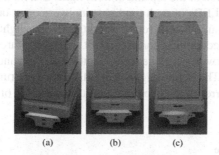

(a)   (b)   (c)

Fig. 4. Signaling behaviors on real robot. (a) Right turn gesture with standard car lights (b) Blinking signal to left (c) Rotating signal [3].

3.2 Experimental Conditions

For a robot operating in a hospital it is important to communicate it intentions to enable humans to anticipate its actions and to minimize conflicts. In the following subsections we will present three implementations of intention signaling: blinking lights, rotating lights and turn gestures as well as their combinations[1].

Table 1. Combination of conditions [3].

	without turn gesture			with turn gesture		
	blink	rotate	none	blink	rotate	none
left	•	•	•	•	•	•
right	•	•		•	•	•

3.2.1 Blinking Lights

This solution for signaling was designed as an analogy with standard signaling on cars for making turns. In this, the outer halves of the top lights were blinking with yellow light at a frequency of about 1 Hz. The blink frequency was designed to comply with automotive industry standards. The inner halves of the top front lights were kept constant white, while the inner parts of the top back lights were constantly red (Figs. 3b, 3c and 4b). These patterns were emulating the front and back lights on cars. Using this setup also adds information about which end is the front of the robot (white inner lights) and which the back (red inner lights), again in analogy with cars. The bottom LED strip was also blinking at the corner position with the same color LEDs [3].

3.2.2 Rotating Lights

We implemented a rotation of the top and bottom lights as a novel signaling method. In this condition only two LEDs of each top light ring were on at one time. The lit LEDs kept changing to create an effect of rotating lights. All four lights were moving in the same direction. This direction was correspondent with the future turn of the robot: the lights were turning clockwise when the robot wanted turn right and anti-clockwise when it intended to turn left. The bottom lights were displaying a "running" pattern around the base of the robot, corresponding to the future turn direction of the robot Figs. 3d, 3e and 4c [3].

3.2.3 Turning Gesture

A final signaling option was implemented in the form of movement: when the robot reached the intersection, it made a turning gesture of about 30° towards the side it wanted to turn to (Fig. 4a). We considered this the strongest signal indicating the intention of the robot: there was no reason why a turn gesture to one side would be interpreted as

---

[1] See a video of the implemented conditions here https://youtu.be/J6jtDH6ZSuw.

an intention to move in the other direction. In the experiment itself we used this signal in two ways: 1) by itself without additional indicators and 2) in combination with the above mentioned two other signaling methods [3].

3.2.4 Combination of Gestures

The main independent variable of our study was the signaling method with conditions: blinking light, rotating light and turn gesture. The last of the conditions could be administered either by itself or in combination with the first two methods. We also wanted to show movements of the robot using a standard car light pattern without any turn signals (none), to establish a baseline behavior. A secondary necessary independent variable we considered was turn direction with levels: left and right. All these combinations of conditions are represented in Table 1.

For the combination of no-turn and no-light the left and right conditions are the same, i.e. the robot just approaches the intersection without any turning lights or gestures. Therefore, these two cases are conjoined into one condition. This give us a total of 11 combinations of conditions [3].

3.3 Experimental Design

We ran a human subject study to investigate which signaling approach would be the most appropriate for our robot. In order to ensure repeatability and efficient gathering of human data, we opted for recording videos of the robot's signaling movements and showing them to human participants via online surveys. As it was essential for all subjects to see exactly the same robot behaviors, video recordings were the best option [3].

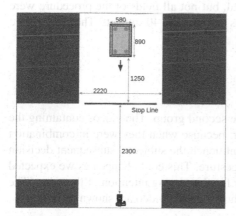

Fig. 5. Video recordings setup layout. Dimensions are in mm [3].

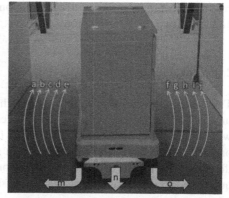

Fig. 6. The last frame of the video, representing the route options in the multiple choice questions [3].

3.3.1 Video Recordings

One video was recorded for each of the 11 combinations of conditions mentioned above. The videos were shot with a mobile phone in 4K resolution with 30 frames per second.

The recording was done from an initial distance to the robot of 3,5 m. At the end of the video the robot approached the intersection and was at a distance of 2,3 m to the camera, see Fig. 5. The camera was mounted on a fixed tripod at a height of 1,7 m, thus simulating the point of view of an average person. The location of the video recording was exactly the same in all clips. We made a careful selection of a location that represents a symmetrical intersection of hallways at the university. The robot always started from the same position of 1,25 m from the intersection. It always ended its movement just at the borderline of the intersection box. It was always in the center of the corridor allowing the same amount of space on both of its sides. The width of the hallway at the entrance to the intersection was 2,22 m. The width of the robot is 0,58 m. This allowed a space of 0,82 m on both sides of the robot for passing around it. In the conditions where the robot also performed a turning gesture, this space somewhat decreased, because of its rectangular geometry. The videos ended at the point when the robot stops at the intersection and has performed the turn gesture and light actions. We intentionally cut it off before the robot performed the actual turn at the intersection, because we wanted to ask our participants to tell us what their prediction would be on what will happen next, thus giving us insight on the effectiveness of our signaling methods in conveying information about the robot's future actions [3] (Table 3).

3.3.2 Online Survey

An online survey was created to test the designed experimental conditions with human subjects. As a survey platform, we selected the site soscisurvey.de which provides many options for randomizing the order of presentation of the videos. The survey started with a quick explanation of the experiment without giving away its scientific purpose. After the initial slide, we presented the 11 videos, each on a separate page, in pseudo-random order. It was designed to be counter-balanced, but not all fields of the procedure were covered because there were 120 combinations of order and 40 subjects. The videos were divided in two randomized groups:

1. With turn gesture,
2. Without turn gesture.

The first group was always shown before the second group. The videos containing the turn gesture were selected to be shown later, because when they were in combination with either of the light signals, they could influence the subjects' subsequent decision on light signals appearing without the turn gesture. This could happen as we expected the turn gesture to be the strongest indicator for the turning intention of the robot. The questions we asked participants right after showing each video are shown in Table 2.

Table 2. Questions about the videos [3].

QA1	Which way would you go around the robot to get to the end of the hallway ahead?
QA2	Which way will the robot turn after the end of the video?

Table 3. Validation questions about the experiment [3].

QB1	What was the color of the robot?
QB2	What was the general shape of the robot?

For the first question we offered multiple choice radio buttons with the labels: a, b, c, d, e, f, g, h, i, j. These labels represented ten possible routes of movement for people to take and corresponded to arrow representations of these paths at the end of the video, which were added in a video editing application, see Fig. 6. The second question's answers were three radio buttons with the labels m, n and o. These were also represented by arrows at the last frame of the video. The videos only played once (of which the subjects were informed at the initial page) and stopped at the last frame with the arrow representations.

Table 4. Likert-scaled questions about the experiment [3].

QC1	The blinking lights on the robot in some of the videos made it very clear which way it would want to go.
QC2	The rotating lights on the robot in some of the videos made it very clear which way it would want to go.
QC3	The turning of the robot at the end of some videos made it very clear which way it would want to go.
QC4	The combination of blinking lights and turning made it very clear which way the robot would go
QC5	The combination of rotating lights and turning made it very clear which way the robot would go.
QC6	The lights on the top of the robot were very useful in understanding where it would go.
QC7	The lights near the bottom of the robot were very useful in understanding where it would go.
QC8	I did not notice any difference between the videos.
QC9	The different signals were insufficient for one to understand which way the robot would go.

After the survey pages with the videos the subjects had two more pages with questions to fill out: one about the experiment and another about demographic information. The experimental page started with two questions for validating if subjects paid attention to the videos.

The first of these questions had an open text field, so people could enter the name of the color they perceived. The second question was a multiple choice one with the following options: cylindrical, box-shaped, ball-shaped, snake-shaped, humanoid, other.

The correct choice was 'box-shaped'. The following 9 questions were in the form of statements with 7-point Likert-scaled answers ranging from $1 =$ 'strongly disagree' to $7 =$ 'strongly agree', see Table 4. With these statements we expected to learn more about people's preference for the conditions we were suggesting. This page ended with a comments section. We asked subjects in a large textual field to let us know about their thoughts, observations, and suggestions concerning the experiment. The last input page asked for demographic information, see Table 5 [3].

Table 5. Demographic information questions [3].

QD1	What is your gender?
QD2	What is your age?
QD3	Are you left-handed or right-handed?
QD4	How many times have you interacted with robots before?
QD5	Do you have a driver's license?
QD6	In your country of residence, which side of the road do cars drive on?
QD7	Have you participated in this experiment before?

3.3.3 Data Collection

We opted for collecting data using Mechanical Turk. For the first part of the experiment that was published in [3] thirty-one participants were recruited with MTurk Master qualification and at least 90% job quality approval rating. They were all located int the United States. We opted for this country as our questionnaire was in English and the USA is the largest English-speaking country (as their native language), thus we could get quick high-quality responses. One of the subjects showed irregular behavior according to our survey collection system: she spent very little time on each slide (around 11,7 s per slide, while the average was 25,7 s), i.e. she didn't pay attention to the videos, thus we eliminated her from the results. Out of the leftover 30, 10 were female and 20 male. The average age was 41,9. After the initial data collection, we realized that if we want to compare gender differences, we need a balanced number of female and male participants. Therefore, we collected 10 more subjects on MTurk with the same qualifications, but we requested only female participants this time. As two participants completed the survey too fast, their results were rejected, and new participants filled out the forms. In the end we had 40 experiment participants for the data reported in this paper. Out of those 20 were women and 20 men. Their average age was 42.9. Three people were left-handed and 37 right-handed. They all had driver's licenses except two. Sixteen subjects never interacted with robots before, 19 a few times, while five experienced robots a number of times.

4   Results

In this section we will present the results of our study performed on 40 participants. In the first subsection we will report on subjective opinions of people on which elements of the different approaches they preferred. The next subsection will present the results of people's opinions on which paths they intend to take in reaction to the robot's movements. In the final subsection it will be discussed what participants predict, which way the robot will continue its motion after the video ends.

Each of these subsections will report the general data with all subjects included, data separated by gender and separated by age.

4.1 Subjective Results

General. First, we report on questionnaire statements QC1, QC2 and QC3, which refer to the clearness of the signaling for each introduced method (rotating, blinking and turning). In accordance with [3], but with the extended number of subjects, the Likert-scaled responses remained very similar, see Fig. 7. To assess the significance of these results we compared them using a Pearson's Chi Squared test. We have found a significant difference between the three signaling approaches $\chi^2(12) = 66.9$; $p < 0.001$. The size of the effect is even more prominent than in our previous study due to the increased number of subjects by 33%. Post-hoc Wilcoxon tests with Bonferroni correction showed significant differences between all three pairs of conditions: rotation-blinking (Z = −4.38, p < 0.001), rotation-turning (Z = −5.037; p < 0.001) and also blinking-turning (Z = −3.4, p < 0.001).

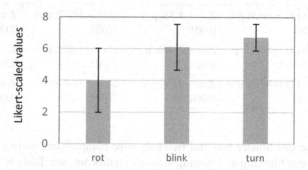

Fig. 7. Averages of opinions on clearness of signaling with rotating lights, blinking lights and turn gesture (± 1SD).

Gender. Next, for the clearness of signaling questions, we divided participants in two groups, based on gender, which resulted in two sections with 20 participants each, see Fig. 8. The green bars represent the combined results between all participants, the red ones stand for female participants' results, while blue show averages for male subjects. We will keep this color coding for the rest of the paper.

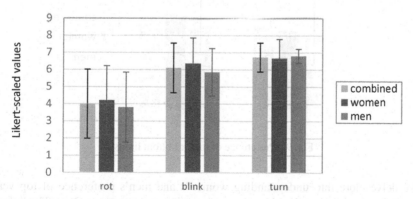

Fig. 8. Averages of opinions about the clearness of different signaling methods divided by gender. (Color figure online)

Statistical analysis (Pearson's Chi Square test) of the data divided by gender showed that for men the differences were significant just as in the general case together with pair-wise comparisons using Bonferroni-corrected Wilcoxon tests ($\chi^2(12) = 43.0$; p < 0.001), see Table 6 for details. However, female participants showed a different result.

Table 6. Gender results for clearness of signals.

	Chi squared	Pair-wise Wilcoxon		
	General	Rot - blink	Rot – turn	Blink - turn
Combined	$\chi^2(12) = 66.9$; p = 0.001	Z = −4.38, p < 0.001	Z = −5.037; p = 0.001	Z = −3.4, p = 0.001
Women	$\chi^2(12) = 30.17$; p = 0.003	Z = −3.406; p = 0.001	Z = −3.533; p = 0.001	Z = −1.89; p = 0.059
Men	$\chi^2(12) = 43.0$; p = 0.001	Z = −2.88; p = 0.004	Z = −3.64, p = 0.001	Z = −2.87; p = 0.004

Even though the Chi Square test and two pair-wise comparisons were significant, the difference between blinking and turning was not significant, see Table 6.

Another subjective question we analyzed was the preference of either the top or bottom signaling lights on the robot, see Fig. 9. Even though none of the differences between top and bottom were significant, similarly as in [3], we report on these results, as it was expected that the top LEDs will be significantly more informative, which proved not to be the case. This was the case not only for the combined results, but also for both gender groups.

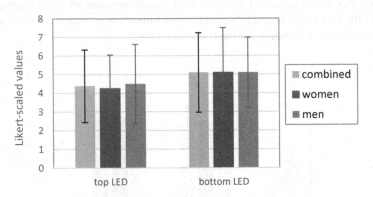

Fig. 9. Preference of top or bottom lights.

We delve more into understanding women's and men's preference of top versus bottom lights if we look at the histograms of reactions to statements QC6 (The lights on the top of the robot were very useful in understanding where it would go.) and QC7 (The lights near the bottom of the robot were very useful in understanding where it would go.), see Fig. 10. It can be noticed that for the top LEDs, women are mostly undecided about its usefulness, as there are many Likert value 4s (neither agree nor disagree). For men this histogram is more evenly spread out. For the bottom lights women either like them a lot (Likert value 7) or not at all (Likert value 1), with no undecided values. For men this is effect is not as pronounced.

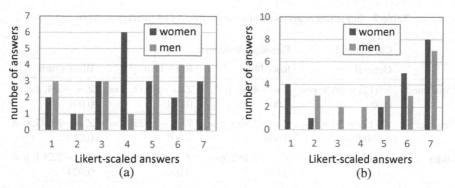

Fig. 10. Histograms for a) The top LED was useful and b) the bottom LED was useful for understanding the robot's intention.

Age. We conducted the analysis of the two age groups in regard of the three basic signaling methods, see Fig. 11. We found that both younger and older participants perform similarly as the combined sample and they show similar statistical differences in a Chi Square test, see Table 7. However, there is one difference: for older participants the pairwise Wilcoxon test for blinking vs turning is not significant even though it has a p = 0.024. This is because of the Bonferroni correction that needs to be applied in multiple comparisons, which changes the required p value to p < 0.05/3. Therefore, although the results for the group of older people follow the trend of the other age groups, they do not allow for the conclusion that the turn gesture is a better signaling method compared to blinking.

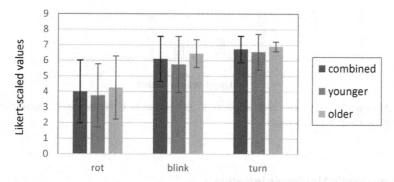

Fig. 11. Averages of opinions about the clearness of different signaling methods divided by age.

Table 7. Statistical analysis results for clearness of signals divided by age.

	Chi squared	Pair-wise Wilcoxon		
	General	Rot - blink	Rot – turn	Blink - turn
Combined	$\chi^2(12) = 66.9$; p = 0.001	Z = −4.38, p < 0.001	Z = −5.037; p = 0.001	Z = −3.4, p = 0.001
Younger	$\chi^2(12) = 34.96$; p = 0.001	Z = −2.866; p = 0.004	Z = −3.529; p = 0.001	Z = −2.585; p = 0.01
Older	$\chi^2(12) = 35.12$; p = 0.001	Z = −3.462; p = 0.001	Z = −3.644, p = 0.001	Z = −2.264; p = 0.024

An interesting outcome can be observed regarding age when looking at question QC9 "The different signals were insufficient for one to understand which way the robot would go", see Fig. 12. The histogram shows a large concentration of answers towards the lower Likert numbers. This means that most participants disagreed with the statement that the signals were insufficient, i.e. they mostly thought that the signals are adequate in general. However, a difference can be noticed in younger and older subjects' opinions: older people (average 2.1) tended to disagree with the insufficiency statement more strongly than younger participants (average: 2.7).

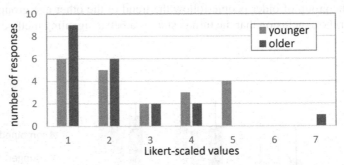

Fig. 12. Histogram of Likert-scaled answers to the question if signals were insufficient for understanding the robot's intention.

4.2 Participant's Movement Intention

This section will discuss participants' responses to the question QA1 "Which way would you go around the robot to get to the end of the hallway?" with ten offered options (a-j paths), out of which 5 would go around the robot from the left-hand side (a–e), while the other half from the right-hand side (f–j). Looking first at a robot which does not display any signals and similar to [3], when all participants were taken together, they were evenly divided between going left (20 people) or right (20 people), see Fig. 13. This was somewhat surprising as it was expected that most people would choose to go around an oncoming robot from the right-hand side in analogy with vehicular traffic.

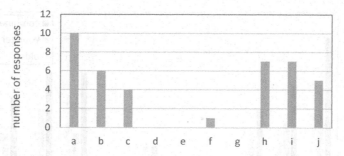

Fig. 13. Histogram of choices between going around the robot from the left (a–e) or right (f–j).

Gender. The same results were further analyzed but this time divided based on gender, see Fig. 14. It can be noticed that there is considerable difference between men and women in this case. Out of 20 men, 12 chose to go around the robot from the left side (paths a–e), while 8 chose one of the 5 right-side passages (f–j). For women this is the opposite: 8 of them took one of the left-side routes, while 12 approached from the right.

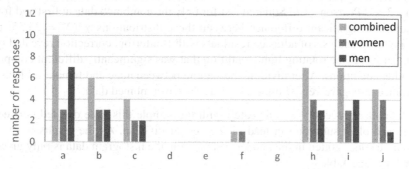

Fig. 14. Histogram of choices between going around the robot from the left or right, divided between genders.

Age. Looking at the same data as in Fig. 13, but divided over age, we see subtler differences where younger subjects choose the left paths 11 times and the right one 9 times. Older participants choose right ways 11 times, while left ways 9 times, see Fig. 15.

It was noticed that these histograms have an irregular bimodal distribution. Therefore we opted to reduce the complexity by clustering all left side paths (a, b, c, d, e) together and all right side paths (f, g, h, i, j) together, thus simplifying the bimodal to a binomial (left, right) distribution. This allowed us to apply simpler statistical methods, while keeping the most important part of the data. With this new approach, we compared which way people want to circumvent the robot when it is signaling to the left and right. Let us look at the combined case in Fig. 16. When the robot makes a blinking signal to its own left side (red bars in figure), people will mostly want to go around it from their own left side to avoid crossing paths and a potential collision. For the turn gesture

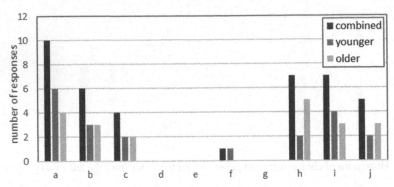

Fig. 15. Histogram of choices between going around the robot from the left or right, divided between younger and older participants.

(green bars) this going left behavior is even more pronounced, as it is an easier signal to interpret. However, for the rotation signal (blue bars), people are divided between going to the left and right as the rotation is not perceived correctly as turning towards the direction that the light rotation indicates. To check the statistical significance of this we ran a 3×2 Pearson's Chi Squared test for only the combined data at first and found that there is a significant difference between these distributions $\chi^2(2) = 23.55$; $p = 0.001$. Post-hoc analysis of adjusted residuals with Bonferroni correction revealed ($p < 0.001$) that it was the rotating light condition that was significantly different compared to the other conditions. After dividing the sample between male and female subjects the significance tests gave very similar results as for the combined data.

Age. A similar procedure was repeated with the sample this time divided between a younger and older subgroup instead of the gender division. As the results were very similar to the ones gotten in the gender comparison, the histogram data is only given in tabular form, see Table 8.

Table 8. Participant's intended binomial movement when distributed over age groups.

	Younger		Older		Combined	
	Left	Right	Left	Right	Left	Right
Rotate left	11	9	9	11	20	20
Blink left	14	6	19	1	33	7
Turn left	18	2	20	0	38	2

4.3 Predicting the Robot's Intentions

In this subsection, we report on the answers to question QA2 "Which way will the robot turn after the end of the video?" It was asked after the end of each video, to gauge

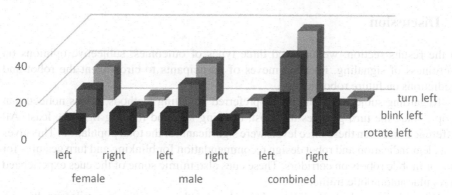

Fig. 16. Histogram of binomial paths (left or right) people take when the robot is signaling a turn to its left divided over genders. (Color figure online)

participants' prediction of the robot's future actions based on the implemented signaling methods. This question had 3 possible answers, paths m, n and o. Path m meant that the robot is predicted to go to its right side, path n meant straight, while path o signifies a left turn. Figure 17a shows the results for all 40 subjects. It can be noticed that as in the previous section, the blinking and turning signals are appropriately interpreted, while the rotation signal still confuses participants. We conducted a Chi Squared test on this dataset too and found significant differences between levels $\chi^2(2) = 18.53$, p = 0.001, indicating that the rotation signal is improperly interpreted. However, when the rotation and blinking signals are presented in combination with the turning gesture, all uncertainties are dispersed, as almost all participants interpret the combination correctly, even when the ambiguous rotation signal is presented, see Fig. 17b.

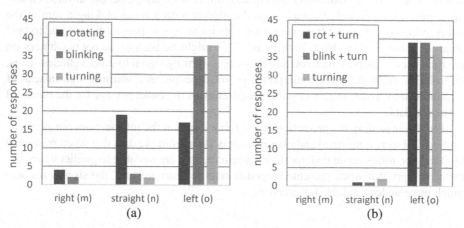

Fig. 17. a) Predicting robot's intentions based only on separate signals and b) signals in combination with turn gesture.

5   Discussion

In the results section, we analyzed three types of outcomes: subjective opinions on usefulness of signaling, intended moves of participants to circumvent the robot and predictions on future robot actions.

Regarding subjective opinions on preferred signaling methods, it was noticed that people liked the turn gestures the most, blinking less and rotating light the least. All differences between these three levels were significant for the total population. This gives us a clear indication and robot design recommendation for blinking and turn gestures for indoor mobile robots on corridors. These cues also mimic some of the cues experienced in regular automobile traffic.

When these results were dissected based on gender, we got very similar results with the only distinction that women did not find blinking lights and turn gestures to be significantly different in terms of signal legibility, i.e. they liked both signal types. This further ensures us that both blinking and turning are good indicators of robot intention. Similarly, when looking at age it was found that older participants also had no distinction between these two signaling methods. Furthermore, we saw that older participants found all signals more informative in general than younger people. One possible explanation might be that older generations in the USA like the car analogy more because they are more reliant on cars, while younger people shift more towards public transportation [20].

Regarding participants' movement intentions to circumvent the robot, we noticed slight differences between women and men: the prior tended to go around the robot from the right side while men have a slight preference for passing on the left. These values are not significantly different but might indicate a tendency. The differences due to age were even less pronounced.

When looking at the binomial reduction of the movement intention data (Fig. 16) it can be clearly noticed that both blinking and turn gesture nudge people towards choosing a path which would avoid a potential collision with a robot making a turn at the intersection. This was not the case for the rotational signal: people did not understand what the robot is trying to do in this case. This might be because heavy machinery on the road need to display such rotating lights as a warning signal to other vehicles. Thus, the rotation might have been interpreted by most people as a warning sign instead of turn indication. There were no significant differences in gender nor age for the binomial reduction data.

Finally, regarding the prediction of the robot's turn at the intersection, our previous findings [3] were confirmed and expanded. It is clear from the data that when presented by itself, the rotation cue underperforms again: people are not able to predict where the robot will go. But when presented together with the turn gesture, the signals become much more understandable for everyone.

In our previous paper [3] we discussed the possibility of expanding our studies on countries with left-hand side driving to see if their preferences for signaling differ than right-hand side drivers. Unfortunately, this was not possible in this iteration, as it seems that our platform of choice for recruiting subjects (Mechanical Turk) is not in wide usage in any of the right-hand side traffic countries. It might also be the case that the reward was not high enough for participants in those countries (e.g. UK, Australia, Ireland, Japan) to spend time on our questionnaires, even though a higher reward was offered (0.8USD per task) than in the USA (0.4USD). We also tried administering the survey to users of Mechanical Turk in India, but the obtained data turned out to suffer from inconsistencies. It was not feasible to integrate sufficiently robust mechanisms to avoid such inconsistent data though.

6   Conclusions

This study was performed with the purpose of finding the best signaling methods for a logistics robot traveling on indoor corridors. It is very important for a robot to efficiently communicate its driving intentions in order to avoid collisions and frustration by people encountering it. We compared three basic signaling methods (rotating light, blinking light and turn gesture) as well as their combinations. In a previous study we already obtained preliminary results which told us that the rotating signal was the least and the turn gesture the most preferred signal. In this paper we expand the power of these findings by adding 33% more people to the batch. It is also confirmed that a combination of signals is much clearer than some of the signals by themselves. This gives a clear recommendation for future robotics direction indication standard that blinking and turning in analogy with vehicular traffic are very understandable indicators for robot movement.

In this study we looked at demographic differences in populations for the first time. As our original dataset contained twice as many male participants than female, we expanded the original 30 people with 10 new female participants, to balance out gender underrepresentation. Regarding gender results, we have found that women find both the blinking signal and turn gesture equally informative as opposed to men who prefer the turn. Female participants also prefer to go around a robot that is not displaying intentions of turning from the right side in analogy with passing by and oncoming car in vehicular traffic. Male subject had a slight preference for passing on the left, unexpectedly. Finally, women were indifferent towards the usefulness of the top LED signals on the robot, while they either liked very much or "hated" the bottom LED strips.

In addition to gender we also looked at age differences. We split the population in two halves by finding the median age (39.5 years). We have found that older participants also did not make distinction in preference between blinking and the turn gesture, unlike younger subjects who did make the distinction. Older people also seem more secure in understanding intention signals with are analogous with car indicators in everyday traffic. This might be because of their stronger connection with driving as opposed to younger people's preference of public transportation.

Acknowledgements. This work was supported by the project Health-CAT, funded by the European Regional Development Fund.

References

1. Riek, L.D.: Healthcare robotics. Commun. ACM **60**, 68–78 (2017)
2. Bodenhagen, L., Suvei, S.-D., Juel, W.K., Brander, E., Krüger, N.: Robot technology for future welfare: meeting upcoming societal challenges–an outlook with offset in the development in Scandinavia. Health Technol. (Berl) **9**(3), 197–218 (2019)
3. Palinko, O., Ramirez, E.R., Juel, W.K., Krüger, N., Bodenhagen, L.: Intention indication for human aware robot navigation. In: VISIGRAPP 2020 - Proceedings of the 15th International Joint Conference on Computer Vision, Imaging and Computer Graphics Theory and Applications (2020)
4. Svenstrup, M., Tranberg, S., Andersen, H.J., Bak, T.: Pose estimation and adaptive robot behaviour for human-robot interaction. In: Proceedings - IEEE International Conference on Robotics and Automation (2009)
5. Hameed, I.A., Tan, Z.-H., Thomsen, N.B., Duan, X.: User acceptance of social robots. In: Proceedings of the Ninth International Conference on Advances in Computer-Human Interactions (ACHI 2016), Venice, Italy, pp. 274–279 (2016)
6. Beer, W.A., Prakash, J. M., Mitzner, A., Rogers, T.L.: Understanding robot acceptance. Georg. Inst. Technol. (2011)
7. Kilner, J.M.: More than one pathway to action understanding. Trends Cogn. Sci. **15**(8), 352–357 (2011)
8. Castiello, U.: Understanding other people's actions: intention and attention. J. Exp. Psychol. Hum. Percept. Perform. **29**, 416 (2003)
9. Ansuini, C., Giosa, L., Turella, L., Altoè, G., Castiello, U.: An object for an action, the same object for other actions: effects on hand shaping. Exp. Brain Res. **185**(1), 111–119 (2008)
10. Gielniak, M.J., Thomaz, A. L.: Generating anticipation in robot motion. In: Proceedings - IEEE International Workshop on Robot and Human Interactive Communication (2011)
11. Duarte, N.F., Raković, M., Tasevski, J., Coco, M.I., Billard, A., Santos-Victor, J.: Action anticipation: reading the intentions of humans and robots. IEEE Robot. Autom. Lett. **3**(4), 4132–4139 (2018)
12. Coovert, M.D., Lee, T., Shindev, I., Sun, Y.: Spatial augmented reality as a method for a mobile robot to communicate intended movement. Comput. Human Behav. **34**, 241–248 (2014)
13. Chadalavada, R.T., Andreasson, H., Krug, R., Lilienthal, A.J.: That's on my mind! Robot to human intention communication through on-board projection on shared floor space (2016)
14. Pörtner, A., Schröder, L., Rasch, R., Sprute, D., Hoffmann, M., König, M.: The power of color: a study on the effective use of colored light in human-robot interaction. In: IEEE International Conference on Intelligent Robots and Systems (2018)
15. Baraka, K., Veloso, M.M.: Mobile service robot state revealing through expressive lights: formalism, design, and evaluation. Int. J. Soc. Robot. **10**, 65–92 (2018)
16. Szafir, D., Mutlu, B., Fong, T.: Communicating directionality in flying robots. In: ACM/IEEE International Conference on Human-Robot Interaction (2015)
17. Hart, J., et al.: Unclogging our arteries: using human-inspired signals to disambiguate navigational intentions. arXiv Preprint arXiv:1909.06560 (2019)
18. Mutlu, B., Shiwa, T., Kanda, T., Ishiguro, H., Hagita, N.: Footing in human-robot conversations: how robots might shape participant roles using gaze cues. Hum. Factors **2**(1), 61–68 (2009)
19. Palinko, O., Fischer, K., Ruiz Ramirez, E., Damsgaard Nissen, L., Langedijk, R.M.: A drink-serving mobile social robot selects who to interact with using gaze. In: ACM/IEEE International Conference on Human-Robot Interaction (2020)
20. Dutzik, T., Inglis, J., Baxandall, P.: Millennials in motion: changing travel Habits of young Americans and the implications for public policy (2014)

Tracking Eye Movement for Controlling Real-Time Image-Abstraction Techniques

Maximilian Söchting$^{(\boxtimes)}$ and Matthias Trapp

Hasso Plattner Institute, Faculty of Digital Engineering, University of Potsdam, Potsdam, Germany
maximilian.soechting@student.hpi.de, matthias.trapp@hpi.de

Abstract. Acquisition and consumption of visual media such as digital image and videos is becoming one of the most important forms of modern communication. However, since the creation and sharing of images is increasing exponentially, images as a media form suffer from being devalued, as the quality of single images are getting less and less important, and the frequency of the shared content turns to be the focus. In this work, an interactive system which allows users to interact with volatile and diverting artwork based on their eye movement only is presented. The system uses real-time image-abstraction techniques to create an artwork unique to each situation. It supports multiple, distinct interaction modes, which share common design principles, enabling users to experience game-like interactions focusing on eye-movement and the diverting image content itself. This approach hints at possible future research in the field of relaxation exercises and casual art consumption and creation.

Keywords: Eye-tracking · Image abstraction · Image processing · Artistic image stylization · Interactive media

1 Introduction

1.1 Temporary Aesthetic Experiences

Providing users with a *temporary* visual and aesthetic experience through an interactive system is not an unprecedented idea. In this work, eye tracking technology and image-abstraction techniques are combined with a novel interaction paradigm (Fig. 1). This approach aims to increase the value of the visual content through volatility and instability, and taking away the decision power of the user. Contradicting the assisting nature of traditional technology, the power dynamic that usually exists between a user and a technical device is reversed.

The presented system takes charge and nudges the user to follow a certain, predetermined behavior by rewarding the user in case of success, and punishing deviating behavior by setting the user back. Such volatile visual content also allows for deeper appreciation of the evolving artwork. The interaction with the art allows it to become more intriguing and provide more enjoyment to observers in contrast to still images.

K. Bouatouch et al. (Eds.): VISIGRAPP 2020, CCIS 1474, pp. 103–123, 2022.
https://doi.org/10.1007/978-3-030-94893-1_5

Fig. 1. The proposed system in a user interaction scenario. Mounted at the bottom side of the monitor, the eye tracker records the eye movement of the user. The application displays the computer-generated artwork that is controlled by the processed sensor inputs.

1.2 Challenges for Eye Tracking Based Interaction Techniques

The presented approach creates a unique interaction experience between the system and the user, by allowing the user to take part in the creation of the computer-transformed visual content that is presented to them. The goal is to create *volatile* artwork, unique to each situation. The interaction aims to be "frictionless" and immersive by using real-time sensors, i.e., especially eye tracking. If the chosen interaction technique requires it, the user may be constrained to certain behavior patterns, e.g., not blinking for a set duration, as a game-like mechanic.

In this work, artistic stylization through image processing gives the interactive system a medium to interact with the user. Processing and interpreting user input, aesthetic changes in the artwork through local and global changes of abstraction parameters, choice of interaction technique, and choice of image are applied. This necessitates strong customizability and high granularity of the image-abstraction techniques to implement the proposed interaction modes successfully. For the proposed approach, a set of different image-abstraction techniques that imitate real mediums such as cartoon or watercolor filtering [12] have been implemented.

Next to the mainstream usage of eye trackers for statistical purposes, e.g., for market research, the application as a direct input device is not usual. Zhai *et al.* observed [22], that eye tracking-based input methods put considerable strain on the user and are less straining and offer more convenient interaction when combined with other input methods. Because the presented work aims to create an intense environment and a particularly inconvenient interaction, using only eye-tracker input and the resulting user strain, benefits the fundamental approach of the system by having the user "work" for his rewards.

Allowing real-time sensor data streams to influence the choice of image-abstraction techniques and its parameters demonstrates unique technical challenges.

Implementing and utilizing the output of sensor data feeds in a real-time application requires the resulting concurrency problems, since both the main application and the sensor threads need to synchronize data access. Additionally, a flexible data model and a dynamic system that adapts these changes during application run-time is required in order to allow system behavior to be influenced by the provided sensor data (*interaction techniques*) in a dynamic and easily exchangeable manner.

1.3   Combining Eye Tracking and Image Abstraction

The image-abstraction techniques utilized by our approach are based on earlier works on the topic of a platform-independent format for image processing effects with parametrization on multiple Level-of-Control (LOC) [5]. Based on this format, a system for capturing and processing sensor data and allowing interaction techniques to be implemented as an interface between sensor data and image abstraction from a previous work by M. Söchting and M. Trapp was extended [19]. The presented approach of that work is developed further in this paper with detailed performance measurements and analysis, more in-depth description of gaze data and its processing, discussion of the platform-independent image abstraction effect format, further conclusions and additional related work and future research directions. It details the concept for an interactive system that manipulates art-work based on Graphics Processing Unit (GPU)-accelerated image-abstraction techniques using eye tracking. For it, a system architecture is described that processes real-time sensor data with exchangeable interaction and image-abstraction techniques. Based on this, observed effects on users using a set of interaction techniques are discussed.

The remainder of this work is structured as follows. Section 2 reviews and discusses related work with respect to fundamentals of eye tracking-based interaction techniques and interactive image processing. Section 3 describes the concept of mapping sensor data to interactions for image-abstraction, the required technical conditions and the interaction techniques themselves. Section 4 presents the parametrization of image and video abstraction techniques (Sect. 4.1) and the mapping of sensor data to their respective behavior. Section 5 highlights aspects of the prototypical implementation of the application and the image-abstraction techniques. Section 6 discusses application and results of the presented approach. Finally, Sect. 7 concludes this paper and presents ideas for future research directions.

2   Background and Related Work

The background of this work mainly concerns interactive image-abstraction techniques with implementations suitable for GPUs (Sect. 2.1) as well as interaction techniques that are based eye tracking technologies (Sect. 2.2) and approaches that apply eye tracking for understanding art (Sect. 2.3).

2.1   Interactive Image-abstraction Techniques

To give the proposed system a medium to interact with the user [17], image processing for the purpose of artistic stylization is used. The system applies aesthetic changes in the artwork, based on user input, through mask-based and global changes of effect parameters, choice of image and choice of image-abstraction effect [8]. This necessitates a high degree of customization of the image-abstraction effects in order to enable the proposed interaction.

Furthermore, the system is required to be highly interactive to prevent user frustration and hold up the immersion of a fluid interaction, which poses to be particularly difficult since the system includes high-frequency eye tracking [20]. Therefore, the described, complex image stylization techniques are implemented in the system through different caching and pre-loading mechanisms. For this work, a set of complex image-abstraction techniques have been selected that imitate real mediums such as cartoon or watercolor filtering [4] and implemented, in the combination with multiple interaction techniques (Sect. 4). More use cases for image processing include medical analysis and enterprise software.

2.2   Interaction Techniques Based on Eye Tracking

Eye tracking has been used prominently in medical and psychological research for recording and studying human visual behavior [13]. Previously, eye tracking devices have been implemented in experimental and business environments in various domains. The field of human-computer-interaction is a prominent example of eye tracking applications, where eye trackers serve mainly two different purposes: statistical analysis and immediate interface interaction.

In interface interaction, projects in human-computer-interaction interpret the user eye movement as an input component for navigating and interacting with interactive systems [11]. The work of Alonso *et al.* on air traffic controllers is one such example [1], in which they show eye tracking can improve interaction convenience even in the complex use case of air traffic control. However, Kasprowski *et al.* concludes that touchpad or mouse input is still superior in interaction accuracy and reaction speed [9] for workloads that necessitate quick and precise interaction. Statistical analysis is more widespread purpose of eye tracking in human-computer-interaction projects, for which users and their eye movement are observed while they fulfill given tasks, e.g., using a web site. The gathered gaze data is then analyzed and conclusions can be drawn, e.g., which parts of the web site attract the most visual attention and which areas the user did not perceive at all. This analysis has the goal of understanding eye movements and human visual behavior, such as in the work by Kiefer *et al.* [10] in which the researchers understand how maps are perceived by the test persons.

The statistical data collected by eye trackers can not only be used for drawing immediate conclusions, but also for creating visualizations. Blascheck *et al.* [3] summarized different approaches to visualizing such eye tracking data. In the visualizations, patterns such as fixations or other repeating eye movements can be identified. From these findings, researchers can draw conclusions about which visual content relates to which eye gaze pattern.

Mishra [15] found that eye tracking as a direct input device lacks precision. As a solution, patents involving prediction systems for improving the precision of interface selections are highlighted. With these improvements, the mainstream usage of eye tracking for interface navigation may be more easily reachable in the future.

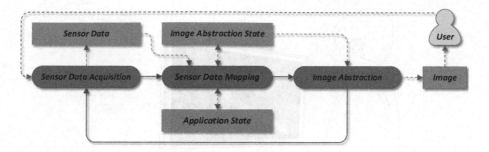

Fig. 2. Overview of the software system's processing stages and control flow (red) as well as data flow (blue) and user interaction (green). (Color figure online)

2.3   Eye Tracking in Understanding and Creating Digital Art

Eye tracking has also found applications in the domain of understanding and creating digital art. For instance, eye tracking as an interaction technique has been used in multiple art exhibitions, allowing to influence the artwork through eye movement. In "Molecular Informatics" by Mikami [14], users can discover a Virtual Reality (VR) environment of 3D molecule structures which are dynamically generated based on the eye movements of the user. Furthermore, statistical analysis of eye tracking data has been utilized for research on how humans process and perceive art. For example, the work of Quiroga and Pedreira [16] has shown that eye movement and visual attention of human observers can be easily manipulated by changing the presented pictures in small areas.

The British artist Graham Fink created many drawings using eye tracking [6]. Using his gaze and an on/off-switch, he draws the lines of his portraits on a digital canvas. He also executed live performances in museums, creating portraits of museum guests. He described using his software as "incredibly difficult" and requiring intense concentration [2].

3   Eye Tracking and Image-abstraction Techniques

Starting with the hardware system setup (Sect. 3.1), this section further describes the software system (Sect. 3.2), required low-level sensor data acquisition (Sect. 3.3), and its mapping to the different levels-of-control for image-abstraction techniques (Sect. 4.3).

3.1   System Setup and Hardware

In the proposed approach, a glasses-free consumer eye tracker (*Tobii Gaming Eye Tracker 4C*) is used to create a natural interaction with the system. Based on the intention of the currently chosen interaction technique, it allows the user to influence the system and the artwork. However, our system does not rely on specific hardware and can be used with different manufacturers. In the following, the requirements and constraints on the environment that need to be met in order for the eye tracker to work in a stable manner is described (Fig. 3).

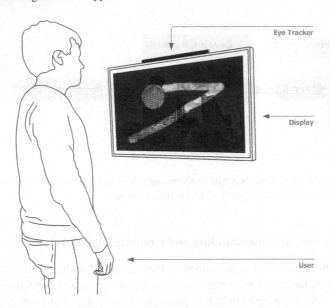

Fig. 3. Overview of system components and the setup environment.

Since the eye tracker can only track one pair of eyes at the same time, a well-lit environment with a single user is required. Furthermore, it is recommended by the manufacturer of the eye tracker to use monitors with a maximum diagonal length of 27 in. with a display ratio of 16:9 and 30 in. with a display ratio of 21:9. Additionally, the distance from the sensor is advised to be kept between 50 cm to 95 cm in order to deliver consistent results. However, in the presented approach, a 43 in. 16:9 display was used with a sensor distance of approx. 1 m and found stable and precise enough for the presented system. Extension cords for the Universal Serial Bus (USB) connection of the eye tracker are advised against while the native cable has a length of 80 cm, therefore constraining the arrangement of the components in the build of the proposed system.

Furthermore, a calibration step that tracks and measures the visual tracking response through varying head position, rotation, and distance is required by the eye tracker to allow for more precise gaze tracking. Ideally, this calibration is repeated on a per-user basis for long-term use, while in a more casual scenario with often switching users, a calibration-less set-up for a frictionless interaction should be aimed towards. A standard calibration for a certain average user position should therefore be used in the latter case. Then, the correct user position could be suggested through ground markers or other physical constraints to guarantee a certain tracking precision. Furthermore, visual feedback the status of eye detection can guide the user to assume the right position.

3.2 Overview of Software System Components

Figure 2 displays a conceptual overview of the software system used for our approach. It comprises three fundamental stages:

Sensor Data Acquisition: This stage acquires, filters, and manages the respective sensor data from the eye tracking device and possibly other real-time sensors (Sect. 3.3). Its main functionality is the conversion of low-level hardware events to high-level software events required by the subsequent stages.

Sensor Data Mapping: Using the derived high-level events, this stage manipulates the respective image-abstraction state and global application state according to the different interaction mappings and modes.

Rendering: In this stage, the behavior of the active interaction modes is executed and the respective rendering and composition steps are executed to generate the complete image that is then displayed to the user.

3.3 Sensor Data Processing

The Tobii Gaming 4C Eye Tracker can be utilized using different Software Development Kits (SDKs), such as Stream Engine, a low-level C++ binding, Core SDK, a high-level C# binding, and a Universal Windows Platform (UWP) preview of the Core SDK. Because the presented approach shares core functionality with related projects written in C# and the low-level binding is presented as the most flexible choice, the Stream Engine SDK was chosen. When connected to an eye tracker device, the SDK allows to register different callbacks, each corresponding to one data point (Table 1). Almost all sensor data feeds are updated and generate an event every 11 ms, calling every corresponding callback handler registered by the developer. Since it is not possible to change the update frequency of 11 ms in the SDK, the only options to reduce the frequency is skipping callbacks or merging them, which results in tick rates of 22 ms, 33 ms, etc.

Even the low-level Stream Engine Application Programming Interface (API) seems to apply interpolation to the sensor values, as around 5 % of user blinks do not seem to invalidate the gaze point data point, suggesting that there could be software interpolation.

4 Eye Tracking Interaction for Image-Abstraction

This section describes the parametrization of the image abstraction techniques (Sect. 4.1) and how they are influenced by the input data of the eye tracking sensor.

Table 1. Overview of low-level and high-level eye tracking events. Each data point can be observed by registering a callback which is called on every sensor capture, i.e., every 11 ms for most points.

Event	Description
Gaze point	Normalized screen coordinates $NDC = [1, 1]^2$ of user's gaze
Gaze origin	3D position of eyes, from the screen center in absolute millimeters
Eye position	Points in 3D space for both eyes, normalized within the tracking area
Head pose	3D position and rotation, from the screen center in millimeters
User presence	Boolean that indicates if a pair of eyes is currently being recognized
Notifications	Various events, e.g., the calibration status or tracking area has changed

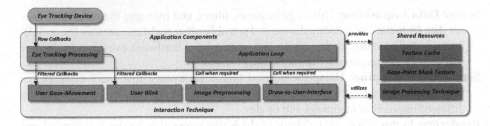

Fig. 4. Overview diagram of the interaction between the application and the interaction technique (Sect. 4.2).

Furthermore, details w.r.t. the context of the interaction techniques (Sect. 4.2) and the implementation itself (Sect. 4.3) are discussed.

4.1 Mapping Sensor Data to Levels-of-Control

Before discussing mappings between sensor data events and state changes of abstraction techniques and the application itself, we briefly review the different LOCs offered by modern, real-time implementation of image and video abstraction techniques [18]. In particular, these are:

Pipeline Manipulation. An image-abstraction pipeline is made up of one or more image-abstraction effects which each have local and global parameters and presets representing certain sets of parameter values. Pipeline presets and pipeline parameters can be used to describe a set of effects and their parameter configuration. In this work, however, only single effects are used, which therefore eliminates the need for pipeline manipulation.

Effect Selection. An image-abstraction effect applies a certain aesthetic change to the processed image. The effect selection for each interaction technique can be either constant, sequentially changing (e.g., on every blink or periodically) or based on randomness.

Preset Selection. Within each effect, different presets represent individual sets of parameters which create certain aesthetic changes. They correspond to specific parameter value configurations that produce a change in the image which is distinctly unique between each other. Presets can be selected in a similar way such as effects: either constant, sequential or random selection. In the case that no preset is selected, a default preset will be used for the effect.

Adjusting Global and Local Parameters. Each effect possesses different parameters that influence the processing and therefore the caused visual change of the effect. These parameters are typically numerical, or an enumeration value. They can be changed on a global basis, i.e., for every pixel in the image, or locally, i.e., for a subset of pixels in the image, usually caused by mask painting [18].

4.2   Interaction Context

The interaction context is given by an input image and an image-abstraction effect. The effect is influenced by its parameter values, which can be locally controlled on a global basis and using masks, and generates the artwork. In order to record (1) the eye position, (2) the gaze movement, and (3) blinks over time, a glasses-free eye tracker is mounted to the display.

Fundamentals for Interaction Techniques. The active abstraction technique uses the parameter values to achieve the desired visual change (Sect. 4.3) by implementing their own behavior in four different points in time (Fig. 4). The interaction techniques are therefore implemented using a Strategy pattern [7] as described in the following.

Gaze Movement Trajectories. In order to abstract from the raw callbacks delivered by the eye tracker API (Sect. 3.3), the gaze tracking values are first interpolated and adjusted to the application window before the interaction technique handles them. Then, these adjusted eye tracking values are processed by the interaction technique regularly (2 to 4 times of the sensor interval, i.e., 22 ms to 44 ms). The eye gaze position paints a circle shape at its position in the Gaze Movement Texture by default. This behavior can be extended and changed by implementing custom behavior based on gaze position.

Blink Events. A blink event is generated by the application whenever the user blinks. For this, the raw gaze movement callbacks and their respective validity are analyzed and processed through a confidence model (Sect. 5.3). By default, this event causes the Gaze Movement Texture to reset, however, this behavior can be overridden and altered similar to the other events. This behavior is common to the design of many implemented interaction techniques, which allows users to understand the fundamental paradigm quickly ("blink = advance, loss", Sect. 6).

Image Loading and Preprocessing. In this stage, the abstract image(s) are rendered into the two provided Cache Textures, effectively preparing for the upcoming user interface update. By pre-processing these images, the need to render them multiple times is eliminated, increasing application performance significantly. In order to achieve the desired behavior (Sect. 4.3), the interaction technique applies the necessary changes to the Processing Effect configuration on different LOCs (Sect. 4.1), e.g., applying effect presets or changing the active effect or image, followed by rendering the effect image(s) to the Cache Texture(s).

Draw-to-User-Interface. Once the main window/the user interface is prompted for an update, i.e., the user interface and the user-side representation of the artwork have to be redrawn, this last stage is called. Usually the two Caching Textures or the Gaze Movement Texture are drawn in a certain order with specific composition modes that achieve the desired effect. This stage, however, can also be restricted to just drawing one of the Cache Textures to the interface.

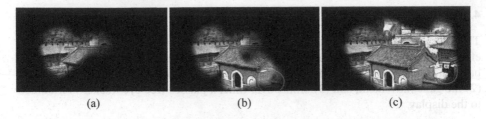

Fig. 5. Successive frames from a spot-light interaction mode session.

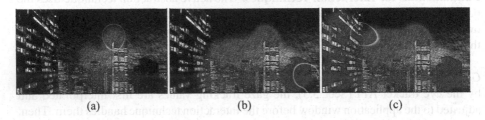

Fig. 6. Successive frames from a shift interaction mode session.

Global Application State. To enable the desired interaction technique and application logic, state information between the different events is stored in the following global resources which are provided to each callback:

Cache Textures: Two textures are provided by the application for rendering and caching the abstracted images. They are stored on the GPU to reduce transfer between GPU and Central Processing Unit (CPU) in the Paint to User Interface phase and are also resized to the rendering resolution automatically. With these two textures, interesting techniques that use blending between different parameter configurations within the same effect or between different effects can be achieved. The application framework can be easily extended to allow for more than two textures, however, not more were considered as required for the implemented, exemplary abstraction techniques.

Gaze-Movement Texture: By default, the Gaze Movement Texture is managed by the application and contains a gray-scale mask of the previous gaze movement of the user since the last time he blinked. It is used during the image preprocessing phase to create compositions together with the abstracted images and reset automatically once the user blinks.

Processing Effect: The Processing Effect represents the interface to the rendering core. It is possible to modify parameters of the active effect, the chosen preset and also change the active effect. It can also be used to combine effects in a pipeline, however, this functionality is not used in this work.

4.3   Exemplary Interaction Modes

In the following, different interaction modes are presented, that each follow similar design principles but represent distinct experiences (Figs. 5, 6 and 7).

Spotlight Interaction Mode. Starting from a black canvas or a highly blurred input photo, the artwork is revealed successively using gaze movement (Fig. 5).

For this, an alpha mask, which blends the gaze canvas with the abstracted image, is manipulated by the abstracted image circle or similar shape at the position where the user's eye is detected. When the user blinks (e.g., a certain number in a certain period of time), the mask is cleared and the revelation process must be performed from the beginning.

Shift Interaction Mode. Using a similar alpha-mask like the Spotlight-Mode, this mode blends between different level-of-abstractions of the same effect (Fig. 6). This means that two sets of parameter combinations or level-of-abstractions are used to create two versions of the image, which are blended to create the effect of transforming one image into the other. For instance, low abstraction (or the original image) could be displayed at the gaze focus area and high abstraction in the remaining area of the image. Through this, the artwork becomes unique dynamic and the user never sees the complete image. Furthermore, the system is capable of reconstructing the creation process and can generate a video for sharing.

Coloring Interaction Mode. In this mode, gaze movement blends from a light pencil sketch of an image to a colored version of the same image at the gaze location (Fig. 7). With this, the Coloring-Mode is a special case of the Shift-Mode, for which two presets of an image-processing technique that imitates watercolor painting are chosen. One preset produces color-less pencil sketches while the other produces softly colored watercolor paintings of the original image. Therefore, blending these two presets results in the desired effect of "coloring-in" the image.

5   Implementation Aspects

In this chapter, the implementation of the proposed concept is discussed. First, an overview of the system architecture is given (Sect. 5.1) and the implementation of the image-abstraction techniques is presented (Sect. 5.2). Finally, the analysis and processing of the eye tracking data is explained (Sect. 5.3).

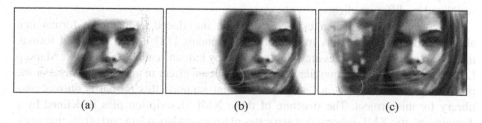

(a)   (b)   (c)

Fig. 7. Successive frames from a coloring interaction mode session.

5.1 Overview of System Architecture

In Fig. 8, an overview of the system architecture is displayed. The *MainWindow* utilizes a *User Interface (UI) Framework* and relies on the respective widgets and rendering management. *CanvasWidget* implements most of the application logic as it described in the previous chapter. Fundamentally, it handles the creation and handling of the respective instance of an *Interaction Technique* by providing the respective events and resources (Fig. 4). It achieves this by collaborating with the *Real-time Image Processor* and handling the *Processing Effect* object that is mainly accessed by the interaction technique. The *Eye Tracking Component* performs the batching, analysis, as well as processing of the eye tracking sensor data (Sect. 5.3) and communicates with the connected Tobii eye tracker using the Tobii Stream Engine library.

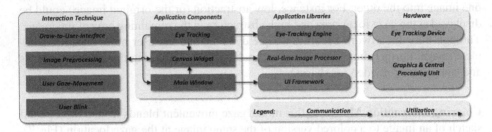

Fig. 8. Overview of the system architecture, external libraries and hardware. The main components of the application collaborate with external libraries and the respective hardware, to achieve the desired behavior of the proposed approach.

5.2 Integration of Interactive Image-abstraction Techniques

The image-abstraction techniques are implemented using a platform independent effect format, which allows parametrization on local and global LOCs. Dürschmid *et al.* stated the following requirements on document formats [5]: first, it should enable platform-independent effect specifications to allow their cross-platform provisioning and sharing. Secondly, it should have a modular structure to allow the reuse of common building blocks. Thereby rapid prototyping of new effects and modification of existing ones even by inexperienced users should be possible. Further, it should be easily parsed and serialized by different clients.

To address these challenges, Semmo *et al.* introduced a document format that allows to decompose effects into several components [18]. In the proposed format, implementation-specific files are complemented by human-readable eXtensible Markup Language (XML) description files, which describe an effect in an abstract way. For the processing of such effects, a C++ processor that supports this format is utilized as a library for this project. The structure of these XML description files is defined by a domain-specific XML scheme that separates platform-independent parts from platform- and implementation-specific parts Fig. 9. Thereby it uses the following components:

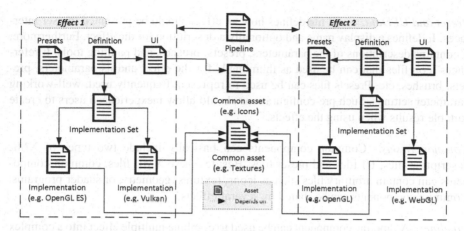

Fig. 9. Structure of an image-abstraction technique in an XML-based document format (after [5]).

Effect Definition. A definition component consists of a single definition XML file, which represents the interface to an effect. The definition file references other XML files and components that are part of the effect description. Additionally, it specifies the inputs, outputs, parameters, brushes, and painting tools. Parameter definitions consist of the parameter name, the data type of the parameter, its value range, and a default value. Brush definitions reference a brush preset and can include specifications of brush strength and stroke width. Specifications of painting tools include a reference to a painting brush and a masking texture. Further, it links to an implementation set, presets, as well as user interface data.

Implementation Set. An implementation set component includes a single implementation set XML file that lists the target platforms and graphic APIs for which implementations of the effect are available. To allow clients to choose an appropriate implementation, the implementation set file provides information regarding the performance of each implementation and lists the graphic API extensions that are required to execute it.

Implementation. The implementation describes how the effect is executed in a specific environment, e.g., following an operating system or graphics API constraint. Implementation components encapsulate the platform-specific parts of an effect description. They include implementation XML files describing the implementation of an effect for one specific target platform. To support different target platforms and graphic APIs, there can be several implementation files for an effect.

In each implementation file, shader programs and textures are specified that are required to execute the respective implementation. Subsequently several rendering passes are defined, each referencing a shader program and defining its inputs and outputs. The effect parameters defined in the corresponding definition XML file are mapped on inputs of these rendering passes. Finally, the control flow of the processing algorithm is defined by specifying an execution order of the rendering passes.

Preset and UI Data. A UI file defines how an effect should be presented in user interfaces. It defines a display name and optionally a description for the effect. Furthermore, it contains descriptions of the parameters, presets, brushes, and painting tools. It references icon files that can be used as thumbnails for the effect and its parameters, presets, brushes, etc. Presets files can be used to represent frequently used, well-working parameter settings. Such pre-configurations should allow inexperienced users to create suitable results when using the effects.

Common Assets. Common components can basically include two types of XML description files, UI files and preset files. Besides these XML files, common components can contain arbitrary files such as icons, textures, geometry, or shader programs. Common components can be shared by several effects.

Pipelines. A Pipeline component can be used to combine multiple effect into a complex one. It includes a pipeline definition XML file and a pipeline presets file. The pipeline definition file specifies a sequence of effects that make up the composite by referencing the respective definition file of each effect. The pipeline presets file is used to store global presets for the composite effect. These global presets consist of a set of presets for the effects that form the foundation the composite.

5.3   Analysis and Processing of Eye Tracking Data

To implement the interaction mode for controlling the respective image abstraction techniques, we distinguish between processing of high-level and low-level eye tracking events for controlling the parameter values of image-processing techniques as follows (Fig. 10).

Low-Level Eye Tracking Events.   Before being used to influence the image-abstraction technique, the low-level eye tracking data is analyzed and converted. At first, the raw callbacks of the Stream Engine API are collected and saved in batches. Then, after a certain time frame, these batches are collectively processed. This way, the raw callbacks are essentially underclocked to an interval set by the application. This allows for more consistent and predictable behavior when implementing an interaction technique.

By default, a circle shape is painted onto the provided Gaze Movement Texture at every valid detected gaze point (Sect. 4.2). The input gaze data is smoothed to achieve a pleasant and non-erratic interaction. If the interaction technique desires such behavior, the gaze point can also be utilized for custom processing. Each interaction technique utilizes the Gaze Movement Texture in a different way, e.g., as a clipping mask. By default, the texture mask is reset once the user blinks in all interaction techniques.

High-Level Eye Tracking Events.   To detect whether the user has blinked or not, a basic confidence model is used. For this, the amount of gaze point callbacks that judged their respective measurement as invalid is analyzed, therefore hinting at the absence of a valid pair of eyes. Through this, the stability of the blink detection is improved

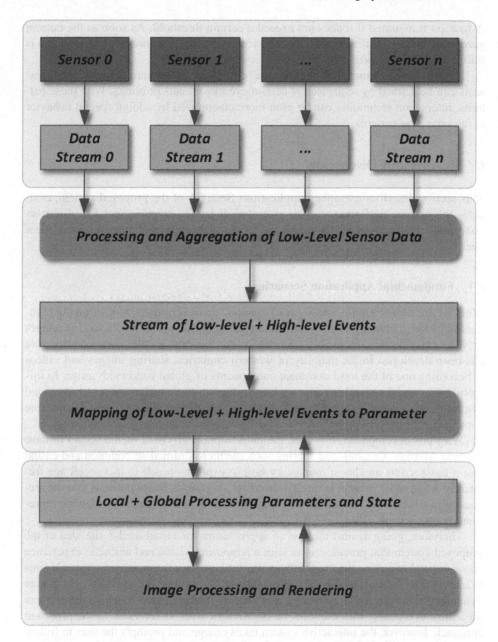

Fig. 10. Overview of the processing pipeline supporting the mapping of low-level and high-level events of multiple sensor streams parameters values of image processing techniques.

significantly, since even during stable measurement periods, some raw invalid callbacks occur, which would produce erroneous blink events without this confidence model.

Sustained gazes, i.e., fixations of the same point, are detected during gaze point processing. For this, the Manhattan distance between the last n gaze points is computed.

A fixation is assumed if it does not exceed a certain threshold. As soon as the current gaze point moves a sufficient amount and exceeds the distance threshold, the fixation is finished and regular gaze point processing commences.

It is possible to summarize high-level eye tracking events into patterns. Such patterns can be defined by sequences of certain eye movements or blinks. With these patterns, interaction techniques can be even more customized by adding special behavior to intricate gaze patterns.

6   Results and Discussion

This section describes exemplary applications Sect. 6.1 of the proposed system, evaluates the runtime performance of its prototypical implementation Sect. 6.2, discusses conceptual and technical challenges Sect. 6.3, and outlines future research ideas Sect. 6.4.

6.1   Fundamental Application Scenarios

With the digital age and the wide-spread usage of smart phones capable of taking high-quality pictures, creating, reproducing, and sharing digital visual media such as images or videos has become incredibly frictionless. As low-cost mobile data infrastructure has been developed in the majority of western countries, sharing images and videos is becoming one of the most dominant components of global bandwidth usage. In this mobile age, social networking apps such as Instagram or Snapchat are centered around communication using images and short videos – such digital visual content has become a major part of modern digital life.

With this development, however, the consumption of visual media seems to have become arbitrary. Creating and sharing such media has turned so common and casual that it has become an almost mandatory task to express oneself in this social age frequently while older content is rarely looked at. This yields the hypothesis that the frequency in which visual media content is created seems more important than the represented content itself.

Therefore, going against the loss of appreciation for visual media, the idea of the proposed system that provides users with a *temporary* visual and aesthetic experience arose. Instead of having the users fully control the system, the proposed approach aims to increase the value of the visual content through instability and volatility. The power dynamic that usually exists between a user and a technical device, in which the user can do almost everything with the tools he is provided with, is reversed. In the proposed approach, however, the interactive system takes charge and prompts the user to follow a certain behavior and, if not successful, takes away from the "reward" for the user, therefore nudging the user into the pre-determined behavior. Furthermore, the volatile visual content can increase the appreciation for the evolving artwork. In contrast to still images, the interaction allows the art to become more intriguing and provide more enjoyment to observers.

Creating a unique interaction experience between the user and the system that enables the user to take part in the creation of the presented, computer-transformed visual content is the main goal. The approach aims to create a *volatile* artwork. The interaction tries to be as frictionless and immersive as possible through the use of sensors, such as eye tracking, while also having the option to constrain the user to a certain behavior, e.g., not blinking for a set amount of time, as a game-like mechanic – in case it is desired by the chosen interaction technique.

6.2   Runtime Performance

Test System. We tested the rendering performance of our implementation using a NVIDIA GeForce GTX 1070 GPU with 4096 MB Video Random Access Memory (RAM) (VRAM) on an Intel Core i7-8700 CPU with 3.2 GHz and 32 GB RAM running Windows 10.

Table 2. Rendering performance results in milliseconds.

	Spotlight		Shift		Coloring		Gaze handling
	(i)	(ii)	(i)	(ii)	(i)	(ii)	(iii)
Average	480.727	4.472	555.910	9.232	514.919	9.231	0.649
Median	478.693	4.426	560.967	9.198	517.438	9.197	0.886
Std. Dev.	8.267	0.088	12.621	0.130	12.137	0.134	0.364

Test Setup. The rendering is performed at a viewport resolution of 1280×720 pixels. The application runs in windowed with vertical synchronization turned on. The spotlight mode comprises a Watercolor effect using a gaze mask and a single input image. The shift-mode comprises a Pencil-hatching effect using a gaze mask and two input images. The coloring mode comprises a Watercolor effect using a gaze mask and two input images as well.

We measured three stages of our system: (i) image abstraction using the gaze mask and the input images, (ii) compositing, (iii) gaze point processing. The performance of the stage (i) comprise: (1) transfer the source image(s) to GPU, (2) run image processing using one (spotlight mode) or two images (other modes), (3) transfer the processing result back to CPU as well as fill the source image buffer (i.e., load image from disk into memory). The performance of the stage (ii) basically comprise the compositing of two or three images differing blending modes to achieve the desired effect. Stage (iii) draws new gaze points into the respective mask. All input images are scaled in a preprocessing to a resolution of 1280×720 pixels.

Test Results. Table 2 shows the performance results in milliseconds. With respect to this, the sample size for step (i) is 10, (ii) is 200 to 350, and (iii) 700 to 1000. The run-time performance mainly depends on the number of processed images that are used. While the Spotlight-Mode uses only one processed image in addition to the gaze point mask, the Shift- and the Coloring-Mode use two images. This difference can be observed in the image abstraction performance (i): the processing of the abstract image(s) takes considerably longer in the Shift- and Coloring-Modes in contrast to the

Spotlight-Mode. Most of the time can be attributed to transfer of data between GPU and CPU, while only a small amount of time is used for the actual image abstraction on the GPU. The difference in the modes also apply to the compositing stage (ii): it takes roughly 9 milliseconds in the Shift- and the Coloring-Mode while it takes about 4.5 milliseconds in the Spotlight-Mode. The gaze handling takes around 0.6 to 0.8 milliseconds on average, independent of the interaction technique. Since the combined time of (ii) compositing and (iii) gaze handling is almost always less than 16 milliseconds, the proposed application is consistently interactive and achieves a frame rate of more than 60 frames per second.

6.3 Observed Effects on Users

Using the proposed system architecture, it was possible to implement the presented concept. With the presented system components, i.e., the Tobii 4C Eye Tracker, all interaction techniques are executed with an interactive frame and response rate. During application run-time, minor lag (<1 s) can occur during blink events, as described in Sect. 6.2, since images are pre-loaded from the hard drive and the effect pipeline may be adapted to change the currently active effect. However, this lag is less noticeable, as the user is blinking at that time.

During the development of the Spotlight-Mode (Sect. 4.3), an interesting observation on the necessity of highly conscious eye movements occurred. In standard human visual behavior, the eye movement is determined by visual interest (interesting patterns or objects) while a lot of information is already gathered from peripheral vision. However, the proposed Spotlight-Mode requires users to repeatedly look at different parts of a black canvas, going strongly against the normal behavior of human eye movement. Even when the user has adapted to the system behavior, the eye movements still feel unnatural. These repeated conscious movements may even be perceived as exhausting when presented with this mode for longer periods of time. Interestingly, conscious eye movements like these are also used in relaxation exercises and even have been trialed for the therapy of mental health conditions [21].

The experienced discomfort is significantly smaller for the other interaction techniques since there is no necessity to look at a black canvas. Yet, triggering direct effects in the presented interface based on eye-tracker input still feels unfamiliar. This is most likely the case because everyday digital devices such as consumer Personal Computers (PCs) and mobile devices operate with touch or mouse/keyboard input, allowing the eyes to look at arbitrary points in the interface without triggering any direct effects.

As most interaction techniques reuse certain interaction patterns, the user forms a common understanding of the interaction principles of the system. With time, the user associates interaction sequences with their respective meaning. For example, blinking usually causes a change in the style of the displayed artwork and a reset in progress. Additionally, the fundamental interaction of causing direct change to the picture wherever the eye movement is directed towards is highly intuitive and quickly learned, while also partially infuriating, since no point in the artwork can be looked at without it transforming into something else.

6.4   Potential Future Research Directions

For future work, complementing the current sensor inputs with additional sensors in order to facilitate interaction techniques which make use of various inputs could be possible. For example, microphones measuring acoustic pressure or reacting to voice commands, ambient light sensors that influence the colors in the artwork, and wearables such as smart watches that transmit the heart rate of the user could be implemented as complementary sensors. In addition, tracking the head position could yield supplementary data that can be used to improve the existing interaction techniques. For example, it could be used to reveal parts of the image while the eye gaze transforms the picture even further, therefore allowing a parallel interaction with two sensory inputs.

To elaborate further on the possibility of creating volatile visual content controlled by eye tracking, future research with respect to user experience evaluations and studies are required. Besides effective interactive techniques for tool selection, these evaluation can take the interaction processes of users with respect content variations in account. Regarding this, an open question is how blink-reflex control impacts the visual content perception and understanding, on the syntactic and semantic level respectively.

Instead of forcing the user into only one certain behavior that is triggered by their gaze, it is possible to give them more control through the selection of a "digital brush". These brushes could influence the artwork in different ways, acting as different manipulators regarding the current interaction technique. In this, also traditional paint brush strokes can be implemented, giving the user the real feel of painting a set picture. Brush attributes such as color, size, opacity or even texture should be correlated to the sensor input. For this purpose, adding additional sensors may allow for a fine-grained control. The brush selection may pose a design dilemma since the current system only includes an eye tracker, for which interface navigation is typically slow and inefficient. Additionally, undo- and redo-functionality may also have to be considered when implementing these brushes and in the interface design.

Finally, to allow for more dynamic shared resources the interaction technique framework could be extended to enable more intricate interaction modes that could even use 3rd-party APIs or libraries for additional sensor or miscellaneous data. Additionally, productive use-cases in the medical domain, such as concentration training and relaxation exercises, could be approached by extensions of the presented approach. Specific interaction techniques that make the user follow certain patterns with their eyes could imitate existing exercises and vision therapies. The approach of gamification can be extended further for a museum showcase. For this, the system could allow users to "color-in" artworks displayed in a museum collection and, after completion, offer detailed information on the artwork and its author. This approach could be implemented by museums to allow for virtual museum tours or as an interactive exhibit.

7   Conclusions

This work reports on techniques for interactive control of image-abstraction techniques using suitable mapping of eye tracking sensor data. For it, eye movement and blinking events are mapped to global and local LOC, that enables different interaction techniques rooted on similar design principles. We found that some interaction techniques, e.g., the spotlight-mode, put significant strain on the user, while others, e.g., the coloring-mode, proved to be more relaxing. Overall, users liked the visual qualities and the temporary visual sensation that is presented by the system. The system has proven to be interactive and useable in real-time without significant processing delays. Such a system can represent a basis for more advanced research w.r.t. recreational or medical applications.

References

1. Alonso, R., Causse, M., Vachon, F., Parise, R., Dehais, F., Terrier, P.: Evaluation of head-free eye tracking as an input device for air traffic control. Ergonomics **56**, 246–255 (2013). https://doi.org/10.1080/00140139.2012.744473
2. Anapur, E., Fink, G.: Drawing with his eyes - graham fink in an interview (2017). https://www.widewalls.ch/magazine/interview-graham-fink
3. Blascheck, T., Kurzhals, K., Raschke, M., Burch, M., Weiskopf, D., Ertl, T.: State-of-the-art of visualization for eye tracking data. In: EuroVis (2014)
4. DiVerdi, S., Krishnaswamy, A., Mech, R., Ito, D.: Painting with polygons: a procedural watercolor engine. IEEE Trans. Vis. Comput. Graph. **19**, 723–735 (2013)
5. Dürschmid, T., Söchting, M., Semmo, A., Trapp, M., Döllner, J.: ProsumerFX: mobile design of image stylization components. In: SIGGRAPH Asia 2017 Mobile Graphics & Interactive Applications, SA 2017, pp. 1:1–1:8. ACM, New York (2017). https://doi.org/10.1145/3132787.3139208. http://doi.acm.org/10.1145/3132787.3139208
6. Fink, G.: Drawing with my eyes (2015). https://grahamfink.com/eye-drawings
7. Gamma, E., Helm, R., Johnson, R., Vlissides, J.: Design Patterns: Elements of Reusable Object-Oriented Software. Addison-Wesley Longman Publishing Co., Inc., Boston (1995)
8. Isenberg, T.: Interactive NPAR: What type of tools should we create? In: Proceedings of the Joint Symposium on Computational Aesthetics and Sketch Based Interfaces and Modeling and Non-Photorealistic Animation and Rendering, Expresive 2016, pp. 89–96. Eurographics Association, Aire-la-Ville (2016). http://dl.acm.org/citation.cfm?id=2981324.2981337
9. Kasprowski, P., Harezlak, K., Niezabitowski, M.: Eye movement tracking as a new promising modality for human computer interaction. In: 2016 17th International Carpathian Control Conference (ICCC), pp. 314–318, May 2016. https://doi.org/10.1109/CarpathianCC.2016.7501115
10. Kiefer, P., Giannopoulos, I., Raubal, M., Duchowski, A.: Eye tracking for spatial research: cognition, computation, challenges. Spat. Cogn. Comput. **17**(1–2), 1–19 (2017). https://doi.org/10.1080/13875868.2016.1254634
11. Kiili, K., Ketamo, H., Kickmeier-Rust, M.: Evaluating the usefulness of eye tracking in game-based learning. Int. J. Serious Games **1**(2) (2014). https://doi.org/10.17083/ijsg.v1i2.15. http://journal.seriousgamessociety.org/index.php/IJSG/article/view/15
12. Kyprianidis, J.E., Collomosse, J., Wang, T., Isenberg, T.: State of the 'art': a taxonomy of artistic stylization techniques for images and video. IEEE Trans. Vis. Comput. Graph. **19**(5), 866–885 (2013). https://doi.org/10.1109/TVCG.2012.160
13. Majaranta, P., Bulling, A.: Eye tracking and eye-based human–computer interaction. In: Fairclough, S.H., Gilleade, K. (eds.) Advances in Physiological Computing. HIS, pp. 39–65. Springer, London (2014). https://doi.org/10.1007/978-1-4471-6392-3_3
14. Mikami, S.: Molecular informatics. morphogenic substance via eye tracking (1996). https://bit.ly/2oezCZv
15. Mishra, U.: Inventions on GUI for eye cursor controls systems. CoRR abs/1404.6765 (2014). http://arxiv.org/abs/1404.6765

16. Quian Quiroga, R., Pedreira, C.: How do we see art: an eye-tracker study. Front. Hum. Neurosci. **5**, 98 (2011). https://doi.org/10.3389/fnhum.2011.00098
17. Schwarz, M., Isenberg, T., Mason, K., Carpendale, S.: Modeling with rendering primitives: an interactive non-photorealistic canvas. In: Proceedings of the 5th International Symposium on Non-photorealistic Animation and Rendering, NPAR 2007, pp. 15–22. ACM, New York (2007). https://doi.org/10.1145/1274871.1274874. http://doi.acm.org/10.1145/1274871.1274874
18. Semmo, A., Dürschmid, T., Trapp, M., Klingbeil, M., Döllner, J., Pasewaldt, S.: Interactive image filtering with multiple levels-of-control on mobile devices. In: Proceedings SIGGRAPH ASIA Mobile Graphics and Interactive Applications (MGIA), pp. 2:1–2:8. ACM, New York (2016). https://doi.org/10.1145/2999508.2999521
19. Söchting, M., Trapp, M.: Controlling image-stylization techniques using eye tracking. In: Chessa, M., Paljic, A., Braz, J. (eds.) Proceedings of the 15th International Joint Conference on Computer Vision, Imaging and Computer Graphics Theory and Applications, VISIGRAPP 2020, Volume 2: HUCAPP, Valletta, Malta, 27–29 February 2020, pp. 25–34. SCITEPRESS (2020). https://doi.org/10.5220/0008964500250034
20. Vandoren, P., Van Laerhoven, T., Claesen, L., Taelman, J., Raymaekers, C., Van Reeth, F.: IntuPaint: bridging the gap between physical and digital painting. In: 2008 3rd IEEE International Workshop on Horizontal Interactive Human Computer Systems, pp. 65–72, October 2008. https://doi.org/10.1109/TABLETOP.2008.4660185
21. Vaughan, K., Armstrong, M.S., Gold, R., O'Connor, N., Jenneke, W., Tarrier, N.: A trial of eye movement desensitization compared to image habituation training and applied muscle relaxation in post-traumatic stress disorder. J. Behav. Ther. Exp. Psychiatry **25**(4), 283–291 (1994). https://doi.org/10.1016/0005-7916(94)90036-1. http://www.sciencedirect.com/science/article/pii/0005791694900361
22. Zhai, S., Morimoto, C., Ihde, S.: Manual and gaze input cascaded (magic) pointing. In: Proceedings of the SIGCHI Conference on Human Factors in Computing Systems, CHI 1999, pp. 246–253. ACM, New York (1999). https://doi.org/10.1145/302979.303053. http://doi.acm.org/10.1145/302979.303053

Information Visualization Theory and Applications

Improving Deep Learning Projections by Neighborhood Analysis

Terri S. Modrakowski[1] , Mateus Espadoto[2,3](✉) , Alexandre X. Falcão[4] ,
Nina S. T. Hirata[2] , and Alexandru Telea[1]

[1] Utrecht University, Utrecht, The Netherlands
t.s.modrakowski@students.uu.nl, a.c.telea@uu.nl
[2] University of São Paulo, São Paulo, Brazil
{mespadot,nina}@ime.usp.br
[3] University of Groningen, Groningen, The Netherlands
[4] University of Campinas, Campinas, Brazil
afalcao@ic.unicamp.br

Abstract. Visualization of multidimensional data is a difficult task, for which
there are many tools. Among these tools, dimensionality reduction methods were
shown to be particularly helpful to explore data visually. Techniques with good
visual separation are very popular, such as those from the SNE-class, but those
often are computationally expensive and non-parametric. An approach based on
neural networks was recently proposed to address those shortcomings, but it introduces some fuzziness in the generated projection, which is not desired. In this
paper we thoroughly explain the parameter space of this neural network approach and propose a new neighborhood-based learning paradigm, which further
improves the quality of the projections learned by the neural networks, and we
illustrate our approach on large real-world datasets.

Keywords: Dimensionality reduction · Machine learning · Neural networks ·
Multidimensional projections

1 Introduction

High dimensional datasets are prominent in many fields of science. However, exploring
such datasets is challenging, especially when the number of dimensions – also called
attributes or variables – is large. This difficulty is particularly salient for visualization
methods that address high-dimensional data [16,21,29].

One major type of techniques used for high-dimensional visualization methods is
formed by so-called *dimensionality reduction* (DR) methods. In contrast to other methods in information visualization, DR methods can handle data having a higher number of dimensions – up to hundreds or even thousands – as the visual space is not
assigned separately for each dimension. Different DR techniques have been developed,
aiming to balance various requirements such as speed, projection quality, and ease of
use [8,29,39,44]. Arguably one of the best known (and used) such techniques is t-SNE
[25], which is able to create scatterplots that capture well data separation in the original

This study was financed in part by FAPESP (2014/12236-1, 2015/22308-2 and 2017/25835-9),
CNPq (303808/2018-7) and the Coordenação de Aperfeiçoamento de Pessoal de Nível Superior
- Brasil (CAPES) - Finance Code 001.

© Springer Nature Switzerland AG 2022
K. Bouatouch et al. (Eds.): VISIGRAPP 2020, CCIS 1474, pp. 127–152, 2022.
https://doi.org/10.1007/978-3-030-94893-1_6

space. Yet, t-SNE is slow to run on datasets of tens of thousands of observations or more, due to its quadratic time complexity; its hyperparameters can be hard to tune to get a good result [47]; its results are quite sensitive to data changes, *e.g.*, adding more samples may result in a completely different projection; and it cannot project out-of-sample data, which is useful for time-dependent data analysis [29,36,46]. Work has been done to address the performance issue, such as tree-accelerated SNE [24], H-SNE [33], A-SNE [34], and UMAP [28], which is a completely different algorithm but with the stated goal of having t-SNE quality at a higher speed. However, in general, there is no technique in the SNE class that jointly addresses scalability, stability, and out-of-sample handling.

A very different approach to projection was recently proposed [6] based on deep learning. Given a high-dimensional dataset and its 2D scatterplot created by the DR technique of choice of the user, a neural network is trained to reproduce the scatterplot. After training, the network can generate projections of high-dimensional datasets that are similar in nature to the ones used during training. This method – referred next as Neural Network Projection (NNP) – is particularly interesting as an alternative to t-SNE, since it is several orders of magnitude faster than classical t-SNE, has out-of-sample capability by design, and is simple to implement and easy to use.

A drawback of the work in [6] is, however, validation: While NNP is shown to work well, in terms of projection quality metrics, on a variety of datasets and able to learn different projection methods, the space of *hyperparameters* used during architecture and training is left unexplored. This leaves two open questions. First, a detailed study of how NNP's results depend on these hyperparameters is needed before being able to claim that the method can consistently generate good projections, as common with other deep learning evaluations [9,13]. A second problem of NNP's results shown in [6] is that these exhibit less sharp separation of data clusters than in the ground-truth (training) projection, compare *e.g.* Figs. 1a and b, a phenomenon referred to next as projection diffusion or fuzziness. Exploring how hyperparameter settings affect, and possibly reduce, diffusion is thus an important open question.

Many potential causes exist for diffusion, *e.g.*: (1) too small training sets or too few training epochs (underfitting); (2) using a suboptimal regularization (overfitting); (3) using an improper optimizer which gets stuck in a local minimum of the cost function. Recently, Espadoto *et al.* [7] studied the causes of diffusion by exploring the *hyperparameter space* of NNP, showing how these influence the results' quality, gauged by projection quality metrics. They showed that NNP is *stable* with respect to

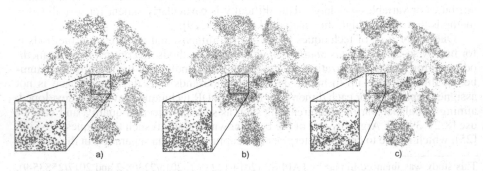

Fig. 1. Example of diffusion introduced by NNP. (a) Ground-truth t-SNE projection (b) Inferred NNP (10K samples) with diffusion. (c) Inferred KNNP (10K samples) showing less diffusion.

hyperparameter settings, thereby completing the claim made by [6] that they can be reliably used for out-of-sample and noisy-data contexts. However, they did not propose a way to *reduce* diffusion.

In this paper, we extend the work in [7] by proposing a novel approach to deep learning projections. Rather than learning from a *single* sample at a time, we project whole groups of related (neighboring) samples at a time. This aids the network to learn how to preserve neighborhoods. To do this, we explore different schemes of efficient nearest-neighbor search in high-dimensional data during both training and inference. We evaluate our method, called K-Nearest-Neighbor Projection (KNNP) against NNP on a variety of datasets and using several quality metrics, and show that our strategy is both computationally scalable and also leads to quality improvements as compared to NNP.

The structure of this paper is as follows. Section 2 discusses related work and introduces NNP. Section 3 details our experimental NNP evaluation. Section 4 presents our results for optimizing NNP via hyperparameter space search, discussed next in Sect. 5. Section 6 presents the new KNNP projection method, whose results are discussed next in Sect. 7. Finally, Sect. 8 concludes the paper.

2 Related Work

2.1 Dimensionality Reduction

We first introduce some notations. Let $D = \{\mathbf{x}_i\}$, $1 \leq i \leq N$ be a dataset of N samples, where each sample $\mathbf{x} = (x^1, \ldots, x^n)$, $x^i \in \mathbb{R}$, $1 \leq i \leq n$ is an n-dimensional (nD) data point. We model a projection method by a function $P : \mathbb{R}^n \to \mathbb{R}^q$ where $q \ll n$. We next consider 2D projections, *i.e.*, set $q = 2$. Hence, the projection of a sample $\mathbf{x} \in D$ is denoted by $P(\mathbf{x})$. For notation ease, we denote the 2D scatterplot obtained by projecting a dataset D as $P(D) = \{P(\mathbf{x}) | \mathbf{x} \in D\}$.

Dimensionality Reduction (DR) techniques implement various versions of the function P, aiming at optimizing different so-called quality metrics such as distance preservation or neighborhood preservation, by using different optimization strategies. Arguably the simplest, and probably earliest, DR method is PCA [15,32], which is simple to implement, fast, and deterministic. More complex techniques include manifold learners, such as MDS [43], Isomap [42], LLE [37], and UMAP [28], which work well when the high-dimensional data is distributed over a manifold surface. These techniques are compared extensively from algorithmic viewpoints [2,5,12,21,39,44,50] and also from practical viewpoints (benchmarking) [8].

The t-Stochastic Neighbor Embedding projection [25] and other similar techniques in the same family [24,33] succeed in creating high-quality projections from a neighborhood preservation perspective, thereby being very effective in exploring cases where data is segregated into similar-sample clusters in unsupervised learning contexts. However, as outlined in Sect. 1, t-SNE is quite slow and, due to its stochastic optimizer, hard to tune so that it produces deterministic results. Obviously, the latter implies it cannot be directly used in out-of-sample contexts. Parametric t-SNE variants help with this latter problem [23] at the expense of more complex, and slower, implementations.

2.2 Deep Learning Projections

Early on, autoencoders [11,18] were proposed to generate a compressed, low-dimensional representation on their bottleneck layers by training the network to reproduce its inputs on its outputs. Typically, autoencoders produce results comparable to PCA. The ReNDA algorithm [1] uses two networks, improving on earlier work from the same authors. One network is used to implement a nonlinear generalization of Fisher's Linear Discriminant Analysis, using a method called GerDA; the other network is an Autoencoder used as a regularizer. The method scores well on predictability and has out-of-sample capability. However, it requires labeled data, which is not always available. Parametric t-SNE (pt-SNE) [23] was proposed to address the out-of-sample limitation of t-SNE. Being of parametric nature (mapping the entire nD input space to the lower-dimensional qD space), it allows out-of-sample behavior by construction. Only few other DR methods are parametric and thus have this ability (*e.g.*, PCA [15], NCA [10], and autoencoders [11]).

Recently, Espadoto *et al.* [6] proposed Neural Network Projections (NNP). Consider a dataset $D \subset \mathcal{D}$, where $\mathcal{D} \subset \mathbb{R}^n$ is a so-called universe of high-dimensional datasets related to a given domain, *e.g.* natural images of people faces. A training subset $D_s \subset D$ thereof is selected, and projected by some DR method (t-SNE or any other) to yield a so-called training projection $P(D_s) \subset \mathbb{R}^2$. Next, D_s is fed into a three-layer, fully-connected, regression neural network which is trained to output a 2D scatterplot $P_{nn}(D_s) \subset \mathbb{R}^2$ by minimizing the mean squared error between $P(D_s)$ and $P_{nn}(D_s)$. After that, the network is used to construct projections of unseen data from the same universe, $D_p = \mathcal{D} \setminus D_s$, by means of 2-dimensional, non-linear regression. This approach is fundamentally different from *autoencoders* [11] which do not learn from a training projection P, but simply aim to extract, in an unsupervised way, latent low-dimensional features that best represent the input data. Also, NNP is different from pt-SNE since it uses *supervised* learning (based on the training projection), has a much simpler network architecture, and a different cost function (distance to 2D ground-truth projection rather than Kullback-Leibler divergence). The NNP pipeline is shown in Fig. 2.

The NNP method is simple to implement, generically learns any projection P for any dataset $D \subset \mathbb{R}^n$, has deterministic (thus, out-of-sample) behavior, and is orders of magnitudes faster than classical projection techniques, in particular t-SNE.

However, as outlined in Sect. 1, designing a quality neural network (in our case, the NNP regressor) is challenging, given the large space of design decisions available. We outline below five such degrees of freedom, all of them relevant for NNP's performance.

Network Architecture: Much of the flexibility of neural networks (NNs) comes from architectural choices. If we follow NNP's design, which restricts itself to fully connected networks, the open choices regard the number of layers and layer sizes.

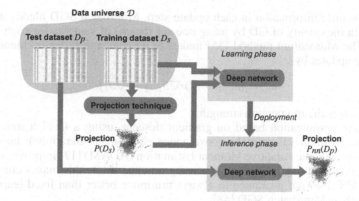

Fig. 2. Pipeline for the Neural Network Projection (NNP) method.

Loss Functions: To start with, one needs to choose a loss function J that describes what the network aims to learn. Typical loss functions for regression are Mean Squared Error (MSE), Mean Absolute Error (MAE), logcosh, and Huber loss (see Table 1, where $\hat{\mathbf{y}} = \{\hat{y}_i\}$ is the NN's output vector and $\mathbf{y} = \{y_i\}$ is the training-set sample that $\hat{\mathbf{y}}$ should infer). These losses differ in several aspects: Smoother ones (MSE, logcosh) are easier to optimize by gradient descent and its variants (discussed further below); MAE is harder to optimize since its gradient is discontinuous. The Huber loss, controlled by a parameter α, behaves in the range of these models – it is close to MAE for low α and close to MSE for larger α. Finally, MAE and Huber losses are typically more robust to outliers than MSE.

Regularization: To address overfitting, regularization techniques are used to make training harder, therefore increasing the number of epochs needed for the NN to achieve convergence and thus increase their generalization power. Such techniques include L_2, L_1, max-norm, early stopping, and data augmentation. The L_k regularization techniques, also known as *weight pruning* ($k = 1$) and *weight decay* ($k = 2$), adds a penalty term $\lambda\|\mathbf{w}\|^k$ to the NN cost function, *i.e.*, the k-norm of the weights $\mathbf{w}$ of a given layer. Here, the parameter λ gives the regularization strength. The L_1 [30] variant sets the weights of less important layers to zero, thereby effectively sparsifying the model. The L_2 [19] variant, in contrast, decreases weights to small but non-zero values, thereby effectively distributing weights over more connections across the model. Both L_1 and L_2 are effective in reducing overfitting. Max-norm [40] regularization caps the norm of layer weights to a maximal value γ. Another way to reduce overfitting is to combine such regularization techniques with early stopping [51]. Hereby training is halted when the validation loss J_V stops decreasing or starts increasing while the training loss J_T keeps dropping, a situation which signals overfitting.

Optimizers: The NN cost can be minimized using Gradient Descent (GD). GD aims to minimize the training error by adjusting the weights $\mathbf{w}_t$ at the current step t by taking steps of size η (also called the learning rate) downwards along the gradient ∇J_t of the current value of the loss function J_t with respect to $\mathbf{w}$ as

$$\mathbf{w}_t = \mathbf{w}_{t-1} - \eta \nabla J_t. \tag{1}$$

Applying GD (Eq. 1) on large datasets is expensive. Stochastic Gradient Descent (SGD) speeds this up by using only one randomly-picked sample per update step t. However, this uses too little information in each update step. Mini-batch SGD blends the speed of SGD with the quality of GD by using one set (batch) of samples for each iteration of Eq. 1. The Momentum method [35] makes SGD converge faster by blending two consecutive updates by

$$\boldsymbol{w}^t = \boldsymbol{w}_{t-1} - \eta(\nu \nabla J_{t-1} + \nabla J_t), \qquad (2)$$

where ν controls the momentum strength.

As in any optimization based on gradient descent, using a fixed learning rate η is not optimal: Small values make convergence slow (many iterations); large values may skip over minima. Adaptive Moment Estimation (ADAM) [17] improves upon this by adaptively computing η by using squared gradients. While this makes convergence faster, ADAM does not guarantee to always minimize better than fixed-learning-rate methods such as Mini-batch SGD [48].

Data Augmentation: Adding data that is similar to existing training data is typically used to make deep learning effective in cases when only small training sets are available. However, data augmentation also creates models that generalize better, thereby being useful for regularization purposes.

Table 1. Typical NN loss functions. (table from [7]).

Function	Definition
MSE	$\frac{1}{n}\sum_{i=1}^{n}(y_i - \hat{y}_i)^2$
MAE	$\frac{1}{n}\sum_{i=1}^{n}|y_i - \hat{y}_i|$
logcosh	$\frac{1}{n}\sum_{i=1}^{n}log(cosh(y_i - \hat{y}_i))$
Huber	$\begin{cases}\frac{1}{2}(y-\hat{y})^2 & \text{if}|y-\hat{y}| \leq \alpha \\ \alpha|y-\hat{y}| - \frac{1}{2}\alpha & \text{otherwise}\end{cases}$

3   NNP Evaluation

While NNP has several advantages, as mentioned in the previous section, its quality and stability *vs* hyperparameter settings has not yet been assessed in detail. We address this by performing a set of experiments that explore the design space of NNP (Sect. 3.1). For each experiment, we evaluate NNP using several quality metrics (Sect. 3.2).

3.1   Hyperparameter Space Exploration

To evaluate NNP's performance, we consider the space spanned by five dimensions: Network architecture, regularization methods, optimizers, data augmentation, and loss functions. We sample every dimension using several values (in terms of both method types and actual values of parameters), aiming to cover typical choices in the literature (Sect. 2) – when these are available – or choices that we deem suitable for the NNP context. All these are detailed below.

Evaluating all combinations of all sample values across all five dimensions is impractical, as it would lead to over 70 thousand of training-and-testing runs. We decrease this search space by optimizing for every dimension in turn. Early stopping was used on all experiments, stopping training if the validation loss stops decreasing for more than 10 epochs. Except when noted otherwise, we used the ADAM optimizer and the MSE loss function. As dataset to project, we use MNIST [20], which has 70K samples of handwritten digits from 0 to 9 represented as 28×28-pixel grayscale images, flattened to 784-element vectors. We use training-sets of 2K, 5K, 10K and 20K samples picked randomly from the full dataset and a 10K test-set sample. This way, we test how *both* the hyperparameter values and the training-set size affect the quality of NNP. Note that MNIST was also used by the original NNP method [6], which makes it easy to compare our results.

We next detail the sampling of our five dimensions, pointing also at sections in the paper where the respective evaluation is detailed.

Network Architecture (Sect. 4.5): The NNP architecture in [6], called next *Standard*, has three fully-connected hidden layers, with 256, 512, and 256 neurons respectively. We created variants of this architecture by using a total of 360 (small), 720 (medium) and 1440 (large) neurons, distributed into three different layouts, called straight (st), wide (wd) and bottleneck (bt). This leads to exploring nine architectures. For each architecture, we list its number of neurons in the first, middle, and final layer below:

- *Small - straight*: 120, 120 and 120 neurons;
- *Small - wide*: 90, 180 and 90 neurons;
- *Small - bottleneck*: 150, 60 and 150 neurons;
- *Medium - straight*: 240, 240 and 240 neurons;
- *Medium - wide*: 180, 360 and 180 neurons;
- *Medium - bottleneck*: 300, 120 and 300 neurons;
- *Large - straight*: 480, 480 and 480 neurons;
- *Large - wide*: 360, 720 and 360 neurons;
- *Large - bottleneck*: 600, 240 and 600 neurons.

All above architectures are fully connected, and use ReLU activation, followed by a 2-unit layer which uses the sigmoid activation function to generate the 2D coordinates of the projected points.

Regularization (Sect. 4.1): Following Sect. 2, we studied three regularization methods:

- L_1 with $\lambda \in \{0, 0.001, 0.01, 0.1\}$ (0 denotes no regularization);
- L_2 with $\lambda \in \{0, 0.001, 0.01, 0.1\}$ (0 denotes no regularization);
- Max-norm, with $\gamma \in \{0, 1, 2, 3\}$, (0 denotes no max-norm constraint).

Optimizers (Sect. 4.2): We explored both ADAM and Mini-batch SGD optimizers with learning rates $\eta \in \{0.01, 0.001\}$ and momentum $\nu = 0.9$. The batch size used was 32 samples in both cases.

Data Augmentation (Sect. 4.3): We used two variants data augmentation with the aim of reducing the diffusion effect present in the original NNP method, as follows:

- *Noise Before:* The t-SNE projection is known to create clear-separated clusters even for relatively noisy data. We aim to leverage this by artificially making the data to project more complex. For this, we add Gaussian noise of zero mean and standard deviations $\sigma \in \{0, 0.001, 0.01\}$, with 0 meaning no added noise, to the high-dimensional training data. We then project this noised data, added to the original (clean) data by t-SNE, and train NNP to mimic this projection;

– *Noise After:* The idea behind this strategy is to 'jitter' the high-dimensional data while keeping its projection fixed to that of the clean data, and train NNP to mimic the (clean) projection. This way, we hope to teach NNP that small-scale jitters in the data should not create diffusion in the projection. For this, add Gaussian noise (same σ as in the Noise Before strategy) to the data and train NNP to project the noised data dataset to obtain the clean projection.

Loss Functions (Sect. 4.4): Following Sect. 2, we experimented with four loss functions: Mean Squared Error (MSE), used by the original NNP; Mean Absolute Error (MAE); logcosh; and Huber, with $\alpha \in \{1, 5, 10, 20, 30\}$.

3.2 Quality Measurement

We measure the quality of the projections created by NNP by four metrics (see Table 2). These are well-known in the DR literature [8]. Moreover, these were also used when assessing the original NNP method.

Trustworthiness T: Gives the fraction of close points in D that are also close in $P(D)$ [45]. Differently put, a low T indicates that a projection exhibits so-called missing neighbors [27]. $U_i^{(K)}$ is the set of points that are among the K nearest neighbors of point i in 2D but not among the K nearest neighbors of point i in $\mathbb{R}^n$; and $r(i, j)$ is the rank of the 2D point j in the ordered set of nearest neighbors of i in 2D. We use $K = 7$ neighbors, following [8,27,44].

Continuity C: Gives the fraction of points in $P(D)$ that are also close in D [45]. A low C indicates that a projection has so-called false neighbors [27]. $V_i^{(K)}$ is the set of points that are among the K nearest neighbors of point i in $\mathbb{R}^n$ but not among the K nearest neighbors in 2D; and $\hat{r}(i, j)$ is the rank of the $\mathbb{R}^n$ point j in the ordered set of nearest neighbors of i in $\mathbb{R}^n$. As for T, we use $K = 7$ neighbors.

Neighborhood Hit NH: For labeled data, NH tells how homogeneous point-clusters are in the projection, ranging from perfect separation ($NH = 1$) to no separation ($NH = 0$) [31]. For data which one knows that consists of well-separated sample clusters, one would want a high NH projection. NH is the number $\mathbf{y}_K^l$ of the K nearest neighbors of a point $\mathbf{y} \in P(D)$, denoted by $\mathbf{y}_K$, that have the same label as $\mathbf{y}$, averaged over $P(D)$. As above, we use $K = 7$ neighbors.

Shepard Diagram Correlation R: Shepard diagrams are scatterplots of Euclidean distances (in nD *vs* 2D) between all point-pairs [14]. Diagrams that are close to the main diagonal indicate that the projection preserves distances well. Following [8], we measure the quality implied by a Shepard diagram by computing the Spearman ρ rank correlation of the respective 2D scatterplot, with $R = 1$ telling a perfect distance correlation.

Table 2. Quality metrics. Right column gives metric ranges, with optimal values in bold.

Metric	Definition	Range
T	$1 - \frac{2}{NK(2n-3K-1)} \sum_{i=1}^{N} \sum_{j \in U_i^{(K)}} (r(i,j) - K)$	$[0, \mathbf{1}]$
C	$1 - \frac{2}{NK(2n-3K-1)} \sum_{i=1}^{N} \sum_{j \in V_i^{(K)}} (\hat{r}(i,j) - K)$	$[0, \mathbf{1}]$
NH	$\frac{1}{N} \sum_{\mathbf{y} \in P(D)} \frac{\mathbf{y}_k^l}{\mathbf{y}_k}$	$[0, \mathbf{1}]$
R	$\rho(\|\mathbf{x}_i - \mathbf{x}_j\|, \|P(\mathbf{x}_i) - P(\mathbf{x}_j)\|), 1 \le i \le N, i \ne j$	$[0, \mathbf{1}]$

4 NNP Evaluation Results

Table 3. Effect of **regularization**. Rows show metrics for t-SNE (*GT* row) *vs* NN projections using different training-set sizes. Bold shows values closest to *GT*. (table from [7]).

a) L_1 regularization

Model	λ	NH	T	C	R	# epochs	Time (s)
GT		0.929	0.990	0.976	0.277		
2K	0	**0.705**	**0.843**	**0.957**	**0.443**	50	6.20
	0.001	0.677	0.827	0.948	0.439	58	7.14
	0.01	0.660	0.815	0.945	0.438	94	10.93
	0.1	0.632	0.806	0.943	0.454	82	9.98
5K	0	**0.738**	**0.871**	**0.962**	**0.423**	26	7.22
	0.001	0.692	0.845	0.953	0.436	38	10.05
	0.01	0.670	0.835	0.947	0.427	68	18.29
	0.1	0.599	0.815	0.945	0.459	53	14.58
10K	0	**0.834**	**0.902**	**0.968**	0.337	45	22.32
	0.001	0.753	0.852	0.958	0.348	31	16.09
	0.01	0.722	0.833	0.951	0.352	39	19.12
	0.1	0.665	0.811	0.947	0.345	61	30.67
20K	0	**0.885**	**0.922**	**0.967**	0.341	49	47.28
	0.001	0.816	0.883	0.960	0.364	30	29.35
	0.01	0.743	0.842	0.954	0.366	28	26.89
	0.1	0.707	0.822	0.946	0.364	25	24.17

b) L_2 regularization

NH	T	C	R	# epochs	Time (s)
0.929	0.990	0.976	0.277		
0.695	0.839	0.956	0.437	35	4.61
0.711	**0.847**	**0.958**	0.432	29	4.27
0.684	0.834	0.954	0.433	42	5.57
0.683	0.830	0.952	**0.428**	68	8.54
0.767	**0.880**	**0.963**	0.422	53	14.33
0.742	0.875	**0.963**	0.419	28	7.71
0.733	0.866	0.959	**0.416**	55	15.24
0.709	0.860	0.958	0.429	45	12.51
0.833	**0.899**	**0.967**	0.342	43	20.93
0.821	**0.899**	0.966	0.340	55	27.88
0.798	0.880	0.963	0.337	34	17.37
0.773	0.865	0.961	**0.336**	36	18.48
0.885	**0.922**	**0.967**	0.341	46	43.49
0.870	0.915	0.966	0.343	34	33.06
0.853	0.902	0.963	0.344	40	38.05
0.826	0.883	0.960	**0.339**	38	37.87

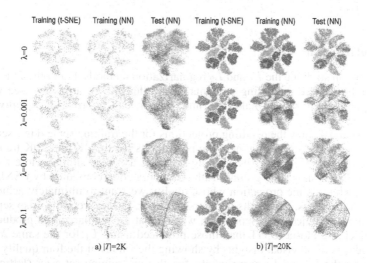

Training (t-SNE) Training (NN) Test (NN) Training (t-SNE) Training (NN) Test (NN)

λ=0 λ=0.001 λ=0.01 λ=0.1

a) |T|=2K b) |T|=20K

Fig. 3. L_1 **regularization:** Effect of λ for different training-set sizes. Compare the ground truth (training-set, projected by t-SNE) with the NN results on the training-set, respectively test-set. (figure from [7]).

We next present the results of the NNP hyperparameter-space exploration performed along the five dimensions described in Sect. 3.

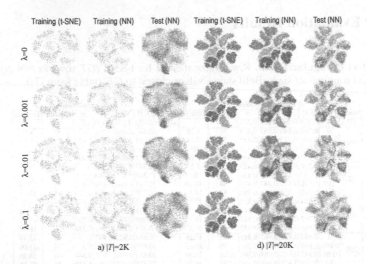

Fig. 4. L_2 **regularization:** Effect of λ for different training-set sizes. Compare the ground truth (training-set, projected by t-SNE) with the NN results on the training-set, respectively test-set. (figure from [7]).

4.1 Regularization

We first focus on studying the L_1 and L_2 regularization methods. For both of them, used independently, we use increasing amounts (controlled by λ), aiming to see whether higher regularization, which makes learning harder, can improve the quality of the inferred projections.

Figures 3 and 4 show the resulting projections for the training set and test set. Given the limited space, we only show here the projections for the 2K and 20K training-set sizes – the ones for 5K and 10K training-set sizes are very similar. Here and next, 'Training (t-SNE)' shows the ground-truth (GT) projection computed by t-SNE on the training set, which is the projection whose quality we want to ultimately achieve. We see that, as λ increases, the results get worse (fuzzier, farther from the crisp separation visible in the GT projection). Separately, we see that L_2 regularization produces projections which are closer to GT than those produced using L_1 for the same λ values. Table 3 confirms these visual insights by showing the values of the four quality metrics (Sect. 3.2) for the L_1 and L_2 experiments, for all four training-set sizes (leftmost column). As noted above, L_2 regularization yields NH, T, and C values closer to the GT ones than L_1 regularization. Separately, Table 3 shows that NNP yields *higher* Shepard correlation R values than GT, for all λ values (slightly higher for L_1 than L_2). In other words, NNP preserves the nD distances in the 2D projection *better* than t-SNE projection (see definition of R, Table 2). This indirectly explains the diffusion we see in NNP: Indeed, since NNP aims to preserve distances, it cannot rearrange points as freely as t-SNE does (which only aims to preserve neighborhoods), thereby yielding a less crisp cluster separation than t-SNE.

The rightmost two columns in Tables 3(a, b) show the *training effort* until convergence (number epochs and seconds). Convergence is reached in under 70 epochs, regardless of the regularization type (L_1 or L_2) or strength λ. L_1 and L_2 regularization require similar effort, with L_2 being slightly faster than L_1 for smaller training sets.

This confirms the initial findings from [6] that NNP converges well, and additionally tells that this happens regardless of regularization.

We next study the max-norm regularization. Figure 5 shows that the projection quality does not strongly depend on the max-norm constraint γ. The metrics in Table 4(a) confirm this. We also see that max-norm yields higher projection quality values (closer to GT) than L_1 and L_2. Effort-wise, max-norm regularization is very similar to L_1 and L_2 (compare rightmost columns in Table 4 (a) with those in Table 3(a, b)). Putting all above results together, we conclude that regularization does not bring a significant benefit to NNP, with max-norm being only slightly better than L_1 and L_2.

Table 4. Effect of **max-norm** (a) and **optimizers** (b). Metrics shown for t-SNE (*GT* row) *vs* NN projections using different training-set sizes. Bold shows values closest to *GT*. (table from [7]).

a) **Max-norm regularization**

Model	γ	NH	T	C	R	# epochs	Time (s)
GT		0.929	0.990	0.976	0.277		
2K	0	**0.701**	0.839	0.956	0.443	44	5.45
	1	0.692	0.836	0.956	**0.431**	32	4.47
	2	0.699	**0.842**	**0.957**	0.441	45	5.80
	3	0.698	0.837	0.956	0.441	31	4.47
5K	0	**0.759**	**0.881**	**0.964**	**0.417**	51	13.34
	1	0.756	0.880	**0.964**	0.421	40	10.70
	2	0.740	0.866	0.961	0.420	24	7.05
	3	0.755	0.879	0.963	0.423	48	13.23
10K	0	0.824	0.898	0.966	**0.337**	37	18.14
	1	**0.840**	0.904	0.967	0.338	31	15.43
	2	0.829	0.903	0.967	0.340	37	18.67
	3	0.837	**0.905**	**0.968**	0.338	53	26.63
20K	0	**0.886**	**0.923**	**0.967**	0.342	56	52.65
	1	0.870	0.918	**0.967**	**0.340**	26	25.22
	2	0.881	0.917	**0.967**	0.341	30	28.88
	3	0.879	0.920	**0.967**	0.345	34	34.11

b) **Optimizers**

Model	Optimizer (η)	NH	T	C	R	# epochs	Time (s)
GT		0.929	0.990	0.976	0.277		
2K	ADAM	0.696	**0.841**	**0.956**	**0.447**	30	3.72
	SGD (0.01)	0.625	0.791	0.938	0.464	97	8.32
	SGD (0.001)	0.610	0.787	0.938	0.464	455	36.56
5K	ADAM	**0.733**	**0.861**	**0.960**	0.421	19	5.27
	SGD (0.01)	0.655	0.817	0.945	0.430	86	16.00
	SGD (0.001)	0.641	0.808	0.942	0.443	402	77.17
10K	ADAM	**0.842**	**0.905**	**0.968**	0.343	56	26.51
	SGD (0.01)	0.707	0.821	0.949	0.362	75	28.55
	SGD (0.001)	0.690	0.812	0.948	0.360	392	147.60
20K	ADAM	**0.882**	**0.920**	**0.968**	0.339	43	40.77
	SGD (0.01)	0.769	0.838	0.952	0.356	129	94.30
	SGD (0.001)	0.754	0.836	0.952	0.370	423	309.19

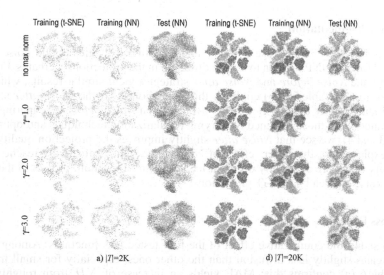

Fig. 5. Max-norm: Effect of γ for different training-set sizes. Compare the ground truth (training-set, projected by t-SNE) with the NN results on the training-set, respectively test-set. (figure from [7]).

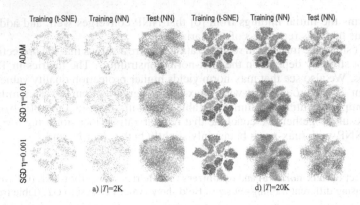

Fig. 6. Optimizer: Effects of different settings (ADAM, SGD with $\eta \in \{0.001, 0.01\}$) for different training-set sizes. Compare the ground truth (training-set, projected by t-SNE) with the NN results on the training-set, respectively test-set. (figure from [7]).

4.2 Optimizer

Following Sect. 3, we trained NNP using the ADAM optimizer with its default settings, and also with Mini-batch SGD with learning rates $\eta \in \{0.01, 0.001\}$. Figure 6 shows that ADAM produces results with far less diffusion than SGD. Table 4(b) confirms this, as ADAM scores better than SGD for all four quality metrics. We also see here that ADAM converges much faster than SGD. Since, additionally, ADAM works well with its default parameters, we conclude that this is the optimizer of choice for NNP.

4.3 Data Augmentation

As outlined in Sect. 3.1, we use two data augmentation strategies to add noise in the attempt of forcing NNP to learn to reduce diffusion in the projections it creates. Figure 7 shows that the *Noise before* and *Noise after* strategies yield similar results, which are also close to GT. Table 5(a, b) confirms this, and shows that the *Noise after* strategy yields slightly higher quality metrics on average than *Noise before*. Comparing these quality values with those obtained by varying regularization techniques and optimizers (Tables 3 and 4), we see that *Noise after* slightly improves the projection quality. This can be explained by the 'jitter' effect of Noise after, which effectively teaches NNP that points which are at slightly different locations (in nD) should project to the *same* location (in 2D, given by the GT projection).

4.4 Loss Function

Figure 8 shows the comparative effect of the four tested loss functions. Among these, MAE creates slightly less diffusion than the other ones, especially for small training sets. Table 6 (a) confirms this: MAE yields an increase of NH from roughly 0.70 (when using the other loss functions) to roughly 0.74 for the smallest test-set of 2K samples; for the largest test-set of 20K samples, the NH increases from roughly 0.87 to 0.88. Also, MAE yields the best quality metrics for all tested configurations. However, Table 6 (a) also shows that the training effort for MAE is higher than for the other loss functions. As the training set increases, the training-effort difference between MAE

Table 5. Effect of **data augmentation**. Rows show metrics for t-SNE (*GT* row)) *vs* NNP (other rows). Right two columns in each table show training effort (epochs and time). Bold shows values closest to *GT*. (table from [7]).

a) **Noise after** strategy

Model	Noise σ	NH	T	C	R	# epochs	Time (s)
GT		0.929	0.990	0.976	0.277		
2K	0	0.717	0.846	0.958	0.448	31	8.84
	0.001	0.726	0.852	**0.960**	**0.430**	37	10.57
	0.01	**0.729**	**0.856**	**0.960**	0.433	54	14.52
5K	0	**0.783**	0.892	**0.966**	**0.401**	43	23.28
	0.001	0.780	**0.895**	**0.966**	0.408	52	29.44
	0.01	**0.783**	0.892	**0.966**	**0.401**	47	26.84
10K	0	**0.849**	0.909	**0.968**	0.339	44	44.06
	0.001	0.844	0.909	**0.968**	0.337	36	37.76
	0.01	0.848	**0.910**	**0.968**	**0.333**	59	60.31
20K	0	0.887	0.924	0.966	0.340	55	105.87
	0.001	**0.888**	0.924	**0.967**	**0.336**	46	88.09
	0.01	0.885	**0.925**	**0.967**	0.339	51	97.06

b) **Noise before** strategy

NH	T	C	R	# epochs	Time (s)
0.929	0.990	0.976	0.277		
0.712	**0.842**	0.957	0.446	23	7.17
0.679	**0.842**	**0.959**	0.422	33	9.57
0.682	0.833	0.956	**0.421**	20	6.86
0.785	**0.894**	**0.966**	**0.401**	62	33.34
0.793	0.884	**0.966**	**0.364**	31	17.91
0.802	0.888	**0.967**	0.366	49	28.68
0.849	**0.908**	**0.968**	0.336	36	35.61
0.798	0.901	0.966	0.304	37	39.58
0.802	0.904	0.966	**0.302**	53	55.58
0.888	**0.925**	**0.967**	**0.337**	40	76.08
0.865	0.920	**0.967**	0.385	42	81.55
0.869	0.920	**0.967**	0.392	41	80.52

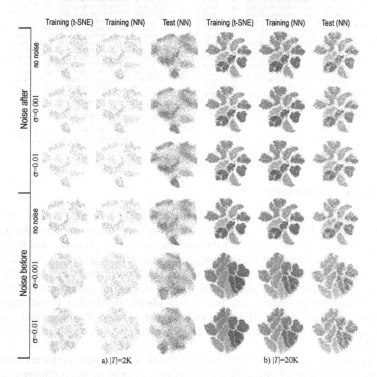

Fig. 7. Noise after and **noise before** data augmentation: Effect of noise strength $\sigma \in \{0, 0.001, 0.01\}$. Compare the ground truth (training-set, projected by t-SNE) with the NN results on the training-set, respectively test-set. (figure from [7]).

and the other loss functions decreases. Hence, for a real-world configuration, MAE is not really more costly than the alternatives. Given all above, we conclude that MAE is the best loss function for NNP.

Table 6. Effect of different **loss functions** (a) and **architectures** (b). Rows show metrics for t-SNE (*GT* row) *vs* NN projections using different training-set sizes. Bold shows values closest to *GT*. (table from [7]).

a) Loss Functions

Model	Loss (α)	NH	T	C	R	# epochs	Time (s)
GT		0.929	0.990	0.976	0.277		
2K	Huber (1.0)	0.706	0.839	0.956	0.445	34	5.94
	Huber (5.0)	0.687	0.827	0.953	0.447	16	3.99
	Huber (10.0)	0.704	0.839	0.957	0.431	45	7.53
	Huber (20.0)	0.692	0.835	0.956	0.442	32	5.88
	Huber (30.0)	0.695	0.836	0.956	0.433	30	5.98
	logcosh	0.704	0.839	0.957	0.434	33	6.37
	MAE	**0.742**	**0.866**	**0.962**	**0.423**	78	11.05
	MSE	0.704	0.842	0.957	0.442	40	6.86
5K	Huber (1.0)	0.762	0.883	0.964	0.420	50	14.50
	Huber (5.0)	0.745	0.871	0.963	0.426	26	8.34
	Huber (10.0)	0.769	0.886	**0.965**	**0.416**	69	19.79
	Huber (20.0)	0.763	0.884	**0.965**	0.420	62	18.18
	Huber (30.0)	0.768	0.883	**0.965**	0.420	55	16.16
	logcosh	0.768	0.883	**0.965**	0.425	54	16.03
	MAE	**0.781**	**0.893**	**0.965**	0.418	57	16.56
	MSE	0.753	0.874	0.963	0.428	30	9.67
10K	Huber (1.0)	0.831	0.898	0.968	0.338	38	19.56
	Huber (5.0)	0.833	0.902	0.968	0.342	40	20.64
	Huber (10.0)	0.837	0.906	**0.969**	0.344	52	26.98
	Huber (20.0)	0.831	0.900	0.968	0.344	38	19.97
	Huber (30.0)	0.831	0.902	0.968	0.348	36	19.55
	logcosh	0.818	0.893	0.967	0.347	25	14.00
	MAE	**0.848**	**0.912**	0.968	**0.333**	58	29.55
	MSE	0.839	0.906	0.968	0.339	65	32.42
20K	Huber (1.0)	0.856	0.907	0.967	0.353	20	19.57
	Huber (5.0)	0.881	0.918	0.967	0.344	44	41.69
	Huber (10.0)	0.882	0.921	**0.968**	0.344	36	34.48
	Huber (20.0)	0.881	0.920	0.967	0.342	45	43.96
	Huber (30.0)	0.877	0.915	0.967	0.341	29	28.71
	logcosh	0.884	0.919	0.967	**0.335**	52	35.46
	MAE	**0.887**	**0.927**	0.966	0.339	47	44.55
	MSE	0.871	0.914	0.967	0.341	23	21.68

b) **Network Architecture**

Model	NN Arch	NH	T	C	R	# epochs	Time (s)
GT		0.929	0.990	0.976	0.277	0	0
2K	small st	0.680	0.827	0.951	0.437	30	5.11
	small bt	0.670	0.819	0.950	0.453	18	3.85
	small wd	0.672	0.820	0.949	0.463	17	3.82
	medium st	0.683	0.827	0.952	0.441	17	3.83
	medium bt	0.690	0.833	0.955	0.456	25	4.96
	medium wd	0.702	0.838	0.956	0.438	44	7.17
	large st	0.692	0.835	0.956	0.447	19	4.66
	large bt	**0.720**	**0.852**	**0.961**	**0.430**	50	8.95
	large wd	0.713	0.847	0.959	0.434	45	8.30
5K	small st	0.744	0.875	0.962	0.414	66	18.31
	small bt	0.719	0.855	0.958	0.423	17	5.78
	small wd	0.726	0.864	0.959	0.424	40	12.21
	medium st	**0.761**	0.879	0.963	0.418	42	12.67
	medium bt	0.742	0.872	0.962	0.426	33	10.54
	medium wd	0.740	0.873	0.963	0.419	40	12.53
	large st	0.752	0.874	**0.964**	**0.408**	29	10.95
	large bt	**0.761**	**0.880**	**0.964**	0.420	34	12.02
	large wd	0.755	0.878	**0.964**	0.423	38	13.87
10K	small st	0.818	0.893	0.966	0.338	43	21.02
	small bt	0.820	0.893	0.966	0.330	54	27.35
	small wd	0.794	0.879	0.963	0.330	28	15.35
	medium st	0.828	0.900	0.968	0.343	45	22.74
	medium bt	0.820	0.895	0.967	0.343	31	16.68
	medium wd	0.825	0.899	0.967	**0.338**	49	25.74
	large st	0.831	0.902	0.968	**0.338**	32	20.34
	large bt	**0.836**	**0.905**	**0.969**	0.341	36	21.97
	large wd	0.830	0.900	0.968	**0.338**	30	19.31
20K	small st	0.865	0.910	0.965	**0.335**	30	30.81
	small bt	0.838	0.891	0.965	0.353	16	15.74
	small wd	0.865	0.910	0.965	0.345	37	34.66
	medium st	0.882	0.922	**0.967**	0.339	45	41.97
	medium bt	0.882	0.921	**0.967**	0.340	45	41.35
	medium wd	0.874	0.917	**0.967**	0.346	34	32.92
	large st	0.886	0.924	**0.967**	0.340	45	50.74
	large bt	**0.890**	**0.925**	**0.967**	0.342	37	42.48
	large wd	0.878	0.917	**0.967**	0.345	29	33.03

4.5 Network Architecture

Our final evaluation considers using different NN architectures. Figure 9 shows that quality increases with the architecture size. This is not too surprising, since larger architectures allow more freedom to learn the desired projection patterns, and in the same time they are not too large to require more training data. Separately, we see that the *Large - bottleneck* architecture produces visual clusters that are slightly sharper than the ones created by the other eight studied architectures. The quality metrics in Table 6 (b) confirm this: *Large - bottleneck* has a NH about 0.04 higher for all training-set sizes. Separately, we see that, while this architecture is larger than the others, its training effort is quite similar to the others. Hence, we choose this architecture as our best one for NNP.

It is interesting to consider why the bottleneck architecture performs better than the others. At a high level, this architecture is reminiscent of the bottleneck structure used by autoencoder (AE) networks, which, as discussed in Sect. 2, are also used for dimensionality reduction. It is possible that NNP's bottleneck layer acts in a conceptually similar way to the AE one, that is, extracts latent features from the data, thereby helping the final layer(s) to create the 2D projection. However, NNP and AE are fundamentally different: While AE is driven *purely* by latent feature extraction, NNP is driven purely by the aim of mimicking a given 2D projection, constructed by completely different mechanisms (*e.g.*, t-SNE). Studying how bottleneck architectures could further improve NNP is a potential future work direction.

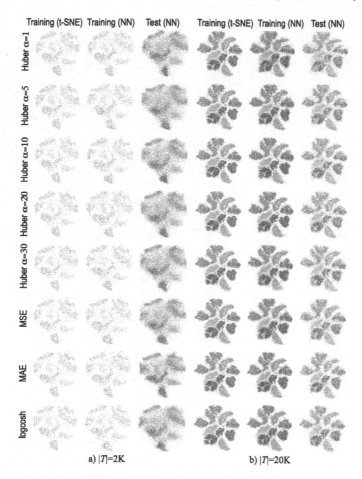

Fig. 8. Loss: Effect of different loss functions. Compare the ground truth (training-set, projected by t-SNE) with the NNP results on the training-set, respectively test-set. (figure from [7]).

5   Insights from Evaluation

We next summarize the insights from the evaluation of NNP along the five dimensions discussed in Sect. 3.

Optimal Settings: We obtain the best quality (that is, closest to the ground-truth t-SNE projection following our four considered quality metrics) with no regularization, ADAM optimizer, *Noise after* data augmentation, MAE loss function, and the *Large - Bottleneck* architecture. The only free parameter in this configuration is σ – the noise standard deviation for the data augmentation step. As Table 5a shows, σ affects the projection quality only very little, so we can in practice fix this parameter. We do this to a default of $\sigma = 0.01$.

As explained at the beginning of Sect. 3, we evaluated the five dimensions of NNP's hyperparameter choices *independently*, to limit the number of tested combinations, and found the above mentioned optimal settings. It is, at this point, important to test that

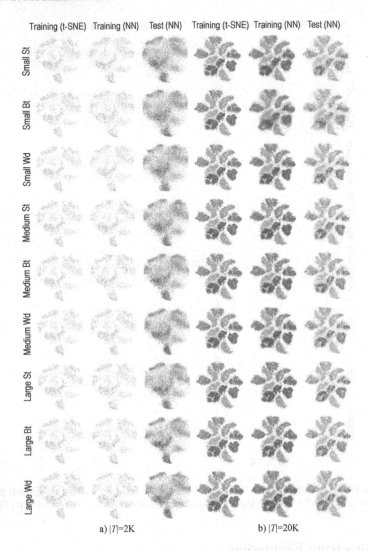

Fig. 9. Arch: Effect of different architectures. Compare the ground truth (training-set, projected by t-SNE) with the NNP results on the training-set, respectively test-set. (figure from [7]).

their *combination* still yields good results. For this, we did a final experiment as follows. We used both NNP's original *Standard* architecture and the *Large - Bottleneck* architecture, both using the optimal settings, to better assess the effect of the architecture change. This is motivated by the fact that the architecture change is the largest deviation from the original NNP parameter values presented in [6]. Table 7 shows that *Large - Bottleneck* performs better than *Standard* on practically all metrics and for all training-set sizes. This improvement can be seen even when compared to the best results of each individual test, especially for smaller training-set sizes. This improvement is also visible in the figure below Table 7 in the form of less fuzziness and better separated

Table 7. Effect of using **optimal settings**. Top: Metrics shown for t-SNE (*GT* row) *vs* NN projections using different training-set sizes. Bold shows values closest to *GT*. Bottom: Optimal settings for *Std* and *Large - Bottleneck* NN architectures. Compare the ground truth (training-set, projected by t-SNE) with the NNP results on the training-set, respectively test-set. (table from [7]).

Model	NN Arch	NH	T	C	R	# epochs	Time (s)
GT		0.929	0.990	0.976	0.277	0	0
2K	std	0.753	0.871	0.963	0.433	73	14.58
	large bt	**0.773**	**0.878**	**0.964**	**0.426**	82	18.44
5K	std	0.794	0.904	0.964	**0.411**	129	60.26
	large bt	**0.813**	**0.906**	**0.966**	**0.411**	70	37.19
10K	std	**0.850**	**0.916**	**0.967**	0.334	113	104.39
	large bt	**0.850**	0.913	0.966	**0.331**	108	112.53
20K	std	0.884	0.923	**0.964**	0.335	121	215.66
	large bt	**0.891**	**0.929**	**0.964**	0.335	101	205.07

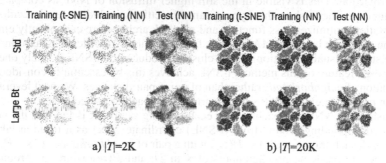

Training (t-SNE) Training (NN) Test (NN)   Training (t-SNE) Training (NN) Test (NN)

Std

Large Bt

a) $|T|$=2K   b) $|T|$=20K

clusters in the images produced with *Large - Bottleneck* (bottom row) as compared to the ones produced by *Standard* (top row).

Quality: We gauged the quality of NNP by measuring four projection quality metrics: neighborhood hit, trustworthiness, continuity, and Shepard diagram correlation. The optimal hyperparameter setting presented in the beginning of Sect. 5 yields quality values that are *closer* to the ground-truth (t-SNE) values than the results presented by the original NNP in [6]. Separately, we see that, as the training-set increases (from 2K to 20K samples), the NNP quality *consistently* approaches the ground-truth quality – see Tables 3, 4, 5 and 6. NNP quality is lower than GT quality, but the difference is under 5% on average for the 20K point training-set. This difference, however small, is still visible in the projections – visual examination of NNP shows still present diffusion as compared to the GT (t-SNE). While this diffusion *decreases* with training-set size, it is still there even for the optimal parameter settings and 20K training samples – compare *e.g.* the inference on unseen data in Fig. 7(b), Test (NN), with Fig. 7(b), Training (t-SNE). To decrease this diffusion further, something more drastic than changing hyperparameters is needed. We present such an alternative next in Sect. 6.

Stability: Our experiments show that NNP is stable with respect to training set sizes and all studied hyperparameter variations. Figures 3, 4, 5, 6, 7, 8 and 9 show that NNP creates practically clusters with the same *shape* and relative *positions* in the test projections (NNP run on unseen data) as the ground-truth t-SNE projections create, for all tested configurations – that is, excluding the diffusion effect already discussed above. The stability of NNP with respect to changes in the training data, hyperparameter settings, and noise added to data is in *stark contrast* with the instability of the t-SNE projection technique with respect to *all* these three factors, and is explained by the deterministic nature of NNP's underlying neural network. This stability is of important practical value in many applications that require predictability and repeatability when creating a projection from data [47].

6 Improving NNP by Neighborhood Analysis

Following our analysis of the NNP evaluation (Sect. 5, we see that NNP scores very well on stability and quality consistency with respect to hyperparameter values. In the same time, the quality is still on average 5% lower than that of the ground-truth (t-SNE) projection. This is visible in the still higher diffusion of NNP as compared to t-SNE. Our experiments show that hyperparameter settings, including regularization, data augmentation, optimizer, loss function and network architecture cannot fully eliminate diffusion, although by using MAE as loss function, quality metrics increased in value.

The strong visual separation of data clusters produced by t-SNE is likely one of the most praised feature of this method. t-SNE achieves this by essentially considering the preservation of *neighborhoods* rather than of point-pair distances. We next leverage this intuition in the context of NNP's deep learning approach to projections.

Consider the NNP approach, where each training sample $\mathbf{x}$ is fed into the network with its corresponding ground-truth (t-SNE) coordinate $P(\mathbf{x})$ as a training label. We replace each such training pair $(\mathbf{x}, P(\mathbf{x}))$ with a pair of *neighborhoods* $(\nu(\mathbf{x}), P(\nu(\mathbf{x}))$. Here, $\nu(\mathbf{x})$ are the K nearest neighbors of $\mathbf{x}$ in D; and $P(\nu(x))$ are the ground-truth projections of these neighbors. We compute neighborhoods ν using both a fast approximate nearest-neighbor search [26] and an exact, slower, brute-force search, to check whether the approximate search has any negative impact on quality. We call our new model K-nearest-neighbors NNP, or KNNP.

During inference, we compute nearest neighbors over points from the training set. There are two reasons for this: (1) The training set is already learned (known) by the network; (2) The training set is already indexed for fast search [26].

We tune the hyperparameters of the KNNP model following the results in Sect. 5. We use MAE as our loss function, which is averaged over the K neighbors as each one is treated as a single sample or label. We chose ADAM as our optimizer. The architecture of the network follows the one in Sect. 3.1 aside from the input and output layers which are scaled so that each input layer containing K nD points outputs a single 2D point.

7 KNNP Evaluation

We next compare the KNNP method introduced in Sect. 6 with the original NNP method using the optimized hyperparameter settings from Sect. 4 and with the ground-truth t-SNE projection. For this, we use the four quality metrics in Sect. 3.2. In addition to the MNIST dataset (Sect. 3.1), we use three more datasets to the comparison, namely:

Fashion MNIST [49]: 70K observations of 10 types of pieces of clothing, rendered as 28×28-pixel grayscale images, flattened to 784-element vectors.

Dogs *vs* **Cats** [4]: 25K images of varying sizes divided into two classes (cats, dogs). We used the Inception V3 [41] Convolutional Neural Network (CNN) pre-trained on the ImageNet data set [3] to extract features of those images, yielding 2048-element vectors for each image.

IMDB Movie Review [22]: 25K movie reviews from which 700 features were extracted using TF-IDF [38], a standard method in text processing.

We next show the performance of KNNP *vs* NNP and t-SNE, for training data (Sect. 7.1) and test data (Sect. 7.2). We also show how quality depends on the training set size (Sect. 7.3) and evaluate KNNP's speed *vs* other techniques (Sect. 7.4). Finally, we show actual projection plots computed by KNNP, NNP, and t-SNE (Sect. 7.5). Due to space restrictions, we present only a subset of our results.

7.1 Quality on Training Data

Figure 10 compares the performance of KNNP, the original method (NNP), and the ground truth (GT, t-SNE) across four quality metrics. Red, yellow, and green indicate that the respective method has a quality lower than, similar to, respectively higher than GT. We see that, for $K = 5$ neighbors, KNNP performs slightly better than NNP, in virtually all cases and for all quality metrics. We also see that quality does not vary much with architecture style or size. Hence, when running on a tight computational budget (where one cannot train or test large architectures), KNNP has a small edge over NNP.

7.2 Quality on Testing Data

So far, we compared both deep learning projections (KNNP and NNP) against each other and against the GT (t-SNE). For testing data, we cannot do the latter comparison, since t-SNE is not a deterministic method, and does not have an out-of-sample capability. Hence, for testing data, we next compare KNNP and NNP – trained on the same data, and tested on the same data – against each other only.

Figure 11 shows that KNNP gets the largest quality boost *vs* NNP for $K = 5$ neighbors again. As in Fig. 10, the style and size of architecture do not influence the results. Overall, KNNP yields better quality than NNP. However, which metric (of the four evaluated) is most improved depends on the dataset. This is expected, since neither NNP nor KNNP do *explicitly* optimize for a given quality metric.

7.3 Quality as Function of Training Set Size

Figure 12 shows how the quality of KNNP compares to that of NNP for different training-set sizes. We see that the added-value of KNNP *vs* NNP is higher for fewer training samples, particularly so for $K = 5$ neighbors. Hence, when the user can only use a small training-set, the relative added-value of KNNP *vs* NNP increases.

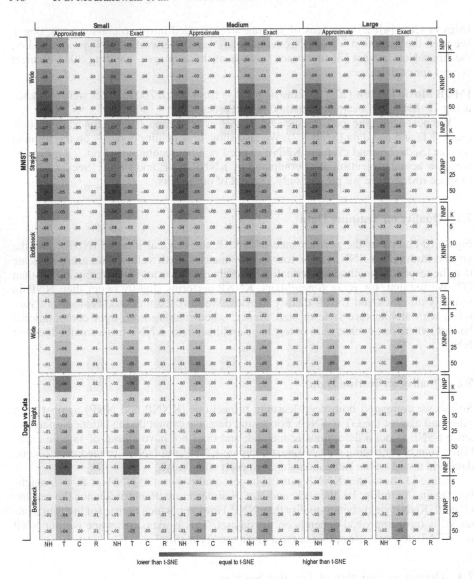

Fig. 10. Comparison of the difference in four quality metrics NH, T, C, and R between t-SNE and NNP, respectively t-SNE and KNNP. The comparison is done on the MNIST and Dogs *vs* Cats datasets, for five K values, using both exact and approximate search, for three architecture styles (wide, straight, bottleneck), each having three sizes (small, medium, large). Red colors indicate cases which are farthest below t-SNE's quality. (Color figure online)

7.4 Computational Scalability

We next compare the speed of KNNP, NNP, and other well-known techniques for up to 1M test samples. All methods were run on a 4-core Intel E3-1240v6 at 3.7 GHz with 64 GB RAM and an NVidia GeForce GTX 1080 Ti GPU with 11 GB VRAM. Figure 13a

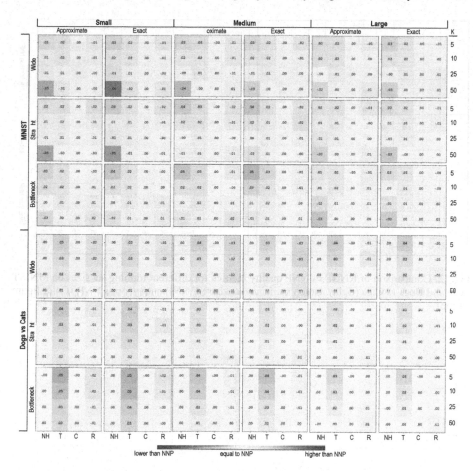

Fig. 11. Comparison of quality metrics of KNNP *vs* NNP for the same datasets, architectures, and parameters as in Fig. 10. Green indicates cases where KNNP performs better than NNP. (Color figure online)

shows the projection time (log scale) as a function of the dataset size for *parametric* techniques. We see that all techniques are linear with dataset size. NNP is the fastest of all compared techniques, with KNNP using approximate nearest-neighbor (ANN) search coming close. Figure 13b adds *non-parametric* techniques to the comparison, specifically MDS [43], t-SNE, LSP [31], and LAMP [14]. We see the same trend as before. Also, we see that KNNP is faster than all non-parametric techniques. Separately, Fig. 14 shows training time for the parametric techniques for up to 1M training samples. Beyond 250K samples, UMAP failed to finish training. NNP and KNNP with ANN search show basically the same speed, being both faster than KNNP with brute-force search.

MNIST (left)

Training Samples	KNN	NN Search	Train NH	T	C	R	Test NH	T	C	R
2k	5	Approx	.04	.01	.00	-.01	.03	.03	.00	-.01
		Exact	.04	.01	.00	-.02	.02	.03	.00	-.02
	10	Approx	.02	.00	.00	-.02	.00	.03	.00	-.01
		Exact	.04	.01	.00	-.01	.01	.02	.00	-.01
	25	Approx	-.01	-.02	.00	.00	-.02	.01	.00	.00
		Exact	-.04	-.03	.00	.01	-.03	.01	.00	.02
	50	Approx	-.06	-.04	.00	-.01	-.05	.00	.00	.00
		Exact	-.05	-.04	.00	.00	-.04	.00	.00	.02
5k	5	Approx	.00	.00	.00	-.01	.00	.01	.00	-.01
		Exact	.02	.01	.00	-.01	.01	.02	.00	-.01
	10	Approx	-.02	-.01	.00	-.01	-.01	.01	.00	.00
		Exact	-.01	-.01	.00	-.01	.00	.01	.00	.00
	25	Approx	-.03	-.02	.00	-.01	-.04	.00	.00	.00
		Exact	-.03	-.02	.00	.00	-.04	.00	.00	.01
	50	Approx	-.05	-.02	.00	.00	-.07	-.01	.00	.02
		Exact	-.04	-.02	.00	-.01	-.05	-.01	.00	.00
10k	5	Approx	.03	.02	.00	.00	.02	.02	.00	-.01
		Exact	.01	.01	.00	.00	.02	.02	.00	.00
	10	Approx	.02	.02	.00	.00	.02	.02	.00	.00
		Exact	.01	.01	.00	.00	.02	.02	.00	.00
	25	Approx	.00	.01	.00	.00	.00	.01	.00	.00
		Exact	-.01	.00	.00	.00	.00	.01	.00	.00
	50	Approx	-.02	.00	.00	.01	-.01	.01	.00	.02
		Exact	-.03	.00	.00	.00	-.02	.01	.00	.00

Dogs vs Cats (right)

Training Samples	KNN	NN Search	Train NH	T	C	R	Test NH	T	C	R
2k	5	Approx	.00	.09	.00	-.03	.01	.06	.00	-.02
		Exact	.00	.09	.00	-.03	.00	.02	.00	-.01
	10	Approx	.00	.08	.00	-.03	.01	.06	.00	-.02
		Exact	.00	.08	.00	-.03	.00	.06	.00	-.02
	25	Approx	.00	.07	.00	-.03	.00	.04	.00	.00
		Exact	.00	.07	.00	-.03	.00	.04	.00	-.01
	50	Approx	.00	.04	.00	-.03	.00	.02	.00	-.01
		Exact	.00	.05	.00	-.03	.00	.03	.00	.00
5k	5	Approx	.00	.02	.00	-.01	.00	.03	.00	-.02
		Exact	.00	.02	.00	-.01	.00	.03	.00	-.02
	10	Approx	.00	.01	.00	-.01	.00	.02	.00	-.01
		Exact	.00	.02	.00	-.01	.00	.03	.00	-.01
	25	Approx	.00	-.01	.00	-.01	.00	.01	.00	-.01
		Exact	.00	-.01	.00	.00	.00	.01	.00	.00
	50	Approx	.00	-.03	.00	.00	.00	-.01	.00	.00
		Exact	.00	-.03	.00	.00	.00	-.01	.00	.00
10k	5	Approx	.00	.02	.00	-.01	.00	.03	.00	-.01
		Exact	.00	.02	.00	.00	.00	.03	.00	.00
	10	Approx	.00	.01	.00	-.01	.00	.03	.00	-.01
		Exact	.00	.01	.00	.00	.00	.03	.00	-.01
	25	Approx	.00	-.01	.00	-.01	.00	.02	.00	-.01
		Exact	.00	.00	.00	-.01	.00	.02	.00	-.01
	50	Approx	.00	-.02	.00	.00	.00	.01	.00	.00
		Exact	.00	-.02	.00	.00	.00	.01	.00	.00

Legend (right margin): higher than NNP / same as NNP / lower than NNP

Fig. 12. Comparison of KNNP *vs* NNP quality metrics for different training set sizes on MNIST (left) and Dogs *vs* Cats (right). Green marks cases where KNNP outperforms NNP. (Color figure online)

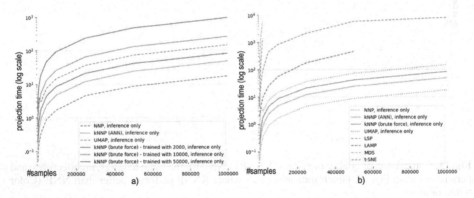

Fig. 13. Projection times for parametric techniques only (a) and for parametric and non-parametric techniques (b).

7.5 Projection Scatterplots

Figure 15 shows samples of scatterplots created with t-SNE, NNP, and KNNP with ANN and brute force search. We see that KNN creates scatterplots which are less fuzzy than NNP, being very close to the ones that t-SNE creates. For test data, note that both NNP and KNNP place point clusters at different locations than t-SNE. This is expected since, as explained, t-SNE is non-parametric. We also see that KNNP delivers visually identical plots for approximate *vs* exact search. Hence, we can use the faster approximate (ANN) search without fear of quality loss.

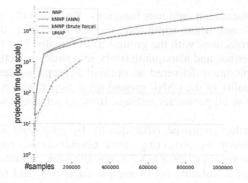

Fig. 14. Comparison of training times between parametric techniques.

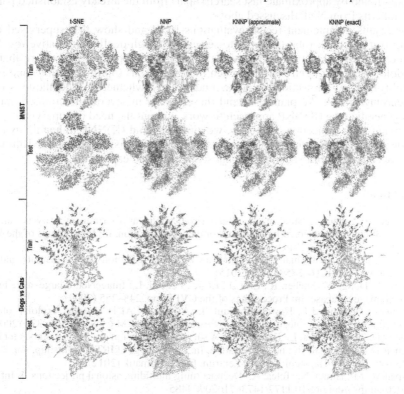

Fig. 15. Projections created by t-SNE, KNN, and KNNP (approximate and exact search variants) on MNIST and Dogs *vs* Cats datasets during training and testing (inference).

8   Discussion and Conclusions

In this paper, we presented an in-depth study aimed at measuring and improving the quality of dimensionality reduction (DR) using deep learning supervised by existing DR techniques. We first explored the design space of a recent deep learning method for DR (NNP, [6]) along six dimensions: training-set size, network architecture, regularization, optimizers, data augmentation, and loss functions. We sampled each dimension using several method types and, where applicable, method parameter values, and compared the resulting NNP projections with the ground-truth (created by t-SNE) quantitatively, using four quality metrics, and also qualitatively by visual inspection of the respective scatterplots. Our exploration delivered an optimal hyperparameter setting that brings NNP closer to the quality of the t-SNE ground truth. Separately, we showed that NNP is stable with respect to all parameter settings, training-set size, and noise added to the input data.

Secondly, we further improved NNP quality by proposing KNNP, a refinement of the method that learns by projecting entire neighborhoods rather than individual samples. While improving quality, KNNP keeps the same attractive features of NNP, namely computational scalability, out-of-sample capability, and robustness to parameter settings. We also inferred optimal parameter settings for KNNP ($K = 5$ nearest neighbors found by approximate fast search) apart from the already established parameters it inherits from NNP discussed above.

Our results complement recent evaluations [6,7] and show that supervised deep learning is a practical, robust, simple-to-set-up, and high-quality alternative to t-SNE for dimensionality reduction in data visualization. More broadly, we believe that our methodology can be directly used to reach the same goals (optimal settings and proof of stability) for any projection technique under study, whether this technique is using deep learning or not. We plan to extend these results in several directions. First, we aim to generalize the (K)NNP approach to work without the need of supervision given by a ground-truth projection. Secondly, we aim to extend (K)NNP to handle dynamic (time-dependent) high-dimensional datasets while keeping its aforementioned attractive points concerning stability, computational scalability, and ease of use.

References

1. Becker, M., Lippel, J., Stuhlsatz, A.: Regularized nonlinear discriminant analysis - an approach to robust dimensionality reduction for data visualization. In: Proceedings of the VISIGRAPP, pp. 116–127 (2017)
2. Cunningham, J., Ghahramani, Z.: Linear dimensionality reduction: survey, insights, and generalizations. JMLR **16**, 2859–2900 (2015)
3. Deng, J., Dong, W., Socher, R., Li, L.J., Li, K., Fei-Fei, L.: ImageNet: a large-scale hierarchical image database. In: Proceedings of the CVPR, pp. 248–255 (2009)
4. Elson, J., Douceur, J.J., Howell, J., Saul, J.: Asirra: a CAPTCHA that exploits interest-aligned manual image categorization. In: Proceedings of ACM CCS, pp. 366–374 (2007)
5. Engel, D., Hüttenberger, L., Hamann, B.: A survey of dimension reduction methods for high-dimensional data analysis and visualization. In: Proceedings of IRTG Workshop, vol. 27, pp. 135–149. Schloss Dagstuhl-Leibniz-Zentrum fuer Informatik (2012)
6. Espadoto, M., Hirata, N., Telea, A.: Deep learning multidimensional projections. J. Inf. Vis. (2020). https://doi.org/10.1177/1473871620909485
7. Espadoto, M., Hirata, N.S.T., Falcão, A.X., Telea, A.C.: Improving neural network-based multidimensional projections. In: Proceedings of the 15th International Joint Conference on Computer Vision, Imaging and Computer Graphics Theory and Applications - Volume 3: IVAPP, pp. 29–41. INSTICC, SciTePress (2020). https://doi.org/10.5220/0008877200290041
8. Espadoto, M., Martins, R.M., Kerren, A., Hirata, N.S., Telea, A.C.: Towards a quantitative survey of dimension reduction techniques. IEEE TVCG (2019). https://doi.org/10.1109/TVCG.2019.2944182
9. Feurer, M., Hutter, F.: Hyperparameter optimization. In: Hutter, F., Kotthoff, L., Vanschoren, J. (eds.) Automated Machine Learning. TSSCML, pp. 3–33. Springer, Cham (2019). https://doi.org/10.1007/978-3-030-05318-5_1

10. Goldberger, J., Roweis, S., Hinton, G.E., Salakhutdinov, R.R.: Neighbourhood components analysis. In: NIPS, vol. 17, pp. 513–520 (2005)
11. Hinton, G.E., Salakhutdinov, R.R.: Reducing the dimensionality of data with neural networks. Science **313**(5786), 504–507 (2006)
12. Hoffman, P., Grinstein, G.: A survey of visualizations for high-dimensional data mining. In: Information Visualization in Data Mining and Knowledge Discovery, pp. 47–82. Morgan Kaufmann (2002)
13. Ilievski, I., Akhtar, T., Feng, J., Shoemaker, C.: Efficient hyperparameter optimization of deep learning algorithms using deterministic RBF surrogates. In: Proceedings of the AAAI (2017)
14. Joia, P., Coimbra, D., Cuminato, J.A., Paulovich, F.V., Nonato, L.G.: Local affine multidimensional projection. IEEE TVCG **17**(12), 2563–2571 (2011)
15. Jolliffe, I.T.: Principal component analysis and factor analysis. In: Jolliffe, I.T. (ed.) Principal Component Analysis, pp. 115–128. Springer, Heidelberg (1986). https://doi.org/10.1007/978-1-4757-1904-8_7
16. Kehrer, J., Hauser, H.: Visualization and visual analysis of multifaceted scientific data: a survey. IEEE TVCG **19**(3), 495–513 (2013)
17. Kingma, D., Ba, J.: Adam: a method for stochastic optimization. arXiv:1412.6980 (2014)
18. Kingma, D.P., Welling, M.: Auto-encoding variational Bayes. CoRR abs/1312.6114 (2013)
19. Krogh, A., Hertz, J.A.: A simple weight decay can improve generalization. In: NIPS, pp. 950–957 (1992)
20. LeCun, Y., Cortes, C., Burges, C.: MNIST handwritten digit database. AT&T Labs, vol. 2 (2010). http://yann.lecun.com/exdb/mnist
21. Liu, S., Maljovec, D., Wang, B., Bremer, P.T., Pascucci, V.: Visualizing high-dimensional data: advances in the past decade. IEEE TVCG **23**(3), 1249–1268 (2015)
22. Maas, A.L., Daly, R.E., Pham, P.T., Huang, D., Ng, A.Y., Potts, C.: Learning word vectors for sentiment analysis. In: Proceedings of the 49th Annual Meeting of the Association for Computational Linguistics: Human Language Technologies, pp. 142–150. Association for Computational Linguistics (2011)
23. van der Maaten, L.: Learning a parametric embedding by preserving local structure. In: Proceedings of the AI-STATS (2009)
24. van der Maaten, L.: Accelerating t-SNE using tree-based algorithms. JMLR **15**, 3221–3245 (2014)
25. van der Maaten, L., Hinton, G.E.: Visualizing data using t-SNE. JMLR **9**, 2579–2605 (2008)
26. Malkov, Y.A., Yashunin, D.A.: Efficient and robust approximate nearest neighbor search using hierarchical navigable small world graphs (2016)
27. Martins, R., Minghim, R., Telea, A.C.: Explaining neighborhood preservation for multidimensional projections. In: Proceedings of the CGVC, pp. 121–128. Eurographics (2015)
28. McInnes, L., Healy, J.: UMAP: uniform manifold approximation and projection for dimension reduction. arXiv:1802.03426 (2018)
29. Nonato, L., Aupetit, M.: Multidimensional projection for visual analytics: linking techniques with distortions, tasks, and layout enrichment. IEEE TVCG (2018)
30. Park, M.Y., Hastie, T.: L1-regularization path algorithm for generalized linear models. J. R. Stat. Soc.: Ser. B **69**(4), 659–677 (2007)
31. Paulovich, F.V., Nonato, L.G., Minghim, R., Levkowitz, H.: Least square projection: a fast high-precision multidimensional projection technique and its application to document mapping. IEEE TVCG **14**(3), 564–575 (2008)
32. Peason, K.: On lines and planes of closest fit to systems of point in space. Phil. Mag. **2**(11), 559–572 (1901)
33. Pezzotti, N., Höllt, T., Lelieveldt, B., Eisemann, E., Vilanova, A.: Hierarchical stochastic neighbor embedding. Comput. Graph. Forum **35**(3), 21–30 (2016)
34. Pezzotti, N., Lelieveldt, B., van der Maaten, L., Höllt, T., Eisemann, E., Vilanova, A.: Approximated and user steerable t-SNE for progressive visual analytics. IEEE TVCG **23**, 1739–1752 (2017)
35. Qian, N.: On the momentum term in gradient descent learning algorithms. Neural Netw. **12**(1), 145–151 (1999)

36. Rauber, P., Falcão, A.X., Telea, A.: Visualizing time-dependent data using dynamic t-SNE. In: Proceedings of the EuroVis: Short Papers, pp. 73–77 (2016)
37. Roweis, S.T., Saul, L.K.: Nonlinear dimensionality reduction by locally linear embedding. Science **290**(5500), 2323–2326 (2000)
38. Salton, G., McGill, M.J.: Introduction to Modern Information Retrieval. McGraw-Hill, New York (1986)
39. Sorzano, C., Vargas, J., Pascual-Montano, A.: A survey of dimensionality reduction techniques. arXiv preprint arXiv:1403.2877 (2014)
40. Srebro, N., Shraibman, A.: Rank, trace-norm and max-norm. In: Auer, P., Meir, R. (eds.) COLT 2005. LNCS (LNAI), vol. 3559, pp. 545–560. Springer, Heidelberg (2005). https://doi.org/10.1007/11503415_37
41. Szegedy, C., Vanhoucke, V., Ioffe, S., Shlens, J., Wojna, Z.: Rethinking the inception architecture for computer vision. In: Proceedings of the CVPR, pp. 2818–2826 (2016)
42. Tenenbaum, J.B., De Silva, V., Langford, J.C.: A global geometric framework for nonlinear dimensionality reduction. Science **290**(5500), 2319–2323 (2000)
43. Torgerson, W.: Theory and Methods of Scaling. Wiley, Hoboken (1958)
44. van der Maaten, L., Postma, E.: Dimensionality reduction: a comparative review. Technical report, Tilburg University, Netherlands (2009). tiCC 2009-005
45. Venna, J., Kaski, S.: Visualizing gene interaction graphs with local multidimensional scaling. In: Proceedings of the ESANN, pp. 557–562 (2006)
46. Vernier, E., Garcia, R., da Silva, I., Comba, J., Telea, A.: Quantitative evaluation of time-dependent multidimensional projection techniques. In: Computer Graphics Forum, vol. 39, no. 20 (2020)
47. Wattenberg, M.: How to use t-SNE effectively (2016). https://distill.pub/2016/misread-tsne
48. Wilson, A., Roelofs, R., Stern, M., Srebro, N., Recht, B.: The marginal value of adaptive gradient methods in machine learning. In: NIPS, pp. 4148–4158. Curran Associates, Inc. (2017)
49. Xiao, H., Rasul, K., Vollgraf, R.: Fashion-MNIST: a novel image dataset for benchmarking machine learning algorithms. arXiv preprint arXiv:1708.07747 (2017)
50. Xie, H., Li, J., Xue, H.: A survey of dimensionality reduction techniques based on random projection. arXiv preprint arXiv:1706.04371 (2017)
51. Yao, Y., Rosasco, L., Caponnetto, A.: On early stopping in gradient descent learning. Constr. Approx. **26**(2), 289–315 (2007)

Scalable Visual Exploration of 3D Shape Databases via Feature Synthesis and Selection

Xingyu Chen[1,2] , Guangping Zeng[1] , Jiří Kosinka[2] ,
and Alexandru Telea[3]( )

[1] University of Science and Technology Beijing, Beijing, China
[2] University of Groningen, Groningen, The Netherlands
[3] Utrecht University, Utrecht, The Netherlands
a.c.telea@uu.nl

Abstract. We present a set of techniques to address the problem of scalable creation of visual overview representations of large 3D shape databases based on dimensionality reduction of feature vectors extracted from shape descriptions. We address the problem of feature extraction by exploring both combinations of hand-engineered geometric features and using the latent feature vectors generated by a deep learning classification method, and discuss the comparative advantages of both approaches. Separately, we address the problem of generating insightful 2D projections of these feature vectors that are able to separate well different groups of similar shapes by two approaches. First, we create quality projections by both automatic search in the space of feature combinations and, alternatively, by leveraging human insight to improve projections by iterative feature selection. Secondly, we use deep learning to automatically construct projections from the extracted features. We show that our three variations of deep learning, which jointly treat feature extraction, selection, and projection, allow efficient creation of high-quality visual overviews of large shape collections, require minimal user intervention, and are easy to implement. We demonstrate our approach on several real-world 3D shape databases.

Keywords: Content-based shape retrieval · Multidimensional projections · Feature selection · Deep learning · Visual analytics

1 Introduction

Recent advances in modeling, authoring, and scanning tools for 3D data have led to wealth of 3D models available to their interested users. As a consequence, this has led to the creation and deployment of specialized *shape databases* [9,26] for managing the available content. A key challenge of these databases is to allow users to easily browse and search them to find models of interest.

As such shape databases grow in size and variability of the stored shapes, so does the users' effort required to explore them [33]. Typical techniques that support exploration include keyword based search, browsing the database along predefined hierarchies or taxonomies, and content-based shape retrieval (CBSR).

© Springer Nature Switzerland AG 2022
K. Bouatouch et al. (Eds.): VISIGRAPP 2020, CCIS 1474, pp. 153–182, 2022.
https://doi.org/10.1007/978-3-030-94893-1_7

While certainly useful, all these techniques have limitations: Keyword search assumes that shapes are labeled with relevant keywords, and that users are familiar with these keywords. Hierarchy browsing is most effective when it matches the user's mental model of how shapes are organized. Finally, CBSR works well when one wants to query for shapes similar to an example that one already avails of.

A particularly important use case which is not well covered by the above mechanisms involves users who want to first get a good overview of what a database contains. This helps understanding whether the database contains shapes of interest to the user – in which case, the user may decide to select a relevant subset thereof to explore in more detail via classical search mechanisms. Keyword, hierarchy, and CBSR techniques are not optimal for the overview task: They either show a small part of the database at a given time and/or ask the user to perform lengthy navigations to create a mental map of the database itself, much like when one navigates a web domain.

To address the overview task, our previous work [4] constructs a visual depiction of a full shape database, with shapes organized by similarity, using a dimensionality-reduction (DR) technique. This method offers *details-on-demand* mechanisms to enable users to control the separation quality of the similar-shape groups in the visual overview, understand what makes selected shapes similar (or different), and find features that have high, respectively little, value for creating the overview. This approach is simple to use, requires no prior knowledge of the organization of a shape database, nor does it require shapes to be labeled. The proposed visualization targets both end users (who aim to explore a shape database) and technical users (who aim to engineer features to create such overviews, or, further, to query or classify shapes in such databases).

However although visually effective, the above approach has a few limitations: (1) The hand-engineered features it uses may not always best capture shape similarity, and also are delicate to compute for poor-quality (non-watertight, self-intersecting, and/or variable-resolution meshes); (2) The feature extraction and DR steps are computationally quite slow, and cannot scale to real-world databases containing tens of thousands of shapes or more; (3) The underlying DR technique used is non-deterministic, meaning that overviews created from the same database (let alone databases where a few shapes change) will be different, which makes it hard for users to maintain their mental map.

In this paper, we improve the approach of [4] with the following contributions to all the above-mentioned limitations:

- We extract features from shapes using deep learning, thereby better capturing the shape's similarities (1);
- We use deep learning for both feature extraction and DR, thereby being able to handle large shape databases efficiently (2);
- We use a deterministic DR projection, thereby ensuring consistent creation of the visual overviews even when the shape database changes (3).

This paper is structured as follows. Section 2 outlines related work in exploring 3D shape databases. Section 3 details our first proposed pipeline, based on hand engineered features which can be interactively selected to construct custom overviews. Section 4 presents results of this pipeline. Section 5 presents our second proposed pipeline, which uses deep learning for jointly addressing the problems of feature extraction and dimensionality reduction, and illustrates the advantages of this approach. Section 6 discusses our overall proposal. Finally, Sect. 7 concludes the paper.

2 Related Work

Several mechanisms for searching and exploring 3D shape databases exist. Most such databases often provide only a subset of them rather than supporting them all. We describe below the most frequently-met such mechanisms.

Keyword search allows users to search for shapes with annotation labels by text words. It is the most popular method for searching for digital data – that is, not only 3D content, but also images and other multimedia types. As such, it is a familiar tool for most users. It is also simple to provide, therefore many 3D databases, such as Aim@Shape [1] and TurboSquid [37] support searching shapes by keywords. On the upload side, shapes can be saved in the database with associated keywords – either picked from a predefined ontology or freely provided by users – to be next searched. Yet, keyword search is not always accurate. One reason is that keyword lists are defined by humans. In many databases, uploaders make the keyword lists of shapes long and/or redundant to increase exposure rate of their favorite content. This mechanism works better for specialized databases, such as [16], which contains only shapes related to space exploration. In this case, keywords are restricted to a predefined dictionary of specialized terms which is easier to use when uploading and/or searching. Another approach to handle keyword search is to allow users to type in search terms freely, and then process these to extract semantic vectors which are used as the actual search keywords. This is the technology underlying several of Google's search mechanisms. While this allows users to search without being aware of the actual ontology used to organize shapes (or other searchable content), topic extraction is typically non-transparent for users and can cause both false positives and false negatives during search, as anyone using text-base search techniques is aware of.

Overall, keyword search is widespread and works well for users familiar with a database's organization (in particular, the ontology defining associated keywords), but also needs large manual effort and is less effective for overall exploration.

Hierarchical exploration systems use a predefined taxonomy of 3D shapes to organize databases. Taxonomies typically come in the form of hierarchies of shape types and included subtypes, which allow the user to directly explore both the shape collection and associated organization of shape types. Such systems often use thumbnail galleries to allow one to explore the database. Users can browse the hierarchy of such databases just like browsing a computer file system. Many databases such as the Princeton Shape Benchmark [29], Aim@Shape [1], and the ITI 3D search engine [9] support hierarchy browsing. However, hierarchical exploration has several limitations. First, it typically only allows one to explore a single *path* in the hierarchy at a given time, and hence is less suited for providing a global overview of a full database. Secondly, unlike keyword indexing – where a shape could be indexed by, and thus searched via, multiple keywords – hierarchical exploration typically only allows using a single such hierarchy at a time. Indeed, it would be confusing and complex to allow one to visually browse multiple interlinked hierarchies. As such, the effectiveness of this method is linked to how well the provided hierarchy matches the user's mental map of the shape universe under exploration.

Content based shape retrieval (CBSR) frees the user from the task of specifying keywords or navigating along the constraints of a predefined (hierarchical) taxonomy. Rather, users specify *content* directly, either in terms of a query shape or a shape proxy, such as a simplified version of the actual shape to search for, for example, a 2D sketch thereof. Next, shapes in the database are ranked based on a computed similarity function to the query, and the best matching ones are returned to the user. Unlike keyword search and hierarchical exploration, CBSR frees users from having to know how shapes and/or their keywords are organized in the database. Many CBSR methods are proposed by previous research [3,33]. At a high level, all these methods extract a high-dimensional feature vector from both the shapes in the database and the query, and then use a suitable distance metric in the descriptor shape to find the most similar shapes to the query. Many methods to extract such shape descriptors exist and each has its own advantages. *Geometric* descriptors aim to capture the actual geometry or form of the shape. They can be divided into global descriptors, such as shape elongation, eccentricity, and compactness; and local descriptors, such as saliency, curvature, shape contexts, and shape thickness. Global descriptors are easy and fast to compute, but cannot separate shapes which differ only at a local levels. As such, they are typically used in a pre-filtering phase to accelerate the search. Local descriptors [24,27,31,34] capture more fine-grained, local, aspects of the shape, and are used to refine the search process. Topological descriptors, such as using 3D curve skeletons [11] or 3D surface skeletons [8] capture the part-whole structure of a shape, and are particularly good for queries which require pose invariance. Finally, view-based descriptors [5,28] describe shapes based on views thereof taken from multiple viewpoints. As such, they do not require shapes to be described by high-quality meshes (which are often required for computing the other aforementioned descriptors). Moreover, view-based descriptors can also integrate additional properties such as color, reflectance, and texture, when these are deemed interesting to drive the search. Descriptors of several of the above types can be combined in the search process [12]. Apart from such hand-engineered descriptors, deep learning solutions have shown to be very effective in all tasks related to processing shape databases by means of extracted feature vectors [22,32]. These include several tasks such as shape classification (which can be used standalone or as a help in designing labels for taxonomy creation) and also shape database querying. One salient method in this area is Point-Net [22] which was used to obtain highly accurate classifications of complex 3D shapes represented as point clouds. We discuss this method, and its adaption to our goals, further in Sect. 5.

As already mentioned, CBSR makes searching easier than keyword search or hierarchical exploration. However, CBSR typically can only be used if one already avails of a query instance to search for. As such, CBSR is not designed to support the more general task of exploration of a shape database. Indeed, while CBSR shows which database shapes are similar to a *given* query, exploration should show how *all* database shapes are similar to *each other*.

Concluding the above, keyword search, hierarchical exploration, and CBSR are complementary tools for exploring a shape database, and optimize each for different tasks and use cases. They can be easily combined in a 3D database exploration system. However, even when combined, none of these methods does offer a compact and detailed overview of an entire database showing how all its shapes relate to each other in terms of similarity. Such an overview functionality is essential in contexts where one does not know what to search for, as it helps 'boostrapping' the search by telling the user upfront what is in the database and how things are organized. Separately, we note that the above mechanisms do not aim to explain *why* a set of shapes – e.g., the ones returned by a query – are found similar. Such explanations are useful for shape-database engineers who want to understand how the search process works to *e.g.* fine tune its underlying feature extraction and/or feature comparison (similarity function) to optimize its accuracy or computational speed. This has been shown by Rauber *et al.* [23] in the context of classification of 2D image databases. Our work in Sect. 4.3 uses similar interactive feature selection mechanisms as Rauber *et al.*. However, as we will discuss there, our goal is entirely different – that is, the creation of customized overviews of 3D shape databases rather than the optimization of an image classifier's accuracy.

3   Feature Selection Method

We detail our first approach to creating visual overviews of shape databases, which uses hand engineered features which can be interactively selected by users to create custom overviews. For simplicity of reference, we call this approach the *feature selection method* next.

Let us introduce a few notations. A shape is described as a mesh $m = (V = \{\mathbf{x}_i\}, F = \{f_j\})$, *i.e.*, a collection of vertices $\mathbf{x}_i \subset \mathbb{R}^3$ and triangular faces f_j. Hence, a shape database is a set of meshes $M = \{m_k\}$. Shapes can be of different kinds, sampling resolutions, and require no extra organization or annotations, *e.g.*, class or hierarchy labels or keywords.

We aim to create a visual *overview* of M in which every shape m_k is depicted by a thumbnail rendering thereof. In this overview, similar shapes should be placed close to each other. Detail views can be invoked interactively via the thumbnails to show specific shape details. This combination of overview and details follows Shneiderman's visual exploration mantra [30] to enable both free and targeted exploration of the shape database along the use-cases outlined in Sect. 2.

We create our visual overview follows. First, we preprocess all meshes in M to normalize their sampling resolution and size (Sect. 3.1). Secondly, we extract local features from each mesh, thereby capturing the geometry of the respective shapes (Sect. 3.2). Next, we extract a fixed-length feature vector from each shape by aggregating the above-mentioned local features (Sect. 3.3). Finally, we use dimensionality-reduction to project the shapes, encoded by their feature vectors, to create a 2D scatterplot (Sect. 3.4). We describe all these steps next.

3.1 Preprocessing

Shapes in a database M can, in general, have any sampling resolution, orientation (pose), and scale. Such variations are typically irrelevant for shape similarity and also induce unwanted variability when computing shape descriptors [3]. To alleviate this, we first remesh all shapes in M to a target edge-length of 1% of m's bounding-box diagonal. Next, we translate and uniformly scale the remeshed shapes to tightly fit in the $[-1, 1]^3$ cube.

3.2 Local Feature Computation

We characterize shapes by several so-called *local features*. These features describe the shape in the neighborhood of every vertex $\mathbf{x}_i \in m$ and are hence good at capturing local geometry characteristics. We compute seven local features, as follows.

Gaussian Curvature (Gc): Gaussian curvature describes the overall deviation from flatness of a shape at a given point. We compute the Gaussian curvature of every vertex $\mathbf{x} \in m$ as

$$Gc(\mathbf{x}) = 2\pi - \sum_{f \in F(\mathbf{x})} \theta_{\mathbf{x},f}, \tag{1}$$

where $F(\mathbf{x})$ is the set of faces in F containing $\mathbf{x}$ and $\theta_{\mathbf{x},f}$ is the angle of the two edges of f that contain $\mathbf{x}$. A perfectly flat triangle-fan around $\mathbf{x}$ will have $Gc(\mathbf{x}) = 0$. Conversely, an infinitely sharp spike on m at $\mathbf{x}$ will have $Gc(\mathbf{x}) = 2\pi$.

Average Geodesic Distance (Agd): Let $d(\mathbf{x}, \mathbf{y})$ be the length of the geodesic curve located on the surface of m between a pair of vertices $\mathbf{x}$ and $\mathbf{y}$ of m. Given this, we estimate the average geodesic distance of a vertex $\mathbf{x}$ as

$$Agd(\mathbf{x}) = \frac{\sum_{\mathbf{y} \in V} d(\mathbf{x}, \mathbf{y})}{|V|}. \tag{2}$$

Intuitively, *Agd* tells how close to a 'tip' or protrusion (or its concave equivalent) a vertex $\mathbf{x}$ is. For example, for a hand model, points on the finger tips will have high *Agd* values, whereas points on the palm will have lower *Agd* values. *Agd* can thus discriminate shapes which have many protrusions (thus, high variations of *Agd* over their points), like the hand model, from overall rounder shapes (thus, very small variations of *Agd* over their points), like a ball.

We approximate the geodesic distance $d(\mathbf{x}, \mathbf{y})$ as the geometric length of the shortest path in the edge connectivity graph of m between $\mathbf{x}$ and $\mathbf{y}$. This length can be easily and efficiently estimated using Dijkstra's shortest-path algorithm with A* heuristics and edge weights equal to edge lengths. More accurate estimations of the geodesic distance between two points on a polygonal mesh exist, including computing the distance transform $DT(\mathbf{x})$ of $\mathbf{x}$ over F and tracing a streamline in $-\nabla DT(\mathbf{x})$ from $\mathbf{x}$ until it reaches $\mathbf{y}$ [20]; minimization of the length of a cut created by a rotating slice plane passing through $\mathbf{x}$ and $\mathbf{y}$ [10]; or hybrid search techniques [38]. While more accurate than the Dijkstra approach we use, these methods are *considerably* more complex to implement, slower to run (except the GPU-based method in [10]), and require careful tuning and/or specialized platforms (GPU support). For a detailed comparison of geodesic estimation methods on polygonal meshes, we refer to [10]. In our case, the added value of accurate geodesic computation is not needed. Indeed, as discussed next in Sect. 3.3, we only use aggregates (histograms) of all Agd values computed over an entire mesh. Hence, less accurate, but fast and easy to compute Dijkstra length estimation is sufficient for our purposes.

Normal Diameter (Nd): This descriptor aims to capture the local thickness of a shape at a given vertex. For this, we first estimate the surface normal at a vertex $\mathbf{x}$ as

$$\mathbf{n}(\mathbf{x}) = \frac{\sum_{f \in F(\mathbf{x})} \mathbf{n}(f)\theta_{\mathbf{x},f}}{2\pi}, \tag{3}$$

where $\mathbf{n}(f)$ is the outward normal of face f. Let $\mathbf{r}$ be a ray starting at $\mathbf{x}$ and advancing in the direction $-\mathbf{n}(\mathbf{x})$. The normal diameter $Nd(\mathbf{x})$ is then the distance along $\mathbf{r}$ from $\mathbf{x}$ to the face $f \in F \backslash F(\mathbf{x})$ that $\mathbf{r}$ intersects. Note that, besides this ray tracing approach, local shape thickness can be computed by other methods, such as medial surfaces [35] or view-based approaches [25]. However, these approaches are not suitable in our context since they require voxel models rather than meshes [35] or require a complex and expensive view-based computation pipeline [25]. As for the Agd estimation, our ray-based Nd estimation is arguably less accurate than alternative approaches but, since ultimately aggregated via histograms, strikes a good balance between quality and computation ease and speed.

Normal Angle (Na) and Point Angle (Pa): These features describe how vertices $\mathbf{x} \in V$ are distributed over the shape's surface. Let $\mathbf{e}_1$ be the major eigenvector of the shape covariance matrix given by all vertices V. As known, $\mathbf{e}_1$ gives the direction in which V spreads the most. For every vertex $\mathbf{x} \in V$, we define the normal angle $Na(\mathbf{x})$ as the dot product between $\mathbf{e}_1$ and the surface normal $\mathbf{n}(\mathbf{x})$; and the point angle $Pa(\mathbf{x})$ as the dot product between $\mathbf{e}_1$ and $\mathbf{c} - \mathbf{x}$, where $\mathbf{c}$ is the barycenter of m, respectively.

Shape Context (Sc): The shape context descriptor [2] is a 2D histogram that describes how distances and orientations of all vertices in V to a fixed, given, vertex $\mathbf{x} \in V$, vary. To compute Sc, we first build a local coordinate system at every vertex $\mathbf{x} \in V$, using the eigenvectors of the shape covariance matrix in the neighborhood of $\mathbf{x}$. This aligns the local coordinate system with the shape, making one of its axes coincide with the normal $\mathbf{n}(\mathbf{x})$ and the two other axes tangent to the surface of m at $\mathbf{x}$. Next, we discretize the orientations around $\mathbf{x}$ into the eight octants of the local coordinate system. We also discretize distances using a set of distance ranges (t_i, t_{i+1}) defined by a distance-set $T = \{0, t_1, t_2, \ldots, t_n, 1\}, n \in \mathbb{N}_+$. In practice, we use $T = [0, 0.1, 0.3, 1]$, given that our shapes are normalized in $[0,1]^3$. Hence, for each vertex $\mathbf{x}$, $Sc(\mathbf{x})$ is a vector with $8 \times 3 = 24$ elements.

Point Feature Histogram (PFH): PFH [24] is a complex descriptor that captures the local shape geometry in the neighborhood of a vertex. Given a pair of vertices $\mathbf{y}$ and $\mathbf{y}'$, where $\mathbf{y}'$ is a neighbor of $\mathbf{y}$, we first define a local coordinate frame $(\mathbf{u}, \mathbf{v}, \mathbf{w})$ as

$$\mathbf{u} = \mathbf{m}, \quad \mathbf{v} = (\mathbf{y}' - \mathbf{y}) \times \mathbf{u}, \quad \mathbf{w} = \mathbf{u} \times \mathbf{v}, \tag{4}$$

where $\mathbf{m}$ is the vertex normal at $\mathbf{y}$. Next, the variation of the shape geometry between $\mathbf{y}$ and $\mathbf{y}'$ is measured by three polar coordinates

$$\alpha = \mathbf{v} \cdot \mathbf{m}', \quad \phi = \mathbf{u} \cdot \frac{\mathbf{y}' - \mathbf{y}}{\|\mathbf{y}' - \mathbf{y}\|}, \quad \theta = \arctan2(\mathbf{w} \cdot \mathbf{m}', \mathbf{u} \cdot \mathbf{m}'), \tag{5}$$

where $\mathbf{m}'$ is the vertex normal at $\mathbf{y}'$. We build three histograms to capture the distributions of α, ϕ, θ for a given vertex $\mathbf{x}$ by considering all pairs $(\mathbf{y}, \mathbf{y}') \in N_{\mathbf{x},k} \times N_{\mathbf{x},k}$ in the k-nearest neighbors $N_{\mathbf{x},k}$ of $\mathbf{x}$. In practice, we set $k = 30$ and use 5 bins for each histogram. This delivers, for each vertex $\mathbf{x}$, a PFH feature vector of $5^3 = 125$ entries.

Fast Point Feature Histogram (FPFH): While PFH models a neighborhood $N_{\mathbf{x},k}$ by all its point-pairs, the Simplified Point Feature Histogram (SPFH) models $N_{\mathbf{x},k}$ by the pairs $(\mathbf{x}, \mathbf{y})|\mathbf{y} \in N_{\mathbf{x},k}$. That is, PFH considers k^2 pairs, whereas SPFH considers only k pairs. To compute FPFH, we proceed analogously to binning the α, ϕ, θ distributions (Eq. 5) in three 11-bin histograms, obtaining a feature vector of $3 \times 11 = 33$ elements. With this vector, we finally compute the FPFH value of a vertex $\mathbf{x}$ following [24] as the distance-weighted average of the SPFH values over $N_{\mathbf{x},k}$ as

$$FPFH(\mathbf{x}) = SPFH(\mathbf{x}) + \frac{1}{k} \sum_{\mathbf{y} \in N_{\mathbf{x},k}} \frac{SPFH(\mathbf{y})}{\|\mathbf{x} - \mathbf{y}\|}. \tag{6}$$

3.3 Feature Vector Computation

The eight features introduced in Sect. 3.2 take different values for every mesh vertex $\mathbf{x} \in V$, as they indeed aim to capture the shape characteristics close to $\mathbf{x}$. To compare entire meshes to each other, we need to abstract from these local descriptors. We do this by computing, from all local descriptors of a shape, a single global descriptor, or feature vector, which (1) has the same length for all shapes, regardless of their vertex count, and (2) is invariant on the ordering (numbering) of vertices in the mesh. For this, we aggregate the values of every local descriptor, at all vertices of a mesh, into a fixed-length (10 bin) histogram. Note that some descriptors are by definition high-dimensional—for instance, the shape context Sc has $d = 24$ dimensions. For such d-dimensional descriptors, we compute a histogram having $10d$ bins, thus using 10 bins per dimension. Table 1 shows the local features, their dimensionality, and the number of bins used to quantize each. Summarizing, we reduce every shape m to a 1870-dimensional feature vector $\mathcal{F}$.

3.4 Dimensionality Reduction

The feature extraction process described so far essentially reduces a shape database M to a set of $|M|$ 1870-dimensional feature vectors. We next achieve our goal of creating a visual overview of the database by projecting these vectors in 2D using the well-known t-SNE dimensionality reduction technique [13].

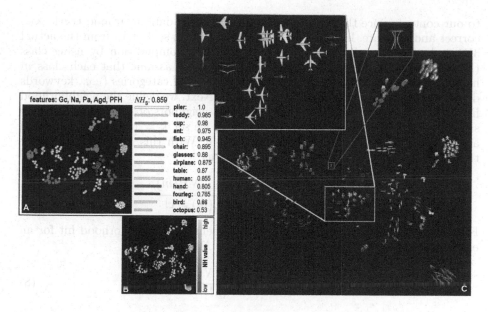

Fig. 1. Three views of the optimal projection scatterplot for the Princeton Shape Database, depicting classes and their NH_c values and the overall plot quality NH_s (A), per-shape NH values (B), and actual shape thumbnails (C). Figure taken from [4].

That is, t-SNE constructs a scatterplot $P(M) = \{P(m_k)\}$, where every shape $m_k \in M$ is mapped to a point $P(m) \in \mathbb{R}^2$, so that the distances between scatterplot points reflect the similarities of their feature vectors. Next, for visual clarity, we render these points $P(m)$ to show thumbnails, or other data attributes, of their respective shapes m.

As outlined in Sect. 1, we aim to use this visual representation to explore the database M. Hence, $P(M)$ should accurately reflect the similarities computed via feature vectors. Many metrics exist that compute the quality of projections – for a detailed overview, we refer to [17]. However, most of these are not applicable

Table 1. Local features, their dimensionalities, and their binning. Table taken from [4].

Name	Dimensionality	Bins
Gaussian curvature (Gc)	1	10
Average geodesic distance (Agd)	1	10
Normal diameter (Nd)	1	10
Normal angle (Na)	1	10
Point angle (Pa)	1	10
Shape context (Sc)	24	240
Point Feature Histogram (PFH)	125	1250
Fast Point Feature Histogram (FPFH)	33	330
Total		1870

to our context, since they assume the feature vector data as ground truth, *i.e.*, correct and accurate. In our case, we actually extract such data from the actual 3D meshes. Hence, we address projection quality computation by using class (label) information from the shapes, as follows. We assume that each class m has a categorical label $c(m) \in C$, where C is a set of categories (*e.g.*, keywords describing the different shapes in a database). Next, we define the neighborhood hit $NH(m)$ as the proportion of the k-nearest neighbors of $P(m)$ that have the same label $c(m)$ as m itself [19]. In practice, we set $k = 10$, following related applications that gauge projection quality [19]. With this, we can next define the neighborhood hit of an entire class $c \in C$ as

$$NH_c(c) = \frac{\sum_{m \in M : c(m)=c} NH(m)}{|m \in M : c(m) = c|}. \tag{7}$$

Finally, at the highest aggregation level, we define the neighborhood hit for an entire scatterplot $P(M)$ for a shape database M as

$$NH_s(M) = \frac{\sum_{m \in M} NH(m)}{|M|}. \tag{8}$$

The intuition behind the above metrics is as follows. $NH(m)$ describes how uniform the projection is, in terms of class labels, around the projection of mesh m. We do not use this metric directly in our evaluation, but only as a means to define the more aggregated NH_c and NH_s metrics. NH_c shows whether a group of points (in the projection) representing same-class meshes is well separated from point groups representing meshes of different classes. This is desirable, since we want next to use the scatterplot to answer questions like "How many shape classes are in a database, and how similar are they to each other?". Finally, NH_s shows how well a whole scatterplot can represent an entire shape database, and is thus a simple metric to use to compare the quality of different scatterplots. Both NH_c and NH_s range between 0 and 1, with higher values indicating better class separation, which is preferred. Note, importantly, that we do not use the class label information for anything related to the *construction* of the visual overview – as mentioned earlier, we can construct such projections using only unlabeled data. We only use class labels as a proxy to gauge the *quality* of the projection for typical tasks involving reasoning about the different types of shapes in a database.

4   Applications

We next illustrate our visual exploration on a subset of the Princeton Shape Benchmark [29] (280 meshes from 14 shape classes, 20 meshes from each class).

4.1   Optimal Scatterplot Creation

As mentioned in Sect. 3.4), creating a high-quality scatterplot is important for all exploration tasks it addresses next. To gauge this, we answer next the following questions:

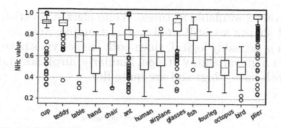

Fig. 2. NH_c statistics for the 14 classes in the shape database for all 255 projection scatterplots. Figure taken from [4].

Q1: How can we create a good projection?
Q2: Which features are best for grouping similar shapes (and separating different shapes) in the projection?
Q3: Which is the minimal set of features needed to generate a good-quality projection?

The easiest way to proceed would be to create a t-SNE projection using the full 1870-dimensional feature vectors we extracted (Sect. 3.3). However, we do not know that all our features effectively capture shape similarity well; some may be redundant, thus only add computational complexity with no extra value; others may be even confusing, that is, decrease the projection quality. Moreover, using high-dimensional feature vectors makes the t-SNE projection task harder [39]. Hence, we first explore the idea of projecting *subsets* of the 1870 feature vector. We have 8 feature types (Table 1), so one idea would be to create all $2^8 - 1 = 255$ possible projections using combinations of these 8 feature types. We compute all these projection and next select the one having the highest NH_s quality. Note that this is related to the well-known scagnostics principle [36,40] of generating a superset of all possible scatterplots from a multivariate dataset and next select for inspection the ones which show interesting details. In our case, however, we do the selection based on the projection quality NH_s.

Figure 1 shows three views of the optimal projection scatterplot. Image A shows the scatterplot with points (shapes $m \in M$) colored by their class value $c(m)$. The title above this image shows the feature subset used for this optimal scatterplot (highest $NH_s = 0.859$ value), namely (Gc, Na, Pa, Agd, PFH). The bar chart in image A shows the NH_c values for all classes, with high values (well separated classes) at the top. We see that *pliers* are perfectly separated from all other classes ($NH_{pliers} = 1$), while *octopus* is least well separated ($NH_{octopus} = 0.53$). Image B shows the optimal scatterplot colored by NH values for all shapes, ranging between red (low NH) to yellow (high NH). Red points show shapes which are not projected well—that is, placed close to different-class shapes. We see that there are such points in a variety of classes. Finally, image C shows the optimal scatterplot with shapes depicted by thumbnails. We see here, better than in image A, that pliers, teddies, cups, ants, and fishes are well projected; but birds are mixed with airplanes, and fourlegs are mixed with humans and hands. The octopus class is visually split in the projection into several parts. While this optimal scatterplot is not perfect, it is the best one we can create by combinations of our 8 available features. While class separation is not perfect, closely-projected shapes are still similar. For example, ants are surrounded by octopuses, which is arguably logical, since both shape types have many thin and spread legs, *i.e.*, a high variability of *Agd*. Similarly, airplanes and birds are close to each other; both have wings and are quite flat.

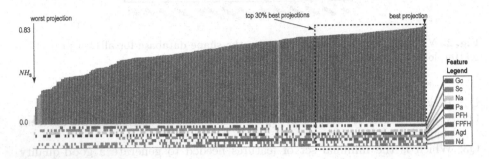

Fig. 3. Bar chart showing the NH_s scores of 255 projections, sorted on increasing value (best projections to the right, worst ones to the left). The color blocks under a bar show which features are used for that projection (the feature color legend on the right). Bars which are not blue only use one feature, whose identity colors the bar. Scanning the color matrix below the bars row-wise tells us which projections use which features. We see that PFH (orange) and FPFH (purple) are good features since their blocks are close to the right. Conversely, Sc (green) is not a very useful feature since its blocks are spread to the left. Figure taken from [4]. (Color figure online)

Besides seeing the optimal projection (Fig. 1), we also want to understand how far are all other 254 projections from this optimum. Figure 2 shows this by whisker plots of the NH_c values for all 255 projections, grouped per class. We see here that some classes (cup, plier) have a low NH_c variance around a very high value. Hence, optimal projection selection is not that relevant for these classes – they would be well separated in virtually any projection computed by any feature combination. However, for other classes (ant, hand), the variance is larger. Hence, computing an optimal projection is important if we want to separate these classes well from the others. We also see that birds and octopuses have quite low NH_c values. This strengthens the insights obtained from Fig. 1, telling that it is hard to separate these classes in any projection.

To address Q2 and Q3, Fig. 3 shows how features affect the quality of all produced projections. Each bar represents one of the 255 projections, with the bar length encoding that projection's NH_s value. Bars are sorted on this value left to right, so best projections are shown right. The matrix plot under the bar chart shows which features (color coded as in the legend at the right) are used in each projection. We also highlight this in the top bar chart: Projections using more than one feature have blue bars; projections that use only one feature have bars colored by that feature. This figure tells us several stories: (1) The difference between the best and worst projections is significant (NH_s 0.831 *vs* 0.38). (2) Some features, *e.g.* PFH (orange) and FPFH (purple), are crucial for high quality, since they appear frequently to the right of the matrix plot; other features actually decrease quality, *e.g.* Sc (green) which appears only in the left half of the matrix plot. (3) The right of the matrix is denser than its left part, *i.e.*, using more features yields better projections, although the relation is not monotonic. (4) The highest-quality projections (roughly, right third of the bar chart) consistently use the same feature mix (Gc, Na, Pa, PFH, FPFH, Agd, Nd). (5) Different features have different patterns in the matrix plot, meaning there are no redundant features in the considered feature set.

Algorithm 1. Computing near-optimal feature sets.

Require: Set of features $\mathcal{F}$; maximal size s, $1 \leq s \leq |\mathcal{F}|$, of feature-set to search for,
Ensure: Near-optimal feature set $\mathcal{C}$,
1: $\mathcal{C} := \varnothing, \mathcal{C}_{new} := \varnothing$;
2: **repeat**
3:     $\mathcal{C} := \mathcal{C}_{new}$
4:     **for each** $\mathcal{F}_{sub} \subseteq \mathcal{F}, |\mathcal{F}_{sub}| \leq s$ **do**
5:         $\mathcal{C}_{temp} := (\mathcal{C} \cup \mathcal{F}_{sub}) - (\mathcal{C} \cap \mathcal{F}_{sub})$
6:         **if** $NH_s(\mathcal{C}_{temp}) > NH_s(\mathcal{C}_{new})$ **then**
7:             $\mathcal{C}_{new} := \mathcal{C}_{temp}$;
8:         **end if**
9:     **end for**
10: **until** $(\mathcal{C}_{new} = \mathcal{C})$;
11: **return** $\mathcal{C}$;

4.2   Fast Computation of Near-optimal Projection Scatterplot

When the feature set $\mathcal{F}$ is large, computing all possible projections to select the optimal one (Sect. 4.1) is expensive. We accelerate this by a greedy algorithm (Algorithm 1). The parameter s gives the maximum size of the feature-set to search for. For every search iteration, $\binom{s}{|\mathcal{F}|}$ feature combinations are examined, retaining the one yielding the highest NH_s value. Better solutions in terms of NH_s are obtained for larger s values, at the expense of higher search times. In the limit, when $s = |\mathcal{F}|$, Algorithm 1 compares all possible $2^{|\mathcal{F}|}$ feature combinations. From our tests, good NH_s values can be obtained by setting $s = 1$. For this setting, the time complexity of our algorithm is $O(|\mathcal{F}|^2)$.

Table 2 shows timing results of our search algorithm, executed 5 times, to account for t-SNE's stochastic nature. For every round, we show the time taken by exhaustive search *vs* our greedy search, and also the number of t-SNE projections being evaluated. We see that our greedy search yields practically the same NH_s as exhaustive search, but is roughly 5 times faster.

4.3   User-Driven Projection Engineering

Section 4.2 showed how to automatically compute a good-quality projection (that separates different-class shapes well) by automatic feature selection. We saw that, even when testing all possible 8-feature combinations, we cannot obtain an ideal projection – some classes are easier to separate than others (see also Fig. 2). This is not surprising, given that our automatic search selects, or discards, all features of the same *type*, *e.g.*, the 24 shape-context Sc features are either all used, or all ignored, when constructing the projection. We next aim to address the creation of a good projection differently. The key observation here is that

Table 2. Performance of the greedy algorithm for near-optimal projection construction. Table taken from [4].

Round	Search method	NH_s	Time (secs)	t-SNE runs
1	Exhaustive	0.831	459.74	255
	Greedy	0.831	103.49	56
2	Exhaustive	0.830	452.12	255
	Greedy	0.830	84.98	48
3	Exhaustive	0.829	453.70	255
	Greedy	0.820	70.24	40
4	Exhaustive	0.832	445.47	255
	Greedy	0.832	111.71	64
5	Exhaustive	0.824	447.66	255
	Greedy	0.824	97.39	55

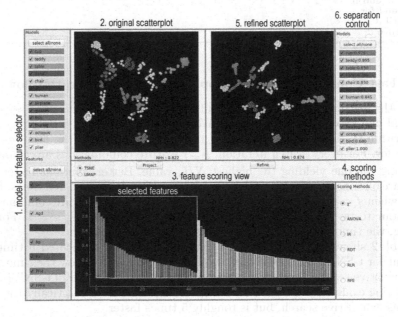

Fig. 4. User-driven projection engineering tool and its six views (Sect. 4.3). Figure taken from [4].

Classes: ● cup ○ teddy ● table ● hand ● ant ○ chair ○ human ● airplane ● glasses ● fish ● fourleg ○ octopus ○ bird ○ pliers

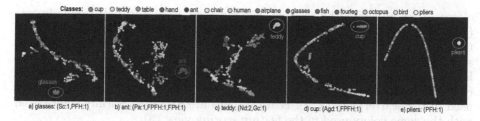

a) glasses: (Sc:1,PFH:1)   b) ant: (Pa:1,FPFH:1,FPH:1)   c) teddy: (Nd:2,Gc:1)   d) cup: (Agd:1,FPFH:1)   e) pliers: (PFH:1)

Fig. 5. Finding the minimal number of feature-bins able to separate five shape classes from the rest of the database. Notation *name:i* indicates that i bins of feature *name* are used. Figure taken from [4].

there are cases when one wants to optimize for separation of certain classes, depending on use-case specifics. Hence, *user input* in deciding which feature combination leads to a good projection is crucial.

We thus rephrase question Q2 as: How can we pick 'good' feature-bins (from the total set of 1870 bins) that separate classes in the way we desire *in a specific context*? To do this, we propose an interactive tool based on feature scoring (Fig. 4) which contains several views (1–6) that allow one to explore how features drive separation of shape classes and also select feature subsets to lead to a customized projection. These views support an overview-and-details-on-demand workflow, as follows:

Model and Feature Selector (1): The user starts by selecting the shape *classes* and feature *types* of interest in this view. If users are interested only in a few classes, these can be selected here; if one wants to separate equally well all

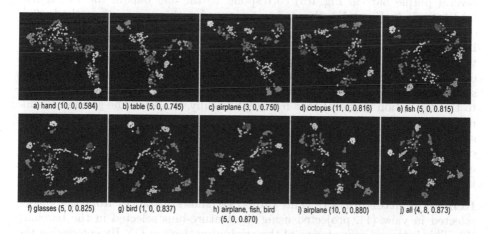

a) hand (10, 0, 0.584)   b) table (5, 0, 0.745)   c) airplane (3, 0, 0.750)   d) octopus (11, 0, 0.816)   e) fish (5, 0, 0.815)

f) glasses (5, 0, 0.825)   g) bird (1, 0, 0.837)   h) airplane, fish, bird (5, 0, 0.870)   i) airplane (10, 0, 0.880)   j) all (4, 8, 0.873)

Fig. 6. Incremental creation of high-quality projection scatterplot that separates all classes well. In each step, a few feature-bins (having high scores, count indicated in green) are selected to separate one or several classes from the rest, and a few feature-bins (having low scores, count indicated in red) are removed from the selection. NH_s at each step are rendered blue. Figure taken from [4]. (Color figure online)

classes, then all should be selected. For instance, from our earlier experiments (Sect. 4.1), we saw that birds are hard to separate from airplanes. The user can then select only these two classes in view (1) to explore how to increase their separation. One can also select feature types (from the 8 computed ones) to use for creating the projection. This helps examining, or debugging, the effect of each feature type. Classes are categorically color-coded, and the same colors are used in the scatterplots (2, 5). Feature types are also categorically color-coded with the same colors used in the feature scoring view (3).

Original Scatterplot (2): This view shows a scatterplot using all shape classes *vs* all feature types chosen in the selector (1). It is used to gauge the effects of the selection performed in view (1) in terms of class separation or overall suitability of the scatterplot to the task at hand. The projection shown here can be next refined to *e.g.* increase separation between desired classes or instances (shapes) using the feature scoring views (3, 4) discussed next. Scatterplots in view (2) are computed either with the t-SNE or UMAP [15] projection methods. t-SNE spreads similar points better over the available 2D space, but is slower. UMAP creates more compact clusters, but is faster than t-SNE. A detailed comparison of these techniques is presented in a recent survey [7].

Feature Scoring Views (3, 4): One can use the feature selector (1) to toggle on or off every feature and gauge its effect on the projection (2). However, this process can be opaque and requires sustained trial and error until a desired effect is obtained. To alleviate this, the barchart (3) shows the *discriminative score* of every element f_i of the 1870-dimensional feature vector, *i.e.*, how much f_i contributes to separating class c_i from a few or from all other classes $c_j \neq c_i$ selected in view (1), depending on the separation control (6, discussed below). Colors show to which feature types the elements f_i belong. For instance, the several purple bars in Fig. 4(3) correspond to the 330 bins of the FPFH feature (purple in Fig. 4(1)). Scores are computed with six scoring methods [23]: chi-squared, one-way ANOVA, Randomized Decision Trees (RDT), Randomized Linear Regression (RLR), iterative relief (IR), and Recursive Feature Elimination (RFE), which are commonly used for assessing classifier performance. The desired scoring method can be chosen by the user in panel (4). This barchart supports two tasks: First, it shows how the many bins of each feature contribute to the separation power of that feature. Secondly, it allows fine-grained examination of the effect of each such bin on class separation: Users can freely *select* specific bins (from the 1870 ones) to create a new projection. Selected bins are outlined with a blue border and listed, in decreasing score order, before the unselected ones, in the barchart. The new projection created by the user-selected bins is shown in view (5).

Refined Scatterplot (5): This projection shows instances from the classes selected in view (1), projected using the feature-bins selected in the barchart (3). This is thus a *refined view* of the original projection (1). By comparing the refined and original scatterplots one can see how the fine-grained selection of each of the 1870 features improves (parts of) the projection. In other words, obtaining an optimal projection is achieved in two steps: First, one selects feature types (in view 1). This is similar to the search process described in Sect. 4.1, except that it is driven by the user rather than automatic. Upon obtaining a suitable projection by this selection, one *refines* it by (de)selecting individual bins for the used feature types. This corresponds to considering or ignoring *ranges* of the values of the features under exploration.

Separation Control (6): As mentioned, feature scoring gauges how well selected features separate a class c_i from other classes $c_j \neq c_i$. The view (6) allows controlling this. The view shows all shape classes c_i in the database. If all classes are selected in (6), scoring measures how well each class c_i is separated from *each* other class $c_j \neq c_i$. If only one class c_i is selected in (6), scoring measures the separation of c_i from *all* other classes $\cup_{j \neq i} c_j$. This allows one to flexibly measure the separation of arbitrary *groups* of classes rather than only the separation of individual classes themselves.

4.4 Use-Cases

We demonstrate our user-driven projection engineering (Sect. 4.3) by answering two practical questions. More use-cases are described in the original paper [4].

A. How to find the smallest number of features that separate a given shape class from all others? (Q3, Sect. 4.1)
Figure 5 answers this question for classes glasses (a), ant (b), teddy (c), cup (d), and pliers (e). We select each of the aforementioned classes in the model selector (Fig. 4(1)) and use the feature scoring view (Fig. 4(3)) and separation control (Fig. 4(6)) to find feature values (bins of the 1870-dimensional feature vector) that best separate this class from the other 13 ones. We gauge separation via the refined projection (Fig. 4(5)) and its NH_s score. For the specific class examples listed here, Fig. 5 shows that these can be separated very well from the rest of the database by *maximally three*, and sometimes just one, feature bin(s) of the 1870 computed ones.

B. How to create a projection that separates well all classes? (Q1, Sect. 4.1)
Figure 6 shows a typical workflow for answering this question. We start with a default projection that uses all 1870 features. Next, we search, using the feature scoring view (Fig. 4(3)), for feature-bins that are most discriminatory, *i.e.*, have highest scores, for each of the classes in our database, starting with the hand class (we can start from any other class). As we study additional classes, we keep adding feature-bins that are discriminatory for them. When we have visited all classes, we have a candidate feature-set. We next clean (reduce) this set by removing from it features that have low scores, *i.e.*, have how discrimination power or even work adversely. The entire process can be done in a few minutes. The images in Fig. 6 show us how the projection quality NH_s almost continuously improves as we add more feature-bins when considering new classes. During this process, we can visit a given class several times (*e.g.* airplane), as features that score high for it can appear several times during the exploration as we study other classes. The final result (Fig. 6j) contains all 14 classes, has a quality score $NH_s = 0.873$, and uses only 51 feature-bins of the total of 1870 ones. It is important to note that our final NH_s value is *higher* than the one found by exhaustive search ($NH_s = 0.831$, Table 1). Indeed, our manual search is more fine-grained, as it allows us to select or discard individual *feature-bins* (of the 1870 ones); in contrast, automatic search only considered entire *features*

(of the 8 in total). Obtaining a similar-quality result to the one manual search led to, by using exhaustive search, would be prohibitively expensive, as it would involve searching all 2^{1870} feature-bin combinations.

5   Feature Learning Method

Our proposal so far showed how we can construct good-quality projections for exploring 3D shape databases, either by exhaustive search or by user-driven projection design. However, our solution has several limitations:

- **input quality:** Computing the features in Sect. 3.2 involves many constraints. For instance, computing Agd requires the meshes to have a single connected component; computing Gc requires meshes to be manifold and water-tight. Overall, poor-quality meshes (containing self-intersections, holes, and/or non-uniform sampling) cause serious problems for feature computation;
- **user effort:** The feature selection process (Sect. 4.1), although able to lead to good-quality projections, is time consuming for the user and involves a non-negligible amount of trial and error;
- **replicability:** The used projections (t-SNE and UMAP) are non-parametric. That is, projecting the same (let alone slightly changed) shape database will lead to different scatterplots, thereby not helping users to maintain their mental map of the database;
- **scalability:** For large databases (more than a few hundred shapes), the feature extraction and projection takes considerable amounts of time; moreover, if we consider using more features, both the greedy search and the user-driven projection engineering become slower and more complex to execute;
- **ease of use:** Implementing and setting up the extraction of hand-engineered features (Sect. 3.2) is a highly involved process. Adding more features to the set of existing ones only complicates this process further.

We address all the above issues jointly by using a deep learning approach for both feature extraction (also next feature learning, following deep learning terminology) and projection. Concretely, we adopt PointNet [22] for feature extraction and NNproj [6] for projection. We next outline this approach and its two main components.

PointNet is a deep-learning model used to classify 3D shapes represented as point clouds with very high accuracy [22] (see Fig. 7, blue part). For our visualization goals, and as a replacement of the hand-engineered features described in Sect. 3.2, we use the latent features extracted by PointNet (see Fig. 7, yellow part), after training it for its original classification task using the labels present in the shape database. NNproj is also using deep learning to create high-quality DR projections of arbitrary high-dimensional data [6]. It is trained by providing it with several 2D scatterplots of corresponding feature vectors, created by any desired DR technique, *e.g.*, t-SNE. NNproj can create projections of nearly the same quality as the ground-truth ones it learns from, is thousands of times faster than t-SNE, has a very simple implementation, and is not sensitive to parameter settings or small changes in the input data. We use NNproj to replace t-SNE and UMAP in our visualization construction.

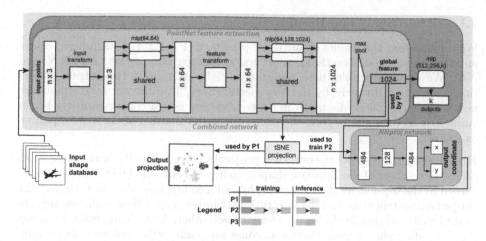

Fig. 7. Architecture of proposed networks P1, P2, P3.

Our framework proposes three pipelines (P1, P2, P3) to create shape-database overviews, as follows. The legend in Fig. 7 shows which models (networks) are part of the training, respectively, inference, of each pipeline. P1 includes PointNet feature-extraction followed by standard t-SNE projection thereof. P1 can already create overviews, but these do not support incremental updating, since t-SNE is non-parametric. Hence, we use P1 mainly for training P2 and P3, as outlined next. P2 runs P1, then trains NNproj to imitate the thus-constructed t-SNE projections, and then uses the trained NNproj instead of t-SNE to create the final projection. P3 drops the classification part of PointNet and trains the joint PointNet-NNProj network. To train P3, we use projections for the training-set shapes created with P1 or P2. In other words: The three pipelines are not different solutions for the same end goal. Rather, P1 is a lower-level pipeline, needed to train PointNet for feature extraction; while P2 and P3 are, functionally identical pipelines that users can choose to use for the final projection construction. The difference between P2 and P3 is simply whether feature extraction and projection are learned separately (P2) or jointly (P3).

For training all models described above, we use the ShapeNet [26] database, which has 14921 shapes from 16 classes. We divide it into a training set (12137 shapes) and a test set (2784 shapes). As this database is quite large, and we have several models to train, we conducted experiments to find how large the training sets of all our deep learning models need to be for sufficient projection accuracy. Specifically, these are:

- NP: the number of shapes for training PointNet,
- NN: the number of feature vectors to train NNProj, and
- NC: the number of shapes for training P3.

We tested 13 values for each of NP, NN and NC, ranging from 320 to 12137. All networks were trained with 250 epochs and early stopping.

5.1 Experiments and Results

We now present the results of our three pipelines (P1, P2, P3) introduced above and how these depend on the sizes of their respective training sets NP, NN, and NC. We evaluate results both qualitatively (by examining the output projections) and quantitatively, by the NH metric (Sect. 3). Since our scatterplots are now larger than those discussed in Sect. 4, we use now a correspondingly larger value $k = 20$ to compute NH. We structure our evaluation along several points, as follows.

Results: Figure 8 shows the overview projection created by P2, with shape icons added to a subset of the database shapes, to limit occlusion. The full projection is shown in the top-left inset as a scatterplot colored by class label. We see that the projection matches our overall expectations: Shapes from different classes are separated well, and similar shapes are close to each other. As with any feature extractor, including the original PointNet, some anomalies exist however. For example, we see a green chair model (A) surrounded by laptop shapes; and a purple lamp model (B) surrounded by table models. This clearly happens since these two shapes are geometrically very similar to the respective classes. Separately, the overview helps us seeing structure *within* classes. For instance, the tables class appears to be visually split into four-legged (FL), round (RO), and bureaus or desks (BU). Note that this information is not available in the original labels of the shape database; it is only the projection that helped us find it.

How much data (NP) is needed to train PointNet? Table 3 shows the test accuracy AC of PointNet for different training-set sizes NP. As NP increases,

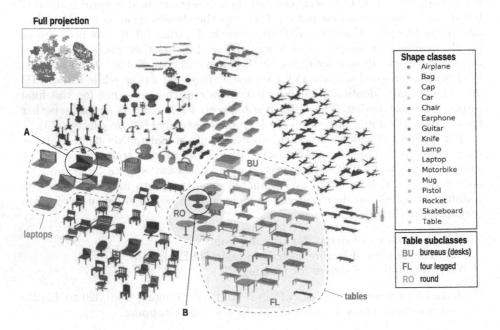

Fig. 8. Overview projection created by pipeline P2.

Table 3. PointNet training accuracy (AC) and NH values for pipeline P1 when training ($P1Train$) and testing ($P1Test$). The two color legends at the bottom show accuracy (green shades) and NH values (yellow-red) respectively in this table and the following ones.

NP	320	1000	2000	3000	4000	5000	6000	7000	8000	9000	10000	11000	12137
AC	0.825	0.935	0.964	0.958	0.962	0.963							
P1Train	0.934	0.970	0.965										
P1Test	0.848	0.915	0.931	0.938	0.942	0.934	0.949	0.932	0.945	0.945	0.94	0.943	0.945

low AC 0.825   0.842   0.859   0.875   0.892   0.909   0.926   0.942   0.959 high AC

low NH 0.703   0.736   0.769   0.801   0.834   0.867   0.9   0.932   0.965 high NH

AC also increases until reaching a local maximum ($AC = 97.1\%$) for $NP = 6000$ shapes. The global maximum $AC = 97.6\%$ is achieved, as expected, when using all $NP = 12137$ shapes in the training set. We also see that for $NP = 2000$ we already get a very good accuracy $AC = 95.4\%$, sufficient for our visualization goals. With the trained PointNet, we next extract features and project them using t-SNE (pipeline P1). Table 3, row $P1Train$ shows the NH projection quality metric for P1 on its training sets of various sizes NP. Next, row $P1Test$ shows the same NH metric, this time for the test set. While NH is slightly higher for the training set (as expected), the NH values for the test set are also quite high, indicating that P1 produces good quality projections.

How much data (NP, NN) is needed to train P2? Training P2 requires training PointNet with NP shapes and next training NNproj with NN feature vectors (Fig. 7). So, P2's quality depends on both NP and NN. Table 4 (a–c) shows this dependency. In detail: Table 4(a) shows the NH value of t-SNE when projecting different sizes NN of feature vector sets extracted by PointNet. We notice that there are some NH fluctuations on the second row where $NN = 320$. However, when NP and NN are both greater than 1000, the t-SNE projections all yield good NH values (above 94%). The highest NH value (99.8%) appears for $NP = NN = 6000$. We also see that the colors in the upper-right triangle half of Table 4(a) are darker than in the lower-left triangle half: NH is slightly higher when $NP \geq NN$. Indeed, when $NP \geq NN$, the input data of t-SNE is a subset of PointNet's training data. In contrast, when $NP < NN$, t-SNE runs with some shapes that are not in PointNet's training set.

After creating the ground-truth scatterplots by t-SNE, we use them to train NNProj. After this, P2 is ready to be used. Table 4(b) shows the NH of P2 trained with different NN and NP values, when projecting NNproj's training-data. The values in Table 4(b) are very close to their counterparts in Table 4(a), being roughly 0.1% to 2% lower. This means that NNproj was trained successfully, so P2 can project well its training data.

Table 4(c) shows NH values when using P2 to project test data (2784 shapes). Although the NH values are slightly lower than those in Tables 4(a) and (b), all of them, except the first one ($NP = 320, NN = 320$) outperform those delivered by our earlier feature engineering. Also, we see that $NN = 2000$ and $NP = 3000$ are already enough to deliver sufficiently high NH values, thus, high-quality projections. The overall highest NH is obtained for $NP = 6000$, same as in Tables 4(a, b). An interesting phenomenon happens when NP is small (320 or 1000). In this case, we train PointNet with few shapes. We can see

Table 4. NH projection quality for (a) ground-truth of pipeline P2; (b) P2 training; (c) P2 testing; and (d) P3, for different values of the respective training-set sizes NP, NN, and NC. Color mapping follows the one in Table 3.

(a) P2 ground-truth

NN\NP	320	1000	2000	3000	4000	5000	6000	7000	8000	9000	10000	11000	12137
320	0.934	0.867	0.889	0.923	0.905	0.824	0.932	0.785	0.866	0.873	0.858	0.843	0.812
1000	0.888							0.942		0.961		0.952	0.957
2000	0.897												
3000	0.9	0.954											
4000	0.901	0.953											
5000	0.905												
6000	0.907		0.963										
7000	0.907	0.954	0.961										
8000	0.911	0.952	0.961										
9000	0.912	0.952											
10000	0.915	0.953											
11000	0.919	0.955	0.966										
12137	0.916	0.955											

(b) P2 training

NN\NP	320	1000	2000	3000	4000	5000	6000	7000	8000	9000	10000	11000	12137
320	0.935	0.865	0.882	0.923	0.906	0.81	0.932	0.782	0.858	0.872	0.858	0.843	0.812
1000	0.886					0.958		0.936				0.939	0.951
2000	0.893					0.964							
3000	0.892	0.951											
4000	0.894	0.947											
5000	0.897	0.95											
6000	0.893	0.948											
7000	0.897	0.945											
8000	0.9	0.943											
9000	0.897	0.943	0.951	0.97	0.968	0.888		0.868					
10000	0.897	0.939	0.952					0.963					
11000	0.896	0.94	0.955										
12137	0.893	0.939	0.952		0.97			0.968					

(c) P2 testing

NN\NP	320	1000	2000	3000	4000	5000	6000	7000	8000	9000	10000	11000	12137
320	0.766	0.829	0.857	0.89	0.858	0.847	0.905	0.812	0.877	0.901	0.88	0.866	0.854
1000	0.809	0.877	0.886	0.9	0.919	0.911	0.927	0.898	0.918	0.914	0.924	0.914	0.924
2000	0.813	0.878	0.888	0.909	0.923	0.911	0.923	0.899	0.916	0.924	0.919	0.916	0.923
3000	0.816	0.887	0.897	0.904	0.909	0.922	0.93	0.908	0.925	0.919	0.928	0.92	0.916
4000	0.823	0.897	0.897	0.905	0.912	0.919	0.925	0.916	0.924	0.917	0.926	0.921	0.912
5000	0.827	0.897	0.897	0.905	0.918	0.919	0.93	0.905	0.92	0.923	0.929	0.925	0.924
6000	0.83	0.897	0.903	0.908	0.91	0.917	0.924	0.907	0.922	0.917	0.916	0.923	0.909
7000	0.83	0.896	0.904	0.908	0.922	0.925	0.929	0.906	0.917	0.923	0.92	0.923	0.917
8000	0.835	0.893	0.908	0.906	0.914	0.916	0.932	0.914	0.917	0.928	0.918	0.917	0.926
9000	0.833	0.895	0.905	0.916	0.913	0.916	0.925	0.911	0.929	0.927	0.917	0.917	0.919
10000	0.836	0.885	0.898	0.901	0.915	0.916	0.925	0.906	0.919	0.925	0.913	0.92	0.918
11000	0.84	0.89	0.911	0.911	0.898	0.905	0.919	0.913	0.919	0.923	0.922	0.931	0.915
12137	0.825	0.895	0.894	0.904	0.92	0.914	0.935	0.912	0.926	0.922	0.915	0.916	0.916

(d) P3

NC	320	1000	2000	3000	4000	5000	6000	7000	8000	9000	10000	11000	12137
P1Train	0.934												
P1Test	0.848	0.915	0.931	0.938	0.942	0.934	0.949	0.932	0.945	0.945	0.94	0.943	0.945
P2Train	0.935												
P2Test	0.766	0.877	0.888	0.904	0.912	0.919	0.924	0.906	0.917	0.929	0.913	0.931	0.916
P3Train	0.927												
P3Test	0.703	0.887	0.879	0.912	0.913	0.921	0.909	0.922	0.918	0.93	0.921	0.92	0.919

| NH | 0.703 | 0.736 | 0.769 | 0.801 | 0.834 | 0.867 | 0.9 | 0.932 | |

that this does not yield high NH values. However, when next using more shapes to train NNproj (NN increases), NH also increases. That is, we can use a small labeled dataset to train PointNet, and then use a larger *unlabeled* dataset to improve P2's performance.

How much data (NC) is enough to train P3? Table 4(d) shows the NH results of P3, trained using P1 for different training set sizes NC, and compares them with those of P1 and P2. To ease comparison, the values in rows $P2Train$ and $P2Test$ in Table 4(d) come from the diagonals of Tables 4(b, c) for $NC = NN = NP$. Rows $P1Train$ and $P1Test$ show the NH values of P1 projecting its training, respectively test, data. Rows $P3Train$ and $P3Test$ show the NH values for P3 on training, respectively test, data. From Table 4(d), we see that P3 performs similarly to P2 on both training and test data, with good NH values when having at least $NC = 3000$ training shapes.

How does PointNet's accuracy influence P1 and P2? As explained, Point-Net was originally designed for *classification*. However, we use here PointNet's feature vectors for *projection*. So, it is interesting to see if the classification-related accuracy (AC) and projection-related quality (NH) are correlated. Separately, we ask ourselves if there is a relationship between the NH of ground truth t-SNE and the NH of projections created with P2 and P3. To explore this, we draw scatterplots of these values and compute their Pearson Correlation Coefficients (PCC). Figure 9(a) shows the AC *vs* P1 NH and AC *vs* P2 NH scatterplots. The plot contains 13 point-groups, one for P1 (blue), and the other 12 for an NN setting of P2 each (green color-coded on NN). These point-groups are visually indicated by different colors and also connected by lines for easing reading. The dotted line shows ideal perfect correlation, for reference. We see that the PCCs of all these lines—each representing an instance of P1 or P2—are close to 1, so P1 and P2's NH metric directly correlates with PointNet's accuracy.

Next, Fig. 9(b) shows scatterplots of P2 and P3's NH *vs* t-SNE's NH values. The plot contains 13 point-groups, one for P3 (red), and the other 12 for a NN setting of P2 each (green color-coded on NN). The PCCs of these lines are also close to 1, so P1 and P2's NH quality is directly correlated with the ground-truth (t-SNE)'s quality. A similar correlation—albeit for a different deep learning model for performing projections—was mentioned in [6], but not formally assessed by means of PCC. The data for P3 (red line) may seem at first sight far worse than that for P2 (green lines). However, this is due to a single point for the lowest t-SNE NH value. For all other values, the red line is practically in the same area as the green lines, telling that P2 and P3 are very similar from the perspective ov t-SNE *vs* deep-learning-network produced NH values.

How can we use classification accuracy to interpret projections? In P1 and P2, we trained PointNet for classification. Besides a feature vector, this delivers a *confidence* value for the classification. We can use this value for our visual exploration goal, as follows. Figure 10 (top) shows the training-set projected by P2, with point luminances encoding their classification confidences (dark = low, bright = high confidence). We immediately see that confidence is high within same-class clusters and low on the cluster borders. Also, as we increase the number of training samples NP for the PointNet classifier, we see how the confidence nears 1.0 for most samples; although, the lowest-confidence ones still remain on

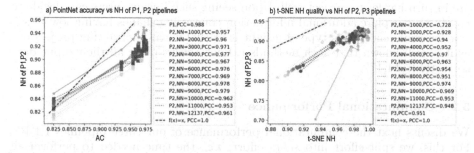

Fig. 9. a) Correlation of PointNet's accuracy AC with the NH quality of pipelines P1 and P2. b) Correlation of t-SNE's NH quality with the NH quality of pipelines P2 and P3.

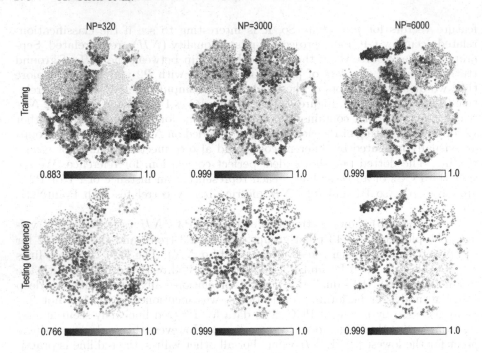

Fig. 10. Classification confidence values (dark = low, bright = high confidence), during training (top) and testing (bottom) for the P2 pipeline trained with three NP values.

cluster borders. Figure 10 (bottom) shows the same visualization for a test-set projected by the trained P2. For a small test set $NP = 300$, we see that confidence is significantly lower than on the training set. For $NP \geq 3000$, test set confidence is basically the same (nearly one) as training set confidence. Importantly, we see that confidence is relatively lowest on the cluster borders also for the test data. We can use these visualizations (on the test data) to assess how confident we are that the shape database projection indeed faithfully reflects the similarities of the underlying shapes. As expected, shapes close to cluster borders are harder to classify, thus, have less discriminant feature vectors and are in turn harder to project well. Upon seeing such images, users can decide to *e.g.* further explore additional information concerning shapes having low classification confidence. This type of insight is crucial when interpreting projections as it is well known that such methods cannot always place all their input data correctly [7,14,17].

5.2   Computational Performance

We discuss next the computational performance of our three pipelines P1-P3. For this, we split effort into *setup* effort, *i.e.*, the time needed to perform all operations required to have the pipeline ready for inference; and *inference* effort, *i.e.*, the time a pipeline needs to create the projection of a shape database.

Table 5. Setup time, pipelines P1–P3 (top). Setup time of P2 as function of NP and NN (bottom).

Setup time P1-P3	NC	320	1000	2000	3000	4000	5000	6000	7000	8000	9000	10000	11000	12137
	P1	347.4	1045.8	2058.2	3001.1									
	P2	361.2	1073.1	2118.0	3068.5									
	P3	301.7	886.8	1743.7										
	P3'	649.1	1932.5											

Setup time details for P2	NN\NP	320	1000	2000	3000	4000	5000	6000	7000	8000	9000	10000	11000	12137
	320	361.2	1062.4	2082.4	3027.8	4079.4	5068.9	6096.0						
	1000	360.9	1073.1	2085.4	3036									
	2000	397.4	1097.5	2118.0	3062	4126.3	5073							
	3000	406.1	1111.8	2155.8	3068.5	4181.0	5141.1	6119.9	7077.2					
	4000	432.0	1126.7	2174.8	3091.7	4128.7	5117.2		7044.2					
	5000	470.6	1178.6	2180.8	3098.0	4234.9	5137.4	6125.6	7625.6					
	6000	444.5	1189.7	2172.0	3161.5	4192.6	5704.1	6157.9	7028.0					
	7000	482.3	1179.0	2198.5	3134.6	4284.4	5235.3	6195.5						
	8000	497.8	1194.9	2214.5	3174.8	4239.6	5241.8	6141.2						
	9000	517.7	1215.4	2205.5	3226.1	4264.8	5150.2	6756.7						
	10000	543.1	1276.0	2262.5										
	11000	451.9	1709.1	2236.9	3238.3	4228.6								
	12137	566.1	1331.4	2324.1	3250.0	4207.2								

| time (secs) | 301 | | | | | | | | | | | | | |

Setup Time: Table 5(top) shows the setup time for all three pipelines. Columns N indicate the training set size for the three pipelines, i.e., NP for PointNet, NN for NNproj, and NC for P3, respectively. Row $P1$ shows the setup time for P1, identical to PointNet's training time. Row $P2$ shows the setup time for P2 when $NN = NP$ (Table 5 (bottom) gives more detailed information, see next). The setup time for P2 includes training PointNet, feature extraction, ground truth generation (t-SNE), and training NNproj. Comparing the first two rows in Table 5 (top), we see that training PointNet is dominating the setup of P2. Row $P3$ shows the setup (training) time of P3 when we already have a ground truth projection. We see that training P3 is slightly faster than training P1 since P3's network is slightly simpler. Finally, row $P3'$ shows the setup time for P3 when we use P1 to create the ground truth needed for training it. Table 5 (bottom) shows the setup time of P2 for all combinations of NP and NN in our experiments. Values in this table increase rapidly with NP and slightly with NN. That is, training NNProj is negligible compared to training PointNet.

Inference Time: Figure 11 shows the projection (inference) time for three pipelines as a function of how many shapes they need to project. We see that all three pipelines have linear time complexity. P1 and P2 are really close and they are about 5 times faster than P1. The high relative cost of P1, and its deviations from a perfect line, are explained by the fact that P1 uses t-SNE, whose cost (a) is high and (b) varies depending on its stochastic initialization, this explaining the wiggles in the blue line in Fig. 11 (for a related analysis, see [7]). In contrast, P2 and P3 show a perfect linear relation with the shape database size, as these are purely deep-learning model executions.

These three pipelines are all much faster than our feature selection method which takes about 127 h to extract the 8 features we listed in Table 1 for 320 shapes.

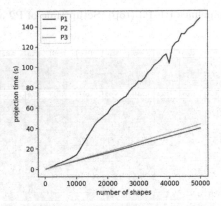

Fig. 11. Projection time comparison for pipelines P1, P2, P3.

6 Discussion

We discuss next several aspects of our proposal, as follows.

Feature Selection *vs* Feature Learning: We have presented two approaches for creating shape-database projections: *selecting* features from a pre-computed set based on feature engineering (Sect. 3) *vs* using an automatically *learned* feature vector using deep learning (Sect. 5). We call these next the feature selection (FS) and the feature learning (FL) approaches. Both approaches share the same aims, listed as Q1-Q3 in Sect. 4.1. From this viewpoint, each approach has its own advantages and limitations. As mentioned at the beginning of Sect. 5, FS has some clear limitations with respect to input shapes, user effort, replicability, scalability, and ease of use – thus, it does not fully address Q1. The FL approach scores very highly on all these points: It accepts any point cloud shape as input, so has no constraints on mesh quality (input shape independence); it works fully automatically, not requiring any specific user input (low user effort); it creates projections deterministically, thus stably upon small-to-medium input changes (replicability); it scales linearly with the input size, being 4 orders of magnitude faster than FS; and it is very easy to deploy, being based on standard deep learning libraries [18]. Also, FL addresses Q2 (Sect. 4.1, *i.e.*, which is the minimal feature-set needed for a good projection, in a different way than FS: Its deep learning approach does not care about feature *selection*, but rather *synthesizes* features which are best for good projection creation. The results in Sect. 5.1 show quite clearly that FL can create high-quality projections this way, without having to worry about feature selection. In contrast, FS *must* consider feature selection, since it is by construction restricted to a fixed number of predefined features.

However, FS has two interrelated advantages upon FL: First, it allows users to see and select how features affect the projection (Q2, Sect. 4.1). The bar chart view (Fig. 3) allows users to find and select features to optimize the projection quality. Secondly, the FL feature scoring view (Fig. 4) interacts with the projection view to enable users to select specific features that explain the similarity of shapes in a group and/or the separation of several groups, and, more importantly, to generate custom projections in which separation of specific classes is favored. Using these views for the same tasks with the FL features is not straightforward, since NNproj is trained on an *entire* feature set and would need re-training if this set changes. Also, the FL features are *abstract*, *i.e.*, they do not have a concrete meaning for users, thereby making reasoning about them extremely challenging. Hence, globally put, FL is better when one wants a full control (and understanding) of how features drive the projection creation; whereas FS is better when one wants a fully automatic, easy to use, and scalable method that creates overall good separation.

Selecting the Best Feature Learning Approach: We have studied and presented two approaches for jointly doing feature learning and projection, called P2 and P3. Which one is best? Our results (Sect. 5.1 shows that P2 and P3 produce very similar results, quality-wise, given the same (amounts of) training data. P3 exhibits slightly higher quality than P2, which makes sense, as P3 trains jointly for both feature extraction and projection. Separately, the results in Sect. 5.1 show very little variation in performance of all pipelines as a function of their training set sizes. In practice, as we discussed there, setting NP, NN, and NC around 3000 shapes gives good results for all pipelines, with only minimal improvements obtained when tweaking these training-set size values.

Learning Projections: Currently, we train NNproj with all the 1024 PointNet features to create projections. We could reduce this dimensionality to a lower value using an intermediate autoencoder stage, or alternatively using a feature-selection optimization technique as presented in Sect. 4.1. This would possibly make NNproj's task of learning projections easier in terms of training set size required to obtain a certain class separation (NH) and/or epochs needed for convergence. Concerning the choice of projection techniques, we used t-SNE to train NNproj. However, learning other projection techniques such as UMAP may lead to ultimately better, easier to interpret, projections.

Scalability: Both the FS and FL approaches depend linearly on the number of *shapes* in the database to be explored and the number of *features* which are extracted from each shape. Yet, as explained already, FS is 4 orders of magnitudes slower. For handling real-world databases of tens of thousands of shapes, like ShapeNet, the FL approach is clearly more suitable. Note that both FS and FL approaches can be applied offline, *i.e.*, when shapes are changed and/or new shapes are added to the database. Shape databases do not change with a high frequency, so offline extraction can be done without highly affecting the performance for the end user. We compute the t-SNE projection using *scikit-learn*, which projects several hundreds of instances in a few seconds; the UMAP implementation, provided by the authors [15], works in real time for this dataset size. If needed, other, faster projections can be used [21]. From a visualization viewpoint, the scatterplot, barchart, and matrix plot metaphors we use scale well to hundreds of thousands of points (shapes) and tens of features.

Evaluation: One important aspect concerning our proposal is evaluating its effectiveness for different types of tasks and users. In detail, we identify *end users*, for whom tasks involve getting an overview of a shape database, finding similar groups of shapes, finding which features make two shape groups similar (or different), and finding outlier shapes; and *technical users*, for whom tasks involve selecting a small set of features able to create effective visualizations for the first user group. We consider such evaluations to be part of future work.

7   Conclusion

We have presented a set of techniques for creating 2D visual representations for exploring 3D shape databases for CBSR applications. Our approach is based, first, on reducing shapes to feature vectors, followed by using dimensionality reduction to create, and explore, 2D scatterplots that encode the shapes' similarities. We support both above steps (feature extraction and projection creation) by two different mechanisms. First, we use a feature engineering approach, followed by a scagnostics approach to create near-optimal projections, and accelerate the automated search for good feature combinations using a greedy technique. To refine the created projections beyond what the automatic search can do, we propose a visual analytics workflow that enables users to customize the obtained projections in terms of separating specific classes or generating high-separation projections for all classes, based on the separation power of all available features. We show that our user-driven approach can create projections with better separation than the automatic one, and also helps finding discriminating features (to be used in a CBSR system) and confusing features (of little value for such systems). Our second approach uses deep learning approach to jointly cover feature extraction and dimensionality reduction. This makes the end-to-end pipeline automatic, easy to use, robust to database changes, and computationally scalable. Both our approaches can be applied to any 3D shape database, allowing CBSR engineers to streamline the process of designing and selecting effective features for shape classification and retrieval. We demonstrate our work on two real-world 3D shape databases.

This work can be extended in several directions, as follows. Performing a user study to measure how well our techniques can support typical exploration tasks related to 3D shape databases, either in opposition to, or as an addition to, existing exploratory tools for such databases, would be of evident added value. Secondly, our techniques are generic, being able to handle any data collections that can be described in terms of high-dimensional feature vectors. Hence, it is interesting to consider its deployment in supporting the exploration of other data types, such as image and/or text collections or scientific data collections.

References

1. Aim@Shape: Aim@shape digital shape workbench 5.0 (2019). http://visionair.ge.imati.cnr.it
2. Belongie, S., Malik, J., Puzicha, J.: Shape context: a new descriptor for shape matching and object recognition. In: Proceedings of the NIPS, pp. 831–837 (2001)
3. Bustos, B., Keim, D., Saupe, D., Schreck, T., Vranic, D.: Feature-based similarity search in 3D object databases. ACM Comput. Surv. **37**(4), 345–387 (2005)
4. Chen, X., Zeng, G., Kosinka, J., Telea, A.: Visual exploration of 3D shape databases via feature selection. In: Proceedings of the 15th International Joint Conference on Computer Vision, Imaging and Computer Graphics Theory and Applications - Volume 3: IVAPP, pp. 42–53. INSTICC, SciTePress (2020). https://doi.org/10.5220/0008950700420053

5. Cyr, C.M., Kimia, B.B.: 3D object recognition using shape similiarity-based aspect graph. In: Proceedings of the IEEE ICCV, pp. 254–261 (2001)
6. Espadoto, M., Hirata, N., Telea, A.: Deep learning multidimensional projections. J. Inf. Vis. (2020). https://doi.org/10.1177/1473871620909485
7. Espadoto, M., Martins, R., Kerren, A., Hirata, N., Telea, A.: Towards a quantitative survey of dimension reduction techniques. IEEE TVCG (2019). https://doi.org/10.1109/TVCG.2019.2944182
8. Feng, C., Jalba, A.C., Telea, A.C.: Improved part-based segmentation of voxel shapes by skeleton cut spaces. Math. Morphol. - Theory Appl. **1**(1) (2016)
9. ITI DB: The informatics & telematics institute database (2019). http://3d-search.iti.gr/3DSearch/index.html
10. Jalba, A., Kustra, J., Telea, A.: Computing surface and curve skeletons from large meshes on the GPU. IEEE TPAMI **35**(6), 783–799 (2013)
11. Jalba, A., Kustra, J., Telea, A.: Surface and curve skeletonization of large 3D models on the GPU. IEEE TPAMI **35**(6), 1495–1508 (2012)
12. Kalogerakis, E., Hertzmann, A., Singh, K.: Learning 3D mesh segmentation and labeling. ACM TOG **29**(4) (2010)
13. van der Maaten, L., Hinton, G.: Visualizing high-dimensional data using t-SNE. J. Mach. Learn. Res. **9**, 2579–2605 (2008)
14. Martins, R., Coimbra, D., Minghim, R., Telea, A.: Visual analysis of dimensionality reduction quality for parameterized projections. Comput. Graph. **41**, 26–42 (2014)
15. McInnes, L., Healy, J., Melville, J.: UMAP: uniform manifold approximation and projection for dimension reduction. arXiv:1802.03426 (2018)
16. NASA: Nasa 3D resources (2019). https://nasa3d.arc.nasa.gov
17. Nonato, L., Aupetit, M.: Multidimensional projection for visual analytics: linking techniques with distortions, tasks, and layout enrichment. IEEE TVCG (2018). https://doi.org/10.1109/TVCG.2018.2846735
18. Paszke, A., et al.: Pytorch: an imperative style, high-performance deep learning library. In: Wallach, H., et al. (eds.) Advances in Neural Information Processing Systems 32, pp. 8024–8035. Curran Associates, Inc. (2019). http://papers.neurips.cc/paper/9015-pytorch-an-imperative-style-high-performance-deep-learning-library.pdf
19. Paulovich, F.V., Nonato, L.G., Minghim, R., Levkowitz, H.: Least square projection: a fast high-precision multidimensional projection technique and its application to document mapping. IEEE TVCG **14**(3), 564–575 (2008)
20. Peyre, G., Cohen, L.: Geodesic computations for fast and accurate surface remeshing and parameterization. In: Bandle, C., et al. (eds.) Elliptic and Parabolic Problems. PNLDE, vol. 63, pp. 151–171. Springer, Heidelberg (2005). https://doi.org/10.1007/3-7643-7384-9_18
21. Pezzotti, N., Lelieveldt, B.P., van der Maaten, L., Höllt, T., Eisemann, E., Vilanova, A.: Approximated and user steerable t-SNE for progressive visual analytics. IEEE TVCG **23**(7), 1739–1752 (2017)
22. Qi, C.R., Su, H., Mo, K., Guibas, L.J.: PointNet: deep learning on point sets for 3D classification and segmentation. In: The IEEE Conference on Computer Vision and Pattern Recognition (CVPR), July 2017
23. Rauber, P.E., da Silva, R.R.O., Feringa, S., Celebi, M.E., Falcão, A.X., Telea, A.C.: Interactive image feature selection aided by dimensionality reduction. In: Proceedings of the EuroVA, pp. 19–23 (2015)
24. Rusu, R.B., Blodow, N., Beetz, M.: Fast point feature histograms (FPFH) for 3D registration. In: Proceedings of the IEEE International Conference on Robotics and Automation, pp. 3212–3217 (2009)
25. Schmidt, W., Sotomayor, J., Telea, A., Silva, C., Comba, J.: A 3D shape descriptor based on depth complexity and thickness histograms. In: Proceedings of the SIBGRAPI (2015)

26. ShapeNet: ShapeNet online repository (2019). https://www.shapenet.org
27. Shapira, L., Shamir, A., Cohen-Or, D.: Consistent mesh partitioning and skeleton-isation using the shape diameter function. Vis. Comput. **24**(4), 249–262 (2008)
28. Shen, Y.T., Chen, D.Y., Tian, X.P., Ouhyoung, M.: 3D model search engine based on lightfield descriptors. In: Eurographics 2003 - Posters. Eurographics Association (2003). https://doi.org/10.2312/egp.20031031
29. Shilane, P., Min, P., Kazhdan, M., Funkhouser, T.: The Princeton shape benchmark. In: Proceedings of the SMI, pp. 167–178 (2004). http://shape.cs.princeton.edu/benchmark
30. Shneiderman, B.: The eyes have it: a task by data type taxonomy for information visualizations. In: Proceedings of the IEEE Symposium on Visual Languages, pp. 336–343 (1996)
31. Shtrom, E., Leifman, G., Tal, A.: Saliency detection in large point sets. In: Proceedings of the IEEE ICCV, pp. 3591–3598 (2013)
32. Su, H., Maji, S., Kalogerakis, E., Learned-Miller, E.: Multi-view convolutional neural networks for 3D shape recognition. In: Proceedings of the IEEE ICCV, pp. 945–953 (2015)
33. Tangelder, J., Veltkamp, R.: A survey of content based 3D shape retrieval methods. Multimed. Tools Appl. **39**(3), 441–471 (2008)
34. Tasse, F., Kosinka, J., Dodgson, N.: Cluster-based point set saliency. In: Proceedings of the IEEE ICCV, pp. 163–171 (2015)
35. Telea, A., Jalba, A.: Voxel-based assessment of printability of 3D shapes. In: Soille, P., Pesaresi, M., Ouzounis, G.K. (eds.) ISMM 2011. LNCS, vol. 6671, pp. 393–404. Springer, Heidelberg (2011). https://doi.org/10.1007/978-3-642-21569-8_34
36. Tukey, J., Tukey, P.: Computer graphics and exploratory data analysis: an introduction. In: The Collected Works of John W. Tukey: Graphics: 1965–1985 (1988)
37. TurboSquid Inc: Turbosquid shape repository (2019). https://www.turbosquid.com
38. Verma, V., Snoeyink, J.: Reducing the memory required to find a geodesic shortest path on a large mesh. In: Proceedings of the ACM GIS, pp. 227–235 (2009)
39. Wattenberg, M.: How to use t-SNE effectively (2016). https://distill.pub/2016/misread-tsne
40. Wilkinson, L., Anand, A., Grossman, R.: High-dimensional visual analytics: interactive exploration guided by pairwise views of point distributions. IEEE TVCG **12**(6), 1363–1372 (2006)

Visual Analysis of Linked Musicological Data with the *musiXplora*

Richard Khulusi[1](✉), Josef Focht[2], and Stefan Jänicke[3]

[1] Image and Signal Processing Group, Leipzig University, Leipzig, Germany
khulusi@informatik.uni-leipzig.de

[2] Musical Instrument Museum, Leipzig University, Leipzig, Germany
josef.focht@uni-leipzig.de

[3] Department of Mathematics and Computer Science, University of Southern Denmark,
Odense, Denmark
stjaenicke@imada.sdu.dk

Abstract. While digitizing data is the first major step for many digital humanities projects, the visual analysis is of high value for humanists, as it brings a
wide range of possibilities to work with data. While rather traditional analysis
often concentrates on standalone or sets of information (close reading), global
inspections of linked data are also requested by today's researchers and made
possible through digital processing. Hence, distance reading approaches are more
and more found in humanities projects. Next to such approaches allowing new
research questions of quantitative analysis, linking previously separate information on a data level is another way of providing humanists with access to further,
previously not reachable, global inspections of faceted datasets.

As a domain with both, faceted data and a rather low level of digitization,
musicology is a prime example of how the digital humanities may improve and
support the daily workflows of humanists. Despite the generally low level of digitization, multiple projects already build a basis to help in digitizing the field. As
an example, the *musiXplora* project collected a vast amount of musicological data
throughout the last 16 years and now offers both, a detailed biography of persons,
places, objects, events, media, institutions and terms and also the linkage between
these kinds of entities to help in giving a user a comprehensible overview in the
traditionally fragmented field of musicology. Supported by a set of visualizations,
the website of the project allows for visual analysis on close reading and distant
reading levels. This does not only help researchers in their daily workflows but
also offers users with a more casual nature an interesting view inside the domain
of musicology.

Keywords: Computer science · Visualization · Visual analysis · Digital
humanities · Musicology

© Springer Nature Switzerland AG 2022
K. Bouatouch et al. (Eds.): VISIGRAPP 2020, CCIS 1474, pp. 183–204, 2022.
https://doi.org/10.1007/978-3-030-94893-1_8

1 Introduction

As a domain for both, theoretical and practical approaches, musicology has a wide set of different subdomains. Each of these domains differs by approaches and goals. Some have specific needs of specialized data, while others need in-depth analysis [16]. Typically known subdomains are namely organology [25] or the instrument restoration. While the former one, as research domain, uses data linked to the *career* of the object to shed light on its history, the latter one, as practical domain, needs information about materials, measurements or temporal aspects to help in preserving or even repairing an instrument. Further, a whole branch of musicology deals with prosopographical research – inspecting or producing biographies of relevant persons, making use of all kinds of metadata and offering different research questions to be answered through data analysis [16].

As a side effect of more than hundred years of work in these different subdomains, today's musicology is not only a field with vast amounts of (analog) data but also quite fragmented. As a result, whole libraries of musicological related books have been published and preserved, normally specifying on a single facet or narrow range of data. Examples may be given with biographical lexicons often containing only persons of a specific profession (like instrument makers) and sometimes even temporal (e.g. medieval) or geographical (working in a specific city) data. While musicologists learned to work with such a degree of fragmentation, caused by a very limited space in manuscripts and books, today's research does begin to shift towards trying to get comprehensible overviews of domains [12,23]. As part of the digital humanities movement, adaptation of digitization, electronically processing, and visual analysis brings distant reading possibilities to the researchers, helping in more global views on the fields and possibilities to work with the growing amount of data [24]. Paired with close reading approaches, more and more projects additionally support their users in daily workflows. Previous work showed this with a focus on musicology and how the digitization of musicological knowledge helped musicologists in generating a comprehensive database of this faceted knowledge [16]. In this publication, we present an extension to the musiXplora tool. Its main goal is to support domain experts in dealing with the fragmented data digitally, aiming to create a more comprehensible musicological knowledge resource. Exemplary, we will present real use cases of our collaborating musicologists, giving insight into the potential a digital knowledge tool with visualizations can offer.

2 Related Work

In the recently published work about the basic concept of the musiXplora [16], the seven facets of musicology are explained in detail. While previous publications of the musiXplora in general focused mainly on the prosopographical aspect [10,11,13–16] only a few works had enough data available for in-detail use cases of other entities [19]. While a continual growth of the database could be seen throughout the years of the project, a shift away from the prioritizing of the persons' data has led to rapid growth in the other facets and especially the linkage between them. In detail, while at the beginning of the year 2020 roundabout 40,000 links existed, half a year later more than 100,000 links between different entities have been added with more to come.

Also non-musiXplora related projects in musicology mirror the fragmentation of the field. In a recent survey on visualization in musicology, more than 120 projects from the last twenty years are included and separated by their focused data type [17]. Again, encountered sub-domains include prosopographical research [4,7,20–22,27], inspection of places linked to musicology [5] or temporal aspects [1]. Facets like the musical objects are inspected in works generating three dimensional data [2,3,8,9,18] and rendered in their volume or surface [26].

2.1 BMLO

A first project trying to link the gaps was started in 2004. The German research project BMLO (short for *Bayrisches Musikerlexikon Online* or *Bavarian Musician Lexicon Online*) [6] began with collecting and digitizing musicological knowledge in a database with lexicon-like web-based access. The project consisted mainly of years of manual work of an editorial team, using different existing online sources or traditional sources like books and magazines and their standardization to fit into a relational database. Due to centuries of research in musicology, an automatic crawling-like process of data is not possible. By far, too few structures can be found within the field. Beginning by missing naming standards and changing definitions – one term having different meanings depending on the temporal context or the same instrument or person having multiple names – [19] and ending by the physical fragmentation of the sources – a division in books specialized on only a small subset of data. Hence, the collection process is especially in need of musicologists and their intellectual knowledge and skills. While in the beginning, the fundamental idea and groundwork for the linkage of the facets were built, the actual process of offering a linked database started with the successor of the BMLO, the *musiXplora*.

2.2 musiXplora

Starting in 2014, ten years after the start of the BMLO, the musiXplora inherited the whole BMLO database and began to open up its boundaries. While previously, a geographical link to Bavaria was required – to reduce the initial gigantic workload of collecting musicological data –, then, musicological relevant data of a worldwide scope was accepted. Also, during the BMLO time, mainly data of persons and places were included. Up to last year, the musiXplora added not only more persons (round about 33,000 today) but also objects (9,000), places (75,000), and institutions (800). While this was already a vast amount of data that took more than 15 years of work, the initial goal of linking facets could still not be met. With the beginning of 2020, the linkage of the facets started. Not only did the editorial team began to include data to all facets but also to include linkage between these types of data entities. For a more detailed description of the musiXplora's data and features, consider Khulusi et al.'s detailed description [16].

3 Data and Linkage

In short, the musiXplora offers seven facets defined by musicologists:

1. MUSICI - Persons
2. CASAE - Institutions
3. LOCI - Places
4. BACCAE - Objects
5. RES - Terms
6. EVENTA - Events
7. CATALOGUS - Media

Table 1 shows a matrix of all facets and which facets are presently reachable through instances of an other facet. Further, the last row shows whether the facet is presently online available for all users[1]. As the structure of the data is inherited from the BMLO project (see Sect. 2.1), existing challenges of the data also apply and have to be considered. Exemplary challenges are the work with uncertainties typical for historical data. While a lot of paper-based information is conserved over the centuries, they are neither always correct nor complete. It is not untypical for persons to be missing crucial information needed for visualizations and analysis like date of birth or even the name, making it hardly possible to put them into relation with others. Also, imprecise information like a birth date of *before 1720* or *around 1300* are frequently encountered. With the dependence on historical sources, such imprecision may never be resolved, as the needed sources may never have existed or could not be preserved through history. As for the temporal data, four kinds of information may be of special relevance: the *first mentioned date*, where a person appeared for the first time in a musicological context, hence, the beginning of the person working in a musicological profession. Second, the *last mentioned date*, analog to the former, but the last time a person is explicitly mentioned. Mostly, this is given with the *date of death*, as most persons have been relevant for musicology until they died. Lastly, a *date of birth* may give insight into the living time of the person. Unlike with the *last mentioned date*, a person was not relevant for musicology beginning with its birth. Thus, the span between *first mentioned date* and *last mentioned date* is the period in which the person was relevant for, or active in, the domain. Nevertheless, the birth date may give useful information and even be used to approximate a *first mentioned date* [13]. In numbers, a *date of birth* is missing for 13,193 out of 33,602[2] persons (39%). Similarly, a *date of death* is not given for 48% of the people. For the *first mentioned date* and *last mentioned date* the missing information is 2.5% and 75%, respectively. This does not include imprecise dates, which do mess with roundabout 14% of the given temporal data. While such uncertainties are known and considered for analysis and visualization inside the musiXplora [16,17], we will not go into more detail in this paper. Instead, we want to shed a bit more light on the available data in general.

---

[1] Due to the work-in-progress-nature of the project and some facets not having a – for the musicologists – satisfying scope, some facets are only available after logging in. Access to these facets may be requested by email.

[2] As of July 2020.

Table 1. Showing connected facets and if they are online available at the moment. A cell is green, when at least one entity links towards the other facet. As example, the person facet is linked to the places facet through naming of places like the place of birth of Beethoven *Bonn*. A click on the *Bonn* label redirects the user to the loci result page of the city. Also, public available facets are marked as green in the last row.

	MUSICI	CASAE	LOCI	BACCAE	RES	EVENTA	CATALOGUS
Type	Persons	Institutions	Places	Objects	Terms	Events	Media
MUSICI	YES	YES	YES	YES	NO	YES	YES
CASAE	YES	NO	YES	YES	NO	YES	NO
LOCI	YES	YES	YES	YES	NO	YES	NO
BACCAE	YES	NO	NO	YES	YES	YES	YES
RES	NO	NO	NO	YES	YES	NO	YES
EVENTA	YES	NO	YES	YES	NO	NO	NO
CATALOGUS	NO	NO	NO	YES	NO	YES	YES
Public Yet	YES	YES	YES	YES	NO	NO	YES

3.1 Musici: Persons

For the set of persons $m_1, m_2, ..., m_n$, with $n = 33,602$, each m_i may have:

1. m_i^{Name} – Naming variants of the person. This may include given and surname, pseudonyms or maiden name
2. m_i^{Date} – Temporal Data as seen above: Life and work years in a range of [0,2020] A.D.
3. $m_i^{Confession}$ – List of Confession(s)
4. m_i^{Gender} – Gender(s)
5. $m_i^{MusicalProfessions}$ – List of musical professions
6. $m_i^{OtherProfessions}$ – List of non-musical professions
7. m_i^{Branch} – List of types of employer. Examples may be concert, court, orchestra or military
8. m_i^r – Lists of relations leading to other facets. A green cell in Table 1 indicates that from this facet an instance of the other facet is included/named.[3]
9. m_i^{IDs} – List of IDs used in related repositories of musicological knowledge [VIAF, GND, Q, ...]
10. m_i^{Links} – List of links using the IDs to reference other resources containing important data of the person (highlighted in red)

---

[3] E.g. a person having worked in the institution *Bayerische Staatsoper* has a list of the to him connected institutions and one entry is the *Bayerische Staatsoper*. A click on the label redirects to the result page of the selected institution in another facet.

3.2   Casae: Institutions

The round about 800 institutions – containing operas, courts and conservatories – may list data of:

1. c_i^m – Members $m_j, ..., m_k$
2. c_i^{Name} – The name
3. c_i^{Date} – Dates of opening and closing
4. m_i^r – Lists of relations leading to other facets. A green cell in Table 1 indicates that from this facet an instance of the other facet is included/named (See Footnote 3).

Compared to the other facets, this list of data is rather short. Nevertheless, the linkage between institutions and persons is of high value and already showed great distant reading analysis in previous works [13].

3.3   Loci: Places

Geographical locations, as places a person was born or worked in or as site an institution was located, are of further interest for musicologists. Mainly, they are linked in other facets' entities and bear useful and interesting results. Already shown examples include the analysis of cities in pre-industrial eras, where specific places were known to be centers of agglomerations. For use cases shedding light on this, consider Khulusi et al.'s paper [16].

Like the prior repositories, given information includes names, links, IDs, and different relations to other facets (See Footnote 3). Further, topological information is given hierarchically, linking e.g. l_i Germany to l_x Europe as a parent and to the German states $l_y, ..., l_z$ as children. More information is given with e.g. longitude and latitude coordinates.

3.4   Baccae: Objects

Objects to generate music are, of course, a further important part of musicological research. This includes mainly instruments and lists different (hierarchical) types, images, sound samples, properties, relations, labels, and internal and external links. Later, in Sect. 5.4, a more detailed description will be found.

3.5   Res: Terms

The repository *Res* includes different terms in musicology. While normally, dictionaries exist that help in understanding terms and offering descriptions, musicology has the unique issue that a lot of terms are uncertain, leading to challenges for automated processing [17, 19]. This ranges from changes in the meaning of a single term in different centuries to almost no endeavors to standardize terminology. For example, the number of strings of a string instrument may have changed due to general changes in music throughout the years. Still, the same term may be used for both types of instruments with a different number of strings. Hence, while using the term, a temporal context may now also change the to be expected features of the object. Especially automated processing encounters difficult challenges due to this lack of standardization. In this facet, terms, and descriptions of musicological labels are collected and described, helping in letting the users get important context information. For this purpose, r, as the set of $r_1, ..., r_n$, contains $r_i^{Variants}$ – labels (in different languages) or synonyms for the term –, describing elements $r_i^{Description}$ for the concept behind the term, and again links and relations to other facets (See Footnote 3) like media containing definitions of it or lists of objects of this term.

3.6 Catalogus: Media and Titles

While *Baccae* contains the physical objects itself, the digital representations of objects (metadata of books, 3D data of objects or contents on CDs) are collected in the *Catalogus* facet. With the piano roll use case (see Sect. 5.4) we will describe in more detail the included data.

3.7 Eventa: Events

The event facet mainly links other facets and can be considered as a kind of interface. Each event has a type, two to be linked IDs and sometimes further to be connected entities like associated persons, temporal context, locations, or more.

4 Connecting Facets

In current work, the musiXplora's editorial team began to include data to link up the different facets and subdomains. While a high coverage of the single facets is mandatory for a useful research tool, the linking of the facets is the heart of the project, offering unique possibilities available through its digital nature.

In general, two kinds of linkage exist. (1) An entity may be linked with a special and internal generated musiXplora ID (mXpID). This ID allows a glance at the type of entity. A mXpID for a person is beginning with the first letter of the surname of the person, followed by a four-digit number combination. The numbers are auto-incremented and do not have a semantic value (as example b1316 for Ludwig van Beethoven). For the other facets, mXpIDs consist of seven-digit combinations, giving more possibilities to help in not running out of combinations. Each of these IDs starts with the facet's index. Hence, all objects have IDs starting with 4, while all terms start with 2. Thus, it is quite easy to know to which facet an ID belongs to. (2) A second way of representation of entities exists for places and terms. While they also have (1) mXpIDs, they also have a *Vorzugsansetzung* (preferred name). This unique name – like *Frankfurt/Oder* or *Frankfurt/Main* – is mainly motivated through the internal editorial work. Some entities have vast lists of data. Additional, the work with digit IDs is prone to errors. Hence, terms and places are internally also linked by their *Vorzugsansetzung*. To illustrate the motivation, Fig. 1 shows the pianist Axel Zwingenberger and his exhaustive list of places he worked at. Maintaining – correcting or adding places to – such a list through digit identifiers has proven to be problematic for the human worker.

Contemporary Title „Boogie-Woogie-Pianist"
Branch Ensemble, Festival, Jazz, Konzert, Medien, Rundfunk/Fernsehen

Place of Activity Hamburg, Aachen, Aalen, Abidjan, Accra, Ägypten, Ahrensburg, Aleppo, Alexandria, Algerien, Algier, Almelo, Alsdorf, Amberg, Amerang, Amman, Ammersbek, Ampflwang, Amsterdam, Amstetten, Ann Arbor, Annecy, Ansbach, Antwerpen, Arnfels, Arnstadt, Arnstein, Arosa, Ascona, Aspach, Asunción, Augsburg, Baabe, Bad Aibling, Bad Aussee, Bad Homburg, Bad Ischl, Bad Kreuznach, Bad Oldesloe, Bad Säckingen, Bad Tölz, Bad Vilbel, Bad Wildungen, Bad Wörishofen, Baden-Baden, Baden/Wien, Bandung, Bangalore, Bangla Desh, Bangui, Bansko, Barcelona, Bargteheide, Basdorf, Basel, Beaune, Beilngries, Beirut, Belfast, Bergen, Berlin, Bern, Beuvron en Auge, Bielefeld, Bietigheim-Bissingen, Binz, Bludenz, Bochum, Bognar Regis, Bolivien, Bonn, Boppard, Bozen, Brounau/Inn, Braunschweig, Brecon, Bregenz, Bremen, Bremerhaven, Bresewitz, Brüssel, Buchholz/Nordheide, Budapest, Bukarest, Burgdorf, Burghausen, Burkina Faso, Burnley, Bussum, Calcutta, Cambrai, Caminha, Campo Bassa, Casablanca, Chaumont, Chemnitz, Chennai, Chibo, Chicago, Chichester, China, Cincinnati, Clermont-Ferrand, Cleveland, Colombo, Crawley, Dacca, Dakar, Damaskus, Deggendorf, Dessau, Detroit, Differdingen, Dijon, Dorsten, Dortmund, Douala, Douglas, Dreieich, Dresden, Düren, Düsseldorf, Eastleigh, Ecaussinnes, Eisenstadt, Elfenbeinküste, Elmau, Emden, Enns, Erding, Erkrath, Erlangen, Ettlingen, Farnham, Feldkirch, Feldkirchen, Ferne, Fischlham, Frankfurt/Main, Freiburg/Breisgau, Freyung, Friedrichshafen, Fürstenfeldbruck, Fürth, Gaggenau, Garching, Gävle, Geisenkirchen, Genf, Gent, Germering, Gernsheim, Ghana, Gleisdorf, Gmunden, Grafenegg, Graz, Great Bardfield, Griechenland, Gütersloh, Hagenbach, Haiger, Hainburg/Donau, Hallein, Hamamatsu, Hamm, Hannover, Harlem/Niederlande, Heide, Heidelberg, Heilbronn, Heiligenhaus, Hell, Herford, Herisau, Hildesheim, Hirschberg, Hongkong, Houston, Husum, Hyannisport, Hyderabad, Icking, Igls, Imola, Imst, Indonesien, Innsbruck, Inverness, Isernhagen, Islamabad, Isle of Man, Itzehoe, Jena, Jordanien, Kairo, Kaltern, Kamen, Kamerun, Karatschi, Kassel, Kathmandu, Kiel, Kirchheim/Teck, Kitakami, Kitzbühel, Klagenfurt, Kochela, Koblenz, Köln, Kopenhagen, Krems, Kreuztal, Kuala Lumpur, Kufstein, Köhlungsborn, Künzelsau, La Chaux de Fonds, La Paz, La Roquebrou, Lagos, Lahore, Lamspringe, Langenzersdorf, Laren, Lauchheim, Leer, Leiden, Leingarten, Leipzig, Leoben, Leutkirch, Leverkusen, Libanon, Liechtenstein, Liège, Lille, Limoges, Lindau, Linz/Donau, Linz/Rhein, Lisboa, Liverpool, Lloret de Vistalegre, Lomé, London, Los Angeles, Louisville, Lübeck, Lüchow, Luckenwalde, Ludwigshafen, Lugano, Luxemburg, Lyme Regis, Lyon, Madrid, Magdeburg, Maison-Laffitte, Malaysia, Malta, Manchester, Manila, Mannheim, Mantua, Maribo, Marlborough, Meinerzhagen, Meiningen, Melk/Donau, Milton Keynes, Minden, Mödling, Moledo, Monaco, Monte Carlo, Mragowo, Mühldorf/Inn, Mülheim/Ruhr, Mumbai, München, Münster, Murau, Mürzzuschlag, Nagoya, Nairne, Nepal, Neuburg/Donau, Neuchatel, Neusäß, New Delhi, New York City, Newcastle upon Tyne, Nigeria, Niigata, Nizza, Nocera, Norderstedt, Norwegen, Nürnberg, Næstved, Oberstaufen, Oberthulba, Oldenburg, Oostende, Osaka, Osnabrück, Österreich, Ottersberg, Ouagadougou, Pakistan, Paraguay, Paris, Passau, Peine, Penang, Perchtoldsdorf, Pilsting, Pinneberg, Porto, Prag, Preston, Pune, Rabat, Radstad, Regensburg, Ried/Innkreis, Ris Orangis, Rochester, Rom, Rosenheim, Roth, Rothenburg/Tauber, Rotterdam, Rügheim, Ruiselede, Rüschlikon, Saarbrücken, Salzburg, Santa Cruz, Sargans, Schaan, Schönberg, Schwarzenbek, Schwaz, Schweinfurt, Seesen, Selb, Sellin, Semarang, Senegal, Seoul, Siegen, Simbach/Inn, Simmerath, Slowakei, Sofia, Southport, Spiekeroog, Sri Lanka, St. Johann/Tirol, St. Pölten, St. Veit/Glan, St. Wolfgang, Starnberg, Stein an der Traun, Steinegg, Steyr, Straßburg, Sturminster Newton, Stuttgart, St⁹ Maria da Feira, Südkorea, Surabaya, Syrien, Tanger, Tegernbach, Terrassa, Thun, Timmendorfer Strand, Töging, Togo, Tokio, Toulouse, Travers City, Trebel, Tripolis, Trittau, Trostberg, Tunis, Uelzen, Ulm, Unna, Utrecht, Valencia, Vannes, Villach, Villingen-Schwenningen, Vilshofen, Vöcklabruck, Vorchdorf, Waidhofen/Thaya, Waidhofen/Ybbs, Watchung, Weiden, Weilheim, Weinstadt, Weiz, Wels, Wendelstein, Wertheim, Westerland, Wetzlar, Wien, Wiener Neustadt, Wilhelmshaven, Wimborne Minster, Winsen/Luhe, Winterthur, Wolfsberg, Worpswede, Wunsiedel, Yaoundé, Yogyakarta, Zeltweg, Zeuthen, Zingst, Zürich, Zwingenberg ◄ less

Venue Aachen, Aalen, Abidjan, Accra, Ägypten, Ahrensburg, Aleppo, Alexandria, Algerien, Algier, Almelo, Alsdorf, Amberg, Amerang, Amman, Ammersbek, Ampflwang, Amsterdam, Amstetten, Ann Arbor, Annecy, Ansbach, Antwerpen, Arnfels, Arnstadt, Arnstein, Arosa, Ascona, Aspach, Asunción, Augsburg, Baabe, Bad Aibling, Bad Aussee, Bad Homburg, Bad Ischl, Bad Kreuznach, Bad Oldesloe, Bad Säckingen, Bad Tölz, Bad Vilbel, Bad Wildungen, Bad Wörishofen, Baden-Baden,

Fig. 1. Snipped showing Axel Zwingenberger's places to illustrate problematic amount of data.

With this in mind, we can have a look at an entity. For the user, the vastness of information is presented with visualizations, helping in grasping and working with even such long lists. The snippet of the musician Axel Zwingenberger's result page (Figs. 1 and 2) shows already multiple links to the other facets, also. Each named place or visualization representative (as long as it is already included in the database) can be clicked, resulting in a call to the places facet and result page of the clicked place. This is indicated by a coloring of the label on mouseover in the facets' color. As the database does not include all places ever mentioned in documentation, not every place is linked. Each place that could not be linked is logged and counted as missing in the database. Hence, the most required missing entities will be the first to be added to the database every month. The linking and logging also apply for all other facets, as seen in Table 1.

With the availability of linked facets, a user may now be able to both, inspecting entities in its facet with all relevant information and also to quickly navigate to other facets. An example and very simple use case may be having a look at a specific person. While we can get a quick overview of the musicological career, like working time, places worked at or professions, the latter one may list *string instrument maker*. Under *Events* we may now see events of this person including the instruments that were built. A click on one of these instruments leads to the objects' facet, showing us detailed information of the instrument, including its type, images, career – especially relevant for organologists –, measurements – for instrument makers and conservators – and more. Hence, the combination of presenting data in its facetted view and still linking them allows the users both, inspecting an entity in its specific subdomain or general context of the musicological knowledge.

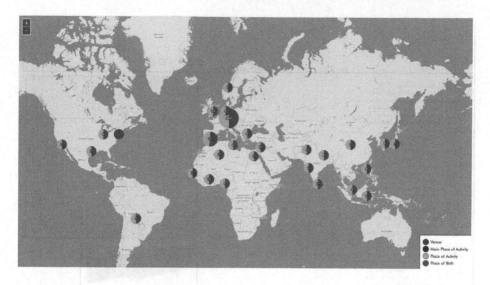

Fig. 2. Map visualization to give an overview of Zwingenberger's places.

4.1 Subsets

Next to this, the collaborating musicologists wanted to also include a more or less traditional view on the data, mirroring the book-like information range. *Teilmengen* (subsets) of specific, relevant entities are predefined. They only include a subset of both, facets and entities within. One subset called *NOVY KINSKY* only contains instrument makers, while another has a geographical range, including only persons who were active in Bavaria (*BMLO*). While the subsets of persons are not disjoint, for objects we see only two disjoint subsets. *MIMUL_OBJECTS* with all objects located in the Musical Instrument Museum of Leipzig University and *FUNDUS* with the objects outside.

While it may seem to be a backward step from a facet containing all available information – especially considering the quantitative global nature of digital humanities inquiries. For musicologists, including of such subsets is highly motivated. Firstly, as discussed in Sect. 6.5 and works by Khulusi et al. [17] and Kusnick et al. [19], musicology's missing standards in terms and definitions lead to quite inhomogeneous data. This inhomogeneity is increased by the described problems of historical data, like uncertainty and imprecision. This makes it hard to reach a global high level of quality within a facet. Using homogeneous subsections allows especially the editorial team to focus on specific aspects of data. Further, like our collaborating musicologists explained, a musicologist, as user, is provided with a tool to work in a similar manner to their traditionally known way. It was stressed as follows: Imagine a user, who already knows analog lexica of information and wants to get information about a lute maker. Such a person wants improvement to the printed media, hence, a digital lexicon showing only the required data and not unnecessarily much information, with also a lower level of quality. Hence, a subset of the whole facet with guaranteed quality is required. This can be offered for typically requested parts of the data through such subsets. Lastly, a practical motivation lies within the funding of humanities projects. Especially state-funding is often limited to the digitization of only a small set of data. The State of Bavaria for

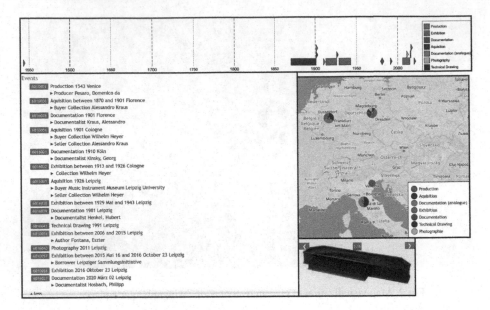

Fig. 3. View on the world oldest clavichord with visualizations of temporal data and geographical data next to a list of all events shaping the career as well as an image browser.

example is funding the digitization of musicians working in its area. Hence, additional manpower may be available, but only to work on the persons within the *BMLO* subset, thus giving the need to separate a facet into different subsets.

5   Use Cases

As a project heavily motivated by musicology and being done in close collaboration, we would like to include further use cases of how our collaborating musicologists work with the tool, to highlight its possibilities and value. Previous works already show a broad spectrum of use cases of mainly the persons' facet (like temporal changes in typical relations found in musicology, time frames of the lute instrument starting to be included in Europe's court, the movement of historism and the changes on instrument production centers due to globalization) [13–16]. Also, different works using the musiXplora database itself, without the tool, highlight the usefulness of the data [10, 11, 19]. With this range of already published use cases, we want to complement the use cases with four newly possible views on the data.

5.1   The Oldest Still Preserved Clavichord

In 1543, Domenicus Pisaurensis, a famous instrument maker, produced the instrument, which is known as the oldest still preserved clavichord. Not only the date of production makes this instrument unique for today's musicology, but also the fact that it consists of mostly original parts, highly uncommon for such old instruments. Figure 3 shows the entry in the musiXplora's web interface, representing the instrument in question.

Next to the images of the instrument, we can also see 15 documented events, shaping the career of the instrument. After its production in the city of Venice, in this time a centre of culture in Europe, it was added to the collection of the wealthy collector Alessandro Kraus in Florence (1870–1900). This collection is known to be one of the earlier collections of music instruments. As part of this collection, it was documented for the first time, by collecting images, measurements and descriptions. In 1901, Wilhelm Heyer bought the whole collection and moved the instruments to Cologne, where it was documented again by Georg Kinsky and then exhibited for 13 years. As of today, the last owner change was the acquisition by the Musikinstrumentenmuseum of Leipzig University in 1926, followed again by being exhibited (1929–1943 and from 2006 onwards). Today, it is placed right at the entrance to the museum's exhibition. Besides this list of events, visualizations can be seen, showing the career of the instrument in time-centered and in geographical context, letting the user get a grasp of not only the geographical space this object travelled but also the time-frame in which it was preserved. Also especially important for musicologists are further references offered by other websites that hold valuable and detailed information about the object, an example being the MIMO (Musical Instrument Museums Online), a shared database of different museums. Here, we can find measurements and descriptive data like the inscription "DOMINICVS PISAVRENSIS MDXXXXIII", which informs on the producer and the year of production. All information on the object's result site is linked to other repositories of the musiXplora. This way, the user can use this page as a starting point for an in-depth research by accessing more detailed information on different points of interest (e.g. related locations, producers or restaurators).

5.2 Jazz Musicians

While scenarios of the musiXplora often refer to historical data [13, 16], some current research projects focus on more contemporary aspects like 20th century jazz, rock and folk musicians in the USA, recently added to the musiXplora. Figure 4 shows a social network graph of banjo players generated by the musiXplora with color-coded relationship types. The musicologist working with these data reported that the different genres of music can be easily seen here. In part A, the folk music genre can be found, centred around Pete Seeger, an essential folk musician. Area B consists of musicians belonging to the country and blue grass genres, who are more connected to each other and less centralized. This is caused by them often playing together in ensembles. The centre of the graph is formed by pop musicians and centered around famous artists like Bob Dylan or Paul Simon. A last genre is given with modern and experimental jazz (D). Here, Tom Waits is a musician to be named and, especially in comparison to the other genres, green edges are dominant, showing that these musicians have mainly worked together as colleagues. A further point of interest is the connection between these sub graphs. The dark nodes are for persons that are inside the result set, hence, banjo players. The lighter ones are their first level neighbours. While for the country musicians, connectivity between dark nodes can be seen (again, caused by their tendency to playing together in performances), the other genres mainly have lighter nodes building connections inside the sub graphs and towards other genres. These are influential people networking as part of their job or by a high level of interest in collaboration. Between folk and country music, a

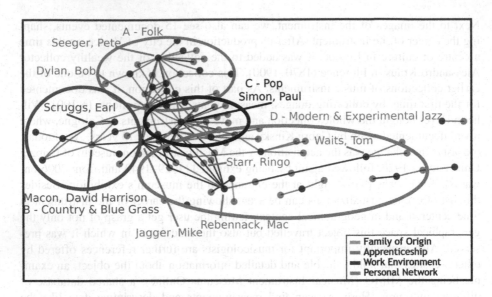

Fig. 4. Network graph of all banjo players currently in the database. Annotated with findings and classifications of the musicologist and prominent musicians.

noticeable connecting node is Bob Dylan, but folk musicians of the 1960s are bridges to country music in general, as we were told by the musicologist. For pop and country music, we can see lesser connecting nodes, indicating less common concepts. The links still found between these subsets relate to studio musicians from the 1950s and 1960s country scene and by people of music research as central nodes. The cluster of modern and experimental jazz shows again a large amount of light nodes connecting to, e.g., the pop genre. Linking musicians in this case are highly connected musicians like Ringo Starr or Mick Jagger, who played in different ensembles. Another view on the data is shown in Fig. 5.

With the help of these pie charts we get an overview of different biographical characteristics. For example, the ratio of female banjo players was very small (A1). As comparison, the ratio for the singer profession was much higher (A2, 32%). The musicologist that we talked to, was quite interested in non-musical professions (C1), showing that the banjo players mainly originated from a lower income class and a creative setting. A background of creative jobs was expected, but the rather high percentage of soldiers in this group surprised him. While this does not mean that these genres are promoted inside these classes, it does highlight the influence of the genre in communities belonging to three specific classes: military, church and agriculture. In the following, he compared them to blues musicians. Here, the non-musical professions indicate a rather low income group (C2). Blues musicians typically had agricultural professions and, especially, a high amount of pastors is shown. This highlights the important role of the church for the rural African American communities in southern states of the United States, typically found for this genre in this time era, and also more rural than creative background in general. Further, the denominations of banjo players were mixed, having a Jewish and Baptist majority (B1), and blues musicians typically had a baptist belief (B2). For a more general

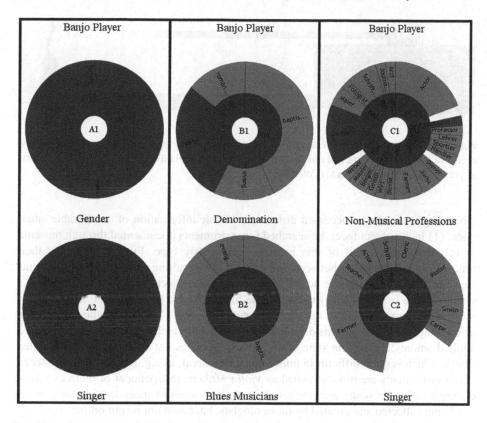

Fig. 5. Pie chart match up of banjo players, singer and blues musicians with their gender, denomination and non-musical profession distribution.

profession like singer, a majority of Roman Catholic musicians can be found, highlighting the specifics of the denominational compositions of sub genres of jazz. Some of these different characteristics are even mirrored in the lyrics of the songs showing their importance for the jazz genres.

5.3 Organological Inspection of a Viola d'amore

Organologists try to shed light on the career of instruments. Figure 6 (B) shows a Viola d'amore, which does not have a typical signature of its builder and is also delivered anonymously. Hence, it is neither known when, nor where, nor who manufactured this instrument. Still, musicologists are interested in knowing the origin of the instrument and its production data. Of course, the musiXplora will not be able to give a guaranteed answer (it cannot recreate lost knowledge), but it may give strong hints and indications on the origin, helping in both, narrowing down the possible answers and directing towards secondary sources where useful information may be hidden/found.

Previous dendochronological inspections of the instrument already pointed on a creation around 1721 in the northern area of the Alps. With this information, a col-

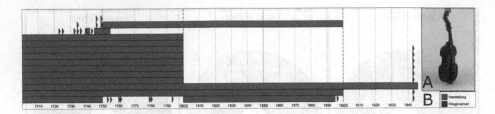

Fig. 6. (A) Timeline showing events of all Viola d'amores. Blue are events of production, yellow events of instruments being lost due to war. (B) Image of a Viola d'amore from the 18th century, as presented in the musiXplora. (Color figure online)

laborating musicologist accessed different available information of comparable situations. (1) In the object facet, he searched for instruments documented through museum or research context and of this baroque and courtly type. Filtered again by their time of production being between 1701 and 1741, resulting in about 20 instruments (see Fig. 6 (A)). Next to the access to each of these objects and their information, a similar search is started for persons. (2) He filtered by the profession of *String Instrument Maker* who worked in the time between 1701 and 1741. While the information of building string instruments does not necessarily only include persons that produced Viola d'amores, the present state of the musiXplora does not allow for a more detailed filter – which is quite difficult in musicology in general, as e.g. persons who produced string instruments are mostly named as *Violin Makers*, independent of them ever producing a violin. Presently a whole set of portfolios – areas of specialization for persons – is being collected and created by musicologists, but could not be put online, yet. Nevertheless, we already have access to the almost 20 instruments that are produced in the relevant period. Through the linkage of the events of the objects, we can directly access the specific instrument makers that could not be reached through the single facet. Hence, through the linkage of the facets, even not yet available, specialized data and functions can be used, which makes us hope that the tool may be used in even more situations than we can imagine (yet). While this lead to an increase in precision in the result set (compared to searching by profession of string instrument maker), the downside is, of course, a low recall, as we only got the rather small set of Viola d'amore builder who's instrument(s) are still preserved/included in the database.

The last step in this use case is now the intellectual work of the musicologist. With access to different relevant instrument makers (2) and instruments (1) similar to the unknown Viola d'amore, he can now use the interactive tool to inspect single data entities in more detail or make use of the various visualizations for visual analytics of the related instruments, giving insight into e.g. single production places or centers typical in the timeline. For this, Fig. 6 shows all Viola d'amores produced in the period of question. Next to the production (blue) events, we can also see a couple of war damage events (yellow). These events describe a loss of the instrument during the Second World War. Therefore, these instruments can be excluded as exactly fitting candidates for the instrument that is still preserved, but can be useful for comparison. With the help of the

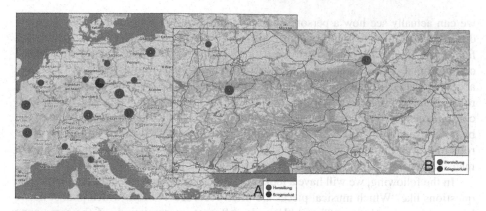

Fig. 7. Maps showing distribution of production places (blue) and war damages (yellow). (A) Overview of middle Europe and (B) locations in the northern Alp region (Mittenwald and Vienna). (Color figure online)

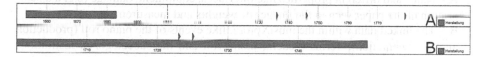

Fig. 8. Timeline showing all Viola d'amores produced in the northern Alp area. (A) The city of Vienna, (B) the city of Mittenwald.

map visualization (Fig. 7) we can see the geographical aspects of the production events. With a zoom on the northern Alp region we find two productions centers of interest: Mittenwald in the lower Bavarian region and Austria's capital Vienna. A match up of both sets of instruments, seen in Fig. 8, shows that only on of the instruments produced in Vienna fits into the temporal scope, while the Mittenwald ones seem all to be promising candidates. With this exemplary delivering of information we conclude this use case. Now, the musicologist would start a more detailed analysis, using information like images and description of the found instruments.

5.4 Piano Rolls: A Special Case

As an entity, piano rolls are a special case in the musiXplora. Normally, an entity can be effortlessly put into one of the seven facets. A piano roll is a long piece of paper (with easily 50 m). Holes indicate sounds to be played and handwritten annotation may be found throughout the roll. These holed papers can be used to recreate musical pieces. In musicology, these objects are known as early ways to document and recreate interpretations. While a typical music notation on paper is by far older, they show a kind of blueprint of a piece and how it should be played. In contrast, piano rolls may be produced as *recorded piano rolls*. These have been recorded in a specialized recording procedure, were – mostly famous – pianists played on a special recording piano. Live, holes were punched into the paper. The difference to musical notations is that here, we can actually see how a person interpreted – played – a song, which may be quite different from its blueprint version. Parts where the rhythm is not followed directly, fingerprint-like and typical keystroke patterns, or parts where the pianist improvised can be found. Thus, a piano roll is a very early way of recording and gives us today access to data and ways how famous persons played piano. For the database, a piano roll is both, an object to create music with (like an instrument, having paper and wood components) and a media to transfer information like a book or note sheet. Hence, it can be put into either the *BACCAE* or the *CATALOGUS* facet. We decided to split the piano rolls to fit well into the categorization. This leads to the physical object and its data like measurements to be put into *BACCAE* and the content like titles into *CATALOGUS*.

In the following, we will have a look at an exemplary piano roll, helping in research questions like "Which musical pieces are often recorded", "From which pianist do we have preserved techniques?" and "How do different interpretations of the same song differ by the pianist recorded?". Figure 9 shows the Object facet's entry for the piano roll, here we can find different kinds of data:

- A – Name and different properties like interfaces, equipment, damage (e.g. a discoloration of the paper seen in the image) or weights and measurements
- B – The linked data within the musiXplora, like events of the piano roll (production and documentation), Terms (general piano roll and the subcategory), institutions linked to the object and media entries.
- C – musiXplora external and internal links. In this case, a hyperlink to the subset of objects in the collection of the Musical Instrument Museum of Leipzig University (*MIMUL_OBJECTS*), where the piano roll is located.
- D – Different kinds of visualization like a scan of the object, a map, and a timeline shaping its career.
- E – Further information like identifiers (only one for this object), a shortcut to give feedback, and information about citing this page.

With a click on the *MIMUL NR6731* label, we move to the media facet entry of the piano roll shown in Fig. 10. While here no visualizations are included (yet), we find again similar entries, more focused on the content of the roll:

- A – Name of the media and different title variants including specification of the key in the – for the production time typical – languages German, French and English, and the specification of the tempo.
- B – List of musiXplora internal links, similar to the Object facet.
- C – List of musiXplora external links, in this case to the German National Library's dataset of the musical piece recorded on this piano roll.
- E – Analog to the Object facet

Like with the clicking on the *MIMUL NR6731* label, all other named labels are linked within the musiXplora as seen in Table 1. Hence, we could also get more information about the composer of the musical piece – Beethoven –, the artist whose musical handwriting is preserved with this piano roll – Pembauer – or general information about the producing firm or project which documented the roll.

In summary, with the availability of piano rolls, a use case may be to inspect different kinds of interpretations and playing techniques by famous pianists from which no

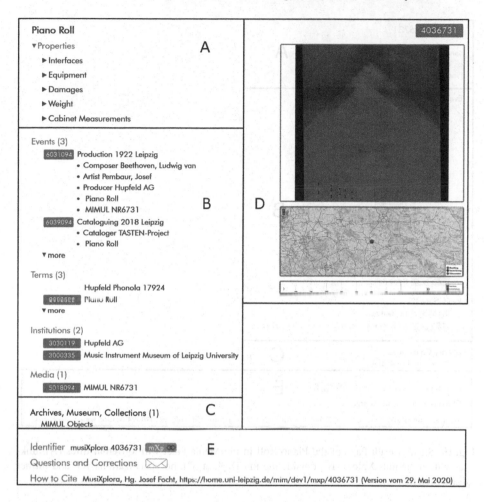

Fig. 9. Single Result Page of the Piano Roll in the Object facet with different properties (A), linkages within the musiXplora (B), outside the musiXplora (C), visualizations (D) and further information (E).

live recordings are preserved otherwise. For this, a musical piece like the *Mondschein-sonate* from Beethoven – from which the musiXplora has 23 different recordings by pianists like Josef Pembaur and Harold Bauer – can be searched for. The found recordings can then be analysed in depth.

For further and future inspections, we presently work on including the whole scans of all piano rolls (1–5 GB per piano roll) next to the already included first part (showing labels and stamps typical on the first few hand-lengths of the paper). Further, sound samples of the musical piece being played through a MIDI interface will be added soon. This will not only allow hearing the exact interpretation but also to choose the instrument on which it is played out of different digitized historical and unique objects

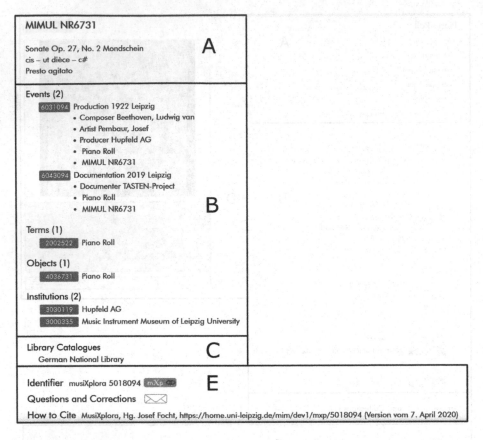

Fig. 10. Single Result Page of the Piano Roll in the Media facet with different titles (A), linkages within the musiXplora (B), outside the musiXplora (C), no visualizations yet, and further information (E).

which a user may never be able to hear from the physical object, due to damages and protections of these instruments.

6 Future Planning

As a longtime project, a lot of effort and time has been put into the planning. While a full list of still open plans would bust the scope of this paper, we would like to include near-future and already being worked on extensions.

6.1 Facets Availability

As seen in Table 1, two facets are still not available for the open public. Mostly, this is caused by a low level of completeness inside this facet's entities' data. An example is given with the newly published facet of institutions and its most important data type of member lists. A lot of institutions only show zero to five persons, which is not representative. Due to working with historical data, it may not be able to extend these data further, as there is just no more detailed information preserved. The editorial team is currently still able to fill the lists of many institutions, but will not be able to deliver a full list for all institutions. Therefore, the facet was put online now, although many entities only have a low level of detail. For the terms, events, and media the situation is different. These three facets are quite new. Existing entities are quite well documented, but the number of entries is rather low. With the focus on these facets now, we expect to be able to put the terms and events online soon, while the media facet has been published together with the institutions facet.

6.2   Connectivity

Table 1 also shows that some connections are not included. For example, the institutions' facet only links to two other facets. With the extending of data in other facets and, hence, the collection of data to be linked, we expect to be able to increase the level of linkage to be able to link all facets. To be added data may be different media about institutions (e.g. books describing an institution), which will create a linkage between media and institutions.

6.3   Complexity

Presently, the musiXplora allows browsing within a facet on a single page and within multiple facets by changing of the page. With the increasing level of complexity, more and more inter-facet ranging questions are arising, leading the musicologists to ask us about ways of visually linking single facets. This directly leads to the visualization subsection.

6.4   Integrating Visualizations

One of the core features of the web-interface is the deploying of visualizations to help users in a distant and close reading of data. While the facets of persons, objects, and places have a whole set of refined visualizations, some of the other facets are missing both, basic visualizations like pie charts, for getting a general overview over sets of data, and specialized visualizations helping in specific analysis approaches. An example of such specialized visualizations are namely the *Musicians Profiling* tool [11], presently available as a stand-alone tool helping in finding similar musicians to a given one by user-chosen and weighted properties. While this is presently accessible through a red link (musiXplora external link) on the person's page, it is planned and allowed to be directly included in the website. Another example is the including of the *Interactive Chart of Biographie* [13], giving the user the possibility to match up groups of persons divided by properties (profession, membership in an institution, confession, ...) and having a look at intra- and inter-group relations and cooperation as well as distributions of properties. Through the persons being positioned on a timeline, it also gives insight into temporal tendencies and time-typical abnormalities of these groups. While these two visualization projects were already included in the persons and institution facets, there is still planning and potential for other visualization tools dedicated to specific research questions.

6.5 Localization

A major future step needed for the tool to be of high value for musicology is the translation to other languages. While the present state only offers the German language (as one of the main languages in musicological research), at least an English translation is desired. Besides the issue of translating a work-in-progress and the high amount of maintenance arising with it, the translation itself is a rather difficult task. With the low level of standardization in musicology, even within a single language, a term may be quite ambiguous. Kusnick et al. tried to deal with a matching of terms between only two different sources and described even this for only a small set of terms in a single language as issue [19]. Nevertheless, localization, as a cooperation project with other universities, is already being planned. The planned localization includes Mandarin, Russian, Arabic and English, although the extent of the intellectual work of multilingual musicologists is still unknown.

6.6 Musicological Motivated Extensions

Next to specific potential, possibilities and ToDos to extend the musiXplora, the close collaboration in which the tool is growing leads to iterative development and evaluation. During these different iterations, more and more aspects of interest for the musicologists showed. Often, these were research questions that were not possible to answer in the musiXplora, at that time. An example has been seen in the organological use case in Sect. 5. While we were still able to get a result with high precision by going through the object facet to instrument makers, we actually want to find specialized instrument makers through the search functionality in the person facet. Due to such needs, the portfolio property of persons is in work, presently. Also, more and more subsets for specialized projects (see Sect. 4.1) are currently evolving through different research projects (*TASTEN* – German for keys –, *KONTRABASS KARTEI* – double bass index – and more).

Due to these real needs of the musicologists towards the tool – arising over time with the work and increasing familiarity –, the actual scope of possible future functions is unknown today. As a user-centred, iterative project, we expected the tool to grow. Nevertheless, we take the actual level of feedback and communication of needs as an indicator for a continued successful collaboration and an, already taken, big step towards a useful tool.

7 Conclusion

Digitizing information on cultural heritage is the first major step in many digital humanities research projects encountered today. This leads not only to a vast amount of data available, bearing a lot of potential for gaining new insights but also to difficulties working with the data [24]. With the rise of the digital humanities, distant reading methods began to revolutionize digital research projects in utilizing the newly found range of data, supporting new kinds of research questions [23]. Musicology has more or less not been a part of this development for the last two decades [17], leading to a rather low quantity of digitized data. Further, in this domain, we encountered unique and general issues related to the fragmentation of the field concerning both, data and the state of research. As part of the new research questions arising with the digital humanities [12], a complete and comprehensive overview of the field began to be of high interest for musicologists. With only few unfragmented data sets being available, offering such a comprehensive overview requires numerous efforts to even be considered. In this paper, we presented the musiXplora project that, including its predecessor, the BMLO, is running since more than 15 years and offers ground building work: Beginning with the editorial work by musicologists, planning and standardizing by digital humanists and providing intuitive access to the data through visualization by computer scientists. These three groups worked hand-in-hand to achieve a general research tool for musicological information. The current state exceeds previous publications of the project [15, 16] by focusing on the newly included linkage between data facets and refined level of data available e.g. musical objects. While the different functions and types of possible use cases were discussed in depth in the conference paper [16], here, we provided more insight into musicological motivated usage scenarios of the musiXplora. One case illustrates how an anonymous instrument, for which only a dendrochronological inspection has been conducted, can be categorized by reviewing information on related instruments and instrument makers. Another scenario provides a look at piano rolls which are part of a current digitization project in the Musical Instrument Museum of Leipzig University, delivering not only descriptive metadata but also high-resolution scans and sound samples, digitally available through the musiXplora.

References

1. André, P., Wilson, M.L., Russell, A., Smith, D.A., Owens, A., Schraefel, M.: Continuum: designing timelines for hierarchies, relationships and scale. In: Proceedings of the 20th Annual ACM Symposium on User Interface Software and Technology, UIST 2007, pp. 101–110. ACM, New York (2007)
2. Borman, T., Stoel, B.: Review of the uses of computed tomography for analyzing instruments of the violin family with a focus on the future. J. Violin Soc. Am.: VSA Papers **22**(1), 1–12 (2009)
3. den Bulcke, J.V., Loo, D.V., Dierick, M., Masschaele, B., Hoorebeke, L.V., Acker, J.V.: Nondestructive research on wooden musical instruments: from macro- to microscale imaging with lab-based X-ray CT systems. J. Cult. Heritage **27**, 78–87 (2017). Wooden Musical Instruments Special Issue
4. Crauwels, K., Crauwels, D.: Musicmap: The Genealogy and History of Popular Music Genres from Origin till Present (1870–2016) (2018). https://musicmap.info/. Accessed 24 June 2019
5. Doi, C.: Connecting music and place: exploring library collection data using geo-visualizations. Evid. Based Libr. Inf. Pract. **12**(2), 36–52 (2017)
6. Focht, J.: Bayerisches Musiker-Lexikon Online (2006). www.bmlo.lmu.de/. Accessed 10 Dec 2019

7. Gleich, M.D., Zhukov, L., Lang, K.: The world of music: SDP layout of high dimensional data. In: Info Vis 2005, vol. 100 (2005)
8. Heller, V.: Methoden zur Untersuchung und Dokumentation der Geigen am Museum für Musikinstrumente der Universität Leipzig; Dissertation (2017). http://nbn-resolving.de/urn: nbn:de:bsz:15-qucosa2-172136
9. Hopfner, R.: Violinforensic (2018). http://www.violinforensic.com. Accessed 24 June 2019
10. Jänicke, S., Focht, J.: Untangling the social network of musicians. In: DH (2017)
11. Jänicke, S., Focht, J., Scheuermann, G.: Interactive visual profiling of musicians. IEEE Trans. Vis. Comput. Graph. **22**(1), 200–209 (2016)
12. Jänicke, S., Franzini, G., Cheema, M.F., Scheuermann, G.: On close and distant reading in digital humanities: a survey and future challenges. In: EuroVis (STARs), pp. 83–103 (2015)
13. Khulusi, R., Kusnick, J., Focht, J., Jänicke, S.: An interactive chart of biography. In: 2019 IEEE Pacific Visualization Symposium (PacificVis), pp. 257–266, April 2019. https://doi. org/10.1109/PacificVis.2019.00038
14. Khulusi, R., Focht, J., Jänicke, S.: Visual exploration of musicians and institutions. In: Data in Digital Humanities 2018: Conference Abstracts, 2018 EADH (2018)
15. Khulusi, R., Jänicke, S.: On the distant reading of musicians' biographies. In: Digital Humanities 2016: Conference Abstracts. Jagiellonian University & Pedagogical University, Kraków, pp. 818–820 (2016)
16. Khulusi, R., Kusnick, J., Focht, J., Jänicke, S.: MusiXplora: visual analysis of a musicological encyclopedia. In: 15th International Joint Conference on Computer Vision, Imaging and Computer Graphics Theory and Applications, VISIGRAPP 2020, pp. 76–87. SCITEPRESS Digital Library (2020)
17. Khulusi, R., Kusnick, J., Meinecke, C., Gillmann, C., Focht, J., Jänicke, S.: A survey on visualizations for musical data. In: Computer Graphics Forum (2020)
18. Konopka, D., Schmidt, B., Kaliske, M., Ehricht, S.: Structural assessment of wooden musical instruments by simulation: models, validation, applicability. In: Proceedings of the 4th Annual Conference COST FP1302 WoodMusICK - Preservation of Wooden Musical Instruments Ethics, Practice and Assessment (2017)
19. Kusnick, J., Khulusi, R., Focht, J., Jänicke, S.: A timeline metaphor for analyzing the relationships between musical instruments and musical pieces. In: Proceedings of the 11th International Conference on Information Visualization Theory and Applications (IVAPP) (2020)
20. Leskinen, P., Hyvönen, E., Tuominen, J., et al.: Analyzing and visualizing prosopographical linked data based on biographies. In: BD, pp. 39–44 (2017)
21. Lu, S., Akred, J.: History of Rock in 100 Songs (2018). https://svds.com/rockandroll/# thebeatles. Accessed 24 June 2019
22. Miller, M., Walloch, J., Pattuelli, M.C.: Visualizing linked jazz: a web-based tool for social network analysis and exploration. Proc. Am. Soc. Inf. Sci. Technol. **49**(1), 1–3 (2012)
23. Moretti, F.: Graphs, maps, trees: abstract models for a literary history. Verso (2005)
24. Saito, S., Ohno, S., Inaba, M.: A platform for cultural information visualization using schematic expressions of cube. In: DH, pp. 365–367 (2010)
25. Tresch, J., Dolan, E.I.: Toward a new organology: instruments of music and science. Osiris **28**(1), 278–298 (2013). https://doi.org/10.1086/671381
26. Tuniz, C., Bernardini, F., Turk, I., Dimkaroski, L., Mancini, L., Dreossi, D.: Did neanderthals play music? X-ray computed micro-tomography of the DIVJE BABE 'Flute'. Archaeometry **54**(3), 581–590 (2012)
27. Vavrille, F.: LivePlasma (2017). http://www.liveplasma.com/. Accessed 24 June 2019

A Research-Teaching Guide for Visual Data Analysis in Digital Humanities

Stefan Jänicke[✉][iD]

IMADA, University of Southern Denmark, Odense, Denmark
stjaenicke@imada.sdu.dk

Abstract. The use of visualization to underpin distant reading arguments on cultural heritage data has established in the digital humanities domain. Novel strategies to represent data visually typically arise from interdisciplinary projects involving humanities and visualization scholars. However, the quality of outcomes might be inhibited as typical challenges of interdisciplinary research arise, and, at the same time, problem solving strategies are missing. I taught a course on visual data analysis in the digital humanities to let students with diverse study backgrounds experience those challenges in their early academic careers. This paper illustrates the research-teaching components of my course. This includes the contents of the theoretical training with active learning tasks, aspects of the practical training and considerations for teachers aiming to compose a related course.

Keywords: Research-teaching nexus · Visual data analysis · Digital humanities

1 Introduction

The importance of visualizations in digital humanities applications has steadily increased in recent years [22]. However, it has been shown that many visual representations are produced from standard tools that are not necessarily tailored for the given research task [24]. On the other hand, interdisciplinary projects can suffer from misunderstandings leading to visual designs that are hardly applicable by domain experts. My intention to offer a visualization course that attracts both computer science and humanities students was to equip them with the necessary knowledge and terminology in order to be able to "speak the same language" in potential future projects on the intersection of visualization and digital humanities. Therefore, students collaboratively conducted visual design projects in which they applied learned theoretical contents and faced typical challenges of interdisciplinary research.

This paper is an extended version of an IVAPP conference paper [32]. In addition, it contains aspects of a report on teaching journalism students [25]. While these publications rather report on the experiences gained in three years of teaching the course with a detailed discussion of conducted research projects, this paper contributes the following aspects:

- *Research-teaching Nexus:* The paper discusses different components of the course, which mainly focuses on conveying the research processes that lead to knowledge construction, referring to the research-teaching nexus by Healey [17].

© Springer Nature Switzerland AG 2022
K. Bouatouch et al. (Eds.): VISIGRAPP 2020, CCIS 1474, pp. 205–222, 2022.
https://doi.org/10.1007/978-3-030-94893-1_9

- *Theoretical Training:* A structured overview of the taught theoretical material is provided, and active learning tasks for individual classes are proposed.
- *Practical Training:* This paper puts a stronger focus on the roles of the teacher in interdisciplinary student projects, and projects that contributed to publications are discussed in detail.
- *Considerations:* Dependent on the cohort of participating students, different aspects that influence structuring course contents are discussed.

2   Terminology

In analogy to my first class in which I present the big picture of the course, this section is dedicated to discussing the terms that compose the title of the paper.

2.1   Digital Humanities

The digital humanities is an interdisciplinary field on the intersection of the humanities and computer science aiming to systematically apply computer-based methods to digital cultural heritage resources. Including a large variety of traditionally grown domains like literary studies, political sciences or computer science, interdisciplinarily oriented fields like computational linguistics, digital history or applied informatics also fall under the umbrella of the digital humanities. This diversity of disciplines makes defining *the digital humanities* a hard task. Heyer and Isenberg [18] describe the terms computational and digital humanities as different strategies to work with digital material. While the digital humanities would focus on creating digital repositories for cultural heritage collections, computational humanities would provide computational methods to analyze and enrich those repositories. The term *eHumanities* stands somewhere in between. Looking at the history of the domain, I use the traditional *digital humanities* term to describe all activities related to gathering and processing digitized material.

A definition for the domain, not aiming to generate a strict boundary, can be rather derived from the methodologies that lead to knowledge construction in the associated areas of research [52]. Whereas the natural sciences are concerned with the systematic study of nature and the discovery of regularities with which (natural) phenomena can be explained, the humanities consider all those phenomena that result from human action, evaluating them in their significance for the individual and society, and thus serving to create human consciousness. Tying those two methodologies together, the *digital humanities* could be defined as an area that generates a quantitative, computationally driven perspective on cultural heritage data, aiming to derive regularities of human action that contribute to creating human consciousness.

This turn from a qualitative to a quantitative analysis of information is depicted in Fig. 1 by the example of comparative literature analysis. The traditional approach includes a close reading of few related works followed by a detailed analysis of the writers intentions. Digital humanities approaches, on the other side, feature distant readings of text. By disrupting the linearity of text and counting occurrences of words, rather universal insights can be gained. In the given example, a literary scholar performed a keyword-based searches on a large text corpus of Latin texts and compared the aggregated contexts in which three synonymous keywords appeared using a comparative

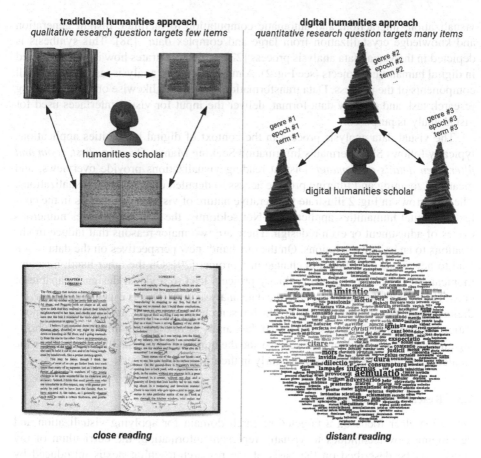

Fig. 1. Traditional and digital humanities approaches for comparative literature analysis. A traditional workflow would be based on close readings of few literary works (close reading image provided by Kehoe [36]), while digital humanities workflows typically involve quantitative distant readings [26].

tag cloud visualization [26]. By comparing shared and non-shared co-occurrences, the scholar was able to clarify and discriminate the meaning of words related to *imitate*. It has to be said that an analysis is typically not done only referring to a distant reading. Visualizations usually aid to generate different perspectives on information and access to close readings is granted interactively.

2.2 Visual Data Analysis

Recent survey papers document the increasing importance of visualizations for digital humanities research [22,62]. Visual interfaces have become indispensable components to generate bridges between a computationally gained result and expert users. Tominski and Schumann describe interactive visual data analysis as a "synthesis of visualization, interaction, and automatic computation to facilitate insight generation and knowledge crystallization from large and complex data" [58]. This synthesis is depicted in the visual data analysis process [22], which illustrates how insight is gained in digital humanities projects (see Fig. 2). A motivating data analysis task influences all components of the process. Data transformation, depending likewise on the underlying research task and the raw data format, deliver the input for visual interfaces used for visual analysis purposes.

The visual data analysis process in the context of digital humanities applications typically follows Shneiderman's Information Seeking Mantra *Overview first, zoom and filter, then details-on-demand*. Distant reading visualizations provide overviews, and means of zooming and filtering provide access to detailed close reading visualizations. The red arrows in Fig. 2 illustrate the iterative nature of visual data analysis in the context of digital humanities applications. Not seldomly, the process includes numerous cycles of adjustment or even redesign. There are two major reasons that induce modifications to an existing solutions. On the one hand, new perspectives on the data might lead to new ideas or a direction change in a project [20]. On the other hand, miscommunications typical for interdisciplinary projects lead to a visual design incapable of constructing knowledge concerning the data analysis task. This is especially crucial for digital humanities collaborations, in which research backgrounds are diverse. My motivation for teaching the course on visual data analysis in digital humanities is to bring together students from computer science and the humanities, so that they experience the challenges of interdisciplinary work early in their academic careers.

2.3   Research-Teaching Nexus

Given the clear focus on a targeted research domain for applying visualization and developing new techniques to visually represent information, the curriculum of my course can be described on the basis of the research-teaching nexus introduced by Healey [17]. As can be seen in Fig. 3, research-teaching can take different forms dependent on the targeted learning outcome and how students engage with the research materials. If a course is *research-led*, research contents and the important results of a domain are central to discussion. This is the rather traditional form of teaching that clearly separates the roles of the active teacher talking to a rather passive audience. Lecturing can also be *research-oriented*, which, instead of research findings, aims to convey research methodologies and best-practices that lead to knowledge construction concerning the taught subject. In *research-tutored* and *research-based* forms of teaching, students more actively participate and engage with research materials. While a *research-tutored* course involves activities such as reading and writing papers, in other words, a critical discussion of research contents, students practically experience research processes themselves when focusing on *research-based* activities.

The major intention of my course is to enable students to investigate research questions on the intersection of digital humanities delivering the research inquiry and visualization tailoring appropriate solutions to support related analysis tasks. Thus, the course focuses primarily on conveying how visual design models can be used to approach a given research task. Related examples from the literature underpin the value of established workflows for knowledge construction in this interdisciplinary field. Therefore, the theoretical training in the first half of the course is mainly *research-oriented*

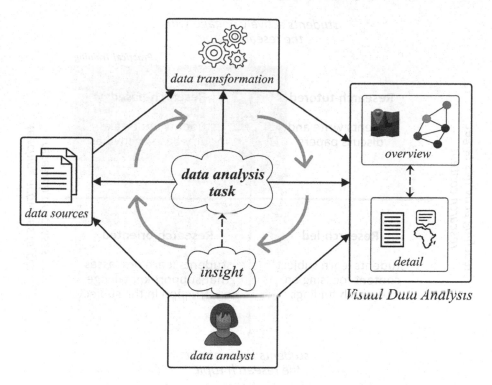

Fig. 2. Visual data analysis process in digital humanities based on [22].

as it teaches on how visualization can be best applied to existing problems to generate knowledge concerning cultural heritage data. The *research-led* part refers to the required basics of information visualization. In order to activate students during the theoretical training in a *research-based* fashion, students can replicate visual data analysis tasks on a small scale. The practical training conducted in the second half of the course is fully *research-based* as students experience real world research scenarios and develop means of visual analysis to investigate the given problem by following taught visual design approaches and workflows. The *research-tutored* part of the practical training refers to publishing promising results of course projects after the course.

3   Theoretical Training

According to the research-teaching nexus [17], the major focus of the theoretical training is to make students understand the processes that support knowledge construction in digital humanities with the aid of visual interfaces. Therefore, the theoretical training is mainly research-oriented. Research-led fragments of the course relate to the discussion of research findings on which visualization scholarship is based on, and research-based *active learning* tasks throughout the theoretical training support the understanding of the theoretical contents and prepare the students for their practical training conducted in the second half of the course.

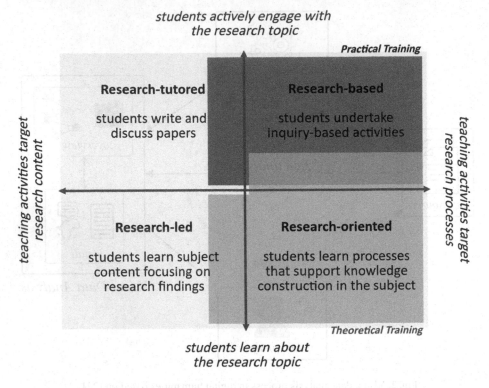

Fig. 3. Curriculum design and the research-teaching nexus based on Healey [17].

The schema of the research-oriented, theoretical training part of the course is depicted in Fig. 4. The syllabus adopts well-established strategies of teaching information visualization [37,51], however, with the digital humanities, focusing on a particular application domain. That means, the course The theoretical training focuses primarily on conveying the processes that lead to knowledge construction in digital humanities using visualization. Therefore, I structured the lecture contents in three blocks.

3.1 Block 1: The Big Picture

The course title included (in my case) the terms *Information Visualization* and *Digital Humanities*. I reserved the first class to give a broad overview of the individual terms and how they play together in the context of applying visualization in digital humanities. The discussion of sample projects that implement the visual data analysis process helped to convey the importance of the taught topic. We discussed four digital humanities projects, all based on raw textual sources, but each with a different research target in mind:

- Geospatial-temporal analysis of places mentioned in Herodotus' Histories with maps and timelines [4]
- Comparative analysis of similarities and differences among text editions with heat maps and variant graphs [29]

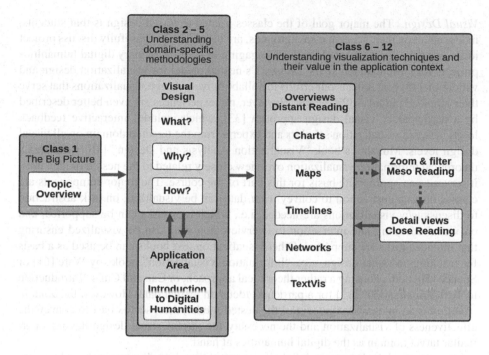

Fig. 4. Suggested structure of the theoretical training.

- Stylometric analysis of a Latin poem collection with graphs [16]
- Quantitative analysis of the Kissinger papers with charts, tag clouds and graphs [35]

3.2 Block 2: Understanding Domain-specific Methodologies

After the students gained an overview of the course topic, they should acquire basic knowledge in the two fields, and they should learn on established research methodologies and process models that lead to knowledge construction.

Application Area. Starting with a concept formation through diverse definitions of digital humanities, we discussed major historical developments that can be seen as the cornerstones of the digital humanities as a research area. One of the early related works, published in 1928, is Wladimir Jakowlewitsch Propp's "Morphology of the Folktale" [47]. Propp analyzed 100 Russian folktales and generated 31 functions, and a subset of which in the given order always defines the plot of a folktale. Another pioneering project is Roberto Busa's "Index Thomisticus". It began in 1948 aiming to create an index of Thomas Aquinas' works that needed to be lemmatized [11]. Recent influential works like Franco Moretti's "Graphs, Maps, Trees" [44], the Culturomics project [43] and Matthew Jocker's "Macroanalysis" [34] lead to defining the term of *distant reading*, which, like no other concept, stands for the importance of visualization for the digital humanities. The collaborative creation of a definition of *digital humanities* and try-out sessions with the Google Books Ngram Viewer[1] are suitable *active learning* tasks.

---

[1] https://books.google.com/ngrams.

Visual Design. The major goal of the classes related to visual design is that students, independent on their academic backgrounds, are capable to purposefully discuss project ideas using the same terminology. I am engaging in interdisciplinary digital humanities projects for more than ten years. Munzner's nested model for visualization design and validation [45] best reflects our efforts to collaboratively design visualizations that serve their intended purposes [23,27,38]. However, my experiences are even better described by a participatory visual design approach [33], which includes interactive feedback loops between visualization scholars and experts from the targeted domain on all visual design levels. Munzner's book "Visualization Analysis and Design" [46] structures a theoretical information visualization overview closely related to the nested model, thus, it serves as an appropriate basis for this part of the course. The major components are classes on data abstraction to convey *what* data can be visualized, on task abstraction to discuss *why* visualizations are needed, i.e., which user tasks can be supported, and on visual encoding and interaction to overview *how* data can be visualized ensuring that intended tasks are supported. Other visualization text books can be used as a basis for teaching on visual design, e.g., "Information Visualization" books by Ware [61] or Spence [56] both choosing a rather theoretical approach, or Cao and Cui's "Introduction to Text Visualization" [12] for a particular focus on textual data. However, the *domain situation* is an integral component of the nested model, thus, serves best to convey the effectiveness of visualization and the necessity for careful visual design having a particular target domain as the digital humanities at hand.

It is not crucial what research field is discussed first. Introducing the digital humanities as the targeted application domain first makes it easier to refer to the targeted application domain when giving an overview of the visual design. However, my introduction to digital humanities ends with the idea of distant reading, which generates a suitable bridge to specialized distant reading visualizations discussed in the third block of the theoretical training.

Active learning activities should aim to foster the understanding of data and task abstraction. Focusing on a single item or an entire cultural heritage collection, student groups can create appropriate data models, and discuss potential user tasks that could be supported by interactive visualization means. In addition, students should be confronted with existing visualizations aiming to evaluate the appropriateness of their visual mapping. A further suitable activity is to let the students participate in a study to assess the error rates across visual channels [14].

3.3   Block 3: Understanding Visualization Techniques and Their Value in the Application Context

The major part of the theoretical training is dedicated to discussing the most frequently used visualization techniques in the context of digital humanities applications. Each discussed technique basically refers to all visual design levels. Focusing primarily on how data of a specific type can be visualized, attention is given to the tasks that can be supported with a particular visual interface by discussing related published digital humanities applications. Block 3 should be organized on the basis of the Information Seeking Mantra [54], which is applied in many digital humanities applications [28]. However, the digital humanities established its own terminology. The terms distant reading and marcoanalysis stand for *overview*, meso reading and zooming comply to *zoom and filter*, and close reading and microanalysis relate to *details on-demand*.

Two strategies can be followed by teaching related contents. Either one strictly structures classes according to the Information Seeking Mantra by starting with overview visualizations. However, when students with a humanities background participate, it is more appropriate to begin with a review of visualization techniques that support digital close reading, as they are familiar with traditional close reading techniques. Moreover, it is easier to motivate overview visualizations necessary when operating with a whole collection instead of a single item. For occurring distant reading patterns, means of interaction are required to reach again individual items that are of potential interest for further investigation.

Detail Views. The course on detail views should be motivated by traditional work procedures of humanities scholars who engage with an object of interest. Especially, if students with different study topics participate, this approach contributes to the mutual exchange of domain knowledge and research workflows fruitful for interdisciplinary projects [45]. As textual data is typically focused in my course, I introduced the traditional close reading technique [10,42] and further discussed the benefits of digital environments for close reading tasks [13,36]. Different means of visualizing information and annotating fragments in a close reading view can be discussed in this context. Performing a traditional close reading individually and a collaborative digital close reading are suitable *active learning* tasks. Next to focusing texts, other data types like artworks [7], media contents [3] or individuals [39] can be the basis for discussion.

Zoom and Filter. Exemplarily, I reserved one course to refer to the task to comparatively analyze different text editions on different scales. In this context, I introduced the concept of meso reading explicitly [23]. However, I chose to discuss the majority of means to interactively navigate large data sources such as zooming, panning or focus+context referring to digital humanities projects implementing related means in the courses on specialized overview techniques.

Overviews. The term of distant reading is one of the main pillars of digital humanities research. Related visualization techniques therefore cover the largest share of the course. In the context of related digital humanities projects, the following techniques should be discussed:

- **Charts:** Motivating with historical examples [49], the power of statistical charts like line or bar charts to communicate a distribution of or trend in numerical data should be taught first. Further, grid-based heat map charts, which are frequently used in the literature [28], should be discussed.
- **Maps:** Many applications offer to analyze geographical data using interactive maps. My course informs on the definition of geovisualization in contrast to cartography [40], on different map projections, and on the various geovisualization techniques applied to point- and region based geographical data like choropleth, heat and glyph maps [55].

- **Timelines:** Temporal information is inherent in most data sets digital humanities scholars deal with. Next to referencing the long history of time-based visual representations of information [50], my course includes a discussion of modeling temporal information [1], a review of visualization techniques referring to the space-time cube [2], and a section on uncertainty, which is often comprised in digital humanities data due to the long historical time frame it refers to [8].
- **Graphs:** Relational data is frequently used to generate insights to digital humanities data in a visual form. After an overview of different graph structures to represent relational data, we discussed the basics of drawing different types of graphs [57], e.g., force-based approaches, radial and tree layouts. As standardized tools like Gephi [5] are often applied to generate graphs, the benefits of careful graph design were discussed on the basis of several related works involving visualization scholars [6, 19, 30].
- **TextVis:** Texts are the most frequently used raw data type in digital humanities applications [28]. Next to basic text processing techniques like part-of-speech tagging and named entity recognition, the course should discuss typical text visualization strategies. First and foremost, this includes traditional [59, 60] and adapted tag cloud representations [15, 31]. Further, hybrid techniques that adopt the idea of communicating the frequency of words with font size like tag maps [48] or tagged stream graphs [53] are related.

Existing ready-to-use domain-specific visualization frameworks can be used for research-based *active learning* activities. Those may include Google Data Studio[2] for charts, Leaflet[3] or GeoTemCo[4] for geographical data visualization, Timeline.js[5] or Sutori[6] for timeline generation, Gephi[7] or Palladio[8] for graph visualization, and Voyant[9] or TAPoR[10] for visual text analysis. Many of such tools offer multiple views for different types of data. Thus, engaging with them further supports the students' understanding of data modeling and multifaceted visual data exploration. Lastly, it bears also the opportunity to discover and discuss the limitations of existing tools, thereby motivating the development of new, sophisticated solutions.

4   Practical Training

While the theoretical training targets to make students understand the techniques, workflows and research methodologies that lead to knowledge construction, in the practical training students conduct related project tasks on their own. On the one hand, they get

---

[2] https://datastudio.withgoogle.com/.

[3] https://leafletjs.com/.

[4] http://www.informatik.uni-leipzig.de/geotemco/.

[5] http://timeline.knightlab.com/.

[6] https://www.sutori.com/.

[7] https://gephi.org/.

[8] https://hdlab.stanford.edu/palladio/.

[9] https://voyant-tools.org/.

[10] http://tapor.ca/.

to know how to apply the learned theoretical contents to practical problems, and on the other hand, students need to engage in interdisciplinary collaborations, in which they face issues typical for a digital humanities project.

4.1 Interdisciplinary Projects

Carried out in a *research-based* format, students need to generate solutions for real world inquiries concerning cultural heritage data. Therefore, they need to form interdisciplinary project groups. Dependent on the study backgrounds of the students of a project group, the teacher (or teaching assistant), who needs to be experienced in digital humanities collaborations, needs to be able to take different roles.

The Mediator. The project involves both students having a computer science or a humanities background. In this constellation, carrying out the project based on an research idea generated within the group is entirely in the hands of the students. However, it is especially considerable to participate in project meetings in the role of a mediator being experienced in interdisciplinary collaborations. This ensures that groups stay together in case of crucial issues, for which students lack appropriate problem solution strategies. In such constellations, students undergo the entire life cycle of a digital humanities project (on a small scale) and face typical pitfalls of interdisciplinary projects, and tackling and reflecting on those is the prior targeted skill to be trained in the course.

The Real Humanities Scholar. The project only involves computer sciences students from the course, but they collaborate with an expert humanities scholar to generate a solution to a real world research problem that is of interest to the expert. Depending on the experience of the humanities scholar in digital humanities projects, the role of the course teacher ranges from being the mediator in case of limited to the observer in case of extensive experience in interdisciplinary collaborations. This project setup produced high quality visual design solutions as students could focus on the development while interdisciplinary exchange is better structured as compared to the mediator role projects.

The Fake Humanities Scholar. The project only involves computer sciences students from the course, and the number of project ideas brought by expert humanities scholars is too low. In such cases, I proposed project ideas and took the role of the domain expert in project discussions. However, as I am not trained in humanities subjects, such projects only generate *fake* interdisciplinary discussions, making them the least preferable setup.

The Helper. The project only involves humanities students from the course, and they require technical support to generate appropriate solutions. The role of the teacher includes discussions on data modeling and assistance for generating visual representations of the data. In such constellations, students generated interesting project ideas and produced high-quality data sets being valuable beyond the duration of the course. For visualization purposes, due to limited programming skills, existing tools and libraries were typically applied instead of new solutions being developed.

The project results were presented by the groups in a block seminar at the end of the course. The outcomes of a project in terms of visualization quality and usability played a secondary role in evaluating the results. Reflections on occurring issues concerning the implementation of standardized design models, reported miscommunications among project members, or problems concerning data acquisition and processing were of particular value not only for me as a teacher, but also for the other groups who experienced similar issues. Previous publications on the course report on individual project outcomes in detail [25,32]. The next section is dedicated to those projects that contributed to related publications.

4.2 Publishing Project Results

The research-tutored fragment of the practical training as depicted in Fig. 3 refers to the publishing of project results. This activity was not part of the actual course curriculum, it was rather offered as a training opportunity for scientific writing. The results of three projects were explicitly published.

On the Impact of the Merseburg Incantations [21]. The idea to publish the results of this project existed before, and an already accepted poster presentation at the upcoming annual digital humanities conference 2017 served as a motivation for two students from the humanities department to participate. In the *helper* role, I discussed data modeling and data gathering strategies targeted to collect and structure metadata of published works that, in any form, refer to the Merseburg Incantations. Next to the data set, the students created a geospatial-temporal browser for the collected references based on Google My Maps. A screenshot, which was included in the poster presentation, can be seen in Fig. 5. Unfortunately, both students were not able to reflect on their experiences gained throughout the project at the conference.

Visual Analysis of Engineer's Biographies and Engineering Branches [41]. The project topic was an extension of a Bachelor thesis. The collaborating historian was interested in quantitatively analyzing taught engineering subjects, and in how the engineering branches *materials, manufacturing* and *construction* evolved geospatially and temporally in Germany. While the Bachelor thesis brought forth interactive visualizations to analyze the related prosopographical database of German engineers[11], the course project focused on the development of an interactive tag cloud that supports the assembling of engineering branches. On mouseover, correlations among subjects taught by the same professors are shown, and subjects can be iteratively added to a branch balancing between appropriate and inappropriate co-taught subjects. A screenshot of the tag cloud is shown in Fig. 6. The computer science student carrying out the *real humanities scholar* project presented his results at the LEipzig symposium on Visualization In Applications 2018.

musiXplora: Visual Analysis of a Musicological Encyclopedia [39]. The musiXplora[12] is an online resource for musicological data of different type, e.g., persons related to music history or musical objects. In the course project, a computer science student

---

[11] https://www.hi.uni-stuttgart.de/gnt/pdm/.

[12] https://home.uni-leipzig.de/mim/musici/.

Fig. 5. The published works are grouped according to time and space. Different icons denote different types of works referring to the Merseburg Incantations. Clicking an icon delivers details on the selected work.

developed in close collaboration with Josef Focht, musicology professor and supervisor of the musiXplora project, a design to analyze the career of musical instrument types, e.g., clavichord instruments registered in the musiXplora with different events (e.g., production, purchase, exhibition) attached to them. The visual depiction shown in Fig. 7 reveals the history of the instrument type, i.e., where instruments have been played and when such instruments have been produced. The description of the design was presented by the student at the International Conference on Information Visualization Theory and Applications 2020.

5 Considerations

In the previous version of this paper [32], I discussed different experiences gained in three years teaching the course, including students' reflections on the conducted projects and grading. What follows is a list of considerations valuable for constructing a related course.

Ensure a Diversity of Study Backgrounds! The composition of students mainly influences contents and learning activities of the course. I experienced all possible constellations resulting in the various project roles for me as a teacher. I recommend to offer the course to all interested students from computer science, humanities and digital humanities. This way, methodological exchange among the students is likely and interdisciplinary projects are formed.

218   S. Jänicke

Fig. 6. Interactive tag cloud supports assembling engineering branches. The selected subject Wärmelehre (thermodynamics) only co-occurs with subjects already assigned to *construction*, denoted by bold, underlined tokens shown on mouseover.

The More Course Time, the Merrier! The three iterations of my course corresponded to 5 ECTS credits each. This limits not only the contents that can be taught, but also the targeted learning outcomes. Sticking to the theme of the course, the focus in my course was conveying how to design a valuable visualization that supports investigating a real world digital humanities task. This setup did not leave room to exhaustively discuss data transformation procedures necessary to turn raw data sources in a format processible by the visualization. In such a case, one should offer pre-processed data sets and project topics should not require sophisticated data transformation efforts. To convey all aspects of the visual design process for digital humanities, a course subject to 10 ECTS credits is better suitable.

Promote Web-based Developments! JavaScript typically does not belong to the studied programming languages of computer science students, and it is often considered a pre-requisite for their studies. However, visualizations used in digital humanities are mostly web-based, and ready-to-use frameworks like D3.js [9] are widely applied. Therefore, I recommend to use widely learned languages such as Python or Java primarily for back end computations, and JavaScript for generating visualizations in a web-based front end. Basics of JavaScript programming could be conveyed in practical sessions parallel to the theoretical training.

Promote Development-driven Visualizations! Digital humanities literature tells us that many visualizations are generated using a standard visualization tool [5]. The generation of arguable visual output in a short amount of time is the main advantage of such ready-to-use frameworks. However, scholars need to learn to operate potentially complex tools and also how to interpret upcoming results. Even more crucial, research interests might deviate from what the tool can provide, which favors new visualization developments. The course should discuss ready-to-use tools, but also point out their limitations.

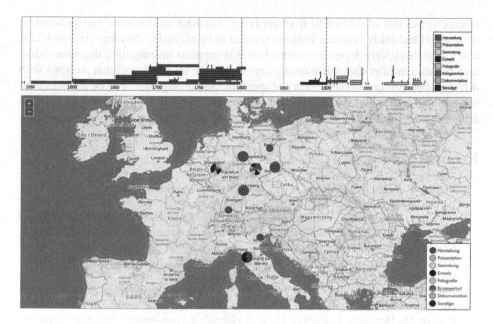

Fig. 7. Geospatial-temporal analysis of the clavichord metadata.

Report on Successes, But, More Importantly, on Failures! As a researcher involved in digital humanities projects, ones own experiences should be discussed thoroughly. This does not only include success stories. Reporting on failures is of particular importance as they document the challenges of interdisciplinary research and diverse merits of generated results. Reporting my failures was important for me being a computer scientist to highlight the necessity to learn more on the research processes and targeted data sources—it is best, if one has a real interest in cultural heritage.

Treat Students Like Researchers! After the theoretical training, students are well equipped with knowledge about visual design and the targeted interdisciplinary research area. Then they are able to implement research ideas in the practical training. Especially participating humanities students generated interesting ideas, and the longer the theoretical training took, the more they used the learned technical terminology to describe their visions. Project discussions, in which the teacher participates, should be perceived and carried out as a meeting among researchers instead of a teacher/student consultation.

6 Conclusion

The insights from my participation in the conducted projects and the students' reflections during project presentations document that a structured research-teaching focusing on understanding and experiencing the research workflows that lead to knowledge construction is worthy for the participating students. While computer science students report on the value to get a detailed overview of a specific application domain for visualization, students of humanities disciplines appreciate to get insights to computational thinking and data modeling making them capable of generating digital humanities research tasks that could benefit from applying visualization solutions. Independent on their individual study subjects, students seemed to be excited to develop a research idea and to collaboratively design a visualization that supports investigating that idea. Informal evaluations after the course finally certify that the intended goal that students with different backgrounds should learn to "speak the same language" can be reached with the outlined course structure. I hope that the given overview will inspire teachers who aim to teach a similar course on the intersection of visualization and digital humanities.

References

1. Aigner, W., Miksch, S., Schumann, H., Tominski, C.: Visualization of Time-Oriented Data, 1st edn. Springer, Heidelberg (2011). https://doi.org/10.1007/978-0-85729-079-3
2. Bach, B., Dragicevic, P., Archambault, D., Hurter, C., Carpendale, S.: A descriptive framework for temporal data visualizations based on generalized space-time cubes. Comput. Graph. Forum **36**(6), 36–61 (2015)
3. Baker, F.W.: Close Reading and What It Means for Media Literacy (2014). https://www.middleweb.com/15929/close-reading-and-media-literacy/
4. Barker, E., Pelling, C., Bouzarovski, S., Isaksen, L.: Mapping the world of an ancient Greek Historian: the HESTIA project. In: Proceedings of the Digital Humanities 2010 (2010)
5. Bastian, M., Heymann, S., Jacomy, M., et al.: Gephi: an open source software for exploring and manipulating networks. In: ICWSM, vol. 8, pp. 361–362 (2009)
6. Bezerianos, A., Dragicevic, P., Fekete, J., Bae, J., Watson, B.: GeneaQuilts: a system for exploring large genealogies. IEEE Trans. Vis. Comput. Graph. **16**(6), 1073–1081 (2010)
7. Binkis, S.: Reading Visual Images: The First World War (2020). https://dcc.newberry.org/teachers/x5lljd50
8. Börner, K., Eide, O., Mchedlidze, T., Rehbein, M., Scheuermann, G.: Network visualization in the humanities (Dagstuhl Seminar 18482). Dagstuhl Rep. **8**(11), 139–153 (2019). https://doi.org/10.4230/DagRep.8.11.139. http://drops.dagstuhl.de/opus/volltexte/2019/10359
9. Bostock, M., Ogievetsky, V., Heer, J.: D data-driven documents. IEEE Trans. Vis. Comput. Graph. **17**(12), 2301–2309 (2011)
10. Burke, B.: A Close Look at Close Reading: Scaffolding Students with Complex Texts (2012)
11. Busa, R.: The Annals of Humanities Computing: The Index Thomisticus. Raccolta delle opere di Roberto Busa, North Holland Publishing Company (1980). https://books.google.dk/books?id=Ph29oAEACAAJ
12. Cao, N., Cui, W.: Introduction to Text Visualization. Atlantis Briefs in Artificial Intelligence. Atlantis Press, Paris (2016). https://cds.cern.ch/record/2230485
13. Cheema, M.F., Jänicke, S., Scheuermann, G.: AnnotateVis: combining traditional close reading with visual text analysis. In: Workshop on Visualization for the Digital Humanities, IEEE VIS 2016, Baltimore, Maryland, USA (2016)
14. Cleveland, W.S., McGill, R.: The many faces of a scatterplot. J. Am. Stat. Assoc. **79**(388), 807–822 (1984)
15. Collins, C., Viegas, F.B., Wattenberg, M.: Parallel tag clouds to explore and analyze faceted text corpora. In: 2009 IEEE Symposium on Visual Analytics Science and Technology, pp. 91–98, October 2009. https://doi.org/10.1109/VAST.2009.5333443
16. Eder, M.: Stylometry, network analysis, and Latin literature. In: Proceedings of the Digital Humanities 2014 (2014)
17. Healey, M.: Linking research and teaching exploring disciplinary spaces and the role of inquiry-based learning. Reshaping the University: New Relationships between Research, Scholarship and Teaching, pp. 67–78 (2005)

18. Heyer, G., Isemann, D.: Digital und computational humanities. In: Book of Abstracts zum DHd Workshop Informatik und die Digital Humanities (2014)
19. Hinrichs, U., Forlini, S., Moynihan, B.: Speculative practices: utilizing infovis to explore untapped literary collections. IEEE Trans. Vis. Comput. Graph. **22**(1), 429–438 (2016)
20. Hinrichs, U., Forlini, S., Moynihan, B.: In defense of sandcastles: research thinking through visualization in digital humanities. Digit. Scholarsh. Hum. **34**, i80–i99 (2018)
21. Jänicke, S.: On the impact of the Merseburg incantations. In: Conference Abstracts of the Digital Humanities 2017 (2017)
22. Jänicke, S., Franzini, G., Cheema, M.F., Scheuermann, G.: Visual text analysis in digital humanities. Comput. Graph. Forum **36**(6), 226–250 (2017)
23. Jänicke, S., Wrisley, D.J.: Interactive visual alignment of medieval text versions. In: 2017 IEEE Conference on Visual Analytics Science and Technology (VAST), pp. 127–138, October 2017. https://doi.org/10.1109/VAST.2017.8585505
24. Jänicke, S.: Valuable research for visualization and digital humanities: a balancing act. In: Workshop on Visualization for the Digital Humanities, IEEE VIS 2016, Baltimore, Maryland, USA (2016)
25. Jänicke, S.: A visualization course for journalism students. In: IEEE VIS 2019 Workshop on Visualization for Communication (VisComm) (2019)
26. Jänicke, S., Blumenstein, J., Rücker, M., Zeckzer, D., Scheuermann, G.: TagPies: comparative visualization of textual data. In: Proceedings of the 13th International Joint Conference on Computer Vision, Imaging and Computer Graphics Theory and Applications, pp. 40–51. INSTICC, SciTePress (2018). https://doi.org/10.5220/0006548000400051
27. Jänicke, S., Focht, J., Scheuermann, G.: Interactive visual profiling of musicians. IEEE Trans. Vis. Comput. Graph. **22**(1), 200–209 (2016)
28. Jänicke, S., Franzini, G., Cheema, M.F., Scheuermann, G.: On close and distant reading in digital humanities: a survey and future challenges. In: Borgo, R., Ganovelli, F., Viola, I. (eds.) Eurographics Conference on Visualization (EuroVis) - STARs. The Eurographics Association (2015)
29. Jänicke, S., Gessner, A.: A distant reading visualization for variant graphs. In: Proceedings of the Digital Humanities 2015 (2015)
30. Jänicke, S., Geßner, A., Franzini, G., Terras, M., Mahony, S., Scheuermann, G.: TRAViz: a visualization for variant graphs. Digit. Scholarsh. Hum. **30**(Suppl. 1), i83–i99 (2015)
31. Jänicke, S., Scheuermann, G.: On the visualization of hierarchical relations and tree structures with TagSpheres. In: Braz, J., et al. (eds.) VISIGRAPP 2016. CCIS, vol. 693, pp. 199–219. Springer, Cham (2017). https://doi.org/10.1007/978-3-319-64870-5_10
32. Jänicke, S.: Teaching on the intersection of visualization and digital humanities. In: Proceedings of the 15th International Joint Conference on Computer Vision, Imaging and Computer Graphics Theory and Applications - Volume 3: IVAPP, pp. 100–109. INSTICC, SciTePress (2020)
33. Jänicke, S., Kaur, P., Kuzmicki, P., Schmidt, J.: Participatory visualization design as an approach to minimize the gap between research and application. In: Gillmann, C., Krone, M., Reina, G., Wischgoll, T. (eds.) VisGap - The Gap between Visualization Research and Visualization Software. The Eurographics Association (2020). https://doi.org/10.2312/visgap.20201108
34. Jockers, M.L.: Macroanalysis: Digital Methods and Literary History, 1st edn. University of Illinois Press, Champaign (2013)
35. Kaufman, M.: 'Everything on paper will be used against me': Quantifying Kissinger. In: Proceedings of the Digital Humanities 2015 (2015)
36. Kehoe, A., Gee, M.: eMargin: a collaborative textual annotation tool. Ariadne (71) (2013)

37. Kerren, A., Stasko, J.T., Dykes, J.: Teaching information visualization. In: Kerren, A., Stasko, J.T., Fekete, J.-D., North, C. (eds.) Information Visualization. LNCS, vol. 4950, pp. 65–91. Springer, Heidelberg (2008). https://doi.org/10.1007/978-3-540-70956-5_4

38. Khulusi, R., Jänicke, S., Kusnick, J., Focht, J.: An interactive chart of biography. In: 2019 IEEE Pacific Visualization Symposium (PacificVis) (2019)

39. Khulusi, R., Kusnick, J., Focht, J., Jänicke, S.: musiXplora: visual analysis of a musicological encyclopedia. In: Proceedings of the 15th International Joint Conference on Computer Vision, Imaging and Computer Graphics Theory and Applications - Volume 3: IVAPP, pp. 76–87. INSTICC, SciTePress (2020). https://doi.org/10.5220/0008977100760087

40. MacEachren, A.M., Kraak, M.J.: Exploratory cartographic visualization: advancing the agenda (1997)

41. Meinecke, C., Jänicke, S.: Visual analysis of engineer's biographies and engineering branches. In: LEVIA 2018: Leipzig Symposium on Visualization in Applications (2018)

42. Mesmer, H.A., Rose-McCully, M.: A closer look at close reading: three under-the-radar skills needed to comprehend sentences. Read. Teach. 71(4), 451–461 (2018). https://doi.org/10.1002/trtr.1639. https://ila.onlinelibrary.wiley.com/doi/abs/10.1002/trtr.1639

43. Michel, J.B., et al.: Quantitative analysis of culture using millions of digitized books. Science 331(6014), 176–182 (2011)

44. Moretti, F.: Graphs, Maps, Trees: Abstract Models for a Literary History. Verso (2005)

45. Munzner, T.: A nested model for visualization design and validation. IEEE Trans. Vis. Comput. Graph. 15(6), 921–928 (2009). https://doi.org/10.1109/TVCG.2009.111

46. Munzner, T.: Visualization Analysis and Design. CRC Press, Boca Raton (2014)

47. Propp, V.: Morphology of the Folktale, vol. 9. University of Texas Press (2010)

48. Reckziegel, M., Cheema, M.F., Scheuermann, G., Jänicke, S.: Predominance tag maps. IEEE Trans. Vis. Comput. Graph. 24(6), 1893–1904 (2018)

49. Rendgen, S.: The Minard System: The Complete Statistical Graphics of Charles-Joseph Minard. Chronicle Books (2018)

50. Rosenberg, D., Grafton, A.: Cartographies of Time: A History of the Timeline. Princeton Architectural Press (2013)

51. Rushmeier, H., Dykes, J., Dill, J., Yoon, P.: Revisiting the need for formal education in visualization. IEEE Comput. Graph. Appl. 27(6), 12–16 (2007)

52. Schwerdtfeger, A.: Erkenntnisgewinn in der Wissenschaft (2020)

53. Shi, L., Wei, F., Liu, S., Tan, L., Lian, X., Zhou, M.: Understanding text corpora with multiple facets. In: 2010 IEEE Symposium on Visual Analytics Science and Technology (VAST), pp. 99–106, October 2010

54. Shneiderman, B.: The eyes have it: a task by data type taxonomy for information visualizations. In: Proceedings of the Visual Languages, pp. 336–343 (1996)

55. Slocum, T.A., McMaster, R.B., Kessler, F.C., Howard, H.H.: Thematic Cartography and Geovisualization. Prentice Hall Series in Geographic Information Science, 3rd international edn. Prentice Hall (2009)

56. Spence, R.: Information Visualization, vol. 1. Springer, Heidelberg (2001)

57. Tamassia, R.: Handbook of Graph Drawing and Visualization (Discrete Mathematics and Its Applications). Chapman & Hall/CRC (2007)

58. Tominski, C., Schumann, H.: Interactive Visual Data Analysis. AK Peters Visualization Series, CRC Press (2020). https://doi.org/10.1201/9781315152707. https://ivda-book.de

59. Viegas, F., Wattenberg, M., Feinberg, J.: Participatory visualization with wordle. IEEE Trans. Vis. Comput. Graph. 15(6), 1137–1144 (2009)

60. Viegas, F., Wattenberg, M., van Ham, F., Kriss, J., McKeon, M.: ManyEyes: a site for visualization at internet scale. IEEE Trans. Vis. Comput. Graph. 13(6), 1121–1128 (2007)

61. Ware, C.: Information Visualization: Perception for Design. Elsevier (2012)

62. Windhager, F., et al.: Visualization of cultural heritage collection data: state of the art and future challenges. IEEE Trans. Vis. Comput. Graph. 25(6), 2311–2330 (2019)

Coherent Topological Landscapes
for Simulation Ensembles

Marina Evers, Maria Herick, Vladimir Molchanov$^{(\boxtimes)}$, and Lars Linsen

Department of Mathematics and Computer Science,
Westfälische Wilhelms-Universität Münster,
Einsteinstr. 62, 48149 Münster, Germany
{marina.evers,m.herick,molchano,linsen}@uni-muenster.com

Abstract. The topological structure is an intrinsic feature of a scalar field of
any spatial dimensionality. The dependence of the topology on the isovalue of
the field can be represented in the form of merge and split trees, which are usually combined to a contour tree. Topological landscapes are algorithmically constructed 2D scalar fields, which have the same topological structure (and, therefore, correspond to the same contour tree) as the given multidimensional scalar
field and serve as an intuitive low-dimensional depiction of its topological features. Topological landscapes computed for a set of scalar fields, e.g., created
by varying over time or by varying simulation parameter values in a simulation
ensemble, are not necessarily coherent among themselves. Therefore, a comparative analysis of topology in an ensemble is hindered. We propose a concept for
the generation of coherent contour trees for simulation ensembles that is based on
merging contour trees of all scalar fields of the ensemble. The coherent contour
tree can be exploited to generate coherent topological landscapes. Visual analysis of varying scalar field topology is, then, supported by animating landscapes
or by volume rendering of a stack of temporal slices representing color-coded
landscapes. We apply the proposed methodology to synthetic data for evaluation
purposes as well as to 2D and 3D simulation ensemble data.

Keywords: Topological landscape · Ensemble visualization · Scalar field
visualization

1 Introduction

A *scalar field* is a scalar-valued function defined over a spatial domain. Examples of
scalar fields include temperature, pressure, and density distributions, which play a crucial role in natural science. For spatial domains of any dimensionality, the topology of
the scalar field captures fundamental properties of the field. The topological structure is
invariant with respect to continuous deformations of the domain and thus can be used
as a powerful descriptor of scalar fields. Knowing the field topology is important for
isosurface extraction [20], segmentation [15], and other visualization and data analysis
algorithms.

A *contour tree* [6] is a popular descriptor to encode topology of a scalar field. However, the direct graph-based visualization of a contour tree can be non-intuitive and hard

© Springer Nature Switzerland AG 2022
K. Bouatouch et al. (Eds.): VISIGRAPP 2020, CCIS 1474, pp. 223–237, 2022.
https://doi.org/10.1007/978-3-030-94893-1_10

to perceive for untrained users. To improve readability of the topology depiction, Weber et al. [40] proposed the metaphor of a *topological landscape*. Topological landscapes are algorithmically constructed fields over a 2D spatial domain, which share the contour tree with the given scalar field of any dimensionality. Thus, both fields have the same topological structure, while visualization, analysis, and interaction with topological landscapes is much simpler.

Scientific visualization is generally concerned with the analysis of spatio-temporal observation and simulation data representing natural phenomena. Simulation data usually depend on a set of input parameters, i.e., characterizing initial conditions. A simulation ensemble consists of several simulation results with varying governing simulation parameters. One core task in the analysis of simulation ensembles is to relate the evolution of the simulation data to the driving parameter values. Topological landscapes are a natural analysis tool when ensemble members are to be compared in terms of their topology. However, when topological landscapes are created for each scalar field individually, it is often impossible to match the identified features and track their changes over time or parameter values. Analysis of the topology dependence on ensemble parameters strongly demands a coherence of computed topological landscapes.

In this paper, we propose an approach for visualizing the changes in topology in varying scalar fields. Our work extends the work by Herick et al. [18], where we analyzed single simulation runs over time using temporally coherent landscapes, to the analysis of simulation ensembles, i.e., we analyze the change of the scalar fields' topology over multiple simulation runs. Thus, we present an algorithm for constructing a family of coherent topological landscapes for simulation runs with changing parameter settings. The temporal variable can be considered as a particular case of such parameters, which has simple linear ordering, i.e., our extended approach naturally embeds the original work in [18].

The proposed method includes several stages. First, we compute contour trees for each ensemble member individually, see Sect. 3 for respective background information. Based on a similarity measure, we merge contour trees into a meta-data structure that stores the topological evolution in dependence of the ensemble's simulation parameter. Then, we generate a sequence of coherent topological landscapes based on information extracted from the meta tree. We propose to either visualize these landscapes by means of an animation or to stack them in form of 2D color images and apply a volume rendering for a static visualization of the evolution. The methodology is detailed in Sect. 4. Finally, we apply the proposed approach to a number of datasets, see Sect. 5. While the original article in [18] used single 2D time-dependent data sets only, we include applications to 3D simulation ensemble data.

Our main contributions can be summarized as follows:

- We extend the approach of temporally coherent topological landscapes to simulation ensembles and, thus, allow for computing coherent topological landscapes over changing simulation parameters.
- We apply the algorithm to analyze synthetic data, 2D simulation data and 3D scalar fields.

2   Related Work

The most common visualizations of scalar fields include isosurfaces and direct volume renderings. However, these techniques require a choice of suitable settings like an isovalue or a transfer function. The choice of these parameters can be supported by different approaches like isosurface similarity maps [4,11], stochastic distributions [27], and isosurface statistics [33]. An effective means to support the scalar field visualization methods are topology-based approaches, which extract and analyze its relevant features [17].

Various aspects of the scalar fields' topology can be visualized. One option is the analysis of critical points and persistent homology using, for example, persistence diagrams or a visualization like barcodes [9]. Another aspect is the *Morse-Smale complex* which partitions the domain into regions with equivalent gradient behavior [14]. The *Reeb graph* [30] shows the evolution of level sets of functions defined on a manifold. If the manifold is simply connected, the Reeb graph becomes a contour tree [6,8]. A wide variety of different methods for topology-based scalar field analysis are available in the Topology ToolKit [37], which we used in our implementation for the creation and simplification of merge and split trees.

A contour tree can be represented in different ways. Conventional visualizations use 2D graph drawing algorithms in the form of vertical node-link layouts, where the vertical axis corresponds to the field value at the nodes of the contour tree [6]. A 3D visualization based on radial graph-drawing algorithms was proposed by Pascucci et al. [26]. Weber et al. [41] extended this approach to a visualization called *topological cacti*. Analysis of such graph-based visualizations generally requires a significant background knowledge related to the construction of contour trees. In order to lower the cognitive complexity of the analysis and provide a more intuitive visualization, topological landscapes were proposed [40].

The information provided by topological landscapes can be enriched by encoding geometrical properties of the topological features as proposed by Beketayev et al. [1]. Harvey and Wang [16] developed volume-preserving topological landscapes that can be constructed for higher-dimensional scalar fields. The metaphor of topological landscapes was also applied to point clouds [23,24] and to general graphs [43]. Topological landscapes for complex datasets might become very complicated. To address this issue, Demir et al. [7] proposed interactive hierarchical renderings of topological landscapes to show deep hierarchies.

Often, it is necessary to explore fields stemming from an ensemble of simulation runs [38] and their interrelations rather than individual scalar fields only. Several approaches based on statistical properties of data, e.g., mean value, were proposed [29,32]. Other approaches aim at the investigation of the parameter space ignoring topological properties [2,5,12,28,34,35].

A range of approaches for topological ensemble exploration focus on uncertainty analysis. Kraus [19] proposed a visualization method for contour trees built for uncertain scalar fields. Other techniques use the mean of all data points for a contour tree-based uncertainty visualization [42] or focus on the analysis of critical points in uncertain scalar fields [13]. Recently, Lohfink et al. [21] presented *Fuzzy contour trees* that allow for easy detecting the outliers. Similar to our previous work in [18] and its extension in this paper, their algorithm is based on the alignment of contour trees. However, Lohfink et al. directly work with contour trees, whereas our approach operates on merge and split trees independently. This comes with the advantage that the algorithm proposed in the current paper is independent of the choice of the root node. Moreover, existing approaches do not allow for tracking changes over variation of parameters, which we present in this paper.

Tracking of temporal changes in Reeb graphs was proposed by Edelsbrunner et al. [10]. Such spatio-temporal topological structures can be used to visualize the evolution of selected topological features [3,39]. Sohn and Bajaj [36] proposed to visualize topological changes over time on an isosurface with a fixed isovalue. However, fixing a single topological feature or an isovalue significantly restricts the capability of the tool. Saikia et al. [31] compared all subtrees of two merge trees to find similar structures and detect temporal periodicity. Oesterling et al. [25] computed time-varying merge trees and visualized their evolution in a bottom-up layout. In our approach, both merge and split trees are involved in the analysis, which allows for constructing parametrized coherent topological landscapes.

3   Background

Let $f(x, t, p)$ be a d-dimensional time- and parameter-dependent scalar function defined on a simply connected set. The function values are given at spatial sample points $\{x_i \in \mathbb{R}^d | i = 1, \ldots, n\}$ at times $t_j, j = 1, \ldots, m$, and for parameter values $p_k, k = 1, \ldots, l$, where n is the number of spatial samples, m is the number of time points, and l is the size of the ensemble, i.e., the number of parameters values used to generate the ensemble. Assuming that $f(x, t, p)$ is a *Morse function* for any time t and parameter value p, we can exclude the existence of degenerate extrema [22]. To guarantee that no two data points have the same value, we preprocess the data and slightly perturb it, if necessary. We follow here the procedure described by Carr et al. [6].

The level set L_z corresponding to isovalue $z \in \mathbb{R}$ at a fixed time t_j and a fixed parameter value p_k is defined by a set of all points $x \in \mathbb{R}^d$ with $f(x, t_j, p_k) = z$. A simply connected component of L_z is called an *isocontour* or *isosurface* for isovalue z. Topological changes of all isocontours for varying isovalues are described by a *contour tree*.

Let $T_{j,k}$ be a contour tree of function $f(x, t_j, p_k)$ for time t_j and parameter value p_k. Its nodes represent critical points of f, i.e., minima (a new isocontour emerges), maxima (an existing isocontour vanishes), or saddle points (isocontours merge or split). The saddle nodes can be classified as *merge nodes*, at which several isocontours merge together, or *split nodes*, at which several isocontours split. The tree nodes are connected by edges which represent the life span of a topological feature. Each point in the contour tree represents an isocontour with an isovalue corresponding to the height in the conventional 2D vertical tree layout.

A *merge tree* (also referred to as join tree) containing only merge nodes and a *split tree* containing only split nodes are computed as intermediate steps for the contour tree construction [6]. Both merge and split trees are rooted trees, whereas the contour tree is an unrooted tree.

Weber et al. [40] proposed a metaphor of *topological landscapes* for an intuitive visual encoding of the topological structure of a scalar field. A topological landscape is a 2D heightfield whose contour tree is identical to the contour tree of f. Thus, the heights of the peaks in the heightfield correspond to the heights in the conventional 2D vertical tree layout. As the position of a peak and the covered area are not determined, these features can be used to encode additional information, for example, the area can encode the volume of the topological feature.

4   Coherent Topological Landscapes

In this paper, we want to visualize the topological changes in a scalar field depending on a parameter p (which can also be time t) by creating coherent topological landscapes. At first, we compute merge and split trees for each scalar field individually, see Sect. 3. For this step as well as for an optional simplification of the trees, we use the Topology ToolKit [37]. Then, we iteratively match the nodes of trees from consecutive steps to combine the merge and split trees. This matching is based on a distance metric, which uses spatial information of the topological feature, see Sect. 4.1. The resulting merge and split trees are combined in a parameter-varying contour tree which is a meta data structure containing contour trees for all parameter values, see Sect. 4.2. Based on this combined contour tree, we compute coherent topological landscapes that visualize the changes in topology over the variation of the parameter value (or over time). For the visualization we propose two alternatives: a dynamic visualization with animated heightfields and a static visualization with direct volume rendering of stacked height-fields (encoded as 2D scalar fields), see Sect. 4.3.

4.1   Distance Metric

To identify, which nodes of two (merge or split) trees match, we define a distance metric between nodes of different trees. Here we differentiate between leaf nodes and inner nodes. It is not necessary to define a distance measure for root nodes as they match by definition.

Leaves of both trees represent either minima or maxima and, thus, isolated critical points. For the distance metric of leaves, the spatial position $\mathbf{x}$ in the scalar field and the function value $f(\mathbf{x}) = f(\mathbf{x}, t, p)$ are taken into account. Hence, the distance $\delta_L(i, j)$ of two leaves i and j can be defined as the weighted sum of the Euclidean distance

$$\delta_{L_1}(i, j) = ||\boldsymbol{x}_i - \boldsymbol{x}_j||$$

and the difference in function values

$$\delta_{L_2}(i, j) = |f(\boldsymbol{x}_i) - f(\boldsymbol{x}_j)|,$$

where both terms are normalized.

The distance for the inner nodes i and j is based on the corresponding spatial region in the field, their position, and on the matches of the leaves of the subtrees S_i and S_j. The single distance measures are combined in a weighted sum, where the weights can be adjusted to increase the influence of individual aspects. Each spatial point x_i associated with an inner node i is surrounded by a connected component R_i. In the merge tree, the region R_i contains all spatial points having lower (or equal) function values as x_i's parent node, in the split tree it contains all points with higher (or equal) values. We compute the distance of the regions $\delta_{I_1}(i, j)$ by first defining an one-sided distance between regions around nodes i and j as

$$\delta'(i, j) = \frac{\sum_{x \in R_i \setminus R_j} \min_{q \in R_j} ||x - q||_2}{|R_i|},$$

where $|| \cdot ||_2$ denotes the Euclidean distance and $| \cdot |$ the cardinality of a set of points. As we are comparing connected components, this calculations can be sped up by only considering the margins of the regions. Based on the one-sided distance metric, we can define a two-sided distance between inner nodes by weighting the one-sided distances with the cardinality of the regions. This leads to

$$\delta_{I_1}(i, j) = \frac{\delta'(i, j) \cdot |R_i| + \delta'(j, i) \cdot |R_j|}{|R_i \cup R_j|}.$$

To take into account how well the leaves in the subtrees S_i and S_j rooted in nodes i and j match, we calculate the average similarity of all possible leaf node pairs by

$$\delta_{I_2}(i, j) = \frac{\sum_{s_i \in S_i, s_j \in S_j} \delta_L(s_i, s_j)}{|S_i| \cdot |S_j|}.$$

Additionally, we assume that the inner nodes i and j would match and calculate the percentage of matched leaf nodes $\delta_{I_3}(i, j)$ in the subtrees S_i and S_j. Together with $\delta_{I_4}(i, j) = ||x_i - x_j||$ we obtain the distance for the inner nodes i and j as the weighted average of the individual distances $\delta_{I_1}(i, j), \dots, \delta_{I_4}(i, j)$.

4.2   Creation of Meta Tree

In the following, we will first describe how two (merge or split) trees T_1 and T_2 can be combined to a meta tree T. Then, we will elaborate on the further considerations necessary to add further trees to the meta tree T and describe the formation of a contour tree.

Let T_1 and T_2 be either two trees $T_{1,k}$ and $T_{2,k}$ for time steps $t_1 < t_2$ with fixed parameter value p_k or two trees $T_{j,1}$ and $T_{j,2}$ for parameter values $p_1 < p_2$ for a fixed time step t_j. If two nodes $a_1 \in T_1$ and $a_2 \in T_2$ correspond to a topological feature existing in both trees, they match and they are combined to a single node $a \in T$. If a node $b_1 \in T_1$ corresponds to disappearing feature or a node $b_2 \in T_2$ corresponds to an appearing feature, they have no matching node in the other tree and should persist in T. Consequently, the life span of a feature in the temporal dimension t or over changing parameter values p is stored in the respective node in T as well as the function values of the feature.

The meta tree T is created by traversing the trees T_1 and T_2 top-down. We start by generating the respective root node in T because the roots of T_1 and T_2 match by

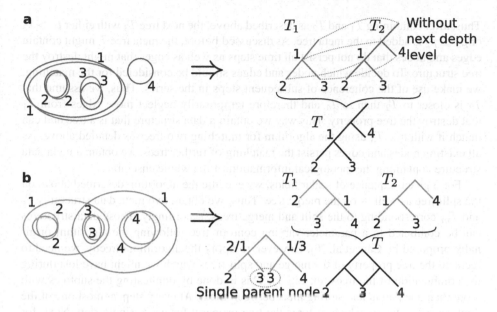

Fig. 1. Examples for combining trees T_1 and T_2 with occurring topological changes. a) Emerging isocontour 4 requires a shift to the next depth level for the subtree matching. b) Change in hierarchical order of isocontour 2 requires storage of two parents for the respective node. (Color figure online)

definition. Next, we iteratively proceed through the next depth level of the tree and use a greedy algorithm for the matching of the nodes. We use the distance metric defined in Sect. 4.1 to calculate the best match between two nodes of trees T_1 and T_2, respectively. However, the best matching node might not be on the same level. Hence, we consider the current and the subsequent depth level in T_2 for a node in T_1 and vice versa. Its necessity can be seen in Fig. 1a, where it is illustrated with the following example: A new isocontour, labeled as 4, emerges in tree T_2 when compared to tree T_1. The matching that would be found without taking the subsequent depth level into account is shown as grey dashed lines. Figure 1a illustrates that the correct matching for the meta tree T is found by shifting the red subtree T_2 one level down. As we assume coherence among subsequent steps, we assume that consecutive trees are sufficiently similar to be properly matched when we only consider the current and the next depth level. Hence, we do not proceed to higher depths level and limit the computational costs.

Another special case occurs if the hierarchical order of topological features changes. One example is depicted in Fig. 1b, where isocontour 1 is the parent node of isocontours 2 and 3 in the orange tree T_1, while isocontour 1 is the parent of isocontours 3 and 4 in the green tree T_2. To correctly combine those trees, isocontour 3 needs two parents in the combined meta tree T (shown in black). However, such a construction destroys the tree property of T which we need to handle appropriately later when creating a contour tree from the combined split and merge trees.

To combine a sequence of trees, the trees are combined iteratively, either in chronological order (if the time t is varied) or ordered depending on the parameter value p.

Thus, after combining T_1 and T_2 as described above, the next tree T_3 with either $t_3 > t_2$ or $p_3 > p_2$ is added to the meta tree. As discussed before, the meta tree T might contain edges and nodes that do not persist all time steps as well as edges that might destroy the tree structure. To decide which nodes and edges should be considered for the matching, we make use of the coherence of subsequent steps in the series. Thus, we assume that T_3 is closer to T_2 than to T_1 and therefore temporarily neglect those edges from T_1 that destroy the tree property. This way we obtain a data structure that is a tree and can match it with tree T_3 using the algorithm for matching two trees as detailed above. As all existing nodes and edges persist the matching of further trees, we obtain a meta data structure containing the topological information of the whole ensemble.

For a given sequence of scalar fields, we execute the algorithm described above on the split tree as well as on the merge tree. Thus, we obtain two meta data structures T_s and T_m corresponding to the split and merge trees, accordingly. Those data structures can be combined to a parameter-varying contour tree following the algorithm originally proposed by Carr et al. [6]. However, to apply the algorithm directly, we need to recreate the tree property of the merge and split trees which we might have lost during the combination of the trees (cf. Fig. 1). This is done by duplicating the subtrees with more than one parent and storing links between them. At every step, at most one of the duplicates is relevant which restores the tree property for every single step. Next, for every step, the split and merge trees can be joined using the original algorithm. In the resulting parameter-varying contour tree, we store all nodes of all time steps, their life spans, the respective contour tree edges, and the links between duplicates.

4.3 Visualization of Changing Landscapes

The parameter-varying contour tree contains joined topology information for all ensemble members. Therefore, we can compute the topological landscape of each ensemble member by using the original algorithm by Weber et al. [40]. Since any landscape is constructed by traversing the same meta tree, the order of extracted common topological features does not change from one landscape to another. This ensures coherency of resulting layouts and allows for their direct comparison.

Since any topological landscape is a 2D scalar-valued function, it can be naturally visualized as a heightfield. A sequence of such heightfields varying with respect to an ensemble's parameter value or time can be shown to the user as an animation. For smooth animation, we interpolate linearly between the heights of two consecutive steps. This provides smoothly changing renderings that also allow for different step sizes between the discrete parameter values as well as covering the right scaling in time if adaptive time steps have been used to generate the ensemble data. Discontinuities may occur when switching between duplicates. Since duplicates represent a change in topology, this is a feature of interest and we consider the fact that sudden changes emphasize these steps as desirable. We support visual matching of topological features by using the same color to highlight them.

Animations are helpful to analyze local topological changes, i.e., when the user focuses on the evolution of a feature of interest. However, for a global overview, animations might demand a high cognitive load. Therefore, we propose as an alternative to use a static visualization based on direct volume rendering, which better supports the global overview. Each topological landscape is transformed into a 2D texture containing the nodes' IDs at each pixel. We stack these 2D textures ordered by parameter value or time to form a 3D texture. In order to take into account different step sizes (if necessary), we again use linear interpolation between topological landscapes. The resulting 3D texture can be visualized using direct volume rendering. By choosing a suitable transfer function, we can assign a unique color to each specific node. For example, we can choose a categorical transfer function following the approach by Weber et al. [40]. The transfer function can be interactively adjusted, which allows for, e.g., accentuating the highest peaks or peaks with a height that lies in a certain range.

5 Results

To show the applicability of our algorithm, we validate it using a synthetic dataset and after that use it to analyze 2D data as well as 3D data.

5.1 Synthetic Data

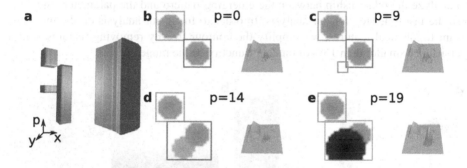

Fig. 2. Validation of our approach using synthetic dataset. (a) Volume rendering of stacked topological landscapes. The x- and y-axes represent the spatial dimensions of the landscapes, while the third dimension reflects parameter p. The green feature persists over the whole parameter range, while the blue one appears at a higher parameter value, then merges with the orange feature, and eventually takes over the orange feature. (b–e) Visualizations of given 2D scalar field using a grayscale color map (left) and the corresponding topological landscapes (right) for four different parameter values. The visualizations show the different phases of topological structures when traversing the parameter space. (Color figure online)

We validate our approach by creating a synthetic 2D dataset that varies over time and depends on one parameter p. The ensemble consists of 20 runs which have 15 times steps each. Each scalar field has a spatial dimension of 30×30 samples over a uniform quadrilateral grid. For $p = 0$, the dataset contains two peaks. Increasing the parameter causes a third peak to emerge and overlap with one of the other peaks. The peaks appear and grow over time. As our main goal here is to study the changes in topology over the variation of p, we use only the last time step. To avoid noise introduced by the creation of the Morse functions, we simplify the landscapes by only keeping features with a persistence larger than 3. The results are shown in Fig. 2. The volume rendering of the stacked landscapes gives a correct overview of the topological changes in the dataset, see Fig. 2a. It can be observed that the green peak persists for all parameter values. The orange peak is the only other peak that is also present for small values of p, which is also shown in Fig. 2b in the form of a greyscale 2D scalar field visualization (left) and the respective topological landscape (right). The blue peak emerges as a separate peak first, as can be seen in the landscape in Fig. 2c. When the parameter value increases further, the blue peak joins the orange peak which causes the blue one to disappear in the stacked visualization and can be seen in Fig. 2d. After a certain parameter range, the blue peak gets higher than the orange one as shown in Fig. 2e. This causes the blue peak to take over the orange one, i.e., the orange peak vanishes and the blue peak reappears.

5.2   Pattern Formation in 2D

We test our algorithm on 2D simulation data ensemble, which is the solution to the Swift-Hohenberg equation describing pattern formation processes. The ensemble consists of 25 time-dependent runs, which differ in one simulation parameter b with values varying between 7.5 and 9.0 in adaptive steps between 0.01 and 0.1. Because we want to analyze the relationship between the emerging pattern and the parameter value, we use the last time step for our analysis. In order to focus our analysis on the most relevant topological features, we simplify the contour tree by removing features with a persistence smaller than 15% of the total function value range.

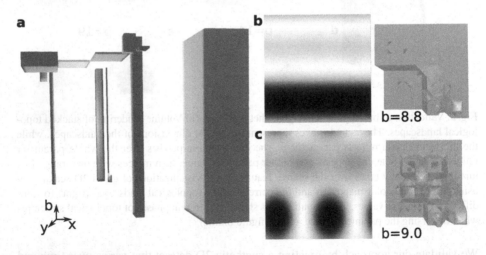

Fig. 3. Analysis of 2D pattern formation simulation ensemble depending on parameter b. (a) Volume rendering of stacked topological landscapes. The x- and y-axes represent the spatial dimensions of the landscapes, while the third dimension reflects parameter b. Some topological features persist for the whole parameter range, while others emerge only for high parameter values. (b, c) Visualizations of the 2D pattern formation scalar field using a luminance color map (left) and the corresponding topological landscapes (right) for two different parameter values. The emerging of additional topological features for higher parameter values corresponds to a change in the pattern.

The visualization of stacked landscapes shown in Fig. 3a demonstrates that some topological features persist over a wide range of parameter values. For higher values of b, new features appear. These changes in topology correspond to changes in the pattern. As further features emerge for higher values, we notice that the pattern gets more complex. A comparison to the scalar fields reveals that we can observe a stripe pattern for smaller parameter values (cf. Fig. 3b), while it changes to spots for higher parameter values, as can be seen in Fig. 3c.

5.3   Cavity Flow in 3D

We also apply our algorithm to an ensemble of 3D simulations describing the lid-driven cavity flow. The ensemble contains 10 simulation runs with different Reynolds numbers Re and 99 time steps each. Each scalar field contains the magnitude of the velocity. For all calculations using this data set, we remove noise by simplifying the data to only keep features with a persistence larger than 1% of the total value range.

We analyze the parameter dependence of the simulation outcome based on the last time step. The results for selected parameter values are shown in Fig. 4. We can observe an increase in the number of mountains in the topological landscapes with an increase of the Reynolds number while other features are existent for every simulation run. This fulfills our expectations, because for larger Reynolds numbers the flow is less laminar and, thus, additional topological structures emerge.

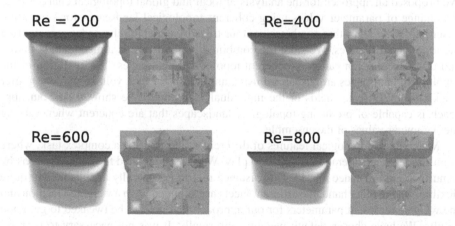

Fig. 4. 3D lid-driven cavity flow simulation ensemble for varying Reynolds numbers (Re): Comparison of last time steps for four different Reynolds numbers by showing a direct volume rendering of the given 3D scalar fields (left) and the corresponding topological landscapes (right), where the landscapes are coherent over the variation of the parameter values. Some topological features exist in all simulation results (e.g., the dark yellow mountain in the topological landscapes), while, in general, the number of topological features increases. (Color figure online)

We also investigate the temporal evolution of the run having Reynolds number of Re = 1000. We can see that some of the topological features persist after they emerged in the beginning. An early time step with few features is shown in Fig. 5a. Over time, further features emerge and vanish until we reach a more complex state as shown in Fig. 5b. Comparing this step to the one shown in Fig. 5a, we see that the three peaks from the beginning persist over time.

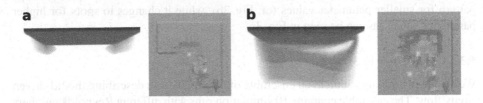

Fig. 5. Analysis of temporal changes for 3D lid-driven cavity flow simulation: (a) After 10 time steps, we see the beginning of the formation of some flow features in the direct volume rendering of the given 3D scalar field (left), which causes the first mountains in the topological landscape to appear (right). (b) At the end of the simulation, the field (left) as well as the topological landscape (right) become more complex, while some initial peaks persist.

6 Conclusion and Discussion

We proposed an approach for the analysis of local and global topological changes over the change of parameter values using coherent topological landscapes for simulation ensembles. The algorithm combines contour trees by matching the nodes representing the topological features. We store the combined contour tree as a meta data structure and use it for the generation of coherent topological landscapes. The evolution of the topological landscapes are visualized using animations or by a volume rendering after stacking the 2D scalar fields of the individual landscapes. We showed that our approach is capable of producing topological landscapes that are coherent when varying the parameter values of the ensemble.

Matching of topological features of different scalar fields is a complex task, where a multitude of considerations come into play. We have integrated the considerations by a multi-faceted distance metric. This distance metric is generally applicable and quite flexible. On the other hand, the different facets are summed up in a weighted fashion and the weights represent parameters for our approach that need to be tweaked to get good results. We have chosen default weights empirically. It was not necessary to perform an extensive parameter tweaking for generating the results presented in this paper, but the role of the different facets of the metric is subject to further investigations in future research.

As discussed in Sect. 4.2, our visualizations introduce sudden changes when a topological feature changes its parent node. We consider this desirable, as such changes shall draw the attention of the analyst. However, one may also argue that the underlying scalar fields do not change suddenly and that the sudden changes in the visualization are, therefore, not desired. In future work, we want to consider ways of avoiding the sudden changes.

The computation times of the current implementation of the generation of the meta tree is in the range of some seconds to a few minutes for the data analyzed in this work. However, this can be considered a pre-processing step to the actual analysis, which can then be performed interactively. Still, there are several ideas of speeding up the meta tree generation. In particular, currently, the new scalar fields are added consecutively one by one. Strategies for performing multiple contour tree joining operations in parallel would surely improve the computational efficiency.

Our approach allows for the analysis of ensembles of simulation runs that vary with respect to a simulation parameter. If a simulation model depends on multiple parameters, we can investigate the parameters with the existing tool one at a time. For future work, it would be desirable to look into how we can investigate multiple parameters simultaneously, including their interplay. This includes the case, where time is considered as a parameter, i.e., we would like to investigate the topological changes with changing parameter values and over time simultaneously. In the current tool, either time or the parameter value is fixed to analyze the ensemble.

Acknowledgements. This work was supported in part by DFG grants MO 3050/2-1 and LI 1530/21-2.

References

1. Beketayev, K., Weber, G.H., Morozov, D., Abzhanov, A., Hamann, B.: Geometry-preserving topological landscapes. In: Proceedings of the Workshop at SIGGRAPH Asia, pp. 155–160 (2012). https://doi.org/10.1145/2425296.2425324
2. Berger, W., Piringer, H., Filzmoser, P., Gröller, E.: Uncertainty-aware exploration of continuous parameter spaces using multivariate prediction. In: Computer Graphics Forum, vol. 30, no. 3, pp. 911–920 (2011). https://doi.org/10.1111/j.1467-8659.2011.01940.x
3. Bremer, P., Weber, G., Pascucci, V., Day, M., Bell, J.: Analyzing and tracking burning structures in lean premixed hydrogen flames. IEEE Trans. Vis. Comput. Graph. **16**(2), 248–260 (2010). https://doi.org/10.1109/TVCG.2009.69
4. Bruckner, S., Möller, T.: Isosurface similarity maps. In: Computer Graphics Forum, vol. 29, no. 3, pp. 773–782 (2010). https://doi.org/10.1111/j.1467-8659.2009.01689.x
5. Bruckner, S., Möller, T.: Result-driven exploration of simulation parameter spaces for visual effects design. IEEE Trans. Vis. Comput. Graph. **16**(6), 1468–1476 (2010). https://doi.org/10.1109/tvcg.2010.190
6. Carr, H., Snoeyink, J., Axen, U.: Computing contour trees in all dimensions. Comput. Geom. **24**(2), 75–94 (2003). https://doi.org/10.1016/S0925-7721(02)00093-7
7. Demir, D., Beketayev, K., Weber, G.H., Bremer, P.T., Pascucci, V., Hamann, B.: Topology exploration with hierarchical landscapes. In: Proceedings of the Workshop at SIGGRAPH Asia, WASA 2012, pp. 147–154. Association for Computing Machinery, New York (2012). https://doi.org/10.1145/2425296.2425323
8. Doraiswamy, H., Natarajan, V.: Computing Reeb graphs as a union of contour trees. IEEE Trans. Vis. Comput. Graph. **19**(2), 249–262 (2012). https://doi.org/10.1109/TVCG.2012.115
9. Edelsbrunner, H., Harer, J.: Persistent homology - a survey. Contemp. Math. **453**, 257–282 (2008). https://doi.org/10.1090/conm/453/08802
10. Edelsbrunner, H., Harer, J., Mascarenhas, A., Pascucci, V., Snoeyink, J.: Time-varying Reeb graphs for continuous space-time data. Comput. Geom.: Theory Appl. **41**(3), 149–166 (2008). https://doi.org/10.1016/j.comgeo.2007.11.001

11. Fofonov, A., Linsen, L.: Fast and robust isosurface similarity maps extraction using Quasi-Monte Carlo approach. In: Wilhelm, A.F.X., Kestler, H.A. (eds.) Analysis of Large and Complex Data. SCDAKO, pp. 497–506. Springer, Cham (2016). https://doi.org/10.1007/978-3-319-25226-1_42

12. Fofonov, A., Molchanov, V., Linsen, L.: Visual analysis of multi-run spatio-temporal simulations using isocontour similarity for projected views. IEEE Trans. Vis. Comput. Graph. 22(8), 2037–2050 (2016). https://doi.org/10.1109/TVCG.2015.2498554

13. Günther, D., Salmon, J., Tierny, J.: Mandatory critical points of 2D uncertain scalar fields. In: Proceedings of the 16th Eurographics Conference on Visualization, pp. 31–40. Eurographics Association, July 2014. https://doi.org/10.1111/cgf.12359

14. Gyulassy, A., Natarajan, V., Pascucci, V., Hamann, B.: Efficient computation of Morse-Smale complexes for three-dimensional scalar functions. IEEE Trans. Vis. Comput. Graph. 13(6), 1440–1447 (2007). https://doi.org/10.1109/TVCG.2007.70552

15. Hahn, H.K., Peitgen, H.O.: IWT-interactive watershed transform: a hierarchical method for efficient interactive and automated segmentation of multidimensional grayscale images. In: Proceedings of the SPIE Medical Imaging: Image Processing, vol. 5032, pp. 643–653 (2003). https://doi.org/10.1117/12.481097

16. Harvey, W., Wang, Y.: Topological landscape ensembles for visualization of scalar-valued functions. In: Computer Graphics Forum, vol. 29, no. 3, pp. 993–1002 (2010). https://doi.org/10.1111/j.1467-8659.2009.01706.x

17. Heine, C., et al.: A survey of topology-based methods in visualization. In: Computer Graphics Forum, vol. 35, no. 3, pp. 643–667 (2016). https://doi.org/10.1111/cgf.12933

18. Herick, M., Molchanov, V., Linsen, L.: Temporally coherent topological landscapes for time-varying scalar fields. In: Proceedings of the 15th International Joint Conference on Computer Vision, Imaging and Computer Graphics Theory and Applications - Volume 3: IVAPP, pp. 54–61. INSTICC, SciTePress, January 2020. https://doi.org/10.5220/0008956300540061

19. Kraus, M.: Visualization of uncertain contour trees. In: IMAGAPP/IVAPP, pp. 132–139 (2010). https://doi.org/10.5220/0002817201320139

20. van Kreveld, M., van Oostrum, R., Bajaj, C., Pascucci, V., Schikore, D.: Contour trees and small seed sets for isosurface traversal. In: Proceedings of the Thirteenth Annual Symposium on Computational Geometry, SCG 1997, pp. 212–220. Association for Computing Machinery, New York (1997). https://doi.org/10.1145/262839.269238

21. Lohfink, A.P., Wetzels, F., Lukasczyk, J., Weber, G.H., Garth, C.: Fuzzy contour trees: alignment and joint layout of multiple contour trees. In: Computer Graphics Forum, vol. 39, no. 3, pp. 343–355 (2020). https://doi.org/10.1111/cgf.13985

22. Milnor, J.: Morse theory. Ann. Math. Stud. 51 (1963)

23. Oesterling, P., Heine, C., Jänicke, H., Scheuermann, G.: Visual analysis of high dimensional point clouds using topological landscapes. In: 2010 IEEE Pacific Visualization Symposium (PacificVis), pp. 113–120 (2010). https://doi.org/10.1109/PACIFICVIS.2010.5429601

24. Oesterling, P., Heine, C., Janicke, H., Scheuermann, G., Heyer, G.: Visualization of high-dimensional point clouds using their density distribution's topology. IEEE Trans. Vis. Comput. Graph. 17(11), 1547–1559 (2011). https://doi.org/10.1109/TVCG.2011.27

25. Oesterling, P., Heine, C., Weber, G.H., Morozov, D., Scheuermann, G.: Computing and visualizing time-varying merge trees for high-dimensional data. In: Carr, H., Garth, C., Weinkauf, T. (eds.) TopoInVis 2015. MV, pp. 87–101. Springer, Cham (2017). https://doi.org/10.1007/978-3-319-44684-4_5

26. Pascucci, V., Cole-McLaughlin, K., Scorzelli, G.: Multi-resolution computation and presentation of contour trees. In: Proceedings of the IASTED Conference on Visualization, Imaging, and Image Processing, pp. 452–290 (2004)

27. Pfaffelmoser, T., Westermann, R.: Visualizing contour distributions in 2D ensemble data. In: EuroVis (Short Papers), pp. 55–59 (2013)

28. Phadke, M.N., et al.: Exploring ensemble visualization. In: Visualization and Data Analysis 2012, vol. 8294, p. 82940B. International Society for Optics and Photonics, January 2012. https://doi.org/10.1117/12.912419
29. Potter, K., et al.: Ensemble-vis: a framework for the statistical visualization of ensemble data. In: 2009 IEEE International Conference on Data Mining Workshops, pp. 233–240. IEEE (2009). https://doi.org/10.1109/ICDMW.2009.55
30. Reeb, G.: Sur les points singuliers d'une forme de pfaff completement integrable ou d'une fonction numerique [on the singular points of a completely integrable pfaff form or of a numerical function]. Comptes Rendus Acad. Sciences Paris **222**, 847–849 (1946)
31. Saikia, H., Seidel, H.P., Weinkauf, T.: Extended branch decomposition graphs: structural comparison of scalar data. In: Computer Graphics Forum, vol. 33, no. 3, pp. 41–50 (2014). https://doi.org/10.1111/cgf.12360
32. Sanyal, J., Zhang, S., Dyer, J., Mercer, A., Amburn, P., Moorhead, R.: Noodles: a tool for visualization of numerical weather model ensemble uncertainty. IEEE Trans. Vis. Comput. Graph. **16**(6), 1421–1430 (2010). https://doi.org/10.1109/TVCG.2010.181
33. Scheidegger, C.E., Schreiner, J.M., Duffy, B., Carr, H., Silva, C.T.: Revisiting histograms and isosurface statistics. IEEE Trans. Vis. Comput. Graph. **14**(6), 1659–1666 (2008). https://doi.org/10.1109/TVCG.2008.160
34. Schneider, B., Jäckle, D., Stoffel, F., Diehl, A., Fuchs, J., Keim, D.: Visual integration of data and model space in ensemble learning. IEEE (2017). https://doi.org/10.1109/VDS.2017.8573444
35. Sedlmair, M., Heinzl, C., Bruckner, S., Piringer, H., Möller, T.: Visual parameter space analysis: a conceptual framework. IEEE Trans. Vis. Comput. Graph. **20**(12), 2161–2170 (2014). https://doi.org/10.1109/tvcg.2014.2346321
36. Sohn, B.S., Bajaj, C.: Time-varying contour topology. IEEE Trans. Vis. Comput. Graph. **12**(1), 14–25 (2005). https://doi.org/10.1109/TVCG.2006.16
37. Tierny, J., Favelier, G., Levine, J.A., Gueunet, C., Michaux, M.: The topology ToolKit. IEEE Trans. Vis. Comput. Graph. **24**(1), 832–842 (2018). https://doi.org/10.1109/TVCG.2017.2743938
38. Wang, J., Hazarika, S., Li, C., Shen, H.W.: Visualization and visual analysis of ensemble data: a survey. IEEE Trans. Vis. Comput. Graph. **25**(9), 2853–2872 (2019). https://doi.org/10.1109/tvcg.2018.2853721
39. Weber, G., Bremer, P.T., Day, M., Bell, J., Pascucci, V.: Feature tracking using Reeb graphs. In: Pascucci, V., Tricoche, X., Hagen, H., Tierny, J. (eds.) Topological Methods in Data Analysis and Visualization, pp. 241–253. Springer, Heidelberg (2011). https://doi.org/10.1007/978-3-642-15014-2_20
40. Weber, G., Bremer, P.T., Pascucci, V.: Topological landscapes: a terrain metaphor for scientific data. IEEE Trans. Vis. Comput. Graph. **13**(6), 1416–1423 (2007). https://doi.org/10.1109/TVCG.2007.70601
41. Weber, G.H., Bremer, P.T., Pascucci, V.: Topological cacti: visualizing contour-based statistics. In: Peikert, R., Hauser, H., Carr, H., Fuchs, R. (eds.) Topological Methods in Data Analysis and Visualization II, pp. 63–76. Springer, Heidelberg (2012). https://doi.org/10.1007/978-3-642-23175-9_5
42. Wu, K., Zhang, S.: A contour tree based visualization for exploring data with uncertainty. Int. J. Uncertain. Quantif. **3**(3), 203–223 (2013). https://doi.org/10.1615/Int.J.UncertaintyQuantification.2012003956
43. Zhang, Y., Wang, Y., Parthasarathy, S.: Visualizing attributed graphs via terrain metaphor. In: Proceedings of the 23rd ACM SIGKDD International Conference on Knowledge Discovery and Data Mining, KDD 2017, pp. 1325–1334. Association for Computing Machinery, New York (2017). https://doi.org/10.1145/3097983.3098130

Computer Vision Theory and Applications

Efficient Range Sensing Using Imperceptible Structured Light

Avery Cole[1,2], Sheikh Ziauddin[1,2], Jonathon Malcolm[1,2],
and Michael Greenspan[1,2,3(✉)]

[1] Department of Electrical and Computer, Engineering, Queen's University,
Kingston, ON, Canada
{avery.cole,zia.uddin,j.malcolm,michael.greenspan}@queensu.ca
[2] Ingenuity Labs, Queen's University, Kingston, ON, Canada
[3] School of Computing, Queen's University, Kingston, ON, Canada

Abstract. A novel projector-camera method is presented that interleaves a sequence of pattern images in the dithering sequence of a DLP projector, in a way that the patterns are imperceptible, and can be acquired cleanly with a synchronized high speed camera. This capability enables the procam system to perform as a real-time range sensor, without affecting the appearance of the projected data. The system encodes and decodes a stream of Gray code patterns imperceptibly, and is deployed on a calibrated and stereo rectified procam system to perform depth triangulation from the extracted patterns. The bandwidth achieved imperceptibly is close to 8 million points per second using a general purpose CPU, which is comparable to perceptible commercial hardware accelerated structured light depth cameras.

Keywords: Range sensing · 3-D · Structured light · Procam

1 Introduction

The temporal multiplexing of a sequence of binary patterns is among the most established forms of *structured light depth mapping*. This method allows each image pixel to be assigned with a unique codephrase, or temporal sequence of high and low illumination, across a series of images. This encoding makes establishing correspondences between image and projector pixels (the heart of any triangulation-based range sensing method) achievable through a simple table lookup, and therefore computationally trivial.

Temporal encoding is highly accurate, dense, and robust when compared with spatial or hybrid spatio-temporal encoding methods. Temporal methods grant the ability to easily achieve pixel or sub-pixel accuracy, while spatial methods often deal in larger blocks. The high contrast of binary patterns makes decoding simple and accurate, even in scenes with varying lighting conditions and less than cooperative radiometric properties, such as non-Lambertian surface reflectance.

One challenge of temporal binary encoding methods has been that they require significantly more data than spatial methods, often resulting in lower speeds and

© Springer Nature Switzerland AG 2022
K. Bouatouch et al. (Eds.): VISIGRAPP 2020, CCIS 1474, pp. 241–267, 2022.
https://doi.org/10.1007/978-3-030-94893-1_11

poorer response to dynamic scenes. For example, a typical temporal encoding sequence requires n images to produce a resolution of 2^n along a single axis, usually necessitating $n \sim 20$ patterns total. As a result, the conventional understanding is that while temporal methods perform better than other methods with respect to depth resolution and quality, their high data transmission requirements are not suited for real-time execution. As a result, temporal methods are generally relegated to applications requiring high accuracy over static scenes, such as industrial inspection.

Recent advances in projector technology have presented an opportunity to revisit temporal encoding, with the potential to achieve high bandwidth transmission that enables real-time performance. Recent developments include using rectification to restrict correspondence to a single axis [43], parallel computing [6], and the emergence of high bandwidth digital light processing (DLP) projection engines [27,29,32]. The characteristics of these projection engines permit a higher data transmission rate, and make them amenable to the imperceptible embedding of patterns, further increasing their attractiveness for real-time applications.

One such application is *dynamic projection mapping* (*DPM*), which is a form of augmented reality (AR) wherein projected content is warped to correspond to the 3-D geometry of the scene [4,33,36,40]. Unlike screen-based systems, which tend to be single-user, DPM creates a shared experience for those present in the environment. One major challenge of DPM lies in intersecting projected content with 3-D geometry. While a projector can overlay its 2-D content over a 3-D scene, a projector is an open-loop system, which cannot be used for meaningful 3-D interaction without added sensing capacity. This capability is most often provided by including a camera, thereby creating a procam system. Adding a camera provides the potential of sensing the 3-D geometry of the scene, and closes the loop by allowing for user interaction, ideally in real-time.

Many different approaches to projection mapping, some dynamic and some static, are presented in Sect. 2. Currently, none of these methods can be used to map projected content onto dynamic scenes without major constraints. Current projection mapping systems include methods for static environments or that use prohibitively complex hardware, highly controlled environments, and/or scene fiducials to function. Some methods can achieve DPM with significant latency or a sub-real-time frame rate. Most methods involve auxiliary hardware, such as depth cameras, or infrared projectors and cameras. These systems can be quite effective, but intersecting the data from multiple systems is a complex and fragile undertaking that often introduces major constraints and adds complexity and cost to the system. The ability for a procam system to incorporate imperceptible structured light projection mapping in real-time and without extra hardware would be highly beneficial to augmented reality pursuits.

The work presented here lays a foundation for such an approach using temporally encoded structured light patterns. A platform is presented for imperceptible, continuous, real-time depth mapping using a calibrated and rectified projector-camera system. Structured light patterns are embedded imperceptibly in projected content and then extracted by a hardware synchronized camera for use in depth scanning. The depth data can then be used for projection mapping, collecting scene data, or other augmented reality pursuits.

This paper extends our earlier work from VISAPP 2020 [7]. In this version, we have made a number of enhancements over the previously published version. The current paper presents additional, distinct and more comprehensive experimental results and evaluation of the system. In particular, instead of a single background image, we have used multiple content images for imperceptible embedding of patterns and showed that the quality of the extracted depth maps was not impacted by the choice of content images. The text of the paper has also been fully rewritten: The sections and headings have been reorganized, and the proposed method as well as the past work have been explained in a greater depth. A number of new figures and tables have also been included.

The main novel contributions of this work are:

- A method of embedding imperceptible structured light patterns into a digital micromirror device (DMD) projection tool without modification to the overall luminous power of projected content. This method also facilitates the extraction of the injected patterns, which are purely binary patterns, rather than scaled greyscale patterns;
- Use of the Texas Instruments Lightcrafter engine [46] and synchronous capture for high speed insertion and recovery of temporally encoded binary patterns suitable for real-time depth extraction;
- Implementation of the method to develop a working prototype combining all software and hardware components for high-speed depth mapping.

The rest of this paper is organized as follows: Sect. 2 gives an outline of the projected augmented reality and the benefits the proposed method could bring to projected AR systems, when compared to the range of currently available methods. Section 3 provides an overview of the hardware and software components of the proposed method, focused on areas where lesser known methods are employed or novelty is presented. Section 4 presents the experimental characterization of the proposed method including the implementation details, hardware listing, demonstration of the method and validation of data. Finally, Sect. 5 concludes the paper by outlining limitations of the proposed system and specifying potential future enhancements in the system.

2   Related Work

A projector is an excellent augmented reality platform by virtue of its capacity to serve as an intersection between the real and virtual worlds and its capacity to be modified in real-time. These characteristics free this technology from the limited area of screen-based AR methods, such as Pokemon GO [2], Snapchat [44] and face swap [47], which require the user to direct their visual attention towards a monitor. Furthermore, projector-based AR does not require wearables, nor is it limited to a single user like currently available holographic AR methods (examples include Google Glass [31], Microsoft's HoloLens [8], Epson's Moverio [9]). For these reasons, data projectors are emerging as the ideal display device for shared, immersive AR experiences.

Projected augmented reality is most commonly seen in consumer entertainment displays such as Touchmagix [37], Brightlink [34], and ARPool [17]. While these systems differ in purpose and execution, the general principle is similar. Each of these systems project content onto a flat surface and use vision sensors to track the user and scene, and modify the projected content accordingly. The choice of sensor differs between these systems: Touchmagix uses range sensing cameras, Brightlink uses a light field generator, and ARPool uses monocular vision. Despite the differences in sensing hardware, all of these systems use the projector in a similar way, i.e. purely as a display device to project dynamic content onto a planar surface.

2.1 Projection Mapping Methods

All projection mapping systems employ a variation of a *sense-compute-display* loop to alter the appearance of projected content according to conditions in the scene. Differences between the various approaches derive from certain assumptions about the environment. Some methods for example assume that the elements in the scene are static, whereas others admit dynamic elements, albeit often with limited motion and other contraints. Yet other methods make use of auxilliary sensors, beyond the primary vision sensor, to detect conditions in the scene.

Static Projection Mapping. The most common projection mapping method is *planar keystone adjustment* [1], which involves transforming the projection plane to be parallel to the projection surface. Almost all commercial projectors provide an interface for manual keystone adjustment, which allows the user to adjust the projection plane in either two or four horizontal and vertical directions to align the projection plane with the scene's planar projection surface. Many projectors also feature automatic keystone adjustment, which is enabled by the assumption that the scene's projection surface is vertical. A gravity acceleration sensor detects the projector's pose relative to gravity, and keystone adjustments are automatically deployed to compensate the projector's tilt. The major disadvantage of this technique is that the modulation transformation has to be determined prior to projection and the system must be recalibrated if changes to the scene occur. The increased complexity and precision required in procam systems usually necessitates a more precise method. Procam keystone systems work by detecting and correcting 2D homographies among three planar surfaces: the camera image, the projector image and the screen [26].

Dynamic Projection Mapping with Constrained Environments. In certain scenarios, the problem of identifying scene geometry can be either greatly simplified, or avoided entirely. Panasonic's real-time tracking demonstration using a large wearable sensor is a visually impressive example of precise, low-latency projection mapping [36]. Their results are achieved by using a large wearable sensor that provides an easily trackable anchor. The projection is centered on this point and constructed to match the subject's physical geometry. This approach, however, is not a general solution to the projection mapping problem. Raskar et al. [39] used projection mapping to animate real scene objects by manually creating a virtual model of the objects. They then reduced the problem to simply registering the object's pose with its virtual counterpart. Bandyopadhyay et al. [4] furthered this method by fusing several projectors to alleviate shadowing, as well as adding another predefined trackable real object (a stylus) to facilitate interaction between the user and the virtual model. Both groups, however, reported limitations in accuracy when matching the virtual to the physical models.

In recent years, the identification of scene geometry has been facilitated by the advent of 3-D printing. Resch et al. [40] presented a new take on shader lamps by leveraging precisely matched virtual and 3-D printed models to great effect. They start by an initial exact pose estimation of the object using projected structured light, followed by a frame-by-frame tracking which is done by matching correspondences between the captured camera image and a virtual camera view based on the current pose prediction. For each frame, a transformation is obtained using Iterative Closest Point (*ICP*) registration, which serves as the pose prediction for the next frame. While these methods do achieve DPM, they are constrained to a single object, which restricts their utility.

Biometric tracking is another approach that reduces the complexity of the mapping problem through approximate knowledge of the tracked scene surface, typically a human face. Examples include the Hypermask [30], which is a white mask worn by an actor that is used as a fixed surface to project facial animations, and techniques that extend biometric projection mapping to the tracking and display of deformable animatronic and real faces [5,19]. These methods make for interesting demonstrations but are constrained to a specific projection environment, and experience significant visible latency due to processing complexity.

Scene fiducial markers are another common way to simplify projection mapping. Lee et al. [25] created a virtual model of a foldable screen and embedded infrared retro-reflectors that, when combined with an infrared illumination source and camera, allowed for simple and accurate registration of the real object's pose. Kagasmi and Hashimoto [22] and Narita et al. [33] proposed similar methods of using infrared-reflective ink with infrared illumination to create a projection surface that can be precisely tracked through complex deformations in real-time. While the use of invisible ink can be effective at facilitating real-time tracking, and lessens the constraint of using pre-defined and prepared objects as projection surfaces, it does not remove this constraint which limits the generality of this approach to DPM.

Auxiliary Projection Mapping. The most common way to achieve non-constrained general projection mapping is through the addition of auxiliary sensors. By auxiliary sensors, we mean the external sensors that are not integrated with the system. These sensors can be used to create a model of the projection scene, which can then be used similarly to the above methods to map projection. Recently, the near-ubiquitous method of scene mapping has been the Kinect V2 [49], which is a time-of-flight sensor that measures the time it takes reflected light to return to the sensor to determine depth.

Packaged depth mapping systems also exist based on structured light. The Zivid One [42] uses visible structured light for depth extraction. The Kinect V1 [49], on the other hand, employs proprietary infrared pattern sequences to achieve imperceptible depth sensing. These systems, and others like them, are able to extract dense and accurate scene maps. However, their drawback is their relatively slow acquisition speed. Despite being deployed on finely tuned custom system-on-a-chip platforms, none of these systems has a capture rate greater than 30 Hz.

For higher speed capture, stereovision systems can be quite effective. The Intel Realsense D435 [20] and the Leap Motion [28] are both stereovision systems: Using two parallel cameras, they capture scene images and compare the disparity of certain keypoints to extract depth. These platforms operate at 90 and 200 Hz, respectively.

However, their visible spectrum operation means projected content can significantly interfere with their operation. In addition, they inherit the fundamental limitation of stereovision, i.e. they do not work well for scenes lacking sufficient texture.

All of the above methods suffer from a fundamental limitation, which is their ability to deliver the extracted data stream for effective real-time processing. A self-contained consumer-available auxiliary sensor usually delivers data over USB, creating a significant bottleneck and precluding their use in high speed capture systems. A method that works inline with a procam system could relieve this bottleneck and significantly improve system responsiveness.

2.2 Structured Light Projection Mapping

Many varieties of structured light procam range sensors have been implemented, all of which aim to efficiently and accurately establish point correspondences between the camera and projector to extract disparities. The first such examples began in the late 1980s with work such as Agin's computer description of curved objects [3] and movable light-stripe sensor [16]. These methods employed simple stripes of illumination for maximum contrast and simple correspondence and disparity determination. Also referred to as coded light, as methods evolved and computing power increased, the bandwidth and precision of active structured light methods improved.

Many variations of and alternatives to binary stripe patterns have been proposed. These methods, some of which employed non-binary structured light, are well-suited for a wide range of problems, but have the fundamental limitation that they require dominion over the visible light spectrum, and so are difficult to implement alongside projected content. Non-binary visible spectrum methods are also limited to the rate at which patterns can be projected, generally 120 Hz. Due to these limitations, these methods will not be further considered here, although Sagawa et al. provide an excellent review [41].

An exception to this bandwidth limitation was presented by Narasimhan et al. [32] and McDowall et al. [29]. Both of these groups created dense, high-speed projection mapping tools by heavily modifying DLP projectors. They both removed the colour filters of these projectors, enabling the projection of 8-bit patterns at three times standard speeds, albeit with only greyscale content. These modifications of course rendered the projectors unsuitable for normal use, and pattern imperceptibility was not considered.

Sagawa et al. [41] also presented a unique structured light method using planar intersections to reconstruct depth with a single binary grid pattern. This method, however, is too computationally expensive for real-time operation, although high frame rate range video segments were demonstrated by capturing a series of projected patterns and then processing the entire sequence offline afterwards.

A recent advance in active binary structured light is Zhang's defocused fringe projection method [27]. This system uses a Lightcrafter engine to display binary stripe patterns at high speeds and a defocused projector lens to create a greyscale fringe pattern shifting sinusoidally from black to white. Frequency transforms are performed on the recovered patterns, and detected alterations to the expected frequencies are then used to recover depth and reconstruct scene geometry. The Lightcrafter engine can project binary patterns at over 9000 Hz, and the defocused projector increases the encoding bandwidth of each pattern from binary (i.e. 2) to the full range of camera intensity levels (usually 256). This method results in an extremely effective single-shot structured light range sensing system. The requirement to defocus the projector lens, however, renders the system unsuitable for regular content projection, and operation within the visible spectrum means that there is no obvious way to add a secondary projector.

Imperceptible Structured Light. The majority of the above-described methods suffer from at least one of two limitations: They either employ external sensors and must be processed and translated into projector coordinates [42,49], or they are perceptible and cannot operate concurrently with normal projection [27,29,32]. A few methods that are free of these limitations can perform projection mapping on a procam system without compromising its normal projection capabilities [18,35,38,45]. The earliest work to describe continuous imperceptible dynamic projection mapping was Raskar et al.'s Office of the Future [38]. They described the use of imperceptible structured light throughout the workspace for AR applications, and they concluded that the idea was sound, but that computational resources at the time were not sufficient.

Their method of embedding patterns used *flicker fusion* [38], in which two distinct frames of luminous powers A and B respectively are modified to detect a single encoded pattern P. The pattern is multiplied by a weighting factor δ and subtracted from A (Eq. 1) and added to B (Eq. 2). This results in no net change to the luminous intensity $A + B$ over the total period (Eq. 3). A synchronized camera can then be used to capture frame A_p (and/or B_p), from which pattern P can then be extracted. These modifications to the projected content A and B become imperceptible if δ is small, and if the total exposure period is sufficiently short so that its corresponding frame rate is over a certain threshold, effectively allowing the human visual system to integrate and therefore negate the subtraction and addition of δP over two consecutive frames. The frame rate to facilitate this effect has been suggested to be as low as 60 Hz [38], and the pattern becomes more imperceptible as the frame rate increases.

$$A_p = A - \delta P \tag{1}$$

$$B_p = B + \delta P \tag{2}$$

$$\overline{A_p + B_p = A + B} \tag{3}$$

Flicker fusion allows virtually imperceptible pattern embedding at half the projector's refresh rate, resolving to 60 patterns per second on a standard 120 Hz projector. Several works have presented similar methods, iterating on the flicker fusion method to improve its effectiveness in varying light and noisy conditions [18,35,45], and a related approach has found footing as an imperceptible anti-piracy watermarking method [15]. None of these methods, however, are designed to increase the operating rate over 60 structured light patterns per second. In addition, selection of the weighting factor δ is also a limitation of flicker fusion-based techniques. Smaller values of δ can make it difficult to detect the pattern and hence lead to noisy depth extraction. On the other hand, larger values of δ result in making the pattern perceptible. This is in contrast to our approach. Instead of modifying the contents of two consecutive frames by adding or subtracting a weighted pattern, we use the Lightcrafter engine's capability to allow the patterns to be exposed for a fraction of a single frame's exposure time. As a result, our system effectively uses a binary δ (0 or 255) by enabling flicker fusion between each individual content frame and embedded pattern. This makes our system more robust against noise. Further details of our imperceptible pattern injection method are presented in Sect. 3.2.

The most significant contribution to high bandwidth imperceptible methods since Raskar's work has been that of Cotting et al. [10], who recognized the potential for exploiting DLP dithering for high-speed pattern embedding. Cotting's method identified the dithering sequences that are proprietary to each family of DLP projector, and leveraged these sequences to embed patterns. Using photodiode circuits, they were able to reconstruct these dithering sequences and isolate a small fraction of the dithering period as their region of interest, which they called the *binary image exposure period* (*BIEP*). Next, they precisely adjusted each pixel of each projected content frame so the light levels during the BIEP encoded the desired pattern. The patterns were then extracted using a hardware-synchronized camera set to capture a single frame during each BIEP. In this way they successfully embedded and extracted patterns, and provided a strong proof of concept. Their method was however somewhat restricted by technology, as the projected content was modified only perceptibly, and the extracted patterns were not free from noise and therefore suffered from distortions.

Since Cotting's work, the major contributions to imperceptible structured light depth mapping have been from Dai and Chung [11, 12], who considered the registration of known objects (such as head or hand tracking, or planar homography mapping) through a sparse point set collected by imperceptible structured light. Jo et al. [21] applied many of the principles of imperceptible content embedding to LCD monitors, and gained the ability to embed and extract data imperceptibly. Their system can be used for various user interface applications such as advertising and tagging objects in museums. Their use of on/off keying and hardware synchronization strongly paralleled the works of Dai and Chung [11, 12], although their use of monitors rather than data projectors removed all geometric considerations that come with structured light projection.

The contributions of the various methods to dynamic projection mapping have been summarized based on the four criteria in Table 1. It can be seen that the method proposed here is the only method that satisfies all four design criteria.

3   Proposed System

The architecture of the proposed system is displayed in Fig. 1. The top block in the architecture diagram shows the pattern generation, projection, capture, and recovery sequence hardware elements, while the bottom block displays different components of the software processing to reconstruct scene depth for projection mapping. Note that the projection mapping component is shown by a dashed box which is to indicate that the proposed system, in its current state, does not perform projection mapping. This is due to the Lightcrafter 6500 engine's inability to dynamically modify projected content. The issue can be addressed in the future upgrades without compromising the key functionality of the system.

The complete pipeline of using structured light patterns to generate disparity is shown in Fig. 2. Patterns were encoded into the image, and then projected onto the scene and captured. Captured images were then filtered into binary patterns. Finally, rectification transforms were performed on both the filtered camera images and the original

Table 1. Summary of previous methods.

	Imperceptible pattern embedding	Dense point cloud	No additional Hardware	Non-planar Scene
Raskar [38]	✓	✗	✓	✓
Zhang [27]	✗	✓	✗	✓
Nayar [21]	✓	✓	✓	✗
Macdowall [29]	✗	✓	✗	✓
Narasimhan [32]	✗	✓	✗	✓
Dai [11, 12]	✗	✗	✓	✓
Kawasaki [41]	✗	✓	✗	✓
Kinect 2 [49]	✓	✓	✗	✓
Zivid One [42]	✗	✓	✗	✓
Proposed method	✓	✓	✓	✓

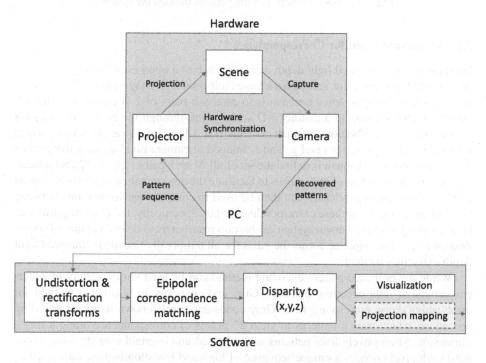

Fig. 1. Proposed system architecture.

pattern. These transformed patterns were then used to establish correspondences with and generate disparity, which was then transformed to 3-D point data using the procam system's calibration parameters. Details of these steps are presented in the following sections.

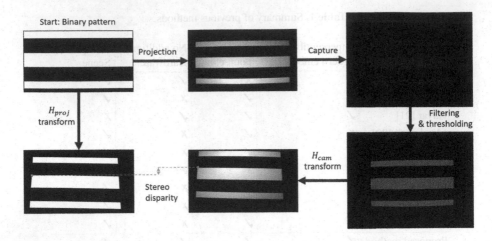

Fig. 2. Pipeline of structured light patterns through the system.

3.1 Structured Light for Correspondence

Fundamentally, structured light depth extraction is based upon establishing correspondences. Both the projector and camera have their own 2-D image planes. The goal of the so-called *correspondence problem* is to establish pairs of 2-D points, one in each plane, which both map to a distinct 3-D scene point, through the projective mapping of each device's calibration parameters. Thus if a 3-D point P_i on the scene surface is illuminated by projector pixel p_i and is imaged at camera pixel q_i, then the goal of the correspondence problem is to find the set of all N such pairs $\{(p_i, q_i)\}_1^N$. Structured light methods are a class of approaches to facilitate the determination of such correspondences. These correspondences can then be used to compute transformations between the 2-D image planes at these corresponding points. Specifically, the pixel disparity can be used along with the known system calibration parameters to determine the 3-D coordinates of P_i. This pipeline forms the basis for all temporally encoded structured light depth extraction methods.

While the proposed pattern encoding method can be used with a variety of different structured light encoding methods, Gray code patterns are a reliable method for establishing dense correspondences. Gray codes are a well-known temporal encoding procedure, which uses n patterns to yield 2^n points of correspondence along a single dimension. Successively finer patterns are projected and overlaid over the same scene until each pixel encodes a unique sequence of high and low illumination values across the image series; this sequence is called a *codephrase*. The locations of the transitions between adjacent codephrases in each image plane are taken as correspondences. Gray code patterns have the desirable property that each adjacent set of codephrases differ by exactly one bit in the temporal sequence. This is in contrast to the binary codes. For example, the binary codes for the decimals 7 (0111) and 8 (1000) differ by all four bits whereas the corresponding Gray codes (0100 and 1100) differ by one bit only so detecting a single bit error using Gray codes is much more efficient than that for binary codes. In our pattern encoding method, we find Hamming distance between adjacent codephrases, and if it is not equal to one, this indicates an error in our reading and we exclude that point from correspondence matching, as it would otherwise result in erroneous correspondence. This significantly reduced noise in the generated point cloud.

Temporally encoded structured light methods are quite effective at establishing correspondences between the projector and image place and ultimately extracting dense depth. Once the codephrase has been identified for a given image pixel, determining its corresponding projector pixel is accomplished through a simple table lookup, which is a constant-time operation, or just $O(N)$ to establish all N correspondences. Despite the computational efficiency of establishing correspondences, temporal encoding methods have seen limited use in real-time and dynamic applications due to their requiring a series of images of a scene to produce a single depth image frame. For Gray codes in particular, the standard method of categorizing each pixel in both the X and Y directions at full 1080p (i.e. 1920 × 1080) resolution requires at least $ceil(log_2(1920)) + ceil(log_2(1080)) = 22$ patterns, as well as ideally an additional all-white and all-black frame for each sequence, for radiometric calibration. To embed the patterns imperceptibly, the flicker fusion method can be used to project this full sequence of 24 patterns at a rate of 2.5 Hz, for a 120 Hz projected frame rate. The reverse-engineered dithering embedding method presented by Cotting et al. [10], can embed a pattern in each frame to display the sequence 5 Hz on the same platform.

The proposed method has allowed a further increase of operating speed by reducing the number of patterns at the expense of resolution along the X and Y axes, as discussed below in Sect. 3.4. The pattern count was further halved by using stereo rectification, which is used so only horizontal (or alternately vertical) Gray code patterns need be projected. This method requires only nine patterns, resulting in a rate of 6.7 Hz, which is a 62% speed-up.

While this rate increase was an improvement, it alone did not achieve real-time rates. The Lightcrafter engine's ability to embed patterns in each content frame colour channel was used to further increase this rate to 26.8 Hz. The Lightcrafter engine allows fine control of the projection period for both binary patterns and 8-bit dithered images in colour. Binary and 8-bit patterns can be exposed for a minimum of 105 μs and 4046 μs respectively, resulting in a total exposure time of 4151 μs for each pattern. For a sequence of 9 patterns, this exposure period corresponds to 26.8 depth frames per second. This rate is slightly below the 30 Hz threshold proposed as the lower bound for real-time operation, but is close enough to demonstrate the principle and potential of the method, and is expected to improve directly with anticipated future increases in hardware processing rates, as discussed in Sect. 4.6.

3.2 Imperceptible Pattern Injection

The relationship between luminous intensity and human visual perception is complex and not completely well-understood. What is apparent is that injected artifacts (such as binary patterns) are easier to notice the greater their deviation from the average background luminous intensity. It is generally accepted that the frame rate at which humans fail to perceive an embedded frame is between 200 and 500 Hz, depending on the exact nature of the frame and the viewer [23]. For example, a bright, high-contrast chessboard pattern interspersed among a dark, still image may be visible at or 500 Hz, while a more subtle, lower contrast pattern in a noisy and/or dynamic image may only become visible below 200 Hz.

Falling below the above rate is the flicker fusion threshold presented in Sect. 2. The flicker fusion method suffers from the fact that two full frames are needed for a single pattern. This constraint limits the pattern embedding rate to half the projection rate, usually 60 Hz. To achieve an improved operating speed, efforts have been made to exploit the aforementioned DLP dithering to embed patterns more frequently. Previous work has involved reverse engineering the proprietary dithering sequences of commercial DMDs, and to leverage that knowledge to embed data [10,35,38]. Such efforts have proved challenging, however, and have not entered widespread use. In commercial projectors, the dithering patterns are complex proprietary sequences, and identifying and exploiting them is imprecise.

The Lightcrafter engine used in this work allows for the circumvention of this issue due to full fine control of the DMD at its maximum functional speed. This capability allows exposing binary patterns for a minimum of 105 μs, corresponding to a refresh rate of >9500 Hz, which is much faster than the standard DLP refresh rate of 120 Hz and allows for the simple and consistent high-speed display of structured light patterns. This functionality can be combined with standard 8-bit dithered projection to achieve increased performance over previous pattern embedding methods. Whereas these methods have involved modifying projected frames so desired binary patterns would be exposed over some identifiable period, the Lightcrafter allows these patterns to be placed as desired, with minimal effect on the projected content. This embedding is achieved by exploiting the human eye as a continuous integrator, such that binary patterns displayed for a short enough time are imperceptible. These patterns are extracted using a hardware-synchronized camera as described in Sect. 4.1 below.

While previous methods used flicker fusion between two consecutive modified content frames, the Lightcrafter engine enabled flicker fusion between each individual content frame and embedded pattern. To illustrate, consider a projected content slide that will display luminous power I over time period T. Over this period, the human eye will expect to see total luminous intensity TI. An embedded pattern of intensity I_p will be exposed over time period $T_p \ll T$. To render this pattern imperceptible, a new content slide I_c is created such that:

$$I_c = \frac{TI - T_p I_p}{T - T_p} \tag{4}$$

The exposure periods for I_c and I_p are set as follows:

$$TI' = (T - T_p)I_c + T_p I_p \tag{5}$$

Thus, the new total amount of light TI' over both slides is as follows:

$$TI' = (T - T_p)(\frac{TI - T_p I_p}{T - T_p}) + T_p I_p = TI \tag{6}$$

so that the total luminous intensity is unchanged.

Empirical testing has led to the observation that a value of $T_p = 105$ μs with a frame rate of 200 Hz results in no perceptible change to projected content, while slight artifacts begin to appear as $T_p > 200$ μs. As the camera we use (PointGrey Blackfly S) is capable of capturing a sequence of patterns at the minimum exposure time of $T_p = 105$ μs, methods to further increase exposure periods were not pursued.

The Lightcrafter engine projects colour by consecutively alternating coloured LED sources. As a result, separate and distinct patterns could be embedded imperceptibly in each colour channel, yielding three embedded patterns per frame. Exemplar modified colour channels are displayed in Fig. 3. The top row ((a)–(c)) displays the colour channels I_c, and the second row ((d)–(f)) displays the corresponding patterns I_p. The summation of the total luminous power of all three channels and patterns is equal to the bottom image I (g) over the same time period $3T$.

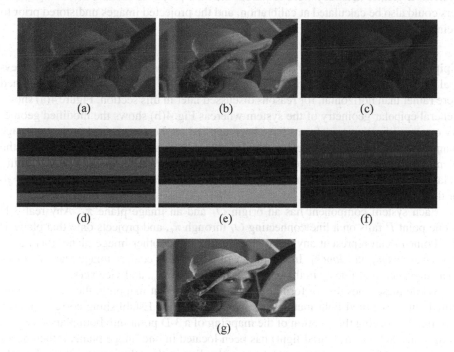

(a)   (b)   (c)

(d)   (e)   (f)

(g)

Fig. 3. Illustration of the pattern embedding method described in Eqs. 4–6; (a)–(c) I_c components, exposed for $T - T_p = 4895$ μs; (d)–(f) I_p components, exposed for $T_p = 105$ μs; (g) All components added, exposed for $3T = 1500$ μs.

3.3 Undistortion and Rectification

Once patterns were successfully embedded and extracted, they had to be processed into a depth map. The first step was to filter, undistort and rectify the images to enable correspondence mapping.

Filtering was a simple binary threshold operation designed to identify the illuminated pixels. The all-white luminous calibration frame was used to determine the threshold. We chose not to use the all-black frame, however, for reasons discussed in Sect. 3.4. Filtering erred strongly on the side of false negatives, as opposed to false positives, because false positives create erroneous correspondences, while each false negative simply reduced the resolution of the frame by a single point.

In this context, *distortion* refers to radial warping of the captured images due to the non-linearities of the camera lens. To undistort, Zhang's well-known method [48] was used to perform intrinsic calibration on the camera. The calculated camera intrinsic parameters were then used to radially undistort each captured image, effectively linearizing the camera's coordinate reference frame. For the projected image, though, we assume that it is not subjected to any radial distortion, which is a valid assumption for the optics of DMD projectors [38], within the accuracy requirements of the proposed system. If greater accuracy were required, then the projector radial distortion parameters could also be calculated at calibration, and the projected images undistored prior to being projected.

Epipolar Geometry. Figure 4 displays the setup of our procam system along with several important geometric entities. The projector and the camera are vertically aligned here rather than horizontal, for reasons discussed later in this section. Figure 4(a) shows general epipolar geometry of the system whereas Fig. 4(b) shows the modified geometry once rectification transforms have been applied on the camera and projector image planes. Here B represents the baseline of the procam system and π_e represents the plane formed by the points P, O_c, O_p, called the *epipolar plane*. Each geometric entity is labelled with a system component $t \in \{p, c\}$ to represent either the projector ($t = p$) or the camera ($t = c$).

Each system component has an origin O_t and an image plane π_t. Any real 3-D scene point P falls on a line connecting O_t through π_t, and projects onto that plane as P_t. Point P_t can represent any point along a line in the other image plane; this line is known as an *epipolar line* e_t. In fact, a line of points e_c in camera image plane π_c maps to a single epipolar line e_p in the projector image plane π_p, and vice versa.

While these lines do not form a precise point-to-point mapping, they can be combined with structured light methods to achieve that goal. Establishing correspondence requires identifying the location of the mapping of a 3-D point into both planes. Once a point (encoded via structured light) has been located in one image plane, it then needs to be located along the corresponding epipolar line in the other image plane. Searching along this line reduces the complexity of the search when compared with searching through the entire second image plane, a speed-up of $O(n^2) \rightarrow O(n)$.

Rectification Transforms. The correspondence problem is facilitated by identifying epipolar lines, and while calculating the conjugate epipolar line corresponding to each point during the search is possible, it is not the most efficient method. To reduce the computational expense of this process, disparity was restricted to a single image plane axis [43]. A transform is computed to warp both image planes so that their epipolar lines were aligned along a single axis and so that the corresponding epipolar lines fell on the same column (or row) index, for a vertical (horizontal) alignment of the projector and camera. As a result, once rectified, any 3-D point in the scene maps to the same column (or row) index in both warped images. The correspondence problem was thus restricted to a single axis, thereby greatly reducing complexity.

The transform H_t that aligned the epipolar lines with the vertical axis is known as a *stereo rectification transform* [14] and can be observed in Fig. 4(c). The transformed

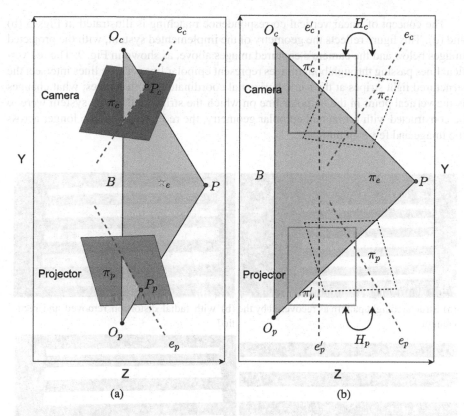

Fig. 4. Exemplar procam stereo system composed of a projector and a camera aligned vertically, (a) epipolar geometry of the system, (b) rectification of the system.

image planes are marked π'_t, and the transformed epipolar lines are marked e'_t. The transformed epipolar lines were aligned with each other and with the vertical axis. The results of stereo rectification transforms on a real projector and camera image are shown in Fig. 5. Once the system has been rectified, structured light encoding becomes much simpler. Rather than encoding along both axes to establish pixel disparities in the X and Y dimensions, only a single axis is encoded. In this way, each codephrase need occur only once per image plane along each epipolar line.

Stereo rectification can align the epipolar lines in either the X or Y dimension, meaning every 3-D scene point will share either the same Y coordinate in both image planes, or the same X coordinate. In the proposed method, vertical alignment of the camera and projector image planes was preferred over horizontal. This orientation aligned the long edges of the image plane (Fig. 5) and created a larger number of shorter epipolar lines when compared with the alternative horizontal rectification, as both the projector's and camera's image widths are greater than their heights. The effect of horizontal vs. vertical rectification on the resolution of depth image for different numbers of patterns is shown in Fig. 6. The figure assumes 1920×1080 resolution, and illustrates the exponential increase in the number of depth points, which doubles for each additional pattern. Both series saturate at 11 patterns as $2^{10} < 1080 < 1920 < 2^{11}$.

The concept of linear vertical correspondence matching is illustrated in Figs. 5 (b) and (d). This figure reflects the geometry of the implemented system, with the projected images below and the camera's captured images above, as shown in Fig. 9. The red vertical lines passing through both images represent epipolar lines. These lines intersect the structured light stripes at the same horizontal coordinate in both images; what changes is the vertical point in the epipolar line on which the stripes fall. If the system were to be constructed with horizontal epipolar geometry, the red lines would be longer across the image and fewer in number.

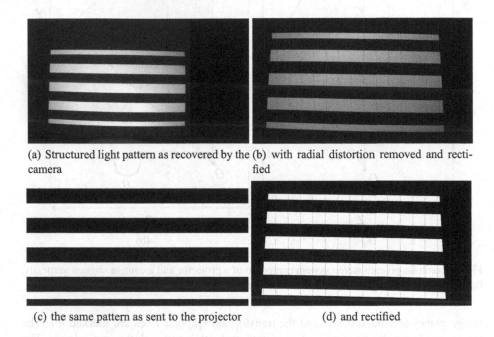

(a) Structured light pattern as recovered by the camera

(b) with radial distortion removed and rectified

(c) the same pattern as sent to the projector

(d) and rectified

Fig. 5. Example of stereo rectification showing vertical epipolar alignment [7].

3.4 Pattern Selection

With the correspondence problem reduced to a single axis, what remained was to encode the points along each axis uniquely so that linear disparity may be determined. Each epipolar line was 1080 pixels long in each image plane. To fully characterize these lines would require $ceil(log_2(1080)) = 11$ patterns, as well as a full black and full white frame for radiometric calibration of luminous intensity levels.

As detailed below in Sect. 4.5, the camera can capture 200 embedded patterns per second. The resulting capture rate would be 15.3 sequences of 13 patterns per second, roughly half the desired target frame-rate. Additionally, fully characterizing 11 patterns would require the camera to recover stripes that are a single camera pixel wide. This would pose a challenge even under perfectly controlled conditions, and would be even more difficult with depth varying scenes that don't perfectly align with the camera's

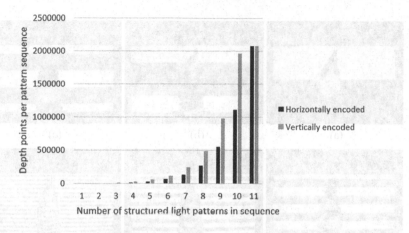

Fig. 6. Chart showing depth points recovered per pattern sequence as a function of the number of patterns in the sequence. Series for both horizontally and vertically aligned systems are shown [7].

field of view. These limitations suggested that full characterization does not maximize the system's bandwidth.

To strike a balance between frame rate and resolution, eight binary patterns were used, providing $2^8 = 256$ points of depth along each epipolar line. Also present is a single white frame for radiometric calibration. A second (black) frame is normally used so that a midpoint between high and low illumination levels can be used for thresholding. To minimize the number of frames employed by the method here, a fraction of the white frame is used in place of the midpoint between white and black. The omission of the data from the black frame renders the system more vulnerable to error from very high or very low reflectance surfaces as well as the effects of strong sources of ambient light; however, experiments have shown this vulnerability to be an acceptable trade-off in this system.

An example of the set of Gray code stripe patterns projected during a single frame is illustrated in Fig. 7, which includes a pure white image as part of the pattern sequence. Using nine patterns yielded an operating rate of 22.2 full sequences per second, which is closer to the design goal of 30 Hz. This rate compared favourably to the Zivid One's 13 Hz and even the Kinect V1 & V2's 30 Hz.

Some of the content images within which these patterns were imperceptibly embedded are shown in Fig. 8(a)–(c). The extracted disparity maps are shown underneath each content image, in (d)–(f) respectively. The disparity maps were substantially similar, irrespective of which content image they were extracted from, the only differences being attributable to system noise. It can be seen that the choice of content image did not impact the quality of the extracted data, or the ability to acquire the imperceptible patterns.

3.5 Disparity, Depth and Visualization

Once encoded patterns were properly undistorted and rectified, the remainder of the process was straightforward. Each column of rectified space was processed indepen-

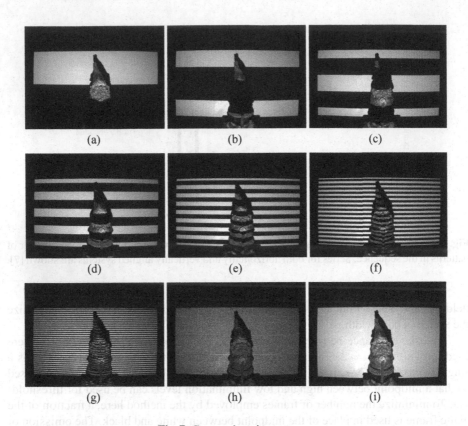

Fig. 7. Gray code stripe patterns.

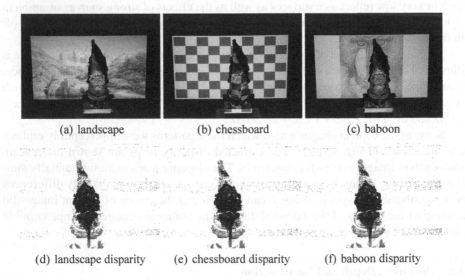

Fig. 8. Content images and extracted disparity maps.

dently. Each transition between adjacent codephrases existed in the same column in both rectified image planes. The difference in the vertical position of this transition in rectified projector and camera space was the stereo disparity. For visualization, no further calculations were required; the disparities could be normalized for a visual display. As depth is linearly dependent on disparity, this was sufficient to show relative depth across the scene.

For projection mapping, the actual metric 3-D coordinates of each point had to be determined. The XYZ coordinates of the point were calculated with respect to the projector origin by applying the well known pixel projection Eqs. 7–9. Here B refers to the baseline distance between the projector and camera origins, f refers to the focal length of the optical system whose coordinate system is the target (the projector in this case), d is the disparity between projected and captured points, and u and v refer to the image plane coordinates of the projection of the real point P.

$$Z = \frac{f \times B}{d} \tag{7}$$

$$Y = B + \frac{v \times Z}{f} \tag{8}$$

$$X = \frac{u \times Z}{f} \tag{9}$$

4   Experimental Results

In this section, we characterize the performance of the proposed method by analysing its current components, and outline opportunities for further improvement of the system. Both software and hardware components are assessed for efficacy. Algorithms are assessed based on their intended function, and for the sake of comparison with future changes. Hardware components are chiefly assessed for speed, as the rate of imperceptible pattern embedding is the major contribution of the proposed method. Limitations caused by the employed hardware are also noted.

4.1   Experimental Setup

The proposed method is deployed on the Optecks RGB LightCrafter 6500 engine, based on the Texas Instruments DLP 6500 module [46]. This device bundles three channel LED illumination with a high-performance DMD and optics to create a powerful and flexible projection platform at 1920×1080 resolution. Its most important characteristics for the purpose of the proposed system are the ability to expose 8-bit patterns for a minimum of 4046 µs and binary patterns for 105 µs, as well as a programmable hardware trigger.

Combined with this projection engine is a PointGrey Blackfly S machine vision camera [13], capable of capturing at 200 Hz at a 1440 × 1080 image resolution. The camera is synchronized with the projector hardware trigger and is capable of a 9 µs response time and a minimum 4 µs exposure time. Processing is performed on an AMD

Ryzen 5 1600 MHz 6-core processor with 2 x 8 Gb 2133 MHz RAM cards and a Samsung SM961 256 Gb solid-state drive.

The hardware synchronized procam system is shown in Fig. 9.

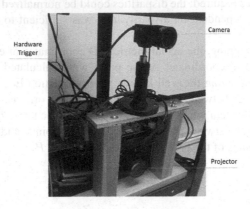

Fig. 9. The hardware synchronized vertically co-axial procam system employed in this work [7].

Calibration. Stereo reprojection was used to determine calibration accuracy. This test began with drawing a line visible in both image planes and then rectifying each image. Under a perfect rectifying transform, both rectified views of the line would match exactly. In practice, some pixel disparity occurs and can provide a measure of the accuracy of the computed transforms. The OpenCV function used to compute the stereo rectification transforms minimizes reprojection error as part of its functionality. It returns the transform associated with the lowest reprojection error, along with the error itself. The test yielded an average error $\epsilon = 1.16$ pixels.

4.2 Depth Reconstruction and Imperceptibility

Figure 10 shows some examples of various processing steps of the method. Several scenes are presented and shown with one of the nine patterns overlaid, and finally, the fully reconstructed depth scene is rendered as a (slightly rotated) point cloud.

The *pipe* represents a near-lambertian curved surface and, as expected, shows strong continuous depth reconstruction. The *gnome* presents dense features with varying colours and reflectivity, but the binary nature of the patterns and high calibration accuracy render these issues inconsequential, and strong continuous depth is present. Finally, the *chessboard* presents a highly reflective surface with stark colour contrast—an extremely challenging scenario for structured light methods. Again, continuous depth points were extracted across all regions of the object.

To test the degree of imperceptibility, patterns were embedded in the perceptible content images, as illustrated in Figs. 7 and 8, respectively. The content images were selected to demonstrate a range of conditions. There are regions that are bright, dark, busy, smooth, gradients, and sharp edges. There is also a significant region in the landscape content image that is dominated by blue, so chosen to test if patterns could still be embedded when some colour channels were barely present.

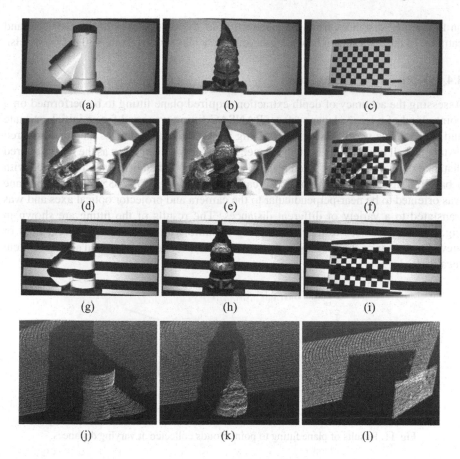

Fig. 10. Several objects presented under flat white illumination (a–c), illuminated by the projected content in which patterns are embedded imperceptibly (d–f), illuminated by an exemplar binary pattern (g–i), and finally reconstructed as a cloud of extracted depth points (j–l) [7].

The resulting pattern embedding was imperceptible. No artifacts or disruptions of any kind were visible to anyone who observed the image (N > 10). In addition, the patterns embedded in red and green channels displayed no loss in quality of recovery. This is due to the high level of contrast in the patterns, which renders them highly resilient to being dimmed.

4.3   Point Density and Resolution

The system collects an average of 280,000 points per depth frame. This count corresponds to the 256 Gy code transitions in the Y direction multiplied by the 1440 camera pixels in the X direction, with about 25% loss due to imperfect overlap in the camera and projector fields of view, transformation quantization, or other error.

The real world z-coordinates of these points form an inversely proportional relationship with the pixel disparity. As a result, the resolution of the points varies depending on the points' distances from the intersection of the optical axes of the projector and camera. In the tests shown below, observed disparities ranged from ∼80 to 200 pixels.

4.4 Depth Extraction Accuracy

Assessing the accuracy of depth extraction required plane fitting to be performed on a point cloud of a large planar surface. RANSAC fitting was used for an initial estimate and then a plane was fit to the inliers using a method that minimizes the mean squared distance of all inlier points from the plane. The error was then taken as the mean squared distance of all points to the fitted plane. The system as tested here was constructed with a baseline distance of 217 mm and a camera focal length of 2035 pixels. The plane was oriented to be near-perpendicular to the camera and projector optical axes and was translated to a variety of different distances. The results of the fitting are shown in Fig. 11. The distances tested were those attainable with the system's current field of view. For longer or shorter ranges, the system geometry could be altered and the system recalibrated.

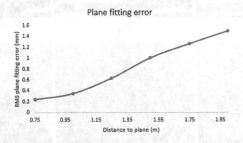

Fig. 11. Results of plane fitting to point clouds collected at varying distances.

4.5 Operating Speed

The system's operating speed can be divided into three sections: pattern projection rate, camera capture rate, and processing speed. The projector and camera speeds are closely aligned. The camera can return the complete set of nine patterns at 22.2 Hz, slightly slower than the 26.8 Hz at which the projector can embed them imperceptibly. The rate at which our software runs and processes all steps of the pipeline for nine patterns stands at 30.2 Hz. Operating perceptibly to display exclusively the binary patterns, the projector could operate at 1038 Hz. However, that would not currently improve the system in the absence of a faster camera and a more powerful computational platform.

Table 2 shows a comparison of the system's current performance in depth points per second as compared with the Kinect V1 and V2 [49] and the Zivid One [42].

4.6 Discussion

Table 2 shows that Zivid One has a much higher bandwidth than the proposed method, however it uses visible structured light for depth sensing which is not suitable for projection mapping applications. The proposed method works at a frame rate of 22.2 Hz,

Table 2. Bandwidth comparison [7].

	Resolution (points)	Frame rate (Hz)	Bandwidth (Mpoints/sec)
Kinect V1	633 × 495	30	9.20
Kinect V2	512 × 424	30	6.51
Zivid One	1900 × 1200	13	29.9
Proposed method	1400 × 256	22.2	7.96

bottlenecked by the camera's capture rate. The other systems used for comparison in Table 2 have been implemented in FPGA and/or VSLI, so presumably have already been optimized for time performance. This fact implies significant potential for our proposed method to further exceed the bandwidth of these other systems.

Table 3 outlines several methods that could provide an increase to the system's depth scanning rate. Gray code was used here to demonstrate the potential for real-time temporal encoding, but many other methods exist. The projector's current speed limitation is due to the need to embed binary patterns in 8-bit content. A method allowing for full speed binary projection would operate much faster. Such a method could involve using a multi-projector system or a proprietary dithering sequence—or simply eliminating the imperceptiblity feature, for applications other than DPM where it is not required.

One-shot methods are generally more sparse but could significantly improve performance. For camera capture, a single-shot method would yield a speedup. In addition, a higher frame rate camera would provide a speedup over the current model. Two such examples are presented in Table 3. The models in question, the EoSens 3 and UHS v2640, are highly specialized and respectively cost approximately 10 and 1,000 times that value of the Blackfly S. They also require complex and costly frame capture cards to deliver content, as opposed to the Blackfly's USB 3.1 interface. Such an advanced interface would be necessary to improve the overall rate of the system, as the USB 3 bandwidth is already the overall limiting factor.

For this work, processing was parallelized on a 6-core 1600 MHz processor. Using more specialized hardware would result in much faster processing. Two previous works were analyzed to approximate the potential speeds: one which employed GPU acceleration, and one which employed an FPGA. First, Chen et al. [6] employed a similar DLP-based depth mapping engine using GPU parallelization and were able to achieve depth scanning at 500 Hz using 16 patterns per frame (although perceptibly). Using nine patterns, that translates to ∼888 Hz. FPGA acceleration is slightly more difficult to approximate, as it must be tailored precisely to the application. Langerman et al. [24] used FPGA acceleration to algorithmically upsample depth scans. They claimed a 40× speedup over CPU parallelization. However, their method is more computationally expensive and handles less data than ours and thus provides an extreme approximation at best. Testing would be required to assess the viability and effectiveness of such a method on structured light depth scanning.

Finally, the system used a single projector and camera. No additional hardware was required to implement the proposed method. This alleviated the data delivery issues found in auxiliary depth mapping systems such as the Kinect or Zivid One. The system did not form a complete closed-loop system in its final state, due to the inability of the

Table 3. Hypothetical frame rates achievable using variations of the proposed method with upgraded hardware.

Method	Depth image rate (Hz)
Projection (Current = 26.8)	
One-shot encoding	240
Deployed perceptibly	1058
One-shot and perceptible	9524
Camera (Current = 22.2)	
One-shot encoding	200
Mikotron EoSens 3	133.3
One-shot with EoSens	1200
Phantom UHS v2640	1388.8
One-shot with UHS v2640	12500
Processing (Current = 30.2)	
GPU acceleration	~888

current hardware to dynamically modify projected content while injecting binary patterns. This is an issue with the particular hardware of the Optecks RGB LightCrafter 6500 engine, and can be addressed in future upgrades without altering the key functionality of the system.

5   Conclusion

In this paper, we presented a method to achieve an imperceptible, continuous, real-time depth mapping using a calibrated and rectified projector-camera system. This work shows that temporally encoded structured light depth sensing methods are suitable for real-time applications, including those that benefit from imperceptibility. Each depth map extracted using our method has more points than a map from the Kinect V2, a platform often used for depth mapping. The extracted points are sufficiently accurate and precise to enable dynamic projection mapping. Approaches to further improve the system's speed have also been presented. The system does not yet form a complete pipeline for use in dynamic projection mapping due to the hardware limitations of the LightCrafter engine we used. In the future, a new pipeline could be put in place to adjust projected content at speeds matching the rest of the system to enable dynamic projection mapping.

References

1. Epson answers automatic keystone correction (2002). https://www.projectorpeople.com/slis/downloads/whtpapers/epson/auto-keystone.pdf
2. Pokemon go (2016). http://itunes.apple.com/us/app/pokemon-go/id1094591345?mt=8

3. Agin, B.: Computer description of curved objects. IEEE Trans. Comput. **C–25**(4), 439–449 (1976). https://doi.org/10.1109/TC.1976.1674626

4. Bandyopadhyay, D., Raskar, R., Fuchs, H.: Dynamic shader lamps: painting on movable objects. In: Proceedings IEEE and ACM International Symposium on Augmented Reality, pp. 207–216. IEEE (2001)

5. Bermano, A.H., Billeter, M., Iwai, D., Grundhöfer, A.: Makeup lamps: live augmentation of human faces via projection. In: Computer Graphics Forum, vol. 36, pp. 311–323. Wiley Online Library (2017)

6. Chen, J., Yamamoto, T., Aoyama, T., Takaki, T., Ishii, I.: Real-time projection mapping using high-frame-rate structured light 3D vision. SICE J. Control Measur. Syst. Integr. **8**(4), 265–272 (2015)

7. Cole, A., Ziauddin., S., Greenspan., M.: High-speed imperceptible structured light depth mapping. In: Proceedings of the 15th International Joint Conference on Computer Vision, Imaging and Computer Graphics Theory and Applications, VISAPP, vol. 4, pp. 676–684. INSTICC, SciTePress (2020). https://doi.org/10.5220/0008955906760684

8. Corporation, M.: Microsoft hololens — mixed reality technology for business (2016). https://www.microsoft.com/en-us/hololens

9. Corporation, S.E.: Moverio - smart glasses - epson (2011). https://moverio.epson.com/

10. Cotting, D., Naef, M., Gross, M., Fuchs, H.: Embedding imperceptible patterns into projected images for simultaneous acquisition and display. In: Proceedings of the 3rd IEEE/ACM International Symposium on Mixed and Augmented Reality, pp. 100–109. IEEE Computer Society (2004)

11. Dai, J., Chung, R.: Head pose estimation by imperceptible structured light sensing. In: 2011 IEEE International Conference on Robotics and Automation, pp. 1646–1651. IEEE (2011)

12. Dai, J., Chung, R.: Making any planar surface into a touch-sensitive display by a mere projector and camera. In: 2012 IEEE Computer Society Conference on Computer Vision and Pattern Recognition Workshops, pp. 35–42. IEEE (2012)

13. FLIR Systems, I.: Machine vision cameras (2019). https://www.flir.ca/browse/industrial/machine-vision-cameras/

14. Fusiello, A., Trucco, E., Verri, A.: A compact algorithm for rectification of stereo pairs. Mach. Vis. Appl. **12**(1), 16–22 (2000). https://doi.org/10.1007/s001380050120

15. Gao, Z., Zhai, G., Wu, X., Min, X., Zhi, C.: DLP based anti-piracy display system. In: 2014 IEEE Visual Communications and Image Processing Conference, pp. 145–148. IEEE (2014)

16. Gerald, J., Agin, P.T.H.: Movable light-stripe sensor for obtaining three-dimensional coordinate measurements, vol. 0360 (1983). https://doi.org/10.1117/12.934118

17. Greenspan, M.: Method and apparatus for positional error correction in a robotic pool system using a cue-aligned local camera (2011). uS Patent App. 12/896,045

18. Grundhöfer, A., Seeger, M., Hantsch, F., Bimber, O.: Dynamic adaptation of projected imperceptible codes. In: Proceedings of the 2007 6th IEEE and ACM International Symposium on Mixed and Augmented Reality, pp. 1–10. IEEE Computer Society (2007)

19. Hieda, N., Cooperstock, J.R.: Digital facial augmentation for interactive entertainment. In: 2015 7th International Conference on Intelligent Technologies for Interactive Entertainment (INTETAIN), pp. 9–16. IEEE (2015)

20. Intel Corporation: Intel realsense depth camera d400-series. https://software.intel.com/en-us/realsense/d400. Accessed 07 June 2019

21. Jo, K., Gupta, M., Nayar, S.K.: Disco: display-camera communication using rolling shutter sensors. ACM Trans. Graph. (TOG) **35**(5), 150 (2016)

22. Kagami, S., Hashimoto, K.: Sticky projection mapping: 450-fps tracking projection onto a moving planar surface. In: SIGGRAPH Asia 2015 Emerging Technologies, p. 23. ACM (2015)

23. Kuroki, Y., Nishi, T., Kobayashi, S., Oyaizu, H., Yoshimura, S.: A psychophysical study of improvements in motion-image quality by using high frame rates. J. Soc. Inform. Display **15**(1), 61–68 (2007)
24. Langerman, D., Sabogal, S., Ramesh, B., George, A.: Accelerating real-time, high-resolution depth Upsampling on FPGAs. In: 2018 IEEE International Conference on Image Processing, Applications and Systems (IPAS), pp. 37–42. IEEE (2018)
25. Lee, J.C., Hudson, S.E., Tse, E.: Foldable interactive displays. In: Proceedings of the 21st Annual ACM Symposium on User Interface Software and Technology, pp. 287–290. ACM (2008)
26. Li, B., Sezan, I.: Automatic keystone correction for smart projectors with embedded camera. In: 2004 International Conference on Image Processing, ICIP'04, vol. 4, pp. 2829–2832. IEEE (2004)
27. Lohry, W., Zhang, S.: High-speed absolute three-dimensional shape measurement using three binary dithered patterns. Opt. Exp. **22**(22), 26752–26762 (2014)
28. Marin, G., Dominio, F., Zanuttigh, P.: Hand gesture recognition with leap motion and kinect devices. In: 2014 IEEE International Conference on Image Processing (ICIP), pp. 1565–1569 (2014). https://doi.org/10.1109/ICIP.2014.7025313
29. McDowall, I., Bolas, M.: Fast light for display, sensing and control applications. In: Proceedings of IEEE VR 2005 Workshop on Emerging Display Technologies (EDT), pp. 35–36 (2005)
30. Morishima, S., Yotsukura, T., Binsted, K., Nielsen, F., Pinhanez, C.: Hypermask talking head projected onto real object. In: Multimedia Modeling: Modeling Multimedia Information and Systems, pp. 403–412. World Scientific (2000)
31. Mouclier, J.: Glasses (2007). uS Patent App. 29/228,279
32. Narasimhan, S.G., Koppal, S.J., Yamazaki, S.: Temporal dithering of illumination for fast active vision. In: Forsyth, D., Torr, P., Zisserman, A. (eds.) ECCV 2008. LNCS, vol. 5305, pp. 830–844. Springer, Heidelberg (2008). https://doi.org/10.1007/978-3-540-88693-8_61
33. Narita, G., Watanabe, Y., Ishikawa, M.: Dynamic projection mapping onto a deformable object with occlusion based on high-speed tracking of dot marker array. In: Proceedings of the 21st ACM Symposium on Virtual Reality Software and Technology, pp. 149–152. ACM (2015)
34. Nelson, S., Ivashin, V.: Method for securely distributing meeting data from interactive whiteboard projector (2014). uS Patent 8,874,657
35. Park, H., Lee, M.-H., Seo, B.-K., Jin, Y., Park, J.-I.: Content adaptive embedding of complementary patterns for nonintrusive direct-projected augmented reality. In: Shumaker, R. (ed.) ICVR 2007. LNCS, vol. 4563, pp. 132–141. Springer, Heidelberg (2007). https://doi.org/10.1007/978-3-540-73335-5_15
36. Projector, P.: Real time tracking & projection mapping (2017). https://www.youtube.com/watch?v=XkXrLZmnQ_M&feature=youtu.be&fbclid=IwAR0pN2j95uxwMvc1fISs_SL5fmWM4Al3zTTnyEiKwmcp2lg0ReEpZfu2c8c
37. Pvt.Ltd., T.M.: Motionmagix^{TM} interactive wall and floor. http://www.touchmagix.com/interactive-floor-interactive-wall
38. Raskar, R., Welch, G., Cutts, M., Lake, A., Stesin, L., Fuchs, H.: The office of the future: a unified approach to image-based modeling and spatially immersive displays. In: Proceedings of the 25th Annual Conference on Computer Graphics and Interactive Techniques, pp. 179–188. ACM (1998)
39. Raskar, R., Welch, G., Low, K.-L., Bandyopadhyay, D.: Shader lamps: animating real objects with image-based illumination. In: Gortler, S.J., Myszkowski, K. (eds.) EGSR 2001. E, pp. 89–102. Springer, Vienna (2001). https://doi.org/10.1007/978-3-7091-6242-2_9
40. Resch, C., Keitler, P., Klinker, G.: Sticky projections-a model-based approach to interactive shader lamps tracking. IEEE Trans. Visual Comput. Graph. **22**(3), 1291–1301 (2015)

41. Sagawa, R., Furukawa, R., Kawasaki, H.: Dense 3D reconstruction from high frame-rate video using a static grid pattern. IEEE Trans. Pattern Anal. Mach. Intell. **36**(9), 1733–1747 (2014)
42. Salmi, T., Ahola, J.M., Heikkilä, T., Kilpeläinen, P., Malm, T.: Human-robot collaboration and sensor-based robots in industrial applications and construction. In: Bier, H. (ed.) Robotic Building. SSAE, pp. 25–52. Springer, Cham (2018). https://doi.org/10.1007/978-3-319-70866-9_2
43. Scharstein, D., Szeliski, R.: High-accuracy stereo depth maps using structured light. In: 2003 IEEE Computer Society Conference on Computer Vision and Pattern Recognition, 2003, Proceedings, vol. 1, pp. I-I. IEEE (2003)
44. Sehn, T.: Apparatus and method for supplying content aware photo filters (2015). uS Patent 9,225,897
45. Silapasuphakornwong, P., Unno, H., Uehira, K.: Information embedding in real object images using temporally brightness-modulated light. In: Applications of Digital Image Processing XXXVIII, vol. 9599, p. 95992W. International Society for Optics and Photonics (2015)
46. Texas Instruments: Lightcrafter 6500 Evaluation Module (2016)
47. den Uyl, T.M., Tasli, H.E., Ivan, P., Snijdewind, M.: Who do you want to be? Real-time face swap. In: 2015 11th IEEE International Conference and Workshops on Automatic Face and Gesture Recognition (FG), vol. 1, p. 1. IEEE (2015)
48. Zhang, Z.: A flexible new technique for camera calibration. IEEE Trans. Pattern Anal. Mach. Intell. **22**, 1330–1334 (2000)
49. Zhang, Z.: Microsoft kinect sensor and its effect. IEEE Multimed. **19**(2), 4–10 (2012)

Hierarchical Object Detection and Classification Using SSD Multi-Loss

Matthijs H. Zwemer[1,2]([✉]) [iD], Rob G. J. Wijnhoven[2] [iD], and Peter H. N. de With[1] [iD]

[1] Eindhoven University of Technology, Eindhoven, The Netherlands
{m.zwemer,p.h.n.de.with}@tue.nl
[2] ViNotion B.V., Eindhoven, The Netherlands
rob.wijnhoven@vinotion.nl

Abstract. When merging existing similar datasets, it would be attractive to benefit from a higher detection rate of objects and the additional partial ground-truth samples for improving object classification. To this end, a novel CNN detector with a hierarchical binary classification system is proposed. The detector is based on the Single-Shot multibox Detector (SSD) and inspired by the hierarchical classification used in the YOLO9000 detector. Localization and classification are separated during training, by introducing a novel loss term that handles hierarchical classification in the loss function (SSD-ML). We experiment with the proposed SSD-ML detector on the generic PASCAL VOC dataset and show that additional super-categories can be learned with minimal impact on the overall accuracy. Furthermore, we find that not all objects are required to have classification label information as classification performance only drops from 73.3% to 70.6% while 60% of the label information is removed. The flexibility of the detector with respect to the different levels of details in label definitions is investigated for a traffic surveillance application, involving public and proprietary datasets with non-overlapping class definitions. Including classification label information from our dataset raises the performance significantly from 70.7% to 82.2%. The experiments show that the desired hierarchical labels can be learned from the public datasets, while only using box information from our dataset. In general, this shows that it is possible to combine existing datasets with similar object classes and partial annotations and benefit in terms of growth of detection rate and improved class categorization performance.

Keywords: SSD detector · Hierarchical classification · Traffic surveillance

1 Introduction

Object detection is one of the fundamental challenges in computer vision, involving the localization of specific objects in images, typically followed by a object categorization step. It has evolved from the early stages of defining handcrafted features and a sliding classification window by Viola and Jones [18] and Dalal and Triggs [2] to the recent design of large neural networks that automatically learn both features and classification from annotated training images. An overview of recent developments in object detection is given by Zou *et al.* [20]. Nowadays, object detectors are based on Convolutional

© Springer Nature Switzerland AG 2022
K. Bouatouch et al. (Eds.): VISIGRAPP 2020, CCIS 1474, pp. 268–296, 2022.
https://doi.org/10.1007/978-3-030-94893-1_12

Neural Networks (CNNs) that learn feature hierarchies and the corresponding classification functions from datasets with object annotations. This approach is called supervised learning and because such CNNs have large learning capacity, they strongly benefit from larger training sets.

In the last years, these datasets have become larger and more diverse, both in terms of scenes and object categories. Most datasets have predefined object categories without a class hierarchy. Each annotated object belongs to one of the predefined categories, while other objects are not annotated at all. For animals, typically the classes 'cat' and 'dog' are annotated, but 'giraffe' and 'whales' are not considered. For traffic objects, the classes 'car' and 'truck' are annotated, but tractors are typically ignored. Such a flat class hierarchy is limiting the options for combining existing datasets or expanding existing datasets with additional object classes, because only the highest level of intersecting object categories can be exploited (adding classes like 'giraffe' or 'whale' for animals), or it is required to provide additional label information for the desired object categories in all datasets. Moreover, it is not possible to divide an existing object class into subclasses, such as different breeds of cats and dogs, without completely revising the class definitions.

In this paper, we focus on object detection with a hierarchical classification tree. This allows to predict object categories at different levels of detail (e.g. 'cats' and 'dogs', but also 'animal', or different breeds of cats). More importantly, it enables to combine existing datasets with different levels of detail in object categories. Moreover, we propose to learn detection and localization separately from classification, by using the concept of *objectness* [15]. Using this concept, the object detector can learn to detect and localize an object, without requiring the availability of its ground-truth category label. To learn the classification function, other annotations (possibly from other datasets) can provide the category label information. Note that for all objects to be recognized, at least a box annotation is required, since the objects are otherwise implicitly labeled as background.

The hierarchical category definition is implemented by adopting the existing Single Shot multibox Detector (SSD) [11]. The detection head of this detector is modified such that it is able to predict *if* there is an object (objectness), where the detection fully separated from the notion of object category. Categories are independently defined and organized in a hierarchical manner, e.g. an object can be classified as a 'car' and 'vehicle' at the same time. The detector is trained using datasets that are labeled with different levels of hierarchical labels, combining the classes from multiple datasets. This allows for incremental and semi-automatic annotation of datasets with a limited amount of label detail. As a result of our proposed method, the obtained classification is completely tailored to our desired hierarchical definition, while it is flexible to the input data and can accept a broad range of datasets with slightly different class definitions, which can have both supplementary and complementary properties.

In this paper, the global objective is on visual object detection and classification. For detailing the classification, we propose the use of an hierarchical category definition, that combines datasets at different levels of detail in classification label definitions. As a result of our method, the obtained classification is completely tailored to our desired hierarchical classification, while our method is flexible to the input data and can accept a broad range of pre-categorized datasets. An important research question is how large the fraction of label information should be for the overall dataset and the robustness behaviour of the performance when that labeled fraction deteriorates.

This paper extends our earlier work [21] by providing much more detailed evaluation of the proposed hierarchical classification model. In the experiments we show that the proposed hierarchical system is suitable for any generic detection problem where a hierarchy can be defined. This finding is based on performing experiments with a much larger dataset with only partial label information, i.e. the PASCAL VOC dataset. Furthermore, we attend to solve a practical case in traffic surveillance, where we combine the public UA-DETRAC [19] and MIO-TCD [12] traffic datasets with our proprietary traffic dataset. From the multiple datasets, a newly defined class hierarchy is learned, while none of the sets contain all required category labels. With the new hierarchy, we analyze specific traffic situations with our proprietary dataset, that does not directly overlap visually (camera viewpoint, angles, vehicle types, etc.) with the other two datasets (UA-DETRAC and MIO-TCD). More specifically, we incrementally learn the scene background, add bus and trucks boxes and labels, involve all object boxes without labels, and all objects with labels from our proprietary dataset. It is found that as expected, adding more label information results in a higher detection and classification accuracy. As a result of the proposed method, the obtained classification is completely tailored to the desired hierarchical definition.

The remainder of this paper is structured as follows. First, an overview of related work is given in Sect. 2. Next, the details of the proposed SSD-ML detector are discussed in Sect. 3. Then, the experimental results on the PASCAL VOC dataset are presented in Sect. 4, followed by the experimental results on the traffic datasets in Sect. 5. The paper is concluded with an in-depth discussion and conclusions.

2   Related Work

State-of-the-art object detectors in computer vision can be divided into two main categories: single-stage and two-stage detectors. Two-stage detectors determine *if* there is an object in the first stage and determine its category and exact location in the second stage. Examples are R-CNN [6], Fast R-CNN [5], Faster R-CNN [15] and Mask R-CNN [7]. The two stages already introduce hierarchy: object vs. background at the top and the different object categories as an indication of the contents. Note that the detector only considers a single level of classification output and does not detail into subcategories. Generally, a disadvantage of two-stage detectors is that they are more computationally complex than recent single-stage detectors. We therefore focus in the remainder on single-stage detectors.

Single-stage detectors perform object localization and classification in a single CNN. The most popular single-stage detectors are YOLO [13, 14], SSD [11], RetinaNet [9] and FCOS [17]. The YOLO detector predicts bounding boxes directly for each cell in a fixed grid on the top-most features of the base network. The SSD detector extends this concept by using multiple default bounding boxes with different aspect ratios. In addition, SSD uses multi-scale versions of the top-most feature map, rendering the SSD detector more robust to large variations in object size. Lin *et al.* propose the Focal Loss function in their RetinaNet detector, to enable better handling of the extreme class imbalance between positive and negative samples. The authors add a Feature Pyramid Network (FPN) for the base network in order to extract information more efficiently from multiple scales. The FCOS model also uses an FPN and removes the anchor boxes completely by computing the detection loss functions directly from the ground-truth annotations, thereby avoiding empirical overlap thresholds with annotation bounding boxes. In our work, we propose to use the SSD detector as the basis of our object detector because it is computationally efficient and software implementations are widely available. Note that the Focal Loss from RetinaNet and the different method from FCOS to estimate bounding boxes can both be adopted for modifying the SSD model.

The SSD detector uses a softmax classification function with an additional label for background classes, while the recent YOLO [14] detector follows a different approach for detection and classification. First, the authors use an *objectness* score $P_{physical\ object}$ to predict *if* there is an object present. In parallel, to estimate the object class, the authors assume that there is an object ($P_{physical\ object} = 1$) and estimate probabilities for each category in a hierarchical tree. For each level in this tree, YOLO uses multinomial classification to estimate the most likely category. The authors assume that performance degrades gracefully on new and unknown object categories, i.e. confidences spread out among the sub-categories. Recent work by Bertinetto *et al.* [1] focuses on image classification without detection, and proposes two different hierarchical loss functions which take hierarchy into account. These loss functions aim to minimize the classification mistakes, e.g. false classifications that are close in the hierarchy result in lower loss than when classifying farther away from the considered hierarchical categorization level. In our classification system, the different levels of hierarchy are learned independently. Our approach to implement hierarchical classification in the SSD detector is based on the concept of separating the objectness and classification, which is also being applied in the YOLO detector. However, instead of multinomial classification, we propose to use independent binary classification, as also performed in RetinaNet and FCOS. This allows each classification output to predict only its object (sub-)category, i.e. predict if the object belongs to *that* category instead of choosing the most likely category as with multinomial classification. The binary classification method is chosen because of its flexibility in defining sub-categories and the ability to handle incompletely defined sub-leafs in a hierarchy. Unknown or new categories will result in a performance degradation for all sub-categories.

3   SSD-ML Detection Model

This section describes our Single Shot multibox Detector, called Multi-Loss SSD (abbreviated as SSD-ML). The proposed SSD-ML detector is a modification of the original SSD detector [11] and differs in the following three aspects. First, we decouple presence detection and classification, leading to more robust classification and detection when the number of object classes increases. This decoupling of detection and classification enables the CNN network to predict *if* there is an object separately from predicting the class of an object and allows the use of different datasets that contain objects with different levels of classification detail for training. Secondly, by using binary cross-entropy loss functions for object classification, we decouple the different

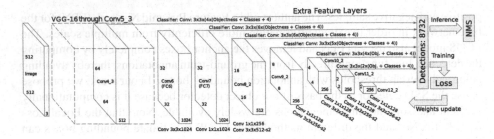

Fig. 1. Design of the SSD detection model (Source: [21], Fig. 1). The modification of the SSD model is visible by the contents of the output branches of the extra feature layers at the top right. The contents involves extra convolutions for objectness. The applied loss function is visualized in more detail in Fig. 2.

classes and enable the use of hierarchical class definitions. In contrary to the multinomial logistic classifications as proposed by [14], we employ independent binary predictions. Finally, we present an improved hard-negative search and the addition of so-called ignore regions, which are used during training of the network. The sequel of this section provides a detailed description of the implementation, separated in sub-sections for the network architecture, inference at test time, and training details including the loss functions.

3.1 Inference

Similar to the original SSD detector, our SSD-ML detector consists of two parts (see Fig. 1). The first part is a CNN base network that computes image features of the input image with an input resolution of 512×512 pixels. Similar to the original SSD network, we use the VGG16 [16] CNN network as a basis. The second part consists of additional feature layers, which form the SSD-specific detection head. The detection head creates several down-scaled versions of the last feature layer of the base network. Detection boxes are then predicted, based on each scaled feature layer. The detection head outputs possible detections at fixed positions in the image using so-called prior-boxes. For each fixed position (prior-box), the detection head estimates location offsets $\delta(cx, cy, w, h)$ and class confidences $[c_0, c_1, c_2, ..., c_N]$. In the SSD-ML model, we extend the detection head by an additional objectness o prediction. All estimates are predicted by a convolution with a kernel of $3 \times 3 \times N_{\text{channels}}$, where the last parameter indicates the number of channels.

Each cell in a feature layer is associated to one or multiple prior-boxes. The relative position of each prior-box to each cell is fixed. Per feature layer there are $m \times n$ locations (cells) and each location has $||\mathcal{P}_r||$ prior-boxes (size or the cardinality of the set $\mathcal{P}_r$). In our work, we use the same configuration for the aspect ratios and sizes of the prior-boxes as the original implementation, further details can be found in the original SSD paper [11].

The objectness score o estimates if a prior-box represents an object. So the objectness score o is predicted for each prior-box in $\mathcal{P}_r$, for all cells in a feature layer. This results in $||\mathcal{P}_r|| \times m \times n$ objectness estimates for a feature layer with $m \times n$ dimensions.

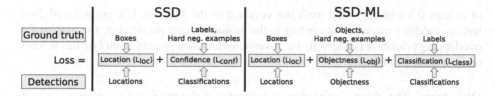

Fig. 2. Loss computation for SSD vs. SSD-ML model. The latter model has modified loss components, using objectness as a novel component and the labels as classification loss instead of confidence.

Object locations are predicted by estimating offsets $\delta(cx, cy, w, h)$ for each prior-box d in the set of prior-boxes $\mathcal{P}_r$, at each location in a feature layer. Parameter estimates $cx, cy, ...$ refer to the offset in x-dimension, y-dimension, etc. Hence, for a feature layer with dimensions $m \times n$, there will be $4 \times ||\mathcal{P}_r|| \times m \times n$ location estimates (4 offset parameters per prior-box).

The classification confidences are predicted per object category. Each classification category prediction is independent from other category predictions using sigmoid activation functions (in contrast to softmax activation functions in the original SSD implementation). The prediction for each category is carried out for each prior-box in $\mathcal{P}_r$. Hence, there are $N_{\text{Categories}} \times ||\mathcal{P}_r|| \times m \times n$ classification confidence predictions per feature layer ($N_{\text{Categories}}$ denotes the number of categories).

The output of the detection head is created by combining the objectness predictions, classification confidences, location offsets and prior-boxes of all feature layers. The prior-box and location offsets are merged to obtain possible detection boxes. Each detection box has its corresponding objectness prediction and classification confidences. This large set of detection boxes, with their corresponding objectness prediction and classification confidences is then filtered by setting a threshold on the objectness prediction scores. The resulting subset contains combinations that are likely to represent any object. The final detection set is created by performing non-maximum suppression, based on the Jaccard overlap of the detection boxes. This suppression approach prevents multiple detections for the same object. The confidence per object category is determined by multiplying each category prediction with all its parent category predictions and the objectness prediction. This ensures that a low parent category prediction results in a low child-category prediction.

3.2 Training

During training, loss functions are used to update the CNN weights. In the SSD-ML detector, individual loss functions for the objectness prediction, classification confidence and location offsets are defined. The newly introduced objectness loss L_{obj} and classification loss L_{class} replace and further detail the confidence loss L_{conf} of the original SSD detector implementation (see Fig. 2). For each loss function, a match between ground-truth boxes from a dataset with the predictions is required. After matching the ground truth with the predicted values, the loss can be computed.

The matching step involves relating the set of ground-truth boxes to prior-boxes and defines a set of positive matches $\mathcal{P}_{\text{Pos}}$. Each prior-box with a Jaccard overlap (IoU) of at least 0.5 with a ground-truth box is added to the $\mathcal{P}_{\text{Pos}}$ set. If a ground-truth box has no matching prior-box according to the minimum Jaccard overlap, the maximally overlapping prior-box is added to $\mathcal{P}_{\text{Pos}}$ to ensure that each ground-truth box has at least one matching prior-box.

Objectness. The objectness prediction estimates *if* the prior-box is an object, e.g. if the prior-box is in the positive matching prior-box set $\mathcal{P}_{\text{Pos}}$. To this end, a negative set of prior-boxes not matching any ground-truth is required to learn the difference. This negative set $\mathcal{P}_{\text{Neg}}$ is a selection of all prior-boxes not in the positive set. A selection is made because only a few prior-boxes are in the $\mathcal{P}_{\text{Pos}}$ set compared to the total set of prior-boxes (mostly negatives). This imbalance is compensated by selecting only the negatives with the highest objectness loss scores. This is comparable to the original SSD implementation in the way the system applies it to the related classification loss. For both SSD and SSD-ML, the amount of negatives is chosen to be a ratio of 3 : 1 with respect to the size of the positive set.

Contrary to the original SSD implementation, we propose to collect negative samples *per batch* instead of per image. The negative-to-positive ratio is kept the same, but the negative samples may come from different images within the same batch. This different approach for negative mining allows us to collect negative samples from background images (not containing any ground-truth boxes) with visually complicated scenes. This approach decreases the number of false-positive detections when applying the detector on novel scenes containing new unseen objects. For example in our traffic application, specific images containing empty city streets, empty highways and all kinds of weather conditions on different (empty) crossings, may be added to the training set.

Although we assume that most of the objects in each image are annotated, there may be regions in a ground-truth image that contain undesirable objects for training. For example, this occurs when only a part of the image is annotated or when static (parked) vehicles are present in multiple training images. To address this aspect, we propose to more carefully select the negative samples by defining and annotating so-called ignore regions in which such undesirable objects are contained. These regions require manual annotation in the training images, but allow fine-grained control over the negative samples used for training. The yellow regions in Figs. 6a and 6c show several ignore regions that cover parked vehicles and vehicles at the back of the scene that should not be involved in the training.

When the set of positive prior-boxes (matching ground-truth) and the set of negative prior-boxes (containing the highest scoring prior-boxes not matching any ground-truth) are both created, the objectness loss is computed. If parameter o_i denotes the objectness estimate for the i-th prior-box for each prior-box in the positive $\mathcal{P}_{\text{Pos}}$ and negative $\mathcal{P}_{\text{Neg}}$ set, then the binary cross-entropy loss for objectness is defined by:

$$L_{\text{obj}}(o_i) = - \sum_{i \in \mathcal{P}_{\text{Pos}}}^{N_{\text{pos}}} \log\left(\hat{o}_i\right) - \sum_{i \in \mathcal{P}_{\text{Neg}}}^{3N_{\text{pos}}} \log\left(1 - \hat{o}_i\right), \tag{1}$$

where $\hat{o}_i$ denotes the sigmoid function on o_i defined by

$$\hat{o}_i = \frac{1}{1 + e^{-o_i}}, \tag{2}$$

where N_{pos} denotes the total number of positive samples in the positive set. This parameter leads also the upper bound of the negative set because of the chosen ratio $1:3$.

Locations. The object locations are predicted (similar to SSD) by estimating offsets $\delta(cx, cy, w, h)$ for each prior-box d. Parameters cx, cy, w and h refer to the offset in the x-dimension, y-dimension, etc. For each i-th prior-box in the positive set $\mathcal{P}_{\text{Pos}}$, there is a location offset prediction l and a matching ground-truth box g. It should be noted that this is the same positive set as used for the objectness loss function. The localization loss is computed by regression of the offsets for the center (cx, cy), width (w) and height (h) of the prior-box d, using a smoothing $L1$ loss function [5], denoted by $\text{Smooth}_{L1}(.)$, leading to:

$$
\begin{aligned}
L_{loc}(l, g) = \sum_{i \in \mathcal{P}_{\text{Pos}}}^{N_{\text{pos}}} \Bigg(& \text{Smooth}_{L1}(l_i^{cx} - \frac{g_j^{cx} - d_i^{cx}}{d_i^{w}}) \\
& + \text{Smooth}_{L1}(l_i^{cy} - \frac{g_j^{cy} - d_i^{cy}}{d_i^{h}}) \\
& + \text{Smooth}_{L1}(l_i^{w} - \log \frac{g_j^{w}}{d_i^{w}}) \\
& + \text{Smooth}_{L1}(l_i^{h} - \log \frac{g_j^{h}}{d_i^{h}}) \Bigg).
\end{aligned}
\tag{3}
$$

Classifications. The hierarchical classification confidences are predicted per object category. The classification loss only uses the positive set $\mathcal{P}_{\text{Pos}}$ of prior-boxes matching with the ground truth. However, within this set, samples are chosen to be used as positive and negative samples for classification. For example, a ground-truth cat sample will be used as a positive sample for output class 'cat', but as a negative sample for output class 'dog'. Hence, a separate negative classification set $\mathcal{P}_{\text{neg,p}} \subset \mathcal{P}_{\text{Pos}}$ is introduced for each output category p. The samples in the negative set $\mathcal{P}_{\text{neg,p}}$ are selected based on the dataset properties (see Table 3). For each classification category, the prediction score $c_{i,p}$ for the i-th prior-box for category p is determined by a binary cross-entropy loss. This means that each category prediction output is independent from other category predictions. More specifically, we define a binary indicator $t_i^p \in \{0, 1\}$ for the i-th prior-box matching a ground-truth box of category p or any of the subcategories of p. Then the subset of the positive set for category p denoted by $\mathcal{P}_{\text{neg,p}} \subset \mathcal{P}_{\text{Pos}}$ is a selection of ground-truth boxes not of category p or any of its super-categories. The classification loss for category p is now defined by

$$
L_{\text{class},p}(t, c) = - \sum_{i \in \mathcal{P}_{\text{Pos}}}^{N_{\text{pos}}} t_i^p \log(\hat{c}_{i,p})) - \sum_{i \in \mathcal{P}_{\text{neg,p}}}^{N_{\text{neg,p}}} \log (1 - \hat{c}_{i,p}),
\tag{4}
$$

where $\hat{c}_{i,p}$ is again the sigmoid function for this prior-box, defined by

$$
\hat{c}_{i,p} = \frac{1}{1 + e^{-c_{i,p}}}.
\tag{5}
$$

The total classification loss becomes now the summation of all losses of the individual categories p.

Training. Training of our model is carried out by combining the different loss functions as a weighted sum, resulting in

$$L(o, t, c, l, g) = \frac{1}{N_{\text{pos}}} \Big(L_{\text{obj}}(o) + \beta \sum_p L_{\text{class},p}(t, c) + \alpha L_{\text{loc}}(l, g) \Big). \tag{6}$$

If an object category is unknown in the ground-truth labels, the classification loss L_{class} is set to zero. Contrary to the original SSD implementation where the loss function is defined to be zero when no objects are present in an image during training, the proposed loss function is only defined zero when objects are absent in a complete batch due to the proposed negative mining technique over a batch instead of per image.

4 Experimental Results: PASCAL VOC

In order to pursue a generic solution, the proposed solution is evaluated for two different cases. More specifically, we evaluate SSD-ML for a generic object detection problem and for a surveillance application considering road traffic (Sect. 5). The current section concentrates on the well-known generic object detection datasets, i.e. the PASCAL VOC 2007 [4] and 2012 [3] datasets.

Three experiments are conducted. First we compare SSD-ML with the original SSD detector and the effect of negative mining. The performance difference between multinomial and binary loss computation is computed. In the second experiment, the proposed classification hierarchy is based on multinomial and binary loss concepts for in-dept evaluation. In the third experiment, the influence of training with less ground-truth label information is investigated. The objective is whether the separated detection (objectness and location) and classification loss functions allow the model to learn effectively when only reduced label information is available.

The remainder of this section is as follows. First, an overview of the PASCAL VOC dataset is presented in Sect. 4.1. Next, the evaluation metrics are discussed in Sect. 4.2 and the training details are given in Sect. 4.3. Then the three outlined experiments are conducted and evaluated in Sects. 4.4, 4.5 and 4.6.

4.1 Dataset: PASCAL VOC

The PASCAL Visual Object Classes (VOC) project published several datasets and organized challenges for evaluating performance on object class recognition from 2005 until 2012. Although the PASCAL VOC challenges have ended, the dataset is still regularly used in evaluation, despite of its relatively small size in the number of images and object classes, as compared to newer datasets such as COCO [10] (80 categories, 330k images) and Open Images [8] (500 categories, ±1.7M images). The PASCAL VOC set contains 20 different object classes and 26k images (2007+2012).

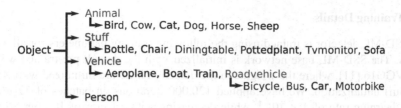

Fig. 3. Original PASCAL VOC classes (black) and our additional hierarchy (red). (Color figure online)

The common practice is to combine the VOC 2007 [4] and VOC 2012 [3] *trainval* sets for training, and use the VOC 2007 *test* set for testing. The PASCAL VOC 2007 *trainval* dataset contains 9, 963 images that contain a total of 12, 608 annotated objects. PASCAL VOC 2012 contains 11, 540 images and 27, 450 object annotations. The testing set (VOC 2007 *test*), contains 4, 952 images and 12, 032 annotations. Figure 4 shows several example images from the PASCAL VOC datasets.

To experiment with our hierarchical classification method, we have defined four extra categories (labels): vehicle, road-vehicle, stuff and animal. Each existing category in PASCAL VOC is assigned to one of these extra categories. Figure 3 shows the hierarchy, where the black labels are the original categories from PASCAL VOC and the red labels are the additional super-categories. Note that the 'person' category remains a separate category because it cannot be captured by any of the other categories.

Fig. 4. Example images with annotations from PASCAL VOC 2007 and 2012. (Color figure online)

4.2 Evaluation Metrics

Detection performance is evaluated using the Average Precision (AP) metric, which is used in the PASCAL VOC challenge [3]. The Average Precision (AP) is computed as the area under the recall-precision curve. The combined performance for all classes is summarized as the mean Average Precision (mAP), which is the mean of the average precision scores per category. Recall $R(c)$ is defined as the fraction of objects that are detected with a confidence value of at least c. Similarly, precision $P(c)$ is defined as the fraction of detections that are correct with a confidence value of at least c. An object is detected if the detected bounding box has a minimum Jaccard index (IoU) of 0.5 with the ground-truth bounding box, otherwise a detection is considered incorrect. All experiments are carried out three times, so that the evaluation metrics are reported by their average value and standard deviation.

4.3 Training Details

Our SSD-ML detector is trained using the following training parameters for all experiments. The SSD-ML base network is initialized with the default pre-trained weights from VGG16 [11], where the weights in the detection head are initialized with Xavier (random) initialization. We have applied 120,000 iterations on batches of 32 images with a learning rate of 4×10^{-4}, while decreasing with a factor of 10 after 80k and 100k iterations, using stochastic gradient descent as the optimizer. We set $\alpha = 1$ and $\beta = 1$ (see Eq. (6)).

4.4 Experiment 1: Non-hierarchical Classification

In this first experiment, we compare the detection and classification performance of the original SSD detector with the proposed SSD-ML detector. For the SSD-ML detector, we evaluate the performance with- and without the proposed negative mining over the batch and evaluate the proposed binary classification method against a multinomial classification method. To enable multinomial classification in SSD-ML, the binary cross-entropy loss function (Eq. (4)) is replaced by a categorical cross-entropy loss (softmax loss) and all sigmoid activations are replaced by a single softmax activation.

Table 1 shows the average precision metric for objectness (ignoring all class labels) and all individual categories. The mAP VOC denotes the mean average precision over the PASCAL VOC categories. In this experiment, the focus is on the SSD512 and SSD-ML models, that are trained on the flat hierarchy (denoted by 'Experiment 1' in the table).

Objectness. When comparing the objectness scores we notice a low score for the original SSD detector of 50.0% versus 72.4% AP for the SSD-ML detector (with negative mining over the batch), while the classification scores and mAP for all classifications are quite similar to our SSD-ML results. This is an inherent consequence of our implementation of the objectness score for the original SSD detector. The original SSD detector does not have an objectness prediction output, but a multinomial classification prediction (including a background class). We have adopted the maximum value over all classification predictions as an objectness score. However, this low score shows that in the original SSD detector a detection threshold should be implemented per category, because a low prediction score for one class may be an actual detection, while for another class this could be a false detection. A more accurate objectness prediction score could be obtained if a normalization factor would be available for each object class, which requires empirical tuning.

Negative Mining. The objectness score results of the SSD-ML detector show that the negative mining over the batch has a positive impact on detection performance. Although the performance improvement of negative mining is only 0.6% AP for both, i.e. binary classification (from 71.8% to 72.4%) and multinomial classification (from 71.6% to 72.2%), there is no additional computational requirement. Apparently, a better distribution of negative samples is found when mining over the batch, as compared to selecting negative samples in a single image. In the original implementation a fixed negative-to-positive ratio is obtained, which leads to a different number of extracted negative samples when very few or many positive annotations are present in an image. Moreover, when no positive annotations are present, negatives do not appear as well in that image. The minor positive impact on the PASCAL VOC set can be explained by the fairly constant number of positive annotations per image.

Table 1. Detection performance of original SSD detector (SSD512) and different variants of our SSD-ML detector.

Hardnegative Classification	Non-hierarchical					Hierachical	
	SSD512	SSD-ML				SSD-ML	
		Experiment 1				Experiment 2	
	Original	Orignal		Batch Neg		Batch Neg	
		Multi	Binary	Multi	Binary	Multi	Binary
Objectness	**50.0 ± 0.1**	**71.6 ± 0.1**	**71.8 ± 0.2**	**72.2 ± 0.0**	**72.4 ± 0.2**	**71.8 ± 0.1**	**72.0 ± 0.2**
Aeroplane	81.2 ± 1.0	80.3 ± 1.6	80.6 ± 0.4	80.3 ± 1.2	82.5 ± 1.6	80.0 ± 0.5	80.6 ± 0.3
Bicycle	80.7 ± 0.8	79.5 ± 1.7	79.4 ± 1.5	79.5 ± 1.0	79.4 ± 0.8	79.3 ± 0.4	80.7 ± 0.6
Bird	71.5 ± 0.8	72.3 ± 0.7	72.6 ± 0.5	73.2 ± 0.6	73.0 ± 0.8	73.4 ± 0.9	72.9 ± 0.3
Boat	62.2 ± 0.7	59.9 ± 1.3	59.6 ± 0.2	60.3 ± 0.9	61.4 ± 0.7	60.6 ± 0.9	60.1 ± 1.6
Bottle	46.1 ± 0.1	44.7 ± 0.8	44.5 ± 1.1	47.0 ± 1.0	45.4 ± 0.6	45.3 ± 0.7	44.5 ± 1.3
Bus	81.2 ± 0.5	82.2 ± 0.5	81.4 ± 0.5	80.9 ± 1.3	82.0 ± 0.8	81.7 ± 0.1	81.7 ± 0.9
Car	82.9 ± 0.2	82.1 ± 0.2	82.9 ± 0.7	82.4 ± 0.1	83.0 ± 0.2	82.2 ± 0.4	82.6 ± 0.2
Cat	91.0 ± 0.5	91.5 ± 0.8	91.4 ± 0.3	91.3 ± 0.8	90.9 ± 0.6	91.3 ± 0.9	91.0 ± 0.4
Chair	54.4 ± 1.1	54.7 ± 0.3	53.5 ± 0.4	53.9 ± 0.9	54.7 ± 0.7	54.4 ± 0.1	54.4 ± 1.0
Cow	79.6 ± 1.4	81.7 ± 0.3	81.5 ± 0.8	81.1 ± 0.3	80.3 ± 0.4	80.8 ± 0.4	80.7 ± 0.8
Diningtable	66.9 ± 0.1	65.5 ± 1.9	66.7 ± 1.0	65.6 ± 0.5	66.8 ± 1.2	64.5 ± 1.0	66.5 ± 1.1
Dog	85.3 ± 0.7	86.3 ± 0.2	86.7 ± 0.5	86.2 ± 0.6	86.6 ± 0.4	85.7 ± 0.3	85.9 ± 0.2
Horse	84.5 ± 0.6	84.7 ± 0.6	84.8 ± 0.9	85.3 ± 0.2	84.9 ± 0.2	85.4 + 0.1	85.3 ± 0.5
Motorbike	80.5 ± 1.4	81.2 ± 1.0	81.7 ± 0.6	82.3 ± 0.7	82.1 ± 0.3	81.8 ± 0.5	80.6 ± 0.3
Person	64.9 ± 0.3	64.2 + 0.0	64.8 ± 0.2	64.8 ± 0.4	65.1 ± 0.2	64.5 ± 0.3	64.8 ± 0.2
Pottedplant	48.8 ± 0.2	47.6 ± 1.2	48.4 ± 0.5	49.0 ± 0.8	49.6 ± 1.3	48.6 ± 1.0	48.1 ± 1.2
Sheep	70.6 ± 0.7	71.0 ± 0.8	71.4 ± 0.7	70.7 ± 0.3	71.6 ± 0.5	70.7 ± 0.9	71.3 ± 0.6
Sofa	72.0 ± 1.0	68.4 ± 0.6	69.3 ± 0.6	68.8 ± 1.0	69.6 ± 1.2	69.6 ± 1.7	70.3 ± 0.7
Train	87.3 ± 1.0	85.5 ± 0.2	86.6 ± 1.1	86.7 ± 1.1	86.6 ± 0.9	87.1 ± 0.7	87.9 ± 0.7
Tvmonitor	75.6 ± 0.8	75.8 ± 0.7	76.4 ± 0.7	76.8 ± 0.5	75.9 ± 0.3	75.2 ± 0.6	75.1 ± 0.8
mAP VOC	**73.4 ± 0.2**	**73.0 ± 0.1**	**73.2 ± 0.1**	**73.3 ± 0.1**	**73.6 ± 0.2**	**73.1 ± 0.2**	**73.3 ± 0.1**
Animal						84.9 ± 0.2	84.8 ± 0.0
Roadvehicle						82.6 ± 0.2	82.8 ± 0.3
Stuff						58.6 ± 0.3	58.8 ± 0.4
Vehicle						80.7 ± 0.0	80.9 ± 0.2
mAP extra cat.						**76.7 ± 0.1**	**76.8 ± 0.2**
mAP						**73.7 ± 0.2**	**73.9 ± 0.1**

Classification Performance. The classification performance of the original SSD detector (73.4% AP) and the SSD-ML detector with negative mining over batch, using multinomial (73.3% AP) or binary classification (73.6% AP), are similar. The SSD-ML detectors not using negative mining over the batch have a minor drop in mAP of 0.3% and 0.4% AP (multinomal and binary) with respect to the versions with negative mining over batch. The difference of 0.3% mAP between multinomial classification (73.3%) and binary classification (73.6%) is negligible, but shows that our binary classification method is equally suited for this problem as the multinomial classification (similar to YOLO9000 [14]). However, note that our binary classification allows for more advanced hierarchies when datasets are combined and therefore we prefer the proposed approach.

4.5   Experiment 2: Hierarchical Classification

This experiment introduces the hierarchical classification tree for the PASCAL VOC categories and measures the impact of the hierarchy on the classification performance of our SSD-ML model. The applied hierarchy is depicted in Fig. 3. The SSD-ML model is trained with multinomial classification and the proposed binary classification. The resulting average precision scores are listed in the two rightmost columns under the 'Experiment 2' header in Table 1. This allows for comparison with the original SSD512 and SSD-ML algorithms without the hierarchical classification tree.

Objectness. From the table, it is observed that the detection performance (objectness score) is slightly lower then when using the SSD-ML detectors trained without the additional hierarchy. Using binary classification, the objectness score drops by 0.4% from 72.4% to 72.0%. For multinomial classification, the drop is 0.4% from 72.2% to 71.8%, respectively. Apparently the additional classes have a small negative impact on object detection. This is unexpected because objectness and classification are computed with different loss functions and use separated convolutions in the detection head. However, it can be explained by the fact that the feature layers are shared, so that the (more complex) classification loss probably influences the weight updates towards these layers more than the objectness loss, causing a slightly lower objectness accuracy.

Classification. The SSD-ML model with binary classification has a slightly higher average accuracy for the VOC classes (0.2%) than the version with multinomial classification (73.3% vs 73.1%). However, this difference is negligible with respect to the standard deviation of 0.1 and 0.2 of that average accuracy, respectively. Compared to not using hierarchy, the multinomial classification has a 0.2% lower accuracy while binary classification performs 0.3% worse, as compared to their non-hierarchical versions. We assume that the additional classes from the hierarchy have a small negative impact on the classification performance because the CNN network effectively has to learn more categories (24+1 vs. 20+1), making the problem more complex.

Hierarchy. The newly added hierarchical categories show similar results for binary and multinomial classification, having an average precision score of 76.8% and 76.7%, respectively. Note that the accuracy for these extra categories is significantly higher (3.5% and 3.6%, respectively) than the mAP for the PASCAL VOC classes. This shows that the network is able to predict more accurately if an object belongs to one of the super-categories. The mAP over all hierarchical classes combined shows similar results for SSD-ML binary (73.9%) and multinomial (73.7%) classification methods.

For the remainder of the experiments, we have chosen to use the SSD-ML variant with negative mining over batch, and binary classification. The binary classification method is adopted because of its flexibility in defining sub-categories and the ability to contain non-fully defined sub-leafs in a hierarchy. For example, in the case of PASCAL VOC this would mean we could add additional animal samples (such as giraffes) without adding an explicit 'giraffe' class, since such samples should be classified as 'animal'. This aspect provides extra flexibility, when combining datasets and expanding categories in existing datasets, because the ground-truth labels do not require to have the same category depth.

4.6 Experiment 3: Less Available Ground Truth for Classification

In our final experiment on the PASCAL VOC dataset, we measure the impact of having less ground truth available for classification, by iteratively removing class labels for each category. Note that ground-truth annotations without class labels are still used to learn the objectness and bounding-box predictions. The results are reported for the SSD-ML model with binary classification and negative mining over batch, however, similar trends in the results are observed for the SSD-ML model with multinomial classification. Table 2 presents the results only for binary classification because multinomial classification offers similar values. The first column (0%) refers to training on the original training dataset without removing any label information.

Objectness. The detection performances of the original detector and the detectors without label information are similar. When 90% of the label information is removed, the average precision is 71.0%, which is only a small drop of 1.0%, compared to having all the label information available (72.0% AP). This is unexpected, as localization is learned separately from the classification in our network. Thus, the availability of label information does not have an impact on the detection performance. However, as also observed in the previous experiments, there is a minor influence because the base CNN is shared for objectness and classification and is effectively trained with less classification samples.

Classification. It can be noticed that for each category, the classification performance drops significantly when 50–60% of the labels is removed. When training with more labels, the impact of removing labels is limited to 2.0% in AP, even for the classes that have the lowest amount of samples (e.g. 'Bus' and 'Train'). When looking at the 'Car' category, which is relatively well represented by a large amount of samples $(4, 008)$ in the dataset, it can be observed that up to 70% of the samples can be removed before experiencing a significant deterioration of the classification performance, e.g. from 82.6% to 81.4%. Moreover, for the best represented 'Person' category $(15, 576$ samples), up to 80% of the person labels can be removed without any significant impact on performance (64.1% AP). A minimum number of samples seems to be required for each object class, where the absolute number is defined by the complexity of that class. Above that absolute number, the classification performance tends to converge.

Apparently, it is not required to have classification labels available for all ground-truth annotations, in order to obtain an acceptable classification performance.

Hierarchical Classification. The average precision results for the extra hierarchical categories denote a similar trend, since the marginal performance drop from 76.8% to 76.0% when 60% of the label information is removed. However, due to the higher amount of samples in these extra categories, the drop in classification performance starts later (between 80–90%). In more detail, for animals up to 70% of the label information can be removed while decreasing the average precision with only 0.6%, going from 84.8% to 84.2%, respectively. Similar drops are noticeable for the other categories. These extra categories contain more samples per category by combining the original PASCAL VOC categories. Although the classification of the super-categories seems intuitively more complicated than classification of the original categories because of higher intra-class variances, this experiment shows that the high-level categories can be trained effectively with less ground-truth label information.

5   Experimental Results: Traffic Surveillance

The object detection and classification challenges for traffic surveillance are clearly different from more generic datasets, such as PASCAL VOC. Common scenes in traffic surveillance include fixed cameras (causing static background), low-light conditions and varying weather conditions, typically resulting in low-resolution objects that can become unsharp and suffer from motion blur. Recently, two large-scale traffic surveillance datasets have been published: UA-DETRAC [19] and MIO-TCD [12]. Both datasets contain multiple vehicle object categories and multiple camera viewpoints.

In this section, we combine these datasets for training SSD-ML with hierarchical categories, as shown in Fig. 5. We propose a novel proprietary dataset specifically for traffic evaluation. The aim is to train the SSD-ML detector with annotations from the public datasets, and evaluate the performance on our proprietary traffic test set. Both datasets do not map perfectly to the desired hierarchy, since they either do not have the 'van' category in their ground-truth labels, or lack detailed truck information ('articulated truck' vs 'single-unit truck'). Moreover, in the desired hierarchy, we have defined the sub-category 'van' as a single sub-category of cars, which is impossible to learn with a multinomial classification method (this would require a subcategory named 'Other' for all cars that are not vans). By combining these datasets, the SSD-ML model can learn classification labels from one dataset while exploiting localization information from another dataset.

Three main experiments are carried out for the traffic application. First, we evaluate the SSD-ML detector trained on each dataset individually and report the cross-validation results, to investigate the difference between the three datasets. In Experiment T2, we aim to increase the detection performance for all object categories by combining the datasets. In multiple iterations, the amount of annotations for training is increased, while measuring the effect on the accuracy. In Experiment T3, this evaluation is repeated while evaluating classification accuracy. All experiments presented in this section are based on employing the SSD-ML detector with negative mining over batch and using binary hierarchical classification. The training parameters and the involved ablation studies are equal to Sect. 4.3 and Sect. 5.2, respectively, we see it gives slightly better results for VOC as compared to ... for the PASCAL VOC dataset (Sec. 5.2).

Prior to going into the details of the experiments, we want to draw ... to our original publication [24] we have ... that sufficient experimental subspace network. This has resulted in some minor differences ... percentage points of ...

Table 2. Detection performance for the proposed SSD-ML detector when increasingly removing the amount of label information from the ground truth.

Objectness	#Samples	Percentage of labels removed									
		0%	10%	20%	30%	40%	50%	60%	70%	80%	90%
Aeroplane	1,285	80.6±0.3	80.6±0.7	81.0±1.0	81.0±0.7	81.5±0.9	79.7±1.1	79.5±1.6	78.4±1.2	77.7±1.0	57.2±1.8
Bicycle	1,208	80.7±0.6	78.2±0.9	78.8±0.1	79.5±0.5	79.1±1.0	78.5±0.6	77.4±0.4	76.1±0.8	72.3±1.6	52.7±0.8
Bird	1,820	72.9±0.3	72.4±1.4	72.0±0.5	72.1±0.4	71.7±1.2	71.6±0.5	71.4±0.4	69.4±1.4	66.1±0.9	55.6±1.6
Boat	1,397	60.1±1.6	59.0±0.6	58.7±0.5	59.3±0.7	58.3±0.4	59.9±2.0	56.9±0.4	55.9±0.3	50.2±1.8	32.5±0.5
Bottle	2,116	44.5±1.3	44.5±0.2	44.2±0.3	44.9±1.0	44.5±0.6	43.4±0.3	44.1±0.4	43.0±0.9	40.8±0.8	38.2±0.1
Bus	909	81.7±0.9	81.5±0.3	80.8±1.0	80.0±1.1	80.1±0.4	79.5±0.3	80.1±0.2	78.2±0.4	73.8±1.9	43.4±2.3
Car	4,008	82.6±0.2	82.7±0.2	82.3±0.3	82.5±0.7	82.0±0.5	82.0±0.3	81.4±0.7	81.4±0.6	79.6±0.7	73.7±0.2
Cat	1,616	91.0±0.4	91.6±1.2	91.5±0.2	90.6±0.5	90.4±0.2	89.6±0.7	88.3±0.5	86.6±0.7	82.8±1.0	57.3±1.6
Chair	4,338	54.4±1.0	54.0±0.6	53.7±0.7	52.7±0.2	53.5±0.8	52.4±0.7	52.1±0.8	52.5±0.5	51.3±0.6	49.3±0.7
Cow	1,058	80.7±0.8	79.8±0.9	79.1±0.5	78.5±1.4	77.7±0.4	76.0±1.7	73.2±1.5	69.9±0.4	58.2±1.6	35.4±0.1
Diningtable	1,057	66.5±1.1	65.3±1.7	66.2±1.1	65.3±1.4	64.4±1.7	62.9±2.0	62.8±1.4	61.5±0.9	54.5±1.0	43.6±1.3
Dog	2,079	85.9±0.2	85.7±0.4	86.0±0.3	83.9±0.6	83.3±0.2	82.8±0.6	82.2±0.4	79.4±0.7	74.0±0.5	44.8±1.0
Horse	1,156	85.3±0.5	85.1±0.3	84.9±0.5	85.0±0.8	83.6±0.5	82.7±0.6	83.1±0.5	81.5±1.0	73.9±0.4	54.9±1.5
Motorbike	1,141	80.6±0.3	81.9±0.4	80.9±0.6	80.8±0.5	80.7±0.6	79.7±0.6	79.0±0.7	78.0±1.9	73.2±0.8	49.0±2.9
Person	15,576	64.8±0.2	64.6±0.3	64.5±0.2	64.4±0.3	64.6±0.0	64.1±0.1	64.6±0.3	63.9±0.3	64.1±0.1	62.8±0.2
Pottedplant	1,724	48.1±1.2	47.3±1.1	47.3±0.5	48.4±0.7	48.1±0.5	46.7±1.5	46.4±0.6	45.7±0.5	42.8±0.7	33.2±1.5
Sheep	1,347	71.3±0.6	71.9±0.8	71.6±1.7	71.3±0.4	70.0±1.4	68.3±0.8	67.2±0.3	64.8±1.2	59.6±0.4	31.0±3.0
Sofa	1,211	70.3±0.7	68.4±0.8	67.7±1.3	67.2±0.8	66.5±0.4	66.0±0.6	64.9±0.7	63.1±0.7	59.9±0.1	41.7±2.0
Train	984	87.9±0.7	88.2±0.6	86.0±0.6	86.2±0.2	85.8±1.1	85.7±0.6	85.3±0.8	84.0±0.7	80.6±0.5	47.1±4.1
Tvmonitor	1,193	75.1±0.8	75.4±0.4	75.2±0.5	74.4±1.5	73.4±0.5	73.9±1.5	73.3±0.3	72.8±0.4	70.6±1.3	64.8±0.8
mAP VOC		**73.3±0.1**	**72.9±0.3**	**72.6±0.3**	**72.4±0.3**	**72.0±0.3**	**71.3±0.3**	**70.6±0.2**	**69.3±0.2**	**65.3±0.5**	**48.4±1.0**
Animal	9,076	84.8±0.0	84.6±0.6	84.8±0.3	84.8±0.4	84.6±0.2	84.5±0.4	84.4±0.2	84.2±0.4	83.5±0.2	79.1±0.5
Roadvehicle	7,266	82.8±0.3	82.8±0.4	82.6±0.4	82.8±0.6	82.5±0.2	82.5±0.2	82.1±0.4	82.0±0.3	81.3±0.5	76.8±0.1
Stuff	11,639	58.8±0.4	58.3±0.1	58.4±0.2	58.3±0.4	58.2±0.2	57.9±0.2	57.4±0.4	57.1±0.3	55.6±0.5	52.2±0.2
Vehicle	10,932	80.9±0.2	80.9±0.3	80.6±0.3	80.8±0.4	80.6±0.2	80.6±0.3	80.1±0.3	80.0±0.2	79.6±0.2	76.8±0.2
mAP extra cat.		**76.8±0.2**	**76.7±0.3**	**76.6±0.3**	**76.7±0.3**	**76.5±0.1**	**76.4±0.2**	**76.0±0.1**	**75.8±0.0**	**75.0±0.2**	**71.2±0.2**
mAP		**73.9±0.1**	**73.5±0.3**	**73.3±0.3**	**73.1±0.3**	**72.7±0.3**	**72.1±0.3**	**71.5±0.2**	**70.4±0.2**	**66.9±0.4**	**52.2±0.8**

and using binary hierarchical classification. The training parameters and involved evaluation metrics are equal to Sect. 4.3 and Sect. 4.2, respectively. We set $\beta = 0.5$ because it gives slightly better results for traffic as compared to $\beta = 1.0$ for the PASCAL experiments (see Eq. (6)).

Prior to going into the details of the experiments, we want to remark that compared to our original publication [21], we have used a different experimental software framework. This has resulted in some minor differences (up to a percent point in order of magnitude) in the provided traffic experiment results reported in this work, but did not change the trends, observations and conclusions.

This section continues with a description of the datasets in Sect. 5.1, followed by the three experiments in Sects. 5.2, 5.3 and 5.4.

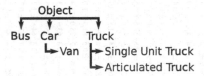

Fig. 5. The proposed hierarchical categories for traffic.

5.1   Datasets

In the traffic experiments, three different traffic-surveillance datasets are used. The first two datasets are the publicly available UA-DETRAC [19] and MIO-TCD [12] datasets. The third dataset is generated by the authors and is used for testing the proposed trained SSD-ML detector. Each dataset has different scene and image characteristics and classification-label definitions. The following paragraphs discuss these characteristics and explain how the datasets are mapped to our single hierarchical classification tree for traffic surveillance. This classification tree is depicted in Fig. 5.

Dataset 1: UA-DETRAC.   The first dataset used is the publicly available UA-DETRAC [19], further referred to as DETRAC in the remainder of this paper. This dataset is recorded at 24 different locations in Beijing and Tianjin in China at an image resolution of 960×540 pixels. Typical scenes contain multiple high-traffic lanes captured from a birds-eye view. Some example images are shown in Fig. 6a. The training set contains 61 video clips with annotated bounding boxes. The videos are sampled at a high temporal resolution (25 fps), resulting in many images of the same physical vehicle with identical scene background. Each bounding box is classified into one of four vehicle categories: 'Car', 'Bus', 'Van', and 'Other'.

Table 3 describes the mapping of the DETRAC dataset to our classification tree. The numbers behind the label names for DETRAC denote the number of sampled physical objects. Note that in our hierarchy 'Van' is a sub-category of 'Car' and in the DETRAC set they are labeled individually, so that we can use the DETRAC 'Car' label as negatives for our 'Van' category. Visual inspection shows that the 'Other' category in DETRAC contains various types of trucks. Because the test-set annotations have not

Table 3. Mapping of the dataset labels to our hierarchical categories. Samples are used as positive (P) or negative (N) during training, otherwise they are ignored.

Input categories			Output categories					
Dataset	Label	#Samples	Car	Truck	Bus	Van	SUT	AT
DETRAC (China)	Car (5,177)	479,270	P	N	N	N		
	Van (610)	55,574	P	N	N	P		
	Bus (106)	29,755	N	N	P			
	Other (43)	3,515	N	P	N			
MIO (North-America)	Articulated Truck	8,426	N	P	N		N	P
	Bus	9,543	N	N	P			
	Car	209,703	P	N	N			
	Motorcycle	1,616						
	Motorized Vehicle	13,369						
	Non-Motorized	2,141						
	Pickup Truck	39,817	P	N	N			
	Single Unit Truck	5,148	N	P	N		P	N
	Work Van	7,804	P	N	N	P		
Ours (Europe)	Car	50,984	P	N	N			
	Bus	2,215	N	N	P			
	Single Unit Truck	1,422	N	P	N		P	N
	Articulated Truck	2,420	N	P	N		N	P

been made publicly available, we construct our own test set for the traffic experiments, based on a part of the original training set. The test set is created from the video clips {MVI_20011, MVI_3961, MVI_40131, MVI_63525} and consists of 4,617 images containing 54,593 annotations. The training set contains the remaining 77,468 images with 568,114 annotations.

Dataset 2: MIO-TCD. The MIO-TCD dataset [12] further referred to as MIO in the remainder of this paper, consists of 137,743 images recorded by traffic cameras all over Canada and the United States. The images cover a wide range of urban-traffic scenarios and typically cover one or two traffic lanes captured from the side of the road with a wide-angle lens, producing noticeable lens distortion. Visual examples are depicted in Fig. 6b. The image resolution is generally low and varies from 342×228 to 720×480 pixels. Each vehicle annotation is categorized into one of 11 vehicle categories, of which we remove the 'pedestrian' and 'bicycle' categories, since we focus on road traffic. The remaining categories are mapped to our hierarchical categories, as shown in Table 3. Note that the classes 'Motorcycle', 'Motorized Vehicle' and 'Non-Motorized Vehicle' are not assigned to any category, because they are used only for the objectness prediction.

(a) UA-DETRAC

(b) MIO-TCD

(c) Ours

Fig. 6. Example images from the UA-DETRAC, MIO-TCD and our dataset (Source: [21], Fig. 4, 5 and 6).

Similar to the DETRAC set, a small part of the annotations is used to create a test set. For this, we select every tenth image from the training set, resulting in a validation set of 11,000 images containing 34,591 annotations. The training set contains the remaining 99,000 images with 307,567 annotations.

Dataset 3: Proprietary Dataset. Our dataset is considerably smaller than the DETRAC and MIO datasets, but contains high-resolution images of 1280 × 720 and 1920 × 1080 pixels, recorded by typical surveillance cameras monitoring different traffic in Europe. The captured scenes contain traffic crossings, roundabouts and highways. In total, 20,750 images are captured at 12 different locations under various lighting and weather conditions, covering 96,600 annotations. All images are annotated with object bounding boxes and labels.

The dataset is split into a test set of 2,075 randomly selected images, containing 6,363 bounding box annotations. Each bounding box is assigned one of the hierarchical categories according to Table 3. Note that all vans in our training set are labeled as cars. The training set contains 90,237 annotations in 18,675 images. In our test set, we have annotated the 'Van' category to also enable the validation of our detector for that class. Table 4 outlines the distribution of the test set.

To validate the performance of our newly introduced batch negative mining, a dataset containing only scene-background images is created. Such a background image is created for every scene in our dataset, by computing the median value for each pixel over every 100 images, thereby effectively removing objects occurring in the individual images. This results in 154 scene-background images in our train set. This background set is relatively small compared to other datasets used for training, therefore each background image is sampled 10 times more often than other images during training. Note that it requires minimal effort to create such a background-image dataset for new scenes compared to annotating new ground truth, e.g. drawing bounding boxes and assigning label categories for each object. Note that images from the same location occur in both train and test set. Therefore, the explicit use of background information from the train set leads to an inherent performance increase for the test images. Although this is not common for validation, in the specific application of traffic surveillance, most variation is covered by the moving traffic objects at the foreground and not the background. This also holds for the normal train/test division, without explicitly adding background images.

Table 4. Our test-set categories and the amount of samples per category.

Label	Car	Truck	Bus	Van	Single Unit Truck	Articulated Truck	Total
#Samples	5,681	438	244	590	160	236	**6,363**
%	89.3%	6.9%	3.8%	9.3%	2.5%	3.7%	**100%**

5.2 Experiment T1: Vehicle Detection, Effect of Datasets

The first experiment provides insight in the variations of objects between the different datasets, because the datasets are recorded in different countries with varying camera viewpoints. To this end, SSD-ML is trained separately on DETRAC, MIO and our dataset, and evaluated on each of the test sets. The objectness and classification performances are reported on each individual test set. The DETRAC dataset does not contain any sub-labels for truck, so that no average precision can be reported for the sub-categories of truck.

The results are presented in Table 5. Each row reports the average precision for a class in our defined hierarchy. "Train" denotes the dataset used for training, while "Test" refers to the dataset used for testing.

Objectness. We observe that the performance for each dataset is optimal when trained with the corresponding training set, which is expected given that vehicle models are different in Europe, America and Asia. The detector trained on DETRAC performs well on our dataset for detection (79.1%) and the detector trained on our dataset performs well on DETRAC (87.3%), suggesting that the vehicle models in Europe and Asia are more similar than in America. Both the detectors trained on DETRAC and on our dataset perform poorly on the MIO set (34.9% and 28.5%, resp.). Surprisingly, when training with MIO, the performance on all sets is quite high. This will be addressed later.

Table 5. Average precision for traffic-object detection and classification.

Train	DETRAC			MIO			Ours		
Test	DETR.	MIO	Ours	DETR.	MIO	Ours	DETR.	MIO	Ours
Objectness	96.9±0.0	34.0±1.1	78.8±0.3	88.6±0.5	91.8±0.2	82.5±0.1	85.7±2.7	26.6±2.0	96.2±0.1
Car	96.5±0.1	36.1±1.2	78.1±0.5	88.8±0.6	91.4±0.2	79.4±0.6	85.3±3.1	31.8±3.0	95.6±0.1
Truck	34.4±10.5	5.1±1.4	26.6±0.4	1.3±0.2	82.8±0.4	63.8±4.0	7.5±3.4	5.2±0.3	95.5±0.2
Bus	98.4±0.3	43.9±1.2	52.7±2.4	86.7±0.3	96.3±0.3	79.3±0.9	93.0±0.3	28.1±3.4	87.8±0.2
Van	54.8±2.3	4.3±0.1	30.1±3.1	3.7±0.1	3.2±0.0	6.4±0.2	6.9±0.6	1.6±0.2	14.3±1.8
SUT		2.7±1.2	10.4±1.4		60.0±0.3	22.0±1.6		1.0±0.1	81.5±0.2
AT		2.3±0.4	11.8±1.6		85.9±0.4	58.6±8.0		5.4±1.5	88.1±1.4
mAP	71.0±2.1	15.7±0.8	34.9±0.6	45.1±0.3	69.9±0.1	51.6±1.7	48.2±1.5	12.2±0.6	77.1±0.3

Classification. The classification scores for cars and buses are very similar to the object-ness scores for all objects. For the 'Van' class, we observe that only the DETRAC dataset has clearly defined vans. In the MIO set, part of the vans are annotated as 'Car'. Therefore, all car samples cannot be used as negative samples during training, which significantly reduces the training set size. Moreover, our set does not have any vans labeled. The classification scores for vans when trained on DETRAC are very low on MIO and our set, concluding that the 'Van' samples from DETRAC are visually different. Trucks in the DETRAC set are apparently not well-defined, as the highest obtained classification accuracy is 30.6%. For DETRAC, single-unit and articulated trucks are not labeled and thus not trained, but a prediction is always made by the detection model for this class, so that noise in the network leads to classifications with very low score. For the MIO and our dataset, for trucks a similar behaviour to cars and buses is observed. Visual inspection of DETRAC results shows that many false positive classifications for busses originate from trucks in the testing set, causing low precision. The low performance for vans results from many larger vehicles, which are being falsely classified (such as station-wagons).

It is remarkable that a relatively high performance is obtained when training on the MIO dataset. This can be potentially explained by the assumption that the MIO set is a super-set of both DETRAC and our set. Probably, the visual variation in the DETRAC and our dataset is also contained in the MIO set (resulting in good performance when training on MIO), but this set has additional variation that is not covered in the other sets (leading to poor performance on MIO when training with the other set). This additional variation can originate from limited image quality, large variations in viewpoint, image roll, lens distortion and potentially different vehicle models.

5.3 Experiment T2: Vehicle Detection

This experiment evaluates the detection performance of our SSD-ML model in more detail. The detection performance is evaluated by measuring the recall at a fixed precision point (90%) in the recall-precision curve (see Sect. 4.2). This provides insight in which class categories are localized better than others. We focus on the contribution of the additional training sets and the effect on the different vehicle categories. Our

Table 6. Evaluation of SSD-ML objectness score (detection only, ignoring classification). The objectness (Obj.) is reported by the average precision (AP), while the per-category scores are reported as the recall for that category at the 90%-precision point for objectness.

	Obj.	Recall@P90					
		Car	Truck	Bus	SUT	AT	Van
DETRAC	**78.8 ± 0.3**	69.7 ± 0.7	57.0 ± 1.0	76.1 ± 2.7	57.3 ± 2.9	56.3 ± 1.5	81.6 ± 0.2
MIO	**82.5 ± 0.1**	69.1 ± 0.1	70.5 ± 0.8	86.1 ± 0.6	72.5 ± 1.2	72.2 ± 0.3	82.5 ± 0.7
D+M	**84.1 ± 0.3**	71.2 ± 1.0	72.8 ± 0.9	84.2 ± 0.6	75.4 ± 1.2	72.5 ± 0.5	85.8 ± 1.0
D+M+Backgr	**84.7 ± 0.4**	75.3 ± 0.4	76.5 ± 1.5	88.1 ± 1.3	75.6 ± 1.5	77.1 ± 1.1	88.6 ± 0.7
D+M+BusTruck	**93.1 ± 0.2**	84.3 ± 0.5	84.0 ± 0.9	93.2 ± 0.4	84.0 ± 0.4	83.1 ± 1.5	93.1 ± 0.3
D+M+Boxes	**94.2 ± 0.3**	86.9 ± 0.3	84.0 ± 0.7	93.4 ± 0.4	83.8 ± 0.7	83.3 ± 0.8	93.3 ± 0.3
D+M+Ours	**94.1 ± 0.1**	86.9 ± 0.2	84.0 ± 0.6	94.3 ± 0.4	84.3 + 0.4	83.1 ± 0.9	93.4 ± 0.3
Ours	**96.2 ± 0.1**	89.0 ± 0.2	84.9 ± 0.4	95.1 ± 0.0	84.5 ± 1.2	84.3 ± 0.7	93.0 ± 0.0

final goal is to obtain the best performance on our specific traffic dataset. Therefore, we evaluate the detection performance only on our test set.

We start by combining the DETRAC and MIO sets. Next, we iteratively add more training data in four sequential steps:

– D+M+Backgr: add train set background images (see Sect. 5.1),
– D+M+BusTruck: add all bus and truck annotations from our train set,
– D+M+Boxes: add all our train set annotations (boxes only, no labels),
– D+M+Ours: add all annotations from our train set (including labels).

The obtained results of all combinations are reported in Table 6, which are discussed below.

DETRAC and MIO. Training with the DETRAC and MIO datasets individually results in an objectness AP of 78.8% and 82.5%, respectively. The recall per object category shows that the MIO dataset has high recall for vans (82.5%) and busses (86.1%) and lower recall for cars (69.1%) and trucks (70.5%). Similarly, the DETRAC dataset has high recall for busses (76.1%) and vans (81.6%) and lower for trucks (57.0%) and cars (69.7%). Combining DETRAC and MIO generally leads to an improved or similar performance on each of the different classes and increases the objectness score to 84.1% AP. For busses, we expect that the low performance is caused by the difference in truck models in the different datasets.

Background. The addition of our background set improves the AP to 84.7% due to our proposed negative mining over the batch method. Although the background set does not contain any objects, it allows for better negative harvesting, causing less false positive detections. This can be observed specifically for cars and vans, of which the scores increase with 4.1% (71.2%–75.3%) and 2.8% (85.8%–88.6%) AP, respectively. Although it seems that the detection of these classes is better, this improvement originates from the fact that the overall precision improves (less false detections because of explicit background data). This automatically results in a higher recall (at precision

90%) which has most effect for objects with a low objectness score, such as cars and vans in this case.

Bus & Truck. In addition to the background images, a subset is added, containing all samples with busses and trucks from our set. This subset forms about 25% of all images in our set. In this 'Bus & Truck' subset, all busses and trucks are labeled with their ground-truth labels while the remaining traffic only has box information (no labels). The created subset is added to the DETRAC and MIO sets. The detection performance increases significantly for each object category when including this subset, while the objectness score improves with 8.4% (84.7%–93.1% AP). This is as expected, despite the fact that only 25% of our dataset was added. Many of the images in the subset contain cars and vans, since these categories are more common than busses and trucks.

Boxes with and without Labels. To improve detection performance even more, our complete dataset is combined with DETRAC and MIO to create the largest possible dataset. First, we add our dataset without labels (denoted by 'D+M+Boxes' in the table). Training without labels improves the detection performance marginally compared to using only the Bus & Truck subset with 0.9% (93.1%–94.2%). This shows that the Bus & Truck subset already contains most variance required to train a detector w.r.t. localization. It can be observed that only the 'Car' class benefits from the additional training samples, as it is apparently a more difficult class. Next, we add our dataset with labels ('D+M+Ours'). The addition of the classification labels does not have a significant effect on the detection performance with respect to having only the bounding-box information. This is as expected because the classification labels do not have an influence on the localization.

Ours. The detector trained on only our dataset outperforms the other combinations with an AP of 96.2% and it also outperforms the detector trained on the combination of DETRAC, MIO and our dataset. However, our training set is very similar to the test set (images from similar scenes/locations) which could lead to over-fitting, benefiting the evaluation on the test set. Note that combining all datasets has an advantage for classification, as we will show in the next experiment.

Note that the results in Table 6 contain significantly higher recall values than in the equivalent experiment in our previous work. This is explained by using so-called ignore regions in the new work of which it is sure that objects are absent. As a consequence, the total number of ground-truth annotations is reduced. By computing the recall only on the areas where objects are present, the recall rate is effectively increased.

5.4   Experiment T3: Vehicle Classification

The final experiment concentrates on the classification performance, obtained on our test set, as an extension of the localization performance from Experiment T2. We employ the same incremental combinations of datasets as in the previous experiment. Hence, the same detection models as in the previous experiment are used, but we measure the classification performance instead of the localization performance. Classification performance is measured for each object class individually and summarized by the

Table 7. Mean Average Precision (mAP) and Average Precision per object category, tested on our dataset.

	Car	Truck	Bus	SUT	AT	Van	mAP
DETRAC	78.1 ± 0.3	26.6 ± 0.4	52.7 ± 2.4	10.4 ± 1.4	11.8 ± 1.6	30.1 ± 3.1	**34.9 ± 0.6**
MIO	79.4 ± 0.1	63.8 ± 4.0	79.3 ± 0.9	22.0 ± 1.6	58.6 ± 8.0	6.4 ± 0.2	**51.6 ± 1.7**
D+M	82.5 ± 0.3	61.4 ± 1.5	73.2 ± 1.3	14.8 ± 3.2	57.2 ± 1.2	35.1 ± 0.7	**54.0 ± 1.0**
D+M+Backgr	83.3 ± 0.4	68.7 ± 1.3	72.9 ± 1.1	18.7 ± 1.5	62.3 ± 1.7	36.8 ± 4.8	**57.1 ± 1.5**
D+M+BusTruck	92.4 ± 0.2	88.9 ± 0.9	89.6 ± 0.3	34.7 ± 2.9	80.8 ± 2.0	49.8 ± 2.1	**72.7 ± 0.8**
D+M+Boxes	93.6 ± 0.3	81.8 ± 2.6	83.0 ± 0.4	35.2 ± 5.1	63.5 ± 2.6	66.8 ± 0.7	**70.7 ± 1.7**
D+M+Ours	93.4 ± 0.1	93.1 ± 0.9	87.9 ± 0.7	62.0 ± 3.1	83.9 ± 1.4	73.0 ± 0.6	**82.2 ± 0.6**
OURS	95.6 ± 0.1	95.5 ± 0.2	87.8 ± 0.2	81.5 ± 0.2	88.1 ± 1.4	14.3 ± 1.8	**77.1 ± 0.3**

mean Average Precision (mAP) over all categories in our hierarchy. Table 7 presents the results. Note that the results on DETRAC, MIO and Our dataset individually are equal to the cross-validation results on our dataset (see Table 5).

DETRAC and MIO. The detector trained on DETRAC and MIO combined increases classification performance for cars by 3.1% (79.4%–82.5%) and vans by 5.0% (30.1%–35.1%) with respect to the maximum score achieved by DETRAC and MIO individually. This hints that the different information from both sets can be effectively combined to improve performance on our dataset. However, the AP for trucks (61.4%) and busses (73.2%) decrease by 2.4% and 6.1%, respectively, with respect to the maximum score achieved by DETRAC or MIO. For these object categories, we expect that combining MIO and DETRAC causes confusion, due to large visual differences for these objects in both datasets.

Background. The addition of background images improves the mAP by 3.1% (54.0%–57.1%). Although the background images are not used for learning object categories, they do improve detection performance (see previous experiment). The increased detection performance originates from less false detections, which also leads to less false classifications. The bus (72.9%) and truck (68.7%) classification performance is low compared to the 'Car' category (83.3%).

Bus & Truck. To improve the classification scores for these objects, we propose to add a subset from our dataset containing only bus and truck annotations. The classification performance is significantly improved by including the Bus & Truck subset. The mAP increases by 15.6% (57.1%–72.7%). The classification performance of trucks has improved by 20.2% to 88.9% AP and busses gain 16.7%, leading to 89.6% AP. Besides the improved classification performance for these two categories, also cars (+9.1%) and vans (+13.0%) benefit from the additional samples. This originates from the increased detection performance, as cars and vans in this subset are only annotated by their bounding box and no label information is available.

Boxes Only. Next, we investigate the effect of additional annotations without any label information (also no bus and truck labels). From the previous experiment, it is known that this significantly improves detection results for all objects. When we focus on clas-

Fig. 7. 'Single-Unit Truck' examples in MIO.

sification performance, it can be observed that the mAP has increased significantly by 13.6% to 70.7% with respect to using background images (57.1%). However, the mAP is 2.0% lower than with the Bus & Truck subset. When looking at the per-category AP scores, it can be noticed that the classification performance of cars and vans have both improved with respect to the Bus & Truck subset, while the Truck and Bus categories have a drop in performance. This is as expected, since the Bus & Truck subset explicitly targets these objects and includes label information. These results imply that it is possible to learn classification information for specific object categories from other datasets when no label information is available in the target dataset. Similarly, localization of object classes can be improved when non-matching class definitions between datasets exist.

Boxes with Labels. The classification performance further increases when our dataset, including label annotations, is combined with DETRAC and MIO. The average gain in performance is significant (70.7%–82.2%). This is mainly caused by an improved performance for the 'Truck' sub-categories. Performance of trucks increases with 11.3%, while the sub-categories 'Single Unit Truck' and 'Articulated Truck' increase with 26.8% and 20.4%, respectively. Visual inspection has shown that this is caused by a difference in vehicle model types but mostly due to inconsistent labeling in the MIO dataset. The 'Single Unit Truck' category contain variations of large vehicles that do not fit the remaining class categories of MIO, such as excavators and tractors. Example images are shown in Fig. 7. The DETRAC set does not contain samples of single-unit trucks. Note that the 'Van' performance is increased from 66.8% to 73.0%, while no additional van labels are presented. We expect this to originate from less confusions with the 'Bus' class. Visual inspection shows that busses were previously misclassified as vans.

Ours. Training with our dataset results in high average precision for all object categories except 'Van'. This is expected, as vans are not present in our training dataset (See Table 3). This shows the benefit of using label information from other datasets.

6   Discussion

The first discussion point is on the choice of binary classification versus multinomial classification for creating classification hierarchy. In our experiments on PASCAL

VOC, it can be observed that multinomial classification and binary classification have similar performance. The preferred classification method depends on the application. When the complete hierarchy is known, and all labels can be categorized into leafs so that the hierarchy is fully described, multinomial classification is a suitable choice. During training, multinomial loss enforces a single class to always be activated, whereas with binary classification none of the output predictions may be activated. The main drawback of multinomial classification is when inter-class confusion occurs, which may cause multinomial classification to output a uniform distribution of output activations with no clearly preferred output class. With binary classification this would not happen and it would allow specific classes to be much higher in score than others. Alternatively, binary classification is attractive when from a main class of objects, not all sub-classes are annotated and available as ground truth, although having a large number of images available.

The second point of discussion is the awareness of hidden inconsistencies in datasets. In our traffic experiments, it can be observed that combining the datasets is not trivial and can imply challenges. One of the challenges is the geographic origin of the datasets. For example, trucks are larger in North America with respect to Asia and Europe. Another pitfall when combining datasets is that the labeled object categories in each dataset should be consistent. For example, the 'Single-Unit Truck' category is defined differently in the MIO dataset than in our dataset. Because we have separated the vehicle presence and classification tasks, inconsistent sub-labels of a class can still be used to improve object localization and classification of the (super-)class. For example, in our case the category 'Single-Unit Truck' in the MIO dataset can still be used for training our objectness prediction without any changes to the dataset to improve detection performance of the general vehicle class.

7   Conclusions

In this paper, we have proposed a novel detection system with hierarchical classification called SSD-Multi Loss (SSD-ML), based on the state-of-the-art Single-Shot multi-box Detector (SSD). Inspired by the recent You Only Look Once (YOLO) detector, prediction of object presence is learned separately from object class prediction. Our implementation uses hierarchical binary classification instead of multinomial classification, leading to independent training of the classification classes. This allows combining datasets that are not labeled with a complete set of object classes. Moreover, we propose an improved negative mining procedure by selecting false-positive examples in a training-batch instead of per image.

We have experimented with this novel SSD-ML detector for two object detection problems: generic objects and traffic surveillance. The experiments on generic object detection are carried out on the PASCAL VOC datasets. In our experiments, we have found that our proposed negative mining improves detection performance with 0.6% AP. The difference between using binary classification and multinomial classification is negligible. The introduction of a hierarchy on this set causes a small drop in performance (-0.4% AP). However, the hierarchy results in the practical flexibility to add additional object categories to the class definitions, without explicit annotation of the whole set. This occurs often in practice when datasets are augmented or combined. A final experiment shows that classification performance converges quickly when only a limited number of ground-truth labels are provided, while exploiting all ground-truth bounding boxes. The detection and classification performance only decreases slightly when a large part of the labels is removed (performance decreases from 73.3% to 71.3%, when removing 50% of all labels). The performance starts to drop significantly after removing 60% to 80% of all labels, depending on the object class and total number of training samples.

Our second type of experiments focus on traffic surveillance, for which different public surveillance datasets with non-overlapping class definitions have been combined. The UA-DETRAC and MIO-TCD datasets are combined with our newly introduced dataset. The datasets have large visual differences and originate from different regions of the world. In a first experiment, we have performed cross-validation over the datasets and have found that the MIO-TCD dataset contains more visual variation than our dataset and UA-DETRAC.

In a second experiment, we have investigated the effect of incrementally adding more datasets and have shown that detection performance (ignoring classification) increases by adding more datasets. The choice of hierarchical binary classification is here highly beneficial, since the partial growth of the annotated ground-truth samples leads to a continuous growth of detection rate and specific category recognition improvements in classification.

In the last experiment, we have measured the classification performance of our hierarchical system. It was found that it is possible to train a detector learning the classification labels only from UA-DETRAC and MIO-TCD, while including only annotation boxes from our set (no labels). Including classification label information from our dataset raises the performance significantly from 70.7% to 82.8%. Although this increase is considerable and valuable, it originates only from two specific classes (busses and mostly trucks). This proves that the previous conclusion on continuous growth on detection and classification rate indeed occurs when datasets are mutually combined.

To explain this improvement, visual inspection has shown that this is mostly caused by inconsistent labeling in the MIO-TCD dataset for trucks. Despite this inconsistency, the hierarchical classification can benefit from the other available labeling. Although vans are not labeled in our dataset, it is apparently possible to learn the classification from the other datasets, achieving a respectable 73.0% average precision score. Alternatively, note that for cars, all required label information has already been learned from the other datasets and adding our car labels does not improve performance.

Summarizing, we have addressed an important practical problem on the combination of existing datasets with partial classification of categories. Our method of hierarchical binary classification has proven to be attractive for this problem because the classification is independent and allows to build classification trees as far as good examples in ground truth are available. Moreover, the combination of datasets shows growth in detection rate and specific categories. With our experiments we have shown that our hierarchical object detection system provides flexibility in combining datasets and enables hierarchically expanding of categories in already existing datasets. Not all objects in a dataset are required to have category labels. In addition, non-labeled object classes in existing datasets can be learned using external datasets providing the labels for at least those classes, while simultaneously also improving the localization performance of the non-labeled objects.

References

1. Bertinetto, L., Mueller, R., Tertikas, K., Samangooei, S., Lord, N.A.: Making better mistakes: leveraging class hierarchies with deep networks. In: Proceedings of the IEEE/CVF CVPR (2020)
2. Dalal, N., Triggs, B.: Histograms of oriented gradients for human detection. In: 2005 IEEE CVPR, vol. 1, pp. 886–893. IEEE (2005)
3. Everingham, M., et al.: The PASCAL visual object classes challenge 2012 (VOC2012) results (2012)
4. Everingham, M., et al.: The PASCAL visual object classes challenge 2007 (VOC2007) results (2007)
5. Girshick, R.: Fast R-CNN. In: Proceedings of the IEEE International Conference on Computer Vision (ICCV) (2015)
6. Girshick, R., Donahue, J., Darrell, T., Malik, J.: Rich feature hierarchies for accurate object detection and semantic segmentation. In: IEEE CVPR (2014)
7. He, K., Gkioxari, G., Dollar, P., Girshick, R.: Mask R-CNN. In: Proceedings of the IEEE International Conference on Computer Vision (ICCV) (2017)
8. Kuznetsova, A., et al.: The open images dataset v4: unified image classification, object detection, and visual relationship detection at scale. IJCV (2020)
9. Lin, T.Y., Goyal, P., Girshick, R., He, K., Dollár, P.: Focal loss for dense object detection. In: Proceedings of the IEEE ICCV, pp. 2980–2988 (2017)
10. Lin, T.-Y., et al.: Microsoft COCO: common objects in context. In: Fleet, D., Pajdla, T., Schiele, B., Tuytelaars, T. (eds.) ECCV 2014. LNCS, vol. 8693, pp. 740–755. Springer, Cham (2014). https://doi.org/10.1007/978-3-319-10602-1_48
11. Liu, W., et al.: SSD: single shot multibox detector. In: Leibe, B., Matas, J., Sebe, N., Welling, M. (eds.) ECCV 2016. LNCS, vol. 9905, pp. 21–37. Springer, Cham (2016). https://doi.org/10.1007/978-3-319-46448-0_2
12. Luo, Z., et al.: MIO-TCD: a new benchmark dataset for vehicle classification and localization. IEEE Trans. Image Proc. 27(10), 5129–5141 (2018). https://doi.org/10.1109/TIP.2018.2848705
13. Redmon, J., Divvala, S., Girshick, R., Farhadi, A.: You only look once: unified, real-time object detection. In: CVPR, pp. 779–788 (2016). https://doi.org/10.1109/CVPR.2016.91
14. Redmon, J., Farhadi, A.: Yolo9000: better, faster, stronger. In: CVPR, pp. 6517–6525 (2017). https://doi.org/10.1109/CVPR.2017.690
15. Ren, S., He, K., Girshick, R., Sun, J.: Faster R-CNN: towards real-time object detection with region proposal networks. In: NIPS (2015)
16. Simonyan, K., Zisserman, A.: Very deep convolutional networks for large-scale image recognition. arXiv:1409.1556 (2014)
17. Tian, Z., Shen, C., Chen, H., He, T.: FCOS: fully convolutional one-stage object detection. In: Proceedings of the IEEE ICCV, pp. 9627–9636 (2019)
18. Viola, P., Jones, M.: Rapid object detection using a boosted cascade of simple features. In: Proceedings of the 2001 IEEE CVPR (2001)
19. Wen, L., et al.: UA-DETRAC: a new benchmark and protocol for multi-object detection and tracking. arXiv CoRR abs/1511.04136 (2015)

20. Zou, Z., Shi, Z., Guo, Y., Ye, J.: Object detection in 20 years: a survey (2019)
21. Zwemer., M.H., Wijnhoven., R.G.J., de With., P.H.N.: SSD-ML: hierarchical object classification for traffic surveillance. In: Proceedings of the 15th International Joint Conference on Computer Vision, Imaging and Computer Graphics Theory and Applications, VISAPP, vol. 5, pp. 250–259 (2020). https://doi.org/10.5220/0008902402500259

Scene Text Localization Using Lightweight Convolutional Networks

Luis Gustavo Lorgus Decker[1]([✉]) [iD], Allan Pinto[1] [iD], Jose Luis Flores Campana[1] [iD],
Manuel Cordova Neira[1] [iD], Andreza Aparecida dos Santos[1] [iD],
Jhonatas Santos de Jesus Conceição[1] [iD], Helio Pedrini[1] [iD],
Marcus de Assis Angeloni[2] [iD], Lin Tzy Li[2] [iD], Diogo Carbonera Luvizon[2] [iD],
and Ricardo da S. Torres[3] [iD]

[1] Institute of Computing, University of Campinas, Campinas 13083-852, Brazil
luisgustavo.decker@gmail.com, {allan.pinto,helio}@ic.unicamp.br,
j209820@dac.unicamp.br
[2] AI R&D Lab, Samsung R&D Institute Brazil, Campinas 13097-160, Brazil
{m.angeloni,lin.tzy.li,diogo.cl}@samsung.com
[3] Department of ICT and Natural Sciences, Norwegian University of Science and Technology
(NTNU), Ålesund, Norway
ricardo.torres@ntnu.no

Abstract. Various research initiatives have been reported regarding highly effective results for the text detection problem, which consists of detecting textual elements, such as words and phrases, in digital images. Text localization is an important step on very widely used mobile applications, for instance, on-the-go translations and recognition of text for the visually impaired. At the same time, edge computing is revolutionizing the way embedded systems are architected by moving complex processing and analysis to end devices (e.g., mobile and wearable devices). In this context, the development of lightweight networks that can be run in devices with restricted computing power and with a minimum latency as possible is essential to make plenty of mobile-oriented solutions feasible in practice. In this work, we investigate the use of efficient object detection networks to address this task, proposing the fusion of two lightweight neural network architectures, MobileNetV2 and Single Shot Detector (SSD), into our approach named MobText. As experimental results in the ICDAR'11 and ICDAR'13 datasets demonstrates that our solution yields the best trade-off between effectiveness and efficiency in terms of processing time, achieving the state-of-the-art results on the ICDAR'11 dataset with an F-measure of 96.09% and an average processing time of 464 ms on a smartphone device, over experiments executed on both dataset images and with images captured in real time from the portable device.

Keywords: Scene text detection · Mobile devices · Object detector networks · MobilenetV2 · Single shot detector

Part of the results presented in this work were obtained through the "Algoritmos para Detecção e Reconhecimento de Texto Multilíngue" project, funded by Samsung Eletrônica da Amazônia Ltda., under the Brazilian Informatics Law 8.248/91.

1   Introduction

Reading text in images is still an open problem in computer vision and image understanding research fields. This problem has attracted a lot of attention to these communities due to a large number of modern applications that can potentially benefit from this knowledge, such as self-driving vehicles [51,56], robot navigation, scene understanding [48], assistive technologies [54], among others. In addition, the ubiquity of mobile and wearable devices led the text detection and recognition problems to a high-order complexity in terms of efficiency and effectiveness, as both are expected to be performed in real-time in several practical usage scenarios. Thereby, the conception of methods for understanding texts in images effectively and at low computation costs is of paramount importance.

Several methods have been recently proposed in the literature towards localizing textual information in scene images. In general, the text reading problem comprises two distinct tasks: localization and recognition. The former seeks to localize delimited candidate regions that contain textual information, while the second is responsible for transcribing the text inside the candidate regions found during the localization task. In both tasks, the inherent variability of a text (for instance, size, color, font style, background clutter, and perspective distortions), as illustrated in Fig. 1, makes the text reading a very challenging problem.

Fig. 1. Examples of scene text images from ICDAR13 [21] with challenging visual properties.

Among the several approaches for localizing text in images, deep learning-based techniques are the most promising strategies to reach high detection accuracy. He et al. [17], for example, presented a novel technique for scene text detection by proposing a Convolutional Neural Network (CNN) architecture that focuses on extracting text-related regions and specific characteristics of a text. The authors introduced a deep multi-task learning mechanism to train the Text-CNN efficiently, in which each level of the supervised information (text/non-text label, character label, and character mask) is formulated as a learning task. Besides, the authors proposed a pre-processing method, which extends the widely used Maximally Stable Extremal Regions (MSERs) [35] by enhancing the local contrast between text and background regions. Although the proposed CNN presented a reasonable efficiency in detecting candidate regions, with a processing time of about 0.5 s per image, the pre-processing step requires about 4.1 s per image, which may prevent a real-time detection.

Another venue that may render outstanding results in terms of effectiveness consists of combining different neural network architectures to benefit from complementary information to make a better decision. In this vein, Zhang et al. [55] introduced an

approach based on two Fully Convolutional Network (FCN) architectures for predicting a salient map of text regions in a holistic manner (named as Text-Block FCN), and
also for predicting the centroid of each character. The main idea of this approach consists of detecting text line blocks, which are more stable in comparison with character
regions. Similarly, Tang et al. also proposed an ensemble of three modified VGG-16 networks [46]: the first extracts candidate text regions (CTR); the second network refines
the coarse CTR detected by the first model, segmenting them into text; and finally, the
refined CTR are served to a classification network to filter non-text regions and obtain
the final text regions. The CTR extractor network is a modified VGG-16 that, in the
training process, receives the edges of the text as supervisory information in the first
blocks of convolutional layers and the segmented text regions in the last blocks. Both
strategies present several issues in terms of computational efficiency that could make
their use unfeasible in restrictive computing scenarios.

Towards having a truthfully single-stage text detection, Liao et al. [29] proposed an
end-to-end solution named TextBoxes++, which handles arbitrary orientation of word
bounding boxes, whose architecture inherits from the VGG-16 architecture. Similarly
to TextBoxes++, Zhu et al. proposed a deep learning approach [56] also based on the
VGG-16 architecture, but for detecting text-based traffic sign. Both techniques pre
sented outstanding detection rates, but they rely on the use of VGG-16 architecture,
which could be considered inadequate for restrictive computing scenarios due to its
model size with about 138 millions of parameters [18], and floating-point operations
per second (FLOPS) that reach about 15.3 billions [15]. In contrast, lighter CNN architectures, such as MobileNet [18], present a very competitive alternative for this scenario,
with a model size of 4.2 millions of parameters and 569 million FLOPS, for instance.

In light of these remarks, we propose a novel method for text localization considering efficiency and effectiveness trade-offs. Our approach, named MobText, combines two light architectures that were originally proposed for object detection –
MobileNetV2 [43] and SSD [32] – and adapts them to our problem. The main contributions of this work are:

1. the proposal of an effective method for text localization task in scene images, which
   presented better or competitive results when compared with state-of-the-art methods
   at a low computational cost in terms of model size and processing time;
2. a comparative study, in the context of text localization, comprising widely used CNN
   architectures recently proposed for object detection;
3. state-of-the-art results on the ICDAR'11 dataset, with F-Measure of 96.09%, and
   competitive results on ICDAR'13 with F-Measure of 73.58%; and
4. experiments on a computationally restricted device to ensure the efficiency and
   effectiveness on the restricted computing scenario.

In summary, we addressed the following research questions:

– Would a general-purpose object detection network, trained for the text detection
  task, achieve competitive results, in comparison with baseline methods?
– Would a mobile-oriented CNN architecture maintain a competitive performance on
  text detection while being light enough to be executed on devices with restricted
  computing power and built-in memory capacity?

We organized the remaining of this chapter as follows. Section 2 introduces the basic concepts related to the text detection problem and an overview of the technologies and techniques employed in this work. Section 3 presents the MobText, the proposed method for text detection, while Sect. 4 describes the datasets, evaluation metrics, and protocols used to validate our approach. Section 5 presents the experimental results, including a comparison with the baselines methods and the usage of our proposed method in a mobile device to evaluate the efficiency and effectiveness of our approach in a real-world scenario. Finally, Sect. 6 provides our conclusions over the results of our research and points out possible future work.

2   Concepts and Related Work

This section provides an overview of the background and concepts related to this work. Section 2.1 introduces the main concepts related to text localization and recognition problem. Next, in Sect. 2.2, we briefly present a background on deep learning and on its use in the context of restricted computing power scenarios. Finally, examples of efficient and effective methods are discussed.

2.1   Text Localization and Recognition

Text localization and recognition in images and videos from diverse sources have received substantial attention recently, as diverse "robust reading" competitions as ICDAR'11 [20], ICDAR'13 [21], and ICDAR'15 [19] emerged as tools to infer the state-of-the-art in methods designed to address this issue.

The objectives of text localization and recognition are:

- to determine if there is a text in a given image;
- to find the text location, obtaining the estimated position in the image; and
- to recognize the text, obtaining the characters or words contained in the text.

Scene Text. Given the huge rise in the availability of portable, accessible image recorders as smartphones and cameras, it is possible to notice an equivalent increase in the size of data archives and datasets composed of images. A very common element in digital images is text. Text in digital images can occur in a variable fashion: as artificially generated graphic text, digitally added to an image as a caption; or even in scenarios related to giving some useful context to the image as a timestamp or subtitles; and in scene images, which is naturally found in the image captured by the camera and is part of the scene, such as a shop facade or a street sign, for example.

Graphic, or born-digital images, as is called in ICDAR'11 competition [20], have some characteristics so that methods can take advantages of them. Commonly, born-digital images have the text horizontally oriented, in the foreground, with high contrast and in a very controlled background. Examples of such images can be found in Fig. 2. Scene text, as shown in Fig. 3, is a lot more complex: the text is usually cluttered with the background, with variable texture, color, illumination and orientation. Furthermore, possible deformations derived from a perspective view and occlusions from other objects can also be found.

Fig. 2. Examples of images from the ICDAR'11 dataset [20] with texts digitally generated.

Fig. 3. Examples of scene text images extracted from the ICDAR'13 dataset [21].

Text Localization. The process of detecting texts present in an image is called text localization. The fundamental goal is to determine which regions of an image contain a textual element, considering the fact that there is no prior information on whether or not the input image contains any text. Found textual elements are often enclosed in bounding-boxes with as minimum background as possible, or the pixels constituting the textual element can be highlighted in a binary mask. In this process, the text in the image is segmented from the background. Figure 4 shows examples of outputs of a text localization algorithm [47].

Fig. 4. Examples of bounding boxes delimiting texts in images, with the recognized words above each bounding box [47].

Text Recognition. The objective of the text recognition process is basically the same as those of Optical Character Recognition (OCR) software. Given input digital images or videos, the goal is to identify alphabets, numbers, punctuation marks or special characters, without any human cooperation, and then convert each of the recognized symbols into an appropriate character code. Figure 4 shows the recognized characters above the bounding box of the located word.

Text Detection and Recognition Methods. A common way of categorizing existing methods for text detection and recognition relies on dividing them into deep-learning and non-deep learning groups. In this chapter, we are assuming that a deep learning method is a machine learning apparatus so that the feature extraction and the classification modules are both trainable. The remaining methods are therefore classified as non-deep methods, even the ones with a trainable classifier but without trainable feature extraction.

Several non-deep methods were proposed to solve the problem of text detection and recognition. One category of non-deep text detection methods is based on connected component analysis (CCA). Being essentially a graph-based algorithm, CCA approaches take a set of connected components of the image, each one of them individually labeled by a heuristic about feature similarity. Pattern recognition methods are often used to analyze the spatial and feature consensus of the connected components and then define text regions. Some approaches [22,24,27] rely on statistical models, such as AdaBoost, to learn the CCA models, which significantly improve their robustness.

Another category of text detection methods consist of the sliding window classification methods. The principle of these methods is sliding a multiscale window through the image, classifying the regions defined by the sliding window as text and non-text regions. Later, positive regions are then grouped into text regions with morphological operations, conditional random fields, or graph methods [26,47]. This class of methods is simple and adaptive. Nevertheless, they are computationally expensive when a complex classifier is used, and a large number of sliding windows needs to be classified.

Regarding the text recognition problem, a branch of proposals adopted feature-based methods. Some adopted recognition algorithms based on character segments [44, 52], others exploited label embedding to match strings and images directly [13,42]. Features such as Stroke [3] and character keypoints [40] are also detected for the classification problem. The other great branch of non-deep text recognition solutions opted by decomposing the task into sub-problems, such as text binarization, text line segmentation, character segmentation, single character recognition, and word correction [28,53].

The last class of methods refers to end-to-end solutions. This category of methods integrates text detection and text recognition problems into a single system responsible for both tasks. In some initiatives such as [9], characters are treated as a special case of object detection, being detected by a Nearest Neighbor algorithm trained with shape descriptors and then grouped into words by using a model that relies on a Pictorial Structure. In another work [38], the authors proposed a delayed decision approach by keeping multiple segmentation samples from each character until the context of each character is known. The segmentation of detected characters was obtained using extremal regions and decoded recognition results in a dynamic programming algorithm.

2.2 Deep Learning

As the method proposed in this work is a deep learning method, in this section a brief introduction on deep learning is presented, and the most commonly used terms are defined.

Deep learning is a subset of the machine learning methods that allows computer systems to improve itself with experience and data. This class of methods learns how to represent the data with a nested hierarchy of representations, with each representation defined in relation to simpler representations of the data. This procedure exploits many layers of non-linear information for feature extraction and transformation, and pattern analysis and classification [6, 12].

Most deep learning methods are defined in the context of Artificial Neural Networks (ANN) [11]. Being inspired by the biological neural network from animal brains [36], ANN's are a powerful, scalable, and versatile machine learning architectures, being suitable for tackling complex problems by learning from the complex data fed to it in its training phase. An ANN with a significant number of hidden layers, that is, layers located between the input and output layers, is called Deep Artificial Neural Network [6].

Convolutional Neural Networks. Being inspired by studies over the visual cortex of the brain, Convolutional Neural Networks (CNN) are an architecture of ANN that are specialized in extracting features and information from images. Proposed back in 1998 [25], the basic building block of CNNs are the convolutional layers. Being based on the mathematical concept of convolution, where a function slides over another, and the integral of the pointwise multiplication is measured, the Convolutional Layer abstracts the same concept: each neuron in a convolutional layer n is connected only to a receptive field in the previous layer $n-1$, not to every pixel in the image. This method allows the network to concentrate on small and localized low-level features in the first layers and then assemble these features at higher-level features on the following layers.

Mobile-Oriented Neural Networks. Since the popularization of CNNs with AlexNet [23], the general trend has been proposing deeper models with more layers of learnable parameters, with even more complicated operations, aiming to achieve better accuracy on their tasks. However, in mobile or restrictive computing scenarios, these models with a high number of operations and computational footprint were unable to perform their tasks in an acceptable time [18].

Some solutions aiming to build smaller and faster CNN architectures were proposed to deal with this problem but maintaining the highly effective detection results observed by state-of-the-art methods. One of the first proposals on the scenario of NN for mobile-oriented applications was the Mobilenet [18], in which the authors aimed at developing a CNN architecture that was competitive to the state of the art at the time but with a lightweight model, focusing first on reducing processing time but also yielding smaller models. This goal was achieved by using depthwise separable convolutions, an alternative to the classical convolutional layer that fragments it into two: the first layer is called a depthwise convolution, that filters each input channel with a single convolutional filter. The second one is called a pointwise convolution, that applies a 1×1 convolution with the objective of computing new features by a linear combination of the input channels. This layer is equivalent to a traditional convolutional layer, but with less computational operations.

Sandler et al. [43] proposed a second version of the Mobilenet architecture, named MobilenetV2. The main contribution of this approach was the Inverted Residual with Linear Bottleneck layer. In this new module, the input is a low-dimensional compressed representation of the data, which is first expanded to a high dimension and filtered with a lightweight depthwise convolution. The results are projected back to a low-dimensional representation with a pointwise convolution. A residual connection is also inserted, connecting each low-resolution representation with the next one. This proposal improves the results of the previous version on various tasks, maintaining its low computational cost nature. The intuition is that the bottlenecks encode the model intermediate inputs and outputs, while the inner layer encapsulates the model ability to transform from lower-level concepts (such as pixels) to higher level descriptors (such as image categories). Finally, as with traditional residual connections, shortcuts enable faster training and better accuracy.

Deep Learning for Text Detection and Recognition. This section describes some of the deep learning-based text detection and recognition methods. The Single Shot Text Detector (SSTD) [16] is a variation of the Single Shot Detector (SSD) [32] architecture focused on text detection. This proposal outputs word-level bounding boxes, and can be divided into three parts: the convolutional module, the box prediction module and the text specific module. The convolutional and text specific modules are directly inherited from the SSD model. The text specific module can be divided into two modules: a text attention module and a hierarchical inception module. The text attention module, which comprises the convolutional layers, is responsible for learning rough spatial text features. The goal is to reduce false detections and improve the detection of ambiguous text. The hierarchical inception module has the task to aggregate multiscale features so that multiscale text can be better detected.

Liao et al. [30] proposed a fully convolutional network adapted for text detection and recognition, named TextBoxes. The authors approach inherits the VGG16 [45] architecture, converting the last two fully-connected layers to convolutional layers by parameter downsampling. Multiple output layers are inserted after the last and some of the intermediate layers, and their outputs are aggregated, afterwards passing in a non-maximal suppression process.

The TextBoxes approach was later extended as the TextBoxes++ [29] proposal. The objective was to support the detection of arbitrary oriented bounding boxes. The proposed architecture is also a fully convolutional network. This approach extends the original proposal by predicting an arbitrary quadrilateral as a text bounding box, not only vertically oriented boxes.

Córdova et al. [4] proposed a fast and lightweight architecture designed for detecting and recognizing multi-oriented and multi-lingual text, taking into consideration a mobile-oriented scenario for its use. This method combines the particularities of the TextBoxes++ network for the text detection problem and the efficiency aspects found in the Pelee network, a real-time object detector [49]. Finally, Campana et al. [10] proposed a strategy to fuse several text localization detectors based on deep learning-based methods. This approach focuses on improving the effectiveness of the text localization task by fusing heavy deep learning-based methods but also presented a fusion of non-deep learning-based methods toward investigating how effective is the fusion of models that do not require high computational costs and that could be used in mobile devices.

3   MobText

In this section, a description of the proposed method is provided. Figure 5 illustrates the overall framework of our approach for text localization, which uses MobileNetV2 as feature extractor and then SSD as multiple text bonding boxes detector. We detail the CNN architectures used, and then explain the learning mechanism used for finding a proper CNN model to the problem. Finally, we present and discuss performed experiments aiming to validate the proposed approach.

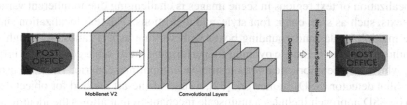

Fig. 5. Overview of the proposed method for text localization [5].

3.1 Characterization of Text Regions with MobilenetV2

The MobilenetV2 is a new CNN specifically designed for restricted computing environments that includes two main mechanisms for decreasing the memory footprints and number of operations while keeping the effectiveness of its precursor architecture, the Mobilenet [43]. Such mechanisms are the linear bottlenecks and the inverted residuals. Besides the depthwise separable convolution operations, which significantly reduce the FLOPS of a neural network, this new version of Mobilenet presents the linear bottleneck mechanism to reduce the number of parameters and keep the accuracy of the network by capturing a low-dimensional subspace (embedded in a manifold formed by a set of activation tensors). The authors claim that non-linearity reduces the capacity of bottleneck features to capture the most representative information. Thus, they decided to use a linear bottleneck, removing the ReLU activation.

The principles that guided the design of the inverted residual layers implemented on MobilenetV2 is that feature maps of the network are able to be encoded in low-dimensional subspaces, and non-linear activation causes some loss of information, notwithstanding their capability to increase representational complexity [43].

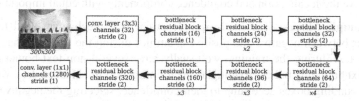

Fig. 6. MobilenetV2 architecture used in this work and its parameters. More details on the bottleneck residual block can be found in [43]. Image extracted from [5].

Figure 6 shows the MobilenetV2 architecture used to characterize text candidate regions. The *bottleneck residual block* implements the optimization mechanisms aforementioned considering the convolutional operations with a kernel of size 3×3. The first bottleneck block uses an expansion factor of 1, while the remaining blocks use an expansion factor of 6, as suggested by Sandler et al. [43].

3.2 Detecting Multiple Instances of Text via SSD

The localization of text regions in scene images is challenging due to inherent variability of texts, such as size, color, font style, and distortions. The text localization should handle multiple scales and bounding boxes with varying aspect ratios. Although several authors consider the image pyramid for performing multi-scale detection, it is quite costly, which may be impractical for a restrictive computing scenario. Thus, we use the Single Shot detector (SSD) framework [32], a state-of-the-art method for object detection. The SSD approach includes a multiscale mechanism that allows the identification of text regions in multiple scales on a single inference. Specifically, in the framework, the authors adopt a top-down fusion strategy to build new features with strong semantics while keeping fine details. Text detections are performed based on multiple new constructed features respectively during a single forward pass. All detection results from each layer are refined by means of a non-maximum suppression (NMS) process [37].

3.3 Learning

The main decisions we took in the learning phase of our network are:

Objective Function. Similar to Liu et al. [32], we use a multi-task loss function to learn the bounding boxes locations and text/non-text predictions, defined as:

$$L(x, c, l, g) = \frac{1}{N}(\mathcal{L}_{conf}(x, c) + \alpha \mathcal{L}_{loc}(x, l, g)). \tag{1}$$

Specifically, x_{ij} indicates a match ($x_{ij} = 1$) or non-match ($x_{ij} = 0$) between i-th default bounding boxes, j-th ground-truth bounding boxes, N is the number of matches, c is the ground truth class of the x_{ij} box and the α parameter is used as a multiplier of $\mathcal{L}_{loc}$ to weight the localization loss ($\mathcal{L}_{loc}$) and the confidence loss ($\mathcal{L}_{conf}$).

We adopted the smooth L1 function for $\mathcal{L}_{loc}$ between the predicted box (l) and the ground truth box (g), and a sigmoid function for $\mathcal{L}_{conf}$. In addition, we set $\alpha = 1$ in order to have the localization and confidence components with equal importance.

Hard Example Mining. The hard example miner is a mechanism used to prevent imbalances between negative and positive examples during the training phase. On the search for text during the training, we usually have several non-text bounding boxes and few text bounding boxes. To mitigate the training with imbalanced data, we sort the negative bounding boxes according to their confidence, selecting the negative samples with higher confidence value, considering a ratio proportion of 3:1 with the positive samples.

4 Experimental Protocol

This section presents the datasets, metrics, and protocols used for evaluating the proposed method.

4.1 Datasets

We evaluated the proposed methods in two datasets widely used for evaluating text localization methods, the ICDAR'11 and ICDAR'13. We also used the SynthText dataset to help training our network due to the small size of the ICDAR's datasets.

SynthText. This dataset comprises 858, 750 synthesized text images, which were generated by blending rendered words with natural images [14]. The synthetic engine proposed by the authors automatically choose the location, in a target image, and transforms a word by using an algorithm that selects contiguous regions based on local color and texture cues. Next, the words were rendered using a randomly selected font, transformed according to the local surface orientation, and finally blended into the scene using the Poisson image editing approach [39].

ICDAR'11. This dataset [20] was introduced in *ICDAR 2011 Robust Reading Competition – "Reading Text in Born-Digital Images (Web and Email)"*. It is an extension of the dataset used for the text locating competitions of ICDAR 2003 [34] and ICDAR 2005 [33], and contains 551 images, which were divided into two subsets, 410 images for training and 141 for test. The images of this dataset have texts digitally created on them, such as headers, logos, captions, among others. The annotations were built in terms of rectangle word bounding boxes and contains 5, 003 words.

ICDAR'13. This dataset was introduced in *ICDAR 2013 – "Focused Scene Text challenge"* and has 462 images divided into two subsets, training and testing sets, which contains 229 and 233 images, respectively [21]. The images in this dataset are born-digital or scene text (captured under a wide variety, such as blur, varying distance to camera, font style and sizes, color, texture, etc.). All the text lines are horizontal or near horizontal. The annotations were built in terms of rectangles word bounding boxes and comprise 1, 943 words.

4.2 Evaluation Metrics

We evaluated the methods in terms of effectiveness and efficiency considering their execution on a dedicated server with a GPU card and on a mobile device. To measure the effectiveness of methods, we used the recall, precision, and F-measure metrics. Similar to the object detection problem, the false positives correspond to textual elements that the detectors localized incorrectly, while the false negatives comprise textual elements that the detectors missed or localized with a low-confidence, considering a threshold 0.5. Consequently, the true positives correspond to the texts that detectors localized correctly, which is determined if the overlap between the ground-truth annotation and detected bounding box has an IoU greater than an threshold (similar to standard practice in object recognition [7]). Otherwise, the detected bounding box is considered an incorrect detection (false positive). Next, we present a brief description of Intersection over Union, as well as the Precision, Recall, and F-measure.

Intersection over Union (IoU). This metric measures the accuracy level between detected bounding boxes and their respective ground-truth annotated bounding boxes. A detected bounding box is considered a correct detection (true positive), if the IoU is greater than 50%. Otherwise, the detected bounding box is considered an incorrect detection (false positive). This protocol was proposed by Everingham et al. in the context of the PASCAL VOC challenge [8], in 2009, and it has been adopted in ICDAR competitions. This metric can be computed as shown in Eq. 2:

$$IoU = \frac{area(B_p \cap B_{gt})}{area(B_p \cup B_{gt})},$$

(2)

where $B_p \cap B_{gt}$ and $B_p \cup B_{gt}$ stand, respectively, for the intersection and the union of the predicted (B_p) and ground truth (B_{gt}) bounding boxes.

Recall (R). This metric refers to the fraction of text regions correctly detected, given the set of all text regions labeled in the dataset:

$$R = \frac{\sum \text{true positive}}{\sum (\text{true positive + false negative})}$$

(3)

Precision (P). This metric is defined as the fraction of text regions correctly detected, given all text regions detected by the text detector:

$$P = \frac{\sum \text{true positive}}{\sum (\text{true positive + false positive})}$$

(4)

F-measure combines P and R, allowing the possibility of having one single effectiveness score to assess the overall quality of a detector. It is defined as:

$$\text{F-measure} = 2 \times \left(\frac{P \times R}{P + R} \right)$$

(5)

Finally, the efficiency aspects considered both the processing time and the disk usage (in MB). We used the Linux *time* command to measure the processing time, while the disk usage considered the size of the learned models. All experiments were performed considering a Intel(R) Core(TM) i7-8700 CPU @ 3.20 GHz with 12 cores, a Nvidia GTX 1080 TI GPU, and 64 GB of RAM.

4.3   Evaluation Protocols

The experiments were divided into three steps: training, fine-tuning, and test. For the training step, we used three subsets of the SynthText dataset. This dataset comprises of images with synthetic texts added in different backgrounds and we selected samples of the dataset considering 10 (9.25%), 20 (18.48%), and 30 (27.71%) images per background. The resulting subsets were again divided into train and validation, using 70% for training and 30% for validation. Using these collections, we trained a model with random initialization parameters until we found no significant variance in the loss function. For the fine-tuning step, we took the model trained in SynthText and continued this training using ICDAR'11 or ICDAR'13 training subsets, stopping when we found no significant variance in the loss function. Finally, for the test step, we evaluated each fine-tuned model in the test subset of ICDAR'11 or ICDAR'13.

Experimental Setup. We conducted the training of the proposed method considering a single-scale input, and therefore, all input images were resized to 300×300 pixels. The training phase was performed using a batch size of 24 and we used the RMSprop optimizer [2] with a learning rate of 4×10^{-3}. We also use the regularization L2-norm, with a $\lambda = 4 \times 10^5$, to prevent possible over-fitting. We conducted the training until the network convergence.

Baselines. For a fair comparison, we selected recent approaches specifically designed for a fast detection, including SqueezeDet and YOLOv3. We also use state-of-the-art methods for text localization as baselines. A brief description of the baseline methods:

- **TextBoxes.** This method consists of a Fully Convolutional Network (FCN) adapted for text detection and recognition [30]. This network uses the VGG-16 network as feature extractor followed by multiple output layers (text-boxes layers), similar to SSD network. At the end, the Non-maximum suppression (NMS) process is applied to the aggregated outputs of all text-box layers. The authors also adopt an extra NMS for multi-scale inputs on the task of text localization.
- **TextBoxes++.** Liao et al. [29] proposed an end-to-end solution able to predict arbitrary orientation word bounding boxes. This architecture is a Fully Convolutional Neural Network (FCN) that detects arbitrary-oriented text. This architecture is inherited from the popular VGG-16 architecture used for the ImageNet competition. First, the last two FCN layers of VGG16 are converted into convolutional layers (conv6 and conv7). Next, other eight convolution layers divided into four stages (conv8 and conv11) with different resolutions by max-pooling are appended after conv7. In the following, multiple output layers (text boxes layers) are inserted after the last and intermediate convolutional layers to predict text presence and bounding boxes. Finally, a non-maximum suppression (NMS) process is applied to the aggregated outputs of all text-box layers.
- **Single-Shot Text Detector (SSTD).** He et al. [16] designed a natural scene text detector that directly outputs word-level bounding boxes without post-processing, except for a simple NMS. The detector can be decomposed into three parts: a convolutional component, a text-specific component, and a box prediction component. The convolutional and box prediction components are inherited from the SSD detector [32] and the authors proposed a text-specific component which consists of a text attention module and a hierarchical inception module.
- **SqueezeDet.** This network was proposed to detect objects for the autonomous driving problem, which requires a real-time detection [50]. The SqueezeDet contains a single-stage detection pipeline, which comprises three components: (i) an FCN responsible for generating the feature map for the input images; (ii) a convolutional layer responsible for detecting, localizing, and classifying objects at the same time; and (iii) the non-maximum suppression (NMS) method, which is applied to remove the overlapped bounding boxes.
- **YOLOv3.** This is a convolutional network originally proposed for the object detection problem [41]. Similarly to SSD network, the YOLOv3 predicts bounding boxes and class probabilities, at the same time. The bounding boxes are predicted using dimension clusters as anchor boxes and predicts an objectness score for each bounding box using logistic regression.

Experiments on Mobile-oriented Environment. To evaluate the use of our proposed solution on real-world usage scenarios and to evaluate the performance on a real constrained computing, an Android application was developed and executed. The developed Android application (APP) utilizes TensorFlow [1]'s Android API so it can load and execute the same model used for inference in our previous evaluations. The chosen portable device for the implementation and execution of our test was a *Xiaomi Redmi Note 5* smartphone, running Android OS version 9 on a *Qualcomm Snapdragon 636* chipset, comprehending a quad-core 1.8 GHz processor alongside a quad-core 1.6 GHz processor and 4 GB of RAM. Two sets of experiments where conducted with the goal of assessing the embedded system:

1. Evaluation of the processing time of the proposed approach when running on a mobile device. Experiments considered the detection of images belonging to the ICDAR'11 and ICDAR'13 datasets; and
2. Evaluation on a real-world mobile-based usage scenarios.

To ensure that the model executed on the mobile device has the same quantitative effectiveness that the one executed on a non-restrictive computing scenario, the same experiments used to evaluate the proposal on the non-restrictive device were executed on the mobile device, conserving datasets and evaluation metric configurations.

The proposed solution was also evaluated in real-world usage scenarios. Given the portability of the embedded APP, the proposed approach was evaluated in detection scenarios involving several images depicting texts in scenes captured using the portable device. To evaluate the efficiency of the proposed method considering a restricted computing environment, we collected 250 images containing text and non-text elements, captured directly from the built-in camera of the mobile device.

5　Results and Discussion

This section presents and discusses our achieved results, considering the described metrics and experimental protocol. The results of our proposal are compared to state-of-the-art methods. Results regarding the developed mobile application are presented alongside visual examples.

5.1　Comparisons with Baselines

This section presents the experimental results of the proposed method (MobText) and a comparison with the state-of-the-art methods for text localization. Figure 7 shows the results for the evaluated methods considering the ICDAR'11 dataset. In this case, the MobText method achieved the best results regarding the evaluated metrics. On the other hand, the SqueezeDet network presented the lowest Precision and F-measure among the evaluated methods (56.36% and 66.01%, respectively). In turn, the TextBoxes achieved the lowest results of Recall (71.93%).

Regarding ICDAR'13 dataset, the SSTD methods presented the highest Recall (82.19%), and F-measure (86.33%), while the YOLOv3 reached the best results in

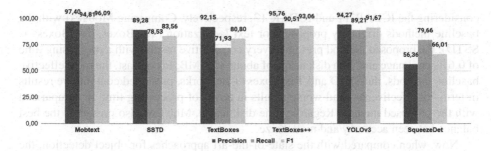

Fig. 7. Comparison of effectiveness among the evaluated deep learning-based methods for the ICDAR'11 dataset.

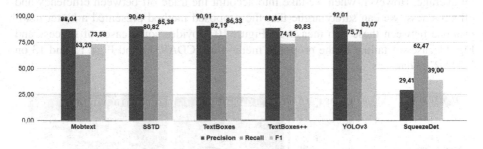

Fig. 8. Comparison of effectiveness among the evaluated deep learning-based methods for the ICDAR'13 dataset.

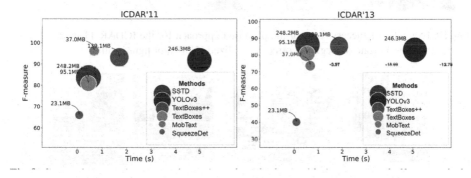

Fig. 9. Comparison results among the evaluated methods considering aspects of efficacy and efficiency [5].

terms of Precision (Fig. 8). Note, however, that the MobText yields very competitive results for this dataset as well, in terms of Precision.

In term of the efficiency of the presented methods, Fig. 9 summarizes the results considering the metrics used to assess the effectiveness of the evaluated methods, in terms of F-measure, along with the metrics for measuring the efficiency of those methods, considering the ICDAR'11 and ICDAR'13 datasets.

Regarding efficiency (processing time and disk usage), the proposed method (MobText) yielded very competitive results, taking only 0.45 and 0.55 s per image, considering the ICDAR'11 and ICDAR'13, respectively. Comparing MobText with the baseline methods originally proposed for text localization (TextBoxes, TextBoxes++, SSTD), the proposed method presented very competitive results with a processing time of 0.67 s per image and with disk usage of about 37.0 MB. In contrast, the most effective baseline methods, the SSTD and TextBoxes++ networks, presented competitive results in terms of effectiveness and worse results in terms of processing time in comparison with the proposed method. Regarding the disk usage, MobText also presented the best balance between accuracy and model size.

Now, when compared with the state-of-the-art approaches for object detection, the proposed method also presented competitive results. In this case, the fastest approach for text localization was the SqueezeDet network, which takes about 0.1 s per image, on average. However, when we take into account the trade-off between efficiency and effectiveness, we can safely argue that the proposed method presented a better compromise between these two measures. Figure 10 provides some cases of success and Fig. 11 cases of failure of the proposed method on ICDAR'11 and Figs. 12 and 13 on ICDAR'13 datasets.

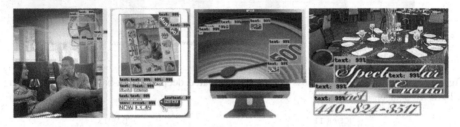

Fig. 10. Examples of success cases of the proposed approach for the ICDAR'11 dataset. Green bounding boxes indicate the regions correctly localized [5]. (Color figure online)

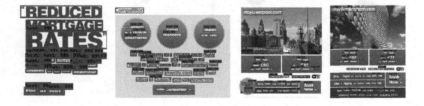

Fig. 11. Examples of failure cases of the proposed approach for the ICDAR'11 dataset. Green bounding boxes indicate the regions correctly localized, while red bounding boxes show candidate regions not detected by our method [5]. (Color figure online)

Fig. 12. Examples of success cases of the proposed approach for the ICDAR'13 dataset. Green bounding boxes indicate the regions correctly localized [5]. (Color figure online)

Fig. 13. Examples of failure cases of the proposed approach for the ICDAR'13 dataset. Green bounding boxes indicate the regions correctly localized, while red bounding boxes show candidate regions were not detected by our method [5]. (Color figure online)

The proposed method is able to detect multi-oriented texts and even texts with textured backgrounds. However, as we could observe, the proposed approach presented some difficulties in localizing scene text in the ICDAR'13 dataset. In comparison with results achieved for the ICDAR'11, the precision and recall rates decreased 9.36 and 31.61% points, respectively, which suggest that our network did not localized several candidate regions containing texts.

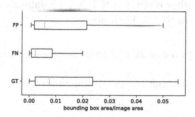

Fig. 14. Comparison among distributions of relative areas of bounding boxes from Ground-Truth (GT), False Negatives (FN) cases, and False Positive (FP) cases. We omitted the points considered outliers for a better visualization. Figure extracted from [5].

To understand the reasons that led the proposed method to have this difficult in localizing text for the ICDAR'13 datasets, we performed an analysis of failure cases taking into account the relative area of missed bounding boxes. Figure 14 presents a box-plot graph that shows the distribution of the relative area of bounding boxes (i.e., ratio of bounding box area to image area) for the ground-truth, false positive cases, and false negative cases.

Fig. 15. Two high resolution examples of ICDAR'13 dataset with both medium-sized text (detected by our method) and small-sized (not detected). Figure extracted from [5].

As we can observe, the missed bounding boxes (false negative cases) have a small relative area. More precisely, 75% of false negative cases (third quartile of FN box-plot) have a relative area up to 0.01 and correspond to 50% of the bounding box present in the ground-truth. This results suggest to us that high resolution images with relatively small text (see Fig. 15) are specially challenging to our method. To overcome this limitation, future investigations can be conducted to devise an architecture to better localize bounding boxes with multiple scales such as Feature Pyramid Networks (FPNs), as proposed by [31].

5.2   Results on Mobile-Oriented Environment

We could observe the same effectiveness as we found considering the execution of our method on a dedicated server with a GPU. Regarding the efficiency of the proposed method, Table 1 shows the processing time spent during inference, considering both datasets. The proposed method spent an average time of 464ms per image for the ICDAR'11, and an average time of 523 ms per image for the ICDAR'13. It is important to notice that ICDAR'11 comprises low-resolution images with an average size of 188×370 pixels. On the other hand, the ICDAR'13 datasets contains high-resolution images with a average size of 882×1115 pixels.

Table 1. Processing time of the embedded application on ICDAR datasets.

Dataset	Processing time (ms)		
	Min.	Max.	Average
ICDAR'11	420	524	464
ICDAR'13	449	602	523

The average time of inference in 250 images was 425 ms, with a minimum inference time of 343 ms and a maximum of 584 ms.

Fig. 16. Example of scene text images captured with a perspective [5].

Figure 16 shows the effect of the capturing angle of the texts in scene text images. As the system was only trained with horizontal aligned text, this kind of perspective lowers the system effectiveness. In Fig. 17, the effects of the size of the text on scene text images is shown. Images with smaller text (top left) are more difficult to detect, while image with medium to large text are easier and have better results, as shown in Fig. 18.

Even though the system was not trained with handwritten text, the results of text detection on handwritten text, such as in Fig. 19, are very promising. Good detection results were obtained on handwritten text on a complex background (top left) and even on multilingual text (bottom left).

Fig. 17. Example of scene text images captured with different zoom levels [5]

Fig. 18. Example of scene text images with good results on our application [5].

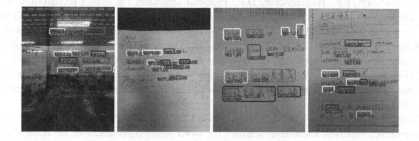

Fig. 19. Example of handwritten text, with complex backgrounds and multilingual text [5].

6   Conclusions and Future Work

This chapter presented a lightweight solution for the text detection problem that can be run on devices with restricted computing power. Our solutions take advantage of two light architectures, MobileNetV2 and Single Shot Detector (SSD), that yield better or comparable effectiveness performance when compared with state-of-the-art baselines. Moreover, our solution enables the detection of textual elements on a low-cost mobile phone device with low processing time. Our findings demonstrated that leverage lightweight object detector networks is a promising research venue to build-up real applications involving the text detection task in scenes. Future work will be dedicated to devise end-to-end text recognition approaches, tailored to constrained processing devices, and also take advantage of our solution to design applications that exploit contextual information provided by text recognition methods.

References

1. Abadi, M., et al.: Tensorflow: large-scale machine learning on heterogeneous distributed systems. arXiv preprint arXiv:1603.04467 (2016)
2. Bengio, Y.: RMSprop and equilibrated adaptive learning rates for nonconvex optimization. Corr Abs/1502.04390 (2015)
3. Busta, M., Neumann, L., Matas, J.: FASText: efficient unconstrained scene text detector. In: IEEE International Conference on Computer Vision, pp. 1206–1214 (2015)
4. Córdova, M., et al.: Pelee-text: a tiny convolutional neural network for multi-oriented scene text detection. In: 18th IEEE International Conference on Machine Learning and Applications, Florida, FL, USA (2019)
5. Decker, L.G.L., et al.: MobText: a compact method for scene text localization. In: 15th International Joint Conference on Computer Vision. Imaging and Computer Graphics Theory and Applications, vol. 5, pp. 343–350. SciTePress, INSTICC (2020)
6. Deng, L., Yu, D.: Deep learning: methods and applications. Found. Trends® Signal Process. 7(3–4), 197–387 (2014)
7. Everingham, M., Eslami, S.M.A., Van Gool, L., Williams, C.K.I., Winn, J., Zisserman, A.: The pascal visual object classes challenge: a retrospective. Int. J. Comput. Vision 111(1), 98–136 (2015). https://doi.org/10.1007/s11263-014-0733-5
8. Everingham, M., Van Gool, L., Williams, C.K., Winn, J., Zisserman, A.: The pascal visual object classes (VOC) challenge. Int. J. Comput. Vision 88(2), 303–338 (2010). https://doi.org/10.1007/s11263-009-0275-4
9. Felzenszwalb, P.F., Huttenlocher, D.P.: Pictorial structures for object recognition. Int. J. Comput. Vision 61(1), 55–79 (2005). https://doi.org/10.1023/B:VISI.0000042934.15159.49
10. Flores Campana, J.L., Pinto, A., Alberto Córdova Neira, M., Gustavo Lorgus Decker, L., Santos, A., Conceição, J.S., da Silva Torres, R.: On the fusion of text detection results: a genetic programming approach. IEEE Access 8(1), 81257–81270 (2020)
11. Géron, A.: Hands-On Machine Learning with Scikit-Learn, Keras, and TensorFlow: Concepts, Tools, and Techniques to Build Intelligent Systems. O'Reilly Media, Sebastopol (2019)
12. Goodfellow, I., Bengio, Y., Courville, A.: Deep Learning. MIT Press, Cambridge (2016)
13. Gordo, A.: Supervised mid-level features for word image representation. In: IEEE Conference on Computer Vision and Pattern Recognition, pp. 2956–2964 (2015)
14. Gupta, A., Vedaldi, A., Zisserman, A.: Synthetic data for text localisation in natural images. In: IEEE Conference on Computer Vision and Pattern Recognition, pp. 2315–2324 (2016)
15. He, K., Zhang, X., Ren, S., Sun, J.: Deep residual learning for image recognition. In: IEEE Conference on Computer Vision and Pattern Recognition, pp. 770–778 (2016)
16. He, P., Huang, W., He, T., Zhu, Q., Qiao, Y., Li, X.: Single shot text detector with regional attention. In: IEEE International Conference on Computer Vision, pp. 3047–3055 (2017)
17. He, T., Huang, W., Qiao, Y., Yao, J.: Text-attentional convolutional neural network for scene text detection. IEEE Trans. Image Process. 25(6), 2529–2541 (2016)

18. Howard, A.G., et al.: MobileNets: efficient convolutional neural networks for mobile vision applications. arXiv preprint arXiv:1704.04861 (2017)
19. Karatzas, D., et al.: ICDAR 2015 competition on robust reading. In: 13th International Conference on Document Analysis and Recognition (ICDAR), pp. 1156–1160. IEEE (2015)
20. Karatzas, D., Mestre, S.R., Mas, J., Nourbakhsh, F., Roy, P.P.: ICDAR 2011 robust reading competition-challenge 1: reading text in born-digital images (web and email). In: International Conference on Document Analysis and Recognition, pp. 1485–1490. IEEE (2011)
21. Karatzas, D., et al.: ICDAR 2013 robust reading competition. In: 12th International Conference on Document Analysis and Recognition, pp. 1484–1493. IEEE (2013)
22. Koo, H.I., Kim, D.H.: Scene text detection via connected component clustering and nontext filtering. IEEE Trans. Image Process. 22(6), 2296–2305 (2013)
23. Krizhevsky, A., Sutskever, I., Hinton, G.E.: ImageNet classification with deep convolutional neural networks. In: Advances in Neural Information Processing Systems, pp. 1097–1105 (2012)
24. Kumuda, T., Basavaraj, L.: Hybrid approach to extract text in natural scene images. Int. J. Comput. Appl. 142(10), 1614–1618 (2016)
25. LeCun, Y., Bottou, L., Bengio, Y., Haffner, P.: Gradient-based learning applied to document recognition. Proc. IEEE 86(11), 2278–2324 (1998)
26. Lee, J.J., Lee, P.H., Lee, S.W., Yuille, A., Koch, C.: AdaBoost for text detection in natural scene. In: International Conference on Document Analysis and Recognition, pp. 429–434. IEEE (2011)
27. Lee, S., Cho, M.S., Jung, K., Kim, J.H.: Scene text extraction with edge constraint and text collinearity. In: 20th International Conference on Pattern Recognition, pp. 3983–3986. IEEE (2010)
28. Lee, S., Kim, J.H.: Integrating multiple character proposals for robust scene text extraction. Image Vis. Comput. 31(11), 823–840 (2013)
29. Liao, M., Shi, B., Bai, X.: Textboxes++: a single-shot oriented scene text detector. IEEE Trans. Image Process. 27(8), 3676–3690 (2018)
30. Liao, M., Shi, B., Bai, X., Wang, X., Liu, W.: Textboxes: a fast text detector with a single deep neural network. In: Thirty-First AAAI Conference on Artificial Intelligence (2017)
31. Lin, T.Y., Dollár, P., Girshick, R., He, K., Hariharan, B., Belongie, S.: Feature pyramid networks for object detection. In: IEEE Conference on Computer Vision and Pattern Recognition, pp. 2117–2125 (2017)
32. Liu, W., et al.: SSD: single shot multibox detector. In: Leibe, B., Matas, J., Sebe, N., Welling, M. (eds.) ECCV 2016. LNCS, vol. 9905, pp. 21–37. Springer, Cham (2016). https://doi.org/10.1007/978-3-319-46448-0_2
33. Lucas, S.M.: ICDAR 2005 text locating competition results. In: Eighth International Conference on Document Analysis and Recognition, pp. 80–84. IEEE (2005)
34. Lucas, S.M., Panaretos, A., Sosa, L., Tang, A., Wong, S., Young, R.: ICDAR 2003 robust reading competitions. In: Seventh International Conference on Document Analysis and Recognition, pp. 682–687. Citeseer (2003)
35. Matas, J., Chum, O., Urban, M., Pajdla, T.: Robust Wide-baseline stereo from maximally stable extremal regions. Image Vis. Comput. 22(10), 761–767 (2004)
36. McCulloch, W.S., Pitts, W.: A logical calculus of the ideas immanent in nervous activity. Bull. Math. Biophys. 5(4), 115–133 (1943). https://doi.org/10.1007/BF02478259
37. Neubeck, A., Van Gool, L.: Efficient non-maximum suppression. In: 18th International Conference on Pattern Recognition, vol. 3, pp. 850–855. IEEE (2006)
38. Neumann, L., Matas, J.: On combining multiple segmentations in scene text recognition. In: 12th International Conference on Document Analysis and Recognition, pp. 523–527. IEEE (2013)

39. Pérez, P., Gangnet, M., Blake, A.: Poisson image editing. ACM Trans. Graph. **22**, 313–318 (2003)
40. Quy Phan, T., Shivakumara, P., Tian, S., Lim Tan, C.: Recognizing text with perspective distortion in natural scenes. In: IEEE International Conference on Computer Vision, pp. 569–576 (2013)
41. Redmon, J., Farhadi, A.: Yolov3: an incremental improvement. arXiv preprint arXiv:1804.02767 (2018)
42. Rodriguez-Serrano, J.A., Perronnin, F., Meylan, F.: Label embedding for text recognition. In: British Machine Vision Conference, pp. 5–1 (2013)
43. Sandler, M., Howard, A., Zhu, M., Zhmoginov, A., Chen, L.C.: MobileNetV2: inverted residuals and linear bottlenecks. In: IEEE Conference on Computer Vision and Pattern Recognition, pp. 4510–4520 (2018)
44. Shi, C., Wang, C., Xiao, B., Zhang, Y., Gao, S., Zhang, Z.: Scene text recognition using part-based tree-structured character detection. In: IEEE Conference on Computer Vision and Pattern Recognition, pp. 2961–2968 (2013)
45. Simonyan, K., Zisserman, A.: Very deep convolutional networks for large-scale image recognition. arXiv preprint arXiv:1409.1556 (2014)
46. Tang, Y., Wu, X.: Scene text detection and segmentation based on cascaded convolution neural networks. IEEE Trans. Image Process. **26**(3), 1509–1520 (2017)
47. Wang, K., Babenko, B., Belongie, S.: End-to-end scene text recognition. In: International Conference on Computer Vision, pp. 1457–1464. IEEE (2011)
48. Wang, L., Wang, Z., Qiao, Y., Van Gool, L.: Transferring deep object and scene representations for event recognition in still images. Int. J. Comput. Vision **126**(2–4), 390–409 (2018). https://doi.org/10.1007/s11263-017-1043-5
49. Wang, R.J., Li, X., Ling, C.X.: Pelee: a real-time object detection system on mobile devices. In: Bengio, S., Wallach, H., Larochelle, H., Grauman, K., Cesa-Bianchi, N., Garnett, R. (eds.) Advances in Neural Information Processing Systems, vol. 31, pp. 1967–1976. Curran Associates, Inc. (2018)
50. Wu, B., Iandola, F., Jin, P.H., Keutzer, K.: SqueezeDet: unified, small, low power fully convolutional neural networks for real-time object detection for autonomous driving. In: IEEE Conference on Computer Vision and Pattern Recognition Workshops, pp. 129–137 (2017)
51. Yan, C., Xie, H., Liu, S., Yin, J., Zhang, Y., Dai, Q.: Effective uyghur language text detection in complex background images for traffic prompt identification. IEEE Trans. Intell. Transp. Syst. **19**(1), 220–229 (2017)
52. Yao, C., Bai, X., Shi, B., Liu, W.: Strokelets: a learned multi-scale representation for scene text recognition. In: IEEE Conference on Computer Vision and Pattern Recognition, pp. 4042–4049 (2014)
53. Ye, Q., Gao, W., Wang, W., Zeng, W.: A robust text detection algorithm in images and video frames. In: Fourth International Conference on Information, Communications and Signal Processing and the Fourth Pacific Rim Conference on Multimedia, vol. 2, pp. 802–806. IEEE (2003)
54. Yi, C., Tian, Y., Arditi, A.: Portable camera-based assistive text and product label reading from hand-held objects for blind persons. IEEE/ASME Trans. Mechatron. **19**(3), 808–817 (2013)
55. Zhang, Z., Zhang, C., Shen, W., Yao, C., Liu, W., Bai, X.: Multi-oriented text detection with fully convolutional networks. In: IEEE Conference on Computer Vision and Pattern Recognition, pp. 4159–4167 (2016)
56. Zhu, Y., Liao, M., Yang, M., Liu, W.: Cascaded segmentation-detection networks for text-based traffic sign detection. IEEE Trans. Intell. Transp. Syst. **19**(1), 209–219 (2017)

Early Stopping for Two-Stream Fusion Applied to Action Recognition

Helena de Almeida Maia[1] ![ORCID], Marcos Roberto e Souza[1] ![ORCID],
Anderson Carlos Sousa e Santos[1] ![ORCID], Julio Cesar Mendoza Bobadilla[1] ![ORCID],
Marcelo Bernardes Vieira[2] ![ORCID], and Helio Pedrini[1(✉)] ![ORCID]

[1] Institute of Computing, University of Campinas, Campinas, SP 13083-852, Brazil
helio@ic.unicamp.br
[2] Department of Computer Science, Federal University of Juiz de Fora,
Juiz de Fora, MG 36036-900, Brazil

Abstract. Various information streams, such as scene appearance and estimated movement of objects involved, can help in characterizing actions in videos. These information modalities perform better in different scenarios and complementary features can be combined to achieve superior results compared to the individual ones. As important as the definition of representative and complementary feature streams is the choice of proper combination strategies that explore the strengths of each aspect. In this work, we analyze different fusion approaches to combine complementary modalities. In order to define the best parameters of our fusion methods using the training set, we have to reduce overfitting in individual modalities, otherwise, the 100%-accurate outputs would not offer a realistic and relevant representation for the fusion method. Thus, we analyze an early stopping technique for training individual networks. In addition to reducing overfitting, this method also reduces the training cost, since it usually requires fewer epochs to complete the classification process. Experiments are conducted on UCF101 and HMDB51 datasets, which are two challenging benchmarks in the context of action recognition.

Keywords: Action recognition · Deep learning · Fusion methods

1 Introduction

Although automatic event recognition is a difficult and challenging task. Nowadays, it is essential, due to the impracticality of carrying out an evaluation of a massive amount of data by human eyes. This becomes even more important in scenarios that need real-time response, for instance, health monitoring, video surveillance, among others [7,10,12,24].

The authors are thankful to FAPESP (grants #2017/09160-1 and #2017/12646-3), CNPq (grants #305169/2015-7 and #309330/2018-7), CAPES and FAPEMIG for their financial support, and NVIDIA Corporation for the donation of a GPU as part of the GPU Grant Program.

In this work, our interest is to classify the activities that were performed by human agents in pre-recorded videos. Task named with recognition of human actions [1,2, 6,17]. Our main focus is on methods that use handcrafted features as input to deep networks. These recent strategies aim to take advantage of our knowledge of traditional methods to improve the convergence of deep learning techniques. Most of these methods use multi-stream architectures based on 2D CNNs, where each stream ideally handles complementary information.

More specifically, we are interested in studying how the strategy of combining stream predictions can influence the final classification performance. Simple weighted mean is typically the strategy for fusing the predictions. In our previous work [26], we proposed and evaluated two variations of integral fuzzy for combining streams using fuzzy integral in the late fusion. In this work, we analyzed other fusion approaches for individual modalities. Besides, we show that techniques for reducing overfitting are essential for fusing streams. Experiments conducted on two well-known challenging datasets, HMDB51 [14] and UCF101 [32], demonstrate that SVM and the weighted average, respectively on these datasets, outperformed the other methods.

The remainder of this text is organized as follows. We review relevant concepts and works that relate to our action recognition method in Sect. 2. We present our fusion method for a two-stream architecture in Sect. 3. We describe and discuss the experimental results achieved with the proposed method in Sect. 4. Finally, we present our conclusions in Sect. 5.

2   Related Work

Action recognition in video sequences has received much research attention over the last years due to its practical applications in several fields, for instance, surveillance systems, health monitoring, sports analysis, smart homes, among others.

Despite its vast range of applications, action recognition remains an open research problem with several challenges, such as occlusion, viewpoint variation, background clutter, camera motion, intraclass variation, and large volume of data.

A variety of methods have been proposed in the literature for action recognition [1,6,25,29,30,49]. Feature extraction is a fundamental task in the process of video analysis. Spatial and temporal features have been used to encode discriminative information extracted from the video frames. Basically, there are two categories of feature descriptors that can be constructed for video representation in the context of action recognition: (i) handcrafted features and (ii) deep learning-based features.

Handcrafted features are obtained through manually designed algorithms. Examples of handcrafted features applied to action recognition include Volume Local Binary Pattern (VLBP) [3], Adaptive Local Motion Descriptor (ALMD) [36], Local Ternary Pattern for Three-Orthogonal Planes (LTP-TOP) [20], Salient Foreground Trajectory (SFT) [47], Space-Time Interest Points (STIP) [15], Gradient Boundary Histograms (GBH) [28], Hierarchical Motion Evolution (HME) [37], Motion Boundary Histogram (MBH) [38], Improved Dense Trajectories (IDT) [39], and Fisher Vectors (FV) [22].

More recently, deep learning-based features have been extracted from the video sequences to address the action recognition problem [5,6,8,11,13,25,30,35,40–43,46,

53]. The main frameworks are based on multiple-stream 2D convolutional networks, 3D convolutional networks, and long short-term memory (LSTM) networks.

In multiple-stream 2D convolutional networks, different information channels are encoded and fused to improve the action recognition efficacy. Examples of streams include spatial features represented as RGB images and temporal features represented as a stack of optical flow images [30], so that the network applies 2D convolution operations during the model training process. Several approaches have extended the use of streams to improve performance, for instance, by adding skeleton [45] and visual rhythm [6] representations.

Many approaches have attempted to improve their performance by extending 2D convolutional networks to 3D convolutional networks and exploring spatio-temporal structures for the learning of action features [5, 12, 50]. Instead of using separate streams, these methods employ end-to-end deep networks to learn powerful features from spatial and temporal dimensions through 3D convolutions.

Another category of approaches uses LSTM networks to learn features through short-term and long-term dependencies in the input videos using gating schemes [9, 16, 21, 27, 51]. Although these networks are generally not easy to train, temporal information can be effectively modeled, especially on longer and more complex video sequences.

Deep learning-based approaches have become state of the art in the action recognition field, especially on recent benchmarks. Nevertheless, handcrafted-based approaches can be still advantageous in certain scenarios, particularly when there is no enough data availability to train the deep models or when combined with deep-learning methods to improve the overall performance.

In order to explore information complementary to improve the classification performance, fusion techniques have been proposed. The fusion can be performed by concatenating information from different video clues, multiple streams, or deep-learning models trained with different data samples. Broadly speaking, fusion strategies [31, 44] can be categorized either as early fusion, when the values for each modality are combined at the beginning of the pipeline, or as late fusion, after computing the prediction values for each of the inputs. In handcrafted-based approaches, a common strategy is to combine the features from different descriptors in an early-fusion scheme. On the other hand, deep learning-based approaches usually adopt the late-fusion scheme by averaging the softmax classification scores from multiple streams.

3   Fusion Methods for Action Recognition

The baseline of our proposal is the two-stream model [30], illustrated in Fig. 1. It consists of two parallel networks: (i) the spatial stream, that classifies RGB frames randomly selected from the video, and (ii) the temporal stream, that classifies stacks of 10 optical flow images also extracted at a random temporal position. Here, we use the modified spatial stream proposed by Concha et al. [6], which it is trained with two RGB frames per video instead of a single one as in the original paper [30]. The temporal stream, on the other hand, is trained with a single stack per video.

During the test stage, the networks receive as input 25 frames/stacks evenly sampled from each test video, and 10 new samples are produced from them using data augmentation techniques. This process results in 250 samples and the final vector of scores are given by the average of the samples outputs.

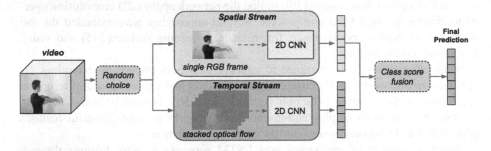

Fig. 1. An illustration of the two-stream architecture [30] for action recognition.

In this work, the training process is divided into two stages in a stacking fashion. First, the CNNs, initialized with ImageNet parameters, are individually trained on the video dataset. Then, we train our fusion method using the scores generated by the trained streams as input. Either the CNNs and the fusion methods are fitted with the same training set. Note that, if the CNNs achieve a perfect score during training, many combinations will be considered correct and the fusion method may not be able to find good parameters for the test stage. For this reason, using a premature model of the CNNs with a smaller score might help the fusion method to consider failure and success cases of each stream. For addressing this issue, we use an early stopping protocol [23] as follows:

1. If the dataset does not have a predefined validation set, we separate 20% of the training set for validation.
2. Every k training epochs, we evaluate the validation loss. If the loss is greater than the best loss found at the moment (that is, the performance has deteriorated), we increment a counter.
3. The counter is reset after any improvement in the best loss. At this point, the best loss and corresponding epoch n are updated.
4. After s consecutive increments in the counter, the training process stops.
5. Then, the stream is retrained using the entire training set (training and validation) for n epochs, resulting in our final model.

With the final model, we extract the score vectors for the entire dataset. The training and validation vectors are used to define the parameters of the fusion methods. It is worth mentioning that each dataset split generates a different model, and both training stages consider the same division, except for the subdivision into training and validation in the first stage.

For fusion, we evaluate 3 strategies: (i) weighted average, (ii) Choquet fuzzy integral and (iii) SVM (Support Vector Machine) classifier. The main advantage of them is the automatic weight assignment that adapts to the inclusion of new streams, datasets and modifications in the approaches. They can learn misclassification patterns from the training scores and take them into account to define the weights.

Weighted Average. The weighted average is the most commonly used fusion in multi-stream networks. In this method, we assign a different weight for each stream and sum the vectors multiplied by the corresponding weight. It produces a final vector, such that the action label is the one with the highest confidence.

We use a grid search strategy to define the weights, in such a way that the best weights for a given split are the ones with the highest score in the combination of the training vectors.

Choquet Fuzzy Integral. Similar to our previous work [26], here we evaluate the Choquet [19] that outperformed the Sugeno integral [18] in our experiments. Fuzzy integral generalizes other common fusion operators, such as average, maximum and ordered weighted average. It is characterized by the use of fuzzy membership functions ($h(x_i)$) as integrands, whereas fuzzy measures are characterized as weights and the type of fuzzy connectives applied.

Fuzzy measures serve as a priori importance for the integrands. They define coefficients for each source, which are denoted as fuzzy densities and also for the union of different sources, characterizing the level of agreement between them. Thus, coefficients $\mu(A_j)$ are defined for all subsets of the set of integrands (χ) in the interval $[0, 1]$ and they must satisfy the monotonicity condition, expressed in Eq. 1.

$$A_j \subset A_k \implies \mu(A_j) \leq \mu(A_k) \quad \forall A_j, A_k \in \chi \tag{1}$$

Choquet integral employs product and addition as fuzzy connectives, as shown in Eq. 2.

$$C_\mu[h_1(x_i), ..., h_n(x_n)] = \sum_{i=1}^{n} h_{(i)}(x_i)[\mu(A_{(i)}) - \mu(A_{(i-1)})] \tag{2}$$

The enclosed sub-index $_{(i)}$ refers to a previous sorting on the integrands, $h_{(1)}(x_1)$ is the source with the highest value, and $A_{(k)}$ is the subset with the k highest values, such that $A_{(n)} = \chi$.

To establish the fuzzy measures and avoid dealing with the monotonicity condition and also narrow down the search space, we explored the particular fuzzy-λ measures [34] that define the coefficients of the union of subsets based on the individual subsets, as shown in Eq. 3.

$$\mu(A_i \cup A_j) = \mu(A_i) + \mu(A_j) + \lambda\mu(A_i)\mu(A_j) \quad \forall A_i, A_j \in \chi \tag{3}$$

where λ is found by considering that the fuzzy measure for the interaction of all sources is equal to 1 ($\mu(\chi) = 1$). Therefore, only two parameters corresponding to the fuzzy densities of each stream need to be defined.

Algorithm 1 summarizes the main steps of using Choquet Integral as the fusion operator. Function get_lambda solves Eq. 4 for λ.

$$\lambda + 1 = \prod_{i=1}^{n}(1 + \lambda \times w_i) \tag{4}$$

Algorithm 1. Fuzzy Fusion (Choquet).

---

input : set of classification scores S, set of fuzzy densities w
output: Final classification score ff

1 $\lambda \leftarrow$ `get_lambda`(w)
    // Decrease sorting
2 $idx \leftarrow$ `argReverseSort`(S)
3 $h \leftarrow S[idx]$
4 $fm \leftarrow w[idx]$
    // initialization of values
5 $A_0 = fm_0$
6 $ff = h_0 \times fm_0$
    // fuzzy integral
7 **for** $i \in 1, ..., |S| - 1$ **do**
8      $A_i = A_{i-1} + fm_i + \lambda \times fm_i \times A_{i-1}$
9      $ff = ff + h_i \times (A_i - A_{i-1})$
10     $A_{i-1} = A_i$
11 $ff = ff + h_{|S|-1} \times (1 - A_{i-1})$
12 **return** ff

The scores for each source of information are sorted from higher to lower and the fuzzy densities (weights) are reorganized to follow their respective sources. After some initial values are defined, the loop in the algorithm performs, at each iteration, the union of the previous fuzzy measure with the current fuzzy density, thus allowing to compute the fuzzy integral, as defined in Eq. 2.

SVM Classifier. In this method, we concatenate the streams outputs and use them as input for an SVM classifier. We apply a standardization preprocessing (i.e. mean removal and variance scaling) in our concatenated vectors. The SVM classifier is trained following a cross-validated grid-search to optimize the parameters.

Complementarity Rate. For a quantitative evaluation of the streams combinations, we can use the complementarity rate between classifiers A and B presented by Brill and Wu [4]:

$$Comp(A, B) = 100 \times \left(1 - \frac{\# \, of \, common \, errors}{\# \, of \, A \, errors}\right) \qquad (5)$$

It estimates the percentage of times that B gives the correct prediction, given that the classifier A is wrong. The complementarity rate is not commutative, that is, $Comp(A, B) \neq Comp(B, A)$. If both rates are low, the classifiers are very similar and combining them will not bring benefits for the method. If one rate is much greater than the other, the second one is not necessary. Therefore, both streams have to contribute in the final model. To combine the two rates, we use a harmonic mean defined as follows:

$$HM(A,B) = \frac{2 \times Comp(A, B) \times Comp(B, A)}{Comp(A, B) + Comp(B, A)} \qquad (6)$$

4   Experiments

In this section, we describe the datasets used in our experiments, relevant implementation details, as well as experimental results for different configurations of our method.

4.1   Datasets

Two challenging datasets that are benchmarks for the human action recognition problem were used in the experiments. The UCF101 [32] dataset is composed of 13,320 video clips distributed in 101 classes. The sequences have a fixed resolution of 320 × 240 pixels, a frame rate of 25 fps and different lengths. The HMDB51 [14] data set is composed of 51 classes and 6,766 sequences extracted mostly from movies. It includes lower quality videos with blur, noise, cuts and actions from unusual points of views.

Both datasets provide a protocol with three splits of the samples, where each split contains 70% of samples for training and 30% for testing for each action class. This is a standard evaluation protocol proposed by the authors of the datasets, which is followed in the literature of action recognition for comparison purposes.

4.2   Experimental Details

Our method was implemented in Python 3 programming language, using Pytorch for deep learning. As baseline, we use the public implementation of the two-stream network [52], inspired by the practices described by Wang et al. [42]. Our implementation is available at https://github.com/helena-maia/multistream_HAR. All experiments were performed on a machine with an Intel® Core™ i7-3770K 3.50 GHz processor, 32 GB of memory, an NVIDIA GeForce®GTX 1080 GPU and Ubuntu 16.04.

The Inception V3 [33] network was the 2D CNN selected in our experiments. It achieved state-of-the-art results on the ImageNet competition and, for this reason, we started with its trained weights in all cases. In addition, the Inception V3 is very compact and easy to converge.

For the temporal stream, images generated with the TV-L1 optical flow estimation method [48] are used as input. The classification network is modified to cope with the 20-channel input, 10 for each x and y direction. The expected number of channels for input to the network is 3, such that it is necessary to change the input layers in order to accept 20 images. This would be as simple as changing one parameter, however, we would lose the pre-trained weights between the input and the first hidden layer. Following the strategy described by Wang et al. [42], the weights of the three-channel version are averaged and copied 20 times.

Two data augmentation techniques were applied: cropping and horizontal flipping. The cropping scheme uses multi-scale crops of the four corners and the central portion of each image. During the training stages, these techniques are randomly applied in the samples, whereas in the test stage all the 10 versions are produced for every sample.

The maximum number of epochs in our early stopping training is 250 for the spatial stream and 350 for the temporal. The validation loss is evaluated at the end of every epoch ($k = 1$), and the training stops after 7 consecutive increases in the loss (patience $s = 7$). In both streams, the stochastic gradient descent optimizer is used with Nesterov momentum equal to 0.9. For all experiments, the used batch size is 25 and the learning rate is 0.001.

The range for the weighted average was $[1, 10]$ with step 1. For the Choquet fusion, the weights need to be in the range $[0, 1]$, so the search range is the same, except that the weight vector is normalized using a L^1-norm. Considering the arithmetic average, the values are based on proportions; for example, the sets of weights $(0.2, 0.4)$ and $(0.4, 0.8)$ are equivalent when performing average because both indicate that a classifier has 2 times more weight than the other. In the fuzzy fusion, these sets of weights represent different combinations, allowing more feasible weights.

Concerning the SVM, for the regularization parameter C and γ, we considered powers of 10 in the range $[10^{-10}, 10^{10}]$. We also tested linear and rbf (radial basis function) kernels with one-vs-one and one-vs-rest decision functions. The grid search is combined with a 3-fold cross-validation.

4.3   Results

In this subsection, we present the accuracies obtained with the fusion methods for the action recognition problem, along with some analysis of the streams complementarity and class performance. Initially, the individual results of each stream, using the early stopping protocol, are shown in Table 1. The spatial stream achieved a slightly better result on UCF101, however, the temporal stream significantly outperformed it on HMDB51.

Table 1. Accuracy rates (%) for individual streams on the UCF101 and HMDB51 datasets.

Stream	Split	UCF101	HMDB51
Spatial	1	85.88	51.96
	2	84.60	49.22
	3	86.09	49.41
	Avg	85.52	50.20
Temporal	1	83.51	56.60
	2	86.02	57.32
	3	86.47	58.37
	Avg	85.33	57.43

In Table 2, we show the best epoch estimated using the early stopping protocol for each dataset, split and stream. Note that, in all cases it took longer to train the temporal stream, probably because the RGB frames are more similar to ImageNet samples. Even with the longest training, the temporal training precisions are far below the perfect score and very much alike its test results from Table 1. In contrast, the spatial stream achieved 20% more precision in training compared to test results.

In Fig. 2, we show the training precision during the early stopping process. We can see that the precision achieved high scores right in the first training epochs, reaching the 90% score around the 8-th epoch. In this split, the early stopping protocol could

Table 2. Training precision of the final model at the best epoch estimated by the early stopping method.

Dataset	Stream	Split	Epoch	Training precision
UCF101	Spatial	1	35	98.81
		2	30	98.46
		3	42	99.12
	Temporal	1	57	79.78
		2	63	81.65
		3	126	90.51
HMDB51	Spatial	1	19	81.25
		2	18	80.38
		3	21	84.60
	Temporal	1	90	61.40
		2	100	64.28
		3	67	53.12

not achieve a training precision similar to the test, however, it could prevent a 100%-accurate training.

From the table, we can also see that the early stopping protocol greatly reduced the number of training epochs compared to the maximum values (250 and 350), leading to a smaller training cost.

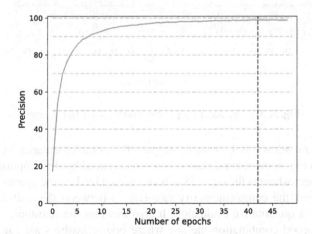

Fig. 2. Precision training during the early stopping process of the spatial stream on the third split of UCF101. The red line indicates the epoch of the best model with the smallest validation loss. The training process reaches 90% of precision around the 8-th epoch. (Color figure online)

Figures 3 and 4 show the average accuracy per class on the UCF101 and HMDB51 datasets, respectively. Although the temporal stream presents a lower accuracy on UCF101, its classes accuracies are above 40%, with the lowest scores near 60%.

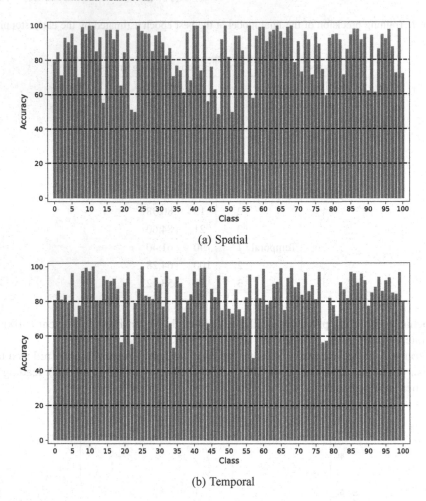

(a) Spatial

(b) Temporal

Fig. 3. Average accuracy per class on the UCF101 dataset.

These histograms allows us to visually inspect the complementarity of the streams. For instance, in Fig. 4, the second class is better recognized by the temporal stream than by the spatial one, whereas the class 38 is better recognized by the spatial stream.

Table 3 shows the complementarity rate (Eq. 5) between the spatial and temporal streams, for a quantitative evaluation. It also includes the harmonic mean (Eq. 6). We consider a good combination the one where both classifiers are capable of complementing each other in a balanced manner. The complementarity rates also indicate a target precision for the combination. For instance, for the spatial stream on UCF101, we have an average precision of 85.52% and an average complementarity rate (*Comp(rgb, flow)*) of 61.52%, which represents a potential accuracy of 94.43% (= 85.52 + 61.52% × 14.48).

Table 4 presents the results of the fusion methods along with the best parameters found in the grid search. The accuracies were very similar, but the weighted

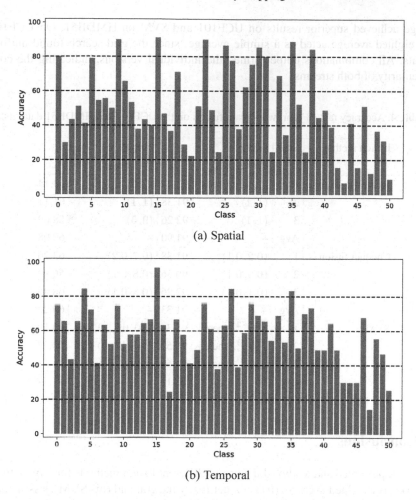

(a) Spatial

(b) Temporal

Fig. 4. Average accuracy per class on the HMDB51 dataset.

Table 3. Complementarity rate of spatial and temporal streams and the harmonic mean (HM) of both values.

Dataset	Split	Comp (rgb, flow)	Comp (flow, rgb)	HM
UCF101	1	58.24	64.26	61.10
	2	65.22	61.69	63.40
	3	61.09	60.00	60.54
HMDB51	1	42.72	36.60	39.42
	2	40.80	29.56	34.28
	3	40.70	27.94	33.14

average achieved superior results on UCF101 and SVM on HMDB51. On UCF101, the weighted average acted as a simple average, since the grid search found uniform weights. All combinations outperformed the individual versions, indicating the complementarity of both streams.

Table 4. Accuracy rate (%) for two-stream fusion on the UCF101 and HMDB51 datasets.

Fusion method	Split	UCF101		HMDB51	
		Parameters	Acc	Parameters	Acc
Weighted average	1	$(1,1)$	92.07	$(7,6)$	63.14
	2	$(1,1)$	91.38	$(1,1)$	61.11
	3	$(1,1)$	92.26	$(9,5)$	58.69
	Avg	–	91.90	–	60.98
Choquet fusion	1	$(0.2,0.1)$	91.38	$(0.7,0.2)$	63.20
	2	$(0.9,0.1)$	90.36	$(0.8,0.1)$	56.99
	3	$(0.1,0.1)$	92.26	$(0.8,0.1)$	60.46
	Avg	–	91.33	–	60.22
SVM	1	$\{10^{-2}, \text{linear}\}$	91.36	$\{10, \text{rbf}, 10^{-2}\}$	63.59
	2	$\{10^{-3}, \text{linear}\}$	90.52	$\{10, \text{rbf}, 10^{-2}\}$	60.52
	3	$\{10^{-3}, \text{linear}\}$	91.64	$\{10^2, 10^{-2}, \text{rbf}\}$	61.11
	Avg	–	91.17	–	61.74

5   Conclusions

This work presented and analyzed the use of different fusion methods for a two-stream network: (i) weighted average, (ii) Choquet fuzzy integral and (iii) SVM classifier. For estimating the parameters of the fusion methods, we have to prevent overfitting on the training stage of the streams. For that, we propose the use of an early stopping protocol to find a premature model without compromising the test accuracies. By using this protocol, we were capable to reduce the difference between the training and test accuracies, specially for the temporal stream, as well as the training cost.

Two well-known and challenging datasets, HMDB51 [14] and UCF101 [32], were used to validate the proposed methods. The methods presented similar performances, but the weighted average and SVM outperformed the others on UCF101 and HMDB51, respectively.

Several action classification methods include additional streams to the two-stream framework adopted in our work. Therefore, a straightforward direction for future work would be to evaluate the proposed fusions to a multi-stream approach. Another aspect of investigation would be a further reduction of the overfitting on the spatial stream.

References

1. Alcantara, M.F., Pedrini, H., Cao, Y.: Human action classification based on silhouette indexed interest points for multiple domains. Int. J. Image Graph. **17**(3), 1750018_1–1750018_27 (2017)
2. Alcantara, M.F., Moreira, T.P., Pedrini, H., Flórez-Revuelta, F.: Action identification using a descriptor with autonomous fragments in a multilevel prediction scheme. SIViP **11**(2), 325–332 (2017)
3. Baumann, F., Ehlers, A., Rosenhahn, B., Liao, J.: Computation strategies for volume local binary patterns applied to action recognition. In: 11th IEEE International Conference on Advanced Video and Signal Based Surveillance, pp. 68–73. IEEE (2014)
4. Brill, E., Wu, J.: Classifier combination for improved lexical disambiguation. In: 36th Annual Meeting of the Association for Computational Linguistics and 17th International Conference on Computational Linguistics, vol. 1, pp. 191–195 (1998)
5. Carreira, J., Zisserman, A.: Quo vadis, action recognition? A new model and the kinetics dataset. In: IEEE Conference on Computer Vision and Pattern Recognition, pp. 4724–4733. IEEE (2017)
6. Concha, D.T., et al.: Multi-stream convolutional neural networks for action recognition in video sequences based on adaptive visual rhythms. In: 17th IEEE International Conference on Machine Learning and Applications, pp. 473–480. IEEE (2018)
7. Cornejo, J.Y.R., Pedrini, H., Flórez-Revuelta, F.: Facial expression recognition with occlusions based on geometric representation. In: CIARP 2015. LNCS, vol. 9423, pp. 263–270. Springer, Cham (2015). https://doi.org/10.1007/978-3-319-25751-8_32
8. Fan, L., Huang, W., Gan, C., Ermon, S., Gong, B., Huang, J.: End-to-end learning of motion representation for video understanding. In: IEEE Conference on Computer Vision and Pattern Recognition, pp. 6016–6025 (2018)
9. Gammulle, H., Denman, S., Sridharan, S., Fookes, C.: Two stream LSTM: a deep fusion framework for human action recognition. In: IEEE Winter Conference on Applications of Computer Vision, pp. 177–186. IEEE (2017)
10. Gori, I., Aggarwal, J.K., Matthies, L., Ryoo, M.S.: Multitype activity recognition in robot-centric scenarios. IEEE Robot. Autom. Lett. **1**(1), 593–600 (2016)
11. Hommos, O., Pintea, S.L., Mettes, P.S., van Gemert, J.C.: Using phase instead of optical flow for action recognition. arXiv preprint arXiv:1809.03258 (2018)
12. Ji, S., Xu, W., Yang, M., Yu, K.: 3D convolutional neural networks for human action recognition. IEEE Trans. Pattern Anal. Mach. Intell. **35**(1), 221–231 (2013)
13. Karpathy, A., Toderici, G., Shetty, S., Leung, T., Sukthankar, R., Fei-Fei, L.: Large-scale video classification with convolutional neural networks. In: IEEE Conference on Computer Vision and Pattern Recognition, pp. 1725–1732 (2014)
14. Kuehne, H., Jhuang, H., Stiefelhagen, R., Serre, T.: HMDB51: a large video database for human motion recognition. In: Nagel, W., Kröner, D., Resch, M. (eds.) High Performance Computing in Science and Engineering, pp. 571–582. Springer, Berlin (2013)
15. Laptev, I.: On space-time interest points. Int. J. Comput. Vis. **64**(2–3), 107–123 (2005)
16. Ma, C.Y., Chen, M.H., Kira, Z., AlRegib, G.: TS-LSTM and temporal-inception: exploiting spatiotemporal dynamics for activity recognition. Signal Process.: Image Commun. **71**, 76–87 (2019)
17. Moreira, T., Menotti, D., Pedrini, H.: First-person action recognition through visual rhythm texture description. In: IEEE International Conference on Acoustics, Speech and Signal Processing, pp. 2627–2631. IEEE (2017)
18. Murofushi, T., Sugeno, M.: Fuzzy measures and fuzzy integrals. In: Grabisch, M., Murofushi, T., Sugeno, M. (eds.) Fuzzy Measures and Integrals - Theory and Applications, pp. 3–41. Physica Verlag, Heidelberg (2000)

19. Murofushi, T., Sugeno, M.: An interpretation of fuzzy measures and the Choquet integral as an integral with respect to a fuzzy measure. Fuzzy Sets Syst. **29**(2), 201–227 (1989)
20. Nanni, L., Brahnam, S., Lumini, A.: Local ternary patterns from three orthogonal planes for human action classification. Expert Syst. Appl. **38**(5), 5125–5128 (2011)
21. Ng, J.Y.H., Hausknecht, M., Vijayanarasimhan, S., Vinyals, O., Monga, R., Toderici, G.: Beyond short snippets: deep networks for video classification. In: IEEE Conference on Computer Vision and Pattern Recognition, pp. 4694–4702 (2015)
22. Peng, X., Zou, C., Qiao, Yu., Peng, Q.: Action recognition with stacked fisher vectors. In: Fleet, D., Pajdla, T., Schiele, B., Tuytelaars, T. (eds.) ECCV 2014. LNCS, vol. 8693, pp. 581–595. Springer, Cham (2014). https://doi.org/10.1007/978-3-319-10602-1_38
23. Prechelt, L.: Early stopping - but when? In: Orr, G.B., Müller, K.-R. (eds.) Neural Networks: Tricks of the Trade. LNCS, vol. 1524, pp. 55–69. Springer, Heidelberg (1998). https://doi.org/10.1007/3-540-49430-8_3
24. Ryoo, M.S., Matthies, L.: First-person activity recognition: feature, temporal structure, and prediction. Int. J. Comput. Vis. **119**(3), 307–328 (2015). https://doi.org/10.1007/s11263-015-0847-4
25. Santos, A., Pedrini, H.: Spatio-temporal video autoencoder for human action recognition. In: 14th International Joint Conference on Computer Vision, Imaging and Computer Graphics Theory and Applications, Prague, Czech Republic, pp. 114–123, February 2019
26. e Santos, A.C.S., de Almeida Maia, H., e Souza, M.R., Vieira, M.B., Pedrini, H.: Fuzzy fusion for two-stream action recognition. In: VISIGRAPP (5: VISAPP), pp. 117–123 (2020)
27. Shahroudy, A., Liu, J., Ng, T.T., Wang, G.: NTU RGB+D: a large scale dataset for 3D human activity analysis. In: IEEE Conference on Computer Vision and Pattern Recognition, pp. 1010–1019 (2016)
28. Shi, F., Laganiere, R., Petriu, E.: Gradient boundary histograms for action recognition. In: IEEE Winter Conference on Applications of Computer Vision, pp. 1107–1114 (Jan 2015)
29. Shi, L., Zhang, Y., Cheng, J., Lu, H.: Skeleton-based action recognition with directed graph neural networks. In: IEEE Conference on Computer Vision and Pattern Recognition, pp. 7912–7921 (2019)
30. Simonyan, K., Zisserman, A.: Two-stream convolutional networks for action recognition in videos. In: Ghahramani, Z., Welling, M., Cortes, C., Lawrence, N., Weinberger, K. (eds.) Advances in Neural Information Processing Systems, vol. 27, pp. 568–576. Curran Associates, Inc. (2014)
31. Snoek, C.G., Worring, M., Smeulders, A.W.: Early versus late fusion in aemantic video analysis. In: 13th annual ACM International Conference on Multimedia, pp. 399–402 (2005)
32. Soomro, K., Zamir, A.R., Shah, M.: UCF101: a dataset of 101 human actions classes from videos in the wild. arXiv preprint arXiv:1212.0402 (2012)
33. Szegedy, C., Vanhoucke, V., Ioffe, S., Shlens, J., Wojna, Z.: Rethinking the inception architecture for computer vision. In: IEEE Conference on Computer Vision and Pattern Recognition, pp. 2818–2826 (2016)
34. Tahani, H., Keller, J.M.: Information fusion in computer vision using the fuzzy integral. IEEE Trans. Syst. Man Cybern. **20**(3), 733–741 (1990)
35. Tran, D., Bourdev, L., Fergus, R., Torresani, L., Paluri, M.: Learning spatiotemporal features with 3D convolutional networks. In: IEEE International Conference on Computer Vision, pp. 4489–4497 (2015)
36. Uddin, M.A., Joolee, J.B., Alam, A., Lee, Y.K.: Human action recognition using adaptive local motion descriptor in spark. IEEE Access **5**, 21157–21167 (2017)
37. Wang, H., Wang, W., Wang, L.: Hierarchical motion evolution for action recognition. In: Asian Conference on Pattern Recognition, pp. 574–578, November 2015
38. Wang, H., Kläser, A., Schmid, C., Liu, C.L.: Dense trajectories and motion boundary descriptors for action recognition. Int. J. Comput. Vis. **103**(1), 60–79 (2013)

39. Wang, H., Schmid, C.: Action recognition with improved trajectories. In: International Conference on Computer Vision, pp. 3551–3558, December 2013
40. Wang, L., Ge, L., Li, R., Fang, Y.: Three-stream CNNs for action recognition. Pattern Recogn. Lett. **92**, 33–40 (2017)
41. Wang, L., Qiao, Y., Tang, X.: Action recognition with trajectory-pooled deep-convolutional descriptors. In: IEEE Conference on Computer Vision and Pattern Recognition, pp. 4305–4314 (2015)
42. Wang, L., Xiong, Y., Wang, Z., Qiao, Y.: Towards good practices for very deep two-stream convnets. arXiv preprint arXiv:1507.02159 (2015)
43. Wang, L., et al.: Temporal segment networks: towards good practices for deep action recognition. In: Leibe, B., Matas, J., Sebe, N., Welling, M. (eds.) ECCV 2016. LNCS, vol. 9912, pp. 20–36. Springer, Cham (2016). https://doi.org/10.1007/978-3-319-46484-8_2
44. Wang, X., Gao, L., Wang, P., Sun, X., Liu, X.: Two-stream 3-D ConvNet fusion for action recognition in videos with arbitrary size and length. IEEE Trans. Multimed. **20**(3), 634–644 (2017)
45. Xu, J., Tasaka, K., Yanagihara, H.: Beyond two-stream: skeleton-based three-stream networks for action recognition in videos. In: 24th International Conference on Pattern Recognition, pp. 1567–1573. IEEE (2018)
46. Yan, S., Xiong, Y., Lin, D.: Spatial temporal graph convolutional networks for skeleton-based action recognition. In: Thirty-second AAAI Conference on Artificial Intelligence (2018)
47. Yi, Y., Zheng, Z., Lin, M.: Realistic action recognition with salient foreground trajectories. Expert Syst. Appl. **75**, 44–55 (2017)
48. Zach, C., Pock, T., Bischof, H.: A duality based approach for realtime TV-L^1 optical flow. In: Hamprecht, F.A., Schnörr, C., Jähne, B. (eds.) DAGM 2007. LNCS, vol. 4713, pp. 214–223. Springer, Heidelberg (2007). https://doi.org/10.1007/978-3-540-74936-3_22
49. Zhang, H.B., et al.: A comprehensive survey of vision-based human action recognition methods. Sensors **19**(5), 1005 (2019)
50. Zhu, J., Zhu, Z., Zou, W.: End-to-end video-level representation learning for action recognition. In: 24th International Conference on Pattern Recognition, pp. 645–650. IEEE (2018)
51. Zhu, W., et al.: Co-occurrence feature learning for skeleton based action recognition using regularized deep LSTM networks. In: Thirtieth AAAI Conference on Artificial Intelligence (2016)
52. Zhu, Y.: PyTorch implementation of popular two-stream frameworks for video action recognition (2017). https://github.com/bryanyzhu/two-stream-pytorch
53. Zhu, Y., Lan, Z., Newsam, S., Hauptmann, A.G.: Hidden two-stream convolutional networks for action recognition. arXiv preprint arXiv:1704.00389 (2017)

RGB-D Images Based 3D Plant Growth Prediction by Sequential Images-to-Images Translation with Plant Priors

Tomohiro Hamamoto, Hideaki Uchiyama[✉️] [ID], Atsushi Shimada, and Rin-ichiro Taniguchi [ID]

Kyushu University, Fukuoka, Japan
{hamamoto,uchiyama}@limu.ait.kyushu-u.ac.jp,
atsushi@ait.kyushu-u.ac.jp, rin@kyudai.jp

Abstract. This paper presents a neural network based method for 3D plant growth prediction based on sequential images-to-images translation. Especially, we extend an existing image-to-image translation technique based on U-Net to images-to-images translation by incorporating convLSTM into skip connections in U-Net. With this architecture, we can achieve sequential image prediction tasks such that future images are predicted from several past ones. Since depth images are incorporated as additional channel into our network, the prediction can be represented in 3D space. As an application of our method, we develop a 3D plant growth prediction system. In the evaluation, the performance of our network was investigated in terms of the importance of each module in the network. We verified how the prediction accuracy was affected by the internal structure of the network. In addition, the extension of our network with plant priors was further investigated to evaluate the impact for plant growth prediction tasks.

Keywords: Images-to-images translation · Plant phenotyping · Future prediction · U-Net · convLSTM

1 Introduction

In agricultural research, one research issue is to design the mathematical model of plant growth to evaluate the degree of plant growth quantitatively and qualitatively. Such model has been useful to manage the cultivation of crops [17]. For example, planned cultivation can be optimized if it is possible to predict plant growth in a plant factory. From the past, plant growth prediction has been a challenging problem because the degree of growth can vary largely due to various factors such as genetic and environmental ones. Plant growth is generally modeled by using phenotype-based indicators such as leaf weight and dry matter [18]. However, the measurement of these indicators often needs plant destruction. Such destructive measurements are unsuitable for monitoring plant growth as sequential observation. As non-destructive ones, image processing applications have been investigated as an attempt to measure plant growth [15].

Supported by JSPS KAKENHI Grant Number JP17H01768 and JP18H04117.

© Springer Nature Switzerland AG 2022
K. Bouatouch et al. (Eds.): VISIGRAPP 2020, CCIS 1474, pp. 334–352, 2022.
https://doi.org/10.1007/978-3-030-94893-1_15

In plant image analysis, image features obtained from plant appearance such as leaf area, leaf length and stem diameter are used as plant growth indicators [16]. Especially, the size of the leaf area is a basic criterion for the plant growth because it is correlated with the growth. It is generally computed as follows. Specific colored pixels in an image are first extracted by using thresholding based binarization. Then, the number of pixels is computed as the size of the leaf area. As aforementioned above, image based approaches for obtaining the growth index of a plant have an significant advantage that the index can be measured non-destructively and non-contactly. In addition, a large number of plants can be processed in parallel. However, it is not possible to observe the three-dimensional deformation of plant growth such as leaf curl and overlap when using RGB images only. This means that there can be a large difference between the actual plant growth and the plant growth estimated from images.

In this paper, we propose a neural network based method for 3D plant phenotyping based on sequential images-to-images translation. As first contribution, we propose to predict the plant growth with a camera that can acquire both RGB and depth images. By using RGB-D images, it is possible to observe plants in 3D space so that 3D plant growth can be predicted. As second contribution, we extend a U-Net based image-to-image translation to images-to-images translation by combining convLSTM with U-Net. With this network, we can predict future images from several past ones. We apply our network to generate the 3D plant growth model from RGB-D images of a plant captured at a bird's eye view [22]. In other words, we aim at predicting future RGB-D plant images that will be captured several hours or several days later from past sequential images, as a future prediction task. As a result, our network can predict a future 3D plant shape by simultaneously predicting both RGB and depth images. In the evaluation, the performance of several variant architectures derived from our basic one was investigated to clarify the importance of each module in the network. Also, the extension of our network with plant priors was evaluated to show the impact of plant priors. This issue is categorized as a future image prediction task for plant phenotyping.

This paper is the extended version of [7]. The main contribution of this paper is the further analysis of our network extended with plant priors for plant image analysis.

2 Related Work

Our goal is to generate future RGB-D images from past ones based on sequential prediction techniques so that plant growth prediction in 3D space can be achieved. In this paper, we propose an images-to-images translation method for neural-network-based plant image analysis. By training the network, the plant growth can be modeled from plant images. In this section, we briefly discuss related work from the following aspects: plant image analysis, image-to-image translation, and sequential predictions.

2.1 Plant Image Analysis

The research on plant image analysis has started since the 1970s. Statistical analysis of plant growth was initially conducted with the size of plant leaves computed in images [14]. As sequential image analysis, plant growth was analyzed by using optical flow [2]. In recent years, predictive analysis based on high-quality or large-scale plant images has been performed [4, 8].

Neural network based approaches have been proposed for image analysis of plants with the progress of deep learning technologies. For instance, detection of plant leaves and measurement of the plant centers [1, 3, 5] and data augmentation for plant images [24] were performed. There was also an attempt to estimate the position of branches from a multi-view plant image by image-to-image translation and reconstruct the original plant shape in 3D space [11].

One work investigated future plant images from the past ones in 2D space [20]. This work predicted future plant images by using both RGB plant images and color-coded leaf label images. In this paper, we extend this work for predicting future plant images in 3D space.

2.2 Image-to-Image Translation

The basic idea of image-to-image translation is to translate an original source image into some target image based on the learning of the characteristics between the domains of each image. In deep learning, the source image was reconstructed by using an auto-encoder [9]. In this research, the network is trained to restore information in the feature layer by inputting and outputting the same original image. The variational auto-encoder [12] enables image style conversion by rewriting the features in the latent space. VAE-GAN [13] is a method that combines the Generative Adversarial Network (GAN) and an encoder-decoder structure, and then generates images with high visual reproducibility.

In addition, U-Net [19] has been proposed as an image-to-image translation structure in the task of image segmentation. Since U-Net uses a skip connection, high-precision image conversion is performed by combining the high-resolution convolution result and the low-resolution convolution result with a channel.

2.3 Sequential Prediction

In sequential prediction with deep learning, one work learns the relationship between images from sequential images and predicts future images. Long-Short Term Memory (LSTM) is a deep neural network with a structure suitable for sequential analysis to learn both short and long-term relationships between sequential information [10]. An effective video representation can be achieved with an encoder-decoder structure that divides LSTM into an encoder capturing the features of a video and a decoder generating a prediction image [21]. Also, convolutional LSTM (convLSTM), which combines spatial convolution with LSTM structure, has been devised to capture spatial features of images [23].

3 Proposed Method

In our work, plant growth prediction is achieved by generating future plant images from past plant ones via deep neural network. Image sequence of the RGB plant images and its corresponding depth images are given as the input of the network. Then, RGB-D image sequence is generated as the output, and is projected into 3D space for visualization.

Our method first takes sequential RGB-D images as input, and then generates future RGB-D images predicted from the input through the network. Therefore, our network can be referred to as images-to-images translation or prediction in 3D space. In this paper, we focus on plant growth prediction as an application of our network even though our network is applicable to other prediction tasks.

3.1 Overview of Network Architecture

U-Net is generally used for image segmentation and image-to-image translation [19]. In our task, we primarily extend U-Net to sequential images-to-images translation to generate multiple future images from past images. Especially, we propose to use an encoder-decoder convLSTM to predict future images by learning sequential changes in plant growth at different layers. Input images are first converted from sequential representation into some latent features by passing through the encoder LSTM. Then, the decoder LSTM reads the features computed in the encoder to reconstruct another sequential representation from the features. In other words, our architecture tries to compress the amount of information by going through the transformation from images to features and allows us to obtain an predicted image sequence independent of the number of input images. In our proposed network, we incorporate convLSTM into U-Net instead of using skip connection in U-Net.

Besides, we propose to incorporate GAN [6] as an error function. We apply GAN to the frames in a generated image sequence to learn the sequential characteristics in the network. In addition, the accuracy of prediction for each image is improved by applying GAN to one image taken at random from the image sequence. In summary, our network utilizes the structure of GAN, which is divided into a generator that generates images and a discriminator that identifies images, as illustrated in Fig. 1. The generator learns the features so that the generated image will be similar to the real image whereas the discriminator learns the ones to distinguish the actual image from the image synthesized provided by the generator. Our motivation is to predict more realistic images by learning these iteratively. In the learning process, the mean squared error (MSE) between pixels of the images is considered as a loss to stabilize the learning, in addition to the loss of GAN. In the following sections, the network structure is explained in the context of GAN.

3.2 Generator

The generator is a U-Net based encoder-decoder structure with convLSTM instead of skip connections in U-Net at some levels, as illustrated in Fig. 2. The encoder performs dimension compression whereas the decoder does reconstruct of the images from the compressed information. In the encoder, the features are computed from input images by using CNN, and then the sequential information is compressed by encoder LSTM. In the decoder, the number of image representations obtained as output is generated

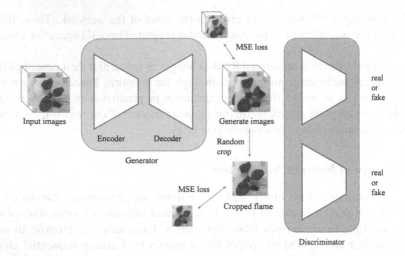

Fig. 1. Overview of network architecture for 3D plant growth prediction [7]. The network converts RGB-D plant images as input through the generator into predicted ones several hours later. In the GAN process, the generated images are discriminated from the correct images in the discriminator.

from the sequential information compressed in the encoder LSTM. Finally, the original image resolution is reconstructed by using deconvolution.

Regarding the computation in CNN, spatial features are obtained by computing weighted sums with surrounding pixels in multiple layers for each image. The size of feature space can generally be compressed by changing the kernel stride. Pixel shuffler increases the size of an image by applying array transformation to the channel. It is generally used for tasks such as generating super-resolution images.

3.3 Encoder-Decoder LSTM in Generator

As illustrated in Fig. 3, the skip connection in U-Net is replaced with convLSTM such that features extracted by CNN are converted into sequential features through two convLSTM structures with different sizes. This design was proposed because the upper convLSTM (LSTM1) reads local changes between features in the high-resolution space whereas the lower convLSTM (LSTM2) does global changes of images in the compressed feature space. In other words, both local and global latent sequential features are generated.

In the encoder, the input is put into the convLSTM in sequential order. The cell state and output are updated by the spatio-temporal weight calculation with the input of the previous time. The output at the encoder is used only for updating the next state, and then the output at the final layer is passed to the decoder along with the cell state.

In the decoder, the output of the encoder is given as the input of the first layer, and then the input of the subsequent layer is given as the output of the previous layer of the decoder itself. The decoder can generate the output in a self-recursive manner, which

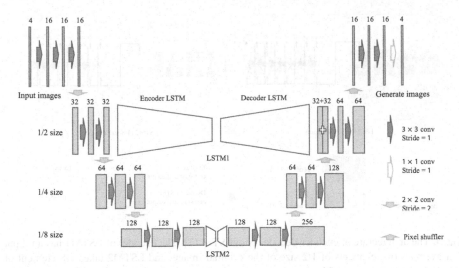

Fig. 2. Network architecture in the generator [7]. Input images are spatially convoluted through CNN, and transformed with sequential information through LSTM. The output/predicted images are reconstructed by using both deconvolution and pixel shuffler.

allows us to generate output independent of the number of inputs. Both the encoder and the decoder are implemented by using convLSTM, which is used for sequential image analysis.

3.4 Discriminator

The discriminator performs discrimination for both a single image and sequential changes between images in parallel, as illustrated in Fig. 4. The sequential discriminator performs the dimensional compression of the image in the 2D convolution part, and then identifies the sequential features by 3D convolution. The single image discriminator takes one random image from the generated sequential images, and performs feature extraction by 2D convolution.

The discriminator classifies the output of the final layer into a binary class of 0 to 1 by activating it with a sigmoid. When learning the generator, it learns so that the output is 1 for the generated image with the weight of the discriminator fixed. When learning the discriminator, the generator weight is fixed so that the output for ground truth is 1 and the output for generated image is 0. Based on this GAN property, the loss function of the generator G and the loss function of the discriminator D are set. Since our network has two discriminators, the loss function of a sequential discriminator is denoted as G_t, D_t, and the loss function of a single image discriminator is denoted as G_s, D_s. In order to stabilize the learning process, MSE loss L_{MSE} is added during generator learning. The loss function of the generator L_G and the loss function of the discriminator L_D in the whole network are as follows. $\alpha = 10^{-3}, \beta = 10^{-3}$ is given as the experimental value.

$$L_G = L_{MSE} + \alpha G_t + \beta G_s \tag{1}$$

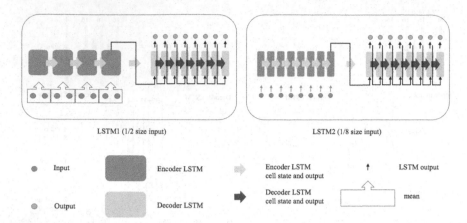

LSTM1 (1/2 size input)   LSTM2 (1/8 size input)

● Input   ▨ Encoder LSTM   ⇨ Encoder LSTM cell state and output   ↑ LSTM output

                                         ➡ Decoder LSTM cell state and output   ⌃ mean

● Output   ▨ Decoder LSTM

Fig. 3. The architecture of encoder-decoder convLSTM [7]. The encoder of LSTM1 has an input that averages two elements of 1/2 size of the original image, and LSTM2 takes 1/8 element of the original image as input. The decoder receives the output and cell state of the final layer of the encoder.

$$L_D = \alpha D_t + \beta D_s \qquad (2)$$

As the learning activation function, relu is used for the final layer of the generator, sigmoid is used for the final layer of the classifier, tanh is used for the LSTM layer, and leaky_relu is used for the other layers.

4 Evaluation

To investigate the performance of our network, the evaluation with both RGB and depth images in the KOMATSUNA dataset [22] was performed. Especially, the effectiveness of each module was investigated by first replacing convLSTM with CNN and then removing GAN from our network for the comparison. Besides, we present the result of the plant growth prediction in 3D space.

4.1 Dataset

We used the KOMATSUNA dataset in this evaluation. This dataset is composed of time-series image sequences of 5 Komatuna vegetables. For each plant, there are 60 frames captured at a bird's eye view every 4 h with lighting for 24 h. In this experiment, both RGB and depth images included in the dataset were used for 3D growth prediction tasks. This dataset assumes an environment where data can be obtained uniformly as in plant factories.

In the experiment, plant data was divided into a training set and a test one. During the network training, four plants were used as a training set, and the remaining one was used as a test set. The resolution of the image was resized into [128, 128]. For each plant, images were not only reversed left and right, and also rotated by 90, 180, and 270°, as data augmentation.

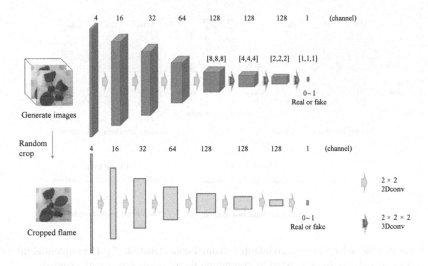

Fig. 4. Network architecture in the discriminator [7]. The discriminator has a single image identification function and a sequential image identification function. 3D convolution is used for the sequential image discrimination.

4.2 Networks for Comparison

As networks for comparison experiments, additional networks were designed by changing our structure at the encoder-decoder part of the network, as similar to ablation study, as illustrated in Fig. 2. The purpose of the design was to investigate the effectiveness of each module in our network.

As illustrated in Fig. 5, one network used the encoder-decoder structure based on the sequential channel concatenation, which was not based on LSTM. Dimensional compression is performed by concatenating input images into channels and convolving them at once. In the subsequent convolution, the amount of information in the image sequence is reconstructed by increasing the number of channels.

Another network for the comparison was illustrated in Fig. 6. This used three stacked LSTM layers, compared with Fig. 3. The difference of the predicted images due to the multiple stacked layers of LSTM was verified. The experiment used the structure in which three layers of different LSTMs were superimposed on each of the encoder and decoder.

Furthermore, the output of the network with and without GAN was investigated to evaluate the usefulness of GAN. As a loss function without GAN, the network only calculated the MSE loss for the generator.

4.3 Result of Network Comparison

In the process of training, we trained each network with an image sequence of four plants. In the test, we predicted the growth of the remaining one plant from the images through the trained network. The input was eight sequential images. Based on the input,

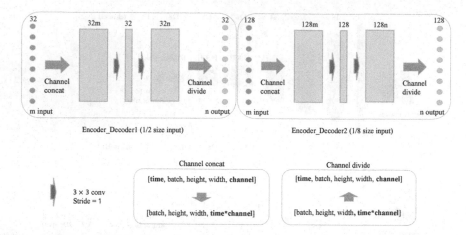

Fig. 5. Encoder-decoder with sequential inter-channel concatenation [7]. The sequential information is compressed and decompressed by combining the sequential axes with channels.

the future growth of the plant was predicted as eight future images. Figure 7 shows the results for each network.

RGB images predicted by channel-concatenation encoder-decoder in Fig. 5 were high reproducible as individual images, and there was blurring of the image for the later prediction. On the other hand, the images predicted by encoder-decoder LSTM tended to maintain the continuity of motion over time, although the image was less sharp due to the prediction in the back. Increasing the stacked layer of LSTM in Fig. 6 improved the sharpness of the image, but overreacted to movement.

As a result of applying a discriminator by GAN, a clearer image was predicted, but a real image could not be predicted. The reason was that the network becomes more sensitive to changes, and the response to minute differences becomes too high. Therefore, GAN did not always act as we expected.

Table 1 shows the MSE loss values computed for each predicted sequence and the average value for the images predicted in the network. The loss values are higher in the later prediction, and this trend is particularly strong when LSTM is not used. In a network with three layers of LSTM, the MSE loss is higher than when only one layer of LSTM is used.

4.4   3D Prediction

By predicting the depth image, the prediction result can be displayed in 3D space. The depth image prediction can be performed simultaneously with RGB prediction by adding a channel for depth image prediction. It should be noted that it is recommended to replace missing values in the depth images with some values such as the median of the image as a preliminary preparation for generating a more natural 3D model.

The 3D model of plants predicted using RGB-D images was displayed, as illustrated in Fig. 8. The surface of the point cloud was reconstructed by using Meshlab's ball pivoting.

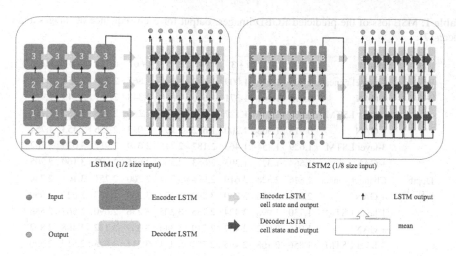

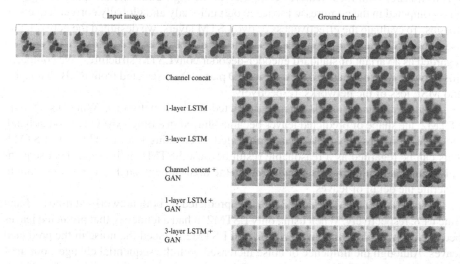

Fig. 6. Three stacked encoder-decoder LSTM layers [7]. The output of the first LSTM is passed to the next one. The output of the last layer of the decoder LSTM is regarded as the output of the entire encoder-decoder.

Fig. 7. RGB image sequence predicted through networks based on given input image sequence [7]. The sequential eight images are input, (left) and the growth was predicted with eight images (right).

4.5 Effectiveness of Two LSTM Layers

We proposed to incorporate two LSTM layers into the feature computations in both high-dimensional space and compressed one such that we used the first LSTM for half-size convoluted features (LSTM1) and the second one for 1/8 size convoluted features (LSTM2), as illustrated in Fig. 2. This is different from the multiple stacked layers of LSTM layer, which was discussed in Sect. 4.2. The motivation of our network design

Table 1. MSE loss of the predicted RGBD images: output for each sequence of images and its mean [7].

Unit	Model	t + 1	t + 2	t + 3	t + 4	t + 5	t + 6	t + 7	t + 8	Mean
RGB (10^{-2})	Channel concat	0.707	1.006	1.009	1.413	1.800	1.867	2.324	2.754	1.610
	+ GAN	0.975	1.364	1.371	1.636	2.060	2.348	2.587	2.949	1.911
	1-layer LSTM	0.866	1.284	1.127	1.759	2.446	2.286	2.228	2.282	1.785
	+ GAN	0.913	1.368	1.200	1.692	2.107	2.043	2.256	2.453	1.754
	3-layer LSTM	1.629	1.454	1.463	2.182	2.745	2.679	2.912	3.029	2.262
	+ GAN	1.564	1.377	1.305	2.053	2.560	2.685	2.993	3.100	2.205
Depth (10^{-4})	Channel concat	1.846	2.328	2.619	2.998	3.264	3.200	2.751	3.107	2.764
	+ GAN	2.994	3.100	3.249	3.292	3.477	3.239	2.577	2.623	3.069
	1-layer LSTM	1.730	1.998	2.424	2.735	3.305	3.236	2.690	2.567	2.586
	+ GAN	1.916	2.072	2.457	2.719	3.344	3.359	3.142	3.408	2.802
	3-layer LSTM	1.856	2.108	2.495	2.781	3.331	3.311	2.826	2.817	2.690
	+ GAN	2.558	2.665	3.050	3.239	3.687	3.614	3.328	3.495	3.204

was to transfer both local features computed in the high-dimensional space and global ones computed in the compressed space to output locally and globally correct sequential images. To evaluate the effectiveness of two LSTM layers, we designed the network that used only LSTM2. In other words, LSTM1 was simply removed in Fig. 2. This can be regarded as a variant of standard encoder-decoder convLSTM structures. We compared this network with our network in terms of 3D plants reconstructed from RGB-D images, and MSE loss of the networks, respectively.

Figure 9 illustrates RGB images predicted by both networks. When using only LSTM2, the shape of predicted leaves became blurred in a time axis. On the other hand, the detail of leaves was more clearly predicted when using both LSTM1 and LSTM2. This can be regarded as a reasonable result because LSTM1 helps learn local sequential features. From the result, convLSTM in the high-dimensional space is important to generate the detail of leaves.

Figure 10a and Fig. 10b show 3D results predicted by both networks at time t + 1 and time t + 8, respectively. When using only LSTM2, it had a tendency that predicted leaves became noisy while using both LSTM1 and LSTM2 reduced the noise in the predicted leaves. Although the influence of noise increased with the sequential changes, our approach using two LSTM layers suppressed the noises in the prediction even after 32 h.

As a quantitative result, Fig. 11 shows the results of MSE loss for both networks. For the long-term prediction, the loss of our network was smaller than the network only with the 2nd convLSTM. This means that the prediction of our network was better. This result was the same as the visualization results. It was confirmed that the results of the loss and those of the comparison of the predicted images were consistent. If there is more training data, more LSTM layers at other levels will be useful.

5   Evaluation with Plant Prior

In the field of plant phenotyping, the methods for leaf counting in a plant image have been proposed as plant image analysis [1]. From such methods, the leaf regions can

Channel concat

1-layer LSTM

3-layer LSTM

Channel concat + GAN

1-layer LSTM + GAN

3-layer LSTM + GAN

Fig. 8. 3D prediction result [7]. 3D point cloud (left) and faceted image by Ball Pivoting (right) are visualized.

be given as a result of instance segmentation. Therefore, we extended our network to utilize the leaf regions represented with labels as plant priors as similar to [20].

5.1 Network Architecture

Labeled images computed by segmenting plant leaves in a pixel-by-pixel manner can be used as the input of the network as plant priors with the RGB images. Such labeled

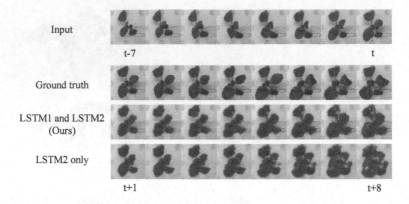

Fig. 9. RGB images predicted by the network. The sequential images of eight plants were input, the growth was predicted as eight images. Predicted images of the network with two LSTM layers (LSTM1 and LSTM2) and the ones only with LSTM2 were compared.

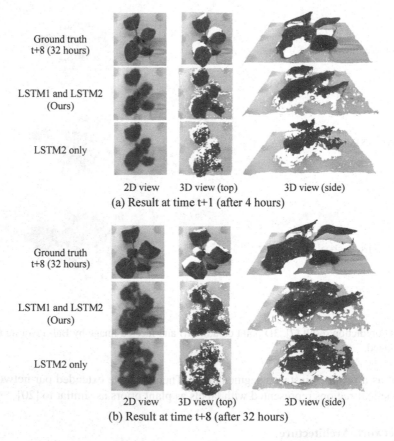

Fig. 10. 3D prediction results by the network with two LSTM layers and the one only with LSTM2. Predicted RGB image and 3D shape are shown for the times at t + 1 and t + 8.

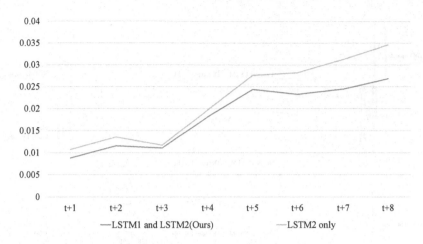

Fig. 11. Comparison of MSE loss results. The MSE loss of RGB-D images predicted in each sequence from t + 1 to t + 8 is compared.

Images were given in the dataset for plant phenotyping. The loss function in our network was extended with four components: the MSE loss of the images, the softmax cross entropy of the labeled images, the difference loss that calculates the differences in leaf motions, and the centroid loss that calculates the differences in leaf centroid positions. The details are described in [20].

Figure 12 show the network extended for incorporating the plant priors in the input. Compared with Fig. 2, the convolution and deconvolution layers were added for labeled images. Also, additional LSTM layer was incorporated to learn more features from labeled images. The number of convolutional layers was determined according to the network noted in [20].

In this experiment, we first evaluated the effectiveness of the plant priors in our network with RGB images and label images. The result of 3D prediction is discussed in Sect. 5.3. For the evaluation, we used with the MSE loss of images only, with the MSE loss of images and the softmax cross entropy loss of labeled images, and with the MSE loss, the softmax cross entropy loss, the different loss, and the centroid loss. The losses used in the final gradient computation were calculated as a linear sum of all the losses. The weights for each loss were determined according to [20]. The weights for MSE loss, softmax cross entropy loss, different loss and centroid loss were set to 1.0, 1.0, 2.0 and 0.5, respectively.

5.2 Result

In the experiment, as a verification of the U-Net structure as in Sect. 4.5, a network using three LSTMs and a network using only LSTM3 were compared. Figure 13 and Fig. 14 show the predicted results of the RGB images and the label images, respectively. Regarding the predicted RGB images, the static areas such as the background area are clearly captured. In the predicted labeled image, details such as plant branches are reproduced. In both predicted images, the locomotion of the leaves of the plant was confirmed, but the exact movement could not be reproduced.

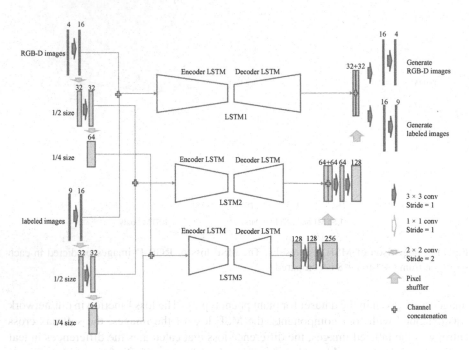

Fig. 12. Network architecture for plant priors. Each of RGB-D and labeled images were convoluted and deconvoluted at different convolution stages, respectively. In the encoder-decoder, the network contained three different LSTMs.

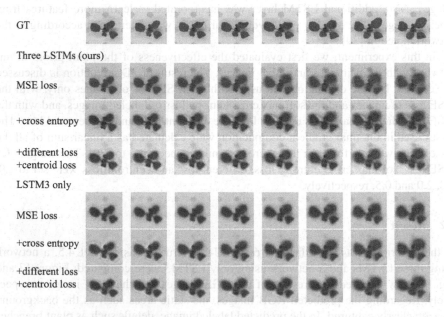

Fig. 13. RGB images predicted by the network. Result of the network with only LSTM3 and with three different LSTMs: LSTM1, LSTM2 and LSTM3.

GT

Three LSTMs (ours)

MSE loss
+cross entropy

+different loss
+centroid loss

LSTM3 only

MSE loss
+cross entropy

+different loss
+centroid loss

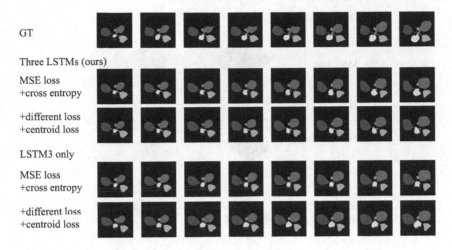

Fig. 14. Labeled image predicted by the network. For each pixel, the label with the highest probability is displayed.

Table 2 shows the loss of the predicted plant images. From the table, losses are improved especially when labeled images are used. On the other hand, MSE loss is getting worse when only MSE loss is used.

Table 2. Loss of the predicted images: MSE loss (for RGB images), softmax cross entropy loss, difference loss and centroid loss (for labeled images).

	Activated loss	MSE	Cross entropy	Different	Centroid
All LSTMs	MSE	0.0121	–	–	–
	+ cross entropy	0.0105	0.163	–	–
	+ different + centroid	0.0103	0.185	0.00791	0.00185
LSTM3 only	MSE	0.0103	–	–	–
	+ softmax cross entropy	0.0121	0.209	–	–
	+ different + centroid	0.0116	0.191	0.00805	0.00157

5.3 3D Prediction

Next, we evaluated the performance of our network that takes both labeled images and RGB-D images as input. In the implementation, the normalized depth image channel was concatenated with the RGB image channel.

Figure 15 shows the result of 3D reconstruction of the plant RGB-D image predicted from the network shown in Fig. 12. When only the MSE of the RGB-D images were used as the loss, the appearance of the plants were roughly predicted. On the other hand, the prediction results became noisy when the loss for the labeled images were used. One of the reasons would be the difference between the MSE loss of the depth image and the

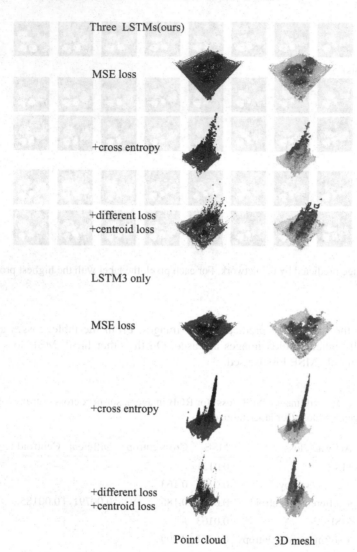

Three LSTMs(ours)

MSE loss

+cross entropy

+different loss
+centroid loss

LSTM3 only

MSE loss

+cross entropy

+different loss
+centroid loss

Point cloud   3D mesh

Fig. 15. 3D reconstruction result of plant images predicted by the network with different LSTM structures. 3D point cloud (left) and 3D mesh by Ball Pivoting (right) are visualized at each network architecture and losses.

cross entropy loss of the labeled image. The simply concatenation with label images did not always improve the prediction results in our experiments. This will be our further issue to be solved.

6 Discussion

In our evaluations, the results may be biased because the amount of dataset was not sufficient. Generally, it is difficult to capture RGB-D images of plants at a high resolution.

The plant growth simulator will be one of the solutions for increasing the size of the dataset in the future. In that case, the difference between real plants and simulated ones may be the subject of research.

Also, it has been confirmed that the prediction of the network becomes unstable, as well as other neural networks. Some differences in the predicted results occurred after several tens of training. For instance, the shape of the plant deviated significantly. The further improvement for stable training would be a remaining issue.

Besides, there is a task that requires the optimization of parameters in the network. Owing to changes in parameters such as the number of channels, the weights related to a loss function, and the training rate, the results may change significantly. When using multiple losses where scales are different, it is not easy to optimize the weights. By using a technique of multi-task learning, this may be solved, as a future work.

7 Conclusion

We proposed a method to generate 3D plant growth model by applying a machine learning framework to plant growth prediction. We applied an image sequence prediction network based on the sequential changes of plant images, and examined how the predicted image changes according to the structure of the network. In the network comparison, it was shown that the prediction can be made with higher accuracy when the low-dimensional image convolution result is introduced into the sequential prediction. We also showed that adding losses of plant priors to the network to make predictions would reduce the ability to restore 3D predictions.

As a future task, it is necessary to investigate the cause of the decrease in 3D prediction accuracy when the network is expanded and work on improving the network structure. We are also considering improving the validity of 3D prediction by adding loss related to 3D shape to the prediction and performing post-processing on the predicted image of the network.

References

1. Aich, S., Stavness, I.: Leaf counting with deep convolutional and deconvolutional networks. In: Proceedings of the IEEE International Conference on Computer Vision, pp. 2080–2089 (2017)
2. Barron, J., Liptay, A.: Measuring 3-D plant growth using optical flow. Bioimaging 5(2), 82–86 (1997)
3. Chen, Y., Ribera, J., Boomsma, C., Delp, E.: Locating crop plant centers from UAV-based RGB imagery. In: Proceedings of the IEEE International Conference on Computer Vision, pp. 2030–2037 (2017)
4. Fujita, M., Tanabata, T., Urano, K., Kikuchi, S., Shinozaki, K.: RIPPS: a plant phenotyping system for quantitative evaluation of growth under controlled environmental stress conditions. Plant Cell Physiol. 59(10), 2030–2038 (2018)
5. Giuffrida, M.V., Minervini, M., Tsaftaris, S.: Learning to count leaves in rosette plants. In: Proceedings of the Computer Vision Problems in Plant Phenotyping (CVPPP) (2015)
6. Goodfellow, I., et al.: Generative adversarial nets. In: Advances in Neural Information Processing Systems, pp. 2672–2680 (2014)

7. Hamamoto, T., Uchiyama, H., Shimada, A., Taniguchi, R.I.: 3D plant growth prediction via image-to-image translation. In: 15th International Joint Conference on Computer Vision, Imaging and Computer Graphics Theory and Applications, VISIGRAPP 2020, pp. 153–161. SciTePress (2020)

8. Hartmann, A., Czauderna, T., Hoffmann, R., Stein, N., Schreiber, F.: HTPheno: an image analysis pipeline for high-throughput plant phenotyping. BMC Bioinform. **12**(1), 148 (2011)

9. Hinton, G.E., Salakhutdinov, R.R.: Reducing the dimensionality of data with neural networks. Science **313**(5786), 504–507 (2006)

10. Hochreiter, S., Schmidhuber, J.: Long short-term memory. Neural Comput. **9**(8), 1735–1780 (1997)

11. Isokane, T., Okura, F., Ide, A., Matsushita, Y., Yagi, Y.: Probabilistic plant modeling via multi-view image-to-image translation. In: Proceedings of the IEEE Conference on Computer Vision and Pattern Recognition, pp. 2906–2915 (2018)

12. Kingma, D.P., Welling, M.: Auto-encoding variational bayes. arXiv preprint arXiv:1312.6114 (2013)

13. Larsen, A.B.L., Sønderby, S.K., Larochelle, H., Winther, O.: Autoencoding beyond pixels using a learned similarity metric. arXiv preprint arXiv:1512.09300 (2015)

14. Matsui, T., Eguchi, H.: Computer control of plant growth by image processing. Environ. Control Biol. **14**(1), 1–7 (1976)

15. Mutka, A.M., Bart, R.S.: Image-based phenotyping of plant disease symptoms. Front. Plant Sci. **5**, 734 (2015)

16. O'Neal, M.E., Landis, D.A., Isaacs, R.: An inexpensive, accurate method for measuring leaf area and defoliation through digital image analysis. J. Econ. Entomol. **95**(6), 1190–1194 (2002)

17. Prasad, A.K., Chai, L., Singh, R.P., Kafatos, M.: Crop yield estimation model for Iowa using remote sensing and surface parameters. Int. J. Appl. Earth Obs. Geoinf. **8**(1), 26–33 (2006)

18. Reuter, D., Robinson, J.B.: Plant Analysis: An Interpretation Manual. CSIRO Publishing (1997)

19. Ronneberger, O., Fischer, P., Brox, T.: U-net: convolutional networks for biomedical image segmentation. In: Navab, N., Hornegger, J., Wells, W.M., Frangi, A.F. (eds.) MICCAI 2015. LNCS, vol. 9351, pp. 234–241. Springer, Cham (2015). https://doi.org/10.1007/978-3-319-24574-4_28

20. Sakurai, S., Uchiyama, H., Shimada, A., Taniguchi, R.I.: Plant growth prediction using convolutional LSTM. In: 14th International Conference on Computer Vision Theory and Applications, VISAPP 2019-Part of the 14th International Joint Conference on Computer Vision, Imaging and Computer Graphics Theory and Applications, VISIGRAPP 2019, pp. 105–113. SciTePress (2019)

21. Srivastava, N., Mansimov, E., Salakhudinov, R.: Unsupervised learning of video representations using LSTMs. In: International Conference on Machine Learning, pp. 843–852 (2015)

22. Uchiyama, H., et al.: An easy-to-setup 3D phenotyping platform for Komatsuna dataset. In: Proceedings of the IEEE International Conference on Computer Vision, pp. 2038–2045 (2017)

23. Xingjian, S., Chen, Z., Wang, H., Yeung, D.Y., Wong, W.K., Woo, W.C.: Convolutional LSTM network: a machine learning approach for precipitation nowcasting. In: Advances in Neural Information Processing Systems, pp. 802–810 (2015)

24. Zhu, Y., Aoun, M., Krijn, M., Vanschoren, J., Campus, H.T.: Data augmentation using conditional generative adversarial networks for leaf counting in Arabidopsis plants. In: BMVC, p. 324 (2018)

ConvPoseCNN2: Prediction and Refinement of Dense 6D Object Pose

Arul Selvam Periyasamy[✉], Catherine Capellen, Max Schwarz, and Sven Behnke

Autonomous Intelligent Systems, University of Bonn, Bonn, Germany
periyasamy@ais.uni-bonn.de

Abstract. Object pose estimation is a key perceptual capability in robotics. We propose a fully-convolutional extension of the PoseCNN method, which densely predicts object translations and orientations. This has several advantages such as improving the spatial resolution of the orientation predictions—useful in highly-cluttered arrangements, significant reduction in parameters by avoiding full connectivity, and fast inference. We propose and discuss several aggregation methods for dense orientation predictions that can be applied as a post-processing step, such as averaging and clustering techniques. We demonstrate that our method achieves the same accuracy as PoseCNN on the challenging YCB-Video dataset and provide a detailed ablation study of several variants of our method. Finally, we demonstrate that the model can be further improved by inserting an iterative refinement module into the middle of the network, which enforces consistency of the prediction.

Keywords: Monocular pose estimation · Fully-convolutional architectures · Robotics

1 Introduction

6D object pose estimation is an important building block for many applications, such as robotic manipulation. While many objects can be grasped without precise pose information, there are many tasks which require 6D pose estimates, for example functional grasping of tools and assembly. Such tasks routinely come up in industrial applications, as evidenced by the Amazon Picking & Robotics Challenges 2015–2017, where pose estimation played a key role for difficult objects, but can also appear in semi-unstructured environments, as in home and assistance robotics.

State-of-the-art pose estimation methods predominantly use CNNs for 6D object pose estimation from RGB(-D) images. One of the notable features of these methods is the joint learning of multiple simultaneous tasks such as object detection, semantic segmentation, and object pose estimation. Although 6D object pose estimation from RGB-D images is an active area of research, for the sake of brevity, we focus on monocular, i.e. RGB only methods. These methods can be broadly classified into two categories: direct regression methods, and 2D-3D correspondence methods. The direct regression methods estimate 6D pose directly from input images, for example in the form of a 3D vector (translation) and a quaternion (orientation). Examples of these methods include Do et al. [4] and Xiang et al. [22]. In contrast, the

© Springer Nature Switzerland AG 2022
K. Bouatouch et al. (Eds.): VISIGRAPP 2020, CCIS 1474, pp. 353–371, 2022.
https://doi.org/10.1007/978-3-030-94893-1_16

correspondence-based methods predict the projection of 3D points in the 2D image and recover the pose of the object by solving the Perspective-n-Point problem. These methods can be further classified into dense correspondence methods and keypoint-based methods. The dense correspondence methods [2,8] predict the projected 3D coordinates of the objects per pixel while the keypoint-based methods [13,16,17,21] predict projection of 3D keypoints in the 2D image.

Since the CNN architecture we propose is closely related to PoseCNN [22], a direct regression method, we review PoseCNN architecture in detail. PoseCNN learns to predict 6D pose objects jointly with semantic segmentation. The CNN uses a pretrained VGG [20] backbone followed by three branches to predict segmentation class probabilities, direction and distance to center, and orientation (represented as quaternions). The orientation prediction branch uses fully connected layers while the other two branches use fully convolutional layers. The orientation prediction branch takes a fixed size image crop as input. From the segmentation class probabilities, a crop containing a single object is extracted and resized to the fixed orientation prediction branch input size using a RoI pooling layer.

Introduced by Girshick [5], RoI pooling is a powerful mechanism for scale normalization and attention and resulted in significant advancements in object detection and related tasks. However, RoI pooling has drawbacks: Especially in cluttered scenes, its cutting-out operation may disrupt flow of contextual information. Furthermore, RoI pooling requires random access to memory for the cutting-out operation and subsequent interpolation, which may be expensive to implement in hardware circuits and has no equivalent in the visual cortex [7].

Redmon et al. [18] demonstrated that simpler, fully-convolutional architectures can attain the same accuracy, while being tremendously faster and having fewer parameters. In essence, fully-convolutional architectures can be thought of as sliding-window classifiers, which are equivalent to RoI pooling with a fixed window size. While the scale-invariance is lost, fully-convolutional architectures typically outperform RoI-based ones in terms of model size and training/inference speed. When addressing the inherent example imbalances during training with a customized loss function [11], fully-convolutional architectures reach state-of-the-art performance in object detection.

Following this idea, we propose a fully convolutional architecture for pose estimation, which can *densely* predict all required information such as object class and transformation. If required, the dense prediction can be post-processed and aggregated per object to obtain a final prediction.

Given the complex nature of the task, instead of directly predicting pose from the given RGB image of a scene, many approaches formulate pose estimation as an iterative refinement process: Given an initial pose estimate and high quality 3D model of the objects, the objects are rendered as per current pose estimate, a refined pose that minimizes difference between the rendered and the observed image is predicted at each step and this step is repeated multiple times. Li et al. [10] trained a CNN that takes RGB image and rendered image of a object as per the current pose estimate as input and predicts the a pose update that refines the current pose update in each step. This step is repeated until the pose update is negligible. Periyasamy, Schwarz, and Behnke [15] used a differentiable renderer to compute pose updates to minimize difference between the

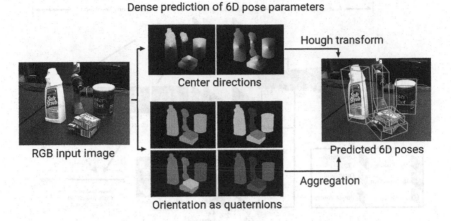

Fig. 1. Dense Prediction of 6D pose parameters inside ConvPoseCNN. The dense predictions are aggregated on the object level to form 6D pose outputs. Source: Capellen., Schwarz., and Behnke [3].

rendered and the observed image. Unlike [10] that refines pose of single object at a time, [15] refined poses for all objects in the scene at each iteration. Krull et al. [8] trained a CNN to predict a matching score—how similar are two images—between the rendered and the observed image. The matching score was used to pick one best pose hypothesis among many available pose hypotheses. One prevalent characteristic among the pose refinement approaches is that refinement is done post prediction–refinement model and pose prediction model are decoupled. In contrast, our proposed iterative refinement module is built into the pose estimator. We enhance the ConvPoseCNN architecture from our previous work [3] with an iterative refinement module to learn representations suitable for both translation and orientation predictions instead of refining the predictions from the estimator (Fig. 1).

In summary, our contributions include:

- A network architecture and training regime for dense orientation prediction,
- aggregation & clustering techniques for dense orientation predictions, and
- an iterative refinement module which increases prediction accuracy.

2 ConvPoseCNN

We propose an extension of the PoseCNN [22] architecture. The PoseCNN network is based on a VGG backbone with three heads: One performing semantic segmentation, one densely predicting object center directions in 2D and object depth, and finally a RoI-Pooling branch with a fully connected head predicting one orientation quaternion for each object. Our proposed network keeps most of this structure, but replaces the orientation prediction branch with a fully convolutional one, which estimates orientation *densely* (see Fig. 2). The architecture of the new branch is modeled after the translation estimation branch.

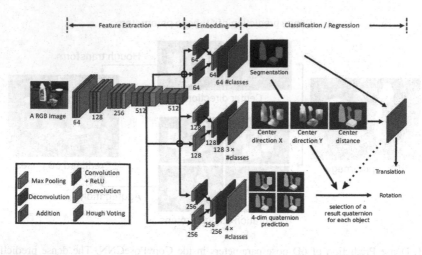

Fig. 2. Our ConvPoseCNN architecture for convolutional pose estimation. During aggregation, candidate quaternions are selected according to the semantic segmentation results or according to Hough inlier information. Source: Capellen., Schwarz., and Behnke [3].

The dense translation prediction is post-processed during inference as by Xiang et al. [22]: The 2D center predictions are fed into a Hough voting layer, which aggregates them into center hypotheses. The predicted object depth is averaged over all inliers. Finally, the 3D position can be computed through ray projection using the camera intrinsics.

2.1 Aggregation of Dense Orientation Predictions

Estimating the final orientation prediction from pixel-wise quaternion predictions is not as straight-forward, however. We investigate two different approaches for this purpose: averaging and clustering.

Quaternions corresponding to a rotation, by definition, have unit norm. But we do not enforce the quaternion predictions to be of unit norm explicitly during the ConvPoseCNN training. Thus, before aggregating the dense predictions, we need to scale them to unit norm. Interestingly, we observe that the norm of the quaternion at a pixel prior to scaling corresponds to quality of the prediction. i.e. pixels in the feature-rich regions of the image have higher quaternion norm. Exploiting this observation, we use the norm of the quaternion prediction $w = ||q||$ as an optional weighting factor in our aggregation step. We extract the quaternions $q_1, ..., q_n$ corresponding to an object using the segmentation predictions and average them following the optimization scheme proposed by [12] using the norm $w_1, ..., w_n$. The average quaternion $\bar{q}$ is given by

$$\bar{q} = \arg \min_{q \in \mathbb{S}^3} \sum_{i=1}^{n} w_i ||R(q) - R(q_i)||_F^2, \qquad (1)$$

where $R(q) - R(q_i)$ are the rotation matrices corresponding to the quaternions, $\mathbb{S}^3$ is the unit 3-sphere, and $|| \cdot ||_F$ is the Frobenius norm. Note that quaternion to rotation matrix conversion eliminates any problems arising from the antipodal symmetry of the quaternion representation. The exact solution to the optimization problem can be found by solving an eigenvalue problem [12]. In case of multiple, overlapping instances of the same object class—here, the predicted segmentation would not be enough to differentiate the instances—we can additionally make use of the Hough voting procedure required for translation estimation to separate the predictions into inlier sets for each object hypothesis.

Averaging based aggregation schemes inherently may from suffer skewed results due to bad outlier predictions. Clustering based aggregation schemes should be less susceptible to outlier predictions.

We follow a weighted RANSAC clustering scheme as an alternative to averaging: For quaternions $Q = \{q_1, ..., q_n\}$ and their weights $w_1, ..., w_n$ associated with one object we repeatedly choose a random quaternion $\bar{q} \in Q$ with a probability proportional to its weight and then determines the inlier set $\bar{Q} = \{q \in Q | d(q, \bar{q}) < t\}$, where $d(\cdot, \cdot)$ is the angular distance. Finally, the $\bar{q}$ with largest $\sum_{q_i \in \bar{Q}} w_i$ is selected as the result quaternion.

2.2 Iterative Refinement

During the prediction of 6D object poses, translation estimates and orientation estimates influence each other. Predicting translation and orientation components using separate branches as in ConvPoseCNN and PoseCNN does not allow the model to exploit the interdependence between translation and orientation estimates. This motivates in designing network architectures that can refine translation and orientation prediction iteratively to enable the network to model the interdependencies between the predictions. One naive way of doing pose refinement would be to perform refinement after prediction. To this end, we experimented with a simple three layered—three blocks of convolutional layer followed by ReLU activation—fully convolutional model to refine the predictions from ConvPoseCNN model iteratively. At each step, segmentation, translation, and orientation predictions along with the features from the VGG backbone model are provided as input and a refined estimate is computed as depicted in Fig. 3. The final predictions are obtained after a small fixed number of iterations. We call this approach post-prediction iterative refinement.

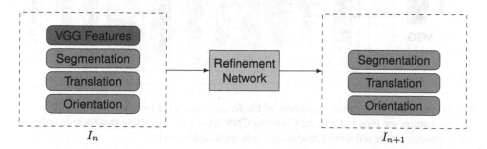

Fig. 3. Naive post-prediction iterative refinement of segmentation probabilities, translation predictions, and rotation predictions. The dense predictions (green) are refined using a small network, which can be applied repeatedly for further refinement. High-level features (blue) can be fed into the network to provide additional context information. (Color figure online)

However, naive post-prediction refinement might be a challenging task because the predictions might be in a suitable form for a simple three layer model. To address this concern, we experimented with a pre-prediction iterative refinement of intermediate representation shown in Fig. 4. The features from the pretrained VGG backbone model as refined before providing them as input to ConvPoseCNN network enabling ConvPoseCNN model to learn joint intermediate representations suitable for both translation and orientation predictions. The refinement module is akin to residual blocks in ResNet architecture (Ren et al. [19]). Each iteration refinement module computes $\Delta(x)$ that is added to the input with the use of skip connections.

$$f^{i+1}(x) = f^i(x) + \Delta(x)$$

In detail, refinement blocks takes two set of features maps F_A, and F_B each of dimension $512 \times 60 \times 80$, and $512 \times 30 \times 40$ respectively as input. F_B is upsampled with transposed convolution and concatenated with F_A. The resulting $1024 \times 60 \times 80$ is passed through a sequence of convolutional, ReLU, and convolutional layers. All the convolutions have a window size of 3 and stride of 1. Zero padding of one pixels is applied to maintain the spatial resolution of the features.

Then the features are split to two equal parts. One of them is downsampled. Thus we arrive at ΔF_A and ΔF_B having same spatial dimensions as of F_A, and F_B respectively. Using skip connections ΔF_A and ΔF_B and added to F_A, and F_B respectively.

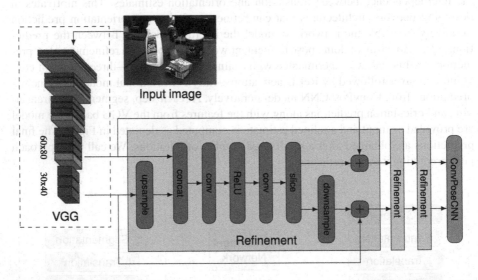

Fig. 4. Pre-prediction iterative refinement of the features extracted from the VGG network. The refined features are then fed into the ConvPoseCNN head networks. Note that there is only one set of weights for the refinement module, i.e. it is applied iteratively.

3 Evaluation

3.1 Dataset

We evaluate our method on the YCB-Video dataset [22]. The dataset contains 133,936 images of VGA resolution (640 × 480) extracted from 92 video sequences. Each image contains a varying number of objects selected from a larger set of 21 objects, some of which exhibit symmetry or are texture-poor. The first frame of each of the 92 video sequences was manually annotated with ground truth pose information, while the rest of the frames were automatically annotated by tracking the camera pose via SLAM. In each sequence, the objects are arranged in various spatial configurations resulting in varying degrees of occlusions making it a challenging dataset. High quality 3D models and downsampled point models containing 2620 points each are made available. The real images are supplemented with simple synthetic renderings of the object models.

3.2 Training Procedure

We implemented ConvPoseCNN using PyTorch [14] framework. Except for the novel dense orientation estimation branch, we based our implementation on the openly available PoseCNN implementation[1]. The openly available official implementation has minor changes compared to the model described by [22]. We noted that these minor design choices were helpful and incorporated them in our implementation as well. Additionally, we implemented Hough voting layer—non differentiable layer that computes inlier pixels—using Numba [9]. Although Numba is CPU only, the Hough Voting layer implementation with Numba is faster than other GPU implementations.

The segmentation and translation branches of ConvPoseCNN are trained with the standard pixelwise negative log-likelihood (NLL) and L2 loss respectively. The depth component of the translation branch is of a smaller scale compared to the other two components. To balance this discrepancy we scale the depth component loss by 100.

We use the ShapeMatch loss (SMLoss) proposed by [22] to train the orientation branch of ConvPoseCNN. SMLoss handles objects with and without symmetry using two different loss definitions as follows.

$$\text{SMLoss}(\tilde{q}, q) = \begin{cases} \text{SLoss}(\tilde{q}, q), & \text{if object is symmetric,} \\ \text{PLoss}(\tilde{q}, q), & \text{otherwise.} \end{cases} \tag{2}$$

Given a set of 3D points $\mathbb{M}$, where $m = |\mathbb{M}|$ and $R(q)$ and $R(\tilde{q})$ are the rotation matrices corresponding to ground truth and estimated quaternion, respectively, and PLoss and SLoss are defined as follows:

$$\text{PLoss}(\tilde{q}, q) = \frac{1}{2m} \sum_{x \in \mathbb{M}} \|R(\tilde{q})x - R(q)x\|^2, \tag{3}$$

$$\text{SLoss}(\tilde{q}, q) = \frac{1}{2m} \sum_{x_1 \in \mathbb{M}} \min_{x_2 \in \mathbb{M}} \|R(\tilde{q})x_1 - R(q)x_2\|^2. \tag{4}$$

---

[1] https://github.com/yuxng/PoseCNN.

Similar to the ICP objective, SLoss does not penalize rotations of symmetric objects that lead to equivalent shapes.

During the training phase, computing SMLoss per pixels is computationally infeasible. Thus, we resort to aggregate dense predictions for each object before computing loss functions. We experimented with the aggregation mechanisms discussed in Sect. 2.1 and observed poor convergence. We hypothesize that this could be because of weighting quaternions with their norm before aggregation results in pixels with smaller quaternion prediction norm receiving smaller gradients. Empirically, we found that using simple numerical averaging to arrive at $\tilde{q}$ alleviates the issue of uneven gradient distribution and contributes to convergence of the training process. Additionally, numerical averaging is computationally less expensive.

Alternatively, we also experimented with training the orientation branch with pixel-wise L2 loss and QLoss [1].

For two quaternions $\bar{q}$ and q it is defined as:

$$QLoss(\bar{q}, q) = \log(\epsilon + 1 - |\bar{q} \cdot q|), \tag{5}$$

where ϵ is introduced for stability. QLoss is designed to handle the quaternion symmetry.

The final loss function used during training is, similarly to PoseCNN, a linear combination of segmentation, translation, and orientation loss:

$$L = \alpha_{seg}L_{seg} + \alpha_{trans}L_{trans} + \alpha_{rot}L_{rot}. \tag{6}$$

where α_{seg}, α_{trans}, are set to 1. α_{rot} is set to 1 and 100 in the case of L2 loss and QLoss, and SMLoss respectively. We train ConvPoseCNN model using SGD with learning rate 0.001 and momentum 0.9.

3.3 Evaluation Metrics

We report area under the accuracy curve (AUC) metrics AUC-P and AUC-S for varying area threshold between 0 and 0.1 m on ADD and ADD-S metrics as introduced along with YCB-Video Dataset [22]. ADD is average distance between corresponding points of the 3D object model in predicted and ground truth pose. ADD-S is the average of distance between each 3D point in predicted pose to the closest point in ground truth pose. ADD-S penalizes objects with symmetry less than ADD metric.

3.4 Results

Prediction Averaging. To aggregate the dense pixel-wise predictions into a single orientation estimate, we use weighted quaternion averaging [12]. In the case of ConvPoseCNN, there are two possible sources of the pixel-wise weighting: segmentation score, and predicted quaternion norm. In Table 1, we show the comparison between the two weighting schemes. The norm weighting showed better results than both no averaging and using segmentation score as weighting. This suggests the predictions with smaller norms are less precise. Encouraged by this observation, we experimented further with pruning the predictions before aggregation We sorted the predictions based on the norm and pruned varying percentile number (λ) of them.

Table 2 shows results of pruning with percentile ranging from 0 (no pruning) to 1 (extreme case of discarding all but one prediction). Pruning improves the results by a small factor overall but considerably for the objects with symmetry. This can be explained by the fact that averaging shape-equivalent orientations might result in an non-equivalent orientation and thus averaging schemes are not suitable for handling objects with symmetry.

Table 1. Weighting strategies for ConvPoseCNN L2.

Method	6D pose[a]		Rotation only	
	AUC P	AUC S	AUC P	AUC S
PoseCNN[b]	53.71	76.12	**78.87**	**93.16**
Unit weights	56.59	78.86	72.87	90.68
Norm weights	**57.13**	**79.01**	73.84	91.02
Segm. weights	56.63	78.87	72.93	90.71

[a]Following Xiang et al. [22].
[b]Calculated from the published PoseCNN model.
Source: Capellen., Schwarz., and Behnke [3].

Table 2. Quaternion pruning for ConvPoseCNN L2.

Method	6D pose[a]		Rotation only	
	AUC P	AUC S	AUC P	AUC S
PoseCNN	53.71	76.12	**78.87**	**93.16**
pruned(0)	57.13	79.01	73.84	91.02
pruned(0.5)	**57.43**	79.14	74.43	91.33
pruned(0.75)	**57.43**	79.19	74.48	91.45
pruned(0.9)	57.37	**79.23**	74.41	91.50
pruned(0.95)	57.39	79.21	74.45	91.50
Single	57.11	79.22	74.00	91.46

[a] Following Xiang et al. [22].
Source: Capellen., Schwarz., and Behnke [3].

Prediction Clustering. As an alternative to averaging schemes we experimented with RANSAC-based clustering schemes where we chose a quaternion at random and cluster the other quaternions into inliers and outliers based on the angular distance between corresponding rotations as the threshold. We repeat the process 50 times and select the quaternion prediction with the maximum inlier count. As opposed to the L2 distance in quaternion space, angular distance function invariant to the antipodal symmetry of the quaternion orientation representation. The results are shown in Table 3. Similar to averaging schemes, weighted variant of RANSAC performs better than non-weighted variants. Overall, clustering schemes outperform averaging schemes slightly on AUC S metric but perform slightly worse on AUC P. This is expected as the clustering schemes can handle object symmetries well.

Table 3. Clustering strategies for ConvPoseCNN L2.

Method	6D pose		Rotation only	
	AUC P	AUC S	AUC P	AUC S
PoseCNN	53.71	76.12	**78.87**	**93.16**
RANSAC(0.1)	57.18	79.16	74.12	91.37
RANSAC(0.2)	57.36	79.20	74.40	91.45
RANSAC(0.3)	57.27	79.20	74.13	91.35
RANSAC(0.4)	57.00	79.13	73.55	91.14
W-RANSAC(0.1)	57.27	79.20	74.29	91.45
W-RANSAC(0.2)	57.42	**79.26**	74.53	91.56
W-RANSAC(0.3)	57.38	79.24	74.36	91.46
Pruned(0.75)	**57.43**	79.19	74.48	91.45
Most confident	57.11	79.22	74.00	91.46

RANSAC uses unit weights, while W-RANSAC is weighted by quaternion norm. PoseCNN and the best performing averaging methods are shown for comparison. Numbers in parentheses describe the clustering threshold in radians. Source: Capellen., Schwarz., and Behnke [3].

Table 4. Results for ConvPoseCNN shape.

	6D pose		Rotation only	
	AUC P	AUC S	AUC P	AUC S
PoseCNN	53.71	76.12	**78.87**	**93.16**
Average	54.27	78.94	70.02	90.91
Norm weighted	**55.54**	79.27	72.15	91.55
Pruned(0.5)	55.33	**79.29**	71.82	91.45
Pruned(0.75)	54.62	79.09	70.56	91.00
Pruned(0.85)	53.86	78.85	69.34	90.57
Pruned(0.9)	53.23	78.66	68.37	90.25
RANSAC(0.2)	49.44	77.65	63.09	88.73
RANSAC(0.3)	50.47	77.92	64.53	89.18
RANSAC(0.4)	51.19	78.09	65.61	89.50
W-RANSAC(0.2)	49.56	77.73	63.33	88.85
W-RANSAC(0.3)	50.54	77.91	64.78	89.21
W-RANSAC(0.4)	51.33	78.13	65.94	89.56

Table from Capellen., Schwarz., and Behnke [3].

Loss Variants. The choice of aggregation method did not have a big impact on the models trained with QLoss and thus we show only the results for Shape variant in Table 4. Among the averaging methods, norm weight improves the result, whereas pruning does not. This suggests that there are less-confident but important predictions with higher distance from the mean and removing them significantly affects the average. This could be an effect of training with the average quaternion, where such behavior is not discouraged. Both RANSAC variants—with and without weighting—resulted in comparatively worse results. We conclude that the pixel-wise losses obtain superior performance, and average-before-loss scheme is not advantageous. Also, a fast dense version of SMLoss would need to be found in order to apply it in our architecture.

ConvPoseCNN Final Results. We start the discussion about ConvPoseCNN with the qualitative result shown in Fig. 5. We visualize the 3D ground truth and predictions for all the objects in the input scene as well as orientation error and predicted orientation norm per pixel. Dense pixel-wise orientation prediction makes it easier to visualize error at each pixel and to analyze them closely. A major observation from the visualizations is that the pixels in the feature-rich regions—close to object boundaries or distinctive textures—have lower orientation error while the pixels in the feature-poor regions exhibit higher angular error. A similar phenomenon is also observed in the prediction norm visualization. The pixels in feature-rich regions have higher norm orientation predictions while the pixels in feature-poor regions have lower norm orientation predictions. We hypothesize that in feature-rich regions, the network is confident of the predictions and thus the predictions are encouraged on one specific direction, whereas in the feature-poor regions, the predictions are pulled towards various possible directions resulting in predictions with a smaller norm.

Table 5. 6D pose, translation, rotation, and segmentation results.

		6D pose		Rotation only		NonSymC	SymC	Transl.	Segm.
		AUC P	AUC S	AUC P	AUC S	AUC P	AUC S	Error [m]	IoU
Full network	PoseCNN	53.71	76.12	78.87	93.16	60.49	63.28	0.0520	0.8369
	PoseCNN[a]	53.29	78.31	69.00	90.49	60.91	57.91	0.0465	0.8071
	Ours, QLoss	57.16	77.08	80.51	93.35	64.75	53.95	0.0565	0.7725
	Ours, Shape	55.54	79.27	72.15	91.55	62.77	56.42	0.0455	0.8038
	Ours, L2	57.42	79.26	74.53	91.56	63.48	58.85	0.0411	0.8044
GT segm.	PoseCNN[a]	52.90	80.11	69.60	91.63	76.63	84.15	0.0345	1
	Ours, QLoss	57.73	79.04	81.20	94.52	88.27	90.14	0.0386	1
	Ours, Shape	56.27	81.27	72.53	92.27	77.32	89.06	0.0316	1
	Ours, L2	59.50	81.54	76.37	92.32	80.67	85.52	0.0314	1

The average translation error, the segmentation IoU and the AUC metrics for different models. The AUC results were achieved using weighted RANSAC(0.1) for ConvPoseCNN QLoss, Markley's norm weighted average for ConvPoseCNN Shape and weighted RANSAC(0.2) for ConvPoseCNN L2. *GT segm.* refers to ground truth segmentation (i.e. only pose estimation). Source: Capellen., Schwarz., and Behnke [3].

[a]Our own reimplementation.

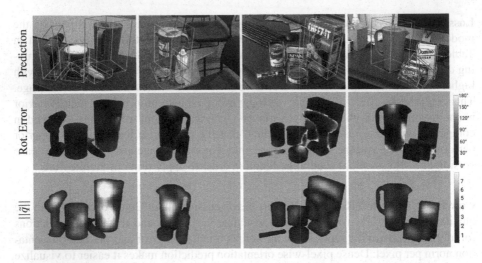

Fig. 5. Qualitative results from ConvPoseCNN L2 on the YCB-Video test set. Top: The orange boxes show the ground truth bounding boxes, the green boxes the 6D pose prediction. Middle: Angular error of the dense quaternion prediction $\tilde{q}$ w.r.t. ground truth, masked by ground truth segmentation. Bottom: Quaternion prediction norm $||\tilde{q}||$ before normalization. This measure is used for weighted aggregation. Note that the prediction norm is low in high-error regions and high in regions that are far from occlusions and feature-rich. Source: Capellen., Schwarz., and Behnke [3]. (Color figure online)

In Table 5, we report the quantitative results of ConvPoseCNN models trained with three different loss functions—L2 and QLoss, and Shape—and compare it with the PoseCNN baseline model provided in the YCB-Video Toolbox[2].

We provide AUC P and AUC S metric for all models including results from our own implementation of PoseCNN model in Table 5. All the three variants of ConvPoseCNN perform slightly better than PoseCNN on both AUC P and AUC S metrics. Moreover, the ConvPoseCNN variant trained with L2 yields the best results among the ConvPoseCNN variants. QLoss variant performed comparative to L2 variant on AUC P metric, whereas Shape variant performed comparative to L2 variant on AUC S loss.

Moreover, to understand the influence of translation and orientation components on the overall AUC P and AUC S metric we report AUC P and AUC S metric computed for rotation only and translation error (computed in Meters) separately. Although all the ConvPoseCNN variants perform slightly better than PoseCNN on the AUC metrics, only QLoss variant performs better than PoseCNN on the rotation only AUC metrics. Analyzing the translation error suggests that the translation estimate influences the AUC losses more than the orientation estimate. However, the models that achieve better translation estimation, performs worse with the orientation estimate.

Furthermore, to analyze the performance of the models on objects with and without symmetry we report the average per-class AUC P metric for objects without symmetry and average per-class AUC S for objects with symmetry. ConvPoseCNN performed a

---

[2] https://github.com/yuxng/YCB_Video_toolbox.

bit better than PoseCNN for the objects without symmetry but worse for the ones with symmetry. This can be explained by the use loss functions—QLoss and L2 loss—that are not designed to handle symmetry. But, surprisingly, the model trained with SMLoss also performs worse for the symmetric objects compared to PoseCNN.

This might be due to different reasons: First, we utilize an average before calculating the loss; therefore during training the average might penalize predicting different shape-equivalent quaternions, in case their average is not shape-equivalent. Secondly, there are only five symmetric objects in the dataset and we noticed that two of those, the two clamp objects, are very similar and thus challenging, not only for the orientation but as well for the segmentation and vertex prediction. This is further complicated by a difference in object coordinate systems for these two objects.

While aggregating the dense pixel-wise orientation predictions to a single orientation prediction per-class, we use segmentation results. Thus, the segmentation results also influence the final metrics. To quantify the influence of segmentation results we report metrics for the all the five models—three ConvPoseCNN, and two PoseCNN variants—using the ground truth segmentation as well. Using ground truth segmentation improves translation and orientation for all the models. Hu et al. [6] also report a similar observation

Table 6. Comparison to related work.

	Total		Average
	AUC P	AUC S	AUC[a]
PoseCNN	53.7	75.9	61.30
ConvPoseCNN L2	57.4	79.2	62.40
HeatMaps without FM			61.41
ConvPoseCNN+FM	58.22	79.55	61.59
HeatMaps with FM			72.79

Comparison between PoseCNN (as reported by Xiang et al. [22]), ConvPoseCNN L2 with pruned(0.75), and HeatMaps [13] without and with Feature Mapping (FM). Source: Capellen., Schwarz., and Behnke. [3].
[a]As defined by Oberweger, Rad, and Lepetit [13].

Comparison to Related Work. In Table 6, we show the comparisons between ConvPoseCNN, PoseCNN, and HeatMaps [13] approaches. Oberweger, Rad, and Lepetit [13] report class-wise area under the accuracy curve metric (AUC) instead of AUC P and AUC S metrics. To make the methods comparable, we provide AUC for both ConvPoseCNN and PoseCNN. [13] proposed Feature Mapping (FM) technique that significantly improves their results. Without feature mapping, we perform slightly better than both PoseCNN and HeatMaps. However, the difference is negligible considering the variations due to the choice of hyperparameters and minor implementations details. Detailed class-wise AUC metrics for both the best performing ConvPoseCNN and PoseCNN models are shown in Table 7.

Table 7. Detailed class-wise results.

Class	Ours		PoseCNN	
	AUC P	AUC S	AUC P	AUC S
master_chef_can	62.32	89.55	50.08	83.72
cracker_box	66.69	83.78	52.94	76.56
sugar_box	67.19	82.51	68.33	83.95
tomato_soup_can	75.52	88.05	66.11	80.90
mustard_bottle	83.79	92.59	80.84	90.64
tuna_fish_can	60.98	83.67	70.56	88.05
pudding_box	62.17	76.31	62.22	78.72
gelatin_box	83.84	92.92	74.86	85.73
potted_meat_can	65.86	85.92	59.40	79.51
banana	37.74	76.30	72.16	86.24
pitcher_base	62.19	84.63	53.11	78.08
bleach_cleanser	55.14	76.92	50.22	72.81
bowl	3.55	66.41	3.09	70.31
mug	45.83	72.05	58.39	78.22
power_drill	76.47	88.26	55.21	72.91
wood_block	0.12	25.90	26.19	62.43
scissors	56.42	79.01	35.27	57.48
large_marker	55.26	70.19	58.11	70.98
large_clamp	29.73	58.21	24.47	51.05
extra_large_clamp	21.99	54.43	15.97	46.15
foam_brick	51.80	88.02	39.90	86.46

Source: Capellen., Schwarz., and Behnke. [3].

We also investigated applying the Feature Mapping technique [13] to our model. Following the process, we render synthetic images with poses corresponding to the real training data. We selected the features from backbone VGG-16 for the mapping process and thus have to transfer two feature maps with 512 features each. We replaced the fullyconnected network architecture for feature mapping as done by [13], with a convolutional set-up and mapped the feature from the different stages to each other with residual blocks based on (1×1) convolutions. The results are presented in Table 6. However, we did not observe the large gains reported by [13] for our architecture. We hypothesize that the feature mapping technique is highly dependent on the quality and distribution of the rendered synthetic images, which are maybe not of sufficient quality in our case.

Table 8. Training performance & model sizes.

	Iterations/s[a]	Model size
PoseCNN	1.18	1.1 GiB
ConvPoseCNN L2	2.09	308.9 MiB
ConvPoseCNN QLoss	2.09	308.9 MiB
ConvPoseCNN SMLoss	1.99	308.9 MiB

[a]Using a batch size of 2. Averaged over 400 iterations.

Source: Capellen., Schwarz., and Behnke [3].

Time Comparisons. We used NVIDIA GTX 1080 Ti GPU with 11 GB of memory to benchmark the training and inference time for ConvPoseCNN and PoseCNN models. In Table 8 we report number of iterations per second. All the variants of ConvPoseCNN are significantly faster. Additionally, size of the saved ConvPoseCNN models are significantly smaller compared to the PoseCNN models.

Unfortunately, this advantage in speed during the training process is not observed during the inference as shown in Table 9. Averaging methods, on average, consume time comparable to the PoseCNN. But the RANSAC based clustering methods more time consuming; the forward pass of ConvPoseCNN takes about 65.5 ms, the Hough transform around 68.6 ms. We attribute the comparable inference time consumption to the highly optimized ROI pooling layers in the modern deep learning frameworks.

Table 9. Inference timings.

Method	Time [ms][a]	Aggregation [ms]
PoseCNN[b]	141.71	
ConvPoseCNN		
- naive average	136.96	2.34
- average	146.70	12.61
- weighted average	146.92	13.00
- pruned w. average	148.61	14.64
- RANSAC	158.66	24.97
- w. RANSAC	563.16	65.82

[a] Single frame, includes aggregation.
[b] Xiang et al. [22].

Source: Capellen., Schwarz., and Behnke [3].

Iterative Refinement. Post-prediction iterative refinement module is trained with segmentation, translation, and orientation estimates from ConvPoseCNN as well as VGG16 features as input. At each iteration, the model refines segmentation, translation, and orientation estimates. VGG16 features provide contextual information about the input scene. We experimented with varying number of refinement steps. Similar

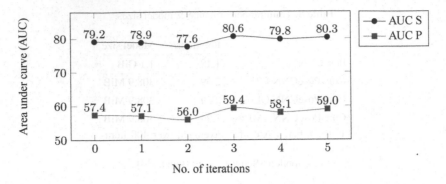

Fig. 6. Results of pre-prediction feature refinement process for various number of iterations. The variant with zero iterations corresponds to ConvPoseCNN without any refinement (Table 6).

to ConvPoseCNN, we used same combined loss function as discussed in Sect. 3.2. But, we observed both training and validation loss plateauing very early on the training process and the resulting model also performed worse quantitatively compared to ConvPoseCNN on the test set.

This could be because the estimates are in a form that is not a suitable for a simple three layer network. Exploring complex architectures is not an option for us since we focus on keeping the overhead of iterative refinement minimal.

In contrast to the post-prediction refinement, pre-prediction refinement not only performed well during but also improved the AUC metrics on the test set. This suggests that in the case of ConvPoseCNN, refining the features at an early stage helps the network in learning representations better suitable for pose estimation. We trained the refinement module with a various number of iterations and in Fig. 6, we present the AUC metrics achieved by various number of refinement iterations. Overall, the iterative refinement improves the prediction and different number of iterations results in slightly different AUC metrics. Interestingly, the performance peaks at three iterations. If there are any gains with more iterations, they are not significant. We attribute this fact to the small depth of our refinement network which limits the operations it can perform. In Table 10 we compare the class-wise AUC metrics for ConvPoseCNN (without refinement), three and five iterations of refinement. For most objects, the AUC metrices are improved but for some objects, there is a drop in accuracy. The maximum gain of 12.48 AUC-P and 9.63 is observed for the *mug* object while a severe drop of 15.05 AUC-P and 5.54 is observed for *cracker_box* and *bleach_cleanser* respectively—both relatively big objects, where information needs to be communicated and fused over larger regions.

Table 10. Class-wise results ConvPoseCNN without refinement, with three iterations of refinement and with five iterations of refinement.

Class	PoseCNN		IR 3		IR 5	
	AUC P	AUC S	AUC P	AUC S	AUC P	AUC S
master_chef_can	62.32	89.55	62.69	90.93	61.58	91.09
cracker_box	66.69	83.78	51.64	79.02	62.48	82.53
sugar_box	67.19	82.51	63.16	80.81	68.95	84.16
tomato_soup_can	75.52	88.05	78.70	90.70	75.12	88.65
mustard_bottle	83.79	92.59	83.66	92.09	83.99	91.65
tuna_fish_can	60.98	83.67	71.10	88.15	72.68	90.37
pudding_box	62.17	76.31	67.72	84.73	66.11	83.25
gelatin_box	83.84	92.92	83.38	91.45	86.98	93.18
potted_meat_can	65.86	85.92	69.52	87.56	68.21	86.22
banana	37.74	76.30	42.96	70.24	42.75	70.34
pitcher_base	62.19	84.63	68.31	86.79	66.51	86.55
bleach_cleanser	55.14	76.92	50.86	71.48	52.28	75.61
bowl	3.55	66.41	7.21	73.04	8.24	69.29
mug	45.83	72.05	58.31	81.68	62.11	82.64
power_drill	76.47	88.26	73.12	86.57	71.60	85.68
wood_block	0.12	25.90	0.785	27.70	1.07	31.86
scissors	56.42	79.01	62.41	80.96	51.22	75.56
large_marker	55.26	70.19	64.16	76.35	60.15	71.96
large_clamp	29.73	58.21	35.66	62.34	33.14	61.93
extra_large_clamp	21.99	54.43	23.16	55.74	23.91	55.91
foam_brick	51.80	88.02	51.31	88.62	47.69	87.08

4 Conclusion

We presented ConvPoseCNN, a fully convolutional architecture for object pose estimation and demonstrated that, similar to translation estimation, direct regression of the orientation estimation can be done in a dense pixel-wise manner. This helps in not only simplifying neural networks architectures for 6D object pose estimation but also reducing the size of the models and faster training. To further the performance of fully convolutional models for pose estimation, scalable dense pixel-wise loss function needs to be explored. As a next step, we plan to evaluate ConvPoseCNN on highly cluttered scenes where we expect the dense predictions to be especially beneficial, since disambiguation of close objects should be more direct than with RoI-based architectures.

Moreover, we demonstrated that the pose predictions can be refined even with a small network to boost the performance, provided the refinement is done at the right level of abstraction. In case of ConvPoseCNN, refining intermediate representations yielded better performance than post-prediction refinement. Thus, network architecture designs that imbue refinement modules should be favoured for object pose estimation. In the future, we plan to combine iterative refinement with other state-of-the-art architectures and further investigate the design of refinement modules. The key challenge is to balance the need for a larger powerful module capable of iterative refinement with keeping the processing time and memory overhead introduced by the refinement module low.

References

1. Billings, G., Johnson-Roberson, M.: SilhoNet: an RGB method for 3D object pose estimation and grasp planning. arXiv preprint arXiv:1809.06893 (2018)
2. Brachmann, E., Michel, F., Krull, A., Ying Yang, M., Gumhold, S., et al.: Uncertainty-driven 6D pose estimation of objects and scenes from a single RGB image. In: IEEE Conference on Computer Vision and Pattern Recognition (CVPR), pp. 3364–3372 (2016)
3. Capellen., C., Schwarz., M., Behnke., S.: ConvPoseCNN: dense convolutional 6D object pose estimation. In: Proceedings of the 15th International Joint Conference on Computer Vision, Imaging and Computer Graphics Theory and Applications, VISAPP, vol. 5, pp. 162–172. INSTICC, SciTePress (2020). https://doi.org/10.5220/0008990901620172
4. Do, T., Cai, M., Pham, T., Reid, I.D.: Deep-6DPose: recovering 6D object pose from a single RGB image. In: European Conference on Computer Vision (ECCV) (2018)
5. Girshick, R.: Fast R-CNN. In: IEEE International Conference on Computer Vision (ICCV), pp. 1440–1448 (2015)
6. Hu, Y., Hugonot, J., Fua, P., Salzmann, M.: Segmentation-driven 6D object pose estimation. In: Proceedings of the IEEE Conference on Computer Vision and Pattern Recognition, pp. 3385–3394 (2019)
7. Kandel, E.R., et al.: Principles of Neural Science, vol. 4. McGraw-Hill, New York (2000)
8. Krull, A., Brachmann, E., Michel, F., Ying Yang, M., Gumhold, S., Rother, C.: Learning analysis-by-synthesis for 6D pose estimation in RGB-D images. In: International Conference on Computer Vision (ICCV), pp. 954–962 (2015)
9. Lam, S.K., Pitrou, A., Seibert, S.: Numba: a LLVM-based python JIT compiler. In: Second Workshop on the LLVM Compiler Infrastructure in HPC. ACM (2015)
10. Li, Y., Wang, G., Ji, X., Xiang, Yu., Fox, D.: DeepIM: deep iterative matching for 6D pose estimation. In: Ferrari, V., Hebert, M., Sminchisescu, C., Weiss, Y. (eds.) ECCV 2018. LNCS, vol. 11210, pp. 695–711. Springer, Cham (2018). https://doi.org/10.1007/978-3-030-01231-1_42
11. Lin, T.Y., Goyal, P., Girshick, R., He, K., Dollár, P.: Focal loss for dense object detection. In: IEEE International Conference on Computer Vision (ICCV), pp. 2980–2988 (2017)
12. Markley, F.L., Cheng, Y., Crassidis, J.L., Oshman, Y.: Averaging quaternions. J. Guid. Control. Dyn. 30(4), 1193–1197 (2007)
13. Oberweger, M., Rad, M., Lepetit, V.: Making deep heatmaps robust to partial occlusions for 3D object pose estimation. In: Ferrari, V., Hebert, M., Sminchisescu, C., Weiss, Y. (eds.) ECCV 2018. LNCS, vol. 11219, pp. 125–141. Springer, Cham (2018). https://doi.org/10.1007/978-3-030-01267-0_8
14. Paszke, A., et al.: Automatic differentiation in PyTorch. In: NIPS (2017)
15. Periyasamy, A.S., Schwarz, M., Behnke, S.: Refining 6D object pose predictions using abstract render-and-compare. In: 2019 IEEE-RAS 19th International Conference on Humanoid Robots (Humanoids), pp. 739–746. IEEE (2019)
16. Rad, M., Lepetit, V.: BB8: a scalable, accurate, robust to partial occlusion method for predicting the 3D poses of challenging objects without using depth. In: International Conference on Computer Vision (ICCV) (2017)

17. Rad, M., Oberweger, M., Lepetit, V.: Feature mapping for learning fast and accurate 3D pose inference from synthetic images. In: IEEE Conference on Computer Vision and Pattern Recognition (CVPR) (2018)
18. Redmon, J., Divvala, S., Girshick, R., Farhadi, A.: You only look once: unified, real-time object detection. In: Conference on Computer Vision and Pattern Recognition (CVPR), pp. 779–788 (2016)
19. Ren, S., He, K., Girshick, R., Sun, J.: Faster R-CNN: towards real-time object detection with region proposal networks. In: Advances in Neural Information Processing Systems, pp. 91–99 (2015)
20. Simonyan, K., Zisserman, A.: Very deep convolutional networks for large-scale image recognition. arXiv preprint arXiv:1409.1556 (2014)
21. Tekin, B., Sinha, S.N., Fua, P.: Real-time seamless single shot 6D object pose prediction. In: IEEE Conference on Computer Vision and Pattern Recognition (CVPR) (2018)
22. Xiang, Y., Schmidt, T., Narayanan, V., Fox, D.: PoseCNN: a convolutional neural network for 6D object pose estimation in cluttered scenes. In: Robotics: Science and Systems (RSS) (2018)

Expression Modeling Using Dynamic Kernels for Quantitative Assessment of Facial Paralysis

Nazil Perveen[1(✉)] 🆔, Chalavadi Krishna Mohan[1] 🆔, and Yen Wei Chen[2] 🆔

[1] Department of Computer Science and Engineering, IIT Hyderabad, Hyderabad, India
{cs14resch11006,ckm}@iith.ac.in
[2] College of Information Science and Engineering, Ritsumeikan University,
Kusatsu, Shiga, Japan
chen@is.ritsumei.ac.jp

Abstract. Facial paralysis is a syndrome that causes difficulty in the movement of facial muscles on either one or both sides of the face. In this paper, the quantitative assessment for facial paralysis is proposed using dynamic kernels to detect facial paralysis and its various effect level's on a person's face by modeling different facial expressions. Initially, the movements of facial muscles are captured locally by spatio-temporal features for each video. Using the extracted spatio-temporal features from all the videos, a large Gaussian mixture model (GMM) is trained to learn the dynamics of facial muscles globally. In order to handle these local and global features in variable-length patterns like videos, we propose to use a dynamic kernel modeling approach. Dynamic kernels are generally known for handling variable-length data patterns like speech, videos, etc., either by mapping them into fixed-length data patterns or by creating new kernels for example by selecting discriminative sets of representations obtained from GMM statistics. In the proposed work, we explore three different kinds of dynamic kernels, namely, explicit mapping kernels, probability-based kernels, and intermediate matching kernels for the modeling of facial expressions. These kernels are then used as feature vectors for classification using the support vector machine (SVM) to detect severity levels of facial paralysis. The efficacy of the proposed dynamic kernel modeling approach for the quantitative assessment of facial paralysis is demonstrated on a self-collected facial paralysis video dataset of 39 facially paralyzed patients of different severity levels. The dataset collected contains patients from different age groups and gender, further, the videos are recorded from seven different view angles for making the proposed model robust to subject and view variations.

Keywords: Facial paralysis · Spatial and temporal features · Gaussian mixture model · Dynamic kernels · Expression modeling · Yanagihara grading scales

1 Introduction

In human beings, there is a single nerve in the face known as a facial nerve that handles all types of facial muscular movements. If there is any damage caused to the facial nerve, the facial muscles start drooping or weakening either on the one half of the face or the full face that results in facial paralysis. The damage to the facial nerve occurs

© Springer Nature Switzerland AG 2022
K. Bouatouch et al. (Eds.): VISIGRAPP 2020, CCIS 1474, pp. 372–393, 2022.
https://doi.org/10.1007/978-3-030-94893-1_17

due to various issues like neurological, surgical, injuries, viral infections, etc. Facial paralysis affects the patient's normal life as it brings difficulty in normal communication and social interaction [1]. Thus, it is very much important to detect facial paralysis and its level of severity for proper diagnosis and clinical aid.

Various subjective assessments approaches are considered in the past years by the skilled clinicians or doctors to diagnose facial paralysis and its severity levels. In western countries like the United States of America (USA), the House-Brackmann (HB) subjective assessment scale [2] is followed by the clinicians. In HB grading scale there are different regions of the face, namely, forehead, eye, and mouth are examined based on the predefined characteristics to grade the patients from grade I, i.e. normal function level to grade VI, i.e. total paralysis. Similarly, in Asian countries like Japan, the Yanagihara grading scale [3] is followed for diagnosis of facial paralysis. In the Yanagihara grading scale, there are ten facial expressions, namely, rest videos (E0), raising of eyebrows (E1), closure of eye gently (E2), closure of eye tightly (E3), closure of paralyzed eye (E4), wrinkle nose (E5), puff out cheeks (E6), toothy movement (E7), whistling movement (E8), and under lip turn down (E9) as shown in Table 1.

Table 1. Yanagihara grading scale with ten facial expressions and two different grading scales.

Facial expressions	5-score grading scale	3-score grading scale
At rest (EP0)	0 1 2 3 4	0 2 4
Wrinkle forehead (EP1)	0 1 2 3 4	0 2 4
Closure of eye lightly (EP2)	0 1 2 3 4	0 2 4
Closure of eye tightly (EP3)	0 1 2 3 4	0 2 4
Blink (EP4)	0 1 2 3 4	0 2 4
Wrinkle nose (EP5)	0 1 2 3 4	0 2 4
Blowing out cheeks (EP6)	0 1 2 3 4	0 2 4
Grin (EP7)	0 1 2 3 4	0 2 4
Whistling (EP8)	0 1 2 3 4	0 2 4
Depress lower lip (EP9)	0 1 2 3 4	0 2 4

These facial expressions are asked to perform by the patients which are further examined by the experts to recognize the severity level of facial paralysis. Different grading from score-0 to score-4 is then assigned to the patients where score-0 denotes total paralysis and score-4 denotes normal facial functional levels. Also, different experts may have their own grading system for diagnosing facial paralysis and its severity levels [4]. However, the Yanagihara grading system is easier for interpreting and conducting the diagnosis of facial paralysis and its different severity levels. However, subjective assessment of the severity levels of facial paralysis is highly based on expert perception and thus different experts might have different opinions on the severity levels of facial paralysis. Thus, the need of quantitative assessment is required for accurate classification of multiple severity levels of facial paralysis for better clinical aid.

With the advancement of computer vision methodologies, a lot of research has been conducted for quantitative assessment of facial paralysis in the past few years. Most of the research work for quantitative assessment of facial paralysis are employed on unilateral facial paralysis (UFP), i.e. when only one half of the face is affected by facial paralysis. Asymmetric distance measurement is the most common practice to detect facial paralysis in UFP [5,6]. However, the approaches used for assessment of UFP does not apply to the scenarios where both sides of the face are affected. Thus, in this paper, we propose to use dynamic kernel modeling for quantitative assessment of facial paralysis. First, we extract the spatial and temporal features from the input video by using dense trajectory features by Wang et al. [7]. Using these local features, a large Gaussian mixture model (GMM) is trained to capture the facial features globally. Once the GMM is trained, the GMM statistics are used to form kernels by using dynamic kernel modeling. Dynamic kernels are known to handle variable-length data patterns by effectively preserving the local and global information of the given input data. Also, the dynamic kernels handle the variable-length data patterns either by transforming it to fixed-length patterns or by designing a novel kernel representation. We use three different types of dynamic kernels, namely, explicit mapping-based, probability-based, and intermediate matching-based dynamic kernels, which uses the GMM statistics, namely, mean, covariances, and posteriors for kernel formation as mentioned in [8] to model different expressions for quantitative assessment of facial paralysis. Once the kernel representations are formed the support vector machine is used as a classifier to detect the different levels of facial paralysis. The experiments are evaluated on the self-collected database of 39 facially paralyzed patients with different degrees of severity levels. The database is collected under three expert supervision to obtain the ground truth for subjective assessment. For the final class label, we select the best two out of three experts labeling. In our work, we evaluate 5-score and 3-score severity levels of facial paralysis based on the Yanagihara grading scale [3]. Furthermore, we use 3D convolution neural network features (3DCNN) to study and compare the deep neural network representations of facial dynamics for quantitative assessment of facial paralysis. We have shown the proposed approach generalized well with fewer input data as compared to deep networks.

The rest of the paper is organized as follows. In Sect. 2, the related literature review is presented for both subjective and quantitative assessment of facial paralysis. Next section, Sect. 3 describes the proposed methodology in detail. The experimental evaluations are illustrated in Sect. 4 with detail analysis of the obtained results. Section 5 concludes the proposed work with future directions.

2   Literature Review

Ngo et al. [6] proposes the spatio-temporal features to capture both spatial and motion information to measure the degree of facial paralysis. Initially, the face is detected using the Adaboost algorithm and then facial markers are manually placed onto the region of interest for computing spatio-temporal features. To capture motion information, these facial markers are tracked using Kanade-Lucas-Tomasi (KLT) tracker. And spatial features were captured by computing asymmetric movement of the facial markers. Using these spatio-temporal features the degree of facial paralysis is computed by comparing asymmetric differences from the normal other side of the face using Yanagihara grading system. Further, to improve the accuracy the 3-dimensional features are computed using camera calibration in extension to the previous work in [5].

Shu et al. [9] proposes an approach known as multi-resolution local binary pattern (MLBP) by computing the uniform local binary patterns at different block levels over the face in both spatial and temporal domain. These extracted MLBP are the facial features, which were further used for computing symmetry between the two halves of the face using resistor average distance (RAD). Support vector machine is then used for the quantitative analysis of facial paralysis based on the House-Brackmann (HB) grading system. The proposed method is evaluated on the self collected bio-medical videos of 197 subjects and achieves 65.3% overall accuracy on HB scale.

With the advancement in deep neural network approaches, Guo et al. proposes a deep assessment approach using Google LeNet model [10]. The face is detected from the given image and transfer learning is used for extraction of deep features for quantitative assessment of facial paralysis on HB grading scale. The deep assessment method obtained 86.17% accuracy on the self-collected unilateral peripheral facial paralysis (UPFP) database of 180 subjects with four expressions.

Yang et al. [1] introduces three levels of long short term memory (LSTM) to capture local and global facial features for recognizing multiple severity levels of facial paralysis automatically. The two LSTM sub-networks are used to capture the local information from both halves of the face and then the third LSTM is used to capture the global facial features from the whole face. The obtained facial features are then used for analysis of severity levels of facial paralysis based on four-levels, namely, normal, mildly ill, moderate ill, and critically ill. The three stream LSTM is evaluated on self collected facial paralysis dataset of 75 subjects posing 5 expression videos that achieves average accuracy performance of 86.35%.

Recent work by Jiang et al. [11] uses conventional laser speckle contrast imaging (LSCI) for capturing blood flow images and RGB images as an input to the image segmentation model for pre-processing. Then three different classifiers, namely, neural network (NN), support vector machine (SVM), and K-NN are employed to compare the best performance model for quantitative analysis of facial paralysis on HB grading scale. The proposed facial paralysis assessment model accuracy is highest using a neural network (NN) classifier with 97.14% on a self collected database of 80 people for 8 expressions.

Xu et al. [4] proposes dual path long short term memory (LSTM) with deep differentiated networks (DP-LSTM-DDN). The dual path LSTM (DP-LSTM) is used for capturing both local and global information from the facial regions and the deep differentiated network (DDN) is used to identify the asymmetry among the two halves of the face for automatic evaluation system of facial paralysis. The DDN is used to extract differentiated features between the two sides of the face to evaluate the asymmetry. Further in DP-LSTM, two LSTM is used where one LSTM is used to capture global facial features and another LSTM is used to capture local facial features. The evaluation of proposed DP-LSTM-DDN is performed using self-collected facial paralysis video data of 143 subjects with seven expressions based on self-prepared facial paralysis grading scale that includes four different levels of facial paralysis severity, namely, normal, mildly ill, moderate ill, and critically ill. The accuracy achieved using DP-LSTM-DDN is 73.47%.

Caroline et al. [12] proposed an application known as eface for quantitative assessment system of facial paralysis. Multiple parameters like static, dynamic, and synkinetic are extracted for disfigurement measurement from both halves of the face. The grading scale from 1 to 100 is applied, where 1 denotes high level of disfigurement and 100 denotes the normal or balanced facial symmetry. The eface application provides the graphical display of each parameter in the form of a bar graph for quantitative assessment by clinicians. The eface application is designed by performing multiple regression analysis on the extracted parameters for computing the overall disfigurement scores from 1–100 based on 74 subjects.

Ali et al. [13] proposed the smart prediction system (SPS) for facial paralysis to remotely detect and monitor the patients suffering from facial paralysis. The SPS involves both hardware and software approach to provide better clinical aid by giving routine based physiotherapy treatment to the patients. The patient is provided by hardware known as headgear which provides the physiotherapy massages to the affected area of the face. Further, a software based smart diagnosis system is proposed by detecting facial paralysis using Google machine learning kit and paralysis prediction neural network (PPNN). Based on the facial paralysis detection, the physiotherapist suggests the facial massages on the required area by routine time suggestion neural network (RTSNN) over the time for providing clinical aid remotely through SPS mobile application.

Another mobile application by Ankit [14], based on self-diagnose of facial paralysis is proposed. Multiple parameters, namely, heartbeat rate, blood pressure, and blood oxygen data are collected from the patient's wrist. Also, facial images, voice recording, and retinal images are collected from the mobile data to provide complete and comprehensive diagnosis of the facial paralysis patients. This self-diagnosing mobile application employ the model trained on 410 facial nerve vascular data points, 520 retinal images, and 100 voice related audio files using various machine learning algorithms, namely, support vector machine (SVM) for facial images, convolution neural network (CNN) for retinal images, and recurrent neural network (RNN) for audio training on 327 subjects. The application achieves 95% accuracy performance to diagnose patients with facial paralysis.

The other work by Park et al. [15] introduces a stroke prediction system using a mobile application named as mFAST. In this the facial paralysis is diagnosed and monitored using image averaging, whitening and histogram matching of facial images. The national institute of health for stroke scale (NIHSS) is used to grade multiple levels of facial paralysis from 0 to 3, with 0 signifies normal facial symmetry and 3 signifies complete facial paralysis. The features selection approach is applied to select dominant features and different machine learning algorithms, namely, naive Bayes, support vector machine, and radial-basis function network are employed for performance comparison of automatic diagnosing system mFAST.

Thus, the observations summarized from the aforementioned literature are given below:

1. Most of the existing works focus only on the frontal view face.
2. Manual processing are extensively involved like placing of facial markers, asymmetric distance calculations, etc.

3. The existing research works detect facial paralysis and its various effect levels only when dominant expressions are posed by the patients so that the facial muscle movements are highly noticeable for example eyes widening, mouth widening, whistling etc. Further, only a 3-score grading scale is explored to gain better accuracy.

Thus, in the proposed approach, we aim to provide the generalized model for quantitative assessment of facial paralysis to provide better clinical aid. The major contribution of the proposed approach are given as follows:

1. A large Gaussian mixture model is trained with seven different view angles and subjects to provide a generalized model for deployability in real world scenarios.
2. Dynamic kernel modeling is introduced in the proposed approach for handling variable length patterns like videos and to effectively preserve features that are learnt and captured both locally and globally.
3. The proposed approach models all the available and existing 10 expressions of Yanagihara grading scales with both 5-score grading assessment and 3-score grading assessment to provide a generalized model for quantitative assessment of facial paralysis.

Thus, in this section we listed the limitations of the existing works and mentioned the objectives of the proposed approach. In the next section, we discuss the proposed methodology in detail.

3   Proposed Methodology

In this section, we present a detailed explanation of the proposed dynamic kernel modeling for the quantitative assessment of facial paralysis. The block diagram of the proposed approach is shown in Fig. 1 where there are four different stages as follows (i) spatio-temporal feature extraction, (ii) training a large GMM also known as Universal GMM (GMM) model, (iii) dynamic kernel formation, and (iv) support vector machine (SVM) classification for 5-score or 3-score grading assessment for quantitative analysis of facial paralysis. Every stage is explained in detail in the below subsections as follows.

3.1   Spatio-Temporal Feature Extraction

For the extraction of spatio-temporal features from the given input video, the improved dense trajectory (IDT) feature extraction method by Wang et al. [7] is employ. The main idea behind using these IDT features are, not all the trajectories of the input video contain important features, for example, trajectories caused due to large and sudden displacements do not contain any useful information and thus could be removed for the final feature representation of the given input video. Hence, only essential trajectories information are stored using IDT in the proposed approach to capture the dynamics of facial movements. Also, existing and commonly used 3D video volume features like HOG3D, 3DSIFT, and LBP-TOP, etc., are computed in a 3D video volume around certain interest points, but they ignore the fundamental dynamic structures of the given

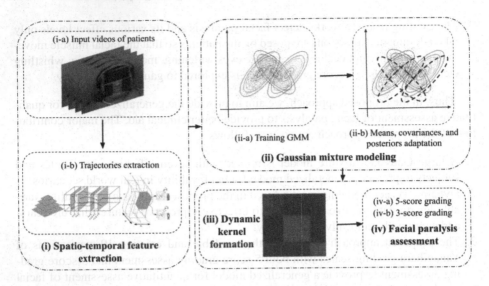

Fig. 1. Block diagram of the proposed dynamic kernel modeling for quantitative assessment of facial paralysis with multiple stages where (i) extracts spatio-temporal feature extraction using IDT features [16], (ii) training of GMM using IDT features of all videos (iii) Dynamic kernel formulation using GMM model and sample adapted statistics (iv) classification using support vector machine for 5-score and 3-score grading scales.

video [16]. Thus, IDT features are far more efficient than commonly existing spatio-temporal features. In the proposed approach, we use IDT features, namely, the histogram of optical flow (HOF) and motion boundary histogram (MBH) to capture the spatial and temporal information of the given input video.

The IDT features are computed at eight different spatial scales such that in each scale, the feature points are densely sampled on a grid space of $W = 5$ pixels. Then each feature point is tracked in the next frame by using median filtering in the dense optical flow field. Further, trajectories obtained by tracking feature points usually drift from the initial location if tracked for a longer period. Thus, to avoid drifting, the frame length of tracking of feature points are fixed to $T = 15$ frames.

Next, the local descriptors are computed around these feature points where these feature points are also known as interest points in 3D video volume. The size of the video volume considered is $P \times P$ pixels, where $P = 32$. To ensure the fundamental dynamic structure of the video volume, the volume is further subdivided into a smaller spatial and temporal grid of $g_h \times g_w \times g_t$, where $g_h = 2$, $g_w = 2$, and $g_t = 3$ are height, width, and temporal segment lengths, respectively of each grid. Each spatio-temporal grid is then used to compute the HOF and MBH descriptors. The size of HOF descriptors obtained is 108 in dimension (i.e., $2 \times 2 \times 3 \times 9$) and the size of MBH descriptors obtained is 192 in the dimension where the MBH descriptors are computed for both horizontal and vertical components of optical flow that is MBH in x and y directions such that each direction contains descriptors of 96 dimension.

3.2   Training of Gaussian Mixture Model (GMM)

The IDT features mentioned in the above subsection is used to extract features from different views of all the input videos for training a large Gaussian mixture model (GMM) that capture all the views and subjects from the given input videos. The GMM contains multiple components define as $q = 1, 2, \cdots, Q$ where different facial muscle movement attributes are captured in the different Q components. For a video, $\mathbf{V}$ the set of IDT features extracted represented as $\mathbf{v}_1, \mathbf{v}_2, \cdots, \mathbf{v}_N$, where N is the total number of local features for the given V. The likelihood of the particular feature $\mathbf{v}_n$ generated from the GMM model is given by

$$p(\mathbf{v}_n) = \sum_{q=1}^{Q} w_q \mathcal{N}(\mathbf{v}_n | \mu_q, \sigma_q), \tag{1}$$

where μ_q, σ_q, and w_q represents the means, covariances, and weights of each component q, respectively, also the GMM mixture weight w_q should satisfy the constraint $\sum_{q=1}^{Q} w_q = 1$. The probabilistic alignment of each feature vector $\mathbf{v}_n$ with respect to the each qth component of the GMM model is evaluated as follows

$$p(q|\mathbf{v}_n) = \frac{w_q p(\mathbf{v}_n | q)}{\sum_{q=1}^{Q} w_q p(\mathbf{v}_n | q)}, \tag{2}$$

where $\mathbf{v}_n$ is the likelihood of a feature vector generated from a component q. Once the GMM training is done for all the given videos, the next step is to adapt to the mean covariances for each video for dynamic kernel representation. The next sub-section describes the formation of different dynamic kernels, based on different adapted GMM statistics.

3.3   Dynamic Kernel Modeling

Kernel methods are one of the extensive research areas in the past few decades as it bridges the gap from linearity to non-linearity. The performance of kernel methods principally depends on the selection of kernel function. There are basically two types of kernels used in the literature, namely, static kernels and dynamic kernels. Static kernels are known to handle the fixed-length data whereas dynamic kernels are known for handing the variable-length data pattern efficiently like video, speech, etc. In the proposed approach, we explore the efficacy of dynamic kernels for video data. Dynamic kernels handle the variable-length data either by mapping it into the fixed-length data or by designing the novel kernel function for the variable-length data. Dynamic kennels are known for effectively preserving the local and global information for better representation of the given input data. In this sub-section, different types of dynamic kernels are discussed in detail based on the GMM statistics.

Explicit Mapping Based Dynamic Kernel: In explicit mapping based dynamic kernel, the variable-length representations are map on two fixed-length representations by using GMM based likelihood. The explicit mapping based dynamic kernel used in the proposed approach is the Fisher kernel, where the variable-length representations are map onto the fixed-length representations by Fisher score. This Fisher score is computed using the first derivative of log-likelihood for GMM means, covariances, and weights obtained from Eq. 2 as follows,

$$\psi_q^{(\mu)}(\mathbf{V}) = \sum_{n=1}^{N} p(q|\mathbf{v}_n)\mathbf{m}_{nq}, \tag{3}$$

$$\psi_q^{(\sigma)}(\mathbf{V}) = \frac{1}{2}\left(\sum_{n=1}^{N} p(q|\mathbf{v}_n)\left[-\mathbf{u}_q + \mathbf{h}_{nq}\right]\right), \tag{4}$$

$$\psi_q^{(w)}(\mathbf{V}) = \sum_{n=1}^{N} p(q|\mathbf{v}_n)\left[\frac{1}{w_q} - \frac{p(q_1|\mathbf{v}_n)}{w_1 p(q|\mathbf{v}_n)}\right]. \tag{5}$$

where $\mathbf{m}_{nq} = \Sigma_q^{-1}(\mathbf{v}_n - \mu_q)$, $\mathbf{u}_q = \Sigma_q^{-1}$ and $\mathbf{h}_{nq} = \left[m_{n1q}\mathbf{m}_{nq}^T, m_{n2q}\mathbf{m}_{nq}^T, \cdots, m_{ndq}\mathbf{m}_{nq}^T\right]$. For any $d \times d$ matrix $\mathbf{A}$ with $a_{ij}, i, j = 1, 2, \cdots, d$ as its elements, $vec(\mathbf{A}) = [a_{11}, a_{12}, \cdots, a_{dd}]^T$.

These first-order derivatives of the gradient of the log-likelihood computed in Eq. 3, 4, and 5 provides the direction in which the GMM parameters are updated for the best fit of the GMM model. We hypothesize that the deviations are occurred due to the facial muscle movement are captured by these gradients. The fixed dimensional feature vector known as the Fisher score vector is then computed by stacking all the gradients from Eq. 3, 4, and 5 given by

$$\Phi_q(\mathbf{V}) = \left[\psi_q^{(\mu)}(\mathbf{V})^T, \psi_q^{(\sigma)}(\mathbf{V})^T, \psi_q^{(w)}(\mathbf{V})^T\right]^T. \tag{6}$$

The Fisher score vector for all the Q components of the GMM is given by

$$\Phi_s(\mathbf{V}) = \left[\Phi_1(\mathbf{V})^T \Phi_2(\mathbf{V})^T \Phi_Q(\mathbf{V})^T\right]^T. \tag{7}$$

The Fisher score vector captures the similarities across two samples, thus the kernel function for comparing two samples V_x and V_y, with given local features is computed by

$$\mathbf{K}(\mathbf{V}_x, \mathbf{V}_y) = \Phi_s(\mathbf{V}_x)^T \mathbf{F}^{-1} \Phi_s(\mathbf{V}_y), \tag{8}$$

Where $\mathbf{I}$ is knows as Fisher information matrix given by

$$\mathbf{I} = \frac{1}{D}\sum_{d=1}^{D} \Phi_s(\mathbf{V}_d)\Phi_s(\mathbf{V}_d)^T. \tag{9}$$

The Fisher information matrix captures the variability's in the facial movement across the two samples. Thus both local and global information is captured using the Fisher score and Fisher information matrix in Fisher kernel computation. However, the computation complexity for the Fisher kernel is highly intensive. The computation of gradient for mean, covariance, and weight matrix involves $Q \times (N_p + N_r)$, each, where Q represents number of GMM components, N is the number of video samples, N_p and N_r are the local feature vectors of two video samples, d_l is the dimension of local feature vector of each input video samples, and d_s is the dimension of the score vector. Then the computation of the Fisher information matrix involves $D \times d_s^2 + D$ computations, where D is the total number of training examples. Similarly, the Fisher score vector requires $d_s^2 + d_s$ computations, where d_s is the dimension of the Fisher score vector. Thus, the total computation complexity of the Fisher kernel is given as $\mathcal{O}(QN + Dd_s^2 + D + d_s^2 + d_s)$ as shown in Table 2.

Table 2. Computation complexity of Fisher kernel where Q represents number of GMM components, N is the number of video samples, N_p and N_r are the local feature vectors of two video samples, d_l is the dimension of local feature vector of each input video samples, and d_s is the dimension of the score vector.

Number of computations	Computational complexity
Computation of gradient vector	$3 \times Q \times (N_p + N_r)$
Fisher information matrix	$D \times d_s^2 + D$
Kernel computation	$d_s^2 + d_s$
Total computational complexity	$\mathcal{O}(QN + Dd_s^2 + D + d_s^2 + d_s)$

Probability-Based Dynamic Kernel: As the computational complexity of explicit mapping based dynamic kernel is very high, therefore, the probability-based dynamic kernel for mapping variable-length representation to fixed-length representation in the kernel space by comparing the probability distribution of the local feature vectors is explored. In order to compute the probability-based dynamic kernel, the maximum a posteriori adaptation (MAP) of GMM statistics, namely, means and covariances of GMM for each clip is adapted from the GMM model, given by

$$\mu_q(\mathbf{V}) = \alpha \mathbf{F}_q(\mathbf{V}) + (1-\alpha)\mu_q. \tag{10a}$$

and

$$\sigma_q(\mathbf{V}) = \alpha \mathbf{S}_q(\mathbf{V}) + (1-\alpha)\sigma_q. \tag{10b}$$

where $\mathbf{F}_q(\mathbf{V})$ is the first-order and $\mathbf{S}_c(\mathbf{V})$ is the second-order Baum-Welch statistics for a clip $\mathbf{V}$, respectively, which is calculated as

$$\mathbf{F}_q(\mathbf{V}) = \frac{1}{n_q(\mathbf{V})} \sum_{n=1}^{N} p(q|\mathbf{v}_n)\mathbf{v}_n \tag{11a}$$

and

$$\mathbf{S}_q(\mathbf{V}) = diag\left(\sum_{n=1}^{N} p(q|\mathbf{v}_n)\mathbf{v}_n\mathbf{v}_n^T \right), \tag{11b}$$

respectively.

The adapted mean and covariance from each GMM component depend on the posterior probabilities of the GMM given for each sample. Therefore, if the posterior probability is high then higher will be the correlations among the facial movements captured in the GMM components. This shows that the adapted mean and covariance for each

GMM mixture will have a higher impact than the full GMM model means and covariances. Based on these GMM statistics there are two different kinds of probability-based dynamic kernels are proposed, namely, super vector kernel (SVK) and mean interval kernel (MIK). The GMM-SVK is computed using first-order statistics of GMM similarly the GMM-MIK is computed using both first-order and second-order statistics of GMM. Thus, the adapted means from Eq. 10a, for sample V is given by

$$\psi_q(\mathbf{V}) = \left[\sqrt{w_q}\sigma_q^{-\frac{1}{2}}\mu_q(\mathbf{V})\right]^T. \tag{12}$$

By stacking the GMM vector for each component, a $Qd \times 1$ dimensional supervector is obtained, which is known as GMM supervector (GMM-SV) represented as $\mathbf{S}_{svk}(\mathbf{V}) = [\psi_1(\mathbf{V})^T, \psi_2(\mathbf{V})^T, \cdots, \psi_Q(\mathbf{V})^T]^T$.

The GMM-SV used for comparing the similarity across two samples, namely, $\mathbf{V}_x$ and $\mathbf{V}_y$ by constructing GMM supervector kernel (GMM-SVK), which is given by

$$K_{svk}(\mathbf{V}_x, \mathbf{V}_y) = \mathbf{S}_{svk}(\mathbf{V}_x)^T \mathbf{S}_{svk}(\mathbf{V}_y). \tag{13}$$

The GMM-SVK kernel formed above only utilizes the first-order adaptations of the samples for each GMM components. Thus, the second-order statistics, i.e., covariance adaptations is also involved in constructing fixed-length representation from variable-length patterns is given by

$$\psi_q(\mathbf{V}) = \left(\frac{\sigma_q(\mathbf{V}) - \sigma_q}{2}\right)^{-\frac{1}{2}} (\mu_q(\mathbf{V}) - \mu_q). \tag{14}$$

Combining the GMM mean interval supervector (GMM-MI) for each component is computed as $\mathbf{S}_{mik}(\mathbf{V}) = [\psi_1(\mathbf{V})^T, \psi_2(\mathbf{V})^T, \cdots, \psi_Q(\mathbf{V})^T]^T$.

Thus, to compare the similarity across the two samples $\mathbf{V}_x$ and $\mathbf{V}_y$, the kernel formation is performed using GMM-GMI kernel also known as GMM mean interval kernel (GMM-MIK) given by

$$K_{mik}(\mathbf{V}_x, \mathbf{V}_y) = \mathbf{S}_{mik}(\mathbf{V}_x)^T \mathbf{S}_{mik}(\mathbf{V}_y). \tag{15}$$

The fixed-length representation formed by using the posterior probabilities in the kernel space is a high dimensional vector, which involves $Q \times (N_p + N_r)$ computations for mean adaptation and $2 \times Q \times (N_p + N_r)$ for mean and covariance adaptations, respectively, where Q represents number of GMM components, N is the number of video samples, N_p and N_r are the local feature vectors of two video samples, d_l is the dimension of local feature vector of each input video samples, and d_s is the dimension of the score vector. And the kernel computation required $Q \times (d_l^2 + 1)$ and d_s^2, where d_l is the dimension of local feature vector. The total computational complexities of GMM-SVK and GMM-MIK kernels are $\mathcal{O}(QN + Qd_l^2 + d_s^2)$ and $\mathcal{O}(QN + Qd_l^2 + Qd_l + Q^2d_s^2)$, respectively as shown in Table 3 and 4. Also, it can be noticed that the GMM-SVK is computationally less expensive than GMM-MIK as GMM-MIK uses both mean and covariance adaptations for kernel computation.

Intermediate Matching Kernel (IMK). The explicit mapping based kernel and the probability-based dynamic kernel aforementioned above are having high computational complexities. Therefore in this sub-section, the alternative approach for the formation of

Table 3. Computation complexity of probability based GMM supervector kernel (GMM-SVK) where Q represents number of GMM components, N is the number of video samples, N_p and N_r are the local feature vectors of two video samples, d_l is the dimension of local feature vector of each input video samples, and d_s is the dimension of the score vector.

Number of computations	Computational Complexity
Computation of mean adaptation	$Q \times (N_p + N_r)$
Computation of supervector	$Q \times (d_l^2 + 1)$
Computation of kernel	d_s^2
Total computational complexity	$\mathcal{O}(QN + Qd_l^2 + d_s^2)$

Table 4. Computation complexity of probability based GMM mean interval kernel (GMM-MIK) where Q represents number of GMM components, N is the number of video samples, N_p and N_r are the local feature vectors of two video samples, d_l is the dimension of local feature vector of each input video samples, and d_s is the dimension of the score vector.

Number of computations	Computational complexity
Computation of mean adaptation	$Q \times (N_p + N_r)$
Computation of covariance adaptation	$Q \times (N_p + N_r)$
Computation of supervector	$Q \times (d_l^2 + d_l)$
Computation of kernel	d_s^2
Total computational complexity	$\mathcal{O}(QN + Qd_l^2 + Qd_l + Q^2 d_s^2)$

the dynamic kernel by designing the new kernel function in order to handle the variable-length representations known as matching based dynamic kernel is introduced. Multiple matching based dynamic kernels are proposed in the literature, namely, summation kernel, matching kernel, etc., however, most of the matching based dynamic kernels are computationally expensive and also does not satisfy the Mercer's theorem. So in the proposed approach, intermediate matching kernel (IMK) is introduced that are computationally better than other dynamic matching based dynamic kernels and also satisfies the theory of Mercer's theorem. The IMK is formed by matching a set of a local feature vector to the closest virtual feature vectors obtained using the training data of all the classes. The virtual features vector could be any attribute, in the proposed approach, the posterior probability is used as the virtual feature vector to form the IMK kernel.

Let $\mathbf{Z} = \{\mathbf{z}_1, \mathbf{z}_2, \cdots, \mathbf{z}_Q\}$ be the virtual feature vectors. Then, the feature vectors $\mathbf{v}_{xq}^*$ and $\mathbf{v}_{yq}^*$ in $\mathbf{V}_x$ and $\mathbf{V}_y$, respectively, that are nearest to q^{th} virtual feature vector $\mathbf{z}_q$ is determined as

$$\mathbf{v}_{xq}^* = \underset{\mathbf{v} \in \mathbf{V}_x}{\arg\min}\, \mathcal{D}(\mathbf{v}, \mathbf{z}_q) \text{ and } \mathbf{v}_{yq}^* = \underset{\mathbf{v} \in \mathbf{V}_y}{\arg\min}\, \mathcal{D}(\mathbf{v}, \mathbf{z}_q), \tag{16}$$

where $\mathcal{D}(.,.)$ is a distance function, which measures the distance of a feature vector $\mathbf{V}_x$ or $\mathbf{V}_y$ to the closest feature vector in $\mathbf{Z}$. We hypothesize that the distance function aid in finding the closest facial muscle movement learned from the clip to one, which is captured by GMM components. Once the closest feature vector is selected, the base kernel will be given by

$$K_{imk}(\mathbf{V}_x, \mathbf{V}_y) = \sum_{q=1}^{Q} k(\mathbf{v}_{xq}, \mathbf{v}_{yq}). \tag{17}$$

In the proposed approach, the GMM parameters like mean, covariance, and weight are used as a set of virtual feature vectors. And, the distance or closeness measure is computed by using the posterior probability of the GMM component generating the feature described in Eq. 2. Thus, the local feature vectors close to the virtual feature vector for the given q is $\mathbf{v}*_{xq}$ and $\mathbf{v}*_{yq}$ for clips $\mathbf{V}_x$ and $\mathbf{V}_y$, respectively, which is computed as

$$\mathbf{v}_{xq}^* = \arg\max_{\mathbf{v} \in \mathbf{V}_x} p(q|\mathbf{v}) \text{ and } \mathbf{v}_{yq}^* = \arg\max_{\mathbf{v} \in \mathbf{V}_y} p(q|\mathbf{v}). \tag{18}$$

The computational complexity of IMK is very low as compared to the aforementioned dynamic kernel that can be defined as (i) $Q \times (N_p + N_r)$ comparisons for selection of closest feature vector, (ii) $Q \times (N_p + N_r)$ required for posterior probability computations, and (iii) Q base kernel computations where Q represents number of GMM components, N is the number of video samples, N_p and N_r are the local feature vectors of two video samples, d_l is the dimension of local feature vector of each input video samples, and d_s is the dimension of the score vector. Thus the total computational complexity of IMK is given by $\mathcal{O}(QN)$ where N is the set of local feature vector as shown in Table 5.

Table 5. Computation complexity of GMM intermediate matching kernel (GMM-IMK) where Q represents number of GMM components, N is the number of video samples, N_p and N_r are the local feature vectors of two video samples, d_l is the dimension of local feature vector of each input video samples, and d_s is the dimension of the score vector.

Number of computations	Computational complexity
Computation of posterior probability	$Q \times (N_p + N_r)$
Comparison required for feature selection	$Q \times (N_p + N_r)$
Computation of base kernel	Q
Total computational complexity	$\mathcal{O}(QN)$

4   Experimental Results

In this section, the experimental results of the proposed approach are discussed in detail with the analysis and comparison of the classification performances of the different dynamic kernels. The comparison and ablation studies of the proposed approach with existing state-of-the-art methodologies are also surveyed to demonstrate the efficacy of the proposed approach for quantitative assessment of facial paralysis to the patients.

4.1   Dataset Description

The dataset used in the proposed approach is the self-collected video data set of 39 facially paralyzed patients. The dataset is collected under three expert supervision who also perform the subjective assessment using Yanagihara 5-score and 3-score grading scale. According to the guidelines of the Yanagihara grading scale, the patients are guided to perform 10 different kinds of expression to detect the different levels of facial paralysis as shown in Fig. 2. The video is recorded with different views using 7 different camera angles place at the angle difference of $\pm 30°$ as shown in Fig. 3.

Expressions	Sample Image	Expressions	Sample Image
At Rest (EP0)		Wrinkle Nose (EP5)	
Wrinkle forehead (EP1)		Blowing out cheeks (EP6)	
Closure of eye lightly (EP2)		Grin (EP7)	
Closure of eye tightly (EP3)		Whistling (EP8)	
Blink (EP4)		Depress lower lip (EP9)	

Fig. 2. Sample image of the collected dataset where the patient is expressing ten different expressions mentioned in the Yanagihara grading scale.

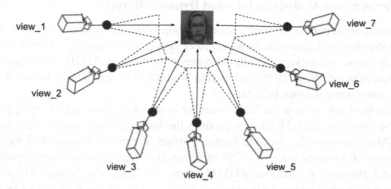

Fig. 3. Sample image of the camera setting to collect video recording from 7 different view angles.

Further, the collected video dataset contains facially paralyzed patients of different age groups and gender. Thus, the main objective of collecting video dataset of multiple subjects and different view angles is to design and develop a robust and generalized model for quantitative assessment of facial paralysis. The total number of 2717 video samples are obtained from 39 subjects, which belongs to the different age group from 17 years to 70 years old. The detailed statistics of the data set age-wise and gender-wise is shown in Fig. 4. Also in Fig. 5 and 6, gives the division of the number of training and testing videos used in the proposed approach for both 5-scores and 3-scores grading assessment using the Yanagihara grading scale.

Total number of video samples collected age-wise

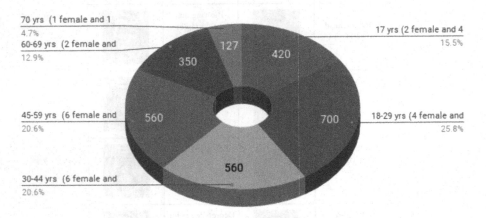

Fig. 4. Age and gender wise statistics of the patients considered during dataset preparation.

Also, the subjects present in the testing videos are not at all present in the training set in any condition during experimentation.

4.2 Performance Analysis on Different Dynamic Kernels

The classification performance of 5-score grading scales for different dynamic kernels used in the proposed approach, namely, Fisher kernel (FK), intermediate matching kernel (IMK), super vector kernel (SVK), and mean interval kernel (MIK), computed using histogram of optical flow (HOF) and motion boundary histogram (MBH) with different GMM components is given in Table 6.

It can be observed from the Table 6 that the best classification performance kernel is the mean interval kernel (MIK), as it captures the first-order and second-order statistics of GMM to compute the dynamic kernel. Further, it can be observed that increasing the number of mixtures from 32 to 256 increases the better generalization capability of the model. However, the number of GMM components cannot be increased beyond 256 components due to the increase in demand of the local features, which cannot be further fulfilled due to the limited size of the dataset.

5-Score Grading Scale

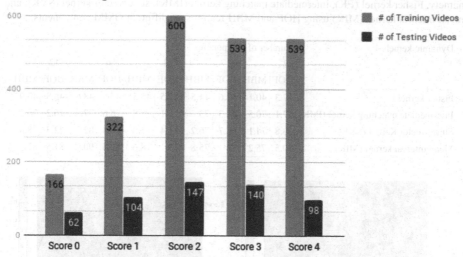

Fig. 5. Training and testing split of the dataset samples for 5-score grading scales.

3-Score Grading Scale

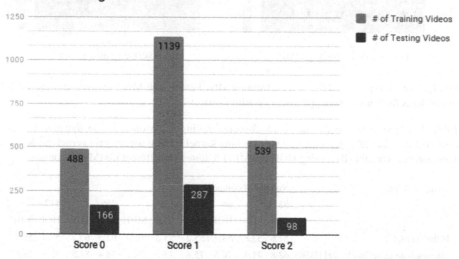

Fig. 6. Training and testing split of the dataset samples for 3-score grading scales.

The confusion matrix of the best classification performance i.e., MBH feature with 256 GMM components and MIK with SVM classifier is shown in Fig. 7. As it can be observed from the Fig. 7(a), most of the misclassified samples are present in the neighboring classes. Therefore, the score 0 class is combined with score 1 class, and score 2 class is combined with score 3 class to construct 3 class grading scale data samples for quantitative assessment of facial paralysis. The classification performance

Table 6. Classification performance for 5-score grading scale on multiple dynamic kernels, namely, Fisher kernel (FK), intermediate matching kernel (IMK), supervector kernel (SVK), and mean interval kernel (MIK) using HOF and MBH features on different GMM components.

Dynamic kernels	Number of components									
	32		64		128		256		512	
	HOF	MBH	HOF	MBH	HOF	MBH	HOF	MBH	HOF	MBH
Fisher kernel	37.3	40.1	43.6	44.5	45.5	45.5	47.9	48.6	46.8	47.9
Intermediate matching kernel (IMK)	67.1	70.5	72.3	73	74.1	75.8	76.6	77.9	76.2	76.2
Super vector Kernel (SVK)	68.8	74.1	69.7	76.2	71.4	77.3	78.4	82.2	72.3	78.4
Mean interval kernel (MIK)	70.5	75.2	72	75.8	73	78.6	86.5	**90.7**	81.5	87.1

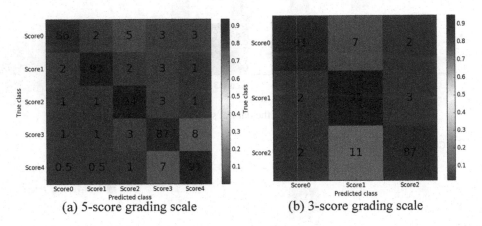

(a) 5-score grading scale   (b) 3-score grading scale

Fig. 7. Confusion matrix of the best performing MIK kernel with MBH features and 256 GMM components for both 5-score and 3-score grading scale.

Table 7. Classification performance for 3-score grading scale on multiple dynamic kernels, namely, Fisher kernel (FK), intermediate matching kernel (IMK), supervector kernel (SVK), and mean interval kernel (MIK) using HOF and MBH features on different GMM components.

Dynamic kernels	Number of components									
	32		64		128		256		512	
	HOF	MBH	HOF	MBH	HOF	MBH	HOF	MBH	HOF	MBH
Fisher kernel	52.6	53.8	53.7	55.2	55.2	58.2	62.3	63.2	55.4	59.9
Intermediate matching kernel (IMK)	68.8	71.4	70.5	75.8	73.2	76.2	78.4	81.5	75.8	78.6
Super-vector kernel (SVK)	71.4	72.3	76.8	79.2	78.8	79.9	82.4	84.1	80.2	81.7
Mean interval kernel (MIK)	85.9	87.2	86.9	89	88.9	90.8	90.2	**92.5**	89.6	91.5

of different kernels on different GMM components for 3 class grading scales is given in Table 7. The confusion matrix for the best classification performances i.e. MBH feature with 256 GMM components and MIK with SVM classifier is given in Fig. 7(b).

4.3   Comparison with Existing Approaches

Comparison with state-of-the-art methods are presented in Table 8. Also, C3D features by Tran et al. [17], for both 5-score grading and 3-score grading scales are extracted to compare the proposed method with deep features. In C3D feature extraction, the features are extracted from fc8 (fully-connected layer 8) and then use a support vector machine (SVM) for a quantitative assessment of facial paralysis. It can be observed from the Table 8 that the proposed approach on both 5-score and 3-score grading scales obtained better classification performance than existing state-of-the-art methods and C3D deep features.

Table 8. Comparison with existing state-of-the-art methodologies and C3D deep features.

Methods	Accuracy (%)
PI [18]	46.55
LBP [9]	47.27
Gabor [19]	55.12
Tracking 2D [6]	64.85
Tracking 3D [5]	66.47
DP-LSTM-DDN [4]	66.47
3-stream LSTM [11]	86.34
C3d (from fc-8 layer and on 5-score grading scales) [17] + SVM	71.5
C3d features (from fc-8 layer and on 3-score grading scales) [17] + SVM	81.3
Proposed approach (on 5-score grading scales)	90.7
Proposed approach (on 3-score grading scales)	92.46

4.4   Quantitative Analysis

To demonstrate the efficacy of the proposed approach the expression wise classification performance for the best model i.e., MBH features with 256 GMM components using MIK kernel with SVM classifier for both 5-score and 3-score grading scale is given in Table 9. It can be noticed that the expression with fewer facial muscle movements like at rest expression has low performance as compared to the expressions with notified facial muscle movements like the closure of the eye tightly, whistling, etc. This is due to the fact that the facial dynamics are difficult to capture with fewer facial movements. Also, as it can be noticed from Table 9 the facial expressions that have notified facial muscle movements are having higher classification performance for the quantitative assessment of facial paralysis.

Further, the existing state-of-the-art methods only explore the proposed approaches on the facial expressions that have notified facial muscle movements and thus achieve better performance as shown in Table 10 and 11 for both 5-score and 3-score grading scales. However, for better quantitative assessment of facial paralysis, the proposed approach models all the 10 expressions to provide a better clinical assessment.

Table 9. Classification performance of each expression used in the Yanagihara grading scale for the best performing MIK kernel with MBH features and 256 GMM components for both 5-score and 3-score grading scale.

Expressions	5-score grading (proposed approach)	3-score grading (proposed approach)
EP0	75.45	81.68
EP1	95.23	94.87
EP2	86.4	93.04
EP3	91.94	97.43
EP4	94.13	92.3
EP5	95.97	95.6
EP6	91.57	91.94
EP7	93.77	95.23
EP8	89.01	87.54
EP9	93.04	95.23

Table 10. Classification performance of each expression used in the Yanagihara grading scale for the best performing MIK kernel with MBH features and 256 GMM components and existing state-of-the-art methods on 5-score grading scale (As it can be noticed the existing methods only evaluate the noticeable facial expressions, namely, wrinkle forehead (EP1), closure of eye tightly (EP3), wrinkle nose (EP5), and grin (EP7)).

Types of expressions	PI	LBP	Gabor	Tracking 2D	Tracking 3D	Proposed approach
EP0	-	-	-	-	-	55
EP1	50.7	58.3	62.4	69.4	70.9	71.25
EP2	-	-	-	-	-	86.25
EP3	48.2	48.9	53.1	62.1	63.3	76.25
EP4	-	-	-	-	-	51.25
EP5	48.1	41.8	50.5	57.3	58.2	75
EP6	-	-	-	-	-	42.5
EP7	39.2	40.1	54.5	70.6	73.5	75
EP8	-	-	-	-	-	48.75
EP9	-	-	-	-		48.75

We further present the t-distributed stochastic neighbor embedding (t-sne) [20] plot in Fig. 8(a) and 8(b), to show the distribution of the kernel matrix representation of the similar and discriminative expressions [8]. The facial expressions having similar facial movements or no facial movements are usually confused with other data samples, thus leads to an increase in misclassification rate for example at rest (EP0) expression and closure of eye lightly (EP2) expression are two visually similar expressions and thus data points are confused with each other. Whereas the facial expressions like closure

Table 11. Classification performance of each expression used in the Yanagihara grading scale for the best performing MIK kernel with MBH features and 256 GMM components and existing state-of-the-art methods on 3-score grading scale (As it can be noticed the existing methods only evaluate the noticeable facial expressions, namely, wrinkle forehead (EP1), closure of eye tightly (EP3), wrinkle nose (EP5), and grin (EP7)).

Types of expressions	PI	LBP	Gabor	Tracking 2D	Tracking 3D	Proposed approach
EP0	-	-	-	-	-	73.75
EP1	50.7	58.3	62.4	69.4	70.9	86.25
EP2	-	-	-	-	-	77.5
EP3	48.2	48.9	53.1	62.1	63.3	88.75
EP4	-	-	-	-	-	71.25
EP5	48.1	41.8	50.5	57.3	58.2	88.75
EP6	-	-	-	-	-	71.25
EP7	39.2	40.1	54.5	70.6	73.5	87.5
EP8	-	-	-	-	-	70
EP9	-	-	-	-	-	80

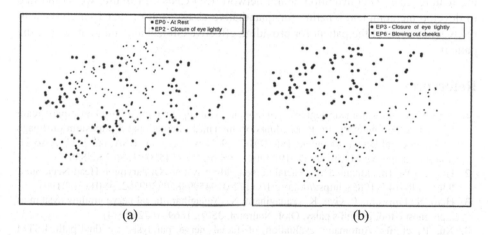

(a)　　　　　　　　　　　　　　(b)

Fig. 8. t-sne plot for the best performing MIK kernel with MBH features and 256 GMM components on 3-score grading scale for the facial expressions data points to distinguish similar and discriminative facial expressions. In (a) expression like at rest expression (EP0) and closure of eye lightly (EP2) are two visually similar expressions and thus data points are confused with each other whereas in (b) facial expressions like closure of eye tightly (EP3) and blowing out cheeks (EP6) are two visually dissimilar expressions having uncommon facial muscle movements and thus less confused with each other.

of eye tightly (EP3) expression and blowing out cheeks (EP6) expression are two visually dissimilar expressions having uncommon facial muscle movements and thus less confused with each other.

5 Conclusion

In this paper, we introduce a quantitative assessment model for facial paralysis using dynamic kernel representation. We capture the local representations using spatio-temporal features and global representations using a large GMM trained with multiple views and subjects. These captured representations are then modeled using dynamic kernels, which are efficient in handling and preserving both local and global features for variable length patterns like videos. In the proposed approach, dynamic kernels use GMM statistics, namely, mean, covariances, and posteriors for mapping variable length patterns to fixed length patterns. These obtained kernel representations are then classified using a support vector machine to detect facial paralysis and its various effect levels. The efficacy of the proposed approach is demonstrated on a self-collected video database of 39 facially paralyzed patients affected with different degrees of facial paralysis. We have shown that the intermediate matching kernel (IMK) has least computational complexity with lower classification performance than probability based matching kernels where both first and second order statistics of GMM are used for dynamic kernel formation. However, the accuracy of the probability based kernels are superior to other dynamic kernels as it uses both first and second order statistics of GMM. Further, we have shown the superior performance of the proposed approach than deep learning features like 3D convolution neural network (3D-CNN). In future, we would like to develop the complete pipeline for quantitative assessment of facial paralysis with recovery analysis of the patient for providing effective clinical aid and treatment to the patients.

References

1. Yang, C., et al.: Automatic degree evaluation of facial nerve paralysis based on triple-stream long short term memory. In: Proceedings of the Third International Symposium on Image Computing and Digital Medicine, ISICDM 2019, New York, NY, USA, pp. 7–11. Association for Computing Machinery (2019). https://doi.org/10.1145/3364836.3364838
2. House, J.W., Brackmann, D.E.: Facial nerve grading system. Otolaryngol. Head Neck Surg. 93(2), 146–147 (1985). https://doi.org/10.1177/019459988509300202. pMID: 3921901
3. Hato, N., Fujiwara, T., Gyo, K., Yanagihara, N.: Yanagihara facial nerve grading system as a prognostic tool in Bell's palsy. Otol. Neurotol. 35(9), 1669–1672 (2014)
4. Xu, P., et al.: Automatic evaluation of facial nerve paralysis by dual-path LSTM with deep differentiated network. Neurocomputing 388, 70–77 (2020). https://doi.org/10.1016/j.neucom.2020.01.014. http://www.sciencedirect.com/science/article/pii/S0925231220300412
5. Ngo, T.H., Chen, Y.W., Seo, M., Matsushiro, N., Xiong, W.: Quantitative analysis of facial paralysis based on three-dimensional features. In: 2016 IEEE International Conference on Image Processing (ICIP), pp. 1319–1323, September 2016. https://doi.org/10.1109/ICIP.2016.7532572
6. Ngo, T.H., Chen, Y.W., Matsushiro, N., Seo, M.: Quantitative assessment of facial paralysis based on spatiotemporal features. IEICE Trans. Inf. Syst. E99.D(1), 187–196 (2016). https://doi.org/10.1587/transinf.2015EDP7082
7. Wang, H., Oneata, D., Verbeek, J., Schmid, C.: A robust and efficient video representation for action recognition. Int. J. Comput. Vis. 119(3), 219–238 (2015). https://doi.org/10.1007/s11263-015-0846-5. https://hal.inria.fr/hal-01145834

8. Perveen, N., Mohan, C.K., Chen, Y.W.: Quantitative analysis of facial paralysis using GMM and dynamic kernels. In: Proceedings of the 15th International Joint Conference on Computer Vision, Imaging and Computer Graphics Theory and Applications, VISAPP, vol. 5, pp. 173–184. INSTICC, SciTePress (2020). https://doi.org/10.5220/0009104801730184

9. He, S., Soraghan, J.J., O'Reilly, B.F., Xing, D.: Quantitative analysis of facial paralysis using local binary patterns in biomedical videos. IEEE Trans. Biomed. Eng. **56**(7), 1864–1870 (2009). https://doi.org/10.1109/TBME.2009.2017508

10. Guo, Z., et al.: Deep assessment process: objective assessment process for unilateral peripheral facial paralysis via deep convolutional neural network. In: 2017 IEEE 14th International Symposium on Biomedical Imaging (ISBI 2017), pp. 135–138, April 2017. https://doi.org/10.1109/ISBI.2017.7950486

11. Jiang, C., et al.: Automatic facial paralysis assessment via computational image analysis. J. Healthc. Eng. **2020**, 2398542 (2020). https://doi.org/10.1155/2020/2398542

12. Banks, C.A., Bhama, P.K., Park, J., Hadlock, C.R., Hadlock, T.A.: Clinician-graded electronic facial paralysis assessment: the eFACE. Plast. Reconstr. Surg. **136**(2), 223e–230e (2015)

13. Ridha, A., Shehieb, W., Yacoub, P., Al-Balawneh, K., Arshad, K.: Smart prediction system for facial paralysis, pp. 321–327, April 2020. https://doi.org/10.1109/ICEEE49618.2020.9102600

14. Gupta, A.: StrokeSave: a novel, high-performance mobile application for stroke diagnosis using deep learning and computer vision. CoRR abs/1907.05358 (2019). http://arxiv.org/abs/1907.05358

15. Park, E., Han, T., Nam, H.S.: mFAST: automatic stoke evaluation system for time-critical treatment with multimodal feature collection and machine learning classification. In: Proceedings of the 2020 12th International Conference on Computer and Automation Engineering, ICCAE 2020, New York, NY, USA, pp. 38–41. Association for Computing Machinery (2020). https://doi.org/10.1145/3384613.3384653

16. Wang, T., Zhang, S., Dong, J., Liu, L., Yu, H.: Automatic evaluation of the degree of facial nerve paralysis. Multimed. Tools Appl. **75**(19), 11893–11908 (2016). https://doi.org/10.1007/s11042-015-2696-0

17. Tran, D., Bourdev, L.D., Fergus, R., Torresani, L., Paluri, M.: C3D: generic features for video analysis. CoRR abs/1412.0767 (2014). http://arxiv.org/abs/1412.0767

18. Wachtman, G., et al.: Measurement of asymmetry in persons with facial paralysis. In: Combined Annual Conference of the Robert H. Ivy and Ohio Valley Societies of Plastic and Reconstructive Surgeons, June 2002

19. Ngo, T.H., Seo, M., Chen, Y.W., Matsushiro, N.: Quantitative assessment of facial paralysis using local binary patterns and Gabor filters. In: Proceedings of the Fifth Symposium on Information and Communication Technology, SoICT 2014, New York, NY, USA, pp. 155–161. ACM (2014). https://doi.org/10.1145/2676585.2676607. http://doi.acm.org/10.1145/2676585.2676607

20. van der Maaten, L., Hinton, G.: Viualizing data using t-SNE. J. Mach. Learn. Res. **9**, 2579–2605 (2008)

Perceptually-Informed No-Reference Image Harmonisation

Alan Dolhasz[✉][iD], Carlo Harvey[iD], and Ian Williams[iD]

Digital Media Technology Lab, Birmingham City University, Birmingham, U.K.
{alan.dolhasz,carlo.harvey,ian.williams}@bcu.ac.uk
http://dmtlab.bcu.ac.uk

Abstract. Many image synthesis tasks, such as image compositing, rely on the process of image harmonisation. The goal of harmonisation is to create a plausible combination of component elements. The subjective quality of this combination is directly related to the existence of human-detectable appearance differences between these component parts, suggesting that consideration for human perceptual tolerances is an important aspect of designing automatic harmonisation algorithms. In this paper, we first investigate the impact of a perceptually-calibrated composite artifact detector on the performance of a state-of-the-art deep harmonisation model. We first evaluate a two-stage model, whereby the performance of both pre-trained models and their naive combination is assessed against a large data-set of 68128 automatically generated image composites. We find that without any task-specific adaptations, the two-stage model achieves comparable results to the baseline harmoniser fed with ground truth composite masks. Based on these findings, we design and train an end-to-end model, and evaluate its performance against a set of baseline models. Overall, our results indicate that explicit modeling and incorporation of image features conditioned on a human perceptual task improves the performance of no-reference harmonisation algorithms. We conclude by discussing the generalisability of our approach in the context of related work.

Keywords: Image compositing · Harmonisation · Artifact detection · End-to-end compositing · Deep learning

1 Introduction

Image harmonisation is an important task in image compositing and synthesis, aiming to minimise appearance-based differences between individual elements of a composite, in order to produce a perceptually plausible end result [32]. An image composite commonly consists of at least one *object*, inserted into a background image, referred to as the *scene*. As the object and scene are commonly captured under different environmental conditions, visible appearance mismatches between them may exist, due to differences in illumination, camera intrinsics, post-processing, encoding or compression. Thus, the goal of image

© Springer Nature Switzerland AG 2022
K. Bouatouch et al. (Eds.): VISIGRAPP 2020, CCIS 1474, pp. 394–413, 2022.
https://doi.org/10.1007/978-3-030-94893-1_18

harmonisation is to minimise such differences and create a realistic result. This process can be performed manually by compositing artists, however, many automatic approaches have been proposed, including alpha matting - linear combinations of object and scene pixel values [23], gradient-domain optimization techniques [1,20,22], statistical appearance transfer [19,25] and multi-scale methods [4,5,29].

With the advent of deep learning (DL), automatic image synthesis techniques have garnered renewed interest and afforded considerable improvements in state-of-the-art image compositing and harmonisation techniques. Methods using variants of convolutional autoencoders (AEs) have been successfully used to directly approximate the harmonisation function, in a supervised learning setting. Notably, Tsai et al. (2017) [30] use a convolutional AE in a multi-task setting to both segment and harmonise an input image, provided the target object mask. Another approach [7] uses a generative adversarial network (GAN) to perform both colour and geometric transformations, pre-training their model on synthetically-generated data. Conditional GANs have also been applied in this context, by learning to model joint distributions of different object classes and their relationships in image space. This allows for semantically similar regions to undergo similar transformations [2]. A more recent method combines state-of-the art attention mechanisms and GAN-based architectures with explicit object-scene knowledge implemented through masked and partial convolutions and provide a dedicated benchmark image harmonisation dataset, dubbed iHarmony [8].

A common requirement of these state-of-the-art techniques is the provision of binary object/scene segmentation masks at input, both during training and inference. These masks serve as an additional feature, identifying the corresponding image pixels that require harmonisation. As such, these methods are applicable to scenarios where new composites are generated, and these masks are available. However, in cases where these ground truth masks are not available, these techniques can not be easily applied without human intervention, limiting their application to scenarios such as harmonisation of legacy composites. Moreover, existing methods do not explicitly leverage human perception - the usual target audience of image composites. This includes human sensitivity to different local image disparities between object and scene, shown to correlate with subjective realism ratings [12]. Lastly, binary object masks used in these techniques provide only limited information about the nature of the required corrections, indicating only the area where corrections are needed. This can result in the harmonisation algorithm over- or under-compensating in different local regions of the composite.

In a recent pilot study [11], the authors argue that explicit modeling of the *perception* of compositing artifacts, in addition to their improvement, would allow for harmonisation algorithms to be used in a *no reference* setting, whereby the input mask is not required at inference time. Thus, the model performs both the *detection* and *harmonisation* task. They also show that combining two off-the-shelf, pre-trained models – a detector [10] and a harmoniser [30] – can achieve comparable results to mask-based state-of-the-art harmonisation algorithms. This enables design of end-to-end harmonisation networks without the need for input object masks, allowing automatic harmonisation of content for which masks are not readily available. The authors also claim that the explicit encoding of the location and perceptual magnitude of errors in the model could allow the process to take advantage of the benefits of multi-task learning, feature sharing and attention mechanism in terms of generalisation [24,26]. The potential applications of such automatic compositing systems are wide-ranging, including improvement of legacy content, detection of image manipulations and forgery, perceptually-based metrics and image synthesis.

In this paper, we recapitulate and extend this work to an end-to-end model designed, trained and evaluated from scratch. First, we present the original proof-of-concept two-stage compositing pipeline [11]. This consists of a *detector* network, which outputs masks corresponding to regions in an input image requiring harmonisation, and a *harmoniser* network, which corrects the detected regions. We then evaluate the performance of the harmoniser based on using object masks predicted by the detector, versus using ground truth object masks. Based on the evaluation of the two-stage model, we then propose a single end-to-end model, and compare its performance to a set of baselines trained from scratch on the challenging iHarmony dataset, as well as the synthetic COCO-Exp dataset from the original study [11]. We show that our end-to-end model outperforms the baselines on both datasets. This indicates the usefulness of the pre-trained perceptual features to the compositing task using two different end-to-end architectures. To our knowledge, this is the first work investigating an end-to-end combination of a DL-based feature extractor, conditioned on a perceptual task, with an image harmonisation network to perform no reference image harmonisation.

The remainder of the paper is structured as follows: Sect. 2 introduces related work and discusses state-of-the-art techniques, Sect. 3 describes the original methodology adopted for the two-stage model evaluation, Sect. 4 presents the results of this evaluation and Sect. 5 discusses the findings [11]. In Sect. 6 we detail the methodology, architecture and optimisation details of the proposed end-to-end models, which are evaluated in Sect. 7. Finally, in Sect. 8, we review our findings in the context of the original study and wider application to image harmonisation. We also discuss the strengths and weaknesses of our approach, before concluding and considering future research directions in Sect. 9.

2   Related Work

2.1   Image Compositing and Harmonisation

Automatic image compositing and harmonisation are both active and challenging problems in the domain of image understanding, synthesis and processing. While, image compositing concerns the entire process of combining regions from different source images into a plausible whole, image harmonisation focuses on the problem of matching the various appearance features between the object and scene, such as noise, contrast, texture or blur, while assuming correctly aligned geometric and illumination properties [29].

Similarly to the problem of image in-painting, compositing and harmonisation are both ill-posed problems [16]. For a given region requiring correction, many different arrangements of pixels could be deemed plausible. This is in contrast to problems where the solution is unique. Depending on the content and context of an image composite, some scene properties, and thus required object corrections, may be inferred from the information contained within the image or its metadata, such as the characteristics of the illuminant [27], colour palette, contrast range or the camera response function. Other properties, such as an object's albedo, texture or shape are often unique to the object and cannot be derived directly from contextual information in the scene. While methods for approximation of these properties do exist [15], they are difficult to integrate into end-to-end systems and can be challenging to parametrise. The recent successes in DL have motivated a number of approaches [2,7,8,30] which attempt to exploit the huge amount of natural imagery available in public datasets in order to learn the mapping between a corrupted composite image and a corrected composite, or natural image.

2.2 Multi-task Learning, Feature Sharing and Attention

Due to the abundance of natural image data and the ill-posed nature of the compositing problem, DL approaches are well-suited for this task. However, supervised DL methods require large amounts of annotated data in order to learn and generalise well. This requirement grows along with the complexity of a problem and the desired accuracy. In order to tackle this issue, many architectural considerations have been proposed, many of which focus on learning good feature representations, which generalise well between tasks.

Multi-task learning approaches rely on performing multiple related tasks in order to learn better feature representations. In recent years many tasks in image understanding have achieved state-of-the-art performance by incorporating multi-task learning [14], for example in predicting depth and normals from a single RGB image [13], detection of face landmarks [36] or simultaneous image quality and distortion estimation [17]. This is afforded by the implicit regularisation that training a single model for multiple related tasks imposes [6], and the resulting improved generalisation. Feature sharing approaches combine deep features from related domains or tasks in order to create richer feature representations for a given task. This is similar to the multi-task paradigm, however instead of sharing a common intermediate feature representation, features from one or multiple layers of two or more networks are explicitly combined. The Deep Image Harmonisation (DIH) model [30] adopts both these paradigms, by combining the tasks of image semgentation and harmonisation and sharing deep features of both task branches. Finally, attention mechanisms [9] can also be used to learn the relative importance of latent features for different combinations of task and input sample.

2.3   No More Masks

State-of-the-art image harmonisation methods focus largely on improving composites in scenarios where the identity of pixels belonging to the object and scene are known a priori. For example, the DIH approach [30] uses a AE-based architecture to map corrupted composites to corrected ones, incorporating a two-task paradigm, which attempts to both correct the composite, as well as segmenting the scene. However, this approach does not explicitly condition the network to learn anything more about the corruption, such as its magnitude, type or location. Instead object location information is explicitly provided at input, using a binary mask. A similar approach [7] inputs the object mask at training time, while also introducing mask segmentation and refinement within a GAN architecture, in addition to learning of geometric transformations of the object. The segmentation network, as part of the adversarial training process, discriminates towards ground truth binary masks as an output - omitting any perceptual factor in the discrimination task. This achieves improved results compared to the AE, however at the cost of a more complex architecture and adversarial training. Due to the many dimensions along which combinations of object and scene may vary, compositing systems should be equipped to encode such differences before attempting to correct them. Kang et al. (2015) [17] show that a multi-task approach is an efficient way to ensure that distortions are appropriately encoded by the model. Other approaches to this problem include self-supervised pre-training to enforce equivariance of the latent representation to certain input transformations [34], which has been used to train perceptually-aligned local transformation classifiers [10], also used in the proposed model.

3   Two-Stage Model: Methodology

3.1   Motivation

Whilst multi-task learning has been shown to be efficient in the coupled process of detecting and correcting arbitrary pixel level transformations within images, perceptually-based encoding of artifacts within masks has not yet been shown to be effective in the image harmonisation field. Before approaching the multi-task model, it is necessary to prove empirically that this end-to-end process is viable. Thus we first design a two-stage approach using two existing standalone networks for both detection and harmonisation to test the efficacy of these perceptual masks in this domain.

3.2   Approach

Our overarching goal is the design of an end-to-end automatic compositing pipeline, capable of detection and correction of common compositing artifacts, without the need for specification of an object mask. In order to evaluate the effectiveness of this approach, we assess predicted, perceptually-informed object

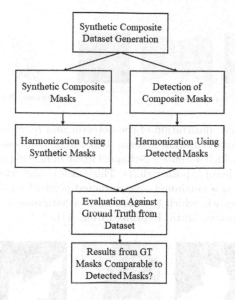

Fig. 1. Illustration of research methodology adopted in the two-stage model evaluation. Reprinted from [11].

masks, rather than ground truth object masks, as input to the deep harmonisation algorithm. We then measure similarity between ground truth images and composites corrected with the harmonisation algorithm, using either the original synthetic binary masks M_s or the perceptually-based masks predicted by the detector M_p. Accordingly, we refer to composites harmonised using ground truth masks as C_s, and composites generated by the end-to-end system as C_p.

We evaluate the hypothesis that the performance of an end-to-end detection and harmonisation model is comparable to a harmonisation model using manually created object masks. Confirmation of this hypothesis would support our case for incorporating explicit detection of composite artefacts into end-to-end image composite harmonisation systems. Our research methodology is summarised in Fig. 1.

3.3 Detector and Harmoniser Models

Both the detector (referred to as the PTC henceforth) [10] and the harmoniser (referred to as the DIH) [30] are deep, image-to-image, fully convolutional autoencoder networks. The PTC takes a single image as input and generates a 2-channel output mask, which encodes probabilities for each pixel, p, in the input image as being affected by a negative (channel 0) or a positive (channel 1) perceptually suprathreshold exposure offset. We combine these two suprathreshold channels by taking a pixel-wise maximum $\max(p_0, p_1)$. This way we generate a single mask of the same resolution as M_s, with the difference that each pixel encodes the probability of a suprathreshold exposure offset. We do not apply

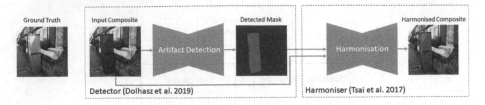

Fig. 2. System overview: illustration of the detector and harmoniser combined into a two-stage composite harmonisation system. A synthetic composite image is first supplied to the detector, which outputs a 2-channel mask indicating detected negative and positive (not pictured here) exposure shifts. This mask is converted to a single-channel representation by taking a maximum over predicted pixel-wise probabilities and fed to the harmonisation network, which then produces a harmonised composite, which we compare against the ground truth. Reprinted from [11].

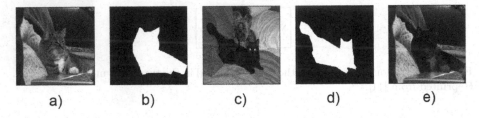

a)   b)   c)   d)   e)

Fig. 3. Dataset generation process adapted from [30]: a) source image sampled from MSCOCO, b) corresponding object mask, c) target image, d) target image object mask, e) result of luminance transfer [25] of source - c), to target - e. Reprinted from [11].

any modifications to the DIH and adopt the authors' original trained implementation. The final detector+harmoniser (PTC+DIH) system can be see in Fig. 2.

3.4 COCO-Exp Dataset

To perform a fair comparison, we follow the composite generation approach of [30]. Specifically, we sample pairs of images containing objects belonging to the same semantic category (e.g. person, dog, bottle etc.) from the MSCOCO dataset [21]. Using their corresponding object masks, we perform statistical colour transfer based on histogram matching, proposed by [25]. This process can be see in Fig. 3. This colour transfer is performed between object regions of the same semantic category. As the detector is only conditioned for exposure offsets, we perform colour transfer only on the luminance channel of Lab colourspace. We generate a total of 68128 composites and corresponding ground truth images. We also extract corresponding ground truth masks for comparison against the masks predicted by the detector. For the sake of brevity, we refer to this dataset as *COCO-Exp* throughout the remainder of this paper.

3.5 Similarity Metrics

To evaluate each of the two approaches, we calculate similarity metrics between ground truth images C_{gt} and harmonised images, corrected by the methods under test: C_s (harmonised using ground truth masks), and C_p (harmonised using predicted masks). We adopt the objective metrics used in the original work, i.e. Mean Squared Error (MSE):

$$MSE = \frac{1}{N} \sum_{i=0}^{n} (Y_i - \hat{Y}_i)^2 \tag{1}$$

where Y is the ground truth and $\hat{Y}$ is the harmonised image (either C_p or C_s), and Peak Signal-to-Noise ratio (PSNR):

$$PSNR = 10 \log_{10} \left(\frac{R^2}{MSE} \right) \tag{2}$$

here R is the maximum possible pixel intensity - 255 for an 8 bit image. In addition, we leverage the Learned Perceptual Image Patch Similarity (LPIPS) [35], which measures similarity based on human perceptual characteristics. We denote these errors with subscripts referring to the method the composite was fixed with, e.g. MSE_p for MSE between the ground truth image and corresponding composite fixed using predicted masks; MSE_s for MSE between ground truth and a composite fixed using the original MSCOCO masks.

3.6 Evaluation Procedure

Using our generated composite dataset we first evaluate the DIH with ground truth masks. We then use the same dataset to generate predicted object masks using the PTC and feed these along with the corresponding composite images to the DIH. We obtain two sets of corrected composites: composites corrected using the ground truth masks C_s and composites fixed using masks predicted by the PTC C_p. We then calculate similarity metrics between the ground truth images used to generate the composites in the first place, and each of the two sets of corrected images C_s and C_p. These are reported in the following section.

4 Two-Stage Model: Results

The results of our evaluation can be seen in Fig. 4, which shows distributions of each of the similarity metrics calculated between ground truth images and composites fixed using C_s and C_p respectively. Mean similarity metrics can be seen in Table 1. Overall, masks predicted by the detector yield higher average errors across all three metrics compared to the ground truth masks, however the magnitude of these differences is small for each of the metrics. Figure 5 shows distributions of image-wise error differentials for both techniques.

Table 1. Means of similarity metrics for both techniques evaluated against ground truth: DIH, and the PTC+DIH. Lower is better for LPIPS and MSE, higher is better for PSNR. Reprinted from [11].

Metric	DIH	PTC+DIH
MSE	19.55	22.65
PSNR	35.81	35.18
LPIPS	0.0227	0.0292

5   Two Stage Model: Discussion

Our results indicate that using detected, instead of ground truth object masks can yield comparable results when performing automatic image composite harmonisation. Errors obtained using ground truth masks are on average lower compared to those obtained using predicted masks, however in a number of cases the situation is reversed. Figure 6 illustrates examples of failure cases, where Figs. 6c 6d show cases of the DIH over-compensating, while the PTC+DIH combination achieves a more natural-looking result. We stress that these results were obtained with no additional training. Further investigation indicates particular scenarios where this occurs. In some cases, the harmonisation algorithm applies an inappropriate correction, rendering a higher error for C_s compared to the un-harmonised input. Then, if M_p does not approximate M_s well, is blank (no detection) or its average intensity is lower than that of M_s, the additional error induced by the harmonisation algorithm is minimised, rendering lower errors for C_p. This can be seen in both images in Fig. 6d. This indicates the benefit of a perceptually motivated approach to mask prediction, allowing the influence over the weight of the transformation applied by the harmoniser. We also notice that the deep harmonisation network tends to apply colour transformations regardless of whether they are required. In some cases, the perceptually-based masks mitigate this problem. Images showing examples of comparable performance of the two methods can be found in Fig. 7. Subfigures c and d show the results of harmonisation using the approaches under test and subfigures e and f show M_p and M_s respectively.

Due to the nature of the PTC currently operating solely on luminance transforms, a further benefit to the multi-task learning paradigm is the generalisability to arbitrary pixel level transforms, for example colour shifts. The binary masks accepted by harmoniser networks currently do not separate across these transforms, they treat them all homogeneously. A perceptually motivated approach to the predicted mask can encode, on a feature-by-feature basis, the perceptual likelihood of harmonisation required. This is not to say, necessarily, that deep harmonisation networks cannot learn this behaviour, but provision of further support to encode this non-linearity at the input to the network, and/or by explicit optimisation at the output, would likely benefit performance and improve generalisation [6]. This is conceptually similar to curriculum learning

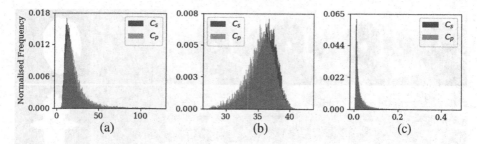

Fig. 4. Similarity metric distributions for both C_s (composites corrected with synthetic ground truth masks) and C_p (corrected with masks predicted by the detector) (a) MSE, (b) PSNR and (c) LPIPS. Larger values indicate poorer performance for MSE and LPIPS, better for PSNR. Reprinted from [11].

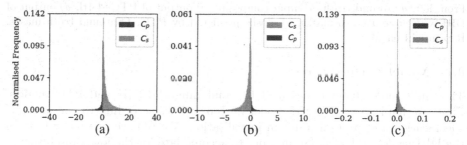

Fig. 5. The image-wise error differentials for C_p-C_s, for each of the three metrics: (a) MSE, (b) PSNR and (c) LPIPS. Note, negative values for MSE and LPIPS indicate images for which C_p (composites corrected with masks predicted by the detector) achieves lower error than C_s (composites corrected with synthetic ground truth masks). For PSNR, the obverse is true. Reprinted from [11].

improving convergence in reinforcement learning problems [3], or unsupervised pre-training techniques improving convergence in general.

6   End-to-End Model: Methodology

In Sect. 4 we illustrated that perceptually-based detection of local image transformations can be leveraged to generate composite masks, achieving comparable results to ground truth masks when evaluated on an image harmonisation task using a state-of-the-art harmonisation model. This indicates that an end-to-end model combining both these tasks could be used to perform *no reference* harmonisation, removing the need for provision of object masks for both training and inference, as opposed to current state-of-the-art approaches. Joint training would also allow for overall performance improvements and enable different combinations of the source models to be evaluated. Thus, to perform a fair evaluation, we implement the end-to-end model and the state-of-the-art baseline from scratch, and train both on the iHarmony dataset [8].

Fig. 6. Examples of the DIH with ground truth masks over-compensating, and applying colour shifts to compensate a luminance transform, resulting in suboptimal output. From left: *a)* ground truth, *b)* input composite, *c)* output of PTC+DIH, *d)* output of DIH with ground truth masks, *e)* masks predicted by PTC, *f)* ground truth masks. Reprinted from [11].

6.1   Model Architectures

The end-to-end model is designed by combining the DIH and PTC models. First, we implement the DIH model in Tensorflow, according to the authors' specification and perform random initialisation. We remove one outer layer of the DIH model, following [8], in order to accomodate for the lower resolution of the PTC and perform all training using a resolution of 256×256.

We evaluate two approaches to combining the source models. The first approach, *PTC-DIH* combines the models sequentially, whereby the PTC generates a mask from the input image, which is then concatenated with the input and fed to the DIH model, as illustrated in Fig. 2. We replace the original 3-class softmax output of the PTC, and replace it with a single-channel sigmoid output, to match the input of the DIH model. We also add up- and downsampling operations in order to adapt the input image to the 224×224 resolution of the PTC, and its output to the 256×256 input of the DIH.

The second approach, *PTC-att-DIH*, inspired by self-attention mechanisms [31], relies on combining the latent features of both models through an attention-like dot product:

$$a_{joint} = fc_3\Big(\sigma\big(fc_1(a_{ptc})\big) \cdot fc_2(a_{dih})\Big) \tag{3}$$

where a_{ptc} is a vector of flattened activations from the bottleneck layer of the PTC, a_{dih} is a vector of activations from the last convolutional layer of the DIH encoder, fc_n are fully-connected layers with 512 neurons each, and σ is a softmax activation.

In both the PTC-DIH and PTC-att-DIH the encoder of the PTC is frozen during training, as in [10], however in the case of PTC-DIH, the decoder of the PTC is allowed to learn, while in the PTC-att-DIH only the encoder is used. The PTC does not receive any additional supervisory signals, such as ground truth object masks, or scene segmentation, only the end-to-end MSE harmonisation loss.

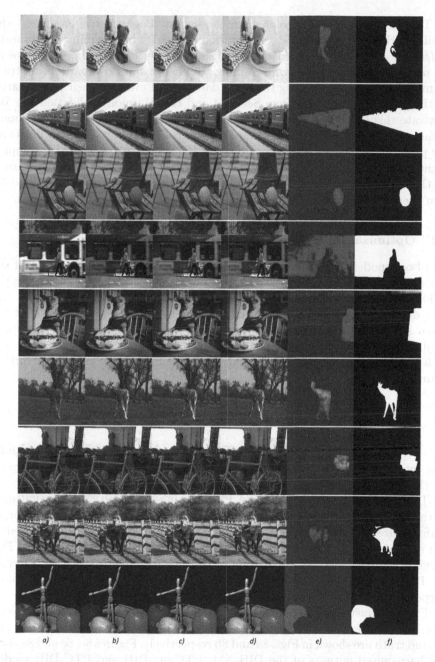

Fig. 7. Comparison of harmonisation outputs from our evaluation. From left to right: a) ground truth, b) input composite, c) corrected with PTC+DIH (C_p), d) corrected with ground truth masks + DIH (C_s), e) Detected masks (M_p), f) ground truth masks (M_s). Masks in colour indicate the raw output of the PTC, where the direction of detected luminance shifts is indicated - red for negative and green for positive shifts. Reprinted from [11]. (Color figure online)

The performance of our joint model is evaluated against two baselines - the vanilla DIH (without semantic segmentation branch), which requires input masks (*DIH-M*), and a no-mask version of the same model (*DIH-NM*), where masks are not provided as input during training. To ensure a fair comparison, we train all models from scratch, using the same dataset and evaluate their performance on the COCO-Exp dataset from Sect. 3.4 and the iHarmony validation set. We motivate this by the fact that the original PTC implementation is only conditioned on exposure shifts, so a comparison across both datasets can illustrate the performance for simple exposure shifts (COCO-Exp) versus more complex colour transformations (iHarmony). If the perceptually-based features learned by the PTC generalise well across image features, an improvement should be seen over the naive DIH-NM model when evaluated on both these datasets.

6.2   Optimization Details

All of our models are trained for 50 epochs using the entire training set of the iHarmony dataset, consisting of 65742 training images and evaluated using the validation set, consisting of 7404 validation images. The Adam optimizer [18] with default parameters and an initial learning rate of 0.001 is used. We set the batch size to 32 and enforce a 256×256 resolution. We apply pre-processing to all input images scaling the pixel intensity range from $[0, 255]$ to $[-1, 1]$. For each training run, we select the model minimising validation loss for further evaluation.

7   End-to-End Model: Results

This section presents the evaluation of the proposed models on both the validation set of the iHarmony dataset, as well as the COCO-Exp dataset generated for the preliminary study.

Table 2 shows average MSE and PSNR values for both datasets and each of the models. We find that both of our proposed end-to-end models improve performance on both the iHarmony and COCO-Exp datasets, as compared to the naive baseline, when performing harmonization with no input mask. This suggests the PTC features are relevant to the image harmonisation task. Overall, the PTC-DIH achieves best performance in harmonisation with no input mask, outperforming the PTC-att-DIH and the DIH-NM baseline.

Figure 8 illustrates the performance of all models under evaluation for several images from the COCO-Exp dataset. Specifically, in each row the input and ground truth are shown in Figs. 8a and 8b respectively. Figures 8c, 8e and 8g show the harmonised outputs of the DIH-NM, PTC-att-DIH and PTC-DIH models respectively, while Figs. 8d, 8f and 8h are difference image heatmaps between the input and the harmonised output predicted by each model. These heatmaps provide an illustration of the magnitude, direction and location of the applied correction. Upon inspection of similarity metrics, the harmonised outputs and the difference heatmaps, it can be seen that the PTC-DIH model outperforms

Table 2. Test metrics for all evaluated models, across the two datasets used in our experiments. Lower is better for MSE, higher is better for PSNR. Best results using no input mask in bold. Results for the input-mask-based baseline (DIH-M) shown for reference. Higher is better for PSNR, lower is better for MSE.

Model	iHarmony		COCO-Exp	
	MSE	PSNR	MSE	PSNR
DIH-M	89	32.56	201	32.18
DIH-NM	153	30.93	276	31.12
PTC-att-DIH	151	31.02	264	31.37
PTC-DIH	**124**	**31.39**	**214**	**31.61**

both the baseline (DIH-NM) and the latent-space-based combination of both models (PTC-att-DIH). This can be seen clearly when comparing the difference images: the PTC-DIH applies corrections more consistently across the region of the target object, compared to the two alternatives. Figure 9 compares the performance of the PTC-DIH to the mask-based DIH-M model for 3 versions of an input image from iHarmony. It can be noticed that the output of both the PTC-DIH and DIH-M closely follow that of the reference. The area corrected by the PTC-DIH aligns with the ground truth mask. Small differeneces in the output images can be noted, particularly around edges, where the PTC-DIH sometimes contribues to softness and smearing (e.g. Figure 9e, middle row). We found this was often related to artifacts around the edges of objects and near edges of images produced by the PTC. Nonetheless, despite the lack of input mask, the PTC-DIH achieves consistent and comparable results for each of the image variations and, in some cases, avoids the colour shifts induced by the DIH (e.g. compare columns d) and e) with column c) of Fig. 9), as discussed in Sect. 5.

Examples of failure cases can be seen in Fig. 10. The top two rows illustrate the most common failure case, where the region requiring harmonisation is not detected, and thus not corrected by the model. The top row illustrates this scenario for a larger object size, while the middle row does so for a small object (one of the sheep near the bottom of the image). The bottom row shows a scenario where the harmonisation is performed on the correct object, however the amount of correction is insufficient. In addition, the model applies harmonisation to a part of the image not requiring harmonisation (the screen). This behaviour is likely due to the fact that the PTC was originally conditioned on exposure shifts, resulting in higher sensitivity to over-exposure, compared to other image distortions.

The impact of object size on harmonisation performance of all models is summarised in Table 3 for both the iHarmony and COCO-Exp datasets. Because the MSE is calculated across the entire image, errors are overall lower for smaller objects. However, when comparing the MSE of harmonised images against their baseline MSE (calculated between the input image and ground truth), the relative MSE improvements are greatest for larger objects. This trend is present

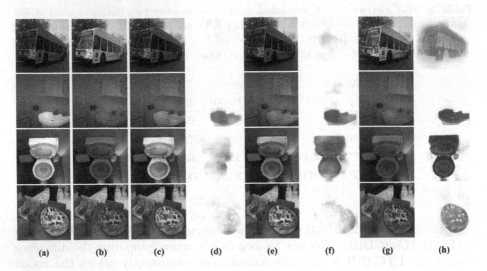

(a)   (b)   (c)   (d)   (e)   (f)   (g)   (h)

Fig. 8. Comparison of outputs from each model under evaluation for a range of images from the COCO-Exp dataset. *a)* input image *b)* ground truth *c)* DIH-NM result *d)* Difference image between input and output for DIH-NM *e)* PTC-att-DIH result *f)* difference image between input and output for PTC-att-DIH *g)* PTC-DIH result h) PTC-DIH difference image. In difference images, red indicates that $\hat{y}_{i,j} - x_{i,j} > 0.0$ whereas blue indicates the opposite. (Color figure online)

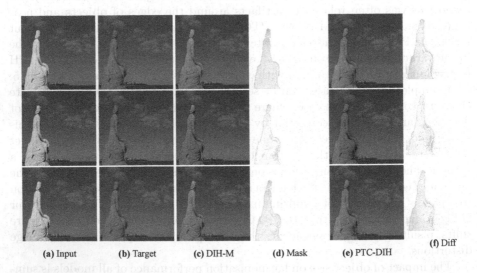

(a) Input   (b) Target   (c) DIH-M   (d) Mask   (e) PTC-DIH   (f) Diff

Fig. 9. Comparison between the corrections applied by PTC-DIH, and the mask-based DIH-M models for multiple variants of the same image. a) input composite, b) ground truth image c) output of DIH-M, d) Difference heatmap between output of DIH-M and ground truth, e) output of PTC-DIH, f) Difference heatmap between output of PTC-DIH and ground truth.

across both datasets. The PTC-DIH achieves lowest errors in each object size category across both datasets. Notably, for objects in the COCO-Exp dataset with areas ranging 20–40% of the image size, the PTC-DIH model achieves lower errors than the mask-based DIH-M baseline. This illustrates the impact of the PTC being conditioned on only exposure shifts, but also indicates that these features are useful when transferred to a different type of transformations, such as those in iHarmony.

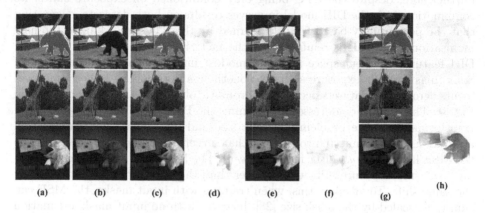

(a)   (b)   (c)   (d)   (e)   (f)   (g)   (h)

Fig. 10. Examples of failure cases. *a)* input image *b)* ground truth *c)* DIH-NM result *d)* Difference image between input and output for DIH-NM *e)* PTC-att-DIH result *f)* difference image between input and output for PTC-att-DIH g) PTC-DIH result h) PTC-DIH difference image.

Table 3. Average MSE on the iHarmony and COCO-Exp datasets for each of the evaluated models, grouped by area of harmonised object as a fraction of image size. *MSE orig* is the MSE between unharmonised inputs and ground truth. Bold values indicate lowest error for each object size, given no mask input. DIH-M model shown for reference.

iHarmony								
Object Size	0–10%	10–20%	20–30%	30–40%	40–50%	50–60%	60–70%	70–80%
DIH-M	33.0	116.1	206.5	335.05	456.2	485.48	484.58	705.12
MSE orig.	47.1	235.02	449.84	642.75	1170.31	1222.97	1151.83	1752.12
DIH-NM	50.73	192.22	360.98	497.42	919.29	1058.39	888.11	1534.94
PTC-att-DIH	50.36	190.2	370.65	462.72	884.22	1001.85	933.02	1659.24
PTC-DIH	**45.02**	**150.04**	**311.72**	**359.99**	**623.03**	**895.33**	**720.82**	**1464.62**
COCO-Exp								
Object Size	0–10%	10–20%	20–30%	30–40%	40–50%	50–60%	60–70%	70–80%
DIH-M	73.74	401.55	655.11	785.35	927.68	1042.68	1119.19	1129.01
MSE orig	86.11	524.29	878.42	1131.53	1503.27	1802.57	2072.08	2097.13
DIH-NM	94.3	502.63	828.69	1045.05	1373.97	1661.55	1876.75	1958.01
PTC-att-DIH	93.26	492.65	802.24	986.49	1271.15	1510.16	1684.99	1806.24
PTC-DIH	**82.35**	**410.08**	**647.13**	**778.76**	**946.99**	**1084.28**	**1240.54**	**1295.38**

8   Discussion

The results of both experiments indicate that, in the context of image harmonisation, perceptually-based detection of harmonisation targets can be used to remove the requirement for input object masks. While the proposed approach does not outperform baseline mask-based approaches, it performs significantly better than the state-of-the-art baseline when trained with no input masks. Furthermore, despite the PTC being only conditioned on exposure shifts, its combination with the DIH model improves results on both datasets, suggesting that the perceptually-based features learned by the PTC are useful to the harmonisation task. This is reinforced by the fact that even combining PTC and DIH features in latent space affords a modest improvement over the baseline. Some bias towards exposure shifts is nonetheless noticeable - largest improvements across both datasets occur for achromatic objects (e.g. the sink or toilet in Fig. 8). This could be addressed by training the PTC on a wider range of local transformations. The problem of object size and its impact on harmonisation accuracy is likely connected to the fact that larger objects tend to contribute to the MSE more, compared to smaller objects. The MSE for a small object requiring a 0.5 stop exposure shift will be lower than that of a larger object requiring the same shift. To alleviate this, when training with input masks, the MSE can simply be scaled by the mask size [28], however with no input mask, estimation of target object area becomes nontrivial and presents and interesting direction for further research.

Not unlike the original DIH implementation, the proposed end-to-end model can suffer from gradient artifacts along mask edges, particularly when the initial error to be corrected is large. This issue could be addressed by adopting masked convolutions and utilising self-attention mechanisms, as in [8] or by explicitly incorporating gradient information, as in [33]. While we plan to address these issues in future work, the advantages of our proposed model demonstrated in this work still hold in the context of image harmonisation with no input mask. Following [10], we argue that in order to improve image harmonisation performance, particularly in scenarios where input masks are not available, detection of target regions for harmonisation should leverage intermediate representations equivariant to the transformations of the input to be harmonised. Input masks used in state-of-the-art harmonisation algorithms mimic this role - they encode the presence and location of all input transformations requiring harmonisation as a local binary feature, thus receiving a form of an extra supervisory signal. Our results show that explicitly incorporating the artifact detection paradigm into the harmonisation process can be beneficial, while alleviating the requirements for presence of object masks at inference time.

9   Conclusions and Future Work

In this paper, we have evaluated a novel method for performing image harmonisation without the need for input object masks. Our approach leverages two state-of-the-art models - an artifact detector and a harmoniser - which, when combined, produce competitive results to mask-based models. We first perform a two-stage evaluation of the original pre-trained models, and based on evaluation results, extend this to a custom end-to-end model in two variants, trained from scratch on the challenging iHarmony dataset. We show that both variants of our end-to-end model outperform the baselines when evaluated on two different datasets. These findings indicate that information about location and magnitude of composite artifacts can be useful in improving the performance of existing compositing and harmonisation approaches. We motivate this by illustrating that ground truth object masks commonly used in harmonisation algorithms essentially substitute the process of detecting local transformations and inconsistencies requiring correction. Accordingly, our results show that the requirement for provision of object masks for such algorithms can be relaxed or removed entirely by the explicit combination of composite artifact detection with their correction. This provides a basis for investigation in future work of joint modeling of both the detection and correction of composite image artifacts, e.g. under a multi-task learning paradigm, where a joint latent representation is conditioned both to be equivariant with respect to input transformations and to encode the structure of the image. In such a scenario, input masks may be used during the training stage, but would not be necessary during inference.

References

1. Agarwala, A., et al.: Interactive digital photomontage. In: ACM Trans. Graph. (ToG) **23**, 294–302. ACM (2004)
2. Azadi, S., Pathak, D., Ebrahimi, S., Darrell, T.: Compositional gan: Learning conditional image composition. arXiv preprint arXiv:1807.07560 (2018)
3. Bengio, Y., Louradour, J., Collobert, R., Weston, J.: Curriculum learning. In: Proceedings of the 26th Annual International Conference on Machine Learning, pp. 41–48 (2009)
4. Burt, P., Adelson, E.: The laplacian pyramid as a compact image code. IEEE Trans. Commun. **31**(4), 532–540 (1983)
5. Burt, P.J., Adelson, E.H.: A multiresolution spline with application to image mosaics. ACM Trans. Graph. **2**(4), 217–236 (1983)
6. Caruana, R.: Multitask learning. Mach. Learn. **28**(1), 41–75 (1997)
7. Chen, B.C., Kae, A.: Toward realistic image compositing with adversarial learning. In: Proceedings of the IEEE Conference on Computer Vision and Pattern Recognition, pp. 8415–8424 (2019)
8. Cong, W., et al.: Dovenet: deep image harmonization via domain verification. In: Proceedings of the IEEE/CVF Conference on Computer Vision and Pattern Recognition, pp. 8394–8403 (2020)
9. Cun, X., Pun, C.M.: Improving the harmony of the composite image by spatial-separated attention module. IEEE Trans. Image Process. **29**, 4759–4771 (2020)
10. Dolhasz, A., Harvey, C., Williams, I.: Learning to observe: approximating human perceptual thresholds for detection of suprathreshold image transformations. In: Proceedings of the IEEE/CVF Conference on Computer Vision and Pattern Recognition, pp. 4797–4807 (2020)

11. Dolhasz., A., Harvey., C., Williams., I.: Towards unsupervised image harmonisation. In: Proceedings of the 15th International Joint Conference on Computer Vision, Imaging and Computer Graphics Theory and Applications - Volume 5: VISAPP, pp. 574–581. INSTICC, SciTePress (2020). https://doi.org/10.5220/0009354705740581

12. Dolhasz, A., Williams, I., Frutos-Pascual, M.: Measuring observer response to object-scene disparity in composites. In: 2016 IEEE International Symposium on Mixed and Augmented Reality (ISMAR-Adjunct), pp. 13–18. IEEE (2016)

13. Eigen, D., Fergus, R.: Predicting depth, surface normals and semantic labels with a common multi-scale convolutional architecture. In: Proceedings of the IEEE International Conference on Computer Vision, pp. 2650–2658 (2015)

14. Evgeniou, T., Pontil, M.: Regularized multi-task learning. In: Proceedings of the tenth ACM SIGKDD International Conference on Knowledge Discovery and Data Mining, pp. 109–117. ACM (2004)

15. Gardner, M.A., et al.: Learning to predict indoor illumination from a single image. arXiv preprint arXiv:1704.00090 (2017)

16. Guillemot, C., Le Meur, O.: Image inpainting: overview and recent advances. IEEE Signal Process. Mag. **31**(1), 127–144 (2013)

17. Kang, L., Ye, P., Li, Y., Doermann, D.: Simultaneous estimation of image quality and distortion via multi-task convolutional neural networks. In: 2015 IEEE International Conference on Image Processing (ICIP), pp. 2791–2795. IEEE (2015)

18. Kingma, D.P., Ba, J.: Adam: A method for stochastic optimization. arXiv preprint arXiv:1412.6980 (2014)

19. Lalonde, J.F., Efros, A.A.: Using color compatibility for assessing image realism. In: 2007 IEEE 11th International Conference on Computer Vision, pp. 1–8. IEEE (2007)

20. Levin, A., Lischinski, D., Weiss, Y.: Colorization using optimization. ACM Trans. Graph. (tog) **23**, 689–694. ACM (2004)

21. Lin, T.-Y., et al.: Microsoft COCO: common objects in context. In: Fleet, D., Pajdla, T., Schiele, B., Tuytelaars, T. (eds.) ECCV 2014. LNCS, vol. 8693, pp. 740–755. Springer, Cham (2014). https://doi.org/10.1007/978-3-319-10602-1_48

22. Pérez, P., Gangnet, M., Blake, A.: Poisson image editing. ACM Trans. Graph. (TOG) **22**(3), 313–318 (2003)

23. Porter, T., Duff, T.: Compositing digital images. In: ACM Siggraph Comput. Graph. **18**, 253–259. ACM (1984)

24. Ranjan, R., Patel, V.M., Chellappa, R.: Hyperface: a deep multi-task learning framework for face detection, landmark localization, pose estimation, and gender recognition. IEEE Trans. Pattern Anal. Mach. Intell. **41**(1), 121–135 (2017)

25. Reinhard, E., Adhikhmin, M., Gooch, B., Shirley, P.: Color transfer between images. IEEE Comput. Graph. Appl. **21**(5), 34–41 (2001)

26. Ruder, S.: An overview of multi-task learning in deep neural networks. arXiv preprint arXiv:1706.05098 (2017)

27. Shi, W., Loy, C.C., Tang, X.: Deep specialized network for illuminant estimation. In: Leibe, B., Matas, J., Sebe, N., Welling, M. (eds.) ECCV 2016. LNCS, vol. 9908, pp. 371–387. Springer, Cham (2016). https://doi.org/10.1007/978-3-319-46493-0_23

28. Sofiiuk, K., Popenova, P., Konushin, A.: Foreground-aware semantic representations for image harmonization. arXiv preprint arXiv:2006.00809 (2020)

29. Sunkavalli, K., Johnson, M.K., Matusik, W., Pfister, H.: Multi-scale image harmonization. ACM Trans. Graph. (TOG) **29**(4), 125 (2010)

30. Tsai, Y.H., Shen, X., Lin, Z., Sunkavalli, K., Lu, X., Yang, M.H.: Deep image harmonization. In: Proceedings of the IEEE Conference on Computer Vision and Pattern Recognition, pp. 3789–3797 (2017)
31. Vaswani, A., et al.: Attention is all you need. In: Advances in Neural Information Processing Systems, pp. 5998–6008 (2017)
32. Wright, S.: Digital Compositing for Film and Video. Routledge, Abingdon-on-Thames (2013)
33. Wu, H., Zheng, S., Zhang, J., Huang, K.: Gp-gan: towards realistic high-resolution image blending. In: Proceedings of the 27th ACM International Conference on Multimedia, pp. 2487–2495. ACM (2019)
34. Zhang, L., Qi, G.J., Wang, L., Luo, J.: AET vs. AED: unsupervised representation learning by auto-encoding transformations rather than data. In: Proceedings of the IEEE Conference on Computer Vision and Pattern Recognition, pp. 2547–2555 (2019)
35. Zhang, R., Isola, P., Efros, A.A., Shechtman, E., Wang, O.: The unreasonable effectiveness of deep features as a perceptual metric. In: CVPR (2018)
36. Zhang, Z., Luo, P., Loy, C.C., Tang, X.: Facial landmark detection by deep multi-task learning. In: Fleet, D., Pajdla, T., Schiele, B., Tuytelaars, T. (eds.) ECCV 2014. LNCS, vol. 8694, pp. 94–108. Springer, Cham (2014). https://doi.org/10.1007/978-3-319-10599-4_7

On-board UAV Pilots Identification in Counter UAV Images

Dario Cazzato[⊠] ⓘ, Claudio Cimarelli ⓘ, and Holger Voos ⓘ

Interdisciplinary Center for Security, Reliability and Trust (SnT), University of Luxembourg,
29, Avenue J. F. Kennedy, 1855 Luxembourg, Luxembourg
{dario.cazzato,claudio.cimarelli,holger.voos}@uni.lu
https://wwwen.uni.lu/snt/research/automation_robotics_research_group

Abstract. Among Unmanned Aerial Vehicles (UAV) countermeasures, the detection of the drone position and the identification of the human pilot represent two crucial tasks, as demonstrated by the attention already obtained from security agencies in different countries. Many research works focus on the UAV detection but they rarely take into account the problem of the detection of the pilot of another approaching UAV. This work proposes a full autonomous pipeline that, taking images from a flying UAV, can detect the humans in the scene and recognizing the eventual presence of the pilot(s). The system has been designed to be run on-board of the UAV, and tests have been performed on an NVIDIA Jetson TX2. Moreover, the SnT-ARG-PilotDetect dataset, designed to assess the capabilities to identify the UAV pilots in realistic scenarios, is introduced for the first time and made publicly available. An accurate comparison of different classification approaches on the pilot and non-pilot images of the proposed dataset has been performed, and results show the validity of the proposed pipeline for piloting behavior classification.

Keywords: Pilot detection · Unmanned aerial vehicles · People detection · Skeleton estimation

1 Introduction

Unmanned Aerial Vehicles (UAVs) are aircraft without a human pilot on-board, and their popularity has exponentially increased as a business opportunity to automate processes and replacing human effort. How aerial robotics can actively benefit from the latest computer vision research results is a matter of fact, as demonstrated by the numerous successful application fields where image understanding has strengthened the autonomous flying system capabilities, from precision agriculture [2] to road traffic monitoring [19], from surveillance and security [3] to autonomous inspection [9]. In this arena, scene understanding is a fundamental component to achieve fully autonomous operational capabilities to flight over real and complex scenarios [22] and, in particular, the detection of the objects of interest that depends on the specific domain. To address this undoubtedly important task, the most employed sensor is by far RGB cameras due to costs, dimensions, and the wide literature on RGB-based object detection.

© Springer Nature Switzerland AG 2022
K. Bouatouch et al. (Eds.): VISIGRAPP 2020, CCIS 1474, pp. 414–430, 2022.
https://doi.org/10.1007/978-3-030-94893-1_19

This advantage is even more evident in the case of UAVs, as it delivers an immediate benefit in terms of smaller payload and overall frame's size, with a clear impact in the production's final cost.

During the last decade, the consumer-grade drone's market has experienced a steep increase in terms of sold units directed towards the hobbyist audience, from photography to racing. Such interest in flying robots develops even further in the popular practice of building customized platforms. Whereas renown drones manufacturers can enforce more easily regulations, for instance, by means of flying restrictions on particular areas through limitations imposed by official software distributions, the air traffic generated from the spread of custom drones is more problematic to control [12]. In fact, in the latter case, it is entirely up to the drone owner to remain updated on the latest local rules and to comply with them even in regions where these are somewhat hazy. Electronic licence plates are envisaged as a possible mean to achieve, in the recent future, remote aircraft's identification using broadcast signals while ensuring the privacy for the pilots through ID code-numbers accessible only to law enforcement's authorized personnel [1,28]. However, the need for appropriate countermeasures is justified by the possibility of rogue drone operators whom often happen to violate restricted and sensible areas, such as airports, as recent news have shown, becoming a threat for the community [16]. Hence, it becomes critical to search for safe and robust countermeasures against potential misuses. As a consequence, UAVs identification represents a very popular research area [6,11,35], based on the optical, acoustical and/or radio-frequency analysis.

Nevertheless, it is important not only the detection and tracking of the UAV intruding restricted airspace, but also to identify the eventual UAV pilot. In fact, despite advances in vision-based surveillance, still very few works have proposed to identify the UAV human operator, especially in scenarios where the pilot can be in crowds or in general with the conjunct presence of other people. This aspect is critical to propose different security and forensic countermeasures, but also to mitigate hijacking risk.

This work presents an investigation of the possibility to use counter UAV on-board processing capabilities to perform UAV(s) pilot(s) identification. The proposed approach employs state of the art neural networks to extract the region and the skeleton of people present in the recorded scene. For each person, the 2D pixel positions of the joints composing the estimated skeleton are extracted and used to discriminate between pilots and non-pilots. Moreover, a labelled dataset consisting of images of different people that perform three behaviors, namely "*pilot*", "*non-pilot*" and "*mobile phone*", is introduced. As the best of our knowledge, this is the first dataset of this type. Finally, different classification approaches are proposed and validated on the aforementioned dataset.

Summing up, the main contributions of this document are:

- a pipeline specifically adapted to exploit the lower on-board computation capabilities of the UAV in order to identify UAV pilots;
- the introduction of the first and publicly available dataset for the task of pilot identification;
- an accurate comparison of different classification approaches on the introduced dataset.

The rest of the manuscript is organized as follows: Sect. 2 reports the related work, while Sect. 3 introduces the proposed pipeline, detailing single blocks. The dataset is introduced in Sect. 4. Section 5 reports the experimental setup used to validate our system. Moreover, different classification approaches are compared, and the obtained results are discussed also with respect to the state of the art. Section 6 has the conclusion.

2 Related Work

The problem of detecting unauthorized UAVs has been massively taken into consideration in the last decades. Typically, many approaches are based on the analysis of signals, e.g. radio-frequency [13] or WiFi fingerprint [6]. Often data coming from multiple sensors is fused [18]. Similar techniques have been recently employed to identify the UAV pilot: main approaches consider vulnerabilities on the communication channel between the remote controller and the UAV [15]. In general, these solutions usually require specialized and expensive hardware [4,25]. Other works try to model the pilot behavior as a sequence of flight commands and to discriminate a specific pilot with machine learning techniques to identify, thus basing on behavioural patterns extracted by radio-control signals [29], but representing more a soft-biometrics based identification approach; moreover, it cannot easily generalized to unseen scenarios.

Instead, computer vision can represent a unique opportunity to reduce costs by exploiting visual information, as shown by pure image processing solutions to identify UAVs [33,34], and for vision-based surveillance in general [20,26]. However, surprisingly, few works have dealt with the vision-based UAV pilot identification challenge. A preliminary work that performs such task using images from a UAV has been recently proposed in [8]. Results are very encouraging, showing the feasibility of using a human-pose estimation method to identify the pilots, but the system necessarily requires to process data offline or to transmit aerial images to a ground processing unit, since computationally expensive neural networks have been employed to guarantee high accuracy. Furthermore, data has not been released.

Finally, the problem of visual pilot identification can be treated as a particular instance of the action recognition problem [36]. Anyway, the main datasets used for evaluating the different approaches, e.g., NTU-RGB+D [24] or UCF101 [30], does not consider the piloting behavior and, consequently, state of the art solutions [14] have never been tested on this specific case.

3 Proposed Method

First of all, images are taken from a camera mounted on a flying UAV. For each frame, people present in the scene are detected: their 2D bounding box is extracted and processed by a skeleton estimator that extracts the 2D position of 25 body joints. The feature vector is normalized and used as the input vector for a classifier that can categorize the person in two possible classes, i.e. "*pilot*" or "*non-pilot*". The classifier has been trained on training sequences recorded by a mobile phone camera and tested on the test sequence of the dataset introduced in Sect. 4. The full processing is performed directly on-board. A block diagram of the proposed pilot detection pipeline is reported in Fig. 1. In the following, each composing block will be detailed.

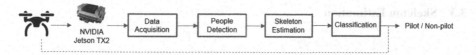

Fig. 1. A block diagram of the proposed approach. The final output is a label to represent the pilot or non-pilot classes. The dashed arrow indicates that data can be transmitted back to take proper countermeasures.

3.1 Data Acquisition

Herein, we assume a scenario with a sensor system to detect and track unauthorized UAVs intruding restricted airspace. This work extends this system with one or more counter UAVs to detect and identify the eventual presence of the pilot(s) in a scene where also other non-pilot people can be present. The counter UAVs fly autonomously and with a pre-planned trajectory, and images are directly taken from the UAV on-board camera. The on-board processing is motivated by the fact that if multiple UAVs are operating at the same time, many data is produced, and a semi-automatic decision system that flag the presence of unauthorized pilots becomes critical for taking proper countermeasures and/or defining human intervention from the legal authorities.

3.2 People Detection

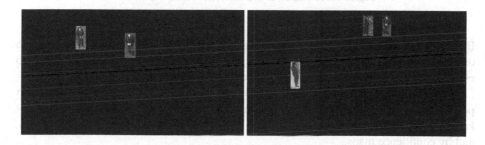

Fig. 2. Outputs of the people detection step.

Differently from [8], in this work, only the 2D bounding box for each people is detected. This change has been implemented to speed up the overall computation. Moreover, a different deep learning architecture is employed in this stage, i.e. *EfficientDet* [32], a weighted bi-directional feature pyramid network (BiFPN) that allows easy and fast multi-scale feature fusion. The authors propose a scaling method that uniformly scales resolution, depth, and width, achieving much better efficiency than prior art across a wide spectrum of resource constraints. In particular, the EfficientDet-D2 version has been employed. From the original 80 MS COCO [23] categories, only occurrences of the *person* class are further processed, and the rest of the image is masked.

In Fig. 2, some output of this processing block is reported.

3.3 Skeleton Estimation

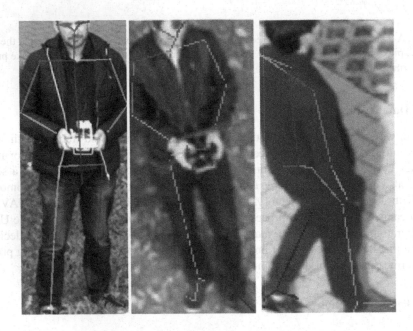

Fig. 3. Three outputs of the skeleton estimation block.

Bounding boxes containing each single detected person are padded of 5 pixels in each direction, and the crop is feed to a second neural network, namely OpenPose [7], to estimate the 2D pixel locations of anatomical keypoints (*skeleton*).

OpenPose uses a multi-task learning approach to detect persons and to estimate their pose in terms of 2D joint's positions. It can detect human body, hand, facial, and foot keypoints by iteratively predicting affinity fields that encode part-to-part association, and by confidence maps.

In this work, the model containing 25 body parts has been employed. Differently from [8], all the estimated skeletons that contain more than 5 joints positions are considered for further processing. The option to track face and hands has not been used and, since the previous block guarantees the presence of only one person in each area, the network is run using this information a priori. According to the authors of the original paper, this information is not used to speed up the computation, and we used instead to increment the accuracy.

The joints' positions, specified by their (x, y) pixel coordinates, are normalized in the range $[0-1]$ with respect to their bounding box size. Instead, if a joint is not detected or its likelihood is below a specific threshold, (x, y) coordinates are set to -1. This way, a feature vector of 50 elements is composed. In Fig. 3, some output of this computational phase is reported.

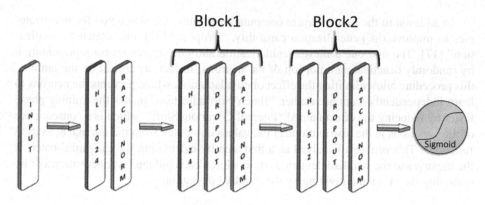

Fig. 4. The neural network model architecture used in the last computational block of the proposed approach.

3.4   Classification

Following from the previous skeleton keypoints' extraction step, the classification of each person into *pilot* or *non-pilot* relies on a sequence of numerically normalized features. Hence, in this work, we explore the application of Artificial Neural Networks (ANNs) as a methodology to create that decision boundary necessary to discriminate between the two classes. The origin of ANNs derives from a biologically inspired simulation of the human brain activity, named "The Perceptron" by Rosenblatt [27], but since then has been popularly adopted to perform non-linear function approximation for the widest variety of classification problems, from intrusion detection [10] to healthcare [21].

In general, a neural network includes a certain number of "Hidden Layers", which enable to learn non-linear separation of the data by projecting it in a high abstract dimensional space whose size depends on chosen numbers of neurons in each layer. In turn, the non-linear boundary shape depends on the choice of the *activation function*, which is computed on each neuron output as:

$$y = W^{\mathbf{T}}x + b \tag{1}$$
$$z = g(y) \tag{2}$$

where W represents the matrix of weights on each input to neuron connection, x is the input, b is an optional bias term, and g is the activation function.

Hence, to assess the different classification capabilities of an increased abstraction level in the network, three models have been created by varying the number of total hidden layers, which we name ANN3, ANN4, and ANN5 to indicate this quantity variation. Figure 4 shows the general architecture, with common aspects to the three models, which includes the number of neurons for each hidden layer (HL). Instead, the input is composed of 50 features, i.e., the number of skeleton keypoints extracted in the previous step. Each hidden layer is followed by a ReLU activation function:

$$g(y) = max(y, 0) \tag{3}$$

In addition to the hidden layers computational units, we also opted for two strategies to improve the generalization capability, "Dropout" [31] and "Batch Normalization" [17]. The first one achieves regularization and encourages sparse representation by randomly deactivating a portion of the neurons. In fact, as argued by the authors, this procedure allows limiting the effect of co-adaptation, which prevents the neurons to learn independently from each other. "Batch Normalization" makes the training phase faster by reducing the effect named "Internal Covariate Shift", which is a consequence of the variations in the distributions of the values computed from the internal activation functions. This problem is solved as a first step by calculating for each mini-batch $\mathcal{B}$ the mean μ and the standard deviations σ, to whiten each hidden layer activation $x^{(k)}$ by removing the mean and dividing by the standard deviation:

$$\mu_{\mathcal{B}} = \frac{1}{m} \sum_{i=1}^{m} x_i^{(k)} \tag{4}$$

$$\sigma_{\mathcal{B}}^2 = \frac{1}{m} \sum_{i=1}^{m} (x_i^{(k)} - \mu_{\mathcal{B}})^2 \tag{5}$$

$$\hat{x}_i^{(k)} = \frac{x_i^{(k)} - \mu_{\mathcal{B}}}{\sqrt{\sigma_{\mathcal{B}}^2 + \varepsilon}} \tag{6}$$

where m is the size of the mini-batch. Then, adding two parameters, i.e. $\gamma^{(k)}$ and $\beta^{(k)}$, the network learns a transformation that shifts and scales the input of the previous layer:

$$y_i^{(k)} = \gamma^{(k)} * \hat{x}_i^{(k)} + \beta^{(k)} \tag{7}$$

This operation introduces a small noise factor during the training that acts as an additional source of regularization and allows to reduce the amount of dropout. In light of this, the probability of dropout has been set to 0.15.

Whereas the first hidden layer with 1024 neurons is directly followed by the Batch Normalization, the two blocks in Fig. 4, which include Dropout, can characterize various possible models by repeating them multiple times. In particular, we build ANN3 and ANN4 by repeating the Block1 once and twice respectively after the first convolution. Instead, ANN5 is built starting from ANN4 and adding Block2 once. Deeper models are possible, but with the risk either of overfitting or to waste unnecessary computations over an already performing model.

Finally, to estimate the probability that an input feature vector x belongs to the class C_i, the Sigmoid function is applied in the last neuron as it normalizes the output of the network between 0 and 1 allowing its interpretation as a posterior probability distribution $P(C_i|x)$ [5]:

$$g(y) = \frac{1}{1 + e^{-y}} \tag{8}$$

Fig. 5. Four images of the SnT-ARG-PilotDetect dataset. The upper row shows two frames of the training sequences, while the bottom row shows frames from the test sequence.

4   Dataset

The SnT-ARG-PilotDetect dataset[1] has been introduced to assess the effectiveness of computer vision algorithms in identifying possible UAV pilots in a realistic scenario. The dataset is composed of six training sequences and one test sequence. For privacy issues, the parts of the images not containing a person have been masked. Figure 5 reports four sample images of the dataset.

The training sequences have been released as part of the dataset to guarantee the reproducibility of the results; to ease the labelling procedure, only one person is present in each sequence. Scenes have been filmed by a consumer camera placed at heights ranging in the interval of $[2 - 3.0]$ m. Two male subjects are framed in total, and both persons act alternatively as pilot or non-pilot to avoid introducing any bias deriving from the body sizes and/or the appearance. In total, 2,959 images at 1280×720 pixels of non-piloting behavior and 3,699 of piloting behavior have been labelled.

The test set represents instead a realistic and long sequence in an urban scenario with a DJI M600 drone recording from a stabilized DJI Zenmuse X5R camera, patrolling the area (remotely controlled by a human pilot). Images are stored at a resolution of 1920×1080 pixels. The UAV changes its orientation and height during the flight, in a height range of $[2.5 - 10.0]$ m. The background varies and it includes buildings, parked cars, a field and an alleyway, and more people can be present at the same time. Similarly, the trajectory of each person is not constrained, implying that several re-appearances can occur and that the bounding boxes can be partially overlapped. In the scene, three people act without constraints in terms of appearance and simulating three types of

---

[1] The dataset is available at https://github.com/dcazzato/SnT-Arg-PilotDetect.

behavior: *pilot*, *non-pilot*, *mobile phone*. The third class mainly shares the poses of the piloting behavior, but the object grabbed by the person is a smartphone. This has been introduced to provide the possibility to detect this third case by analyzing the texture of the area around the detected hands, and in general to leave to the final user to decide whether to use these images and if the latter case should be classified as pilot or non-pilot.

The phase of the bounding boxes' extraction has been facilitated by applying EfficientDet-D2 object detection network to automatically detect people, which are successively manually labelled. If the person turns away or only a small part is visible we used the following convention: if this happens after that the person in charge of the dataset labelling procedure has previously identified the class label, then these frames are stored. If this happens when the person enters the scene for the first time, we waited that the human operator was able to clearly identify the class label before beginning to store the frames.

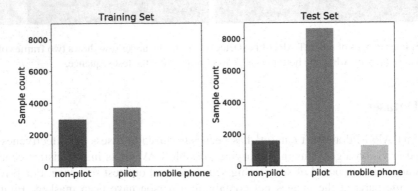

Fig. 6. The number of the samples for each class for the training (left) and the test (right) sets.

As shown in Fig. 6, 11,476 labelled samples (8,628 for the *pilot*, 1,579 for the *non-pilot* classes) have been provided in the test sequence with a noticeable imbalance towards the *pilot* class. Instead, in the training set, about 45% of the samples are labeled as *non-pilot*. The *mobile phone* class presents relatively few samples only in the test set. Hence, for correctly classifying those samples it could be needed to employ additional data at training time.

Furthermore, we note a divergence between the training and test sets distribution of the area size in pixels of the detected bounding boxes. Particularly, referring to the plot in Fig. 7, the test set presents a larger number of small boxes and a wider dispersion of the size, whereas the training set has a narrower band within which the boxes' areas lie.

The released dataset consists of the images with the regions containing the persons in the scene with a padding of 5 pixels in each dimension, and a command separated values (CSV) structure where each line contains the information regarding the frame name and the bounding box of each detected person and the label. Also the normalized (in 0–1 interval, with −1 for a missing joint) skeleton coordinates have been added. Bounding boxes without a detected skeleton or the case of less than 5 estimated joints have been removed from the dataset. The CSV presents the following structure:

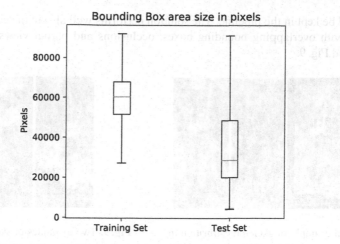

Fig. 7. Box plots of the bounding boxes area size in pixels for the training and test sets.

- Column 1: frame name;
- Column 2–5: bounding box of the person;
- Column 6–55: normalized detected joints;
- Column 56: class label (0 for *non-pilot*, 1 for *pilot*, 2 for persons using a *mobile phone*).

5   Experimental Setup and Results

In this Section, the proposed approach has been evaluated with the SnT-ARG-PilotDetect dataset, and results are reported. Only samples of the pilot and non-pilot classes have been considered. The number of samples for each class used for the following experiments in the training and test dataset is summarized in Table 1.

Table 1. The number of images used for the validation for each class label, in the training (second column) and test (third column) sequences.

Class label	Training	Test
Pilot	3699	8628
Non-pilot	2959	1579
Total	6658	11476

About person and skeleton estimation performance, it is worth to note that the usage of EfficientDet upstream to OpenPose did not generate any false positive. Nevertheless, the introduction of EfficientDet becomes of critical importance to reproduce the proposed pipeline also from images directly coming from the UAV.

Differently from [8], there are no cases of multiple skeleton estimation in the same patch, even without the need of ad-hoc ratio and dimension filters. This result has been achieved by estimating only one skeleton in each patch, thanks to the performance of the upstream block. Notwithstanding, noisy skeletons can be sometimes generated, and they will be kept in the pipeline. The solution performs well also in the case of multiple people with overlapping bounding boxes, occlusions and partial views, as shown in Fig. 8 and Fig. 9.

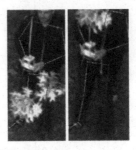

Fig. 8. An example of skeleton estimation in the presence of 2D bounding box overlapping.

Fig. 9. Two examples of skeleton estimation in the presence of occlusions and incomplete view.

In the second experimental phase, the classification performance obtained on the SnT-ARG-PilotDetect dataset has been evaluated. Different classification strategies have been proposed and compared, as well as different metrics.

Our classification results are evaluated as:

- True Positives (TP): correctly predicted pilot class instances.
- True Negatives (TN): correctly predicted non-pilot class instances.
- False Positives (FP): pilot instances wrongly classified as non-pilot instances.
- False Negatives (FN): non-pilot instances wrongly classified as pilot instances.

The proposed metrics are *accuracy, precision, recall* and *F1 score*, defined as:

$$Accuracy = \frac{TP+TN}{TP+FP+FN+TN} \tag{9}$$

$$Precision = \frac{TP}{TP+FP} \tag{10}$$

$$Recall = \frac{TP}{TP+FN} \tag{11}$$

$$F1\,score = \frac{2 \times (Recall \times Precision)}{Recall+Precision} \tag{12}$$

In details, we have evaluated the three proposed ANNs introduced in Sect. 3.4. Moreover, the neural network's performance has been compared with k-Nearest Neighbors (k-NN), Logistic Regression (LR), and Support-Vector Machines (SVM). For the k-NN classifier, the parameter k has been set to 5. For the SVM, the parameters proposed in [8] for the same task have been used, i.e.:

- $C = 2.6049$
- $\gamma = 0.02759$

Table 2. Classification results on the SnT-ARG-PilotDetect dataset in terms of accuracy, precision, recall and F1 score. The best results are highlighted in bold.

Classifiers	Accuracy	Precision	Recall	F1 score
ANN3	**0.873**	0.983	0.865	**0.920**
ANN4	0.868	**0.986**	0.856	0.916
ANN5	**0.873**	**0.986**	0.862	**0.920**
KNN	0.826	0.951	0.837	0.891
LR	0.837	0.980	0.824	0.895
SVM	0.870	0.976	**0.867**	0.918

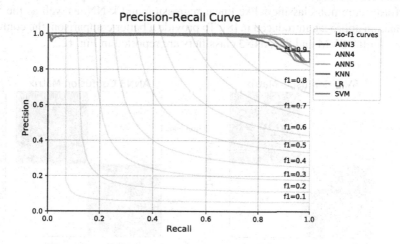

Fig. 10. Precision-Recall curves of the compared classifiers.

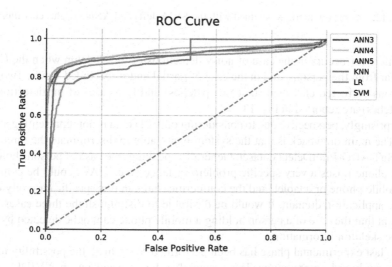

Fig. 11. ROC curves of the compared classifiers.

The obtained results are summed up in Table 2, while the Precision-Recall and the Receiver Operating Characteristic (ROC) curves are reported in Figs. 10 and 11 respectively.

From an analysis of the results, it is possible to note the validity of classifying the pilots by using the human body pose information, and this can be achieved in general, independently from the different adopted machine learning approach. Nevertheless, it is possible to observe how the introduced ANNs achieve in general best performances on the SnT-ARG-PilotDetect dataset. In particular, using the ANN3 architecture, the system achieves the remarkable value of 87.3% of accuracy and 98.3% of precision. Adding more layers does not significantly improve the performance; in fact, values obtained with ANN3 and ANN5 are similar, thus we selected ANN3 to ease the computational load during the inference. It is worth noting how the proposed neural network outperforms common classifiers like linear regression and k-NN, as well as the SVM classification approach introduced in [8]. To provide a better comparison, the confusion matrices for the SVM and the ANN3 classifiers are reported in Fig. 12.

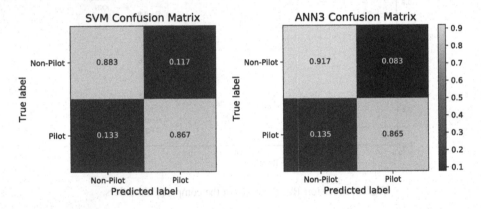

Fig. 12. Confusion matrices obtained with the SVM (left) and ANN3 (right) classifiers.

Some error occurs in the case of noisy detections of the skeleton when the UAV is flying far from the persons, and in the case of partial and/or occluded views. Two cases of persons corrected classified (first two patches) and two cases of misdetection (last two patches) are reported in Fig. 13.

Surprisingly, perspective due to considering only 2D data is not representing a major issue. The main drawback is that the system is not able to discriminate the three cases of the SnT-ARG-PilotDetect dataset. Generally speaking, the case of persons holding a mobile phone raises a very specific problem instance since UAVs could be controlled by a mobile phone or a tablet, and the countermeasures in this specific case rely on the specific application domain. It would be desirable to distinguish the three cases, but it is evident that the case of a person holding a mobile phone cannot be detected by using only the skeleton information.

The last experimental phase has been performed to evaluate the possibility to fully perform on-board computation. The system has been tested on an NVIDIA Jetson TX2. To improve the performance of EfficientDet, the model has been converted using

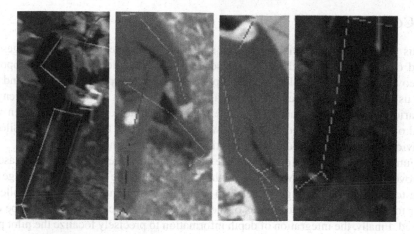

Fig. 13. Examples of classification outputs of the proposed approach. From left to right: a true positive, a true negative, a false positive, a false negative.

NVIDIA TensorRT with an FP32 representation for the weights and a specified input image resolution of 768 × 432. Table 3 offers an overview of the required computation times for each block of the proposed pipeline. Notably, EfficientDet-D2 and Openpose run approximately at the same speed. Furthermore, all the three phases, namely object detection, keypoint estimation, and classification, relies on fully differentiable method, i.e., neural network, that could be learned jointly in a single end-to-end pipeline, thus improving the performances. Finally, we consider that merging these methods would also be beneficial both to the memory footprint and to the overall latency.

Table 3. Running times of the proposed pilot detection method on an NVIDIA Jetson TX2.

Method	Latency (sec)	FPS
EfficientDet-D2	0.177	5.6
Openpose	0.197	5.1
ANN3	0.11	8.9

This is a very encouraging result that demonstrates that it is possible to adopt faster network pipelines to solve the task under consideration even in challenging conditions and with limited computational resources.

This section is concluded with the implementation details. The software has been developed using the Python language. The official implementation of EfficientDet[2] has been used for the people detection step. To estimate the skeleton, the Python wrapper of OpenPose [7] has been used, with pre-trained weights for 25-keypoints body/foot estimation. The proposed ANN models have been implemented with TensorFlow.

---

[2] Available at https://github.com/google/automl/tree/master/efficientdet.

6   Conclusion

In this work, a computer vision pipeline specifically designed to process images on-board of a flying UAV to detect the presence of UAV(s) pilot(s) has been proposed. Moreover, the SnT-ARG-PilotDetect composed by images of pilots, non-pilots and persons using mobile phone, recorded from a flying UAV and in realistic and challenging scenarios, has been introduced and made publicly available. Results have been validated on the aforementioned dataset, showing the validity of the approach for piloting behavior classification based on the detection of the human and his skeleton.

Future works will merging the people detection and skeleton estimation phases to improve the overall speed. Moreover, methods that exploit the texture of the image part close to the hands to distinguish between a mobile phone and a remote controller, in order to discriminate the three cases of the SnT-ARG-PilotDetect dataset, will be considered. Finally, the integration of depth information to precisely localize the pilot position in the space will be investigated, providing a complete input for person following and trajectory planning schemes.

Acknowledgments. We thank Prof. Dr. Miguel Angel Olivares-Mendez for his technical support in the creation of the dataset.

References

1. Al Abkal, S., Talas, R.H.A., Shaw, S., Ellis, T.: The application of unmanned aerial vehicles in managing port and border security in the us and Kuwait: reflections on best practice for the UK. Int. J. Marit. Crime Secur. **1**(1) (2020)
2. Alsalam, B.H.Y., Morton, K., Campbell, D., Gonzalez, F.: Autonomous UAV with vision based on-board decision making for remote sensing and precision agriculture. In: 2017 IEEE Aerospace Conference, pp. 1–12. IEEE (2017)
3. Avola, D., Foresti, G.L., Martinel, N., Micheloni, C., Pannone, D., Piciarelli, C.: Aerial video surveillance system for small-scale UAV environment monitoring. In: 2017 14th IEEE International Conference on Advanced Video and Signal Based Surveillance (AVSS), pp. 1–6. IEEE (2017)
4. Biallawons, O., Klare, J., Fuhrmann, L.: Improved uav detection with the mimo radar miracle ka using range-velocity processing and tdma correction algorithms. In: 2018 19th International Radar Symposium (IRS), pp. 1–10. IEEE (2018)
5. Bishop, C.M., et al.: Neural Networks for Pattern Recognition. Oxford University Press, Oxford (1995)
6. Bisio, I., Garibotto, C., Lavagetto, F., Sciarrone, A., Zappatore, S.: Unauthorized amateur uav detection based on wifi statistical fingerprint analysis. IEEE Commun. Mag. **56**(4), 106–111 (2018)
7. Cao, Z., Hidalgo, G., Simon, T., Wei, S.E., Sheikh, Y.: OpenPose: realtime multi-person 2D pose estimation using Part Affinity Fields. In: arXiv preprint arXiv:1812.08008 (2018)
8. Cazzato, D., Cimarelli, C., Voos, H.: A preliminary study on the automatic visual based identification of uav pilots from counter uavs. In: VISIGRAPP (5: VISAPP), pp. 582–589 (2020)
9. Cazzato, D., Olivares-Mendez, M.A., Sanchez-Lopez, J.L., Voos, H.: Vision-based aircraft pose estimation for uavs autonomous inspection without fiducial markers. In: IECON 2019–45th Annual Conference of the IEEE Industrial Electronics Society, vol. 1, pp. 5642–5648. IEEE (2019)

10. Chen, W.H., Hsu, S.H., Shen, H.P.: Application of svm and ann for intrusion detection. Comput. Oper. Res. **32**(10), 2617–2634 (2005)
11. Christnacher, F., et al.: Optical and acoustical uav detection. In: Electro-Optical Remote Sensing X, vol. 9988, p. 99880B. International Society for Optics and Photonics (2016)
12. Dolan, A.M., et al.: Integration of drones into domestic airspace: selected legal issues (2013)
13. Ezuma, M., Erden, F., Anjinappa, C.K., Ozdemir, O., Guvenc, I.: Micro-uav detection and classification from rf fingerprints using machine learning techniques. In: 2019 IEEE Aerospace Conference, pp. 1–13. IEEE (2019)
14. Feichtenhofer, C., Pinz, A., Wildes, R.P.: Spatiotemporal multiplier networks for video action recognition. In: Proceedings of the IEEE Conference on Computer Vision and Pattern Recognition, pp. 4768–4777 (2017)
15. Hartmann, K., Steup, C.: The vulnerability of uavs to cyber attacks-an approach to the risk assessment. In: 2013 5th International Conference on Cyber Conflict (CYCON 2013), pp. 1–23. IEEE (2013)
16. Huttunen, M.: Civil unmanned aircraft systems and security: the European approach. J. Transp. Secur. **12**(3–4), 83–101 (2019)
17. Ioffe, S., Szegedy, C.: Batch normalization: Accelerating deep network training by reducing internal covariate shift. arXiv preprint arXiv:1502.03167 (2015)
18. Jovanoska, S., Brötje, M., Koch, W.: Multisensor data fusion for uav detection and tracking. In: 2018 19th International Radar Symposium (IRS), pp. 1–10. IEEE (2018)
19. Kanistras, K., Martins, G., Rutherford, M.J., Valavanis, K.P.: A survey of unmanned aerial vehicles (UAVs) for traffic monitoring. In: 2013 International Conference on Unmanned Aircraft Systems (ICUAS), pp. 221–234. IEEE (2013)
20. Kim, I.S., Choi, H.S., Yi, K.M., Choi, J.Y., Kong, S.G.: Intelligent visual surveillance-a survey. Int. J. Control Autom. Syst. **8**(5), 926–939 (2010)
21. Leo, M., Carcagnì, P., Mazzeo, P.L., Spagnolo, P., Cazzato, D., Distante, C.: Analysis of facial information for healthcare applications: a survey on computer vision-based approaches. Information **11**(3), 128 (2020)
22. Li, L.J., Socher, R., Fei-Fei, L.: Towards total scene understanding: Classification, annotation and segmentation in an automatic framework. In: 2009 IEEE Conference on Computer Vision and Pattern Recognition, pp. 2036–2043. IEEE (2009)
23. Lin, T.-Y., et al.: Microsoft COCO: common objects in context. In: Fleet, D., Pajdla, T., Schiele, B., Tuytelaars, T. (eds.) ECCV 2014. LNCS, vol. 8693, pp. 740–755. Springer, Cham (2014). https://doi.org/10.1007/978-3-319-10602-1_48
24. Liu, J., Shahroudy, A., Perez, M.L., Wang, G., Duan, L.Y., Chichung, A.K.: Ntu rgb+ d 120: a large-scale benchmark for 3d human activity understanding. IEEE Trans. Pattern Anal. Mach. Intell., 2684–2701 (2019)
25. May, R., Steinheim, Y., Kvaløy, P., Vang, R., Hanssen, F.: Performance test and verification of an off-the-shelf automated avian radar tracking system. Ecol. Evol. **7**(15), 5930–5938 (2017)
26. Morris, B.T., Trivedi, M.M.: A survey of vision-based trajectory learning and analysis for surveillance. IEEE Trans. Circuits Syst. Video Technol. **18**(8), 1114–1127 (2008)
27. Rosenblatt, F.: The perceptron: a probabilistic model for information storage and organization in the brain. Psychol. Rev. **65**(6), 386 (1958)
28. Schneider, D.: Electronic license plates for drones [spectral lines]. IEEE Spectr. **54**, 8 (2017). https://doi.org/10.1109/MSPEC.2017.7906882
29. Shoufan, A., Al-Angari, H.M., Sheikh, M.F.A., Damiani, E.: Drone pilot identification by classifying radio-control signals. IEEE Trans. Inf. Forensics Secur. **13**(10), 2439–2447 (2018)
30. Soomro, K., Zamir, A.R., Shah, M.: Ucf101: A dataset of 101 human actions classes from videos in the wild. arXiv preprint arXiv:1212.0402 (2012)

31. Srivastava, N., Hinton, G., Krizhevsky, A., Sutskever, I., Salakhutdinov, R.: Dropout: a simple way to prevent neural networks from overfitting. J. Mach. Learn. Res. **15**(56), 1929–1958 (2014). http://jmlr.org/papers/v15/srivastava14a.html

32. Tan, M., Pang, R., Le, Q.V.: Efficientdet: scalable and efficient object detection. In: Proceedings of the IEEE/CVF Conference on Computer Vision and Pattern Recognition, pp. 10781–10790 (2020)

33. Unlu, E., Zenou, E., Riviere, N.: Using shape descriptors for uav detection. Electron. Imaging **2018**(9), 1–5 (2018)

34. Unlu, E., Zenou, E., Riviere, N., Dupouy, P.-E.: Deep learning-based strategies for the detection and tracking of drones using several cameras. IPSJ Trans. Comput. Vis. Appl. **11**(1), 1–13 (2019). https://doi.org/10.1186/s41074-019-0059-x

35. Wang, B., Peng, X., Liu, D.: Airborne sensor data-based unsupervised recursive identification for uav flight phases. IEEE Sens. J. **20**(18), 10733–10743 (2020)

36. Zhang, H.B., et al.: A comprehensive survey of vision-based human action recognition methods. Sensors **19**(5), 1005 (2019)

Exploring Tele-Assistance for Cyber-Physical Systems with MAUI

Philipp Fleck[1($\boxtimes$)], Fernando Reyes-Aviles[1], Christian Pirchheim[1], Clemens Arth[1,2], and Dieter Schmalstieg[1]

[1] ICG, Graz University of Technology, Inffeldgasse 16/2, 8010 Graz, Austria
{philipp.fleck,fernando.reyes-aviles,pirchheim,arth,
dieter}@icg.tugraz.at
[2] AR4 GmbH, Strauchergasse 13, 8020 Graz, Austria

Abstract. In this paper we present an improved version of MAUI [9] (*MAUI - Maintenance Assistance User Interface*), extending the user-study, giving detailed insight into the implementations and introducing a new User-Interface for mobile use. MAUI is a novel take on tele-assisted tasks on cyber-physical systems. In its core we do not only provide real-time communication between workers and experts, but also allow an expert to have full control over the worker's user-interface.

By precisely separating levels of our software-stack, we enable features like hot-patching and hot-loading of any content or web-based application. Our results show reduced error-rate on task performance once an expert takes over virtual task to relieve the worker. Conditions evaluated include the worker operating on his own and the worker being actively supported. While in operation gauges have to be read, switches to be press and virtual user-interfaces of machinery have to be controlled. Furthermore, we explore the creation of user-interfaces through a developer-study and use the feedback to create a mobile version of MAUI.

Keywords: Remote collaboration · Telepresence · Augmented reality

1 Introduction

Almost every industrial machinery (especially in production) and many customer devices are inter-connected nowadays. They can be summarized as Cyber-Physical Systems (CPS) because of their dual nature: they often have a physical interface like buttons and switches, and a virtual representation like companion Apps or Web-Interfaces for additional controls.

With increasing complexity, CPS become more and more difficult to operate, repair and maintain. Such tasks exceed the use of simple tools and often require diagnostic instruments or virtual controls *e.g.,* for re-booting machinery. Furthermore, for precise error-cause detection sensor telemetry data has to be checked and verified *e.g.,* malfunctioning valve showing increased pressure. Such situation (*e.g.,* a broken machinery with physical damage and virtual configuration) are often combined with stress and can quickly overwhelm maintenance personal.

K. Bouatouch et al. (Eds.): VISIGRAPP 2020, CCIS 1474, pp. 431–452, 2022.
https://doi.org/10.1007/978-3-030-94893-1_20

Fig. 1. Facility for production. (*top-left*) an expert in the control center dispatching; (*top-right*) mission control with an dedicate expert Laptop; (*bottom-left*) a worker trying to fix an IT-mess wearing a HoloLens; (*bottom-right*) a worker on the shop floor, wearing a Microsoft Hololens, to fix machine downtime problems, taken from [9].

In particular with respect to industrial use cases, an important aspect is that machine manufacturers are not the actual machine operators usually. The engagement of support personnel from the manufacturer side in fixing maintenance problems on the operator side is a huge cost factor, which drives the inclusion of the tele-assistance concept in the maintenance workflow. Figure 1 depicts and experts and workers operating such facilities. In its most simple form, this is realized through a regular phone-call and through picture sharing using smartphones and services like email. An even more evolved concept includes apps like *WhatsApp*, video-conferencing and remote-desktop systems like *TeamViewer*. Overall, remote support is used as problem solving and guidance tool.

The pure implementation of a tele-presence concept like this does not solve all problems automatically, however. One of the critical issues remaining is establishing context: *This button? – no the left one! The side where the red light is? – No, on the other side!* On the one hand, there is the spatial context, *i.e.,* the relation of objects in the environment, and on the other hand the virtual context, *i.e.,* any interact-able user-interfaces. Using simple audio calls or even picture sharing, context is still establishing through audio communication, instructions and human interpretation. Traditional remote-desktop software in turn does not allow for *integrated* operation like swapping user-interface of the worker to a more task-related one. Control inputs are only allowed including mouse or keyboard. These concepts leave a lot of room for errors and are solutions not as efficient as required by most tasks.

In this work, we present a tele-assistance concept and implementation, that allows a remote expert to further support the worker by taking over virtual tasks and therefore freeing mental capacities. In this regard, to guarantee hands-free operation, we let the worker wear a Head-Mounted-Display (HMD) with built-in camera and microphone like the Microsoft Hololens. Thereby the remote expert is provided with the video- and audio-feed from the worker and a rich data connection to be used for additional content. Support can be given by sharing annotation in the shared video, by spoken instructions and by interaction with the workers virtual environment *directly*.

Since we hereby extend our previous work *MAUI - Maintenance Assistance User Interface* [9], we further focus on industrial use cases, but remain in the same way applicable to applications involving consumer grade hardware. We illustrate the ease to write commands, also giving details on technical solutions to enable real-time performance on the Hololens. Such commands allow the expert to send almost any content to the worker, to directly visualize or open it and to manipulate the UI of the worker. Because of the complexity of CPS, workers can be overwhelmed at handling it. It comes as a relief that the expert can take over the virtual interaction. We demonstrate that by extending common concepts of remote desktop software into AR, UI manipulation is entirely doable beyond keyboard and mouse controls through such a concept allowing hot-patching. Finally we performed an extended user-study focusing on the mental and physical demand of a typical maintenance task and give insights into occurred task-error-rates of the participants.

MAUI was designed with the intention of more efficient subdivision of work between expert and worker, providing the following contributions:

- We analyze the requirements of AR tele-assistance for industrial jobs, where remote operation and configuration of a user interface by a remote expert is required.
- We present implementation details of MAUI, which address the aforementioned requirements with its robust abilities for sharing audio, video, digital content and control state in harsh industrial environments.
- We discuss results of a user study demonstrating lower task completion times, reduced cognitive load, and better subjective comfort on performing a maintenance task.
- We discuss the results of an exploratory study, orthogonal to the first one [9], analyzing how web developers perform when creating user interface content in the MAUI framework.

2   Related Work

AR can help a worker by purely displaying digital information. Henderson *et al.* [18] have shown the benefits of AR in the maintenance and repair domain. However, such pre-configured information sources are often unavailable. In this case, a good alternative is to link the worker to a remote expert providing live support. Dealing with a CPS adds the dimension of a digital interface, which can be controlled locally by the worker, or alternatively by the remote expert. Thus, our work is at the nexus of remote collaboration, interaction with cyber-physical systems and remote desktop user interfaces. Background to each of these topics is provided in the remainder of this section.

2.1 Remote Collaboration

Video transmission is the enabling technology for tele-assistance since the pioneering work of Kruger [23]. Early works in this space [2,34] were mostly constrained to desktop computers due to technical limitations. Recent progress in mobile and wearable computing has brought video conferences abilities to the factory floor, *i.e.,* primarily leveraging mobile handheld devices like smartphones and tablets.

However, establishing a shared spatial presence at the task location is still a challenging topic. Experts need to visually experience the worker's environment. The video stream from a camera worn by the worker will only show the worker's actual field of view [3,5,19,20,24]. Giving the remote expert independent control of a robotic camera [15,25] is usually not economically feasible.

Apart from spoken instructions, most tele-assistance solutions let the expert provide visual-spatial references, either via hand gestures [19,21,28], remote pointing [3,5,12,20], or hand-drawn annotation on the video [6,12,15,20,30]. Hand-drawing is either restricted to images from a stationary camera viewpoint [3,6,12,15,19–21,24] or requires real-time 3D reconstruction and tracking [5,13,14,26].

2.2 Cyber-Physical System Interaction

None of the remote collaboration systems mentioned in the last section takes into account the special requirements of a task that must be performed on a cyber-physical system. The dual nature of a cyber-physical system implies that each task will commonly consist of a physical task (*e.g.,* physical part mounted with screws) and a virtual task (*e.g.,* re-initializing a device after repair). It is crucial for the worker to receive support on both aspects of cyber-physical tasks.

Recent work in interaction design is starting to consider such interactions with CPSs. Rambach *et al.* [31] propose that every cyber-physical system serves its own data (*e.g.,* sensor information, control interface) to enable new ways of interaction. Alce *et al.* [1] experimentally verify different methods of device interaction while increasing the number of devices. A common design are device-specific controls embedded in the AR user interface [7,8].

Other recent work investigates AR in production and manufacturing industries. Kollatsch *et al.* [22] show how to control an industrial press simulator within an AR application by leveraging its numerical interface, *i.e.,* a device interface allowing to run simulations which are partially executed on the machine. Han *et al.* [16] concentrate on automated situation detection and task generation to give better and more responsive instructions, *e.g.,* for fixing paper jams in printers.

Cognitive conditions during task performance are a key element to success in many industrial situations. Maintenance workers must frequently perform multiple repair tasks during one shift, requiring a high level of flexibility and concentration. Therefore, recent research has considered how reducing factors like frustration, stress and mental load can improve overall performance. For instance, Baumeister *et al.* [4] investigate mental workload when using an AR HMD. Funk *et al.* [10,11] compare instructions delivered via HMD to tablet computers and plain paper. Recently, Tzimas *et al.* [33] reported findings on creating setup instructions in smart factories.

2.3 Remote Desktop User Interfaces

Remote desktop tools, such as Skype[1] or TeamViewer[2], combine video conferencing with remote operation. In theory, these tools have the features required for worker-expert collaboration and can be made to run on AR headsets such as the HoloLens. However, a closer inspection reveals that the similarities to the desired solution are shallow. Desktop user interfaces are operated using mouse and keyboard. They do not work very well when one user has reduced resources (*e.g.*, when using a phone with a small screen) or when network connectivity is unstable. Workers do not want to retrieve files and navigate them manually, while they are tending to a task. Moreover, shared spatial presence between worker and expert is not considered at all in desktop tools. Even re-using parts of desktop tool implementation in an AR applications turns out to be hard because of the differences between desktop and mobile operating systems.

Perhaps closest to our approach in this respect is the work of O'Neill *et al.* [29] and Roulland *et al.* [32]. Like us, they present a concept for remote assistance, focused on office printer maintenance. However, unlike ours, their work relies on schematic 3D rendering of a printer device, delivered on the printer's built-in screen, and very few details are provided on the implementation and extensibility of the system. In contrast, MAUI is a comprehensive tele-assistance framework. We describe details about its implementation, and evaluate the system's development and use.

3 Requirement Analysis

3.1 Analysis of Collaborator Feedback

First, we need to discuss a few relevant questions important for the design process, supported by collected statements from our collaborators, operators of multiple production facilities around the world manufacturing 24/7.

What kind of problems do we face? Within manufacturing industries time is precious and costs caused by unexpected stalls are high. Therefore on-call staff (*i.e.*, workers) is always ready to jump in an fix any occurring problems. Broken machinery usually signals some alarm and state, and in certain cases production will stall. As a consequence, downtimes are kept short to reduce costs and additional failures. Increasing the efficiency of repair personal is key in such situations. Unfortunately, knowing about the downtime costs even increases the mental pressure on the individual and can lead to less concentration and further errors.

How Are Common Tasks in Industries Performed? Often workers call and negotiate with remote personal on how the repair is done, what exactly is the issue and if other systems are affected. The identified tasks are problem explanations, collaborative solution finding, data observation and (guided) problem solution. Since all machinery nowadays is interconnected and represents a CPS, solving tasks does not only include manual fixing but also interaction with virtual interfaces of devices. Workers need to be knowledgeable in both areas.

---

[1] Skype: https://www.skype.com.
[2] TeamViewer: https://www.teamviewer.com.

What Are the Most Important Features? Due to the complexity of installations, while performing operations machine telemetry and on-machine gauges have to be monitored constantly. Therefore this information have to be ideally visualized in the field-of-view of an operator at all times.

Obviously, it is counter-productive to replace a complex system (CPS) with an another complex one. By slowly introducing new features through levels of expertise, it is possible to pick everyone up at his own learning speed. AR enabled and hands-free solutions are considered a particularly important feature. As a consequence, minimizing interactions with gaze-based controls (including air-taping and Bluetooth clickers) enables a further improvement and acceptance of solutions.

Finally, in industries the use of established software technologies is favored over proprietary solutions. A web-centric approach, inspired by Argon [27], leveraging existing developer skills and allowing for run-time extensibility is considered important.

What Kind of Content is Mostly Used? Remote support stuff contains well trained experts in their fields. Those usually have a good understanding of CAD models and how CPS operate and behave, forming the ideal counterpart to the workers in the field. Often sharing an instruction manual or a cross-section of a part can drastically improve understanding and support the solution finding process. This fact suggests that experts have precise control about the worker's UI and other contents for supporting the work in solving a common problem. The desktop application (*i.e.,* the expert side) can be more complex and offer more gradual controls, while the operator side should be as lightweight as possible.

What About Non-technical Challenges? As a somewhat surprising outcome, bi-directional video feeds (as opposed to one-directional from the worker to the expert) were considered of utter importance. The most important argument was that this establishes trust between the expert giving instructions, and the operator on the shop floor.

Another challenge, but also opportunity, was identified to be significant age distribution, which ranges from some *digital* natives to more workers in their mid fifties, also with varying educational background. In western countries this gives us ten more years of the same workers with an, in part, antiquated view for digital contents. On the one hand, to on-board all groups of workers, features have to be easy to handle not to overwhelm the individual. On the other hand, designing an easy-to-use system enables the formation of an expert pool consisting of those operators most experienced in practice, essentially increasing their efficiency through sharing their knowledge as experts themselves.

3.2 MAUI Design Decisions

Following this feedback, we distilled a set of core requirements and made a few design decisions for MAUI. Our system primarily aims at helping workers while being in a stressful situation solving an unknown problem. Using a HMD frees the worker's hands and allows any interaction with machinery and tools utilizing a minimal design to reduce distractions. While having a Audio-Video face-to-face conversation, the expert should be capable to manipulating (change, alter, replace, control) the worker's user-interface, share multimedia contents (images, PDF, screen-capture) and point within the video feed. Any UIs should be as easy as possible to understand.

On the technical level, this relates to the following tasks to be solved for the worker side:

- Initiating an audio/video connection with easy connection management including a phonebook and online user discovery;
- 3D mesh transfer functionality to enables the worker to send a scanned 3D model of the current environment to the expert, including the worker's current position (Leveraging device capabilities *e.g.*, accessing the HoloLens mesh, but also allowing to plugin other 3D-reconstruction systems);
- Functionality to visualize information, and corresponding methods to manipulate this information, *i.e.*, the UI, remotely.

In turn, for the expert application, the following list of features is important:

- screen capture functionality, to allow the expert to share screenshots of running applications (*e g , CAD* model viewer showing a cross section of a broken machinery part) with the worker;
- use of multimedia content in a representation-agnostic form (PDF, HTML, images, links) to be transferred and displayed;
- use of multi-page documents, such as PDF files, respectively synchronized navigation between an expert and the worker; optionally enriching this content with shared annotations;
- functionality to control the worker's UI, including web content, but also to trigger native interfaces of the cyber-physical system.

The last feature, remote UI control, implies that a custom UI must be dynamically embedded in the tele-assistance application. This discharges the worker from switching apps or configuring the user experience. The ability to change the UI without touching the underlying application makes it also easy to embed tutorial functions into the UI itself, which can be step-by-step enabled. As an advantageous side-effect, this also facilitates a gentle learning curve for the worker. Once the worker is sufficiently familiar with the UI, more features can be enabled, *e.g.*, transitioning from 2D to 3D visualizations or enabling additional controls for physical devices.

4   Implementation Details

Head-worn AR devices like the HoloLens have not reached mass-adoption yet, and will remain expert tools for a couple of years. In the smartphone and tablet sector however, new AR technology is introduced more frequently, including *e.g.*, ARKit and ARCore SDK features. This implies that MAUI should be able to handle a wide range of current and future devices and to be inherently cross-platform.

4.1 Basic Software Design

We chose Unity3D as our 3D Engine because of its wide support for many devices (AR, VR, iOS, Android, Windows and others). We thereby ensure reuse-ability of our code base. Performance hungry components like Audio/Video streaming in real-time are implemented as native libraries with hardware-acceleration, which becomes especially important on mobile platforms. Direct data-paths to such modules are used to reduce latency by surpassing Unity's Cs layer. MAUI is deployed as UWP (Universal Windows Application) for the HoloLens (Worker) and Windows10 on a desktop Computer (expert).

Dynamic libraries can be loaded at run-time to add new functionality *e.g.*, to enable platform specific features. Such native libraries can be scripted from C# and Javascript allowing not only direct calls but also asynchronous communication via callbacks and message passing. The C# and the native layer represent the core framework offering minimally defined functionality and interfaces for tasks like calls, data-transmission and remote UI-commands. Also support for native device functions like enabling the camera and turning on the flashlight.

4.2 Data Transmission

The foundation of remote assistance is the communication between involved parties. Time critical tasks require real-time capable communication. Given a somewhat capable up- and downlink, the software has to be powerful and efficient enough to ship the data in time to the network driver.

Our communication module implements state-of-art C++ techniques (multi-threaded, state-less, smart-pointer, single-allocations) to achieve such. We utilize a modified version of Raknet[3] library to interface the network stack. Experiments showed, especially on the HoloLens, bad performance of higher level implementations. Within our native layer we establish direct data-paths between the Audio/Video capturing, the hardware accelerated H.264 encoding and the communication library. Additionally we introduce a secondary data-channels between peers with soft real-time constrains to transmit non real-time related data. Coping with variable bandwidth, we can gradually control the data-flow rate attributes like video compression to optimise for the current connection characteristics.

4.3 Web Based User-Interface in Unity

Our web-based UI is fully implemented in Js/Html/Css. It thereby allows us to use well established techniques and concept from the web community. Since Unity lacks an in-game Html-Engine, we use a modified Html-renderer and Js-interpreter[4] to bring web into Unity.

Unfortunately, we do not get full browser support which limits the use of some external libraries. Created UIs are rendered into texture maps displayed on any polygonal structure inside Unity. Responsive designers and applications can easily be created

---

[3] RakNet: https://github.com/facebookarchive/RakNet.
[4] PowerUI: https://powerui.kulestar.com.

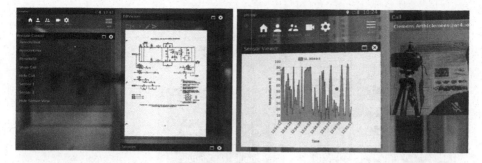

Fig. 2. Example of a remote maintenance demo application. (left) Expert interface with an open document and shortcuts of remote commands, (right) worker UI within a call (A/V, data, commands) and live view of telemetry data shown as a graph, as presented in our previous work [9].

by web-developers and others following web-principles. Written applications (UI and business logic) for our framework are comparable to different web-sites each serving a dedicated purpose and user-loadable at any time. Figure 2 shows the UI run on an desktop computer (left) and on the HoloLens (right). Icons are as well supported, as Css to create appealing themes. Furthermore, widgets are spawned using the data driven template library json2html[5].

For ease of use we created a Js framework to directly bind functionality from our intermediate layer (C#) to Js-objects, allowing us *e.g.,* for code-autocompletion in VisualStudio for even faster prototyping. Features like an Audio/Video call are done simply by calling MAUI.Com.Call(id); in Js. Additionally the Js-interpreter allows to import namespaces at run-time allowing us to call Unity-related functions like spawning a cube:

```
var UE = importNameSpace("UnityEngine");
var go = UE.GameObject.CreatePrimitive(PrimitiveType.Cube);
```

Thus, combining the 2D and 3D world we allow Html-DOM-elements to interact with GameObjects. Still being web-centric we can use REST, AJAX and others to connect to any services and CPS.

4.4   Remote UI Orchestration

A well known and often used practice in web-development is dynamically loading functionality from external sources, where *Lazy loading* is a common technique to load when needed. Utilizing the described Js-interpreter we implement such techniques in Unity, allowing us to hot-fetch code and data. Therefore transmitted data is either a audio/video stream or a message wrapped in JSON. In Js we can directly access the wrapped object and start using its contents. Commands are transmitted or received JSON objects. Since we can store Js-code in JSON objects, we can wrap data in a self-presenting manner *e.g.,* by shipping an visualization command together with an image. Since we can interpret the command at run-time we do not have to enforce a distinction between code and data at all.

---

[5] json2html: http://json2html.com.

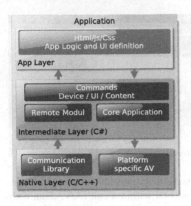
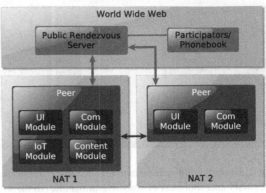

Fig. 3. *(left)* The application stack of MAUI. Data can be bi-directional passed up and down across software layers. The native layer *(purple)* holds hardware close modules for real-time communication and Audio-Video access. The intermediate layer *(blue)* holds wrappers for native libraries and modules for higher level functionality like special 3D Engine commands. The application layer *(turquoise)* holds all business logic and UI implementation. *(right) shows peer-to-peer and peer-2-server communication across the world wide web, where the server (orange) establishes the direct connection between peers (green).* (Color figure online)

Fundamental to commands is the generic web-based structure by using JSON objects. Our UI implementation allows us to append new JS code the current instance for later use. This is done either by adding <script> tags, by writing .js files which are linked within the DOM, by appending with jQuery.loadScript or by just adding it to a JS-runtime-object as function:

```
var receivedFct = "function(x) {return x+1;}";
var myFunc = new Function("return " + receivedFct)();
var res = myFunc(1); // res = 2
```

For single time use, we can run external code through eval() or create a function object for instant execution. In practice, the expert can alter, extend or replace the worker's UI. Thereby, functionality can be added ad-hoc and the UI can be controlled on a very granular level. The experts application provides shortcuts to common functions, like hide widgets, load an instruction application, bring back the worker's UI. For instance, an annotated captured frame of the video stream is send as ShowAnnotatedImage which translates to the following:

```
{
    "type":"CMD", "cmd":"ShowAnnotatedImage",
    "args":[ b64ImageData, AnnotationObject ]
}
```

A cmd-type message is consumed by ShowAnnotatedImage, a function defined in the Js-framework, which takes the args as arguments. Internally the function renders the image into a <img>-tag and draws an optional stroke-based annotations over it. Since we can vary the structure of the sent JSON, we can choose to be more specific or more general. Additionally, we can store any object for later using *e.g.*, like an email. Of course, this concepts allows to control the CPS directly from the expert side by calling available functions. In contrast to traditional remote desktop software, the expert does not have to navigate to a button and click it, instead he can directly activate its functionality.

In the current implementation, we categorize commands into three distinct categories: *UI Commands*, including command manipulating the UI like loading new content, where the experts replace the default-worker-UI (Fig. 2, right) with interactive step-by-step instructions; *Device Commands* including commands controlling the hardware like the RGB-camera; and *Content Commands*, including commands adding new contents like PDFs and images.

4.5 Backend

In order to keep track about users participating in a maintenance session, we use a phone-book similar to any modern real-time messaging application (Fig. 3, right). Furthermore, peer-to-peer calls are established between peers using RakNet's builtin functionality for NAT-Translation.

The beauty of our concept enabling hot-swapping of content unfolds in the management stage of AR, respectively UI content. We can simply host different UI versions, workflows and even application functionality remotely. These contents are downloaded by the clients when needed (*e.g.*, when new update are available, or the local cache runs out of date). This enables fully transparent and easily maintainable representations.

All components are included in Docker[6] containers, such that deployment of components on a distributed server infrastructure is straightforward.

5 Extended User Study

In our previous work [9], we performed a user study showing significant benefits when an experts takes over parts of the virtual interaction, freeing more mental capacities for physical tasks of the worker. In this work we extend the user-study to cover a larger diversity amongst participants from different occupations, including teachers and students in marketing, economics, psychology and other non-computer-science topics.

In the following we summarize our procedures to conduct the extended user-study and discuss our findings in detail. Following the target use-case (tele-assisted maintenance tasks), we analyze how a worker performs a multi-step procedure of repairing a CPS with and without the help of a remote expert. In particular, We focus on errors made under each condition to represent crucial real-world situations.

5.1 Evaluated Conditions

Two conditions of interest where evaluated where the worker has to repair a broken CPS following step-by-step instructions: *SelfNavigation* and *ExpertHelp*.

---

[6] Docker: https://www.docker.com/.

SelfNavigation (SN). All interactions are done by worker himself. There is no external support whatsoever. The worker can decide on his/her own without any feedback or confirmation. As far as the UI of the worker allows it, the worker can use all available windows, but cannot alter them. The focus is on how well the worker can follow written instructions across the virtual and the physical world.

ExpertHelp (EH). While performing the task and working along the step-by-step instructions, the worker is connected to the remote expert with audio/video and can ask for support at any time. The expert gives advice and takes over interactions with the workers UI inside the HMD. Following, the worker can spent more time and attention to the physical task and neglect most of the UI-interactions in the virtual world. Furthermore, the expert can decide which information is presented to the worker. This can be a dedicated control window for a CPS or a new UI(Application) designed around single purpose *e.g.,* interactive step-by-step instruction. Reducing the amount of tasks of the worker, we expect to free (mental) capacities, which reflects in reduced time-to-start(as discussed in [9]) and reduced error-rates.

The extended user-study has the main focus on evaluating the process of task completion, in particular if any error occurred. Since workers are instructed to follow step-by-step instruction, occurring errors caused by lack of concentration can tell a lot about cognitive load and the stress level. In the real-world, such tasks are often mentally demanding, are conducted under high time pressure and often tolerate no errors (manufacturing, power plants, and others).

5.2 The Repair Task

We want to examine the impact of a shared virtual and physical task on a worker. Our theory is that the expert help in controlling the UI should reduce the worker's mental workload and cognitive effort while maintaining a machine. Our prototypical CPS (the faulty device) is represented by a smart light-bulb[7], which includes a virtual control interface. A software-module was added to the application stack to control a variety of smart-home appliances and to capture user-based telemetry data like click-events. We created one app for each condition along with a look-and-feel alike training app to make users comfortable with the system.

The task contains both physical and virtual actions. Physical actions contain unplugging and re-plugging a power cord, pressing buttons and typing on a keyboard. Virtual actions include searching for the device, controlling the device (light-bulb), interacting with the device and reading instructions. Figure 4 depicts the faulty device (light-bulb in the box), the outlet and a participant successfully mastering the task. The task is divided into 5 stages:

1. At first, the faulty device lights up red.
2. In both conditions (*SN* and *EH*), the worker has to open the instructions within the UI (a list with nine step-by-step instructions) for the task.

---

[7] https://www2.meethue.com/.

Fig. 4. (left) User study equipment: faulty device (electronics box with light-bulb, with device id label on top, HoloLens and Bluetooth keyboard), (center) Power cord with labeled outlets Labeled outlets, (right) The worker wearing the HoloLens has completed the task, and the light-bulb turns green, as presented in our previous work [9]. (Color figure online)

3. The worker has to open the "light-bulb" widget to control the smart light-bulb. In *SN*, the worker must do this by searching through the menu. In *EH*, the list is opened by the remote expert.
4. While following the instruction, the worker has to perform a sequence of operations: switching off power, unplugging, re-plugging, and switching power on again. Power outlets are labeled by ID, and the instructions refer to particular outlet IDs for the re-plugging step.
5. The worker has to press the start button in the device-interface widget of the UI. The task finishes when the device lights up green.

5.3   Experimental Procedure

The conditions *SN* and *EH* were tested using a within-subject design. The tasks were alternated in the order of the conditions and between participants. Additionally the position of the power-plug was altered to further balance the study. Before starting the actual study, a quick training task was performed by each participant. The training was aimed to get used to the UI (same kind of widgets, but with different naming and contents) and to understand how to control the smart-light. No power-cord interaction where performed while training.

The study procedure included pre- and post-study questionnaires to elaborate on personal experience, the preferred method and subjective difficulty. Each participant was asked to comfortably put on the HoloLens and adjust it accordingly. Furthermore, they were put in the role of the worker instructed to repair the faulty device. At start the device lights up red and the app starts.

According to the description in our previous work, Fig. 4 depicts the faulty device and its device-id, the HoloLens with the bluetooth keyboard and the switch with the labeled outlets. A participant completing the task (green light) is shown on the far right of Fig. 4. A NASA TLX [17] questionnaire was conducted after each condition.

This user-study acts as an foundation to future studies planned in this field with MAUI. Therefore we are simply interested in the performance of the worker and his cognitive state. *Will the study follow our assumptions generated from conversations with our collaborators and their workers?*. We avoided using a volunteer expert in this first study, due to the big efforts of training, especially regarding consistency and the big unknown in operating the expert application. We decided to have an author play the

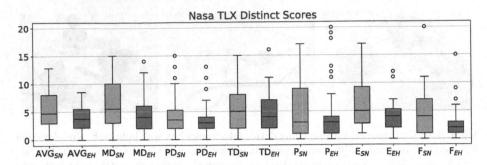

Fig. 5. A one-way ANOVA across all categories of the NASA TLX questionnaire show stastistical significance in the favor of **EH** in the categories **AVG** (Total Score, $p < 0.05$, $F_{1,86}, = 6.713$), **MD** (Mental Demand, $p < 0.05$, $F_{1,86}, = 6.712$), **E** (Effort, $p < 0.05$, $F_{1,86}, = 6.973$) and **B** (Frustration, $p < 0.05$, $F_{1,86}, = 5.947$). The categories PD (Physical Demand), TD (Temporal Demand) and P (Performance) showed not statistical difference whatsoever. (*Orange*) show distributions of *SN* and (*green*) distribution of *EH*. (Color figure online)

expert role in a passive and consistent way, offering just as much help as needed to the worker. In *EH*, the expert performed the device search using the vocally communicated device-ID, pointing out to carefully read through the step-by-step instructions and ask if help was wanted.

5.4   Extended Results

We tested 44 participants (6f), aged 21–40 (avg 28.95, median 29). As shown in [9], the age distribution is below the current[8] (approx. ~10 years), but is a representative cut through future generations. To check the technical fitness of participants, we specifically asked about the familiarity with PCs and step-by-step instructions. All participants performed step-by-step instructions and all of them use PCs on a regular basis. Half of the participants never used a HoloLens or a similar device before and a quarter never repaired or disassembled a PC. All participants found the training procedure suitable to get used of to the system.

A one-way repeated measures ANOVA was performed and we found main effects on NASA TLX scores supporting our hypothesis, *EH* being less mentally demanding and easier to operate over *SN*. We found statistical significance (significance level of 5%) towards *EH* in the overall average NASA TLX score ($p < 0.05$, $F_{1,86}, = 6.713$) and partially in its sub-scores Mental Demand (MD with $p < 0.05$, $F_{1,86}, = 6.712$), Effort (E, with $p < 0.05$, $F_{1,86}, = 6.712$) and Frustration (F with $p < 0.05$, $F_{1,86}, = 5.947$). No significance was found for Physical Demand (PD), Temporal Demand (TD) and Performance (P). However, our extend result supports the hypothesis of MAUI with *EH* relieving the worker while performing CPS heavy tasks. Furthermore, we see noteworthy improvements in a decreased Frustration and a reduced Effort, as well in a lower Mental demand. Figure 5 depicts the distribution over all measured NASA TLX Category scores pairwise for *SN* (orange) and *EH* (green).

---

[8] Workforce Age Distribution.

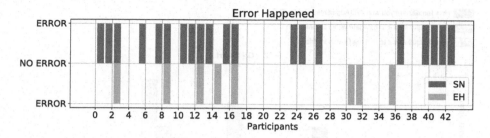

Fig. 6. Occurred errors over all 44 participants. The orange bars show occurred error while performing *SN* and green bars show errors when performed *EH*. Overall, *EH* shows far more occurred error compared to *SN*. No pattern was found correlated with which method was first performed. (Color figure online)

A more detailed look on the error-rate shown in Fig. 6 we find more often errors done while performing *SN* over *EH*. Since we alternate the order of *EH* and *SN*, we can exclude the first condition being more error-prune than the second one. Throughout the whole study participants make more errors when performing *SN*. Common errors include, error due to inattentively reading, pressing the wrong start-sequence for the device in the UI and unplugging without turning off. This errors are not directly related to this specific scenario, but are common mistakes when operating machinery, which goes hand-in-hand with experiences from industry. Counting any occurred error results in 45% of the participants making an error in SH and 18% making an error in *EH*. This results coincide with our previous work, where me only evaluated critical errors (such as missing a step from the instruction) where 25% of the participant made an error while performing *SN* where only 15% errors happened in *EH*.

Questionnaire Results. At the end of the study, each participant was asked to answer selective and Likert-style questions about his or her perceived impressions. 90.6% preferred *EH* over *SN* when asked about which method was easier to operate. Following this trend, 86.36% found it easier to retrieve information needed to complete the task from the system in *EH*. In some cases participant preferred *SN* over *EH*. A possible reason is low trust in the expert combined with being overzealous. Such aspects have a bigger HR (Human Resources) aspect to it, especially in industries like manufacturing.

Likert-style questions at the end of the examination give further insights. Most of the participants where somewhat familiar with AR or had heard about it. We did not find any correlation between being familiar with AR and the performance of participants, however. Over 30 participants found it neutral to easy to navigate within the UI, concluding that the UI is not an obstacle at first-time use. Just 5 out of 44 participants found it difficult to find the device interface (the widget for controlling the device, showing up only when entering the correct device-ID into the device search). Figure 7 depicts the distribution of the Likert question with trends towards easy/moderately familiar. Some of the participants did not read careful enough through the instructions and produced easily avoidable errors like wrong order or jump over an instruction. One participant pointed out that he was *tired to look for an outlet device-ID* where it took him a while to find it. Such cases showed up in small numbers, but more often in *SN* slightly proving

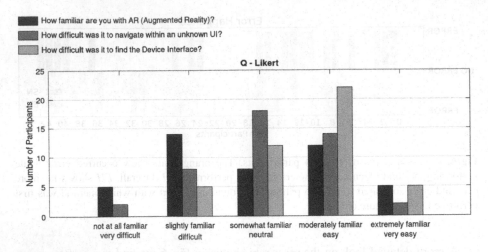

Fig. 7. Likert questionnaire results: Most of the participants where slightly familiar to moderately familiar with AR (dark green); Most of the participants found it neutral to easy to navigate an unknown UI (green); Most of the participants found i neutral to easy to find the device interface (yellow). (Color figure online)

that they did not spend enough attention. Following results from [9], problems caused due to the lack of concentration are avoidable (*e.g.*, caused through tiredness) and the cost of expert support can be better justified.

User Feedback. It was the first time using a device like the Hololens for half of the participants. It turned out, that air-taping with the head-locked cursor (dot as crosshair) was not always well perceived, cumbersome and tiring to use. Our UI design was liked and text was clear to read. Their perceived behaviour was homogeneous and in most case their performance matched with what they believed. Better hand tracking [35] will further improve the experience and make it less cumbersome to use for participants. No errors occurred because of miss-clicking.

Further findings based on our observations show that smaller widgets are good for seated (static) use, but too small for standing experiences. Clutter within the narrow field of view of the HoloLens is always tricky to handle. In MAUI the expert can take care of that by *e.g.*, turning of unused parts of the UI or by locking the UI to the environment.

6   Building a Mobile UI

In our previous work [9] we performed a qualitative developer user-study about the ease of use of the presented framework and to assess how easy it is for a new developer to extend and write new features or applications.

6.1   Use Case

A worker faces an issue with a personal computer, which fails to boot. Therefore, the worker uses an AR-enabled device (in our case a HoloLens) and calls the expert by

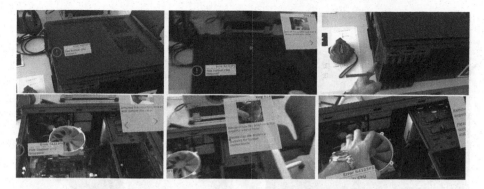

Fig. 8. Workers view of an PC repair: error reported by the CPS (*top-left*) and step-by-step instruction are enabled by the expert (*top-center*). Step-1: turn off the power (*top-right*) and remove the case-cover (Step-2, *bottom-left*); Step-3: remove the fan under instructions of the expert (*bottom-center*) and (*bottom-right*).

selecting the experts ID in the phonebook. First, an audio-video call is established. The expert can perceive the workers outfacing camera view, while the worker sees a live image of the expert.

After identifying the malfunctioning PC, the expert is able to obtain a diagnostic message from the PC over the network: "the fan is stalled". The expert raises the error to the worker by selecting the corresponding command in the remote commands menu. The remote command is shipped to the worker and displayed. The worker, however, is unfamiliar with this error and not really knowledgeable in disassembly of personal computers, so he asks for help and further guidance.

The expert in turn replaces the error message with step-by-step-instructions, depicted in Fig. 8. While going through the steps the worker requires more detailed instructions. To better describe the actual location (*i.e.*, transfer spatial understanding from the expert side to the worker), the expert decides to take a screenshot of the worker's view and to annotate the important areas where the fan-mounts are placed. By pressing the *Send* button, the annotation is sent and displayed in the workers view.

6.2 Developers

Each of both developers (*A* and *B*) was instructed to use our UI-framework to improve or modify the application of repairing a stuck fan in a PC (see Fig. 8). This application follows the same principles (UI exchangeable and controllable by the expert, step-by-step instructions, A/V connectivity), but with a more tangible use case.

Both had a web-development background in creating web-applications (Html, Css, Js). No inputs where given on what task to perform at any time and both participants had free choice. The procedure consisted of a one hour workshop as introduction into the framework followed by three hours of development. Due to the lack of an exhaustive documentation, one author answered typical documentation questions like *Where can I find this function?* Both were in there 30's and work in a technical field.

Fig. 9. Top: comparison of the default expert UI layout (left) *vs.* *A*'s improved layout (right, as shown in [9]). *A*'s version shows a better use of screen-space. Bottom: *B*'s improved layouts vs the default ones. *Close* separated from *maximize* (left) and a more ergonomic placement of the controls (right) to increase usability.

Changes by A: A chose to improve the layout of the expert application due to the bad usage of available screen space. Figure 9 top left depicts our version of the expert's application with a two-column design, smaller content widgets and navigation-bar in the top section on the left and *A*'s improved version on the top right. By re-arranging the navigation-bar vertically to the left hand side of the screen, it allows us to have floating widgets in different sizes unbound from the two column design.

Changes by B: B chose to tackle usability issues found. One being *close* and *maximize* being next to each in the Workers UI (Fig. 9, bottom-left) and the other being the placement of the controls in the step-by-step instructions. By moving *close* to the far left and keeping *maximize* on the right B could increase usability for the worker. Furthermore he updated the widget template to apply the change to all widgets. Step-by-step instructions were improved by moving the controls left and right of the center part instead of heaving them below (Fig. 9, bottom right). This improved aesthetics and the use of space, allowing for more uncluttered content. Slight improvements like this have an big impact in usability, especially the first one can reduce frustration when using the application.

Both participants were able to produce reasonable results in the given time-frame and even surpassed our expectations. The overall feedback was that it was easy to use with some knowledge on web-technologies. They could use the framework and its provided functions and templates to produce reasonable results. The assessed NASA TLX questionnaires showed little Frustration for *B* and a higher level for *A*, correlating with the bigger modifications. Both had a good estimate of their performance, even if the authors would judge them less self critical.

Fig. 10. Mobile UI based on the feedback and outcome of the user-studies. (top-left) main-menu for various functions; (top-right) Incoming call screen; (bottom-left) active widgets within the scroll-able ticker-style view; (bottom-right) the settings widgets with tabs and toggles.

6.3 Handheld AR

The promising outcome of the developer study and the feedback of the user-study let us to rethink concepts of the UI for mobile handheld use. Therefore we ported our application to mobile phones and tablets, implementing a new mobile UI for Android and iOS use, respectively.

Figure 10 depicts the main-menu, an incoming call, the ticker view with multiple widgets open and the settings widget. One of the main reasons to reconsider handheld usage is the inherent request for this by industries, allowing for mobile use at-sight. We increased the icon-size and implemented a scrolling widgets approach (ticker-view), allowing widgets to pop-up either at the end or at the beginning of the ticker-view. Incoming calls and messages are shown in full-screen and need to be acknowledged.

The core changes include modifying the web templates (JSON-transforms for json2html), modifying Css-stylesheets for small screen use and adding. Those changes did not affect the application-framework and only utilized our Js-framework. Icon size where fit to be finger-friendly and font-sizes adapt to the actual handheld device. Again, the beauty of our UI management approach fully unfolds, as minor changes are sufficient to move between head-worn and handheld devices.

7   Discussion and Conclusion

Easy-to-adapt and *easy-to-extend* are key aspect in the industrial world. A hand full of web-developers are always part of development teams at factories to realize custom in-house solutions. Our extendable approach allows such teams to add their content and business logic and to fully integrate into existing infrastructure.

We have extended our previous work MAUI, where we introduce an new mobile UI implemented by only using our Js-framework, an extended user-study showing that repairing a CPS is more error-prone when a worker has to handle all virtual and physical tasks and we given important details about our implementation and show how easy it is to extend and modify MAUI. Furthermore, applications can easily be hot-loaded and live-patched allowing for continuous deploy- and development.

The extended quantitative user-study covered more participants from non-technical professions like teaching. The majority of the participants preferred EH over SN, which is further supported by less errors made in EH. NASA TLX shows a higher demand when operating alone all physical and virtual tasks (SN).

Results of the developer study and inputs were used to create a mobile version of MAUI capable of running on Android and iOS. Insights on how to use our framework have been described, making it easy to create new applications. The developer study shows that developers with basic web knowledge can perform meaningful changes to existing applications and, given enough time, could rather easily create whole applications themselves. Furthermore, all modifications can be implemented using web-technologies and do not require special knowledge in Unity, C#, C++ or `compilation` which was also observed by MacIntyre *et al.* [27]. Furthermore, we showed how to use `Js` running inside Unity to write code which interacts with the 3D world of Unity.

In the future, we plan run further tests in production facilities to gather more insights and further improve MAUI. Additionally, UI experts can further improve the usability and support improved user-interfaces with user-studies. We can further improve the widget-placement and behaviour to allow for bigger flexibility of the worker and the expert. A user interface management to improve continuous delivery will further smooth the process.

Acknowledgements. The authors wish to thank Denis Kalkofen. This work was supported by FFG grant 859208.

References

1. Alce, G., Roszko, M., Edlund, H., Olsson, S., Svedberg, J., Wallergård, M.: [POSTER] AR as a user interface for the internet of things - comparing three interaction models. In: ISMAR-adj, pp. 81–86, October 2017. https://doi.org/10.1109/ISMAR-Adjunct.2017.37
2. Barakonyi, I., Fahmy, T., Schmalstieg, D.: Remote collaboration using augmented reality videoconferencing. In: Proceedings of Graphics Interface (GI), pp. 89–96. Canadian Human-Computer Communications Society (2004). http://dl.acm.org/citation.cfm?id=1006058.1006070
3. Bauer, M., Kortuem, G., Segall, Z.: "Where are you pointing at?" A study of remote collaboration in a wearable videoconference system. In: ISWC, pp. 151–158, October 1999. https://doi.org/10.1109/ISWC.1999.806696
4. Baumeister, J., et al.: Cognitive cost of using augmented reality displays. TVCG **23**(11), 2378–2388 (2017). https://doi.org/10.1109/TVCG.2017.2735098
5. Chastine, J.W., Nagel, K., Zhu, Y., Hudachek-Buswell, M.: Studies on the effectiveness of virtual pointers in collaborative augmented reality. In: 3DUI, pp. 117–124 (2008)
6. Chen, S., et al.: SEMarbeta: mobile sketch-gesture-video remote support for car drivers. In: Augmented Human International Conference (AH) (2013)

7. Ens, B., Hincapié-Ramos, J.D., Irani, P.: Ethereal planes: A design framework for 2D information spaces in 3D mixed reality environments. In: SUI. ACM (2014)
8. Feiner, S., MacIntyre, B., Haupt, M., Solomon, E.: Windows on the world: 2D windows for 3D augmented reality. In: UIST, pp. 145–155. ACM (1993). https://doi.org/10.1145/168642. 168657. http://doi.acm.org/10.1145/168642.168657
9. Fleck, P., Reyes-Aviles, F., Pirchheim, C., Arth, C., Schmalstieg, D.: MAUI: tele-assistance for maintenance of cyber-physical systems. In: VISIGRAPP 2020 - Proceedings of the 15th International Joint Conference on Computer Vision, Imaging and Computer Graphics Theory and Applications (2020). https://doi.org/10.5220/0009093708000812
10. Funk, M., Bächler, A., Bächler, L., Kosch, T., Heidenreich, T., Schmidt, A.: Working with AR?: a long-term analysis of in-situ instructions at the assembly workplace. In: PETRA, pp. 222–229. ACM (2017). https://doi.org/10.1145/3056540.3056548. http://doi.acm.org/10.1145/3056540.3056548
11. Funk, M., Kosch, T., Schmidt, A.: Interactive worker assistance: comparing the effects of in-situ projection, head-mounted displays, tablet, and paper instructions. In: UBICOMP, pp. 934–939. ACM (2016). https://doi.org/10.1145/2971648.2971706. http://doi.acm.org/10.1145/2971648.2971706
12. Fussell, S.R., Setlock, L.D., Yang, J., Ou, J., Mauer, E., Kramer, A.D.I.: Gestures over video streams to support remote collaboration on physical tasks. Hum.-Comput. Interact 19(3), 273–309 (2004)
13. Gauglitz, S., Nuernberger, B., Turk, M., Höllerer, T.: In touch with the remote world: remote collaboration with augmented reality drawings and virtual navigation. In: VRST, pp. 197–205. ACM (2014). https://doi.org/10.1145/2671015.2671016. https://doi.acm.org/10.1145/2671015.2671016
14. Gauglitz, S., Nuernberger, B., Turk, M., Höllerer, T.: World-stabilized annotations and virtual scene navigation for remote collaboration. In: UIST, pp. 449–459. ACM, New York (2014). https://doi.org/10.1145/2642918.2647372. https://doi.acm.org/10.1145/2642918.2647372
15. Gurevich, P., Lanir, J., Cohen, B., Stone, R.: TeleAdvisor: a versatile augmented reality tool for remote assistance. In: CHI, pp. 619–622. ACM (2012). https://doi.org/10.1145/2207676. 2207763. http://doi.acm.org/10.1145/2207676.2207763
16. Han, F., Liu, J., Hoff, W., Zhang, H.: [poster] planning-based workflow modeling for AR-enabled automated task guidance. In: ISMAR-adj, pp. 58–62, October 2017. https://doi.org/10.1109/ISMAR-Adjunct.2017.32
17. Hart, S.G., Staveland, L.E.: Development of NASA-TLX (task load index): results of empirical and theoretical research. Hum. Ment. Workload 1(3), 139–183 (1988)
18. Henderson, S., Feiner, S.: Exploring the benefits of augmented reality documentation for maintenance and repair. TVCG 17(10), 1355–1368 (2011). https://doi.org/10.1109/TVCG. 2010.245
19. Huang, W., Alem, L.: HandsinAir: a wearable system for remote collaboration on physical tasks. In: CSCW, pp. 153–156. ACM (2013). https://doi.org/10.1145/2441955.2441994. http://doi.acm.org/10.1145/2441955.2441994
20. Kim, S., Lee, G.A., Sakata, N.: Comparing pointing and drawing for remote collaboration. In: ISMAR, pp. 1–6, October 2013. https://doi.org/10.1109/ISMAR.2013.6671833
21. Kirk, D., Stanton Fraser, D.: Comparing remote gesture technologies for supporting collaborative physical tasks. In: CHI, pp. 1191–1200. ACM (2006). https://doi.org/10.1145/ 1124772.1124951. http://doi.acm.org/10.1145/1124772.1124951
22. Kollatsch, C., Schumann, M., Klimant, P., Lorenz, M.: [poster] industrial augmented reality: transferring a numerical control connected augmented realty system from marketing to maintenance. In: ISMAR-adj, pp. 39–41, October 2017. https://doi.org/10.1109/ISMAR-Adjunct. 2017.27

23. Krueger, M.W., Gionfriddo, T., Hinrichsen, K.: VIDEOPLACE - an artificial reality. In: CHI, pp. 35–40. ACM, New York (1985). https://doi.org/10.1145/317456.317463. http://doi.acm.org/10.1145/317456.317463

24. Kurata, T., Sakata, N., Kourogi, M., Kuzuoka, H., Billinghurst, M.: Remote collaboration using a shoulder-worn active camera/laser. In: ISWC, vol. 1, pp. 62–69, October 2004. https://doi.org/10.1109/ISWC.2004.37

25. Kuzuoka, H., Oyama, S., Yamazaki, K., Suzuki, K., Mitsuishi, M.: GestureMan: a mobile robot that embodies a remote instructor's actions. In: CSCW, pp. 155–162. ACM, New York (2000). https://doi.org/10.1145/358916.358986. http://doi.acm.org/10.1145/358916.358986

26. Lee, T., Hollerer, T.: Viewpoint stabilization for live collaborative video augmentations. In: ISMAR, pp. 241–242. IEEE Computer Society (2006). https://doi.org/10.1109/ISMAR.2006.297824. https://doi.org/10.1109/ISMAR.2006.297824

27. MacIntyre, B., Hill, A., Rouzati, H., Gandy, M., Davidson, B.: The argon AR web browser and standards-based AR application environment. In: ISMAR, pp. 65–74, October 2011. https://doi.org/10.1109/ISMAR.2011.6092371

28. Oda, O., Sukan, M., Feiner, S., Tversky, B.: Poster: 3D referencing for remote task assistance in augmented reality. In: 3DUI, pp. 179–180, March 2013. https://doi.org/10.1109/3DUI.2013.6550237

29. O'Neill, J., Castellani, S., Roulland, F., Hairon, N., Juliano, C., Dai, L.: From ethnographic study to mixed reality: a remote collaborative troubleshooting system. In: CSCW, pp. 225–234. ACM (2011). https://doi.org/10.1145/1958824.1958859. http://doi.acm.org/10.1145/1958824.1958859

30. Ou, J., Fussell, S.R., Chen, X., Setlock, L.D., Yang, J.: Gestural communication over video stream: supporting multimodal interaction for remote collaborative physical tasks. In: ICMI, pp. 242–249. ACM, New York (2003). https://doi.org/10.1145/958432.958477. http://doi.acm.org/10.1145/958432.958477

31. Rambach, J., Pagani, A., Stricker, D.: [POSTER] augmented things: enhancing AR applications leveraging the internet of things and universal 3D object tracking. In: ISMAR-adj, pp. 103–108 (Oct 2017). https://doi.org/10.1109/ISMAR-Adjunct.2017.42

32. Roulland, F., Castellani, S., Valobra, P., Ciriza, V., O'Neill, J., Deng, Y.: Mixed reality for supporting office devices troubleshooting. In: VR, pp. 175–178, March 2011. https://doi.org/10.1109/VR.2011.5759458

33. Tzimas, E., Vosniakos, G.C., Matsas, E.: Machine tool setup instructions in the smart factory using augmented reality: a system construction perspective. IJIDeM (2018). https://doi.org/10.1007/s12008-018-0470-z

34. Wellner, P., Freemann, S.: The double DigitalDesk: shared editing of paper documents. Technical report EPC-93-108, Xerox Research (1993)

35. Xiao, R., Schwarz, J., Throm, N., Wilson, A.D., Benko, H.: Mrtouch: Adding touch input to head-mounted mixed reality. TVCG 24(4), 1653–1660 (2018). https://doi.org/10.1109/TVCG.2018.2794222. https://doi.ieeecomputersociety.org/10.1109/TVCG.2018.2794222

On the Use of 3D CNNs for Video Saliency Modeling

Yasser Abdelaziz Dahou Djilali[1]([✉]), Mohamed Sayah[2], Kevin McGuinness[1], and Noel E. O'Connor[1]

[1] Insight Center for Data Analytics, Dublin City University, Dublin 9, Ireland
yasser.dahoudjilali2@mail.dcu.ie
[2] Laboratory LITIO, FSEA Faculty, University Oran1, Oran, Algeria

Abstract. There has been emerging interest recently in three dimensional (3D) convolutional neural networks (CNNs) as a powerful tool to encode spatio-temporal representations in videos, by adding a third temporal dimension to pre-existing 2D CNNs. In this chapter, we discuss the effectiveness of using 3D convolutions to capture the important motion features in the context of video saliency prediction. The method filters the spatio-temporal features across multiple adjacent frames. This cubic convolution could be effectively applied on a dense sequence of frames propagating the previous frames' information into the current, reflecting processing mechanisms of the human visual system for better saliency prediction. We extensively evaluate the model performance compared to the state-of-the-art video saliency models on both 2D and 360° videos. The architecture can efficiently learn expressive spatio-temporal representations and produce high quality video saliency maps on three large-scale 2D datasets, DHF1K, UCF-SPORTS and DAVIS. Investigations on the 360° Salient360! and datasets show how the approach can generalise.

Keywords: Visual attention · Video saliency · Deep learning · 3D CNN

1 Introduction

Human attention is the key underpinning consideration in saliency research. In fact, the terms "attention" and "saliency" are highly correlated in most psychological definitions, and are often used interchangeably in the computer vision community. However, attention is an old concept which was investigated first in philosophy, later in psychology and neuroscience, and most recently as a computer vision problem in the field of computer science [64]. Early advances in psychology [38] related attention to the focalization and concentration of consciousness, opposed to the concept of distraction. [92] framed the question of attention into five main levels, that build upon one another in a hierarchical manner:

- **Focused Attention:** the ability to bring an amount of information into conscious awareness;
- **Sustained Attention:** the vigilance to maintain the cognitive resources allocated to a continuous phenomenon;

© Springer Nature Switzerland AG 2022
K. Bouatouch et al. (Eds.): VISIGRAPP 2020, CCIS 1474, pp. 453–476, 2022.
https://doi.org/10.1007/978-3-030-94893-1_21

- **Selective Attention:** implies withdrawal from some competing stimuli to effectively deal with others;
- **Alternating Attention:** the ability to shift between different tasks running in parallel;
- **Divided Attention:** dealing with multiple tasks requiring different sensory resources.

The feature integration theory proposed by [97] stands out as the pioneering work describing which visual features direct human attention. Indeed, this formed the starting point of many computational models. Furthermore, computer vision approaches mainly consider the selective mechanism when modeling attention, where the subtle definition of saliency would relate to the gaze policy on the scene i.e. characterizing some subsets of the space on which a human subject would focus. The term "salient" emerged in the context of bottom-up computations [36,49], while attention refers more broadly to scene-driven bottom-up (BU) or expectation-driven top-down (TD) mechanisms. It should be noted that computational models have been proposed for imitating the attentional mechanisms of the Human Visual Systems (HVS) for both dynamic and static scenes.

How, when, and why human behavior selects pertinent image regions are key questions when modeling attention. Inspired from anatomical findings, and the early understanding of how the human visual system functions, many interesting results were derived demonstrating that visual attention could be influenced by the regions maximizing a reward in a task driven scenario [93], which are typically the most informative or surprising regions [10,34]. This in turn led to pioneering seminal works in saliency prediction [6,36,69,85,86,88,98]. For an extensive eye movements survey, readers are referred to [82]. Despite the deep thinking behind these methods, and the elegant mathematical formulation of the mathematical prediction models, all these approaches share the paradigm of learning the representation in one step, which does not reflect the way in which humans process the sensory data in multiple cognitive layers. Consequently, the performance of these approaches were far from the "infinite humans" baselines [44].

Thanks mainly to advances in deep learning, the development of computational models of human attention has received renewed research interest in recent years [64] – see [101] for a comprehensive recent review. Dynamic fixation prediction, or video saliency prediction, is very useful for understanding human attentional behaviors for video content and has multiple practical real-world applications, e.g. tracking [21,63], video shot detection [2,104], image and video compression [29,33,76], video summarization [23,62,65], and object segmentation [37,102]. The reader is referred to [84] for a detailed survey of saliency applications. It is thus highly desirable to have robust high-performance video saliency prediction models.

Recently introduced saliency benchmarks for images and videos, such as DIEM [71], UCF-SPORTS [67], HOLLYWOOD-2 [67], MIT300 [11], SALICON [43], CAT2000[9], DHF1K [100] and LEDOV [41], have allowed researchers to effectively train deep learning models in an end-to-end manner by formulating saliency as a regression problem. However, the reported performances on video (dynamic scene) datasets according to commonly used saliency metrics are still far from those reported for images (static scene). This is most likely due to the rapid transition of video frames that makes dynamic saliency prediction very challenging. Many video saliency deep learning based models separate spatial features from temporal features. This is implemented, for example, by a CNN module to extract spatial features, which can then be aggregated into an LSTM module to capture the temporal features [30].

In this chapter we present the details of our proposed video saliency predction model, 3DSal, originally published in [16], that uses a 3D CNN architecture [39]. When performing a cubic convolution, our model captures spatio-temporal features in one 3D CNN module. The dimensions r and s of the cube extract the spatial features while the t axis extracts the temporal features. In this way, the model learns saliency by fusing spatio-temporal features for calculating the final saliency map. Our key contribution is a 3D CNN architecture for predicting human gaze in dynamic scenes, which explicitly learns the hidden relationship between adjacent frames for accurate saliency prediction. In this chapter we extend the work originally presented in [16] in the following ways:

- We present a more detailed description of the 3DSal architecture, arguing the importance of the weighting function.
- We reviewed the most recent saliency works.
- We discussed the saliency task adaptability from a fixed viewport to multiple viewports prediction in the case of 360° videos.
- We investigated the state-of-the-art models performance of low level attention situations, as one of the most prominent Human Visual System features.

The remainder of this chapter is organized as follows. Section 2 provides an overview of related video saliency models. Section 3 gives a detailed description of the proposed deep saliency framework. Section 4 compares the experimental results to state-of-the-art methods. Finally, we conclude this work in Sect. 5. The results can be reproduced with the source code and trained models available on GitHub: link.

2   Computational Models for Saliency Prediction

In this section we review important works related to attention modelling for both static and dynamic scenes. We consider both heuristic and data-driven approaches.

2.1   Static Saliency Models

Heuristic Approaches. Saliency prediction for images has been widely studied during the last few decades. As pioneers Itti et al. [36] derived bottom-up visual saliency using center-surround differences across multi-scale image features. The conspicuity maps are obtained from linearly summed and normalized feature maps where three features are considered: color C, orientation l, and intensity I:

$$C_I = f_I, \quad C_C = \mathcal{N}(\sum_{l \in L_C} f_l), \quad C_O = \mathcal{N}(\sum_{l \in L_O} f_l). \tag{1}$$

Where $\mathcal{N}(.)$ is the map normalisation operator. The final saliency map is the average of the three conspicuity maps: $S = \frac{1}{3}\sum_{k \in \{I,C,O\}} C_k$. A more advanced bottom-up saliency approach based on other HVS features, namely, contrast sensitivity functions, perceptual decomposition, visual masking, and center-surround interactions, was proposed in [56].

Other static saliency models e.g. [10,22,24,26,50,72,73,90] are mostly cognitive based models relying on computing multiple visual features such as color, edge, and orientation at multiple spatial scales to produce a saliency map. Other approaches used Bayesian models built on top of the cognitive models to add a layer of prior knowledge (e.g., scene context or gist), using a probabilistic approach such as Bayes rule for combination [20,34,75,95,110]. These models have the ability to unify many factors in a principled manor. Other report approaches, albeit not considered to be within the scope of this chapter, include graphical models, information theoretic models, and decision theoretic models.

Data-Driven Approaches. Known also as pattern classification models, the essence of data-driven approaches is learning models from recorded eye-fixations or labeled salient maps. [47] introduced a non-parametric bottom-up approach for learning saliency from human eye fixation data. The model consists of a support vector machine (SVM) to determine the saliency using the local intensities and was the first method not requiring any prior assumptions on HVS features to encode saliency. Similarly, [46] trained a linear SVM on 1003 labelled images using a set of low, mid, and high-level image features. More recent deep learning based static saliency models e.g. [15,32,52,53,61, 77,78] have achieved remarkable improvements relying on the success of deep neural networks and the availability of large-scale saliency datasets for static scenes, such as those described in [9,11,43].

The authors of [99] and [52] were the first to use CNNs for saliency prediction when introducing eDN and DeepFix, respectively. DeepFix initialized the first 5 convolution blocks with VGG-16 weights, then added two novel Location Based Convolutional (LBC) layers to capture semantics at multiple scales. Pan et al. [77] used Generative Adversarial Networks (GANs) [27] to build the SalGAN model. The network consists of a generator model whose weights are learned by back-propagation computed from a binary cross entropy (BCE) loss over existing saliency maps. The resulting prediction is processed by a discriminator network trained to solve a binary classification task between the saliency maps generated at the generative stage and the ground truth ones in a min-max game, using the following adversarial loss:

$$\mathcal{L} = \alpha \mathcal{L}_{BCE} + L(D(I,S),1). \tag{2}$$

The objective is to optimise $L(D(I,S),1)$, where $D(I,S)$ is the probability of fooling the discriminator network by producing saliency maps that looks very similar to the Ground truth coming from the data distribution. [32] proposed SALICON, the model optimizes an objective function based on the saliency evaluation metrics, from two parallel streams at different image scales. [60] trained the deep spatial contextual long-term recurrent convolutional network (DSCLRCN), incorporating both global spatial interconnections and scene context modulation. EML-NET proposed by [40] consists of a disjoint encoder and decoder trained separately. Furthermore, the encoder can contain many networks extracting features, while the decoder learns to combine many latent variables generated by the encoder networks. These deep models achieves results closer to the human baseline results on the SALICON [43], MIT300 [11], and CAT2000 [9] datasets.

2.2 Dynamic Saliency Models

Models for dynamic scenes need to take into account egocentric movements or the motion of the scene being observed, as well as accounting for the short amount of time available to view a video frame ($\sim$1/30 s) compared to static images (typically 5 s). Dynamic saliency is usually formulated as bottom-up feature extraction with an ad-hoc temporal domain adaptation from previous time points [8]. This, in addition to the need for high computational and memory resources means that video saliency prediction is an extremely more challenging research question than static saliency prediction [7]. In contrast to static stimuli, few hand-crafted dynamic approaches have been proposed [5,25,28,55,66,75,87,108]. Boccignone [5] proposed a non-parametric Bayesian technique, namely variational inference on a mixture of Dirichlet processes. Based on HVS biology, [66] extracted two signals from a video corresponding to the outputs of the retina: parvocellular and magnocellular, to predict spatio-temporal saliency. [55] extended [56] to the spatio-temporal domain by combining chromatic, achromatic, and temporal priors. These methods all apply some linear/nonlinear algorithms to fuse spatial and temporal features. However, such a straight forward approach to combine spatial and temporal information often forces the model to lose the intrinsic correlation between these two complementary aspects.

Deep Saliency Models. More recent works have demonstrated the potential of learning saliency from large eye-fixation data distributions [1,4,16,19,42,54,59,70,100]. These are mainly based on two distinct network modules to deal with spatial and temporal fields separately. These works exhibit strong performance and show the potential of using neural networks for the video saliency problem. Bak et al. [4] were the first to leverage deep learning when they used a two-stream CNN architecture for video saliency prediction. Video frames and motion maps were fed to the two streams. [100] proposed a CNN-LSTM network architecture with an attention mechanism to explicitly encode static saliency information, thus allowing the LSTM to focus on learning a more flexible temporal saliency representation across successive frames. [79] introduced a temporal regularization for their previous model SalGAN [77] for static saliency prediction. In terms of architecture, they added a convolutional LSTM layer on top of the frame-based saliency prediction to adapt it for dynamic saliency prediction. SalEMA [59] added a conceptually simple exponential moving average of an internal convolutional state to the SalGAN network [77], arguing that saliency tends to be relatively consistent across successive frames, arguing that the use of ConvLSTM is not necessary. [54] proposed a composite attention mechanism that learns multi-scale local and global features priors end-to-end, designed in a two-stream approach with models learning appearance and motion features separately. UNISAL [19] proposed four novel domain adaptation techniques to enable strong shared features: Domain-Adaptive Priors, Domain-Adaptive Fusion, Domain-Adaptive Smoothing and Bypass-RNN. UNISAL achieved the state-of-the-art results on the DHF1K benchmark [100] (e.g. AUC-J: 0.901, NSS:2.776).

All these works consider the spatial domain as the most influential aspect, and use very little accumulated knowledge from the past ($\sim$70 ms), while the average human eye reaction time is of the order of 284 ms [89]. We propose that more importance needs to be given to the temporal domain for video saliency prediction. To this end, we exploit the temporal and spatial domain in an equal manner via the use of a 3D CNN, with a view to more appropriate spatio-temporal feature learning (see Fig. 1). Furthermore, we smooth adjacent frames to obtain good eye fixation quality saturation by introducing the tangent hyperbolic weighting function on the input sequence frames.

Spatio-temporal feature map

Fig. 1. 3D Convolution operation over adjacent frames [16].

2.3 Saliency Prediction for 360° Video/Image

360° video, referred to as panoramic, spherical, or omnidirectional video (ODV), is a new type of multimedia that provides the user with an immersive experience. The content of ODV is rendered to cover the entire 360 × 180 viewing space. Humans, however, naturally focus on the most attractive and interesting field-of-views (FoV) while ignoring others in their visual field. Despite significant advances in the field of saliency modelling on a fixed 2D viewport (see [7,35] for a comprehensive review), saliency prediction methods on 360° video/image are still in their infancy. A recent survey conducted by Xu et al. [105] reviewed many works for predicting the Head and eye movements saliency maps of 360° images and video that model the probability distribution of viewports/regions of interest (RoIs) of multiple subjects. Rai et al. [83] derived the volcano-like distribution of EM within the viewport. Results show that eye-gaze fixations are quasi-isotropically distributed in orientation, typically far away from the center of the viewport. Furthermore, ODV presents some statistical biases, as investigated in [106]. Human attention on 360° video is biased toward the equator and the front region, known as the equator bias, which could be leveraged as priors in modelling. Along with the statistical bias, a subject's attention is driven by the most salient objects in the scene.

Datasets and Models. Trained on recently published datasets [17, 106, 107, 111], a number of deep learning based saliency prediction approaches for 360° video have been proposed [14,94,106,109,111]. Zhang et al. [111] proposed a spherical convolutional neural network, spherical U-NET, trained following the teacher forcing technique, for applying a planar saliency CNN to a 3D geometry space, where the kernel is defined on a spherical crown, and the convolution involves the rotation of the kernel along the sphere. Mai et al. [106] applied deep reinforcement learning (DRL) to predict HM positions by maximizing the reward of imitating human HM scanpaths through the agent's actions. The reward, which measures the similarity between the predicted and ground-truth HM scanpaths, is estimated to evaluate the action made by the DRL model. The reward is then used to make a decision on the action through the DRL model: i.e., the HM scanpath in the current frame. Please refer to [105] for an extensive review.

3 3DSal Model

3.1 Overview

Figure 2 represents the overall architecture of our 3DSAL video saliency model. We consider i consecutive input frames: $\{F_{-i} \in \mathbb{R}^{224 \times 244 \times 3} : i \in \{0, ..., 5\}\}$. This is motivated by the psychological studies arguing that the latency for saccadic eye movement is about 284 ms [89], when watching a 30 fps video. The human eye is sensitive to exactly (0.284 ms × 30 fps) $\simeq 8$ frames. Thus, we set the batch size to six in order to approximate the ideal threshold and reflect the human visual system (HVS) process. The feature extractor function, modeled with a pre-trained VGG-16 [91] after removing the fully connected layers, outputs the feature maps of each frame separately. This design was motivated by the reduction of complexity while improving accuracy. Trained on the large-scale ImageNet dataset (1.4M images) [18], VGG-16 guarantees robust feature extraction performance. The output of the spatial feature extraction function is six feature cuboids: $F_{t-5}^*, z_{t-4}^*, ..., z_t^* \in \mathbb{R}^{14 \times 14 \times 512}$, and where the function G_Θ is modelled by the truncated VGG-16 model (for more details see [91]).

$$G_\Theta(\Gamma_x) - z_x^*, \tag{3}$$

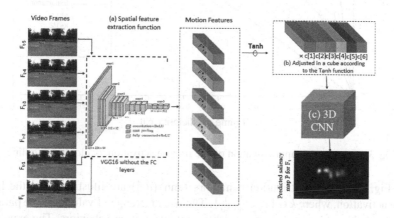

Fig. 2. Network architecture of 3DSAL [16]. (a) Feature extraction function with the truncated VGG-16. (b) Composition of adjacent feature maps via the use of tanh activation function. (c) Spatio-temporal feature fusion with a 3D CNN.

3.2 Cuboid Weights Tuning

Several questions related to the configuration of the cuboid array weights or coefficients $c[\,]$ could be discussed to better approximate the eye motion activation. Also, it is worth noting that one could develop new optimization algorithm or implement learning techniques to estimate these cuboid parameters $c[\,]$ to better fit the eye motion activation.

In our context, we are concerned with analysing the dispersion index of the experimental used coefficients $c[\,]$. First, the eye motion on a given object has been intuitively considered as a tangent hyperbolic activation function [74]. Also, to further preserve the consistency of human vision and avoid time and space computing complexity, we considered the previous six frames from the necessary eye sensitivity threshold. This enables us to approximately define the motion features for human eye movement.

Second, as we have used holistically a tangent hyperbolic behavior of the eye motion, different function curves $\tanh^k$ with respect to a parameter k were proposed (see Fig. 3). Thus, a k-distribution $[\tanh^k(c_i)_{,i\in[1,6]}]$ is associated to each coefficient array $c[\ ]$ to design a curve behavior of the eye motion.

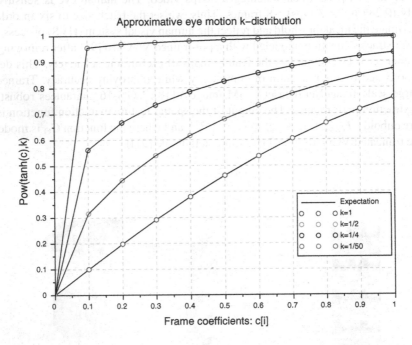

Fig. 3. k-distribution approximation of eye motion activation. (Color figure online)

In Fig. 3, some k-distribution behaviors $\tanh^k(c[\ ])$ are illustrated for the human motion activation, where $k \in \{1, \frac{1}{2}, \frac{1}{4}, \frac{1}{50}\}$. The use of a range of values for the parameter k is motivated by our concern to cover different eye motion behaviors. The expectation eye motion for a given k is represented by the continuous black curve, while the experimental values are marked by colored circles. Hence, different k parameter values can be proposed to approximately model the eye motion behavior, and for each k there exists multiple configuration $c[\ ]$. Also, it is noteworthy that for a configuration $c[\ ] = [c_i]_{,i=1\cdots6}$ where $c_i \in [0, 1]$ the $\lim_{k\to 0} \tanh^k(c[\ ]) = [1]$ and $\lim_{k\to\infty} \tanh^k(c[\ ]) = [0]$.

To strengthen and to refine the quality of the experimental parameters used $c[\ ]$, we have estimated the dispersion index of the k-distribution behavior $\tanh^k$ for each set of experimental coefficients $c[\ ]$. This characterization for the k-distribution using the mean μ, the standard deviation σ and the dispersion index σ^2/μ, should give a better approximation of the eye motion activation and sensitivity behavior on real frames.

When the dispersion index (σ^2/μ) is equal to 1, the k-distribution $\tanh^k(c[\ ])$ represents *well-dispersed* frames. If the dispersion index is less than 1, the frames are defined to be *under-dispersed*. This indicates that the values $\tanh^k(c[i])_{i=1\cdots6}$ are highly dependent. In the case where the values $\tanh^k(c[\,])$ are *over-dispersed*, the k-distribution is over diversified and the frames should be completely independent. In our context, we should avoid two borderline cases including equal weight coefficients $c[\,]$ or independent highly disparate $c[\,]$ parameters. This means a dispersion index equal to zero with the mean $\mu = 1$ and a standard deviation $\sigma = 0$.

Let us consider the k-distribution approximates for the eye motion considering the suite of k values in $[1, \frac{1}{2}, \frac{1}{4}, \frac{1}{50}]$, resulting in seven (07) experimental configurations $c_\#[\,]$ in the following Table 1. Firstly, we consider the under-dispersed k-distribution terms (representing approximately the eye motion) for each configuration $c_j[\,]_{,j \in \{1,2,\cdots,7\}}$ characterised by the smallest dispersion index σ^2/μ and a standard deviation σ far from zero. It is clear that for all the configurations in $k = \frac{1}{50}$ and in particular for $c_7[\,]$, the k-distribution terms are strongly linked, this is because the dispersion index and the standard deviation tend both to zero. Secondly, let us consider the configurations with the minimum index dispersion and (10^{-2}) scale deviation sensitivity in Table 1. We notice that the candidate configurations are $c_4[\,]$, $c_5[\,]$, and $c_6[\,]$.

Finally, the analysis of the dispersion index for the $\tanh^k$ distributions on the experimental configurations $c_\#[\,]$ enables us to use a suitable weight $c[i]_{i=1,\cdots 6}$ for the motion frames – see bold weights in Table 2. Considering for example the vector of parameters $c_5 = [0.4, 0.5, 0.6, 0.7, 0.8, 1.0]$ as illustrated in Table 2, we can reach the eye fixation quality saturation in the 6th spatial frame. As such, the temporal dimension is defined as a continuation of six c-weighted latent representations. In each step, the 6th spatial frame is determined via an iterative process in which the spatial frames $F_{t-5}, F_{t-4}, F_{t-3}, F_{t-2}$, and F_{t-1} are used to compute the F_t saliency map. Finally, each of the six cuboids, weighted with respect to their importance in the learning process, are adjusted in a temporary order to construct one spatio-temporal feature map. Note that the six frames do not represent a large variation of space and that their concatenation preserves the spatial information when finding the correlation in time for each pixel location. Later, a spatio-temporal feature map of $6\times$ frames determines the spatio-temporal latent variable $\mathbb{S} \in \mathbb{R}^{6 \times 14 \times 14 \times 512}$. The 3D CNN takes $\mathbb{S}$ as an input, to perform a spatio-temporal fusion, in order to learn saliency. Then, a saliency map $P \in \mathbb{R}^{224 \times 224}$ is generated to represent the saliency map for F_t.

3.3   3D CNN Architecture

3D ConvNets have shown the potential for spatio-temporal feature learning. Compared to a 2D ConvNet, a 3D ConvNet has the ability to better model temporal information by virtue of 3D convolutions and 3D pooling operations. In 2D ConvNets, convolution and pooling operations are only performed spatially. 3D ConvNets perform those operations spatio-temporally to preserve temporal information in the input signals resulting in an output volume (see Fig. 1). The same phenomena is applicable for 2D and 3D pooling [96].

As shown in Table 3, we built a five block decoder 3D CNN network to learn saliency in a *slow fusion* manner. Each block consists of Two 3D convolutions, followed by 3D transpose convolution operations, with a ReLU (Rectified Linear Unit) activation function. The role of Deconv3D is to up-sample the feature map resolution and Conv3D to construct the spatio-temporal features for saliency learning. We denote the triplet (t, r, s) as the kernel size for Deconv3D and Conv3D layers. We use the t axis

Table 1. k-distribution $\tanh^k$ dispersion for configurations $c_\#[\,]$.

k parameter in $tanh^k$	$c_\#$	Configuration $c_\#[\,]$	Stdeviation σ	Mean μ	Index σ^2/μ
k = 1	c_1	[0.1, 0.2, 0.3, 0.4, 0.5, 0.6]	0.1642754	0.3279119	0.0822977
	c_2	[0.2, 0.3, 0.4, 0.5, 0.6, 0.7]	0.1528469	0.4120286	0.0567004
	c_3	[0.3, 0.4, 0.5, 0.6, 0.7, 0.8]	0.1399626	0.4898055	0.0399945
	c_4	**[0.4, 0.5, 0.6, 0.7, 0.8, 0.9]**	**0.1262893**	0.5606364	**0.028448**
	c_5	**[0.4, 0.5, 0.6, 0.7, 0.8, 1.0]**	**0.1382436**	0.5681857	**0.0336356**
	c_6	**[0.5, 0.6, 0.7, 0.8, 0.9, 1.0]**	**0.1124326**	0.6242439	**0.0202503**
	c_7	[1.0, 1.0, 1.0, 1.0, 1.0, 1.0]	0.0	0.7615942	0.0
k = 1/2	c_1	[0.1, 0.2, 0.3, 0.4, 0.5, 0.6]	0.1553874	0.554789	0.0435215
	c_2	[0.2, 0.3, 0.4, 0.5, 0.6, 0.7]	0.1245755	0.6317405	0.0245655
	c_3	[0.3, 0.4, 0.5, 0.6, 0.7, 0.8]	0.1030524	0.6935097	0.0153131
	c_4	**[0.4, 0.5, 0.6, 0.7, 0.8, 0.9]**	**0.0861881**	0.7446113	**0.0099762**
	c_5	**[0.4, 0.5, 0.6, 0.7, 0.8, 1.0]**	**0.0928244**	0.749003	**0.0115038**
	c_6	**[0.5, 0.6, 0.7, 0.8, 0.9, 1.0]**	**0.0723342**	0.7873269	**0.0066456**
	c_7	[1.0, 1.0, 1.0, 1.0, 1.0, 1.0]	0.0	0.8726936	0.0
k = 1/4	c_1	[0.1, 0.2, 0.3, 0.4, 0.5, 0.6]	0.1093411	0.7381234	0.0161971
	c_2	[0.2, 0.3, 0.4, 0.5, 0.6, 0.7]	0.0803508	0.7914293	0.0081577
	c_3	[0.3, 0.4, 0.5, 0.6, 0.7, 0.8]	0.0628804	0.8307916	0.0047592
	c_4	**[0.4, 0.5, 0.6, 0.7, 0.8, 0.9]**	**0.050516**	0.8616756	**0.0029615**
	c_5	**[0.4, 0.5, 0.6, 0.7, 0.8, 1.0]**	**0.0540083**	0.8640441	**0.0033759**
	c_6	**[0.5, 0.6, 0.7, 0.8, 0.9, 1.0]**	**0.0411112**	0.8865204	**0.0019065**
	c_7	[1.0, 1.0, 1.0, 1.0, 1.0, 1.0]	0.0	0.9341807	0.0
k = 1/50	c_1	[0.1, 0.2, 0.3, 0.4, 0.5, 0.6]	0.0121518	0.9752978	0.0001514
	c_2	[0.2, 0.3, 0.4, 0.5, 0.6, 0.7]	0.0081761	0.9811395	0.0000681
	c_3	[0.3, 0.4, 0.5, 0.6, 0.7, 0.8]	0.0060624	0.9851023	0.0000373
	c_4	[0.4, 0.5, 0.6, 0.7, 0.8, 0.9]	0.0046868	0.9880547	0.0000222
	c_5	[0.4, 0.5, 0.6, 0.7, 0.8, 1.0]	0.0049795	0.9882579	0.0000251
	c_6	[0.5, 0.6, 0.7, 0.8, 0.9, 1.0]	0.0037049	0.9903441	0.0000139
	c_7	[1.0, 1.0, 1.0, 1.0, 1.0, 1.0]	0.0	0.994568	0.0

in the kernel to cover the temporal dimension in the kernel, while, (r,s) denotes the spatial kernel size. Consider a convolutional layer l and the input spatio-temporal units $\mathbb{S}$. The ith output unit $V_{i,K}{}^{(l)}$ for the layer l is computed as:

$$
\left(V_{i,K}^{(l)}\right)_{(x,y,z)} = \sum_{c=1}^{C}\left(\sum_{t=1}^{T}\sum_{r=1}^{R}\sum_{s=1}^{S}\left(W_{i,K,c}^{(l)}{}_{(t,r,s)} \times U_{i,c}^{(l-1)}{}_{(x+t,y+r,z+s)}\right)\right) + \left(B_{i,K}^{(l)}\right),
\tag{4}
$$

where C is the channel number for the layer (l) and x, y, z are the cubic spatial dimensions. The parameter K is considered as the channel dimension for the output unit $V^{(l)}$.

Table 2. Fixation quality motion.

Frames F_t	Weight $c[\,]$	Fixation $\tanh^k(c[i])$	Variation $\Delta(\tanh^k(c[i]))$	Saturation $\sum_{l=1}^{i}\tanh^k(c[l])$	Eye motion $\frac{\sum_{l=1}^{i}\tanh^k(c[l])}{i}$
–	$c_4[\,]$	–	–	–	–
F_{t-5}	0.4	0.380	0.0	0.38	**0.38**
F_{t-4}	0.5	0.462	0.082	0.84	**0.42**
F_{t-3}	0.6	0.537	0.075	1.38	**0.46**
F_{t-2}	0.7	0.604	0.067	1.98	**0.50**
F_{t-1}	0.8	0.664	0.060	2.65	**0.53**
F_t	0.9	0.716	0.052	3.36	**0.56**
–	$c_5[\,]$	–	–	–	–
F_{t-5}	0.4	0.380	0.0	0.38	**0.38**
F_{t-4}	0.5	0.462	0.082	0.84	**0.42**
F_{t-3}	0.6	0.537	0.075	1.38	**0.46**
F_{t-2}	0.7	0.604	0.067	1.98	**0.50**
F_{t-1}	0.8	0.664	0.060	2.65	**0.53**
F_t	1.0	0.762	0.098	3.41	**0.57**
–	$c_6[\,]$	–	–	–	–
F_{t-5}	0.5	0.462	0.082	0.84	**0.46**
F_{t-4}	0.6	0.537	0.075	1.38	**0.50**
F_{t-3}	0.7	0.604	0.067	1.98	**0.53**
F_{t-2}	0.8	0.664	0.060	2.65	**0.57**
F_{t-1}	0.9	0.716	0.052	3.36	**0.60**
F_t	1.0	0.762	0.045	4.13	**0.62**

The $W_{i,K,c}^{(l)}$ term denotes the weights connecting the ith unit at position (x,y,z) in the feature map of layer $(l-1)$ and the ith unit in the layer l with K channels. Finally, the $B_{\forall i,K}^{(l)}$ term is the bias vector with length K.

It has been demonstrated that the most suitable kernel size for 3D convolution is $3 \times 3 \times 3$ [58,96]. Hence, we set the 3D convolution kernel size to $3 \times 3 \times 3$ with stride $1 \times 1 \times 1$. Since the ground truth saliency map can be seen as a multimodal Gaussian distribution, where each pixel represents the probability to be fixated by a human, at the final block, we use the sigmoid as an activation function to get a normalized predicted saliency map in $[0,1]$ with a size 224×224.

Loss Function. The saliency loss is computed on a per-pixel basis, where each value of the predicted saliency map is compared with its corresponding peer from the ground truth map. We denote the predicted saliency map as $P \in [0,1]^{224 \times 224}$ and the continuous saliency map as $G \in [0,1]^{224 \times 224}$. The continuous saliency map G is obtained by blurring the binary fixation map FM with a 2D Gaussian kernel. The fixation map FM is a binary image with:

$$FM_{ij} = \begin{cases} 1 & \text{if location } (i,j) \text{ is a fixation} \\ 0 & \text{otherwise,} \end{cases}$$

and the variance of the Gaussian is selected so the filter covers approximately 1-degree of visual angle, as done in [45]. The saliency task can be seen as a similarity measure between the predicted saliency map P and the ground truth G. The loss function must be designed to maximise the invariance of predictive maps and give higher weights to locations with higher fixation probability. An appropriate loss for this situation is the binary cross entropy, defined as:

$$\mathcal{L}_{BCE}(G,P) = -\frac{1}{N}\sum_{i=1}^{N}(G_i \log(P_i) + (1-G_i)\log(1-P_i)) \tag{5}$$

Table 3. Architecture of the 3D CNN [16].

Layer	Depth	Kernel/Pool	Output shape	Params #	Act
Conv3D_1_1	512	$3 \times 3 \times 3$	(6, 14, 14, 512)	7078400	ReLU
Conv3D_1_2	512	$3 \times 3 \times 3$	(6, 14, 14, 512)	7078400	ReLU
MaxPool3D_1	–	$4 \times 2 \times 2$	(3, 7, 7, 512)	0	–
Batch-Norm	–	–	(3, 7, 7, 512)	2048	–
Deconv3D_1	512	$1 \times 3 \times 3$	(3, 14, 14, 512)	2359808	ReLU
Conv3D_2_1	512	$3 \times 3 \times 3$	(3, 14, 14, 512)	7078400	ReLU
Batch-Norm	–	–	(3, 7, 7, 512)	2048	–
Deconv3D_2	256	$3 \times 3 \times 3$	(3, 28, 28, 256)	3539200	ReLU
Conv3D_2_1	256	$3 \times 3 \times 3$	(3, 28, 28, 256)	179728	ReLU
Conv3D_2_2	256	$3 \times 3 \times 3$	(3, 28, 28, 256)	179728	ReLU
MaxPool3D_2	–	$3 \times 1 \times 1$	(1, 28, 28, 256)	0	–
Batch-Norm	–	–	(1, 28, 28, 256)	1024	–
Deconv3D_3	128	$1 \times 3 \times 3$	(1, 56, 56, 128)	295040	ReLU
Conv3D_3_1	128	$1 \times 3 \times 3$	(1, 56, 56, 128)	147584	ReLU
Conv3D_3_2	128	$1 \times 3 \times 3$	(1, 56, 56, 128)	147584	ReLU
Batch-Norm	–	–	(1, 56, 56, 128)	512	–
Deconv3D_4	64	$1 \times 3 \times 3$	(1, 112, 112, 64)	73792	ReLU
Conv3D_4_1	64	$1 \times 3 \times 3$	(1, 112, 112, 64)	36928	ReLU
Conv3D_4_2	64	$1 \times 3 \times 3$	(1, 112, 112, 64)	36928	ReLU
Batch-Norm	–	–	(1, 112, 112, 64)	2048	–
Deconv3D_5	32	$1 \times 3 \times 3$	(1, 224, 224, 32)	18464	ReLU
Conv3D_5_1	32	$1 \times 3 \times 3$	(1, 224, 224, 32)	9258	ReLU
Conv3D_5_2	16	$1 \times 3 \times 3$	(1, 224, 224, 16)	4624	ReLU
Conv3D_5_3	1	$1 \times 3 \times 3$	(1, 224, 224, 1)	145	Sigm

Total Params: 31, 447, 841

4   Experiments and Results

4.1   Experimental Setup

Datasets. DHF1K [100], LEDOV [41], HOLYWOOD [68], UFC-SPORT [68] and DIEM [71] are the five datasets widely used for video saliency research. DHF1K com-

Table 4. Comparative performance study on: DHF1K, UFC-SPORT datasets.

Dataset	DHF1K					UFC-SPORT				
	AUC-J ↑	SIM ↑	s-AUC ↑	CC ↑	NSS ↑	AUC-J ↑	SIM ↑	s-AUC ↑	CC ↑	NSS ↑
# OBDL [31]	0.638	0.171	0.500	0.117	0.495	0.759	0.193	0.634	0.234	1.382
# AWS-D [57]	0.703	0.157	0.513	0.174	0.940	0.823	0.228	0.750	0.306	1.631
OM-CNN [42]	0.856	0.256	0.583	0.344	1.911	0.870	0.321	0.691	0.405	2.089
Two-Stream [4]	0.834	0.197	0.581	0.325	1.632	0.832	0.264	0.685	0.343	1.753
ACLNET [100]	0.890	0.315	0.601	0.434	2.354	0.897	0.406	0.744	0.510	2.567
SalEMA [59]	0.890	**0.466**	0.667	0.449	2.574	0.906	0.431	0.740	0.544	2.639
STRA-Net [54]	0.895	0.355	0.663	0.458	2.558	0.910	0.479	0.751	0.593	3.018
TASED-Net [70]	0.895	0.361	**0.712**	0.470	2.667	0.899	0.469	0.752	0.582	2.920
UNISAL [19]	**0.901**	0.390	0.691	**0.490**	**2.776**	**0.918**	**0.523**	**0.775**	**0.644**	**3.381**
3DSAL-Base [16]	–	–	–	–	–	0.811	0.326	0.609	0.321	1.712
3DSAL-Weighted [16]	0.850	0.321	0.623	0.356	1.996	0.881	0.498	0.701	0.595	2.802

(#) Not deep learning models. The best score is marked in bold. The second best score is marked in red.

prises a total of 1,000 video sequences with 582,605 frames covering a wide range of scenes, motions and activities. HOLLYWOOD-2 is a dynamic eye tracking dataset. It contains short video sequences from a set of 69 Hollywood movies, containing 12 different human action classes, ranging from answering a phone, eating, driving and running. The UCF-Sports dataset consists of 150 videos covering 9 sports classes like golf, skateboarding, running and riding. LEDOV contains videos with a total of 179,336 frames covering three main sub-categories: Animals, Man-made-Objects and Human activities varying from social activities, daily actions, sports and art performance.

We have chosen DHF1K and UFC-SPORT to train our 3DSAL model. DHF1K characterises the free viewing approach, in which subjects freely watch the stimuli so that many internal cognitive tasks are engaged, thereby making the generated saliency map more difficult to predict. UFC-SPORT is a task driven dataset, where subjects are more likely to follow the main objects in the scene, affording the model precision. Training on these two different paradigms helps ensure more robust prediction.

Training. We have two training modes: (1) *3DSAL-base*: Training the model without regression, where all frames are fed into the 3D CNN in an equal manner, without multiplying by the weighting coefficients. (2) *3DSAL-weighted*: The use of weighting coefficients, to indicate the frame importance in the prediction process.

For DHF1K, we respect the original training/validation/testing partitioning (600/100/300). For UFC-SPORT, as proposed by the authors in [68], the training/testing is split (103/47). We test our model on: DHF1K, UFC-SPORT and DAVIS [80] for both quantitative and qualitative results.

Technical Specification. We implemented our model in Python using the Keras API running a TensorFlow backend. Due to the huge size of the training data (550k frames), we used the early stopping technique on the validation set for optimal generalization performance [81]. The Adam Optimizer [48] initial learning rate was set to 10^{-4} and was dropped by 10 each 2 epochs. The network was trained for 33 epochs. The entire training procedure took about 7 days (160 h) on a single NVIDIA GTX 1080 GPU, which has a total of 8 GB global memory and 20 multiprocessors, and i7 7820 HK 3.9 GHZ Intel processor.

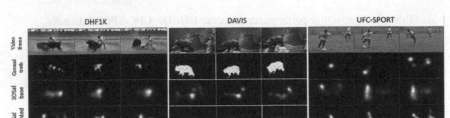

Fig. 4. Saliency map predictions over three datasets [16].

Metrics. To test the performance of our model, we utilize the five widely used metrics: AUC-Judd (AUC-J), Similarity metric (SIM), Linear Correlation Coefficient (CC), shuffled AUC (s-AUC) and Normalized Scanpath Saliency (NSS). A detailed description of these metrics is presented in [8].

Competitors. We compare the performance of the introduced 3DSal model [16] according to the different saliency metrics, with nine video saliency models: OM-CNN [42], Two-stream [4], AWS-D [57], OBDL [31], ACLNet [100], [79], SalEMA [59], STRA-Net [54], TASED-Net [70], UNISAL [19]. Benefiting from the work of [100], which tested the performance of the previous models in three datasets (DHF1K, HOLYWOOD-2, UFC-SPORT), we add our results to this work, to compare the performance of our model with these works. Please note that the last four models are more recent works that were published after our work was originally published 3DSal [16].

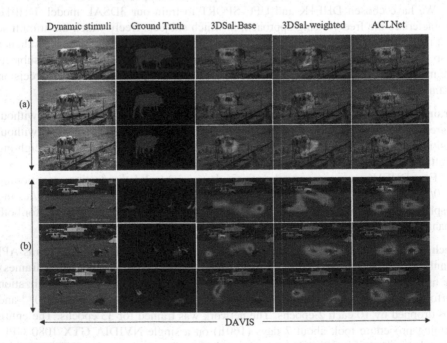

Fig. 5. Qualitative results of the 3DSAL model [16] and the ACLNet model [100] on two validation video samples from the object segmentation dataset DAVIS. It can be observed that the proposed 3DSAL-weighted is able to capture the main objects in the scene.

4.2 Evaluation

Table 4 shows the comparative study with the aforementioned models according to the different saliency metrics on DHF1K and UFC-SPORT datasets (300/47) test videos. Our model still very competitive in the two datasets. The 3DSAL-weighted repeatedly appears in the range of the best scores, and exhibits the second best score for certain metrics. Also, it is clear that deep learning approaches outperform classic hand-crafted video saliency methods.

DHF1K. The diversity of this dataset makes the prediction task very challenging, our model remains very competitive since our scores are close to the state of art model (ACLNet [100]). This is due to the inclusion of temporal domain exploration via the use 3D CNN for adjacent frames.

UFC-SPORT. On the 47 test videos of UFC-SPORT dataset, our model exhibits much better performance than other techniques. This demonstrates the capacity of our model to predict task driven saliency, when observers are more likely to track the main object in the scene e.g. soccer player, horse rider, skateboarder, etc. Most UFC-SPORT fixations are located on the human body zone.

The 3DSAL-weighted model outperforms the 3DSAL-base model in all situations for the UFC-SPORT dataset. 3DSAL-base faces the problem of a centered saliency in the middle and considering the same weight for all frames ($c[] = [1]$) confuses the model to predict saliency map in a highly correlated space, which increases the false positive rate. We solved this problem by using the tanh weighting function, which helped the 3D CNN learn more accurate relationships between the features of adjacent frames (e.g. AUC-J: $0.8111 \rightarrow 0.8813$, NSS: $1.7119 \rightarrow 2.8023$).

Figure 4 illustrates the prediction task on a sample of frames from three datasets: DHF1K, DAVIS, UFC-SPORT. It can be seen that the generated saliency maps with 3DSAL-weighted are more comprehensive and look remarkably similar to the Ground truth saliency maps in terms of fixations. DAVIS [80] is a video object segmentation dataset, thus, the various saliency metrics are not applicable. However, it is used in the qualitative study to show the effectiveness of our model to capture the main objects in the scene.

For more qualitative results, Fig. 5 and Fig. 6 show the overlaid saliency maps on sample videos/frames from DAVIS and DHF1K datasets for the 3DSAL-Base, 3DSAL-weighted, and ACLNet. Two main points can be noted from these figures:

- In Fig. 5, as the scene progresses, the 3DSAL-weighted ignores some static objects and only focuses on other moving objects, while ACLnet [100] still considers them salient. In video (b), both models considered the car as a salient object in the first frame. Since the car was static all over the scene, the 3DSAL-weighted considered it as a background, and only focused on dynamic objects (dog, ducks), while ACLNet [100] took it as salient during the whole scene. This demonstrates the effectiveness of 3D convolutions to capture motion.
- In Fig. 6, it is noticeable that the generated saliency maps using 3DSAL-base are sparse, this is due to the large number of features in the latent space. The model tends to give a high probability to a given pixel, which makes it salient. In the 3DSAL-weighted version, the use of the weighting function forces the model to generate a more focused and consistent saliency regions.

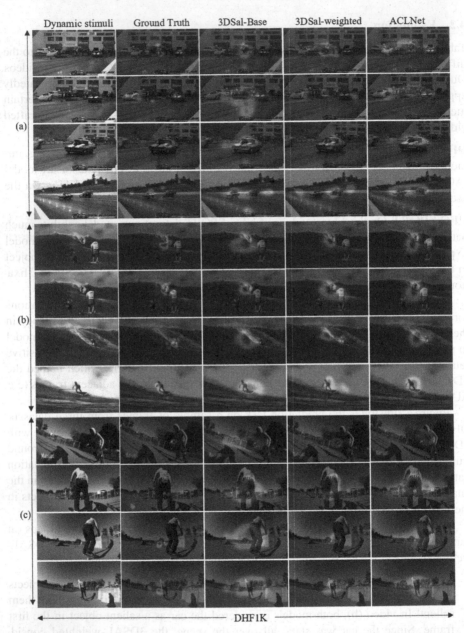

Fig. 6. Qualitative results of the 3DSal model [16] and ACLNet [100] on three validation video samples from DHF1K dataset. It can be observed that the proposed 3DSal-weighted is able to handle various challenging scenes well and produces consistent video saliency results.

Images	Labels	ACLNet	SalEMA	UniSal	3DSal

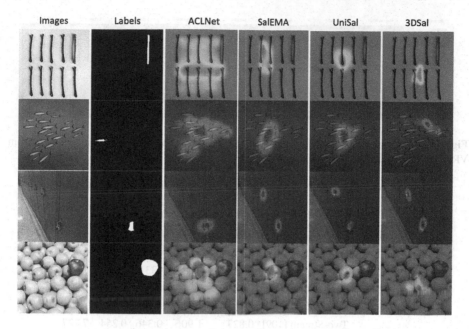

Fig. 7. Results on realistic low level attention images. (Color figure online)

4.3 360° Adaptation

We also want to understand how our approach performs on 360° video as an emerging form of multimedia that is quickly growing in popularity. To this end 3DSal is compared with six models. Two state-of-the-art 2D video saliency models: UNISAL [19], SalEMA [59], and four 360 specialized models: U-NET [111], CP360 [14], SalGAN360 [13], and Two-Stream [109]. This choice is motivated by the publicly available code. The VR-EyeTracking were used for evaluation, the testing set consists of 75 ODV.

Table 5 shows the comparative study with the aforementioned models according to five different saliency metrics: Normalized Scanpath Saliency (NSS), Kullback-Leibler Divergence, Similarity (SIM), Linear Correlation Coefficient (CC), and AUC-Judd (AUC-J) (Please refer to [12] for an extensive description of the metrics), on the VR-EyeTracking datasets (75) test ODVs. Surprisingly, 2D approaches achieve mostly the same results as 360° specialized models; this presents opportunities for further investigation of the transfer of the well verified visual attention features from 2D to 360° video. However, it may also point to the lack of large scale well-annotated 360° datasets that might enable 360° specialized models to perform better. Figure 8 represents a the visual overlaid predictions on a sample of 360° frames from two datasets: Salient360! and VR-EyeTracking. It can be seen that the generated saliency maps with 3DSal remain consistent and look remarkably similar to the Ground truth saliency maps in terms of saliency distribution. It is worth noting that 3DSal was not fine-tuned on 360° datasets.

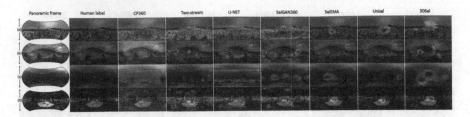

Fig. 8. Qualitative results of our 3DSal model and six other competitors on sample frames from VR-EyeTracking and Salient360! datasets.

Table 5. Comparative performance study on VR-EyeTracking [107] dataset.

Type	Models	AUC-J ↑	NSS ↑	CC ↑	SIM ↑	KLD ↓
2D models	UNISAL [19]	0.764	1.798	0.314	0.281	6.767
	SalEMA [59]	0.772	1.790	0.320	0.284	6.532
360° models	U-NET [111]	0.818	1.430	0331	0.247	7.070
	Cheng et al. [14]	0.735	0.914	0.171	0.179	8.879
	Salgan360 [13]	0.704	1.267	0.236	0.238	7.625
	Two-Stream [109]	0.827	1.906	0.346	0.254	7.127
	3DSal [16]	0.679	1.229	0.228	0.232	8.317

4.4 Some Considerations Around Low Level Attention

Most deep saliency models are based on feature extractors trained on ImageNet. This gives the model the ability to capture high level features such as cars, humans, etc. However, these kinds of approaches may fail to adequately capture a number of other crucial features that describe aspects of human visual attention that have been extensively investigated in psychology and neuroscience. Visual search, often couched in relation to Feature Integration Theory (FIT), is one of the most prominent processes shaping human attention. This is where a subject's brain parallel processes regions that differ significantly in one feature dimension i.e. Color, Intensity, Orientation. These correspond to low level features, that operate as the basic mechanisms of the HVS. Deep learning approaches, however, are trained with gaze recorded data, making the models data-dependent and thus it is not clear how well these low-level features are captured.

We close this chapter with some preliminary investigations of this phenomenon. We conducted evaluations of the performance of ACLNet, SalEMA, UNISAL, and 3DSal on samples of low level attention using images from a recently proposed dataset [51]. As shown in Fig. 7, all deep models fail to respond to simple features. For example, considering colour (4th row in Fig. 7), only ACLNet captured the red apple as the most salient object and even then overestimates saliency because of the high receptive field used that captures global visual attention. The models do not discriminate a different orientation (3rd row in Fig. 7). Similar to color and orientation features, a differently shaped object to others should capture the viewer's attention, but all of the approaches fail to do so (1st and 2nd rows in Fig. 7). Unlike the other two scenarios, the evaluated models do not encode orientation neither implicitly as a pattern, or explicitly through multi-scale or domain adaptation. These features affect a primary metric in the psychology literature [3, 103], called the response time (RT), which the ability to initiate quick responses to certain stimuli. This has major impact on the decision making and planning, necessary in many scenarios (e.g. the suddent appearance of a predator whilst walking in a forest). The results shown here demonstrate the inability of recently introduced deep saliency models to capture low level features in realistic scenarios. This points to a need to review the design of models to not only correlate with the gaze data, but to also incorporate characteristics of the visual system as important priors.

5   Conclusion

Visual saliency prediction falls at the intersection of psychology, neuroscience and computer vision. In this chapter, we adapted 3D ConvNets to the problem of learning spatio-temporal features for video saliency prediction, trained on large-scale video saliency datasets. The architecture embeds a 3D CNN decoder, which fuses the spatio-temporal features from adjacent frames to accurately learn the hidden relationship that affects human behavior when watching videos. We reported the performance of our model compared with the state-of-the-art video saliency models, on three large benchmarks: DHF1K, UFC-SPORT and DAVIS datasets. Furthermore, we investigated the direct transfer of the well verified video saliency models from 2D to 360° video. We also evaluated the performance of models on the special case of low level attention modelling, highlighting a need to re-consider how we design saliency prediction models. Finally, it has been shown that most 2D fixed viewport models do not generalize to the task of prediction saliency over multiple viewports. For the latter issue, even the best saliency models tend just to assign a high probability density on text, human, etc., without any causal reasoning. Thus, saliency predictors will need to reason to reflect the human visual system, constructing the visual attention at multiple levels as parallel processes.

References

1. Adel Bargal, S., Zunino, A., Kim, D., Zhang, J., Murino, V., Sclaroff, S.: Excitation back-prop for RNNs. In: Proceedings of the IEEE Conference on Computer Vision and Pattern Recognition, pp. 1440–1449 (2018)
2. Amudha, J., Radha, D., Naresh, P.: Video shot detection using saliency measure. Int. J. Comput. Appl. **975**, 8887 (2012). Citeseer
3. Arun, S.: Turning visual search time on its head. Vis. Res. **74**, 86–92 (2012)
4. Bak, C., Kocak, A., Erdem, E., Erdem, A.: Spatio-temporal saliency networks for dynamic saliency prediction. IEEE Trans. Multimed. **20**(7), 1688–1698 (2018)
5. Boccignone, G.: Nonparametric Bayesian attentive video analysis. In: 2008 19th International Conference on Pattern Recognition, pp. 1–4. IEEE (2008)
6. Boccignone, G., Ferraro, M.: Modelling gaze shift as a constrained random walk. Phys. A **331**(1–2), 207–218 (2004)
7. Borji, A.: Saliency prediction in the deep learning era: an empirical investigation. arXiv preprint arXiv:1810.03716 (2018)

8. Borji, A., Itti, L.: State-of-the-art in visual attention modeling. IEEE Trans. Pattern Anal. Mach. Intell. **35**(1), 185–207 (2013)

9. Borji, A., Itti, L.: CAT 2000: a large scale fixation dataset for boosting saliency research. arXiv preprint arXiv:1505.03581 (2015)

10. Bruce, N., Tsotsos, J.: Saliency based on information maximization. In: Advances in Neural Information Processing Systems, pp. 155–162 (2006)

11. Bylinskii, Z., et al.: MIT saliency benchmark (2015)

12. Bylinskii, Z., Judd, T., Oliva, A., Torralba, A., Durand, F.: What do different evaluation metrics tell us about saliency models? IEEE Trans. Pattern Anal. Mach. Intell. **41**(3), 740–757 (2018)

13. Chao, F.Y., Zhang, L., Hamidouche, W., Deforges, O.: Salgan360: visual saliency prediction on 360 degree images with generative adversarial networks. In: 2018 IEEE International Conference on Multimedia & Expo Workshops (ICMEW), pp. 01–04. IEEE (2018)

14. Cheng, H.T., Chao, C.H., Dong, J.D., Wen, H.K., Liu, T.L., Sun, M.: Cube padding for weakly-supervised saliency prediction in 360 videos. In: Proceedings of the IEEE Conference on Computer Vision and Pattern Recognition, pp. 1420–1429 (2018)

15. Cornia, M., Baraldi, L., Serra, G., Cucchiara, R.: A deep multi-level network for saliency prediction. In: 2016 23rd International Conference on Pattern Recognition (ICPR), pp. 3488–3493. IEEE (2016)

16. Dahou Djilali, Y.A., Sayah, M., McGuinness, K., O'Connor, N.E.: 3DSAL: An efficient 3D-CNN architecture for video saliency prediction. In: Proceedings of the 15th International Joint Conference on Computer Vision, Imaging and Computer Graphics Theory and Applications - Volume 4: VISAPP, pp. 27–36. INSTICC, SciTePress (2020). https://doi.org/10.5220/0008875600270036

17. David, E.J., Gutiérrez, J., Coutrot, A., Da Silva, M.P., Callet, P.L.: A dataset of head and eye movements for 360 videos. In: Proceedings of the 9th ACM Multimedia Systems Conference, pp. 432–437 (2018)

18. Deng, J., Dong, W., Socher, R., Li, L.J., Li, K., Fei-Fei, L.: ImageNet: a large-scale hierarchical image database. In: 2009 IEEE Conference on Computer Vision and Pattern Recognition, pp. 248–255. IEEE (2009)

19. Droste, R., Jiao, J., Noble, J.A.: Unified image and video saliency modeling. arXiv preprint arXiv:2003.05477 (2020)

20. Ehinger, K.A., Hidalgo-Sotelo, B., Torralba, A., Oliva, A.: Modelling search for people in 900 scenes: a combined source model of eye guidance. Vis. Cogn. **17**(6–7), 945–978 (2009)

21. Frintrop, S., Jensfelt, P.: Attentional landmarks and active gaze control for visual SLAM. IEEE Trans. Rob. **24**(5), 1054–1065 (2008)

22. Gao, D., Vasconcelos, N.: Discriminant saliency for visual recognition from cluttered scenes. In: Advances in Neural Information Processing Systems, pp. 481–488 (2005)

23. Gao, J., Huang, Y., Yu, H.H.: Method and system for video summarization, 31 May 2016. US Patent 9,355,635

24. Garcia-Diaz, A., Fdez-Vidal, X.R., Pardo, X.M., Dosil, R.: Decorrelation and distinctiveness provide with human-like saliency. In: Blanc-Talon, J., Philips, W., Popescu, D., Scheunders, P. (eds.) ACIVS 2009. LNCS, vol. 5807, pp. 343–354. Springer, Heidelberg (2009). https://doi.org/10.1007/978-3-642-04697-1_32

25. Garcia-Diaz, A., Fdez-Vidal, X.R., Pardo, X.M., Dosil, R.: Saliency from hierarchical adaptation through decorrelation and variance normalization. Image Vis. Comput. **30**(1), 51–64 (2012)

26. Goferman, S., Zelnik-Manor, L., Tal, A.: Context-aware saliency detection. IEEE Trans. Pattern Anal. Mach. Intell. **34**(10), 1915–1926 (2012)

27. Goodfellow, I., et al.: Generative adversarial nets. In: Advances in Neural Information Processing Systems, pp. 2672–2680 (2014)

28. Guo, C., Ma, Q., Zhang, L.: Spatio-temporal saliency detection using phase spectrum of quaternion fourier transform. In: 2008 IEEE Conference on Computer Vision and Pattern Recognition, pp. 1–8. IEEE (2008)

29. Guo, C., Zhang, L.: A novel multiresolution spatiotemporal saliency detection model and its applications in image and video compression. IEEE Trans. Image Process. **19**(1), 185–198 (2009)

30. Hochreiter, S., Schmidhuber, J.: Long short-term memory. Neural Comput. **9**(8), 1735–1780 (1997)

31. Hossein Khatoonabadi, S., Vasconcelos, N., Bajic, I.V., Shan, Y.: How many bits does it take for a stimulus to be salient? In: Proceedings of the IEEE Conference on Computer Vision and Pattern Recognition, pp. 5501–5510 (2015)

32. Huang, X., Shen, C., Boix, X., Zhao, Q.: SALICON: reducing the semantic gap in saliency prediction by adapting deep neural networks. In: Proceedings of the IEEE International Conference on Computer Vision, pp. 262–270 (2015)

33. Itti, L.: Automatic foveation for video compression using a neurobiological model of visual attention. IEEE Trans. Image Process. **13**(10), 1304–1318 (2004)

34. Itti, L., Baldi, P.: Bayesian surprise attracts human attention. Vision. Res. **49**(10), 1295–1306 (2009)

35. Itti, L., Koch, C.: A saliency-based search mechanism for overt and covert shifts of visual attention. Vis. Res. **40**(10–12), 1489–1506 (2000)

36. Itti, L., Koch, C., Niebur, E.: A model of saliency-based visual attention for rapid scene analysis. IEEE Trans. Pattern Anal. Mach. Intell. **11**, 1254–1259 (1998)

37. Jacobson, N., Lee, Y.L., Mahadevan, V., Vasconcelos, N., Nguyen, T.Q.: A novel approach to FRUC using discriminant saliency and frame segmentation. IEEE Trans. Image Process. **19**(11), 2924–2934 (2010)

38. James, W.: The Principles of Psychology, vol. 1. Cosimo, Inc. (1950)

39. Ji, S., Xu, W., Yang, M., Yu, K.: 3D convolutional neural networks for human action recognition. IEEE Trans. Pattern Anal. Mach. Intell. **35**(1), 221–231 (2013)

40. Jia, S., Bruce, N.D.: EML-NET: an expandable multi-layer network for saliency prediction. Image Vis. Comput. **95**, 103887 (2020)

41. Jiang, L., Xu, M., Liu, T., Qiao, M., Wang, Z.: DeepVS: a deep learning based video saliency prediction approach. In: Proceedings of the European Conference on Computer Vision (ECCV), pp. 602–617 (2018)

42. Jiang, L., Xu, M., Wang, Z.: Predicting video saliency with object-to-motion CNN and two-layer convolutional LSTM. arXiv preprint arXiv:1709.06316 (2017)

43. Jiang, M., Huang, S., Duan, J., Zhao, Q.: SALICON: saliency in context. In: The IEEE Conference on Computer Vision and Pattern Recognition (CVPR), June 2015

44. Judd, T., Durand, F., Torralba, A.: A benchmark of computational models of saliency to predict human fixations. MIT Technical report (2012)

45. Judd, T., Durand, F., Torralba, A.: A benchmark of computational models of saliency to predict human fixations (2012)

46. Judd, T., Ehinger, K., Durand, F., Torralba, A.: Learning to predict where humans look. In: 2009 IEEE 12th International Conference on Computer Vision, pp. 2106–2113. IEEE (2009)

47. Kienzle, W., Franz, M.O., Schölkopf, B., Wichmann, F.A.: Center-surround patterns emerge as optimal predictors for human saccade targets. J. Vis. **9**(5), 7 (2009)

48. Kingma, D.P., Ba, J.: Adam: a method for stochastic optimization. arXiv preprint arXiv:1412.6980 (2014)

49. Koch, C., Ullman, S.: Shifts in selective visual attention: towards the underlying neural circuitry. In: Vaina, L.M. (ed.) Matters of intelligence. Synthese Library (Studies in Epistemology, Logic, Methodology, and Philosophy of Science), vol. 188, pp. 115–141. Springer, Dordrecht (1987). https://doi.org/10.1007/978-94-009-3833-5_5

50. Kootstra, G., Nederveen, A., De Boer, B.: Paying attention to symmetry. In: British Machine Vision Conference (BMVC2008), pp. 1115–1125. The British Machine Vision Association and Society for Pattern Recognition (2008)

51. Kotseruba, I., Wloka, C., Rasouli, A., Tsotsos, J.K.: Do saliency models detect odd-one-out targets? New datasets and evaluations. arXiv preprint arXiv:2005.06583 (2020)

52. Kruthiventi, S.S., Ayush, K., Babu, R.V.: DeepFix: a fully convolutional neural network for predicting human eye fixations. IEEE Trans. Image Process. **26**(9), 4446–4456 (2017)

53. Kümmerer, M., Theis, L., Bethge, M.: Deep gaze i: Boosting saliency prediction with feature maps trained on ImageNet. arXiv preprint arXiv:1411.1045 (2014)

54. Lai, Q., Wang, W., Sun, H., Shen, J.: Video saliency prediction using spatiotemporal residual attentive networks. IEEE Trans. Image Process. **29**, 1113–1126 (2019)

55. Le Meur, O., Le Callet, P., Barba, D.: Predicting visual fixations on video based on low-level visual features. Vis. Res. **47**(19), 2483–2498 (2007)

56. Le Meur, O., Le Callet, P., Barba, D., Thoreau, D.: A coherent computational approach to model bottom-up visual attention. IEEE Trans. Pattern Anal. Mach. Intell. **28**(5), 802–817 (2006)

57. Leboran, V., Garcia-Diaz, A., Fdez-Vidal, X.R., Pardo, X.M.: Dynamic whitening saliency. IEEE Trans. Pattern Anal. Mach. Intell. **39**(5), 893–907 (2017)

58. Li, X., et al.: DeepSaliency: multi-task deep neural network model for salient object detection. IEEE Trans. Image Process. **25**(8), 3919–3930 (2016)

59. Linardos, P., Mohedano, E., Nieto, J.J., O'Connor, N.E., Giro-i Nieto, X., McGuinness, K.: Simple vs complex temporal recurrences for video saliency prediction. arXiv preprint arXiv:1907.01869 (2019)

60. Liu, N., Han, J.: A deep spatial contextual long-term recurrent convolutional network for saliency detection. IEEE Trans. Image Process. **27**(7), 3264–3274 (2018)

61. Liu, N., Han, J., Zhang, D., Wen, S., Liu, T.: Predicting eye fixations using convolutional neural networks. In: Proceedings of the IEEE Conference on Computer Vision and Pattern Recognition, pp. 362–370 (2015)

62. Ma, Y.F., Hua, X.S., Lu, L., Zhang, H.J.: A generic framework of user attention model and its application in video summarization. IEEE Trans. Multimed. **7**(5), 907–919 (2005)

63. Mahadevan, V., Vasconcelos, N.: Saliency-based discriminant tracking. In: 2009 IEEE Conference on Computer Vision and Pattern Recognition, pp. 1007–1013. IEEE (2009)

64. Mancas, M., Ferrera, V.P., Riche, N., Taylor, J.G.: From Human Attention to Computational Attention, vol. 2. Springer, Heidelberg (2016). https://doi.org/10.1007/978-1-4939-3435-5

65. Marat, S., Guironnet, M., Pellerin, D.: Video summarization using a visual attention model. In: 2007 15th European Signal Processing Conference, pp. 1784–1788. IEEE (2007)

66. Marat, S., Phuoc, T.H., Granjon, L., Guyader, N., Pellerin, D., Guérin-Dugué, A.: Modelling spatio-temporal saliency to predict gaze direction for short videos. Int. J. Comput. Vis. **82**(3), 231 (2009)

67. Mathe, S., Sminchisescu, C.: Actions in the eye: dynamic gaze datasets and learnt saliency models for visual recognition. IEEE Trans. Pattern Anal. Mach. Intell. **37**(7), 1408–1424 (2014)

68. Mathe, S., Sminchisescu, C.: Actions in the eye: dynamic gaze datasets and learnt saliency models for visual recognition. IEEE Trans. Pattern Anal. Mach. Intell. **37**(7), 1408–1424 (2015)

69. Milanese, R.: Detecting salient regions in an image: from biological evidence to computer implementation. Ph. D Theses, the University of Geneva (1993)

70. Min, K., Corso, J.J.: TASED-net: temporally-aggregating spatial encoder-decoder network for video saliency detection. In: Proceedings of the IEEE International Conference on Computer Vision, pp. 2394–2403 (2019)
71. Mital, P.K., Smith, T.J., Hill, R.L., Henderson, J.M.: Clustering of gaze during dynamic scene viewing is predicted by motion. Cogn. Comput. 3(1), 5–24 (2011)
72. Murray, N., Vanrell, M., Otazu, X., Parraga, C.A.: Saliency estimation using a non-parametric low-level vision model. In: CVPR 2011, pp. 433–440. IEEE (2011)
73. Navalpakkam, V., Itti, L.: An integrated model of top-down and bottom-up attention for optimizing detection speed. In: 2006 IEEE Computer Society Conference on Computer Vision and Pattern Recognition (CVPR 2006), vol. 2, pp. 2049–2056. IEEE (2006)
74. Nwankpa, C., Ijomah, W., Gachagan, A., Marshall, S.: Activation functions: comparison of trends in practice and research for deep learning. CoRR abs/1811.03378 (2018). http://arxiv.org/abs/1811.03378
75. Oliva, A., Torralba, A., Castelhano, M.S., Henderson, J.M.: Top-down control of visual attention in object detection. In: Proceedings 2003 International Conference on Image Processing (Cat. No. 03CH37429), vol. 1, p. I-253. IEEE (2003)
76. Ouerhani, N., Hügli, H.: Real-time visual attention on a massively parallel SIMD architecture. Real-Time Imaging 9(3), 189–196 (2003)
77. Pan, J., et al.: SalGAN: visual saliency prediction with generative adversarial networks. arXiv preprint arXiv:1701.01081 (2017)
78. Pan, J., Sayrol, E., Giro-i Nieto, X., McGuinness, K., O'Connor, N.E.: Shallow and deep convolutional networks for saliency prediction. In: Proceedings of the IEEE Conference on Computer Vision and Pattern Recognition, pp. 598–606 (2016)
79. Panagiotis, L., Eva, M., Monica, C., Cathal, G., Xavier, G.i.N.: Temporal saliency adaptation in egocentric videos (2018)
80. Perazzi, F., Pont-Tuset, J., McWilliams, B., Van Gool, L., Gross, M., Sorkine-Hornung, A.: A benchmark dataset and evaluation methodology for video object segmentation. In: Proceedings of the IEEE Conference on Computer Vision and Pattern Recognition, pp. 724–732 (2016)
81. Prechelt, L.: Early stopping - but when? In: Orr, G.B., Müller, K.-R. (eds.) Neural Networks: Tricks of the Trade. LNCS, vol. 1524, pp. 55–69. Springer, Heidelberg (1998). https://doi.org/10.1007/3-540-49430-8_3
82. Privitera, C.M., Stark, L.W.: Algorithms for defining visual regions-of-interest: comparison with eye fixations. IEEE Trans. Pattern Anal. Mach. Intell. 22(9), 970–982 (2000)
83. Rai, Y., Le Callet, P., Guillotel, P.: Which saliency weighting for omni directional image quality assessment? In: 2017 Ninth International Conference on Quality of Multimedia Experience (QoMEX), pp. 1–6. IEEE (2017)
84. Ren, Z., Gao, S., Chia, L.T., Tsang, I.W.H.: Region-based saliency detection and its application in object recognition. IEEE Trans. Circ. Syst. Video Technol. 24(5), 769–779 (2013)
85. Rimey, R.D., Brown, C.M.: Controlling eye movements with hidden Markov models. Int. J. Comput. Vis. 7(1), 47–65 (1991)
86. Rosenholtz, R.: A simple saliency model predicts a number of motion popout phenomena. Vis. Res. 39(19), 3157–3163 (1999)
87. Rudoy, D., Goldman, D.B., Shechtman, E., Zelnik-Manor, L.: Learning video saliency from human gaze using candidate selection. In: Proceedings of the IEEE Conference on Computer Vision and Pattern Recognition, pp. 1147–1154 (2013)
88. Salvucci, D.D.: An integrated model of eye movements and visual encoding. Cogn. Syst. Res. 1(4), 201–220 (2001)
89. Saslow, M.: Effects of components of displacement-step stimuli upon latency for saccadic eye movement. Josa 57(8), 1024–1029 (1967)

90. Seo, H.J., Milanfar, P.: Static and space-time visual saliency detection by self-resemblance. J. Vis. **9**(12), 15 (2009)
91. Simonyan, K., Zisserman, A.: Very deep convolutional networks for large-scale image recognition. arXiv preprint arXiv:1409.1556 (2014)
92. Sohlberg, M.M., Mateer, C.A.: Introduction to Cognitive Rehabilitation: Theory and Practice. Guilford Press (1989)
93. Sprague, N., Ballard, D.: Eye movements for reward maximization. In: Advances in Neural Information Processing Systems, pp. 1467–1474 (2004)
94. Suzuki, T., Yamanaka, T.: Saliency map estimation for omni-directional image considering prior distributions. In: 2018 IEEE International Conference on Systems, Man, and Cybernetics (SMC), pp. 2079–2084. IEEE (2018)
95. Torralba, A.: Modeling global scene factors in attention. JOSA A **20**(7), 1407–1418 (2003)
96. Tran, D., Bourdev, L., Fergus, R., Torresani, L., Paluri, M.: Learning spatiotemporal features with 3D convolutional networks. In: Proceedings of the IEEE International Conference on Computer Vision, pp. 4489–4497 (2015)
97. Treisman, A.M., Gelade, G.: A feature-integration theory of attention. Cogn. Psychol. **12**(1), 97–136 (1980)
98. Tsotsos, J.K., Culhane, S.M., Wai, W.Y.K., Lai, Y., Davis, N., Nuflo, F.: Modeling visual attention via selective tuning. Artif. Intell. **78**(1–2), 507–545 (1995)
99. Vig, E., Dorr, M., Cox, D.: Large-scale optimization of hierarchical features for saliency prediction in natural images. In: Proceedings of the IEEE Conference on Computer Vision and Pattern Recognition, pp. 2798–2805 (2014)
100. Wang, W., Shen, J., Guo, F., Cheng, M.M., Borji, A.: Revisiting video saliency: a large-scale benchmark and a new model. In: Proceedings of the IEEE Conference on Computer Vision and Pattern Recognition, pp. 4894–4903 (2018)
101. Wang, W., Shen, J., Xie, J., Cheng, M.M., Ling, H., Borji, A.: Revisiting video saliency prediction in the deep learning era. IEEE Trans. Pattern Anal. Mach. Intell. (2019)
102. Wang, W., Shen, J., Yang, R., Porikli, F.: Saliency-aware video object segmentation. IEEE Trans. Pattern Anal. Mach. Intell. **40**(1), 20–33 (2017)
103. Wolfe, J.M.: Guided search 2.0 a revised model of visual search. Psychon. Bull. Rev. **1**(2), 202–238 (1994)
104. Wu, X., Yuen, P.C., Liu, C., Huang, J.: Shot boundary detection: an information saliency approach. In: 2008 Congress on Image and Signal Processing, vol. 2, pp. 808–812. IEEE (2008)
105. Xu, M., Li, C., Zhang, S., Le Callet, P.: State-of-the-art in 360 video/image processing: perception, assessment and compression. IEEE J. Sel. Top. Signal Process. **14**(1), 5–26 (2020)
106. Xu, M., Song, Y., Wang, J., Qiao, M., Huo, L., Wang, Z.: Predicting head movement in panoramic video: a deep reinforcement learning approach. IEEE Trans. Pattern Anal. Mach. Intell. **41**(11), 2693–2708 (2018)
107. Xu, Y., et al.: Gaze prediction in dynamic 360 immersive videos. In: Proceedings of the IEEE Conference on Computer Vision and Pattern Recognition, pp. 5333–5342 (2018)
108. Zhang, J., Sclaroff, S.: Saliency detection: a boolean map approach. In: Proceedings of the IEEE International Conference on Computer Vision, pp. 153–160 (2013)
109. Zhang, K., Chen, Z.: Video saliency prediction based on spatial-temporal two-stream network. IEEE Trans. Circ. Syst. Video Technol. **29**(12), 3544–3557 (2018)
110. Zhang, L., Tong, M.H., Marks, T.K., Shan, H., Cottrell, G.W.: SUN: a Bayesian framework for saliency using natural statistics. J. Vis. **8**(7), 32 (2008)
111. Zhang, Z., Xu, Y., Yu, J., Gao, S.: Saliency detection in 360 videos. In: Proceedings of the European Conference on Computer Vision (ECCV), pp. 488–503 (2018)

CNN-Based Deblurring of THz Time-Domain Images

Marina Ljubenović[1]([✉])[iD], Shabab Bazrafkan[2][iD], Pavel Paramonov[2][iD],
Jan De Beenhouwer[2][iD], and Jan Sijbers[2][iD]

[1] Center for Cultural Heritage Technology, Italian Institute of Technology, Venice, Italy
marina.ljubenovic@iit.it
[2] imec-Vision Lab, Department of Physics, University of Antwerp, Antwerp, Belgium
{shabab.bazrafkan,pavel.paramonov,jan.debeenhouwer,
jan.sijbers}@uantwerpen.be

Abstract. In recent years, terahertz (THz) time-domain imaging attracted significant attention and become a useful tool in many applications. A THz time-domain imaging system measures amplitude changes of the THz radiation across a range of frequencies so the absorption coefficient of the materials in the sample can be obtained. THz time-domain images represent 3D hyperspectral cubes with several hundred bands corresponding to different wavelengths i.e., frequencies. Moreover, a THz beam has a non-zero beam waist and therefore introduces band-dependent blurring effects in the resulting images accompanied by system-dependent noise. Removal of blurring effects and noise from the whole 3D hyperspectral cube is addressed in the current work. We will start by introducing THz beam shape effects and its formulation as a deblurring problem, followed by presenting a convolutional neural network (CNN)-based approach which is able to tackle all bands jointly. To the best of our knowledge, this is the first time that a CNN is used to remove the THz beam shape effects from all bands jointly of THz time-domain images. Experiments on synthetic images show that the proposed approach significantly outperforms conventional model-based deblurring methods and band-by-band approaches.

Keywords: THz imaging · THz-TDS · CNN · Deblurring

1 Introduction

Terahertz (THz) imaging has attracted increasing interest in recent years driven by the immense progress in the development of more affordable THz sources [14]. The THz frequency range, between the microwave and the infrared regions, enabled THz imaging to become an established tool for non-destructive testing [19] and material analysis [15]. Many imaging applications in security [20], conservation of cultural heritage [7], medicine [31], biochemistry [37], and in many other fields, find their place within the THz frequency range, i.e., from 0.1 to 10 THz. Such increasing interest is additionally attributed to the fact that the THz radiation is non-ionizing and can be applied to dielectric materials (e.g., paper, plastic, canvas) providing an alternative to X-ray in many applications (e.g., computed tomography (CT) [33]).

© Springer Nature Switzerland AG 2022
K. Bouatouch et al. (Eds.): VISIGRAPP 2020, CCIS 1474, pp. 477–494, 2022.
https://doi.org/10.1007/978-3-030-94893-1_22

THz time-domain spectroscopy (THz-TDS), is a technique that can be used for spectroscopy, i.e., for testing and analysing of different materials [2] and imaging in the THz domain [16]. In a THz-TDS system, the radiation is generated in the form of short pulses with the duration of 1 ps or less. A typical system employs an ultra-short pulsed laser and an antenna (e.g., low-temperature grown GaAs). The laser generates a series of pulses which is split into two halves: one for THz beam generation and the second to gate a detector. A THz detector receives the incoming radiation only for very brief periods of time which leads to sampling of the THz field at various delays: on the detector side, we are measuring a THz electric field as a function of time. The resulting pulse is transformed into the frequency domain covering a broad spectrum (e.g., a range of frequencies from 0.076 to 2 THz). For more information about the THz-TDS system and beam-forming we refer to [5] and references therein.

One of the main advantages of THz-TDS is its ability to measure both spectral amplitude and phase through a broad spectral range. The amplitude of a THz signal corresponds to the material absorption properties and the phase corresponds to the thickness and density of the sample. The broad bandwidth of the THz radiation is valuable for spectroscopy since many materials have a unique spectral fingerprint in the THz domain [2].

Although THz imaging is a powerful tool in many applications, several challenges need to be addressed. Here, we will start by briefly introducing two main challenges and then bring a focus on the latter one, followed by a strategy for tackling it. Firstly, the propagation of a THz beam through the object leads to the diffraction effect [29] and Fresnel losses [40]. Several methods are proposed to tackle these losses by employing different approaches. Mukherjee *et al.* in [29] developed a method to deal with Fresnel reflection power losses and steering of the THz beam through the sample for THz-CT reconstruction of cylindrical shaped objects. Recently, Tepe *et al.* in [40] adapted an conventional CT reconstruction technique, namely, algebraic reconstruction technique (ART), by including refraction and reflection losses for THz-CT. Secondly, the effects of a THz beam shape additionally limit the achievable resolution. These effects cannot be neglected as the THz beam has a non-zero waist (minimum beam radius), and therefore introduces a blurring effect to the resulting image.

1.1 Related Work

In the literature, several methods were proposed to deal with the aforementioned blurring effects in order to increase the spatial resolution of THz images. In [43], the authors employed several well-known super-resolution approaches to tackle blur in a single-band THz image: projection onto a convex set, iterative backprojection, Richardson-Lucy iterative approach [27,34], and 2D wavelet decomposition reconstruction [28]. In [32], the authors applied a specially designed phantom to perform the beam point-spread function (PSF) estimation, followed by the deconvolution process based on a well-known Wiener technique [10]. To deal with THz beam shape effects in THz-CT, Recur *et al.* primarily modelled a 3D THz beam and further incorporated it in several well-established CT reconstruction approaches as a deconvolution filter [33]. All the above-mentioned methods are based on the well-established deconvolution approaches, tailored to a single THz image or a specific application (e.g., THz-CT). Furthermore, conventional deconvolution approaches require one or more input parameters that, in many cases, need to be hand-tuned.

The past decade is witnessing the rapid development of neural network-based approaches for various computer vision tasks [23,41]. The convolutional neural network (CNN) is arguably the most common class of deep neural networks applied to image restoration tasks, such as denoising [45], super-resolution [11], and deblurring [42].

Here, we introduced a CNN-based method for beam shape effects removal from THz-TDS images that represent a hyperspectral (HS) cube composed by several hundred bands. The problem of beam shape effects removal is formulated as a deblurring task, also known as deconvolution, with a known, band-dependant, PSF modelled as a Gaussian distribution [33]. We extended the previous work from [26], THzNet-2D, by introducing a novel CNN-based deblurring approach which performs deblurring on all bands jointly, taking into consideration connections between bands during training.

By using CNN-based deblurring, we avoid hand-tuning of the input parameters as network weights can be learned from a set of training images. In our previous work [26], we considered bands of a THz-TDS hyperspectral cube as independent, which is not the case in the practice: the bands show the same objects on different frequencies and capture the interconnected nature of the degradation effects (e.g., blur and noise). Therefore, the network extension proposed in this work is the natural step forward for tackling beam shape effects in THz-TDS images.

1.2 Outline

In Sect. 2, we start by explaining the effects of different THz beam shape parameters and noise levels. Next, we show how the CNN-based deblurring is designed and introduce a novel approach which considers all bands of a THz-TDS image jointly. Furthermore, we show how THz-TDS images are synthesized applying the Gaussian beam modelling approach. Finally, we compare results obtained by conventional deblurring approaches with the proposed CNN-based methods and demonstrate the superiority of the extended version of the proposed method. To the best of our knowledge, this is the first time that a CNN or any other deep learning approach is applied to deblur THz time-domain images.

2 Beam Shape Effects

To be suitable for imaging and to increase the spatial resolution, a typical THz imaging system includes focusing optics. With the introduction of the focusing optics and with the fact that THz system forms a non-zero beam waist, the focal spot of the THz beam at the place of the object has a complicated characteristic which strongly depends on the system design and frequencies.

In a THz-TDS system, an image is formed from the full dataset which contains a complete THz time-domain waveform i.e., THz pulse transformed to the frequency domain, its amplitude and phase, corresponding to each pixel of the image. To additionally analyze the sample, we may calculate transmittance and phase-difference images by measuring a reference background when the optical path is left open. The resulting THz-TDS images represent a 3-dimensional (3D) hyperspectral data cube (2d spatial +

spectral domain) where every band represents an image on a different frequency in a given range.

Images formed from lower frequencies are more blurry as the beam waist increases together with the wavelength. The high frequency bands on the other hand are less blurry due to the smaller beam waist. However, due to lower amplitudes of these higher frequency bands, signal-to-noise (SNR) ratio drastically decreases [12]. This effect is illustrated in the upper row of Fig. 1. Additionally, we show selected bands of a phase image (bottom row). Note that the leaf is placed in the black envelope during scanning visible as a stripe (i.e., intensity change) on the right hand side of phase images corresponding to different bands.

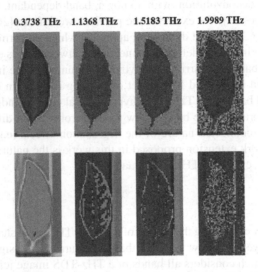

Fig. 1. The THz-TDS amplitude (upper row) and phase (bottom row) images of a leaf at different frequencies.

The THz beam of the THz-TDS system is usually modelled as a Gaussian distribution characterized by a beam waist which depends on a frequency of the THz system [33]. Following the Gaussian beam modelling formulation, the radius at the position x from the beam waist w_0 is

$$w(x) = w_0 \sqrt{1 + \left(\frac{x}{x_R}\right)^2},\qquad(1)$$

where $x_R = \frac{\pi w_0^2}{\lambda}$ is the Rayleigh range with λ representing a wavelength. The intensity of the beam over cross-section in 3D is modelled as

$$I(x, y, z) = I_0 \left(\frac{w_0}{w(x)}\right)^2 \exp\left(\frac{-2(y^2 + z^2)}{w^2(x)}\right),\qquad(2)$$

with I_0 representing the beam intensity at the centre of w_0 and y and z are distances from the beam axes in two directions. We model the blurring artifacts present in a single band of THz-TDS images as the convolution between an underlying sharp image and a PSF that corresponds to the considered frequency:

$$g = f \circledast h + n, \tag{3}$$

where g, f, h, and n represent one band of an observed THz-TDS image, one band of an unknown sharp image, a PSF (blurring operator), and noise respectively. $\circledast$ represents the convolution operator. The goal of the proposed method is to estimate the underlying sharp image f.

From (2) it is clear that several parameters define the intensity within the beam: the wavelength (λ), the beam waist (w_0), and the intensity of the beam at w_0 (I_0). To control the PSF model h in (3), we may tune these parameters. Note that the PSF represents an intersection of the 3D THz beam in a position of the scanned object (see Fig. 2).

Fig. 2. Influence of a beam waist on PSF: Examples of PSF for 1 THz, $I_0 = 1$, and different w_0 in mm (numbers in the upper-left corner) as presented in [26].

The removing of the blurring effects from THz-TDS images is a challenging task as not only we have a different blur (PSF) but also an unknown noise type and different noise levels for different bands. Moreover, the size of each THz image band is usually only hundreds of pixels (e.g., 61×41 pixels) which additionally complicates a deblurring process as a blurring filter covers a too large portion of the underlying sharp image. The differences in blur and noise over bands accompanied by the small image size inspired us to propose a CNN-based deblurring approach: the proposed network is learned from a training dataset which contains all of these differences and therefore it is arguably more robust than conventional deblurring approaches.

3 Deblurring Based on CNN

In the last few years, Deep Learning techniques have been extensively applied to almost every machine learning problems from consumer electronic applications [24] to medical [25,36] and industrial [18,35] use cases. They provide superior results for highly non-linear and not self-contained problems compared to classical machine learning techniques. Deep Learning is the science of designing, training, and implementing Deep Neural Networks (DNN). DNNs are defined as neural networks with more than three layers. These layers are processing units such as fully connected, convolution, deconvolution, pooling, and unpooling layers accompanied by regularization techniques such as Batch Normalization [17], and/or drop out [38]. These networks are widely used to process different types of signals such as text, voice, still images, and videos. Based on the application, the neural network design differs for different use cases. One of the most popular types of DNN is 2 dimensional Fully Convolutional Deep Neural Network (FCDNN) wherein the input and output of the network is a 2D image. They have several applications such as segmentation [1,3] and image restoration [4,30,46]. These networks consist of convolution, deconvolution, and different types of pooling operators. There are no fully connected layers in FCDNNs.

In this work, a FCDNN is utilized to perform the deblurring operation to THz time-domain images. All layers in CNN perform the convolution operation with a learnable kernel which is given by:

$$S^m(x, y, c) = \sigma\Big(\sum_{k=1}^{n_c^{m-1}} \sum_{j=-[n_w/2]}^{[n_w/2]} \sum_{i=-[n_h/2]}^{[n_h/2]} H_c^m(i, j, k) \cdot$$
$$S^{m-1}(x - i, y - j, k) \Big), \tag{4}$$

where $S^m(i, j, c)$ is the pixel signal at (x, y), located in channel c in layer m, H_c^m is the kernel associated with the channel c of layer m. Namely, this kernel maps every channel in layer $m - 1$ to channel c in layer m. n_h and n_w are the width and height of the kernel and n_c^{m-1} is number of channels in layer $m - 1$. The activation function σ represents the nonlinearity of the layer.

3.1 THzNet-2D

To perform band by band deblurring of THz-TDS images, we introduced a CNN architecture [26]. The proposed architecture is based on the work of [42] and illustrated in Fig. 4. The first two layers consist of horizontal and vertical kernels and the last layer performs convolution with a large square kernel. This design resembles the Singular Value Decomposition (SVD) technique used in conventional deblurring methods, with the difference that the CNN filters could be learned during training (Fig. 3).

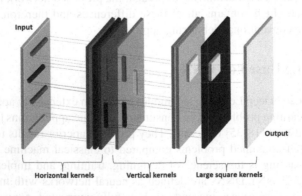

Fig. 3. THzNet-2D architecture as presented in [26].

There are several other approaches for utilizing DNNs to perform image deblurring [39,44]. Nevertheless, we choose to use the approach from [42] for two reasons i) the proposed network design is supported by the model-based method (i.e., SVD) commonly used for image restoration and therefore well studded. ii) By making the horizontal and vertical kernel in the first two layers, the additional blurring of the intermediate outputs is minimized.

3.2 THzNet-HS

In a typical THz signal, the images in different sub-band are not independent of each other. In other words, the information in each sub-band could be utilized to restore other sub-bands. In order to take advantage of this interdependence, we designed a new FCDNN wherein the network accepts all the sub-bands at the same time and the output of the network is the restoration of all frequencies in a single sample. Training this network provides the opportunity to capture the sharpness of high-frequency bands and low noise property of low-frequency bands in a single architecture. The new network accepts a 263 channel tensor and returns a same size one. Since in the new model, there is more information to be processed at each layer, the number of convolution kernels is significantly increased compared to THzNet-2D. Namely, for the first layer, we went from 64 to 512 channels, for the second layer from 32 to 256 channels, and for the third one from 1 to 263 channels.

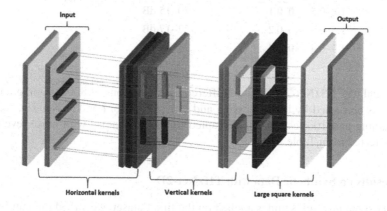

Fig. 4. THzNet-HS architecture.

4   Experiments

The proposed CNN-based approaches, both THzNet-2D and THzNet-HS, contains two steps: in the first step, we perform denoising as preprocessing followed by the second step, CNN-based deblurring. Denoising is performed using a state-of-the-art hyperspectral image denoiser FastHyDe [47] tailored to both Gaussian and Poisson noise. Deblurring is performed band by band in the case of THzNet-2D, namely input and output of the network is an image corresponding to one band of a THz-TDS cube. In the case of THzNet-HS, after preprocessing step, we deblur all bands jointly.

For the proposed CNN-based approachs, an ADAM optimizer [21] was utilized to update the network parameters with learning rate, β_1, β_2 and ϵ are equal to 0.00001, 0.9, 0.999, and 10^{-8}, respectively. The MXNET 1.3.0 [6][1] framework was used to train the network on a NVIDIA GTX 1070 in all the experiments.

4.1 Creating Synthetic Data

To train and test the network, we created in total 10000 training and 300 test images corrupted by Gaussian and Poisson noise and different blurs. We used two different noise types to make the CNN more robust as THz-TDS images in practice may be corrupted by noise from several sources [12]. Synthetic THz-TDS images (size: 61 × 41 × 263 pixels) are created by corrupting bands with different blurs (controlled by different w_0 and λ as described by Eq. (1)) and noise levels. Frequencies over bands are always set from 0.0076 to 1.9989 THz. The beam waists w_0 and input noise levels over bands are randomly chosen from sets presented in Table 1.

Table 1. Variations of w_0, noise level for Gaussian noise, and noise level for Poisson noise as presented in [26].

w_0 [mm]	Gaussian noise level	SNR in [dB] (Poisson noise)
1.5–0.5	0	68–13 dB
1.8–0.5	0–0.1	70–15 dB
1.5–0.3	0–0.2	72–17 dB
1.7–0.4	0–0.4	74–19 dB

To train and test THzNet-2D we used different combinations of 8000 training and 200 test images corrupted by both Gaussian and Poisson noise. For THzNet-2D, we used 2000 training and 100 test images corrupted by Poisson noise with noise levels randomly selected from Table 1.

4.2 Results on Synthetic Data with THzNet-2D

To find optimal network settings applied on the first dataset, we varied the number and texture of training data and the approach to weights initialization. These variations are listed in Table 2. Note that in Table 2, $6k\_r$ stands for 6000 training images (6k THz-TDS cubes) from which 4k is without texture and 2k is with background texture that is extracted from real THz-TDS images. Similarly, THzNet-2D-6k_t contains 4k training data without texture and 2k with synthetic texture (e.g., stripes, dots). In every experiment, 20% of training images are used for validation. Comparison of the variations of THzNet-2D from Table 2 in terms of PSNR is shown in Fig. 5.

Figure 5 shows the effect of the number and structure of a training data. Note that the results from the figure are obtained on the last band of the hyperspectral cube. We

---

[1] https://mxnet.apache.org/.

Table 2. THzNet-2D variations. NoI: Number of training images; Init: Weights initialization method.

THzNet-2D	No. of training images	Texture	Initialization
1k	1000	No	Uniform
2k	2000	No	Uniform
4k	4000	No	Uniform
6k_r	6000	Yes - 2k realistic	Uniform
6k_t	6000	Yes - 2k stripes	Uniform
4k_x	4000	No	Xavier

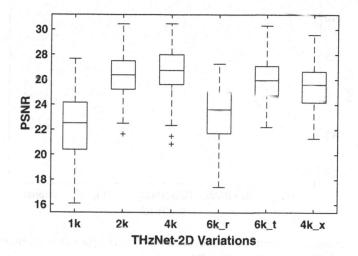

Fig. 5. Comparison of different variations of THzNet-2D (PSNR values obtained on the last band of 100 images) as presented in [26].

may see how the number of training data influences the results (compare the results for THzNet-2D-4k and THzNet-2D-2k). Further, the introduction of training data with additional texture does not necessarily have a positive influence on the results even if a test dataset contains both images with and without texture. Finally, we tested the influence of a different initialization approach for network weights, a so-called Xavier method [13] compared to the standard uniform initialization.

Furthermore, to remove the effects of the THz beam we employed conventional model-based deblurring/deconvolution approaches and compare results with the proposed network THzNet-2D. We tested five conventional deblurring approaches: 1) Richardson-Lucy method (RL) [27,34]; 2) RL followed by a state-of-the-art denoiser, BM3D [8] (RL+BM3D); 3) an extension of BM3D for non-blind deblurring, IDD-BM3D [9]; 4) a state-of-the-art deblurring method with a hyper-Laplacian image prior (H-L) [22]; and 5) a well-known Wiener deconvolution technique (Wiener) [10].

The conventional methods were tested on 100 synthetic THz-TDS images created following the same procedure applied to training data. Deblurring of THz-TDS images was performed band-by-band. Same as previously, before performing deblurring, to remove noise, we denoise the whole THz-TDS cube employing the FastHyDe method. Furthermore, we chose optimal parameters for all conventional deblurring approaches by measuring *mean squared error* (MSE) and *peak signal-to-noise ratio* (PSNR). Results in terms of PSNR obtained with the model-based deblurring approaches applied to the last band (band 263) of 100 THz-TDS test images are presented in Fig. 6.

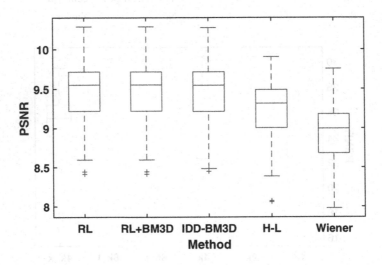

Fig. 6. Comparison of conventional model-based deblurring approaches (deblurring results obtained on the last band) as presented in [26].

Figure 6 shows that RL, RL+BM3D, and IDD-BM3D give the best results in terms of PSNR. The rationale behind this lies in the fact that these approaches are not imposing a prior tailored to natural images: RL is searching for a maximal likelihood solution without the use of any prior knowledge and BM3D and IDD-BM3D are based on self-similarity of non-local image patches. Here, we argue that this self-similarity is present in THz images and therefore the non-local patch-based method will show the promising results. On the contrary, the H-L method imposes a hyper-Laplacian prior on image gradients tailored to natural images. The Wiener method expects an input parameter, noise-to-signal power ratio, which is very difficult to tune for images corrupted by moderate to strong noise.

To compare performance of THzNet-2D and the conventional deblurring approaches, in Fig. 7 we show the results obtained with two representatives: the RL method and THzNet-2D-4k. The results are obtained for different bands (namely bands 50, 100, 150, 200, and 263) and 100 THz-TDS images. We choose RL and THzNet-2D-4k as they are arguably the best tested model-based and CNN-based methods respectively. Moreover, the average difference in performance for the last band of the same 100 images measured by three metrics, MSE, PSNR, and *structural similarity index* (SSIM) is shown in Table 3.

Table 3. THzNet-2D vs Richardson-Lucy as presented in [26].

Method	MSE	PSNR	SSIM
Richardson-Lucy	0.113	9.475	0.544
THzNet-2D	**0.002**	**26.673**	**0.929**

Figure 7 and Table 3 show that THzNet-2D significantly outperforms the model-based methods for several tested bands in terms of three measurement metrics. The results additionally show that for higher bands there is a better performance which is expected as they are less blurry and the noise is mostly removed during pre-processing.

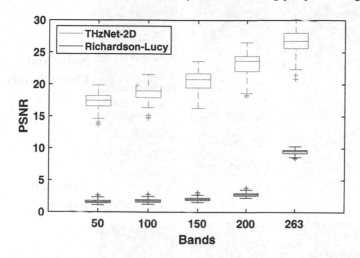

Fig. 7. THzNet-2D vs Richardson-Lucy in terms of PSNR for different bands (50, 100, 150, 200, and 263) as presented in [26].

Figure 8 illustrates the performance of THzNet-2D for three selected bands: 50, 150, and 263. The first row shows the ground truth bands and the second represents the same bands with added blur and noise. In the third row, we show the results after preprocessing/denoising and finally, the fourth and fifth row show results obtained by the Richardson-Lucy (RL) method and THzNet-2D, respectively. The results obtained by the RL method indicates strong ringing and boundary artifacts. Boundary artifacts are most likely due to the incorrect assumption of cyclic convolution in (3). THzNet-2D output bands do not suffer from the same degradation effects. Nevertheless, we see that for the lower band (band 50), the network output shows some missing pixels especially visible on one-pixel thick squared objects.

To show the influence of texture introduced in training and test data on deblurring results, we tested THzNet-2D on an image without any texture and with added texture pattern. Figure 9 shows the obtained results on these two images. In the first row, we see the original ground truth image without texture (A), followed by the texture pattern (B), and the ground truth image with the added pattern (C). Note that the contrast in the image C is increased for the illustration purpose. The second row represents the

band 50   band 150   band 263

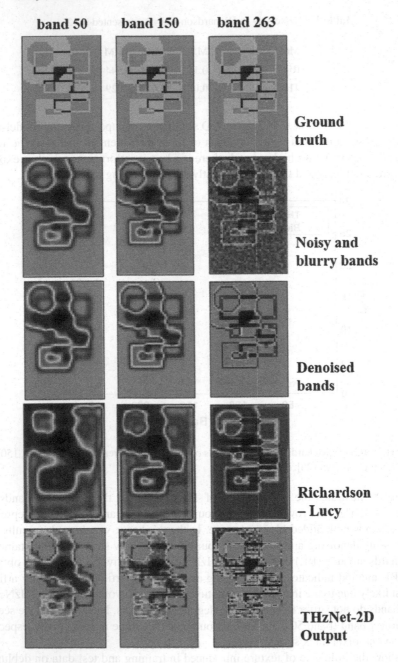

Ground truth

Noisy and blurry bands

Denoised bands

Richardson – Lucy

THzNet-2D Output

Fig. 8. THzNet-2D visual results for bands 50, 150, and 263 (first, second, and third columns respectively).

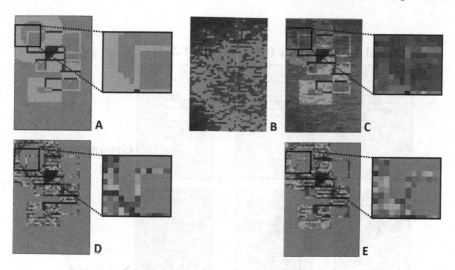

Fig. 9. Influence of texture on deblurring results as presented in [26] A; Ground truth without texture; B: added texture pattern; C: Ground truth with texture; D: THzNet-2D output tested on image A (the last band); E: THzNet-2D output tested on image C (the last band).

THzNet-2D output obtained on the last band of the two THz-TDS images synthesized from the above ground truths (D and E). The network outputs are comparable with the small differences visible near the object edges.

4.3 Results on Synthetic Data with THzNet-HS

Figure 10 shows the results obtained with THzNet-HS compared to THzNet-2D. The proposed THzNet-HS shows more constant output over bands, being able to reconstruct even one-pixel objects from the lower bands (see one pixel sized square objects corresponding to THzNet-HS output, band 50).

Figure 11 illustrates the comparison of THzNet-2D and THzNet-HS in terms of SSIM. The SSIM is calculated for three bands (i.e., 50, 150, and 263) over 100 test images. The same as previously, we see more constant performance of THzNet-HS over bands and significant improvement when compared to band by band deblurring.

Finally, we compare the outputs of THzNet-2D and THzNet-HS in terms of PSNR, calculated for three bands (i.e., 50, 150, and 263) over 100 test images. The results presented in Fig. 12 show that THzNet-HS significantly outperforms the band by band version. Additional, we see that the slightly lower results are obtained for higher bands (e.g., band 263). The same effect is visible in Fig. 10 as the noise artifacts present in the output increase with bands. The reason behind these artifacts in the output is most likely due to the presence of remaining noise after the preprocessing step.

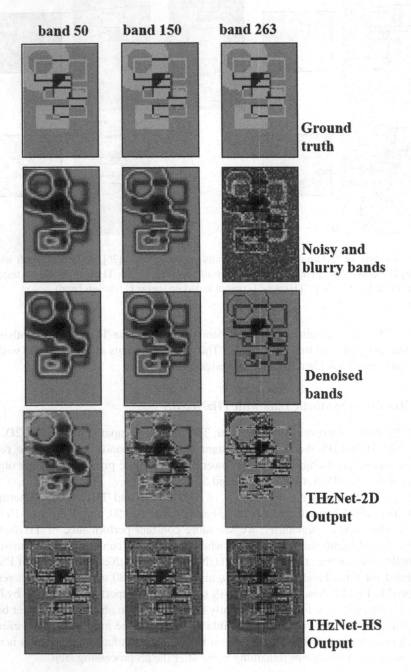

Fig. 10. THzNet-HS visual results for bands 50, 150, and 263 (first, second, and third columns respectively).

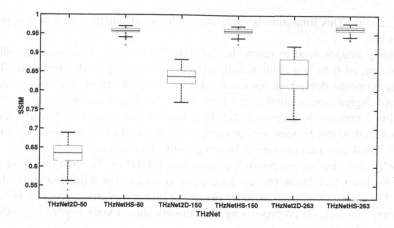

Fig. 11. THzNet-HS vs THzNet-2D results in terms of SSIM for bands 50, 150, and 263 over 100 test images.

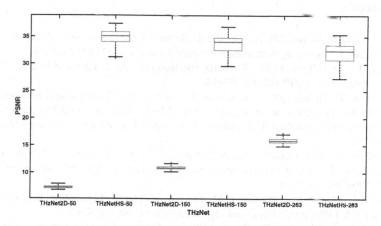

Fig. 12. THzNet-HS vs THzNet-2D results in terms of PSNR for bands 50, 150, and 263 over 100 test images.

5   Conclusion

In this work, we extended the previously proposed CNN-based approach for deblurring THz-TDS images introduced in [26], tacking into consideration deblurring of all HS bands jointly. We demonstrated the superiority of the proposed CNN-based method tested on synthetic images and compared to conventional model-based deblurring methods in performing 2D-based deblurring. The rationale behind choosing a CNN-based approach is reflected in several ways. to name only two: 1) CNNs are robust to small-size and low-resolution images and 2) there is no need for parameter settings as the network weights are learned from training data. A limitation of the previously proposed THzNet-2D network is reflected in the fact that it considers the HS bands independently during training. This limitation is overcome with the introduction of a new approach, THzNet-HS.

Training images need to resemble real THz-TDS images as close as possible in terms of size, artifacts (e.g., blur, noise), texture, and intensity levels over bands. Therefore, the proposed deblurring approach takes into consideration changes of intensity levels and degradation relation over bands. This is an important step as it will open a possibility for testing the proposed CNN-based approach on real data. Nevertheless, the proposed method can be seen as a proof of concept: we show that employing a neural network-based approach improve deblurring results significantly.

Finally, there are several possible extensions of THzNet. The first one is an extension of the beam simulation process taking into consideration refraction and reflection losses. The second extension includes denoising into a deblurring process: instead of performing denoising as preprocessing, the network should learn to perform both tasks denoising and deblurring.

References

1. Badrinarayanan, V., Kendall, A., Cipolla, R.: Segnet: A deep convolutional encoder-decoder architecture for image segmentation. arXiv preprint arXiv:1511.00561 (2015)
2. Baxter, J.B., Guglietta, G.W.: Terahertz spectroscopy. Anal. Chem. **83**(12), 4342–4368 (2011). https://doi.org/10.1021/ac200907z
3. Bazrafkan, S., Thavalengal, S., Corcoran, P.: An end to end deep neural network for iris segmentation in unconstrained scenarios. Neural Netw. **106**, 79–95 (2018). https://doi.org/10.1016/j.neunet.2018.06.011, http://www.sciencedirect.com/science/article/pii/S08936080 1830193X
4. Bazrafkan, S., Van Nieuwenhove, V., Soons, J., De Beenhouwer, J., Sijbers, J.: Deep neural network assisted iterative reconstruction method for low dose ct. arXiv preprint arXiv:1906.00650 (2019)
5. Chan, W.L., Deibel, J., Mittleman, D.M.: Imaging with terahertz radiation. Rep. Prog. Phys. **70**(8), 1325–1379 (2007). https://doi.org/10.1088/0034-4885/70/8/r02
6. Chen, T., et al.: Mxnet: A Flexible and Efficient Machine Learning Library for Heterogeneous Distributed Systems. arXiv preprint arXiv:1512.01274 (2015)
7. Cosentino, A.: Terahertz and cultural heritage science: examination of art and archaeology. Technologies **4**(1) (2016). https://doi.org/10.3390/technologies4010006, https://www.mdpi.com/2227-7080/4/1/6
8. Dabov, K., Foi, A., Katkovnik, V., Egiazarian, K.: Image denoising by sparse 3-D transform-domain collaborative filtering. IEEE Trans. Image Process. **16**(8), 2080–2095 (2007). https://doi.org/10.1109/TIP.2007.901238
9. Danielyan, A., Katkovnik, V., Egiazarian, K.: BM3D frames and variational image deblurring. IEEE Trans. Image Process. **21**(4), 1715–1728 (2012). https://doi.org/10.1109/TIP.2011.2176954
10. Dhawan, A., Rangayyan, R., Gordon, R.: Image restoration by wiener deconvolution in limited-view computed tomography. Appl. Opt. **24**, 4013 (1986). https://doi.org/10.1364/AO.24.004013
11. Dong, C., Loy, C.C., He, K., Tang, X.: Image super-resolution using deep convolutional networks. IEEE Trans. Pattern Anal. Mach. Intell. **38**(2), 295–307 (2016). https://doi.org/10.1109/TPAMI.2015.2439281

12. Duvillaret, L., Garet, F., Coutaz, J.L.: Influence of noise on the characterization of materials by terahertz time-domain spectroscopy. JOSA B **17**, 452–461 (2000). https://doi.org/10.1364/JOSAB.17.000452
13. Glorot, X., Bengio, Y.: Understanding the difficulty of training deep feedforward neural networks. In: Proceedings of the International Conference on Artificial Intelligence and Statistics (2010)
14. Guillet, J.P., et al.: Review of terahertz tomography techniques. J. Infrared Millim. Terahertz Waves **35**(4), 382–411 (2014). https://doi.org/10.1007/s10762-014-0057-0, https://hal.archives-ouvertes.fr/hal-00968839
15. Haddad, J.E., Bousquet, B., Canioni, L., Mounaix, P.: Review in terahertz spectral analysis. Trends Anal. Chem. **44**, 98–105 (2013). https://doi.org/10.1016/j.trac.2012.11.009, http://www.sciencedirect.com/science/article/pii/S0165993613000022
16. Hu, B.B., Nuss, M.C.: Imaging with terahertz waves. Opt. Lett. **20**(16), 1716–1718 (1995). https://doi.org/10.1364/OL.20.001716, http://ol.osa.org/abstract.cfm?URI=ol-20-16-1716
17. Ioffe, S., Szegedy, C.: Batch normalization: Accelerating deep network training by reducing internal covariate shift. arXiv preprint arXiv:1502.03167 (2015)
18. Kato, N., et al.: The deep learning vision for heterogeneous network traffic control: proposal, challenges, and future perspective. IEEE Wirel. Commun. **24**(3), 146–153 (2016)
19. Kawase, K., Shibuya, T., Hayashi, S., Suizu, K.: THz Imaging techniques for nondestructive inspections. Comptes Rendus Physique **11**(7), 510–518 (2010). https://doi.org/10.1016/j.crhy.2010.04.003, http://www.sciencedirect.com/science/article/pii/S1631070510000423, terahertz electronic and optoelectronic components and systems
20. Kemp, M.C., Taday, P.F., Cole, B.E., Cluff, J.A., Fitzgerald, A.J., Tribe, W.R.: Security applications of terahertz technology. In: Terahertz for Military and Security Applications, vol. 5070, pp. 44–52 (2003). https://doi.org/10.1117/12.500491, https://doi.org/10.1117/12.500491
21. Kingma, D.P., Ba, J.: Adam: A Method for Stochastic Optimization. arXiv preprint arXiv:1412.6980 (2014)
22. Krishnan, D., Fergus, R.: Fast image deconvolution using hyper-laplacian priors. Adv. Neural Inf. Process. Syst. 1033–1041 (2009). http://papers.nips.cc/paper/3707-fast-image-deconvolution-using-hyper-laplacian-priors
23. LeCun, Y., Bengio, Y., Hinton, G.E.: Deep learning. Nature **521**(7553), 436–444 (2015). https://doi.org/10.1038/nature14539, https://doi.org/10.1038/nature14539
24. Lemley, J., Bazrafkan, S., Corcoran, P.: Deep learning for consumer devices and services: pushing the limits for machine learning, artificial intelligence, and computer vision. IEEE Consum. Electron. Mag. **6**(2), 48–56 (2017)
25. Litjens, G., et al.: A survey on deep learning in medical image analysis. Med. Image Anal. **42**, 60–88 (2017)
26. Ljubenović., M., Bazrafkan., S., Beenhouwer., J.D., Sijbers., J.: CNN-based deblurring of terahertz images. In: Proceedings of the 15th International Joint Conference on Computer Vision, Imaging and Computer Graphics Theory and Applications - Volume 4: VISAPP, pp. 323–330. INSTICC, SciTePress (2020). https://doi.org/10.5220/0008973103230330
27. Lucy, L.B.: An iterative technique for the rectification of observed distributions. Astron. J. **79**(6), 745–754 (1974)
28. Mallat, S.: A Wavelet Tour of Signal Processing, Third Edition: The Sparse Way, 3rd edn. Academic Press Inc., Orlando, FL, USA (2008)
29. Mukherjee, S., Federici, J., Lopes, P., Cabral, M.: Elimination of Fresnel reflection boundary effects and beam steering in pulsed terahertz computed tomography. J. Infrared Millim. Terahertz Waves **34**(9), 539–555 (2013). https://doi.org/10.1007/s10762-013-9985-3
30. Pelt, D., Batenburg, K., Sethian, J.: Improving tomographic reconstruction from limited data using mixed-scale dense convolutional neural networks. J. Imaging **4**(11), 128 (2018)

31. Pickwell-MacPherson, E., Wallace, V.P.: Terahertz pulsed imaging - a potential medical imaging modality? Photodiagn. Photodyn. Ther. **6**, 128–134 (2009)
32. Popescu, D.C., Hellicar, A.D.: Point spread function estimation for a terahertz imaging system. EURASIP J. Adv. Signal Process. **2010**(1), 575817 (2010). https://doi.org/10.1155/2010/575817, https://doi.org/10.1155/2010/575817
33. Recur, B., et al.: Propagation beam consideration for 3D THz computed omography. Opt. Express **20**(6), 5817–5829 (2012). https://doi.org/10.1364/OE.20.005817, http://www.opticsexpress.org/abstract.cfm?URI=oe-20-6-5817
34. Richardson, W.H.: Bayesian-based iterative method of image restoration. J. Opt. Soc. Am. **62**(1), 55–59 (1972). https://doi.org/10.1364/JOSA.62.000055, http://www.osapublishing.org/abstract.cfm?URI=josa-62-1-55
35. Shang, C., Yang, F., Huang, D., Lyu, W.: Data-driven soft sensor development based on deep learning technique. J. Process Control **24**(3), 223–233 (2014)
36. Shen, D., Wu, G., Suk, H.I.: Deep learning in medical image analysis. Annu. Rev. Biomed. Eng. **19**, 221–248 (2017)
37. Song, Z., et al.: Temporal and spatial variability of water status in plant leaves by terahertz imaging. IEEE Trans. Terahertz Sci. Technol. **8**, 520–527 (2018)
38. Srivastava, N., Hinton, G., Krizhevsky, A., Sutskever, I., Salakhutdinov, R.: Dropout: a simple way to prevent neural networks from overfitting. J. Mach. Learn. Res. **15**(1), 1929–1958 (2014)
39. Tao, X., Gao, H., Wang, Y., Shen, X., Wang, J., Jia, J.: Scale-recurrent network for deep image deblurring (2018)
40. Tepe, J., Schuster, T., Littau, B.: A modified algebraic reconstruction technique taking refraction into account with an application in terahertz tomography. Inverse Probl. Sci. Eng. **25**(10), 1448–1473 (2017). https://doi.org/10.1080/17415977.2016.1267168, https://doi.org/10.1080/17415977.2016.1267168
41. Voulodimos, A., Doulamis, N., Doulamis, A., Protopapadakis, E.: Deep learning for computer vision: a brief review. Comput. Intell. Neurosci. **2018**, 1–13 (2018). https://doi.org/10.1155/2018/7068349
42. Xu, L., Ren, J.S.J., Liu, C., Jia, J.: Deep Convolutional Neural Network for Image Deconvolution. Adv. Neural Inf. Process. Syst. **27**, 1790–1798. Curran Associates, Inc. (2014). http://papers.nips.cc/paper/5485-deep-convolutional-neural-network-for-image-deconvolution.pdf
43. Xu, L.M., Fan, W., Liu, J.: High-resolution reconstruction for terahertz imaging. Appl. Opt. **53** (2014). https://doi.org/10.1364/AO.53.007891
44. Zhang, J., et al.: Dynamic scene deblurring using spatially variant recurrent neural networks. In: 2018 IEEE/CVF Conference on Computer Vision and Pattern Recognition, pp. 2521–2529 (2018). https://doi.org/10.1109/CVPR.2018.00267
45. Zhang, K., Zuo, W., Chen, Y., Meng, D., Zhang, L.: Beyond a gaussian denoiser: residual learning of deep CNN for image denoising. IEEE Trans. Image Process. (2017). https://doi.org/10.1109/TIP.2017.2662206
46. Zhang, K., Zuo, W., Gu, S., Zhang, L.: Learning deep cnn denoiser prior for image restoration. In: Proceedings of the IEEE Conference on Computer Vision and Pattern Recognition, pp. 3929–3938 (2017)
47. Zhuang, L., Bioucas-Dias, J.M.: Fast hyperspectral image denoising and inpainting based on low-rank and sparse representations. IEEE J. Sel. Topics Appl. Earth Obs. Remote Sens. **11**(3), 730–742 (2018). https://doi.org/10.1109/JSTARS.2018.2796570

Thermal Image Super-Resolution: A Novel Unsupervised Approach

Rafael E. Rivadeneira[1]([✉])[iD], Angel D. Sappa[1,2][iD], and Boris X. Vintimilla[1][iD]

[1] Escuela Superior Politécnica del Litoral, ESPOL, Facultad de Ingeniería en Electricidad y Computación, CIDIS, Campus Gustavo Galindo Km. 30.5 Vía Perimetral, P.O. Box 09-01-5863, Guayaquil, Ecuador
{rrivaden,asappa,boris.vintimilla}@espol.edu.ec

[2] Computer Vision Center, Edifici O, Campus UAB, Bellaterra, 08193 Barcelona, Spain

Abstract. This paper proposes the use of a CycleGAN architecture for thermal image super-resolution under a transfer domain strategy, where middle-resolution images from one camera are transferred to a higher resolution domain of another camera. The proposed approach is trained with a large dataset acquired using three thermal cameras at different resolutions. An unsupervised learning process is followed to train the architecture. Additional loss function is proposed trying to improve results from the state of the art approaches. Following the first thermal image super-resolution challenge (PBVS-CVPR2020) evaluations are performed. A comparison with previous works is presented showing the proposed approach reaches the best results.

Keywords: Thermal image super-resolution · Thermal images · Datasets · Challenge · Unpair thermal images

1 Introduction

Single Image Super-Resolution (SISR) is a challenging ill-posed problem that refers to the task of restoring high-resolution (HR) images from a low-resolution (LR) image of the same scene, usually with the use of digital image processing or Machine Learning (ML) techniques. Super-Resolution is wide used in several applications, such as medical imaging (e.g., [25]), object detection (e.g., [12]), security (e.g., [31,39]), among others. In recent years deep learning techniques have been applied to SISR problem achieving remarkable results with respect to state-of-the-art approaches. Most of these techniques are focused on the visible domain—i.e., RGB images. Long-wavelength infrared (LWIR) images, also referred to in the literature as thermal images, have become very important in several challenging fields (e.g., dark environments for military security, medicine for mama cancer detection [14] or for car driving assistance [8] are just three examples where these images can be used). Thermal cameras capture the information of LWIR spectra, which is the radiation emitted by the object's surface when their temperature is above zero [11].

Unfortunately, most of the thermal cameras in the market have poor resolution, due to the technology limitation and the high price of that technology. Thermal cameras

© Springer Nature Switzerland AG 2022
K. Bouatouch et al. (Eds.): VISIGRAPP 2020, CCIS 1474, pp. 495–506, 2022.
https://doi.org/10.1007/978-3-030-94893-1_23

with a high-resolution are considerably expensive with respect to low-resolution ones. Due to this limitation and a large number of applications based on their use, single thermal image super-resolution (SThISR) has become an attractive research topic in the computer vision community.

In the visible spectrum exists thousands of images captured with HD cameras, which are very useful for training networks used in the SISR problem. On the contrary to the visible spectrum domain, thermal images tend to have a poor resolution and there are a few HD datasets. Due to the lack of thermal images, a novel dataset was recently proposed in [29] containing images with three different resolutions (low, mid, and high) obtained with three different thermal cameras. This dataset has been used in the first thermal image super-resolution challenge on PBVS-CVPR2020 conference, where several teams have participated and a baseline has been obtained. The current work is focused on two topics; firstly, a novel CycleGAN architecture is proposed, which makes use of a novel loss function (SOBEL cycle loss) to achieve better results than the ones obtained in PBVS-CVPR2020 challenge [28]; secondly, the dataset presented in PBVS-CVPR2020 is enlarged with new images that help to generalize the training phase to ensure that the architecture is enough to SR any thermal image characteristics.

The manuscript is organized as follows. Section 2 presents works related to the topics tackled in the current work. The used datasets and the proposed architecture are detailed in Sect. 3. Results are provided in Sect. 4. Finally, conclusions are given in Sect. 5.

2   Related Work

Single Image Super-Resolution (SISR) is a classic problem in the computer vision community, most often for images from the visible spectrum. In this section, common thermal image datasets used as benchmarks by the community, together with the state of the art SISR approaches in the thermal image domain, are reviewed.

2.1   Benchmark Datasets

Visible spectrum HD images, for training SR networks and evaluating their performance, is not a problem due it large variety of datasets available in the literature (e.g., [1,2,15,22,23,34,37], among others). These HR images have been acquired in different scenarios covering a large set of objects' category (e.g., building, people, food, cars, among others) at different resolutions. On the contrary to the visible spectrum, in the thermal image domain, there are just a few datasets available in the literature, most of them in low resolution (e.g., [7,16,26], among others); actually, thermal image datasets available in the literature have been designed for other specific applications (e.g., biometric domain, medical, security) but used to tackle the thermal image super-resolution problem. Up to our knowledge, [36] is the largest HR thermal image dataset available in the literature; this dataset consists of full-resolution 1024 × 1024 images, collected with a FLIR SC8000, containing 63782 frames; the main drawback of this dataset is that all the images come from the same scenario.

Trying to overcome the lack of datasets intended for thermal images SR task, in [30] a novel dataset is presented. It consists of 101 images acquired with a HR TAU2 FLIR camera, with a native resolution of 640 × 512 pixels of different scenarios (e.g. indoor, outdoor, day, night). A very large dataset (FLIR-ADAS) has been released by FLIR[1], it provides an annotated thermal images set for training and validation object detection neural networks. This dataset was acquired also with a TAU2 thermal camera but mounted on a vehicle. Provided images are with a resolution of 640 × 512. It contains a total of 14452 thermal images sampled from short videos taken on streets and highways. This dataset was intended for driving assistance applications, although can be used for the super-resolution problem.

Most of these datasets are not large enough to reach good results when heavy SR learning-based approaches are considered; furthermore, the datasets mentioned above contain images obtained from just one thermal camera. Having in mind all these limitations, recently [29] presents a novel dataset that consists of a set of 1021 thermal images acquired with three different thermal cameras, which acquire images at different resolutions. The dataset contains images of outdoor scenarios with different daylight conditions (e.g., morning, afternoon, and night) and objects (e.g., buildings, cars, vegetation), mounting the cameras in a rig trying to minimize the baseline distance between the optical axis to get an almost registered image. This dataset has been used as a benchmark in the first thermal image super-resolution challenge organized on the workshop *Perception Beyond the Visible Spectrum* of CVPR2020 conference [28].

2.2 Super-Resolution

The image SR is a classical issue, and still a challenging problem in the computer vision community and can be categorized as single-image SR (SISR) and multi-image SR (MISR), where SISR task is more challenging than MISR due to the lack of features that can be obtained in just one image rather than multiple images of the same scene. SISR has been studied in the literature for years and can be roughly classified as interpolation-based SR (conventional and traditional methods) and deep learning-based SR.

SRCNN [9] for the first time introduced deep learning in the SR field, showing the capability to improve the quality of SR results in comparison to traditional methods. Inspired in SRCNN, [18] proposes a VDSR network showing significant improvement. The authors propose to use more convolutional layers, increasing the depth of the network from 3 to 20 layers, and adopt global residual learning to predict the difference between generated image from the ground-truth (GT) image instead pixel-wise. FSR-CNN [10] gets better computational performance by extracting the feature maps on a low-resolution image and just in the last layer up-sampled it reducing the computational cost. Inspired by these works, different approaches to the image SR problem have been published using deeper networks using more convolutional layers with residual learning (e.g., [18,38]). Recently, several SR approaches using CNN (e.g., SRFeat-M [27], EDSR [20], RCAN [40]) have been proposed obtaining state-of-the-art performance for visible LR images. The CNNs mentioned above aim to minimize the difference between

---

[1] FREE FLIR Thermal Dataset for Algorithm Training https://www.flir.in/oem/adas/adas-dataset-form/.

SR and GT images by using a supervised training process with a pair of images having a pixel-wise registration. In general, the strategy followed by these approaches is to down-sample the given HR image, add random noise or blur it, and then use it as the input LR image.

To overcome the limitation of having a pixel-wise registration between SR and GT images, unsupervised approaches have been proposed. For instance, [32] proposes a single image super-resolution approach, referred to as SRGAN, which achieves impressive state-of-the-art performance. This approach is inspired by the seminal Generative Adversarial Network (GAN) presented in [13]. In recent literature, different unsupervised training processes have been presented for applications such as transferring style [3], image colorization [24], image enhancement [4], feature estimation [33], among others. All these approaches are based on two-way GANs (CycleGAN) networks that can learn from unpaired data sets [41]. CycleGAN can be used to learn how to map images from one domain (source domain) into another domain (target domain). This functionality makes CycleGAN models appropriate for image SR estimation when there is not a pixel-wise registration.

Most of the SR approaches mentioned above are focused on images from the visible spectrum. Based on SRCNN, [5] propose the first approach named Thermal Enhancement Network (TEN). Due to the lack of thermal image dataset, TEN uses RGB images for training. In [30], a dataset of 101 HR thermal images have been considered and, in conclusion, the authors state that better results are obtained if the network is trained using images from the same spectral band. Recently, [21] uses a concept of multi-image SR (MISR) for thermal imaging SR. As mentioned above, in [29] a novel dataset using three different camera resolutions has been proposed; this dataset is used to train a CycleGAN architecture that makes a transfer domain from a LR image (from one camera) to a HR image (of another camera), without pairing the images. Using this dataset as a reference, in [28] two kinds of evaluations are proposed, the first evaluation consists of down-sampling a HR thermal images by ×2, ×3 and ×4 and comparing their SR results with the corresponding GT images. The second evaluation consists in obtaining the ×2 SR from a given MR thermal image and comparing it with its corresponding semi registered HR image. Results from this work are considered as baseline measures for future works in the thermal images super-resolution—MLVC-Lab [6] and Couger AI [17] corresponds to the approaches with the best results according to the mentioned evaluations.

3 Proposed Approach

In Sect. 3.1, details of the proposed architecture are given together with information about the proposed loss function. Additionally, in Sect. 3.2, the datasets used for training and validation are described. Finally, the process followed to evaluate the performance of the proposed approach is introduced.

3.1 Architecture

The proposed approach is based on the usage of Cycle Generative Adversarial Network (CycleGAN) [41], widely used for map feature maps from one domain to another domain. In the current work, this framework is used to tackle the SR problem by mapping information from the mid-resolution (MR) to the high-resolution (HR) domain. As shown in Fig. 1, the proposed approach consists of two generators (MR to HR and HR to MR), with their corresponding discriminators (DISC MR and DISC HR) that validate the generated images. As generators, a ResNet with 6 residual blocks (ResNet-6) is considered. It uses optimization to avoid degradation in the training phase. The residual blocks have convolutional layers, with instant normalization and ReLu, and skip connections. As discriminators a patchGAN architecture is considered; the generated image and a non paired GT image are used to validate if the output is real or not.

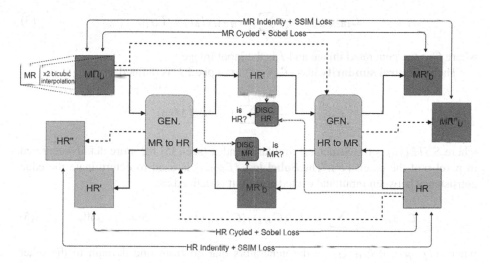

Fig. 1. CycleGAN architecture with 6 blocks ResNet for MR to HR generator and for HR to MR; with cycled + Sobel Loss and Identity + SSIM loss, and it respective discriminators.

Following the architecture presented in [29], a combination of different loss functions is used: i) adversarial loss $\mathcal{L}_{Adversarial}$, ii) cycle loss $\mathcal{L}_{Cycle}$, iii) identity loss $\mathcal{L}_{Identity}$, and iv) structural similarity loss $\mathcal{L}_{SSIM}$; additionally, another loss term, Sobel loss $\mathcal{L}_{Sobel}$, is proposed. Sobel loss consist in apply Sobel filter edge detector [19] to the input image and the cycled generated image, and get the mean square difference between both images, helping to evaluate the contour consistency between the two images. Details on each of these loss terms are given below—Fig. 1 illustrates these terms.

The **adversarial loss** is designed to minimize the cross-entropy to improve the texture loss:

$$\mathcal{L}_{Adversarial} = -\sum_i logD(G_{M2H}(I_M), I_H), \tag{1}$$

where D is the discriminator, $G_{M2H}(I_M)$ is the generated image, I_M and I_H are the low and high-resolution images respectively.

The **cycled loss** ($\mathcal{L}_{Cycled}$) is used to determinate the consistency between input and cycled output; it is defined as:

$$\mathcal{L}_{Cycled} = \frac{1}{N} \sum_i \|G_{H2M}(G_{M2H}(I_M)) - I_M\|, \qquad (2)$$

where G_{M2H} and G_{H2M} are the generators that go from one domain to the other domain.

The **identity loss** ($\mathcal{L}_{Identity}$) is used for maintaining the consistency between input and output; it is defined as:

$$\mathcal{L}_{Identity} = \frac{1}{N} \sum_i \|G_{H2M}(I_M) - I_M\|, \qquad (3)$$

where G is the generated image and I is the input image.

The **structural similarity loss** ($\mathcal{L}_{SSIM}$) for a pixel P is defined as:

$$\mathcal{L}_{SSIM} = \frac{1}{NM} \sum_{p=1}^{P} 1 - SSIM(p), \qquad (4)$$

where $SSIM(p)$ is the Structural Similarity Index (see [35] for more details) centered in pixel p of the patch (P). The **Sobel loss** ($\mathcal{L}_{Sobel}$) is used to determinate the edge consistency between input and cycled output; it is defined as:

$$\mathcal{L}_{Sobel} = \frac{1}{N} \sum_i \|Sobel(G_{H2M}(G_{M2H}(I_M))) - Sobel(I_M)\|, \qquad (5)$$

where G_{M2H} and G_{H2M} are the generators that go from one domain to the other domain and Sobel gets the contour of the images.

The **total loss function** ($\mathcal{L}_{total}$) used in this work is the weighted sum of the individual loss function terms:

$$\mathcal{L}_{total} = \lambda_1 \mathcal{L}_{Adversarial} + \lambda_2 \mathcal{L}_{Cycled} + \lambda_3 \mathcal{L}_{Identity} + \lambda_4 \mathcal{L}_{SSIM} + \lambda_5 \mathcal{L}_{Sobel}, \qquad (6)$$

where λ_i are weights empirically set for each loss function.

3.2   Datasets

The proposed approach is trained by using two datasets. The novel dataset from [29] and the FLIR-ADAS mentioned in Sect. 2.1. For the first dataset, only mid-resolution (MR) and high-resolution (HR) images, acquired with two different cameras at different resolutions (mid and high resolution) are considered; each resolution set has 951 images and 50 images are left for testing. Figure 2 shows some illustrations of this dataset, just images from the mid-resolution and high-resolution are depicted.

For the second dataset, which contains 8862 training images, just one out of nine images have been selected, resulting in a sub-set of 985 images. This subsampling process has been applied in order to have more different scenarios since these images correspond to a video sequence, consecutive images are quite similar. Figure 3 shows some illustrations from this second dataset.

Fig. 2. Examples of thermal images. (*top*) MR images from Axis Q2901-E. (*bottom*) HR images from FC-6320 FLIR [29].

Both datasets have HR images with a native resolution of 640 × 512; these images have been cropped to 640 × 480 pixels, centered, to be exactly x2 of MR images; both datasets have 8bits and are saved in jpg format, so both have similar scenarios but acquired in different places and conditions.

The main idea is to train the network with a shuffle mix of images between these two datasets, having the same proportion of images, sizes, and the same condition's scenarios. As mention in Sect. 3.3, the validation is done with the same set of images used in the PBVS-CVPR2020 challenge [28], to compare the results with the most recent results in the state-of-the-art literature.

Fig. 3. Examples of the *Free FLIR Thermal Dataset for Algorithm Training* (FLIR-ADAS).

3.3 Evaluation

The quantitative evaluations of the proposed method are performed as proposed in [29] for MR to HR case; this evaluation has been adopted in the PBVS-CVPR2020 Challenge [28], referred to as *evaluation2*, which consists in getting the average results of PSNR and SSIM measures on the generated SR of mid-resolution images and compared with the semi registered high-resolution image obtained from the other camera. This process is illustrated in Fig. 4. Just a centered region containing 80% of the image is considered in order to use these measures. For a fair comparison, the images from the validation set are the same ones used in the previous works mentioned above. Results from this *evaluation2* are compared with those presented in [29].

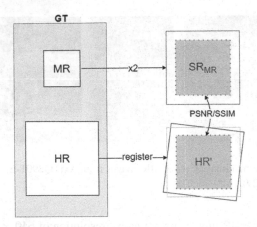

Fig. 4. PBVS-CVPR2020 challenge evaluation2 approach [28].

4   Experimental Results

This section presents the results obtained with the unsupervised SThISR architecture proposed in this work. Section 4.1 describes the settings used for training the proposed approach, while Sect. 4.2 presents the quantitative results.

4.1   Settings

The proposed approach is trained on a NVIDIA Geforce GTX mounted in a workstation with 128 GB of RAM, using Python programming language, Tensorflow 2.0, and Keras library. Only the two datasets mentioned in Sect. 2.1 are considered, no data-augmentation process has been applied to the given input data.

Images are up-sampled by bicubic interpolation, due to the CycleGAN transfer domain (from mid to high resolution) needs images at the same resolution. Images are normalized in a $[-1, 1]$ range. The network was trained for 100 epochs without dropout since the model does not present overfit. The generator is a ResNet with 6 residual blocks (ResNet-6) using Stochastic AdamOptimizer to prevent over fittings and lead to faster convergent and avoiding degradation in the training phase. The discriminators use a patchGAN architecture, and it validates if the generated image together with the GT images is real or not. For each epoch in the training phase, input images were shuffle random mix. The hyper-parameters used were 0.0002 for learning rate for both the generator and the discriminator networks; epsilon = 1e−05; exponential decay rate for the 1st moment momentum 0.5 for the discriminator and 0.4 for the generator. For λ_i values weights in losses, the set of values that obtain the best results were: for $\mathcal{L}_{Cycled}$ = 10, $\mathcal{L}_{Identity}$ = 5, $\mathcal{L}_{SSIM}$ = 5 and $\mathcal{L}_{Sobel}$ = 10. The proposed architecture has been trained twice, one with just the first dataset and once with both datasets.

4.2   Results

The quantitative results obtained for each training, together with previous works and other approaches from the PBVS-CVPR2020 Challenge are shown in Table 1 using

PSNR and SSIM measures comparison. The best results are highlighted in bold and the second-best result is underline. As can be appreciated, the proposed SThISR approach achieves better results than other works. Between both current work results, using just one dataset gets seven-tenths better PSNR results rather than using both datasets. SSIM measure gets higher result using the two datasets buts just by one-thousandth. These results show that using just the first dataset the proposed approach archive better results, meaning that this dataset is varied enough to train a network and that it is possible to do a Single Thermal Image Super-Resolution between two different domains using images acquired with different camera resolutions and without registration.

Table 1. Quantitative average results of evaluation detail in Sect. 3.3. [+]Winner approaches at the PBVS-CVPR2020 Challenge. Work[1] using just first dataset; Work[2] using both datasets. Bold and underline values correspond to the first and second best results respectively.

Approachs'	PSNR	SSIM
Bicubic interpolation	20,24	0,7515
[29]	22,42	0,7989
MLVC-Lab[+]	20,02	0,7452
COUGER AI[+]	20,36	0,7595
Current work[1]	**22,98**	0,8032
Current work[2]	22,27	**0,8045**

Regarding the quality of the obtained results, Fig. 5 shows the worst and best super-resolution results from the validation set. The worst result gets 20.11/0.6464 PSNR and SSIM measures respectively; it should be mentioned that although it is the worst

Fig. 5. Examples quality results. (*top*) from left to right, MR image, HR image, worst results. (*bottom*) best results.

result from the whole validation set, it is considerably better than the results obtained with a bicubic interpolation: 17.36/0.6193 PSNR and SSIM respectively. In the case of the best result, a 26.06/0.8651 PSNR and SSIM measures respectively are obtained, in this case, the bicubic interpolation reaches 19.41/0.8021 PSNR and SSIM respectively. In conclusion, it could be stated that the most challenging scenarios are those with objects at different depth and complex textures, on the contrary, it can be appreciated that scenes with planar surfaces are more simple to obtain their corresponding super-resolution representation.

5   Conclusions

This paper presents an extended version of the work presented at VISAPP 2020. Two datasets are considered during the training stage, and adjusting different hyper-parameters values on loss function in CycleGAN and adding a Sobel loss. The proposed approach has shown an improvement on previous work and achieved better results on state-of-the-art values comparing to the results from the first challenge on SR thermal images in terms of PSNR and SSIM measures. It should be mentioned that the proposed SThISR architecture is trained using an unpaired set of images. The first dataset has large variability, showing that its not necessary the use of other datasets.

Acknowledgements. This work has been partially supported by the Spanish Government under Project TIN2017-89723-P; and the "CERCA Programme/Generalitat de Catalunya". The first author has been supported by Ecuador government under a SENESCYT scholarship contract.

References

1. Arbel, P., Maire, M., Fowlkes, C., Malik, J.: Contour detection and hierarchical image segmentation. IEEE Trans. Pattern Anal. Mach. Intell. **33**(5), 898–916 (2011)
2. Bevilacqua, M., Roumy, A., Guillemot, C., Alberi-Morel, M.L.: Low-complexity single-image super-resolution based on nonnegative neighbor embedding (2012)
3. Chang, H., Lu, J., Yu, F., Finkelstein, A.: PairedCycleGAN: asymmetric style transfer for applying and removing makeup. In: Proceedings of the IEEE Conference on Computer Vision and Pattern Recognition, pp. 40–48 (2018)
4. Chen, Y.S., Wang, Y.C., Kao, M.H., Chuang, Y.Y.: Deep photo enhancer: unpaired learning for image enhancement from photographs with GANs. In: Proceedings of the IEEE Conference on Computer Vision and Pattern Recognition, pp. 6306–6314 (2018)
5. Choi, Y., Kim, N., Hwang, S., Kweon, I.S.: Thermal image enhancement using convolutional neural network. In: 2016 IEEE/RSJ International Conference on Intelligent Robots and Systems (IROS), pp. 223–230. IEEE (2016)
6. Chudasama, V., et al.: TheriSuRNet-a computationally efficient thermal image super-resolution network. In: Proceedings of the IEEE/CVF Conference on Computer Vision and Pattern Recognition Workshops, pp. 86–87 (2020)
7. Davis, J.W., Keck, M.A.: A two-stage template approach to person detection in thermal imagery. In: 2005 Seventh IEEE Workshops on Applications of Computer Vision (WACV/MOTION 2005), vol. 1, pp. 364–369. IEEE (2005)

8. Ding, M., Zhang, X., Chen, W.H., Wei, L., Cao, Y.F.: Thermal infrared pedestrian tracking via fusion of features in driving assistance system of intelligent vehicles. Proc. Inst. Mech. Eng. Part G: J. Aerosp. Eng. **233**(16), 6089–6103 (2019)
9. Dong, C., Loy, C.C., He, K., Tang, X.: Image super-resolution using deep convolutional networks. IEEE Trans. Pattern Anal. Mach. Intell. **38**(2), 295–307 (2015)
10. Dong, C., Loy, C.C., Tang, X.: Accelerating the super-resolution convolutional neural network. In: Leibe, B., Matas, J., Sebe, N., Welling, M. (eds.) ECCV 2016. LNCS, vol. 9906, pp. 391–407. Springer, Cham (2016). https://doi.org/10.1007/978-3-319-46475-6_25
11. Gade, R., Moeslund, T.B.: Thermal cameras and applications: a survey. Mach. Vis. Appl. **25**(1), 245–262 (2013). https://doi.org/10.1007/s00138-013-0570-5
12. Girshick, R., Donahue, J., Darrell, T., Malik, J.: Region-based convolutional networks for accurate object detection and segmentation. IEEE Trans. Pattern Anal. Mach. Intell. **38**(1), 142–158 (2015)
13. Goodfellow, I., et al.: Generative adversarial nets. In: Advances in Neural Information Processing Systems, pp. 2672–2680 (2014)
14. Herrmann, C., Ruf, M., Beyerer, J.: CNN-based thermal infrared person detection by domain adaptation. In: Autonomous Systems: Sensors, Vehicles, Security, and the Internet of Everything, vol. 10643, p. 1064308. International Society for Optics and Photonics (2018)
15. Huang, J.B., Singh, A., Ahuja, N.: Single image super-resolution from transformed self-exemplars. In: Proceedings of the IEEE Conference on Computer Vision and Pattern Recognition, pp. 5197–5206 (2015)
16. Hwang, S., Park, J., Kim, N., Choi, Y., So Kweon, I.: Multispectral pedestrian detection: benchmark dataset and baseline. In: Proceedings of the IEEE Conference on Computer Vision and Pattern Recognition, pp. 1037–1045 (2015)
17. Kansal, P., Nathan, S.: A multi-level supervision model: a novel approach for thermal image super resolution. In: Proceedings of the IEEE/CVF Conference on Computer Vision and Pattern Recognition Workshops, pp. 94–95 (2020)
18. Kim, J., Kwon Lee, J., Mu Lee, K.: Accurate image super-resolution using very deep convolutional networks. In: Proceedings of the IEEE Conference on Computer Vision and Pattern Recognition, pp. 1646–1654 (2016)
19. Kittler, J.: On the accuracy of the Sobel edge detector. Image Vis. Comput. **1**(1), 37–42 (1983)
20. Lim, B., Son, S., Kim, H., Nah, S., Mu Lee, K.: Enhanced deep residual networks for single image super-resolution. In: Proceedings of the IEEE Conference on Computer Vision and Pattern Recognition Workshops, pp. 136–144 (2017)
21. Mandanici, E., Tavasci, L., Corsini, F., Gandolfi, S.: A multi-image super-resolution algorithm applied to thermal imagery. Appl. Geomat. **11**(3), 215–228 (2019). https://doi.org/10.1007/s12518-019-00253-y
22. Martin, D., Fowlkes, C., Tal, D., Malik, J., et al.: A database of human segmented natural images and its application to evaluating segmentation algorithms and measuring ecological statistics. In: ICCV, Vancouver (2001)
23. Matsui, Y., et al.: Sketch-based manga retrieval using manga109 dataset. Multimed. Tools Appl. **76**(20), 21811–21838 (2016). https://doi.org/10.1007/s11042-016-4020-z
24. Mehri, A., Sappa, A.D.: Colorizing near infrared images through a cyclic adversarial approach of unpaired samples. In: Proceedings of the IEEE Conference on Computer Vision and Pattern Recognition Workshops (2019)
25. Mudunuri, S.P., Biswas, S.: Low resolution face recognition across variations in pose and illumination. IEEE Trans. Pattern Anal. Mach. Intell. **38**(5), 1034–1040 (2015)
26. Olmeda, D., Premebida, C., Nunes, U., Armingol, J.M., de la Escalera, A.: Pedestrian detection in far infrared images. Integr. Comput.-Aided Eng. **20**(4), 347–360 (2013)

27. Park, S.J., Son, H., Cho, S., Hong, K.S., Lee, S.: SRFeat: single image super-resolution with feature discrimination. In: Proceedings of the European Conference on Computer Vision (ECCV), pp. 439–455 (2018)
28. Rivadeneira, R.E., et al.: Thermal image super-resolution challenge-PBVS 2020. In: Proceedings of the IEEE/CVF Conference on Computer Vision and Pattern Recognition Workshops, pp. 96–97 (2020)
29. Rivadeneira, R.E., Sappa, A.D., Vintimilla, B.X.: Thermal image super-resolution: a novel architecture and dataset. In: VISIGRAPP (4: VISAPP), pp. 111–119 (2020)
30. Rivadeneira, R.E., Suárez, P.L., Sappa, A.D., Vintimilla, B.X.: Thermal image superresolution through deep convolutional neural network. In: Karray, F., Campilho, A., Yu, A. (eds.) ICIAR 2019. LNCS, vol. 11663, pp. 417–426. Springer, Cham (2019). https://doi.org/10.1007/978-3-030-27272-2_37
31. Shamsolmoali, P., Zareapoor, M., Jain, D.K., Jain, V.K., Yang, J.: Deep convolution network for surveillance records super-resolution. Multimed. Tools Appl. 78(17), 23815–23829 (2018). https://doi.org/10.1007/s11042-018-5915-7
32. Shi, W., Ledig, C., Wang, Z., Theis, L., Huszar, F.: Super resolution using a generative adversarial network, 15 March 2018. US Patent App. 15/706,428
33. Suarez, P.L., Sappa, A.D., Vintimilla, B.X., Hammoud, R.I.: Image vegetation index through a cycle generative adversarial network. In: Proceedings of the IEEE Conference on Computer Vision and Pattern Recognition Workshops (2019)
34. Timofte, R., Agustsson, E., Van Gool, L., Yang, M.H., Zhang, L.: NTIRE 2017 challenge on single image super-resolution: methods and results. In: Proceedings of the IEEE Conference on Computer Vision and Pattern Recognition Workshops, pp. 114–125 (2017)
35. Wang, Z., Bovik, A.C., Sheikh, H.R., Simoncelli, E.P., et al.: Image quality assessment: from error visibility to structural similarity. IEEE Trans. Image Process. 13(4), 600–612 (2004)
36. Wu, Z., Fuller, N., Theriault, D., Betke, M.: A thermal infrared video benchmark for visual analysis. In: Proceedings of the IEEE Conference on Computer Vision and Pattern Recognition Workshops, pp. 201–208 (2014)
37. Zeyde, R., Elad, M., Protter, M.: On single image scale-up using sparse-representations. In: Boissonnat, J.-D., Chenin, P., Cohen, A., Gout, C., Lyche, T., Mazure, M.-L., Schumaker, L. (eds.) Curves and Surfaces 2010. LNCS, vol. 6920, pp. 711–730. Springer, Heidelberg (2012). https://doi.org/10.1007/978-3-642-27413-8_47
38. Zhang, K., Zuo, W., Gu, S., Zhang, L.: Learning deep CNN denoiser prior for image restoration. In: Proceedings of the IEEE Conference on Computer Vision and Pattern Recognition, pp. 3929–3938 (2017)
39. Zhang, L., Zhang, H., Shen, H., Li, P.: A super-resolution reconstruction algorithm for surveillance images. Signal Process. 90(3), 848–859 (2010)
40. Zhang, Y., Li, K., Li, K., Wang, L., Zhong, B., Fu, Y.: Image super-resolution using very deep residual channel attention networks. In: Proceedings of the European Conference on Computer Vision (ECCV), pp. 286–301 (2018)
41. Zhu, J.Y., Park, T., Isola, P., Efros, A.A.: Unpaired image-to-image translation using cycle-consistent adversarial networks. In: Proceedings of the IEEE International Conference on Computer Vision, pp. 2223–2232 (2017)

Regression-Based 3D Hand Pose Estimation for Human-Robot Interaction

Chaitanya Bandi[✉] and Ulrike Thomas

Technical University of Chemnitz, 09126 Chemnitz, Germany
chaitanya.bandi@etit.tu-chemnitz.de

Abstract. In shared workspaces where humans and robots interact, a significant task is to hand over objects. The process of hand over needs to be reliable, a human must not be injured during the process, hence reliable tracking of human hands is necessary. To avoid collision, we apply an encoder-decoder based 2D and 3D keypoint regression network on color images. In this paper, we introduce a complete pipeline with the idea of stacked and cascaded convolutional neural networks and tune the parameters of the network for real-time applications. Experiments are conducted on multiple datasets, with low and high occlusions and we evaluate the trained models on multiple datasets for the human-robot interaction test set.

Keywords: Regression · HRI · Pose · Region of interest

1 Introduction

Human-robot interaction (HRI) has gained much attention in recent years. Applications range from industrial setup to service scenarios where elderly people might have contacts with robots. The challenges on robot's behavior are increasingly high, they should be able to interact without hurting humans. Thus for common HRI task like the handover of objects, robots should not come into collision with humans. The robot needs to know the exact position of human hand joints to avoid hurting. Thus, in this paper we provide a solution for continuous tracking of human fingers in such demanding tasks. Figure 1 left shows the interaction-workspace for the evaluation of trained models. We consider a tabletop scenario where the objects are handed to the robot and the camera is located on the right side as in Fig. 1 right image perspective. In such workspaces, cameras must be well calibrated with respect to robot. Besides in HRI, 3D hand pose estimation can be applied in virtual reality, gesture recognition, and sign language recognition. The research work on pose estimation has gained huge advancement over the past decade, nevertheless, the dexterity of hand makes it complex to fully embrace the learned models with real-time demands. Dexterity increases the challenge for detecting self-occluded hand and during the handover process, objects increase occlusion. Such issues create the need for hardware equipment like sensors, markers, and gloves for either data generation or tracking during complete application. In recent years, many research works introduced

---

The original version of this chapter was revised: The acknowledgements section and grant number have been added. The correction to this chapter is available at
https://doi.org/10.1007/978-3-030-94893-1_26

K. Bouatouch et al. (Eds.): VISIGRAPP 2020, CCIS 1474, pp. 507–529, 2022.
https://doi.org/10.1007/978-3-030-94893-1_24

convolutional neural networks (CNNs) based approaches that perform well under self-occlusions. Low-cost RGB-D sensors like Kinect and Intel Realsense make dataset generation easy and for this work, we use Intel Realsense D435 camera as it is flexible in mounting and calibration. The goal is to estimate the 3D hand pose using RGB images for human-robot interaction scenario as seen in Fig. 1, an Intel Realsense camera is attached to the right-hand side in the scene to avoid having more than 60% of the hand being occluded at a time. From this viewing angle using the Realsense camera, the hand is only partially occluded even when holding an object in this HRI workspace. To estimate the 3D hand pose, we make advancements to the architecture mentioned in our previous work [1]. Besides, we evaluate the architecture with new occluded datasets, analyze the robutness with new metrics and tune the network parameters for real-time HRI application. The approach consists of a cascaded convolution neural network where the first network is the region of interest (ROI) detector and the confined region is passed as input to the second network for 2D and 3D hand pose regression. The regressed 3D hand pose is normalized, so further post-processing is necessary to extend the normalized coordinates to camera coordinates and then transform to the robot coordinate system. A key component of CNNs is the dataset and especially for the HRI application dataset must be occluded and contain high variance. In the next section, related works that are most relevant are mentioned with existing benchmarks. Later, the proposed architecture is trained with multiple datasets and evaluated their performance on the validation set. Finally, we test the trained models in realtime HRI scenarios.

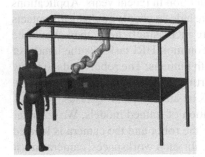 

Fig. 1. Left: tabletop human-robot interaction-workspace, right: the interaction workspace from the prespective of the camera.

2 Related Works

Many research works have been published on pose estimation. In this section, we briefly review the state-of-the-art works on pose estimation. In the early research works, the pose was estimated on the human body and a successful approach can be observed in [2]. The authors in [2] directly regressed the 2D skeleton joint on RGB images. With the idea of belief-maps or heatmaps, [3] recovers the hand pose continuously on depth images using CNNs and inverse kinematics. As an advancement, [4] propose convolutional pose machines with the idea of belief-maps, later many improved works are based on the idea of heatmaps and joint coordinates regression. Initial research works propose an idea of detecting 2D keypoints in RGB images and then extending them to 3D space as in [5, 6]. In the first stage, authors in [5] propose a CNN architecture for 2D pose estimation and in the next stage, the detected keypoints are extended to 3D using a database of 2D to 3D correspondence matching. To extend to 3D, the authors in [13] introduce a probabilistic 3D pose model based upon a mixture of probabilistic PCA bases and [14] propose optimization techniques to improve reprojection error of 3D joint locations and 2D predictions. The most of above-mentioned works are related to human pose estimation.

The authors in [3] are one of the first methods who published a CNN for detection of 2D keypoints on hands, and the 3D poses are recovered by applying inverse kinematics. Since the invention of low-cost RGBD cameras, the approaches in [14, 15] proposes the idea of regressing the 3D coordinates in depth images. Instead of using either cartesian coordinates or correlations, [14] proposed angle relations between bones of the kinematic chain and trained the model. The works mentioned in [16–18] explores the point cloud-based 3D hand pose estimation, and [19–21] used complete depth-based 3D regression models. The method in [8], introduces 3d hand pose estimation from single RGB images and a rendered hand pose dataset but this model struggles to generalize on occluded data. [9] introduces a new large scale GANerated dataset that resembles realistic images with high occlusions and it is evaluated in real-time applications. In their approach, once the 3D joints are regressed, the skeleton fitting model is applied to lower the errors. As an advancement for augmented reality, the approach in [22, 23] propose shape estimation of the hand in addition to 3D poses of finger joints. hand shape estimation is dependent on the detection of keypoints, to this end we focus on the regression of keypoints to track human hand position in real-time HRI scenarios.

2.1 Existing 3D Hand Pose Benchmarks

There are only few pre-existing datasets with accurate anotatations for hand pose estimation. The ICVL dataset [24] is one of the first benchmarks and the data is collected by using a skeletal tracking technique and then they are manually corrected the data to reduce the error. The NYU hand dataset is one of the earliest large-scale datasets published in [3]. It contains samples from a single user with variable gestures. The data has been annotated by using model-based tracking on depth images from multiple cameras. Although authors managed to automate the process of annotation, the method produces result that often deviates from correct poses hence the manual interception is necessary. The NYU dataset is most widely used for depth-based approaches for hand pose estimation, [8] provides information on why this dataset cannot be applicable for a color-based approach. The MSRA15 dataset [25] implemented with an iterative approach using optimization technique, which is published in [7] and then manually adjusted for better results. In one way or another, all these datasets are limited regarding low variability, scale, and incorrect/missing annotations. Later, a first-person hand action benchmark [26] with daily actions were recorded by attaching sensors to each finger. Since we estimate the pose using RGB images in their dataset are not applicable as the sensors are visible in RGB images.

In this work, we consider color images for 3D hand pose regression and one of the largest color datasets that is available for research as the GANerated dataset [9]. This dataset consists of over 300k color images with and without occlusions. This dataset is synthetically generated to bridges the gap between real and purely synthetic images. In [10], the authors introduces a complete markerless way of capturing the 3D hand pose data in color images called the FreiHAND dataset. They introduce a semi-automatic iterative approach on multi-view camera images for annotation of a large-scale dataset. The approach estimates not only the 3D pose but also the shape parameters of the hand. The dataset contains 32560 training samples and 3960 validation/evaluation samples. This dataset consists of high occlusions with objects holding in hands. As an improvement to [10], a new dataset with a fully automatic markerless dataset generation approach is presented in [11]. This dataset consists of over 77k images with hand plus object annotations (HO-3D dataset) with high occlusions. The dataset consists of 3D hand pose, shape parameters, and 6D object pose in hand. For HRI scenarios, it is highly significant to have the 3D hand pose annotations when occlusions occur. Since the datasets in [9, 11] consist of highly occluded data, we consider these datasets for evaluation of our architecture. In our previous work [1], we introduce a manually annotated dataset of 15k with multi-camera setup and we train the model with that SSMH dataset but labeling by hand is a costly and time taking process, so we rely on the approach mentioned in [11] for only test dataset generation and evaluation in HRI setting.

3 Proposed Architecture

We aim to infer 3D joints of the hand given a color image. Since the hand size in images is variable, a two-staged cascaded CNN helps to reduce the search space for the second network. The architecture is similar to the one in our previous work [1] with few parameter modifications, at first, we apply localization technique to obtain the ROI of a human hand and body, then the preprocessed ROI is forwarded to a cascaded convolutional network to regress the 2D heatmaps of joints and 3D normalized coordinates. 2D keypoints are regressed from 2D heatmaps and the normalized coordinates are converted with respect to 3D camera coordinates, and repectively to robot coordinates. The proposed architecture with a complete process can be seen in Fig. 2.

There is a possibility to regress both body and hand joints using a single pipeline when we have a single dataset containing both hands and body annotations. In this work, we trained the model twice as two different datasets are utilized one for body pose and another for hand pose during training. Based on the detection of persons or hands, the proposed architecture forwards the ROI to the respective block. Besides cropping the ROI, images are resized before forwarding to the pose network so that the batch training is possible and for faster convergence.

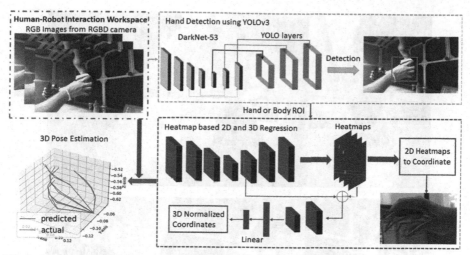

Fig. 2. The proposed architecture in the human-robot interaction scenario, the blue block represents the region of interest detection, the red block represents the pose regression network using heatmaps for 2D and 3D joint regression. (Color figure online)

3.1 Region of Interest (ROI) Detector

ROI detection is a well-researched topic, so we apply the idea of transfer learning to the existing model. Widely used backbones of ROI detection are the VGG [27], the ResNet [28], and the MobileNet [29]. Most approaches proposed in the early stages use a two-staged object detection process, for example, R-CNN [31], fast R-CNN [30], faster R-CNN [32]. Later, YOLO [34], SSD [33], and RetinaNet [35] was introduced that uses a single stage. The research on YOLO continued to improve and multiple versions were proposed with improved accuracy and real-time detection speed.

YOLOv3 [36] showes a huge advancement to its predecessors, the DarkNet-53 architecture is fast and accurate. Recently versions, YOLOv4 [37] and YOLOv5 [38] show improvement to the previous version but in this work, we utilize the YOLOv3 [36] architecture to learn the model for ROI detection of human hand. Two different datasets are utilized for training the YOLOv3 [36] architecture. The EgoHands [39] dataset is a first-person interaction dataset obtained using google glass. The dataset consists of over 15k labeled hands, a few samples from the dataset can be seen in Fig. 3 top. The annotations of EgoHands [39] dataset is a mask polygon segmenting the region of hands, but in out application, we need rather bounding boxes, to this end extrema features with offset are extracted. To avoid the complete dataset being ego-centric, we combined with a SSMH dataset containing 10k samples from distinct views, a few samples can be observed in Fig. 3 bottom.

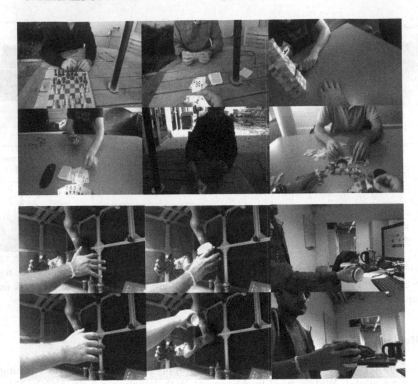

Fig. 3. Top: few samples from EgoHands dataset [39], bottom: samples from the SSMH dataset presented in our previous work [1].

3.2 Pose Regression Network

Once the region of hand is cropped and resized, we pass it as input to pose regression network to obtain the 2D heatmaps of joints. The heatmaps are further processed to regress the 2D pixel coordinates. Besides the 2D heatmaps, we obtain the intermediate features from the network and process it using convolution and pooling layers to match the 2D size of heatmaps. The processed intermediate features are concatenated with heatmaps and further reduced by convolution and pooling layers followed by linearization to regress the 3D normalized coordinated of all joints in N × 3 format. The regression network can also be stacked like an hourglass model [40]. Refer to our previous work [1] to understand the stacked encoder-decoder process and layers. The single encoder-decoder based simplified architecture of 3D regression can be seen in Fig. 2 red block. The cropped region from YOLOv3 is resized to 128 × 128 with three channels. The input information is forwarded through encoder to extract features as low as 512 × 4 × 4, then bilinear interpolation is applied to decode the features. Since the heatmaps must have similar shape as input, the output of decoded network is 128 × 128 × N heatmaps. Where N is the number of joints, N varies depending on input joints, N is 21 for hand pose in this work and N is 17 for body pose. In the next sections, we experiment on this network.

4   Experiments

In this section, pose regression network is trained with multiple datasets and calculate the robustness on validation dataset. In addition to validation dataset, we evaluate the models in human robot workspace for real-time HRI scenarios.

4.1   Fast Region of Interest Detection

As mentioned in Sect. 3.1, The images taken from egocentric and non-egocentric view are considered for training the YOLOv3 [36] architecture. Originally this architecture is implemented for detecting a large number of classes but in this work, we modify the input parameters so that it is applicable for either single class detection (Hand detection) or two class detection (both person and hand) based on application. Since the YOLO network parameters are perfectly adjusted, we modify only the necessary parameters like learning rate, batch size, number of epochs for training the network. We modified the YOLO architecture provided in this repository [12] using the Pytorch library in Python. The dataset for training the hand detection consists of 25k images and the network is trained for 200 epochs with 500 iterations. We do not show any in-depth results regarding the accuracy estimation for this network as it is highly researched. The bounding box regressions from the learned model can be seen in Fig. 4. The top row images are from the EgoHands dataset [39] and other images are taken in the human-robot interaction environment, provided in this paper.

Fig. 4. The 2D hand ROI detection using YOLOv3 approach [35].

4.2   Pose Estimation from Heatmaps and 3D Regression

Training Parameters and Evaluation Metrics. The pose network is implemented using the Pytorch library in Python. Datasets are the key for training the network and specifically for HRI scenarios, we require a dataset that contains both occluded and non-occluded data. To evaluate the proposed model in a human-robot interaction workspace, we consider three different datasets known as GANerated, HO3D and SSMH datasets. The training parameters of all the datasets are mentioned in Table 1. Since the SSMH dataset consists of 15k images, we included on the fly data augmentation technique during the training process. Closely cropped and resized hands are the inputs to pose estimation network. Weights initialization for the training process are completely randomized. The first output from the network is a 2D heatmaps (see Fig. 2) of joints where intersection over union (IoU) loss is utilized for training. IoU loss is widely used in object detection, and this metric will test the similarity between two inputs. In this case, we test the similarity between predicted heatmap and ground truth heatmap, the difference is used for improving the loss by backpropagation.

$$IoU = \frac{\left| Heatmap_{predicted} \cap Heatmap_{groundtruth} \right|}{\left| Heatmap_{predicted} \cup Heatmap_{groundtruth} \right|} \tag{1}$$

$$Loss_{IoU} = 1 - IoU \tag{2}$$

$$Loss_{MSE} = \frac{1}{n} \sum_{i=1}^{n} \left(predicted_i - actual_i \right)^2 \tag{3}$$

$$Loss_{total} = Loss_{IoU} + Loss_{MSE} \tag{4}$$

By calculating IoU, we get similarity information predicted heatmap and groundtruth heatmap for all joints and calculate mean, but we need the difference in IoU for backward propagation, so we subtract with 1 as in Eq. (2). In addition to heatmaps, we train 3D normalized coordinates of all joints where the mean squared error (MSE) loss is calculated. The MSE loss is calculated between 3D coordinates of predicted value and ground truth value for backpropagation and optimization. To optimize RMSprop [44] is suitable in this case. The network is trained on Nvidia 1080Ti 12 GB graphical processing unit. The training loss versus validation loss on the HO3D dataset can be observed in Fig. 5. The loss values presented in Fig. 5 is the total loss. We can observe that the training loss and validations loss constantly improving over each epoch.

Table 1. Training parameters for all datasets.

Dataset	GANerated	HO3D	SSMH
Training data	290k	70k	13k
Test data	10k	7k	2k
Learning rate	0.00025	0.0001	0.001
Epochs	500	500	100
Iterations	500	500	500
Batch size	32	32	16
Optimizer	RMSprop	RMSprop	RMSprop
Loss	IOU/MSE	IOU/MSE	IOU/MSE
Augmentation	False	False	True

For evaluation, the percentage of correct keypoints (PCK) and root mean squared error (RMSE) are most widely used metrics. Both these metrics can be used for 2D and 3D pose evaluation. PCK considers the detected joint as correct if the distance between the predicted joints and the ground truth joint is within a certain threshold. PCK@0.9 with 5-pixel threshold means 90% of keypoints are correct and the error is within 5 pixel range.

- For 2D keypoints, PCK is calculated from 2 to 20-pixel threshold
- For 3D keypoints, PCK is calculated from 10 to 150-mm threshold

The RMSE metric is used to calculate the error of each joint for a set of validation data. The RMSE gives the measure of pixel error in 2D and distance in 3D. The RMSE of each joint can report on error distribution for further tuning the network. The RMSE error is:

$$error_{RMSE} = \sqrt{\frac{\sum_{i=1}^{n}\left(predicted_i - true_i\right)^2}{n}} \tag{5}$$

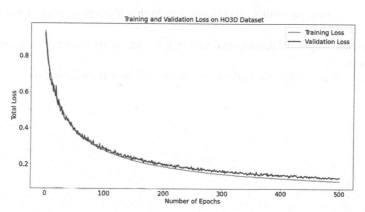

Fig. 5. The total loss curve during the training process and validation on the HO3D dataset.

Body Pose Estimation. The inputs of body pose is similar to the hand pose we test the network by applying transfer learning for 3D body pose regression. The self-occlusion of body joints is lower compared to hand joints as degress of freedom of body joints are lowe than hand joints. There exists a multitude of datasets for human pose estimation, but we decided to apply NTU-RGBD [42] data. Although the data is recorded for action recognition, the dataset consists of high variations of actions. The data is recorded using Kinect camera and the annotation errors exist. We manually pick 25k images with low annotation error. The network is trained with this dataset and the obtained 3D pose estimation results can be observed in Fig. 6. From this, it is concluded that the pose estimation network work for body pose estimation. We can regress both body and hand joints as single output when the dataset consists of both hands and body annotations.

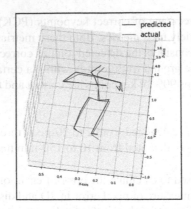

Fig. 6. 3D pose estimation on NTU RGB dataset.

2D Hand Pose Estimation. The Fig. 7 shows the performance of the regression network on 2D joint regression and reports on PCK values with distinct thresholds. We evaluated on three validation datasets:

1. HO3D, a dataset containing real images with high self-occlusions and object in hand occlusions.
2. GANerated, a hybrid dataset containing significantly high self-occlusions and object occlusions.
3. SSMH, a small-scale custom dataset containing low self and object occlusions.

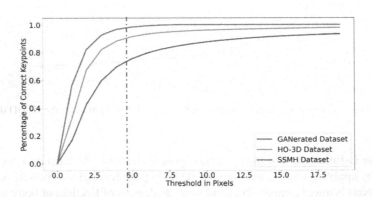

Fig. 7. Percentage of correct keypoint estimation on three different validation datasets.

In Fig. 7, x-axis represents the threshold values in pixels and y-axis represents PCK in decimals and we can observe that the PCK@0.9 for the 5-pixel threshold for HO3D dataset and SSMH dataset and PCK@0.8 for GANerated dataset. The SSMH dataset performs much better as the dataset does not contain high occlusions. The other two datasets consist of high occlusions and we can notice the difference in PCK values of HO3D dataset and GANerated dataset.

To get a clear understanding of the high occlusion datasets, we calculate RMSE values for each joint on images from the validation dataset. The distribution of error on the HO3D, the GANerated and the SSMH values can be seen in Fig. 8. The joint order is different for HO3D and other two datasets and the joint order can be observed in Fig. 8 right image with numbering. Based on the keypoint order, we can conclude that the fingertip locations have high self-occlusion and hard to detect. In the GANerated and the SSMH graph, joints 4, 8, 12, 16, and 20 have high RMSE value and in HO3D graph, joints 16, 17, 18, 19, and 20 have high RMSE value compared to others. From the HO3D graph, we notice that the thumb joint has a high RMSE value compared to others. This is due to the dataset occlusions and similarly, for the GANerated dataset, joint 20 has high occlusion and a high error value.

The 2D detections on the validation dataset can be seen in Fig. 9. The first row consists of HO3D validation data and the trained model was able to generalize well on validation images. For these images, error was lower than 5 pixels. In the next row, 2D detections on GANerated hands validation images can be observed. The model was

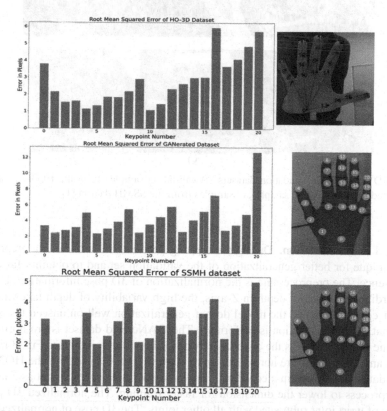

Fig. 8. RMSE calculation, top left: RMSE of HO3D dataset, top right: joint order used for training, middle left: RMSE of GANerated dataset, middle right: joint order used for training the model, bottom left: RMSE of SSMH dataset, bottom right: joint order.

able to achieve high accuracy even in self occlusions. Finally, 2D detections on SSMH validation images can be seen in bottom row. For all these images RMSE value is lower than 5-pixels.

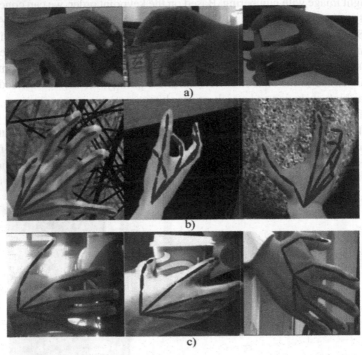

a)

b)

c)

Fig. 9. 2D detection on validation datasets, a) validation samples from the HO3D dataset, b) GANerated hands validation samples, c) samples from the SSMH dataset [1].

3D Hand Pose Estimation. During the training process, we performed a preprocessing technique for better generalization of the validation set and to obtain a faster loss convergence. The preprocessing is the normalization of 3D pose information. Usually, 3D coordinates consist of depth in Z-axis, the high variability of depth takes a longer time for convergence and the model do not generalization well on unseen test set. To avoid that, the normalization is performed. The GANerated dataset is pre-normalized where the normalization is the distance between joint 0 and joint 9 (see Fig. 8 right) is set to 1 and other joints are normalized in relation to joint 0 and 9. For the HO3D and SSMH dataset, we perform a coordinate conversion with respect to wrist as a normalization process to lower the dimension for faster training. The normalized 3D pose is the pose of wrist joint subtracted with all other joints. The 3D pose of normalized joints $P_{norm\_joints_i}$ are:

$$P_{norm\_joints_i} = \left[P_{joint_{wrist}} - P_{joint_i}\right] \forall i \, (1, 2, \dots 21) \tag{6}$$

We apply this normalization as the wrist joint is the most visible compared to others. During the testing process, we apply the denormalization for validation of error in millimeters. Since the GANerated dataset is pre-normalized, we cannot compare it with other datasets. The PCK estimation on the HO3D dataset and SSMH dataset can be observed in Fig. 10. Without any post-processing techniques PCK@0.7 for 50 mm and PCK@0.9 for 100 mm on the HO3D and since the SSMH dataset has low occlusion PCK@0.9 for 50 mm threshold.

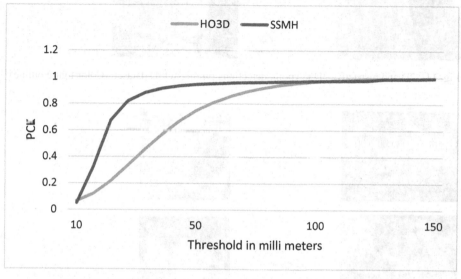

Fig. 10. 3D PCK estimation on the HO3D dataset and SSMH dataset.

The 2D detections and their corresponding 3D detections of the HO3D validation color images can be seen in Fig. 11, both predicted values, and actual values are plotted. Low error achieved on highly occluded images, the 2D predicted values are plotted with red color and ground truth values are plotted with green colored lines. The corresponding 3D detections are attached to the right of the color image and actual values are plotted with a blue line. The 3D RMSE error is less than 40 mm for all these predictions.

GANerated and SSMH dataset follow the same joint order and 3D detection samples can be seen in Fig. 8. The predicted values are represented with red lines and the green lines are the actual values. In Fig. 12, images to the left are from the SSMH dataset, and images to the right are from the GANerated hands dataset. Both low occlusion and self-occlusion images are presented with respective 3D normalized predictions. The resulting image is directly taken from previous work [1].

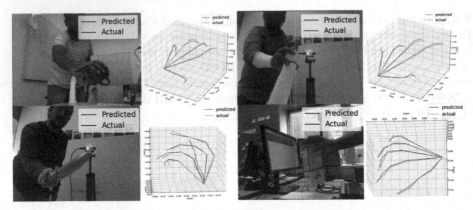

Fig. 11. 2D and respective 3D keypoint detections on the HO3D dataset. (Color figure online)

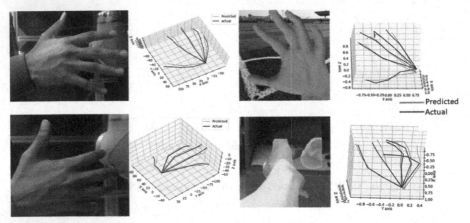

Fig. 12. Left: 3D detections on the SSMH dataset, right: 3D detections on the GANerated dataset. (Color figure online)

4.3 Evaluation in HRI Environment

The goal of this approach is to regress the 3D coordinates in human-robot interaction workspaces seen in Fig. 1. From Sect. 4.2 we obtain three trained models for three different datasets and we test these three model with HRI test dataset. Since the datasets consist of highly occluded data, we check the performance of three different models on a completely new test set collected from the HRI workspace. Few test scenario images can be observed in Fig. 13, to annotate the dataset, we followed a similar approach as the HO3D dataset [11] using this repository [41].

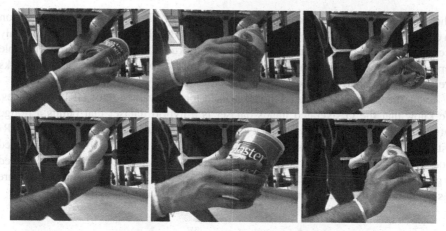

Fig. 13. Test dataset captured in HRI workspace.

Although the complete markerless annotation approach works better on a multi-camera setup, the performance on a single-camera setup is not perfectly accurate due to segmentation error at fingertips and the 2D keypoint detections for annotations are limited to CPM hand pose model [4].

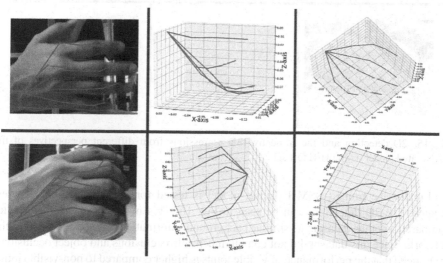

Fig. 14. 2D detections and respective 3D regression from multiple perspectives of the HO3D trained model on the HRI test set.

First, we consider the HO3D trained model for testing in the HRI scenario. Since the dataset is well occluded, we expect the model to generalize well on completely new test set. The generalization of the HO3D model on the test set can be observed in Fig. 14. First lets look at 2D detections, although the model is detecting wrist and knuckle joints, the other joints fail to generalize. The performance on the thumb joint is much worse than other joints and a similar issue can be observed in RMSE Fig. 8 joint 16. The detection on complete open hand did not perform well either as the HO3D dataset consists of only occlusion images. In the figure, respective 3D information is captured from multiple perspectives and the results are much better compared to 2D detections and it works even in for open hand scenarios.

Later, the trained GANerated model is used for the evaluation of HRI test images. We know that the GANerated hands dataset is a hybrid dataset that builds a bridge between real and synthetic images. We check the performance of the model on the HRI test dataset and the 2D results can be seen in Fig. 15. For open hands, the GANerated model performed much better compared to the HO3D model in 2D but completely failed to generalize in 3D coordinates as the fingertips are false. The bottom row in the figure has occlusion in the HRI setting and the result is in an acceptable range.

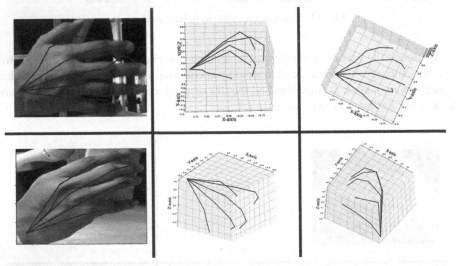

Fig. 15. 2D detection and the respective 3D regressions from different perspectives of the GANerated model on the HRI test set.

Finally, the trained SSMH dataset model is tested for performance on HRI test images. The 2D detections can be seen in Fig. 16. This model perform much better compared to other datasets as similar background information is used for training the network. Since this dataset did not contain much self-occlusions and object occlusions, we noticed that the performance of visible joints is higher compared to non-visible joints like a thumb.

In summary, the HO3D trained model and GANerated trained model did not perform well on the test set and the model trained on SSMH dataset performed well on visible joints and resulted in high errors for non-visible joints. HO3D dataset consists of high occlusions but not many open hand images, so as a final evaluation process, we combined the SSMH dataset images with the HO3D dataset and trained using pose regression network to check for further improvements. The 70k HO3D images are combined with 15k SSMH dataset images and trained with similar parameters mentioned in Table 1

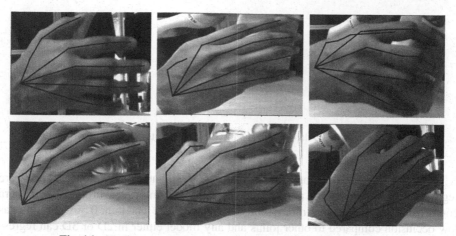

Fig. 16. 2D detection of the trained SSMH model in HRI workspace.

HO3D column. The resulting 2D detection in HRI setting without any object in hand occlusion can be seen in Fig. 17. From the figure, we can observe that the 2D detection works well for open hands as well as self-occlusions.

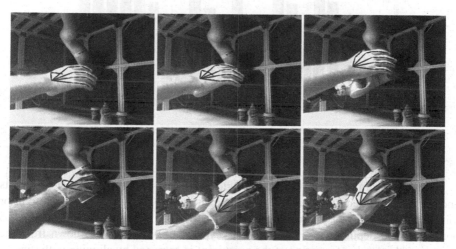

Fig. 17. Low occlusion detections on a model trained using HO3D and SSMH dataset.

The 3D pose estimations can be seen in Fig. 18. The images are taken from a continuous video clip and few frames are shown in the figure. From this, we can observe that even in object occlusions the model is performing well. We achieved a RMSE value of 5 pixels for 2D detections and less than 39 mm error for 3D coordinates of all joints on test set. The RMSE value of each joint can be seen in Fig. 19.

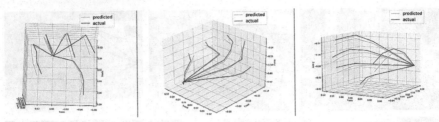

Fig. 18. Self-occlusion 3D detections on a model trained with HO3D and SSMH dataset.

Once the 2D keypoints and 3D normalized coordinates with respect to wrist are regressed, denormalization is performed to lift the 3D normalized coordinated to camera coordinated using the depth information of the wrist joint. The joint 0 or wrist joint has low occlusion compared to other joints and any model either in 2D or 3D can regress this joint accurately.

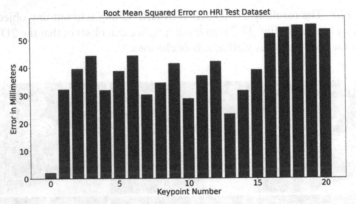

Fig. 19. RMSE value of each joint on HRI test set.

We tested from this (Fig. 18 camera angle) perspective for the handover of objects and we can understand the reason for normalization of 3D keypoints to wrist joint or joint 0 as the visibility is high and occlusion is low. Intel Realsense D435 camera has both color and depth sensor, since the 2D keypoint of wrist joint is known from the heatmaps, the depth information of the wrist joint is extracted by aligning both sensors at that 2D pixel location. 3D coordinates with respect to camera can be extracted by:

$$P_{joints\_camera_i} = -P_{norm_{joints_i}} + P_{joint\_wrist_{cc}} \ \forall \, i \, (1, 2, \ldots 21) \tag{7}$$

Where $P_{joints\_camera_i}$ is predicted joints with respect to camera coordinates, $P_{joint\_wrist_{cc}}$ is 3D position of wrist joint with respect to camera coordinates leveraging 2D pixel location. A image with transformed with respect to wrist can be observed in Fig. 20. Initially the X, Y, and Z values are zeros and then converted to camera coordinates in millimeters where Z-axis is 561 mm from camera center. Besides estimating the 3D keypoint coordinates, the complete process must be applicable in real-time and after testing the complete process we achieved 18 frames per second (fps) with visualization. By tuning further and without visualization, the complete process works at an average of 20 fps on Nvidia GTX 1050Ti GPU.

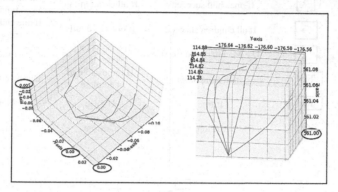

Fig. 20. Left: 3D normalized prediction, right: predictions with respect to camera coordinates.

Interaction Modeling Through Behavior Trees. Once the 3D normalized coordinates are extended to 3D camera coordinates, the coordinates are further transformed to a robot coordinate system for grasping applications. In an interaction-workspace, different tasks are probable and the ability to switch between tasks can be performed using behavior trees (BTs). Most common task-switching is performed using finite state machines (FSMs) but the reactiveness and modularity of BTs have a huge advantage in robotics applications. FSMs have one-way control transfer where the execution of code moves to another part code as the statement is a success, but the BTs have a two-way control transfer where function calls are used, once the program is executed, the reply goes back to the function call. A BT has a root node and multiple children based on application, execution of root node generates signals (also known as ticks). Execution of node takes place if ticks are received. If the node is under execution it returns running, success if the goal is reached, or failure back to the parent. There exist different kinds of nodes in BTs and are mentioned in Table 2.

For the handover object, BT with sequence and fallback nodes can be observed in Fig. 21. The conditional statements are mentioned in curved and actions are mentioned in rectangular boxes. This BT is created as an example of the handover of an object to the robot. Once the tick is active, nodes execute in sequential order from left to right. First, it checks if hand pose retrieved, if it fails then the action estimate hand pose is executed, and it returns succeed if the pose is retrieved else running or failed. Similarly, object pose is retrieved, and it checks if the object is in hand. Then the execution moves to the next node in the sequence and checks if the robot gripper is empty and it follows the other node for collision-free trajectory and grasping. The advantage of BTs is that it can further be divided into subtasks and later recombine. Such BTs help run the systems without any complexities. The introduction to BTs will work as a future advancement in better handling of interaction tasks in collaboration workspace.

Table 2. The node types of BT from [43].

Node type	Symbol	Succeeds	Fails	Running
Fallback	?	If one child succeeds	If all children fail	If one child returns running
Sequence	→	If all children succeed	If one child fails	If one child returns running
Parallel	⇉	If ≥ M children succeed	If > N-M children fail	else
Action	Text	Upon completion	If impossible to complete	During completion
Condition	Text	If true	If false	Never
Decorator	◇	Custom	Custom	Custom

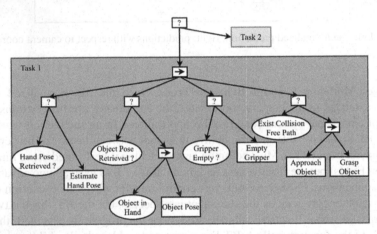

Fig. 21. A simple behavior tree for the handover of an object.

Discussion. In this work, the stacked CNN architecture we propose can generalize well on different datasets. The advantage is that the model is applicable in realtime with low end GPU. To apply the model in real-time only single encoder-decoder architecture is considered without compromising accuracy. Normalization of all joints with respect to wrist joint in 3D space is considered as the wrist joint occlusion is low in HRI workspace. One limitation is that, the model fails to generalize when the wrist joint is occluded or if depth value is inaccurate. In a human-robot workspace, multiple tasks exist like handover of objects, pointing at an object and other interactions states. The reactiveness and modularity of BTs make them a powerful tool for task handling in robotic applications. To be able to switch between interaction states, behavior trees can be applied and we are currently working on more adaptable BTs modeling. In addition, we are also working on fully markerless automated dataset generation for HRI applications.

5 Conclusion

In this work, we proposed a complete architecture for 3D hand pose estimation using a cascaded and regression network. We extensively validated the pipeline with multiple datasets by training to obtain the individual models. Performance on indiviual validation dataset achieved high accuracy. PCK achieved 0.9 for 5-pixel threshold for 2D keypoint regression and 0.8 for 50 mm threshold in 3D coordinates. Later, the individual models are tested in human-robot interaction-workspace and noticed the 2D detections did not perform as expected on certain datasets, but the 3D keypoint regression performed well. To further improve both 2D and 3D keypoint detections, two datasets with low occlusions and high occlusion are combined and trained the model, resulting in improved accuracy 2D and 3D detections. Finally, 3D keypoints are extended to robot coordinates for interactions and the complete process is applicable in real-time with an average of 18 fps. The behavior trees are further used for keeping track of all the processes in the human-robot collaboration workspace.

Acknowledgements. The project is Funded by the Deutsche Forschungsgemeinschaft (DFG, German Research Foundation) - Project-ID 416228727 - SFB 1410.

References

1. Bandi, C., Thomas, U.: Regression-based 3D hand pose estimation using heatmaps. In: 15th International Conference on Computer Vision Theory and Applications. SCITEPRESS, Malta (2020)
2. Toshev, A., Szegedy, C.: DeepPose: human pose estimation via deep neural networks. In: Proceedings of the IEEE Conference on Computer Vision and Pattern Recognition (CVPR), pp. 1653–1660 (2014)
3. Tompson, J., Stein, M., Lecun, Y., Perlin, K.: Real-time continuous pose recovery of human hands using convolutional networks. ACM Trans. Graph. **33**, 1–10 (2014)
4. Wei, S., Ramakrishna, V., Kanade, T., Sheikh, Y.: Convolutional pose machines. In: Proceedings of the IEEE Conference on Computer Vision and Pattern Recognition (CVPR), pp. 4724–4732 (2016)
5. Chen, C.-H., Ramanan, D.: 3D Human pose estimation = 2d pose estimation + matching. arXiv preprint arXiv:1612.06524 (2016)
6. Chen, X., Yuille, A.L.: Articulated pose estimation by a graphical model with image dependent pairwise relations. In: Proceedings of the Conference on Neural Information Processing Systems (NIPS), pp. 1736–1744 (2014)
7. Qian, C., Sun, X., Wei, Y., Tang, X., Sun, J.: Realtime and robust hand tracking from depth. In: Proceedings of the IEEE Conference on Computer Vision and Pattern Recognition (CVPR) (2014)
8. Zimmermann, C., Brox, T.: Learning to estimate 3D hand pose from single RGB images. arXiv:1705.01389v3 [cs.CV] (2017)
9. Mueller, F., et al.: GANerated hands for real-time 3D hand tracking from monocular RGB. In: Proceedings of the IEEE Conference on Computer Vision and Pattern Recognition (2018)
10. Zimmermann, C., Ceylan, D., Yang, J., Russell, B.C., Argus, M.J., Brox, T.: FreiHAND: a dataset for markerless capture of hand pose and shape from single RGB images. In: The IEEE International Conference on Computer Vision (ICCV), pp. 813–822 (2019)

11. Hampali, S., Oberweger, M., Rad, M., Lepetit, V.: HOnnotate: a method for 3D annotation of hand and object poses. In: Proceedings of CVPR (2020)
12. Github source. https://github.com/eriklindernoren/PyTorch-YOLOv3. Accessed 29 July 2020
13. Tome, D., Russell, C., Agapito L.: Lifting from the deep: convolutional 3D pose estimation from a single image. arXiv preprint arXiv:1701.00295 (2017)
14. Bogo, F., Kanazawa, A., Lassner, C., Gehler, P., Romero, J., Black, M.J.: Keep it SMPL: automatic estimation of 3D human pose and shape from a single image. In: Leibe, B., Matas, J., Sebe, N., Welling, M. (eds.) ECCV 2016. LNCS, vol. 9909, pp. 561–578. Springer, Cham (2016). https://doi.org/10.1007/978-3-319-46454-1_34
15. Oberweger, M., Wohlhart, P., Lepetit. V.: Hands deep in deep learning for hand pose estimation. arXiv preprint arXiv:1502.06807 (2015)
16. Ge, L., Ren, Z., Yuan, J.: Point-to-point regression pointnet for 3D hand pose estimation. In: Ferrari, V., Hebert, M., Sminchisescu, C., Weiss, Y. (eds.) ECCV 2018. LNCS, vol. 11217, pp. 489–505. Springer, Cham (2018). https://doi.org/10.1007/978-3-030-01261-8_29
17. Liuhao, G., Yujun, C., Junwu, W., Junsong, Y.: Hand pointnet: 3D hand pose estimation using point sets. In CVPR (2018)
18. Li, S., Lee, D.: Point-to-pose voting based hand pose estimation using residual permutation equivariant layer. In: CVPR (2019)
19. Ren, P., Sun, H., Qi, Q., Wang, J., Huang, W.: SRN: stacked regression network for real-time 3D hand pose estimation. In: Proceedings of BMVC, pp. 1–14 (2019)
20. Yuan, S., Stenger, B., Kim, T.-K.: RGB-based 3D hand pose estimation via privileged learning with depth images. arXiv preprint arXiv:1811.07376 (2018)
21. Huang, W., Ren, P., Wang, J., Qi, Q., Sun. H.: AWR: adaptive weighting regression for 3D hand pose. In: AAAI (2020)
22. Boukhayma, A., Bem, R.-D., Torr, P.-H.S.: 3D hand shape and pose from images in the wild. In: IEEE Conference on Computer Vision and Pattern Recognition (CVPR) (2019)
23. Zhang, X., Li, Q., Mo, H., Zhang, W., Zheng, W.: End-to-end hand mesh recovery from a monocular RGB image. In: ICCV (2019)
24. Tang, D., Chang, H.J., Tejani, A., Kim, T.-K.: Latent regression forest: structural estimation of 3D articulated hand posture. In: Proceedings of IEEE Conference on Computer Vision and Pattern Recognition (CVPR), Columbus, Ohio, USA (2014)
25. Sun, X., Wei, Y., Liang, S., Tang, X., Sun, J.: Cascaded hand pose regression. In: CVPR (2015)
26. Garcia-Hernando, G., Yuan, S., Baek, S., Kim, T.-K.: First-person hand action benchmark with RGB-D videos and 3D hand pose annotations. arXiv preprint arXiv:1704.02463 (2017)
27. Simonyan, K., Zisserman, A.: Very deep convolutional networks for large-scale image recognition. arXiv preprint arXiv:1409.1556 (2014)
28. He, K., Zhang, X., Ren, S., Sun, J.: Deep residual learning for image recognition. In: Proceedings of the IEEE Conference on Computer Vision and Pattern Recognition (CVPR), pp. 770–778 (2016)
29. Howard, A.-G, et al.: MobileNets: efficient convolutional neural networks for mobile vision applications. arXiv preprint arXiv:1704.04861 (2017)
30. Girshick, R.: Fast R-CNN. In: Proceedings of the IEEE International Conference on Computer Vision (ICCV), pp. 1440–1448 (2015)
31. Girshick, R., Donahue, J., Darrell, T., Malik, J.: Rich feature hierarchies for accurate object detection and semantic segmentation. In: Proceedings of the IEEE Conference on Computer Vision and Pattern Recognition (CVPR), pp. 580–587 (2014)
32. Ren, S., He, K., Girshick, R., Sun, J.: Faster R-CNN: towards real-time object detection with region proposal networks. In: Advances in Neural Information Processing Systems (NIPS), pp. 91–99 (2015)

33. Liu, W., et al.: SSD: single shot multibox detector. In: Leibe, B., Matas, J., Sebe, N., Welling, M. (eds.) ECCV 2016. LNCS, vol. 9905, pp. 21–37. Springer, Cham (2016). https://doi.org/10.1007/978-3-319-46448-0_2

34. Redmon, J., Divvala, S., Girshick, R., Farhadi, A.: You only look once: unified, real-time object detection. In: Proceedings of the IEEE Conference on Computer Vision and Pattern Recognition (CVPR), pp. 779– 788 (2016)

35. Lin, T.-Y., Goyal, P., Girshick, R., He, K., Dollar, P.: Focal loss for dense object detection. In: Proceedings of the IEEE International Conference on Computer Vision (ICCV), pp. 2980–2988 (2017)

36. Redmon, J., Farhadi, A.: YOLOv3: an incremental improvement. arXiv preprint arXiv:1804.02767 (2018)

37. Bochkovskiy, A., Wang, C.-Y., Mark Liao, H.-Y.: Yolov4: optimal speed and accuracy of object detection. arXiv preprint arXiv:2004.10934 (2020)

38. Github source. https://github.com/ultralytics/yolov5. Accessed 29 July 2020

39. Bambach, S., Lee, S., Crandall, D.-J., Yu, C.: Lending a hand: detecting hands and recognizing activities in complex egocentric interactions. In: ICCV (2015)

40. Zhou, X., Huang, Q., Sun, X., Xue, X., Wei, Y.,: Towards 3D human pose estimation in the wild: a weakly-supervised approach. Shanghai Key Laboratory of Intelligent Information Processing School of Computer Science, Fudan University, The University of Texas at Austin, Microsoft Research arXiv:1704.02447v2 [cs.CV] (2017)

41. Github source. https://github.com/shreyashampali/HOnnotate. Accessed 29 July 2020

42. Shahroudy, A., Liu, J., Ng, T.-T., Wang, G.: NTU RGB+ D: a large scale dataset for 3D human activity analysis. In: CVPR, pp. 1010–1019 (2016)

43. Colledanchise, M., Ögren, P.: Behavior trees in robotics and AI: an introduction. arXiv preprint arXiv:1709.00084 (2018)

44. Tieleman, T., Hinton, G.: Lecture 6.5 - RMSProp, COURSERA: neural networks for machine learning. Technical report (2012)

Detection and Recognition of Barriers in Egocentric Images for Safe Urban Sidewalks

Zenonas Theodosiou[1]([⊠]), Harris Partaourides[1], Simoni Panayi[2], Andreas Kitsis[2], and Andreas Lanitis[1,2]

[1] CYENS Center of Excellence, Nicosia, Cyprus
{z.theodosiou,h.partaourides,a.lanitis}@cyens.org.cy
[2] Department of Multimedia and Graphic Arts, Cyprus University of Technology, Limassol, Cyprus
https://www.cyens.org.cy

Abstract. The impact of walking in modern cities has proven to be quite significant with many advantages especially in the fields of environment and citizens' health. Although society is trying to promote it as the cheapest and most sustainable means of transportation, many road accidents have involved pedestrians and cyclists in the recent years. The frequent presence of various obstacles on urban sidewalks puts the lives of citizens in danger. Their immediate detection and removal are of great importance for maintaining clean and safe access to infrastructure of urban environments. Following the great success of egocentric applications that take advantage of the uninterrupted use of smartphone devices to address serious problems that concern humanity, we aim to develop methodologies for detecting barriers and other dangerous obstacles encountered by pedestrians on urban sidewalks. For this purpose a dedicated image dataset is generated and used as the basis for analyzing the performance of different methods in detecting and recognizing different types of obstacle using three different architectures of deep learning algorithms. The high accuracy of the experimental results shows that the development of egocentric applications can successfully help to maintain the safety and cleanliness of sidewalks and at the same time to reduce pedestrian accidents.

Keywords: Pedestrian safety · First-person dataset · Egocentric dataset · Barrier detection · Barrier recognition · Deep learning

1 Introduction

Walking has been recognized as the most environmentally sustainable, financially free form of transportation with many benefits in urban settings [24]. However, urban environments are becoming increasingly more dangerous for pedestrians enumerating several injuries and deaths over the last years. The number of pedestrians who lost their lives worldwide in 2013 was equal to 270,000 and increased to more than 350,000 in 2016 as reported by the World Health Organization (WHO) [26,27]. In European Union countries, 21% of road accidents recorded in 2017 involved pedestrians, with 40% involving accidents in urban areas [9].

K. Bouatouch et al. (Eds.): VISIGRAPP 2020, CCIS 1474, pp. 530–543, 2022.
https://doi.org/10.1007/978-3-030-94893-1_25

Urban areas are faced with serious problems caused by the frequent occurrence of various barriers and damages on sidewalks that put the lives of pedestrians at risk [34]. Ensuring day-to-day urban safety has always been a central issue for society, addressing significant human, social and economic aspects. Obtaining clean, well-maintained and continuous sidewalks without barriers and damages is imperative.

The development of automated methods for detecting and recognizing people, barriers and damages to create safe urban environments has been of particular concern to the research community in recent years. Pedestrian detection [38] is one of the main research areas focused on developing efficient systems with the ultimate aim of eliminating deaths in traffic accidents. The safety in roads has attracted a large interest in the last years and a number of studies have been presented for both pedestrians [24,45] and drivers [43]. A study on pothole detection was presented by Prathiba et al. [29] for the identification of different types of cracks on road pavements. Wang et al. [45] developed the WalkSafe, a smartphone application for vehicles recognition to help pedestrians cross safely roads. Jain et al. [16] presented an approach based on smartphone images for recognizing the texture of the surfaces in pedestrians' routes to be used for safety purposes. A mobile application which uses phone sensors was also presented to enhance the safety of the distracted pedestrians [44]. On the other hand, Maeda et al. [22] proposed an approach for the detection of several road damages in smartphones using convolution networks.

Wearable cameras can efficiently tackle the important issue of safety by providing useful information for both pedestrians and city authorities. The analysis of the uninterrupted visual data acquisition can provide real-time detection of urban hazards to both citizens and public authorities. By warning the former about the potential dangers and alerting the latter for their maintenance and mitigation, the vision of a safe sidewalk can be achieved. The majority of the automatic egocentric vision analysis methods nowadays use deep learning algorithms. Thus, the availability of large annotated egocentric datasets are more essential than ever before.

Among the available datasets created using data collected via wearable or smartphone cameras, there is a number of datasets related to road safety. Taking into account that none of those was solely about pedestrian safety on sidewalks, we created the first-person database dedicated to barriers and other damages that pose safety issues to the pedestrians [42]. In [42], we presented the new dataset consisting of 1976 images and the initial results of its performance in a classification scheme using a well-known deep Convolutional Neural Network (CNN). More specifically, the VGG-16 architecture was used as a baseline classifier for 15 barriers objects with encouraging results.

We continued our experiments on the egocentric dataset and in this paper we present the results of our work in regard to the detection and recognition of barriers. When compared to the work described in [42] the annotation process was refined and cross checked by different annotators and then, in order to establish the baseline classification performance, 3 different algorithms were used to detect and recognize several barrier classes. The remainder of the paper is organized as follows: Sect. 2 reviews related work. Section 3 presents the egocentric vision dataset while Sect. 4 presents and discusses the experimental results. Finally, conclusions and further work hints are given in Sect. 5.

2 Literature Review

2.1 Wearable Cameras

Nowadays, wearable cameras have gained a great attention due to the advances in wearable and sensing technologies [41]. The ideal size of wearable cameras which facilitates their use without burdening the carrier as well as the widespread use of smartphone devices have built the framework for visual lifelogging through the uninterrupted acquisition of the carrier's daily life [3]. The analysis of collected data can give useful insights which can be utilized for improvements in several domains such as health, protection, security, etc. The new domain of computer vision focusing on the analysis of data collected through wearable cameras, is known as Egocentric or First-person Vision.

Exploiting the great potential of wearable cameras and egocentric vision, several research efforts have been presented for indoor and outdoor applications. The idea of using wearable cameras for monitoring nutrition habits proposed by Bolanos et al. [4] through a method for food localization and recognition in visual lifelogging data. Among others, a study for the automatic recognition of locations in the daily activities of the wearer is presented in [10] and the analysis of social interactions and lifestyle patterns in egocentric data are studied in [2] and [13] respectively.

The use of visual lifelogging in ambient assisted living applications has been extensively studied focusing on monitoring daily activities and detecting and recognizing several hazards such as falls [6]. The role of visual lifelogging in creating digital memory for improving the life of people with memory problems has been thoroughly researched [25] and a broad range of dedicated techniques for recording, storage and retrieval of digital memories have been presented in the last years [35].

In addition, the development of methods for improved and safer citizen navigation with the help of mobile cameras has attracted the interest of the research community. A wearable system for assisting blind and people with vision impairments was presented by Jiang et al. [17] while a smartphone application for driver safety through road damages' detection was developed by Maeda et al. [22].

2.2 Available Datasets

Due to the broad use of deep learning algorithms in automatic analysis of data collected through wearable cameras, the availability of related datasets is essential for the successful development of new egocentric vision applications. According to Penna et al. [28], the challenges that need to be addressed for the successful interpretation of egocentric data are related to the limitations of data quality and their availability. Deep learning algorithms perform better when trained and tested on better qualitative and quantitative data.

The first egocentric vision dataset created by Mayor and Murray [23], consists of 600 frames captured by a wearable camera which was installed on the left shoulder of the wearer and was used to train algorithms for recognizing hand actions. Recently, the widespread use of portable cameras and smartphones has led to the creation of several egocentric datasets [3], including datasets for object recognition [5], activity recognition [12], and social interaction analysis [2]. Nonetheless, few of them are publicly available for further use by the research community.

The larger and one of the most popular available dataset is the Epic-kitchens that contains 100 h (20 million frames) of high-definition camera recordings in the wearers' environment covering daily activities in 32 kitchens [7]. Another example of a large set available is the KrishnaCam [37] which concerns daily outdoor activities captured using google glasses. The dataset consists of a total of 7.6 million frames created through 460 video recordings, lasting from a few minutes to about half an hour.

The need for improving road safety led to the creation of relevant egocentric vision datasets capable of being used for covering road and pavement cracks detection [11]. Zhang et al. [46] proposed a dataset of 500 images created using a low-cost smartphone which was then used to detect cracks on pavements with the aid of deep convolutional networks. Maeda et al. [22] created a large-scale dataset related to road damages. The dataset was created using includes 9,053 images collected by a smartphone attached on a car.

Concerning pedestrian's safety, a large-scale dataset was created by Jain and Gruteser [16] who combined recordings collected by 8 people through their smartphones while walking in 4 large cities (i.e. New York, London, Paris and Pittsburg). The dataset was utilized for training an algorithm to recognize pedestrians' walking surfaces. Despite the great potential of the dataset to be used in pedestrians' safety applications, it only covers the different types of walking surfaces and is not publicly available yet. The first egocentric vision dataset dedicated on the barriers and damages which endanger walkers was proposed in a previous work [42]. The data set consists of 1796 images which were collected through a smartphone camera while a pedestrian was walking in the center of Nicosia, Cyprus.

2.3 Visual Content Analysis

The effective analysis of visual egocentric data is dependent upon the ability of algorithms to robustly handle their indicative features which include large numbers of objects with varying sizes, intra-object variations, blurring, motion artifacts, lighting variations, etc. Over the past years, deep learning algorithms, specifically CNNs [30], have emerged as formidable methods to overcome these limitations and successfully analyze the visual content of egocentric data for different image interpretation tasks. Great attention has been given to the multi-task problem of object detection which aims to locate and classify via bounding boxes all objects of interest within a given image.

In the last few years, research on object detection has achieved great success due to the rapid evolutionary progression of CNN architectures, the advancements in computer hardware (powerful Graphics Processing Units) and the availability of large public image datasets, with which the efficiency of the object detection models can be improved. Currently, the Microsoft Common Objects in Context (MS-COCO) [32] dataset has been extensively used for object detection and often serves as the benchmark dataset for developing methods above the state-of-the-art. More specifically, it contains approximately 300 000 images with 90 different object classes and their precise bounding box locations. Transfer learning approaches in object detection tasks typically make use of large datasets, for instance MS-COCO, for pretraining their models.

The object detection literature broadly divides the available architectures into groups of two-stage models and single-stage models [47]. While two-stage detectors were the first to enter the object detection field and achieved groundbreaking accuracies, single-stage detectors have proven to be worthy competitors with exceptionally faster training speeds and easier parameter adjustment.

Prevalent models of the two groups are Faster Region based CNN (Faster R-CNN) [31] for a two-stage model and the Single Shot MultiBox Detector (SSD) [20] for a single-stage model. The feature extractor in these architectures can be easily replaced by any preferred CNN component thus obtaining a wide scope of performances.

In the context of the Faster R-CNN, the process of detection is split between the class-agnostic Region Proposal Network (RPN) and the box classifier network in an end-to-end manner. In the first stage of detection, the RPN, which is a fully convolutional network (FPN) [21], extracts features to produce a convolutional feature map and slides a window across it to generate candidate Regions of Interest (RoIs). The number of candidate RoIs predicted at each window position is dependent upon the number of anchor boxes used for reference. Typically in literature, 9 anchor boxes are used in order to produce sufficient overlapping with the ground truth boxes and generate accurate predictions. The lower-dimensional features produced by the RPN are then fed into the second-stage fully connected layer which performs adjacent multi-task classification and bounding box regression. The backbone feature extractor in a Faster R-CNN can take the form of different established CNN families such as VGG, Inception, ResNet and MobileNet [14,32,36,39].

The SSD model consists of a single feedforward CNN backbone that directly predicts the object classes and anchor offsets without the need for an intermediate RPN module. In the early layers, the network has the form of a standard feature extraction architecture which is called the base network. At the end of the base network, additional convolutional feature layers are added which progressively decrease in size to support detection at multiple scales. Each of these added layers generate a fixed set of predictions given by the set of convolutional filters (3×3 kernels) used. These kernels in return can produce a score for a class and a bounding box offset. The bounding box offset is predicted relative to a set of default bounding boxes associated with each scale in a similar manner as the Faster R-CNN anchor boxes. To produce the final detections, the ground truth boxes are first matched to the default boxes that produce the largest overlap and then the default boxes are matched to any ground truth with overlap higher than a specified threshold. This allows for a prediction of high scores for multiple overlapping default boxes instead of a single prediction with the maximum overlap. However, using this matching procedure, one undesired by-product emerges: most default boxes are marked as negative examples which leads to a significant class imbalance in the training examples. To alleviate this effect, the negatives are filtered by highest confidence loss for each default box so that the remaining account for at most 75% of training examples.

The most popular metric of interest in object detection is the mean Average Precision (mAP) [1] calculated at a specified Intersection over Union (IoU) threshold (e.g. mAP@0.5 is the literature standard). The IoU is defined as the fraction of overlap between the predicted and ground truth bounding boxes over the union of the two and its value at the specified threshold determines whether a prediction is a true positive. Using the IoU, the mAP can be acquired by calculating the average of interpolated precisions obtained from 101 equally spaced recall values r where $r \in \{0.0, \ldots, 1.0\}$. Concretely:

$$p_{interp}(r) = \max_{\tilde{r}:\tilde{r} \geq r} p(\tilde{r}) \qquad (1)$$

$$mAP = \frac{1}{101} \sum_{r \in \{0.0, \ldots, 1.0\}} p_{interp}(r) \qquad (2)$$

3 Barriers Egocentric Dataset

During walking people have to face various obstacles that put their safety at risk as several static barriers (e.g. badly designed pavements, dustbins, furniture, etc.), short-term barriers (e.g. construction work, illegal parking, and dense crowds, etc.) and damages (e.g. cracks, holes, broken pavers, etc.) in the infrastructure. In many cases the differences between harmless and dangerous obstacles are imperceptible making them even more difficult to be located and identified. Obstacles can become dangerous when they prevent free access to urban infrastructure or appear in front of pedestrians without warning. Based on our observation that there was no available dataset related to the obstacles that impair pedestrians' safety while walking, we presented the first egocentric dataset dedicated on the barriers and damages occurred on city sidewalks [42].

The dataset consists of 1976 images collected using a smartphone camera while a pedestrian walked around the Nicosia city center. The dataset was initially annotated using the VGG Image Annotator tool [8] and a structured lexicon (Table 1) was developed specifically to cover the several types of barriers and damages occurring in urban sidewalks. While having undergone testing by means of object classification and achieved very good results, the annotation process was repeated and cross checked, aiming to increase the annotation accuracy following the same procedure: the three closest obstacles of the lexicon categories which were within, or started at, the bottom part of the image, were labelled using the relevant bounding box.

The created dataset consists of a total of 2165 bounding boxes which correspond to 25 different classes of barriers. In 6 of the 31 classes of the lexicon used for the annotation, no barrier was detected. The classes concern the following: *Bench, Flower, Public Art-statue, Kiosk, Play Area,* and *Scaffolding.* On the other hand, *Tree,* and *Parking Prevention Barriers* were the most popular classes with 337 and 329 bounding boxes respectively covering together the 30% of the given bounding boxes. Concerning the 3 main categories, 983 of the bounding boxes are related to barriers of the Infrastructure, 561 are related to barriers of Physical Condition and the remaining 620 to Temporary barriers. One bounding box was not related with any category and was labelled as *Other.* Figure 1 presents examples of the annotation on different types of barriers while the number of instances per barrier type is shown in Fig. 2.

Fig. 1. Examples of the used annotated dataset.

Table 1. Barrier types.

Category	Barrier Type	Detail	Class
Physical Condition	Damage	Crack	B00
		Hole/Pot-hole	B01
		Paver (broken)	B02
	Layout	Narrow Pavement	B10
		No Pavement	B11
Infrastructure	Street Furniture	Bench	B20
		Light	B21
		Bin	B22
		Parking Meter	B23
		Plant Pot	B24
	Street Decor	Tree	B30
		Shrub	B31
		Flower	B32
		Parking Prevention Barrier	B33
		mail Box	B34
		Public art, Statue Box	B35
	General Interest	Bus Stop	B40
		Kiosk	B41
		Play Area	B42
Temporary	Vehicles	4-wheels	B50
		2-wheels	B51
	Construction	Scaffolding	B60
		Boulder	B61
		Safety Sign	B62
		Fence	B63
		Traffic Cone	B64
	Other	Litter	B70
		Chair	B71
		Table	B72
		Advert. Sign	B73
		Other	B80

4   Experimental Results

To perform object detection and evaluate our dataset we employ Tensorflow's object detection API [15]. This open source framework allows for a seamless implementation of numerous out-of-the-box training pipelines such as Faster R-CNN [31] and Single Shot Detection [20] (SSD).

Our experiments are performed on three architectures:

- Faster R-CNN with InceptionV2 [40] feature extraction,
- Faster R-CNN with ResNet-50 feature extraction, and
- SSD with MobileNetV2 [33] feature extraction

The first two are deep networks to evaluate the peak performance of our dataset, and the third one is a lighter model architecture more suited for mobile devices. These baselines are some of the typical choices in the object detection literature.

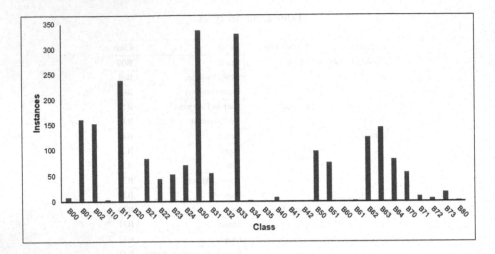

Fig. 2. Instances per barrier type.

Table 2. Train-validation-test dataset split.

Class	Train	Validation	Test	Total
B01	139 (87%)	13 (8%)	8 (5%)	160
B02	122 (80%)	15 (10%)	15 (10%)	152
B11	192 (81%)	27 (11%)	19 (8%)	238
B21	63 (75%)	9 (11%)	12 (14%)	84
B22	38 (86%)	4 (9%)	2 (5%)	44
B23	44 (83%)	3 (6%)	6 (11%)	53
B24	54 (76%)	5 (7%)	12 (17%)	71
B30	273 (81%)	30 (9%)	34 (10%)	337
B31	45 (75%)	7 (12%)	8 (13%)	60
B33	264 (80%)	31 (9%)	34 (10%)	329
B50	71 (72%)	14 (14%)	13 (13%)	98
B51	62 (82%)	5 (7%)	9 (12%)	76
B62	103 (82%)	7 (6%)	15 (12%)	125
B63	112 (78%)	18 (13%)	14 (10%)	144
B64	70 (84%)	7 (8%)	6 (7%)	83
B70	48 (84%)	4 (7%)	5 (9%)	57
Total	1700 (81%)	199 (9%)	212 (10%)	2111

During training we subsample the images to a fixed size of 800×600 for Faster R-CNN and 300×300 for SSD. Additionally, we initialize the models with the pretrained weights of MS-COCO dataset [19]. To avoid overfitting we used the default data augmentation of each architecture (as defined by the framework) and dropout value 0.2. The models are trained by means of Adam [18] with learning rate 1e−4 on a subset of the complete dataset. The subset excludes classes that have less than 20 instances, resulting to 16 out of 25 classes and 2111 out of 2165 available objects. We split the revised dataset in conventional 80-10-10 training-validation-test set. However, since in each image there is a variable amount of classes and objects, the split is not perfectly balanced among the classes. Table 2 depicts the instances of each class in each set. We use mean Average Precision(mAP) and Intersection Over Union (IOU) for our performance metrics with IOU thresholds 0.5 and 0.75.

The best performing model is Faster R-CNN with InceptionV2 feature extraction with mean average precision 88.4% on the test set. SSD with MobileNetV2 exhibits a suboptimal performance of 75.6% but with a fraction of the computation time. More details on the performance of each architecture are shown in Table 3. As expected taking a more strict IOU of 0.75 reduces the performance of the best performing model at 72.4%. A closer look at the confusion matrix of the best performing model, presented in Table 4, shows no obvious difficulties to distinguish between obstacles. For completeness, within the confusion matrix table we included the precision and recall for each class. Additionally, we show in Fig. 3 a representative sample of object detection predictions. We argue that the performances depict the maturity of object detection architectures to tackle real world problems. However, the suboptimal performance of the lighter architecture shows that more training examples are needed to achieve real-time predictions on memory restrictive mobile devices.

Table 3. Performance metrics.

Model	Features	Validation		Testing		Time (ms)
		0.5IOU	0.75IOU	0.50IOU	0.75IOU	
Faster R-CNN	Inception V2	0.8371	0.6897	0.8842	0.7242	106.7
Faster R-CNN	ResNet-50	0.8167	0.6320	0.8754	0.6953	161.3
SSD	MobileNetV2	0.6713	0.3968	0.756	0.436	36.1

Table 4. Validation confusion matrix of best performing model.

	B01	B02	B11	B21	B22	B23	B24	B30	B31	B33	B50	B51	B62	B63	B64	B70	Recall
B01	11	1	0	0	0	0	0	0	0	0	0	0	0	0	0	1	0.84
B02	0	15	0	0	0	0	0	0	0	0	0	0	0	0	0	0	1.00
B11	0	0	23	0	0	0	0	1	0	0	0	0	0	0	0	3	0.85
B21	0	0	0	8	0	0	0	0	0	0	0	0	0	0	0	1	0.89
B22	0	0	0	0	3	0	0	0	0	0	0	0	0	0	0	1	0.75
B23	0	0	0	0	0	3	0	0	0	0	0	0	0	0	0	0	1.00
B24	0	0	0	0	0	0	4	0	0	0	0	0	0	0	0	1	0.80
B30	0	0	0	0	0	0	0	30	0	0	0	0	0	0	0	0	1.00
B31	0	0	0	0	0	0	0	0	2	0	0	0	0	0	0	1	0.67
B33	0	0	0	0	0	0	0	0	0	30	0	0	0	0	0	1	0.97
B50	0	0	0	0	0	0	0	0	0	0	12	0	0	0	0	2	0.86
B51	0	0	0	0	0	0	0	0	0	0	0	4	0	1	0	0	0.80
B62	0	0	0	0	0	0	0	0	0	0	0	0	7	0	0	0	1.00
B63	0	0	0	0	0	0	0	0	0	0	0	0	0	17	0	1	0.94
B64	0	1	0	0	0	0	0	0	0	0	0	0	0	0	6	0	0.86
B70	0	0	0	0	0	0	0	0	0	0	0	0	0	0	0	4	1.00
Precision	1.00	0.88	1.00	1.00	1.00	1.00	1.00	0.96	1.00	1.00	1.00	1.00	1.00	0.94	1.00	0.25	

Fig. 3. Object detection predictions.

5   Conclusions and Future Work

This work presents the performance of our first-person dataset on pedestrians' barriers in automatic detection and recognition of barriers. Three state-of the art deep learning algorithms were used to detect and classify the barriers in predefined classes. Faster

R-CNN with InceptionV2 and Faster R-CNN with ResNet-50 feature extraction were used to analyze the maximum performance of our dataset while SSD was utilized to test the possibility of incorporating such technologies in a smartphone application for improving pedestrians' safety while walking in urban sidewalks. Our experiments reach an average accuracy of 88.4% in the case of Faster R-CNN with InceptionV2 feature extraction, while the corresponding value for the case of SSD is 75.6%. The encouraging performance results show the possibility of developing systems and methods based on wearable cameras and smartphone devices for the automatic reporting of barriers and damages. Such systems can be part of a broader framework such as a science-citizen program to maintain free and safe walking in urban environments with great social and economic impact. Currently, we are working on the development of a smartphone application for reporting the barriers to a crowdsourcing platform and informing pedestrians and public authorities in real time. The CNN models for automatic detection and recognition were embedded in the application aiming to help the users to report easier the detected obstacles. Besides the creation of knowledge, the application can be used for increasing the number of images in the proposed dataset, overcoming the limitations of the collection process.

Our future plans include the improvement of the dataset in regard to: (1) the number of images by collecting more data and balancing the number of instances for the less popular barrier types, (2) the annotation by utilizing different tools and methods including crowdsourcing. The performance of the dataset will be further tested with more algorithms and different frameworks with the ultimate goal of increasing the detection and recognition accuracy. We will carry out all necessary evaluations and follow all requisite steps so as to make the egocentric dataset publicly available. In addition, the smartphone application which utilizes the proposed automatic detection and identification methods will be completed and tested before being released in app stores.

Acknowledgements. This project has received funding from the European Union's Horizon 2020 research and innovation programme under grant agreement No 739578 complemented by the Government of the Republic of Cyprus through the Directorate General for European Programmes, Coordination and Development.

References

1. Microsoft common objects in context, detection evaluation, metrics. https://cocodataset.org/#detection-eval. Accessed 16 July 2020
2. Bano, S., Suveges, T., Zhang, J., McKenna, S.: Multimodal egocentric analysis of focused interactions. IEEE Access **6**, 1–13 (2018)
3. Bolaños, M., Dimiccoli, M., Radeva, P.: Toward storytelling from visual lifelogging: an overview. IEEE Trans. Hum. Mach. Syst. **47**, 77–90 (2015)
4. Bolaños, M., Radeva, P.: Simultaneous food localization and recognition. In: 23rd International Conference on Pattern Recognition (ICPR), pp. 3140–3145 (2016)
5. Bullock, I.M., Feix, T., Dollar, A.M.: The yale human grasping dataset: grasp, object, and task data in household and machine shop environments. Int. J. Robot. Res. **34**(3), 251–255 (2015)
6. Climent-Pérez, P., Spinsante, S., Michailidis, A., Flórez-Revuelta, F.: A review on video-based active and assisted living technologies for automated lifelogging. Expert Syst. Appl. **139**, 112847 (2020)

7. Damen, D., et al.: Scaling egocentric vision: the epic-kitchens dataset. In: European Conference on Computer Vision (ECCV) (2018)
8. Dutta, A., Zisserman, A.: The VIA annotation software for images, audio and video. arXiv preprint arXiv:1904.10699 (2019)
9. EU: 2018 road safety statistics: what is behind the figures? (2019). https://ec.europa.eu/commission/presscorner/detail/en/MEMO_19_1990. Accessed 14 July 2020
10. Furnari, A., Farinella, G.M., Battiato, S.: Recognizing personal locations from egocentric videos. IEEE Trans. Hum. Mach. Syst. **47**(1), 6–18 (2017)
11. Gopalakrishnan, K.: Deep learning in data-driven pavement image analysis and automated distress detection: a review. Data **3**(3), 28 (2018)
12. Gurrin, C., Joho, H., Hopfgartner, F., Zhou, L., Albatal, R.: Overview of ntcir-12 lifelog task (2016)
13. Herruzo, P., Portell, L., Soto, A., Remeseiro, B.: Analyzing first-person stories based on socializing, eating and sedentary patterns. In: Battiato, S., Farinella, G.M., Leo, M., Gallo, G. (eds.) ICIAP 2017. LNCS, vol. 10590, pp. 109–119. Springer, Cham (2017). https://doi.org/10.1007/978-3-319-70742-6_10
14. Howard, A.G., et al.: Mobilenets: Efficient convolutional neural networks for mobile vision applications. arXiv preprint arXiv:1704.04861 (2017)
15. Huang, J., et al.: Speed/accuracy trade-offs for modern convolutional object detectors. In: Proceedings of the IEEE Conference on Computer Vision and Pattern Recognition, pp. 7310–7311 (2017)
16. Jain, S., Gruteser, M.: Recognizing textures with mobile cameras for pedestrian safety applications. IEEE Trans. Mob. Comput. **18**(8), 1911–1923 (2019)
17. Jiang, B., Yang, J., Lv, Z., Song, H.: Wearable vision assistance system based on binocular sensors for visually impaired users. IEEE Internet Things J. **6**(2), 1375–1383 (2019)
18. Kingma, D.P., Ba, J.: Adam: A method for stochastic optimization. arXiv preprint arXiv:1412.6980 (2014)
19. Lin, T.-Y., et al.: Microsoft coco: common objects in context. In: Fleet, D., Pajdla, T., Schiele, B., Tuytelaars, T. (eds.) ECCV 2014. LNCS, vol. 8693, pp. 740–755. Springer, Cham (2014). https://doi.org/10.1007/978-3-319-10602-1_48
20. Liu, W., et al.: SSD: single shot multibox detector. In: Leibe, B., Matas, J., Sebe, N., Welling, M. (eds.) ECCV 2016. LNCS, vol. 9905, pp. 21–37. Springer, Cham (2016). https://doi.org/10.1007/978-3-319-46448-0_2
21. Long, J., Shelhamer, E., Darrell, T.: Fully convolutional networks for semantic segmentation. In: Proceedings of the IEEE Conference on Computer Vision and Pattern Recognition, pp. 3431–3440 (2015)
22. Maeda, H., Sekimoto, Y., Seto, T., Kashiyama, T., Omata, H.: Road damage detection and classification using deep neural networks with smartphone images: road damage detection and classification. Comput. Aided Civ. Infrastruct. Eng. **33**, 1127–1141 (2018)
23. Mayol, W.W., Murray, D.W.: Wearable hand activity recognition for event summarization. In: Ninth IEEE International Symposium on Wearable Computers (ISWC 2005), pp. 122–129 (2005)
24. Nesoff, E., Porter, K., Bailey, M., Gielen, A.: Knowledge and beliefs about pedestrian safety in an urban community: implications for promoting safe walking. J. Community Health **44**, 103–111 (2018)
25. Oliveira-Barra, G., Bolaños, M., Talavera, E., Gelonch, O., Garolera, M., Radeva, P.: Lifelog retrieval for memory stimulation of people with memory impairment, pp. 135–158 (January 2019)
26. Organization, W.H.: A road safety manual for decision-makers and practitioners. Technical report (2013)

27. Organization, W.H.: Global status report on road safety 2018. Technical report (2018)
28. Penna, A., Mohammadi, S., Jojic, N., Murino, V.: Summarization and classification of wearable camera streams by learning the distributions over deep features of out-of-sample image sequences. In: 2017 IEEE International Conference on Computer Vision (ICCV), pp. 4336–4344 (2017)
29. Prathiba, T., Thamaraiselvi, M., Mohanasundari, M., Veerelakshmi, R.: Pothole detection in road using image processing. Int. J. Manag. Inf. Technol. Eng. 3(4), 13–20 (2015)
30. Rawat, W., Wang, Z.: Deep convolutional neural networks for image classification: a comprehensive review. Neural Comput. 29(9), 2352–2449 (2017)
31. Ren, S., He, K., Girshick, R., Sun, J.: Faster r-cnn: towards real-time object detection with region proposal networks. Adv. Neural Inf. Process. Syst. 28, 91–99 (2015). NIPS
32. Russakovsky, O., et al.: Imagenet large scale visual recognition challenge. Int. J. Comput. Vis. 115(3), 211–252 (2015)
33. Sandler, M., Howard, A., Zhu, M., Zhmoginov, A., Chen, L.C.: Mobilenetv 2: inverted residuals and linear bottlenecks. In: Proceedings of the IEEE Conference on Computer Vision and Pattern Recognition, pp. 4510–4520 (2018)
34. Sas-Bojarska, A., Rembeza, M.: Planning the city against barriers. Enhancing the role of public spaces. Procedia Eng. 161, 1556–1562 (2016)
35. Silva, A.R., Pinho, M., Macedo, L., Moulin, C.. A critical review of the effects of wearable cameras on memory. Neuropsychol. Rehabil. 28, 1–25 (2016)
36. Simonyan, K., Zisserman, A.: Very deep convolutional networks for large-scale image recognition. arXiv preprint arXiv:1409.1556 (2014)
37. Singh, K.K., Fatahalian, K., Efros, A.A.: Krishnacam: using a longitudinal, single-person, egocentric dataset for scene understanding tasks. In: 2016 IEEE Winter Conference on Applications of Computer Vision (WACV), pp. 1–9 (2016)
38. Szarvas, M., Yoshizawa, A., Yamamoto, M., Ogata, J.: Pedestrian detection with convolutional neural networks, pp. 224–229 (July 2005)
39. Szegedy, C., et al.: Going deeper with convolutions. In: Proceedings of the IEEE Conference on Computer Vision and Pattern Recognition, pp. 1–9 (2015)
40. Szegedy, C., Vanhoucke, V., Ioffe, S., Shlens, J., Wojna, Z.: Rethinking the inception architecture for computer vision. In: Proceedings of the IEEE Conference on Computer Vision and Pattern Recognition, pp. 2818–2826 (2016)
41. Theodosiou, Z., Lanitis, A.: Visual lifelogs retrieval: state of the art and future challenges. In: 2019 14th International Workshop on Semantic and Social Media Adaptation and Personalization (SMAP) (2019)
42. Theodosiou, Z., Partaourides, H., Atun, T., Panayi, S., Lanitis, A.: A first-person database for detecting barriers for pedestrians. In: Proceedings of 15th The International Conference on Computer Vision Theory and Applications, pp. 660–666 (2020)
43. Timmermans, C., Alhajyaseen, W., Reinolsmann, N., Nakamura, H., Suzuki, K.: Traffic safety culture of professional drivers in the state of qatar. IATSS Res. 43(4), 286–296 (2019)
44. Tung, Y., Shin, K.G.: Use of phone sensors to enhance distracted pedestrians' safety. IEEE Trans. Mob. Comput. 17(6), 1469–1482 (2018)
45. Wang, T., Cardone, G., Corradi, A., Torresani, L., Campbell, A.T.: Walksafe: a pedestrian safety app for mobile phone users who walk and talk while crossing roads. In: Proceedings of the Twelfth Workshop on Mobile Computing Systems & #38; Applications, pp. 5:1–5:6. HotMobile 2012 (2012)
46. Zhang, L., Yang, F., Zhang, Y., Zhu, Y.: Road crack detection using deep convolutional neural network (Sep 2016)
47. Zhao, Z.Q., Zheng, P., Xu, S.T., Wu, X.: Object detection with deep learning: a review. IEEE Trans. Neural Netw. Learn. Syst. 30(11), 3212–3232 (2019)

Correction to: Regression-Based 3D Hand Pose Estimation for Human-Robot Interaction

Chaitanya Bandi and Ulrike Thomas

Correction to:
Chapter "Regression-Based 3D Hand Pose Estimation for Human-Robot Interaction" in: K. Bouatouch et al. (Eds.): *Computer Vision, Imaging and Computer Graphics Theory and Applications*, CCIS 1474, https://doi.org/10.1007/978-3-030-94893-1_24

In the originally published version of chapter 24, the acknowledgements section was erroneously omitted. The acknowledgements section and grant number have been added.

The updated original version of this chapter can be found at
https://doi.org/10.1007/978-3-030-94893-1_24

Correction to: Regression-Based 3D Hand Pose Estimation for Human-Robot Interaction

Chengyu Bandi and Ulrike Thomas

Correction to:
Chapter "Regression-Based 3D Hand Pose Estimation
for Human-Robot Interaction," in: K. Bouatouch et al. (Eds.):
Computer Vision, Imaging and Computer Graphics Theory
and Applications, CCIS 1474,
https://doi.org/10.1007/978-3-030-94893-1_24

In the originally published version of Chapter 24, the acknowledgements section was erroneously omitted. The acknowledgements section and grant number have been added.

The updated original version of this chapter can be found at
https://doi.org/10.1007/978-3-030-94893-1_24

© Springer Nature Switzerland AG 2022
K. Bouatouch et al. (Eds.): VISIGRAPP 2020, CCIS 1474, p. C1, 2022.
https://doi.org/10.1007/978-3-030-94893-1_26

Author Index

Angeloni, Marcus de Assis 297
Arnaldi, Bruno 3
Arth, Clemens 431

Bandi, Chaitanya 507
Bataille, Guillaume 3
Bazrafkan, Shabab 477
Beenhouwer, Jan De 477
Behnke, Sven 353
Bobadilla, Julio Cesar Mendoza 319
Bodenhagen, Leon 83

Campana, Jose Luis Flores 297
Capellen, Catherine 353
Cazzato, Dario 414
Chen, Xingyu 26, 153
Chen, Yen Wei 372
Cimarelli, Claudio 414
Cole, Avery 241
Conceição, Jhonatas Santos de Jesus 297

Dahou Djilali, Yasser Abdelaziz 453
de Almeida Maia, Helena 319
de With, Peter H. N. 268
Decker, Luis Gustavo Lorgus 297
Dolhasz, Alan 394

e Santos, Anderson Carlos Sousa 319
e Souza, Marcos Roberto 319
Espadoto, Mateus 127
Evers, Marina 223

Falcão, Alexandre X. 127
Fayolle, Pierre-Alain 53
Fleck, Philipp 431
Focht, Josef 183
Friedrich, Markus 53

Gouranton, Valérie 3
Greenspan, Michael 241

Hamamoto, Tomohiro 334
Harvey, Carlo 394

Herick, Maria 223
Hirata, Nina S. T. 127

Illium, Steffen 53

Jänicke, Stefan 183, 205

Khulusi, Richard 183
Kitsis, Andreas 530
Kosinka, Jiří 153
Krüger, Norbert 83

Lacoche, Jérémy 3
Lanitis, Andreas 530
Li, Lin Tzy 297
Linnhoff-Popien, Claudia 53
Linsen, Lars 223
Ljubenović, Marina 477
Luvizon, Diogo Carbonera 297

Malcolm, Jonathon 241
McGuinness, Kevin 453
Modrakowski, Terri S. 127
Mohan, Chalavadi Krishna 372
Molchanov, Vladimir 223

Neira, Manuel Cordova 297

O'Connor, Noel E. 453

Palinko, Oskar 83
Panayi, Simoni 530
Paramonov, Pavel 477
Partaourides, Harris 530
Pedrini, Helio 297, 319
Pelé, Danielle 3
Periyasamy, Arul Selvam 353
Perveen, Nazil 372
Pinto, Allan 297
Pirchheim, Christian 431

Ramirez, Eduardo Ruiz 83
Reyes-Aviles, Fernando 431
Rivadeneira, Rafael E. 495

Santos, Andreza Aparecida dos   297
Sappa, Angel D.   495
Sayah, Mohamed   453
Schmalstieg, Dieter   431
Schwarz, Max   353
Shimada, Atsushi   334
Sijbers, Jan   477
Söchting, Maximilian   103

Taniguchi, Rin-ichiro   334
Telea, Alexandru   26, 127, 153
Theodosiou, Zenonas   530
Thomas, Ulrike   507
Torres, Ricardo da S.   297
Trapp, Matthias   103

Uchiyama, Hideaki   334

Vieira, Marcelo Bernardes   319
Vintimilla, Boris X.   495
Voos, Holger   414

Wijnhoven, Rob G. J.   268
Williams, Ian   394

Yu, Lingyun   26

Zeng, Guangping   153
Zhai, Xiaorui   26
Ziauddin, Sheikh   241
Zwemer, Matthijs H.   268